Standard	Key Elements of the Standard	Chapter and Topic	MyEducationLab Topic
3: Observing, Documenting, and Assessing to Support Young Children and Families	3a. Understanding the goals, benefits, and uses of assessment	10: Fig. 10.1: Purposes of Assessment, p. 271 10: Fig. 10.3: Observation Processes and Methods, p. 275 10: Fig. 10.6: Your Multiple Assessment Roles, p. 284	3: Family/ Community 4: Observation/ Assessment 7: Curriculum/ Content Areas
	3b. Knowing about and using observation, documentation, and other appropriate assessment tools and approaches	1: Fig. 1.8: Teacher Reflection on a Behavior Issue with a Child, p. 17 7: Ask The Expert: Thelma Harms, Assessing Learning Environments, p. 188 10: Fig. 10.4: Materials for Recording Observations, p. 276 10: Fig. 10.7: Key Features of Documentation, p. 287	
	3c. Understanding and practicing responsible assessment to promote positive outcomes for each child	10: Fig. 10.2: Major Errors in Observation, p. 274 10: Fig. 10.5: Test Preparation and Test Anxiety, p. 278	
	3d. Knowing about assessment partnerships with families and with professional colleagues	10: Collaborating with Families: A Question-and-Answer Session with Parents on Portfolios, p. 285	
4: Using Developmentally Effective Approaches to Connect with Children and Families	4a. Understanding positive relationships and supportive interactions as the foundation of their work with children	6: The Importance of Learner-Centered Experiences, p. 136 12: Fig. 12.4: Tips for Communicating Effectively with Families, p. 328 12: Fig. 12.5: Practical Ways to Build Rapport with Families, p. 329 12: Collaborating with Families: Respecting Parents'/Families' "Funds of Knowledge," p. 338 13: Collaborating with Families: Sending Supportive Messages to Families, p. 359	5: Program Models 6: Curriculum Planning 8: DAP/Teaching Strategies 9: Guiding Children 10: Cultural & Linguistic Diversity 11: Special Needs/ Inclusion
	4b. Knowing and understanding effective strategies and tools for early education	6: Features of Authentic Learning Experiences, p. 132 6: Assessment Activity 2: Learning Through Multiple Intelligences, p. 161	
	4c. Using a broad repertoire of developmentally appropriate teaching/learning approaches	6: The Central Role of Play in Children's Learning, p. 139 6: Table 6.1: Play and Learning, p. 143 6: Fostering Learning Through Technology, p. 144 7: Table 7.1: Guidelines for Selecting Appropriate Materials for Children of All Ages, p. 183 8: Ask The Expert: Sue Bredekamp, Developmentally Appropriate Practice, p. 202 8: Thematic Units, p. 221 8: Projects, p. 222 9: Project Approach, p. 252 9: Ask the Expert: Sylvia Chard, The Project Approach, p. 257 9: Fig. 9.1: Questions to Ask for Effective Planning, p. 235 9: Fig. 9.2: Strategies to Meet Learners' Diverse Needs, p. 238	
	4d. Reflecting on their own practice to promote positive outcomes for each child	1: Fig. 1.3: Categories of Pedagogical Knowledge, p. 7 6: Assessment Activity 1: Alexander's Struggle to Learn to Read as an English Language Learner, p. 160 7: Pause and Reflect: About the Indoor Environment, p. 184 9: Assessment Activity 2: Planning for Diverse Learners, p. 265 13: Fig. 13.4: Evaluating Your Role in a Conference, p. 357	

continued

Suggested Correlation of Chapter and MyEducationLab Content with *NAEYC Standards for Early Childhood Professional Preparation Programs*

Standard	Key Elements of the Standard	Chapter and Topic	MyEducationLab Topic
5. Using Content Knowledge to Build Meaningful Curriculum	5a. Understanding content knowledge and resources in academic disciplines	8: Entire Chapter, Developing Curriculum, p. 198 8: The Importance of the Curriculum, p. 200 8: Content Standards, p. 206 8: Content Areas of the Early Childhood Curriculum, p. 207 8: Table 8.1: Overview of Early Childhood Curriculum Content-Area Standards, p. 208	1: History 6: Curriculum Planning 7: Curriculum/ Content Areas
	5b. Knowing and using the central concepts, inquiry tools, and structures of content areas or academic disciplines	3: Ask The Expert: Douglas H. Clements, Early Math Education, p. 59 8: Table 8.2: Examples of Age-Appropriate Learning Experiences, p. 211 8: Teaching a Meaningful Curriculum, p. 220 8: Curriculum Theories, p. 223 8: Assessment Activity 2: Brainstorming with Curriculum Webs, p. 227	
	5c. Using their own knowledge, appropriate early learning standards, and other resources to design, implement, and evaluate meaningful, challenging curricula for each child	3: Defining Early Childhood Programs, Standards, and Models, p. 50 3: Fig. 3.2: National, State, and Program-Specific Standards for Early Childhood Education, p. 52 8: Standards-Based Curriculum, p. 206 8: Fig. 8.1: Developmental Domains as a Curriculum Organizer, p. 213 8: Integrated Curriculum, p. 214 8: Emergent Curriculum, p. 216 8: Culturally Responsive Curriculum, p. 216 8: Characteristics of Meaningful Curriculum, p. 217 8: Pause and Reflect: About Meaningful Curriculum, p. 219	
6: Becoming a Professional	6a. Identifying and involving oneself with the early childhood field	1: Fig. 1.7: Characteristics of Effective Early Childhood Educators, p. 13 10: Assessment Activity 2: Evaluation of Preservice Early Childhood Educators, p. 290 13: Fig. 13.5: Characteristics of Outstanding Early Childhood Educators, p. 358	4: Observation/ Assessment 12: Professionalism/Ethics
	6b. Knowing about and upholding ethical standards and other professional guidelines	2: Assessment Activity 1: Reporting Suspected Child Abuse, p. 44 3: Assessment Activity 1: Giselle's After-School Care, p. 69 4: Fig. 4.5: Ethical Reasoning Process, p. 82 4: Ask The Expert: Stephanie Feeney, NAEYC Code of Ethics, p. 83	
	6c. Engaging in continuous, collaborative learning to inform practice	1: Fig. 1.6, Stages in Teacher Concerns, p.11 13: Fig. 13.2, Stages in Teachers' Development, p. 349 13: Fig. 13.3, Influences on Teachers' Professional Development, p. 351 13: Assessment Activity 2: Becoming a Valued Colleague, p. 361	
	6d. Integrating knowledgeable, reflective, and critical perspectives on early education	1: Fig. 1.1: A Self-Questioning Framework, p. 4 1: Fig. 1.2: Four Dimensions of Complexity in Teaching, p. 6 1: Figure 1.4: The Basic Dispositions for Reflection, p. 9 4: Assessment Activity 1: Autumn Is Sent Home by the School Nurse, p. 89 5: Assessment Activity 1: Angelica's Baby Pictures, p. 126 7: Assessment Activity 1: Creating a Sensory-Rich Environment for Robert, p. 195 8: Assessment Activity 1: Benjamin's Kindergarten Play, p. 226	
	6e. Engaging in informed advocacy for children and the profession	2: Assessment Activity 2: Getting Started with Advocacy, p. 45	

EXPLORING YOUR ROLE
IN EARLY CHILDHOOD EDUCATION

Fourth Edition

Mary Renck Jalongo
Indiana University of Pennsylvania

Joan Packer Isenberg
George Mason University

Boston   Columbus   Indianapolis   New York   San Francisco   Upper Saddle River
Amsterdam   Cape Town   Dubai   London   Madrid   Milan   Munich   Paris   Montreal   Toronto
Delhi   Mexico City   São Paulo   Sydney   Hong Kong   Seoul   Singapore   Taipei   Tokyo

Vice President and Editor in Chief: Jeffery W. Johnston
Senior Acquisitions Editor: Julie Peters
Development Editor: Bryce Bell
Editorial Assistant: Penny Burleson
Vice President, Director of Marketing: Margaret Waples
Senior Marketing Manager: Christopher D. Barry
Senior Managing Editor: Pamela D. Bennett
Senior Project Manager: Linda Hillis Bayma
Senior Operations Supervisor: Matthew Ottenweller
Senior Art Director: Diane C. Lorenzo
Text Designer: Element, LLC

Photo Researcher: Carol S. Sykes
Cover Designer: Ali Mohrman
Cover Image: Fotosearch
Media Producer: Autumn Benson
Media Project Manager: Rebecca Norsic
Full-Service Project Management: Michael B. Kopf, S4Carlisle Publishing Services, Inc.
Composition: S4Carlisle Publishing Services, Inc.
Printer/Binder: R.R. Donnelley & Sons Company
Cover Printer: Lehigh-Phoenix Color/Hagerstown
Text Font: Slimbach

Credits and acknowledgments borrowed from other sources and reproduced, with permission, in this textbook appear on appropriate page within text.

Every effort has been made to provide accurate and current Internet information in this book. However, the Internet and information posted on it are constantly changing, so it is inevitable that some of the Internet addresses listed in this textbook will change.

Photo Credits: Krista Greco/Merrill, pp. x (top), 296, 325, 344; Lori Whitley/Merrill, pp. x (bottom), 214; David Mager/Pearson Learning Photo Studio, pp. xii, 92, 235, 273, 281, 328, 357; © Bill Bachmann/Alamy, p. 2; Superstock Royalty Free, p. 8; Scott Cunningham/Merrill, pp. 10, 48, 72, 153, 181, 218, 237, 333, 347, 354; David Young-Wolff/PhotoEdit Inc., p. 20; Jupiterimages, p. 24; Corporation for National & Community Service, p. 29; courtesy of the Library of Congress, pp. 35, 167 (top); Anthony Magnacca/Merrill, pp. 54, 60, 97, 111, 116, 138, 189, 201, 223, 282, 284, 299, 301, 308, 349, 350; Laura Bolesta/Merrill, pp. 75, 130; Pearson Learning Photo Studio, p. 79; Annie Pickert/Pearson, pp. 84, 124, 164, 198; Alan Oddie/PhotoEdit Inc., p. 86 (left); Shutterstock, pp. 86 (right), 147; Todd Yarrington/Merrill, p. 105; Jo Hall/Merrill, p. 122; Bob Nichols/USDA/NRCS/Natural Resources Conservation Service, p. 134; Kenneth P. Davis/PH College, p. 135; Michelle Pearlstein, pp. 144, 245; Mike Peters/Silver Burdett Ginn, p. 167 (bottom); Jennifer Isenberg Blacker, p. 184; Mac H. Brown/Merrill, p. 205; Pearson Scott Foresman, pp. 232, 268; Laura Dwight/PhotoEdit Inc., p. 243; Marilyn Ornstein, p. 256; Elena Rooraid/PhotoEdit Inc., p. 292; Michael Newman/PhotoEdit Inc., p. 318; UPI/CORBIS -NY, p. 322 (top left); iStockphoto.com, p. 322 (bottom left); Skip Nall/Getty Images, Inc. -Photodisc/Royalty Free, p. 322 (right). All Ask the Expert photos provided by the subjects.

Library of Congress Cataloging-in-Publication Data
Jalongo, Mary Renck.
   Exploring your role : an introduction to early childhood education/Mary Renck Jalongo,
Joan Packer Isenberg.—4th ed.
      p. cm.
   ISBN 978-0-13-231047-5
   1. Early childhood education—United States.   2. Early childhood teachers—United States.
I. Isenberg, Joan P.   II. Title.
   LB1139.25.J35 2012
   372.210973—dc22   2010043245

10 9 8 7 6 5 4 3 2 1

www.pearsonhighered.com

ISBN-13: 978-0-13-231047-5
ISBN-10:   0-13-231047-3

I dedicate this book to educators throughout the world who devote their lives to the care and education of the very young. Through the concerted efforts of professionals in the field of early childhood education, people learn to appreciate the importance of the early years and recognize the enduring benefits that high-quality programs make to the lives of all young children and their families.

M.R.J.

I lovingly dedicate this book to my children, Jennifer, Scott, Michelle, and Dave, and to my grandchildren, Jacob, Sara, and Samantha, who exemplify the uniqueness and beauty in every child.

J.P.I.

About the
AUTHORS

MARY RENCK JALONGO is a professor at Indiana University of Pennsylvania, where she earned the university-wide outstanding professor award and coordinates the Doctoral Program in Curriculum and Instruction. She is a co-editor of Springer's *Educating the Young Child* book series and has written, co-authored, or edited more than 25 books, including *Early Childhood Language Arts* (6th ed.) and *Creative Thinking and Arts-Based Learning* (5th ed.) with Pearson, and *Major Trends and Issues in Early Childhood Education: Challenges, Controversies, and Insights* (2nd ed.). In addition, she has written two books for NAEYC (*Learning to Listen, Listening to Learn; Young Children and Picture Books*), edited two for ACEI, and earned various national awards for writing. Since 1995, Dr. Jalongo has served as editor-in-chief of the *Early Childhood Education Journal*.

JOAN PACKER ISENBERG is Professor of Education at George Mason University in Fairfax, Virginia, where she has twice received the distinguished faculty award for teaching excellence and also served as an Associate Dean. She received her bachelor's and master's degrees in early childhood education from Wheelock College and her doctorate in elementary education from Rutgers University. She has taught preschool-, primary-, and elementary-age children and held administrative positions in both public and private school settings. As a writer, Dr. Isenberg has authored or co-authored 15 books and more than 50 journal articles. She has been a Visiting Scholar for the National Board for Professional Teaching Standards (NBPTS), where she led higher education initiatives and the reform of advanced master's degrees for practicing teachers, and has served on the NCATE Board of Examiners, as President and in other elected offices of the National Association of Early Childhood Teacher Educators (NAECTE), and in offices of the Metro Area Branch of the Association for Childhood Education International (ACEI). Her research interests are in teachers' professional development, arts integration, and early childhood curriculum. She was the 2006 NAECTE recipient of the Pearson/Allyn and Bacon Outstanding Early Childhood Teacher Educator Award.

PREFACE

The fourth edition of *Exploring Your Role in Early Childhood Education* is designed to inaugurate your investigation into the lives of children, your research in the field of early childhood education, and your inquiry into the multiple roles that you will need to play as someone who cares deeply about nurturing and educating young children, ages birth through 8. This book addresses the critical issues in the field of early childhood education with an emphasis on the transformational roles of all early childhood professionals. Each chapter discusses these roles in depth so you will be best prepared to face realities of the field, such as how to be accountable to standards, to collaborate with families, to develop intentional and meaningful curriculum and assessment, to teach children in a diverse and inclusive classroom environment, and to use developmentally appropriate principles and practices so that every child you teach will learn and succeed.

New to This Edition

This fourth edition has been completely updated, both in the content and presentation. This major revision included condensing the text, reorganizing the content, adding two new chapters and completely revising a third, expanding the visual material in every chapter, and incorporating the latest research and the current professional standards. The substantive changes include:

- **More accessible and usable learning aids.** Each chapter begins with easy-to-understand learning outcomes that are aligned with the chapter headings, the chapter summary, and three sets of national standards. Each chapter concludes with two different end-of-chapter assessments that offer an opportunity to apply what students have learned from reading each chapter. We have streamlined and reorganized chapters for better comprehension, added authoritative online resources for instructor and student use, designed several new figures to depict the key concepts, and updated features such as "Did You Know?," "Ask the Expert," and "Meet the Teachers" to portray the types of work, challenges, and joys of today's early childhood professional. In addition, we updated and replaced material with the most current references within the field of early education and key related fields.

- **New chapters on history and ethics and early childhood programs and curriculum models.** Although information on these topics is interspersed throughout the text, the fourth edition devotes an entire chapter to each. *The new chapter on history and ethics* examines the time-honored precepts of our field, the code of ethical conduct, and influential leaders from ancient to modern times. *The new chapter on program and curriculum models* elaborates on the general indicators of high-quality programs and describes various career paths for early childhood educators. In addition, each of the five most widely implemented program models is discussed more specifically in terms of goals and mission, theoretical underpinnings, background for the program, role of the teacher, and specific approach to working with children and their families.

- **Completely new chapter on diversity, inclusion, and cultural competence.** Although the third edition included a chapter on diversity, for the fourth edition, the chapter is completely new. This chapter integrates the topics of anti-bias education, ethical

reasoning, the National Association of Young Children's Code of Ethical Conduct, and includes more practical suggestions on ways to integrate diversity across the curriculum.

- **Updated coverage of content, standards, accountability, and assessment.** Throughout the text, there is expanded coverage of brain-based learning, the latest version of developmentally appropriate practice, intentional teaching, the importance of healthy social and emotional development, evidence-based practices, and learning standards, to name a few. More and more early childhood educators are expected to be accountable for children's learning through the standards that children and programs must meet.

- The **Glossary** is a new addition to the book. It is designed to aid the reader in expanding her or his professional vocabulary and it focuses on the key terminology that is introduced in each chapter. Key words are introduced in context and in bold type within each chapter and are highlighted in each chapter. The Glossary provides clear, "standalone" definitions in alphabetical order that students can refer to if the terminology remains unclear as they read. It is also useful for review purposes and as a check for understanding. Each definition in the Glossary is also keyed back to the specific chapter in which it is discussed for ease of reference.

- **Online resources** are included in every chapter. A short list of authoritative sources that complement the chapter content is supplied as a resource. In addition, each website is annotated so that readers will know what is available there.

- **Seven new appendices of resources and materials** help student teachers and beginning teachers locate and organize materials and resources for their curriculum. There are updated online resources for instructor and reader use and expanded web links for additional reference, research, and information relative to each topic. These helpful appendices reflect best practices and provide teachers with practical information and an important reference tool that can be used across the curriculum.

Each of these changes addresses current issues in early childhood education and implementation. Their inclusion should better prepare readers to face the realities of teaching young children on a day-to-day basis.

Motivation for Teaching

Why do people decide to make the care and education of young children their life's work? When we ask undergraduate students this question, their answers vary. Some will simply say, "I love children." Others will be more specific and say things like the following:

"I idolized my second-grade teacher, Ms. Cardill. When I was in second grade, I found out that I had a learning disability. Ms. Cardill helped me learn how to cope and inspired me to become a teacher in the process."

"My mother and sisters are teachers, so is one of my uncles. I grew up with teaching and come from a teaching family. I guess you could say that I am carrying on the family tradition."

"Because I am the oldest and my family lives nearby, my job when I was growing up was to babysit for my little brother, nieces, and nephews. There were always kids around the house and I found that I really enjoyed their company."

By way of introduction, here is what we have to say about what precipitated our decisions to pursue a career in early childhood:

Mary: "I've always wanted to be a teacher just like Ms. Klingensmith, my kindergarten teacher. Throughout early childhood, my favorite play theme was playing school and, when I did, I was always Miss K. When I was in high school, my little sister was in first grade. After six months with a mean teacher who was a former Marine sergeant, my sister was crying and throwing up every morning before school started. At age 7, she developed a stomach ulcer. Her teacher was fired at the end of that year, but when I saw the damage that one bad teacher could do, I made the commitment to go into teaching and become a good teacher."

Joan: "As the oldest of four siblings, I spent much of my childhood and adolescence with young children. When I was a teenager, my best friend and I planned and organized children's birthday parties. In the summers, I worked at a camp and was a swimming instructor for young children who were learning to swim for the first time. These experiences helped me to see many different ways to teach things that children really wanted to learn. These experiences also differed dramatically from the kind of in-school learning I remembered from my early childhood days, where I was expected to sit quietly, memorize information, and tolerate boredom. My work at the camp and in my neighborhood allowed me to see children's delight in learning and led me to become an early childhood teacher."

Whether you are a beginner or a veteran in the field of early childhood, the underlying message is clear: We decide to teach young children because we believe that early childhood is one of the most delightful periods in life, because we are intrigued and charmed by the newcomer's perspective the young child has of the world, and because we feel well suited to fulfill the early childhood educator's multiple roles. In short, we seek careers in early childhood education because we believe that we can exert a powerful and positive influence on the lives of the very young.

How does a college student move from dreams of teaching well to becoming an effective professional educator? One thing is certain: In that journey from imagining ourselves as effective teachers to actually becoming outstanding teachers, good intentions are not enough. It is almost inconceivable that anyone would enter into teaching with the thought, "I plan to be a terrible teacher and make children's lives miserable," yet there are many examples of teachers who have drifted from a firm commitment to fostering students' healthy development and learning. Generally speaking, they are the teachers who have neglected their own learning, who became jaded by the futile search for one method that works equally well with all children, who waited to be told what to do, or who failed to put children at the center of their practice.

General Focus and Purpose

Traditionally, introductory textbooks in early childhood education have been organized by curriculum area. The typical introductory text begins with a history of the field and a chapter on developmental theory followed by one chapter on each major subject area—language, mathematics, science, the arts, and so forth. *Exploring Your Role in Early Childhood Education* takes a more integrated and innovative approach. This text is organized around the essential roles and responsibilities that effective early childhood educators must fulfill. Another fundamental difference between *Exploring Your Role in Early Childhood Education* and other introductory textbooks is that it is interactive. This means that readers are encouraged to respond to what they are reading while they are reading it. We rely upon case material and verbatim comments from students to make the content come alive. As you look through the book, you will notice sections called "Pause and Reflect About . . ." in the margins. This material will encourage you to relate what you have read to your own experiences and guide you to reflect more deeply on important topics.

The National Association for the Education of Young Children (NAEYC) *Standards for Early Childhood Professional Preparation Programs* state:

> professional preparation for early childhood teachers is more than a list of competencies to be assessed or a course list to complete. Early childhood students in well-designed programs develop professional knowledge, skills, and dispositions in a community of learners making sense of readings, observations, field experiences, and group projects through their interactions with others. They make connections between life experiences and new learning. They apply foundational concepts from general education course work to early childhood practice. They learn to self-assess and to advocate for themselves as students and as professionals. They strengthen their skills in written and verbal communication, learn to identify and use professional resources, and make connections between these "college skills" and lifelong professional practice. (NAEYC, 2009, p. 5)

As a contemporary early childhood educator, you will need to fulfill at least 13 important roles that correspond to the contents of *Exploring Your Role.* These roles that NAEYC (2009) identifies and that we have adapted here include:

1. The **reflective practitioner** who carefully considers educational issues and is capable of intentional decision making (Chapter 1);

2. The **ethical professional** who puts children and families first, behaves in accordance with a code of ethics, and understands the traditions of the field (Chapter 2);

3. The professional who is **knowledgeable about early childhood programs and career paths for teachers of young children** (Chapter 3);

4. The **professional with a commitment to diversity, equity, and justice** for children and families (Chapter 4);

5. The **professional with knowledge of child development** who understands young children's characteristics and needs and uses this professional knowledge to promote all children's learning (Chapter 5);

6. The **facilitator of learning** who understands the multiple influences on young children and fosters children's engagement in learning (Chapter 6);

7. The **environment designer/arranger** who uses knowledge of child development to create a safe, healthy, supportive, respectful, and engaging environment for learning (Chapter 7);

8. The **curriculum developer** who can design, implement, and assess learning across the content areas and provide meaningful programs that respect diversity and promote positive child outcomes (Chapter 8);

9. The **educational planner** who understands different types and levels of collaborative planning/organization and uses a wide array of effective approaches, strategies, and tools that respond to children's needs and interests and yield positive learning outcomes (Chapter 9);

10. The **professional skilled in assessment and documentation** who works in partnership with families and other professionals to document children's learning using appropriate assessment strategies (Chapter 10);

11. The **professional who guides children's behavior** by building a sense of community in early childhood settings and teaching the skills of self-regulation (Chapter 11);

12. The **collaborator with families** who builds trust and respect between, among, and with families and the larger community (Chapter 12); and

13. The **emerging professional** who seeks and self-monitors professional growth through research-based practice and professional collaboration (Chapter 13).

From this list alone, it is clear that working effectively with young children is a challenging and demanding avocation. As Johnson (2006) points out,

> For all of its potential rewards, teaching is uncertain work. In some professions goals are clear and explicit, and success is easily measurable.
>
> The purposes of schooling extend well beyond the intellectual; schools are also charged with the social, emotional, and moral development of children. Given the various purposes of education, teaching's goals are hard to define, in turn making their attainment hard to measure.
>
> Teachers receive multiple, sometimes conflicting, messages about their roles. They are supposed to build skills while nurturing creativity and a love for learning, foster development of the "whole child" while closing the achievement gap, and respond to the individual needs of students while managing the group. The goals are overarching; one of the "givens" of being a teacher is knowing you will not be able to do all the society asks of you. (pp. 71–72)

Teaching young children is qualitatively different from the way it was 20, 10, or even 5 years ago. Our field has been profoundly affected by changes in families, advances in cognitive psychology, perspectives on the preparation of teachers, political influences on early childhood education, and a new era of sensitivity to cultural diversity and young children with exceptionalities (Isenberg & Jalongo, 2009). As you enter early childhood education, you will be engaged in the rigorous work of figuring out who you are as a professional and flexibly adapting to a wide array of early childhood settings.

Audience for This Book

The fourth edition of *Exploring Your Role in Early Childhood Education* is written for college students who are relatively new to formal study of the field of early childhood education. Typically, these students are enrolled in specialized programs at 2- or 4-year colleges or universities that prepare them to work with children ages birth through 8. This comprehensive introduction to the field is most appropriate as the primary textbook for the initial course. It will meet the needs of instructors who teach in baccalaureate (4- or 5-year) programs as well as the needs of instructors who teach in online colleges or 2-year associate degree programs at community colleges.

UNIQUE Features

The fourth edition of *Exploring Your Role in Early Childhood Education* has numerous features that set it apart from other introductory texts in the field of early childhood education. Descriptions of these features follow.

FOCUS ON ACADEMIC STANDARDS AND PROGRAM ACCREDITATION

Early childhood education today is more standards-based than ever before (Hyson & Biggar, 2006). From its inception, *Exploring Your Role* was built around the NAEYC standards. The fourth edition addresses not only the 2009 NAEYC standards for early childhood preparation programs serving children from birth through age 8, but also the standards of the Association for Childhood Education International (ACEI) and the Interstate New Teacher Assessment and Support (INTASC). A complete listing of the ACEI standards is available online at www.acei.org/standhp.htm and a complete listing of the INTASC standards is available at www.ccsso.org/intasc. Chapter content is keyed to specific standards through the learning outcomes at the beginning of every chapter. The first learning outcome of each chapter matches that chapter's content to the three sets of standards (NAEYC, ACEI, INTASC), and the grid at the beginning of the text shows how the chapter content is aligned with these sets of program evaluation criteria.

❶ Meet the TEACHERS

Readers will "Meet the Teachers" through case material that describes one infant/toddler caregiver, one preschool teacher, and one kindergarten or primary-grade teacher. In this way, we provide a balance of all three age groups every early childhood teacher needs to know—infants/toddlers (0–2), preschoolers (3–5), and children in the primary grades (5 or 6–8). Unlike some introductory textbooks that focus almost exclusively on 3- to 5-year-olds, our emphasis is on the education and care of young children ages birth through 8. Each Meet the Teachers is followed by an invitation to *compare* the three teachers, *contrast* the three teachers, and *connect* the teachers' experiences with the reader's experience.

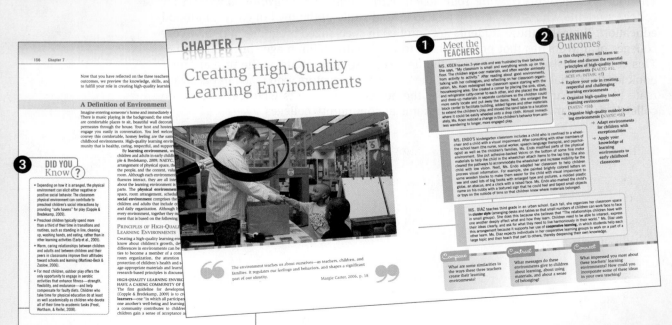

❷ LEARNING Outcomes

Every chapter includes a list of outcomes for the student, linked to the professional standards. This shift away from behavioral objectives to outcomes statements is consistent with current program accreditation requirements. Increasingly, teacher educators are being asked to provide more holistic and performance-based evidence that their early childhood programs make significant contributions to college students' growth as professionals.

❸ DID YOU Know?

Each chapter begins with four or five recent facts or research findings related to the topic/professional role of the chapter. Instructors will find this material useful when introducing the chapter because much of this information is not what students might expect, based on their personal experience.

BODY OF THE CHAPTER

As the Table of Contents details, the chapters follow a clear organizational pattern. Most chapters define the professional role, discuss the principles underlying that role, lead the student in reflecting about how she or he will fulfill that role, provide a rationale for its importance, and address the classroom practices that support that role. The body of the chapter then moves to the most influential paradigms that have resulted from theory and research.

❹ COLLABORATING WITH Families

Families figure prominently in any successful childhood program. Therefore, we have not only devoted an entire chapter to this topic, but also include a recommended strategy for working more successfully with families in all of the chapters. Collaborating with Families illustrates specific ways that skillful practitioners we know convey information on a variety of topics to the significant adults in each child's life.

❺ Chapter Summary

To support the students in reviewing the chapter content, each chapter concludes with a bulleted list of the key points that are aligned with the chapter learning outcomes and major headings.

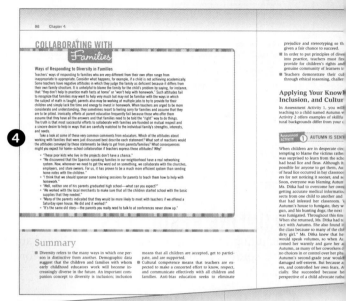

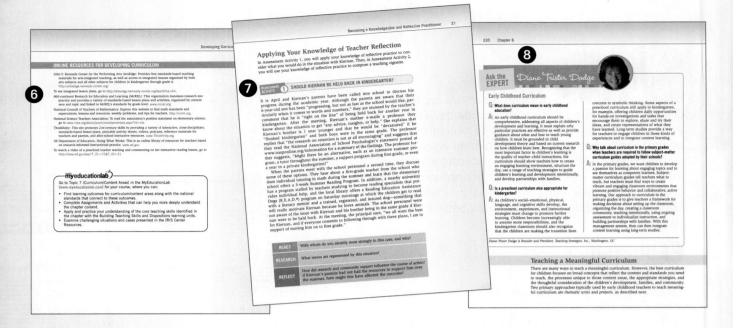

❻ ONLINE RESOURCES

Concluding each chapter is an annotated list of authoritative sources related to each chapter's focus for both instructors and students.

❼ Assessment ACTIVITIES

Each chapter concludes with two Assessment Activities that provide application-level practice with the chapter's content. Some of these Assessment Activities have been adapted from the third edition's end-of-chapter materials entitled "One Child, Three Perspectives" or "In-Class Workshop"; others are completely new. Assessment Activity 1 is a case study followed by discussion questions that analyze the situation from different perspectives. Included among the perspectives are the views of parents, classroom teachers, social workers, school administrators, child guidance experts, health-care professionals, and others who are committed to helping the child. This approach is in keeping with the new NAEYC standards that call for the preparation of early childhood professionals who have developed the skills of collaboration necessary to work with teams consisting of parents, families, colleagues, and professionals from many different fields who are committed to the education and care of young children. One of the complaints of highly regarded professionals in virtually every field is that nobody ever told them how challenging it would be to work in the "real world" of the profession for which they were prepared. In *Exploring Your Role* in *Early Childhood Education,* we present a wide array of challenging situations that early childhood educators are likely to encounter.

Assessment Activity 2 is designed as a mini-workshop and is an application activity of the chapter content. It addresses NAEYC's Standard 6 that calls for teachers to be "continuous, collaborative learners who demonstrate knowledgeable, reflective, and critical perspectives on their work, making informed decisions that integrate knowledge from a variety of sources" (NAEYC, 2009). Both assessment activities can be used with the total group or small groups to give readers a chance to apply the basic principles they have acquired from reading the chapter. In the professional development chapter, for example, we lead you in beginning to develop a teaching portfolio. All of these activities have been extensively field-tested with students in our classes over the years and have been well received in presentations at professional conferences.

❽ Ask the EXPERT

Each chapter has one to three "Ask the Expert" pieces authored by leading authorities in the field of early childhood education that are linked to the chapter content. As you scan through the chapters, you will see the photographs of highly respected early childhood educators who have made major contributions to the field. In this way, *Exploring Your Role* provides the most up-to-date and authoritative information available by incorporating the insights and voices of contemporary leaders and experts.

The Power of Classroom Practice

In *Preparing Teachers for a Changing World,* Linda Darling-Hammond and her colleagues point out that grounding teacher education in real classrooms—among real teachers and students and among actual examples of students' and teachers' work—is an important, and perhaps even an essential, part of training teachers for the complexities of teaching in today's classrooms. MyEducationLab is an online learning solution that provides contextualized interactive exercises, simulations, and other resources designed to help develop the knowledge and skills teachers need. All of the activities and exercises in MyEducationLab are built around essential learning outcomes for teachers and are mapped to professional teaching standards. Utilizing classroom video, authentic student and teacher artifacts, case studies, and other resources and assessments, the scaffolded learning experiences in MyEducationLab offer preservice teachers and those who teach them a unique and valuable education tool.

For each topic covered in the course you will find most or all of the following features and resources:

Connection to National Standards

Now it is easier than ever to see how coursework is connected to national standards. Each topic on MyEducationLab lists intended learning outcomes connected to the appropriate national standards. And all of the activities and exercises in MyEducationLab are mapped to the appropriate national standards and learning outcomes as well.

Assignments and Activities

Designed to enhance student understanding of concepts covered in class and save instructors preparation and grading time, these assignable exercises show concepts in action (through video, cases, and/or student and teacher artifacts). They help students deepen content knowledge and synthesize and apply concepts and strategies they read about in the book. (Correct answers for these assignments are available to the instructor only under the Instructor Resource tab.)

Building Teaching Skills and Dispositions

These learning units help students practice and strengthen skills that are essential to quality teaching. After presenting the steps involved in a core teaching process, students are given an opportunity to practice applying this skill via videos, student and teacher artifacts, and/or case studies of authentic classrooms. Providing multiple opportunities to practice a single teaching concept, each activity encourages a deeper understanding and application of concepts, as well as the use of critical thinking skills.

IRIS Center Resources

The IRIS Center at Vanderbilt University (http://iris.peabody.vanderbilt.edu—funded by the U.S. Department of Education's Office of Special Education Programs [OSEP]) develops training enhancement materials for pre-service and in-service teachers. The Center works with experts from across the country to create challenge-based interactive modules and case study units that provide research-validated information about working with students in inclusive settings. In your MyEducationLab course we have integrated this content where appropriate.

Teacher Talk

This feature emphasizes the power of teaching through videos of master teachers telling their own compelling stories of why they teach. These videos help teacher candidates see the bigger picture and consider why what they are learning is important to their career as a teacher. Each of these featured teachers has been awarded the Council of Chief State School Officers Teachers of the Year award, the oldest and most prestigious award for teachers.

Course Resources

The Course Resources section on MyEducationLab is designed to help students, put together an effective lesson plan, prepare for and begin their career, navigate their first year of teaching, and understand key educational standards, policies, and laws.

The Course Resources Tab includes the following:

- The **Lesson Plan Builder** is an effective and easy-to-use tool that students can use to create, update, and share quality lesson plans. The software also makes it easy to integrate state content standards into any lesson plan.

- The **Preparing a Portfolio** module provides guidelines for creating a high-quality teaching portfolio.

- **Beginning Your Career** offers tips, advice, and other valuable information on:

  - *Resume Writing and Interviewing:* Includes expert advice on how to write impressive resumes and prepare for job interviews.
  - *Your First Year of Teaching:* Provides practical tips to set up a first classroom, manage student behavior, and more easily organize for instruction and assessment.
  - *Law and Public Policies:* Details specific directives and requirements teachers need to understand under the No Child Left Behind Act and the Individuals with Disabilities Education Improvement Act of 2004.

Certification and Licensure

The Certification and Licensure section is designed to help students pass their licensure exam by giving them access to state test requirements, overviews of what tests cover, and sample test items.

The Certification and Licensure tab includes the following:

- **State Certification Test Requirements:** Here students can click on a state and will then be taken to a list of state certification tests.

- Students can click on the **Licensure Exams** they need to take to find:

  - Basic information about each test
  - Descriptions of what is covered on each test
  - Sample test questions with explanations of correct answers

- **National Evaluation Series**™ by Pearson: Here students can see the tests in the NES, learn what is covered on each exam, and access sample test items with descriptions and rationales of correct answers. They can also purchase interactive online tutorials developed by Pearson Evaluation Systems and the Pearson Teacher Education and Development group.

- **ETS Online Praxis Tutorials:** Here students can purchase interactive online tutorials developed by ETS and by the Pearson Teacher Education and Development group. Tutorials are available for the Praxis I exams and for select Praxis II exams.

Visit *www.myeducationlab.com* for a demonstration of this exciting new online teaching resource.

INSTRUCTOR
Resources

All supplements are available online. To download and print supplement files, go to www.pearsonhighered.com and then click on "Educators."

Online Instructor's Manual—This manual contains chapter overviews and activity ideas to enhance chapter concepts, as well as instructions for assignable MyEducationLab material.

Online Test Bank—The Test Bank includes a variety of test items, such as multiple-choice, true/false, and short-answer items.

Pearson MyTest—This powerful assessment-generation program helps instructors easily create and print quizzes and exams. Questions and tests are authored online, allowing ultimate flexibility and the ability to efficiently create and print assessments anytime, anywhere! Instructors can access Pearson MyTest and their test bank files by going to www.pearsonmytest.com to log in, register, or request access. Features of Pearson MyTest include:

Premium assessment content
- Draw from a rich library of assessments that complement your Pearson textbook and your course's learning objectives.
- Edit questions or tests to fit your specific teaching needs.

Instructor-friendly resources
- Easily create and store your own questions, including images, diagrams, and charts, using simple drag-and-drop and Word-like controls.
- Use additional information provided by Pearson, such as the question's difficulty level or learning objective, to help you quickly build your test.

Time-saving enhancements
- Add headers or footers and easily scramble questions and answer choices—all from one simple toolbar.
- Quickly create multiple versions of your test or answer key, and, when ready, simply save to MS-Word or PDF format and print!
- Export your exams for import to Blackboard 6.0, CE (WebCT), or Vista (WebCT).

Online PowerPoint Slides—PowerPoint slides highlight key concepts and strategies in each chapter and enhance lectures and discussions.

A FINAL WORD

In writing this, the fourth edition of *Exploring Your Role in Early Childhood Education*, we drew upon our many years of teaching toddlers, preschoolers, and children in the primary grades; supervising student teachers; as well as our work with practitioners in child care, nursery school, Head Start, and public school so that we could offer a useful, contemporary, and comprehensive perspective on the field.

Welcome, then, to an exploration of your role as an early childhood educator. You are joining the ranks of a profession with a long and distinguished history of dedication to the care and education of children. You are becoming a member of a field characterized by compassion, commitment, enthusiasm, and joy in the growth, development, and learning of young children.

Acknowledgments

Over 20 years ago Joan and I were in Atlanta attending an NAEYC conference and standing in line, waiting to be seated for dinner. We saw Dave Faherty, then Merrill's Senior Editor, walk in with Joanne Hendrick, an early childhood educator and Merrill author whose books we both greatly admired. At the time, I dreamed aloud that that might be us some day as we approached the end of our careers. I imagined us celebrating with our editor after the successful publication of our book with Merrill. Little did we know that we would be thinking about an introductory textbook going into its fourth edition with our current editor, Julie Peters, and our former editor, Ann Davis. We thank them for their faith in us as thinkers, their support of us as authors, and their willingness to try a very different type of introductory textbook in early childhood education. We thank them also for their creativity and expert knowledge of the publishing field. Their support has enabled us to revise our introductory text more extensively and more frequently than we ever expected.

We also want to express our gratitude to the reviewers of this book: Johnny Castro, Brookhaven College; Kathleen DeVries, Red Rocks Community College; Andrew S. Forshee, Portland Community College; Christopher Meidl, Towson University; and Janet M. Melton, University of Texas at Arlington, for their thoughtful criticisms and many contributions that refined and polished *Exploring Your Role in Early Childhood Education*. Two graduate assistants, Jamie D'Amico and Magge Cales, provided support in developing the new glossary as we went to press with the fourth edition. We also want to thank our former graduate assistants, Natalie K. Conrad and Ruth Steinbrunner, who helped with the ancillary materials and suffered through the early drafts of the manuscript. Ruth contributed primarily to the Collaborating with Families feature. We also want to thank Michelle Amodei, who revised the Instructor's Manual and Test Bank, and Mary Beth Chaney, who revised the PowerPoint Slides for this edition. And, of course, we want to thank our families for tolerating our passion to try to make a contribution to the early childhood field through writing and for supporting us in many ways, ranging all the way from taking care of household duties to reading and critiquing drafts of chapters so that we could be more productive textbook writers.

BRIEF
Contents

Appendices

CONTENTS

Chapter 6   Fostering Children's Engagement
in Learning   **130**

Chapter 7   Creating High-Quality Learning
Environments   **164**

EXPLORING YOUR ROLE
IN EARLY CHILDHOOD EDUCATION

Fourth Edition

CHAPTER 1

Becoming a Knowledgeable and Reflective Practitioner

Possibly no goal of education is more important—or more neglected—than self-understanding. . . . We need to ask not only what we believe but why we believe it. Similarly, we need to ask, What do I feel? Why? What am I doing? Why? And even, what am I saying and, again, why?

Nel Noddings, 2006, p. 10

Meet the TEACHERS

DARLENE has been a toddler caregiver for 7 years. She arrives at a Saturday workshop wearing a sweatshirt that shows a cartoon face shouting the word, "Mine!" If you spent the day with Darlene's toddler group, you would see that, much of the time, she is seated on the floor interacting with the six toddlers for whom she is responsible. Darlene explains her perspective this way: "Toddlers need, first and foremost, to learn social skills. At this age, disputes over toys are common, and a frustrated toddler tends to respond physically—hitting, crying, or biting—because the words aren't there yet. I see my primary roles as caring deeply about them, teaching them to get along with one another, and meeting their basic needs. I know that parents trust me to do what is right for their little ones, and I take that trust very seriously."

MS. THOMAS and her aide, Mrs. Grant, teach in a special public school prekindergarten program for children from low-income backgrounds. After children arrive, the day begins with a breakfast served in the school cafeteria. As they eat, the 4-year-olds engage in informal conversations with their teachers and peers. After cleanup, the children return to the classroom and gather on the carpet for a planning session. They preview the day's events and choose the centers that they will visit. Each day, one child is responsible for drawing a picture depicting a classroom event and dictating a sentence. The picture and caption become part of a journal that chronicles the school year. Following center time the children meet in small groups to review their accomplishments. Some of their comments are, "I made a farm with a fence out of blocks" and "We put together a big dinosaur puzzle."

MRS. GOMI teaches first grade in a small, rural elementary school. Because she believes that the transition from kindergarten to first grade is an important one, she collaborates with the kindergarten teacher to create a "buddy system." In the late spring, each kindergarten child is paired with a first-grader buddy and has the opportunity to spend a day in first grade; that way, the children are familiar with the routines and expectations for the next year well before the start of school (Laverick & Jalongo, 2011).

LEARNING Outcomes

In this chapter, you will learn to:

→ Become familiar with national standards and guidelines that address the knowledge, skills, and dispositions of effective early childhood educators (NAEYC #5, ACEI #5b, INTASC #9)

→ Describe categories of knowledge that are essential for teachers and define reflective practice

→ Understand the principles and processes of reflective practice

→ Explore your role in becoming a reflective practitioner

→ Apply your knowledge of reflective practice to case material and composing a teaching vignette

Compare

What are some commonalities that these three teachers share, even though they are working with children of various ages?

Contrast

How do these teachers think about teaching? How would you characterize the outlook of each one?

Connect

What aspect of these teachers' experiences made the greatest impression on you, and what might you incorporate into your teaching?

Now that you have reflected on the three teachers' perspectives and noted the learning outcomes, we preview the knowledge, skills, and dispositions you will need to acquire in order to become a reflective practitioner.

Definition of Pedagogy and Reflective Practice

What led you to pursue a career working with young children? When we ask our students that question, their answers often include their love of children, descriptions of teachers who inspired them, and expressions of their enthusiasm about supporting children's development and learning. As a starting point, look through the Self-Questioning Framework in Figure 1.1 and jot down some of your responses.

Figure 1.1 A Self-Questioning Framework

What led me to this career choice?

- Why do I want to work with young children?
- What do I believe about how young children learn?
- How do I think about concepts such as equality, freedom, individuality, and honesty as they relate to teaching and learning?
- What personal qualities and abilities do I possess that will make me successful in working with young children?
- What kind of early childhood teacher do I want to become?
- How will I demonstrate my commitment to young children and families through my work?

How are my personal characteristics matched to the job?
Am I . . .

- Convinced that all children can learn?
- Committed to maximizing the potential of each and every one of my students?
- Dedicated to principles of inclusion and fairness in all of my dealings with children, families, and colleagues?
- Responsible in fulfilling my duties and capable of exercising sound judgment?
- Reliant on ethical principles in my decision making?
- Enthusiastic about and able to sustain a lifelong interest in learning?
- Willing to take constructive criticism and use it to improve?
- Passionate about becoming a teacher and determined to pursue continuous improvement in my effectiveness?
- Genuinely interested in young children, their development, ways to help them achieve high standards, and strategies for assessing their progress?
- Proud to be entering the field of early childhood education and eager to contribute to it?

There are many misconceptions about what it means to teach, particularly where early childhood is concerned. When most people hear the word "teacher," a mental image of an adult presenting academic content to a group of attentive children seated at desks often springs to mind. This happens because there is

> a widespread confusion about what teaching really is. It is commonly thought that teaching involves the transmission of knowledge to students, knowledge defined by curriculum. In this view, teachers transmit knowledge more or less successfully, depending on their own skills and also on their students' capacities and receptivity. This is what teachers look like they do.
>
> What teachers really do, however, is more complicated than [this] . . . teachers want their students to achieve certain kinds of understandings. To encourage the development of their students' understandings in the right direction, teachers create relationships with the students anchored in explorations of particular material. It is not just the scope and sequence of the explorations, but also the quality of the relationships that determines how much understanding the students reach. (McDonald, 2001, pp. 210–211)

Many people assume that working with young children is "natural," just an extension of maternal or paternal instincts. While care and concern for children is essential, it is not enough. For example, teachers often enter the field thinking that their success will depend on caring about children, working independently, and knowing the right answers but soon discover that they must learn how to help children attain academic standards, collaborate with many different adults, and accept that the inherent nature of teaching is uncertainty (Blank, 2009; Helsing, 2006). As Figure 1.2 illustrates, teaching is a complex, dilemma-ridden professional role.

TEACHER KNOWLEDGE AND PEDAGOGY

Sometimes people dismiss early childhood teaching as being "easy" because the content to be covered is not as sophisticated as that in middle school or high school. Actually, an extensive body of research confirms that teachers need expansive knowledge in order to produce quality outcomes for young children (Early et al., 2007; Fukkink & Lont, 2007; LoCasale–Crouch et al., 2007; Lowe Vandall, & Wolfe, 2000; Marshall, 2004).

Early childhood educators are expected to know about:

- Children's play and development—physical, social, emotional, cognitive (Trawick-Smith, 2009)
- Curriculum planning/educational programming (Eliason & Jenkins, 2007; Kostelnik, Soderman, & Whiren, 2010)
- Children's health, safety, and nutrition (Marotz, Cross, & Rush, 2008)
- Working with parents, parenting, and social services for families (Berger, 2007; Keiff, 2008)
- Interventions for young children and families (Perry, Kaufmann, & Knitzer, 2007)
- Classroom management and child guidance (Essa, 2002)

DID YOU Know (?)

- Teachers make hundreds of decisions every day, so it is particularly important that those decisions are thoughtful, focused on promoting every child's learning, and respectful of families, colleagues, and the community (Falk, 2008; MacDonald, 2009).

- Research in neuroscience suggests that when professionals consider what they do (or have done) and why, they stimulate many different areas of the brain (Esslen, Metzler, Pascual-Marqui, & Jancke, 2008; Zull, 2006).

- The ability to critically analyze professional behavior reveals values (Orstorga, 2006), exposes biases, shapes a teacher's philosophy (Paris & Lung, 2008), and enhances success in teaching (Belton, Thornbury Gould, & Scott, 2006; Bygdeson-Larsson, 2006; Davis, 2004; Harle & Trudeau, 2006; Li, 2007; Peters, 2000).

- Four variables crucial to the success of new teachers are (1) a match between their expectations and the realities of the workplace, (2) evidence of having exerted a positive impact on their students, (3) use of effective strategies to manage their students' behavior, and (4) awareness of the professional culture of the school (Kardos, Johnson, Peske, Kauffman, & Liu, 2001).

Figure 1.2 Four Dimensions of Complexity in Teaching

Teaching is not routine and predictable.

Teachers must cope with changing situations, learning needs, challenges, questions, and dilemmas in different contexts. It is not possible to exercise a high level of control over all of the variables.

Teaching has muliple goals that must be addressed simultaneously.

At the same time that teachers are teaching content, they are also considering students' social and intellectual development. Teachers need to think about the total group at the same time that they are attending to the needs of individual students within the group.

Teaching involves relationships with diverse groups.

Children, families, and colleagues differ in cultural background and prior experience as well as learning needs, strengths, areas of challenge, range of abilities, interests, and expectations.

Teaching requires the integration of multiple kinds of knowledge.

Teachers have to integrate their knowledge of child development, subject matter, group interaction, and students' cultures/backgrounds with their teaching strategies and child guidance strategies.

Sources: Darling-Hammond, 2006; Lampert, 2001; Snow, Griffin, & Burns, 2005.

- Child assessments and evaluation (Wortham, 2007)
- Multicultural education, diversity, inclusion, and anti-bias curriculum (Sparks & Edwards, 2010)
- Implications of brain research for early childhood education (Jensen, 2006; Zambo, 2007)
- Working with colleagues and professionals from other fields (Stacey, 2009)
- Personal/professional growth, including what increases competence and effective ways of coping with stress (De Schipper, Riksen-Walraven, Geurts, & deWeerth, 2009)

Pause and Reflect
About First Teachers

Think about your first teachers. How did they influence your ideas about your talents and capabilities? How did they affect your sense of belonging to the group? What were the most important lessons that you learned from them? How will you exert a powerful, positive influence on the lives of children and families?

In addition to knowledge of this wide range of topics, teachers also need **pedagogy,** defined as specific knowledge about teaching children. A teacher's pedagogical knowledge includes four broad categories: case knowledge, procedural knowledge, conceptual understandings, and emotional intelligence, as highlighted in Figure 1.3.

REFLECTIVE PRACTICE

In order to put that knowledge into practice, teachers also need to thoughtfully consider what they do—and why (Nieto, 2005; Schon, 1983). **Reflective practice** is taking the time to rethink and rework teaching plans, strategies, words, and actions—and scrutinizing them through the lens of ethical decision making, all the while considering the effects of your behavior on self and others

Figure 1.3 Categories of Pedagogical Knowledge

Case Knowledge

Acquired through direct experience with actual events that become part of a teacher's "case file." Teachers compare/contrast these cases to new cases they encounter. Case knowledge often is pursued in response to personally meaningful, deeply affecting events.

Example:

The teacher may have had experience working with a child who has cerebral palsy during student teaching and draw upon that experience to work with other children who have the condition. In the absence of prior personal experience, the teacher may also "borrow" a case from a published source or a colleague.

Conceptual Understandings

Application of terminology, facts, principles, and strategies to more thoughtfully observe, analyze, discuss, and improve real-world teaching.

Example:

A student teacher who has experienced difficulty during circle time tries different strategies (e.g., such as sitting close to a child who has difficulty with self-control, making group times more interactive, keeping large-group sessions short, providing a small carpet square to keep each child's space distinct, and restating the rules).

Procedural Knowledge

Insight into the physical sequence of events associated with a particular task.

Example:

A teacher who has learned the proper procedure for taking children on a field trip, including such things as permission forms, adequate adult supervision, safety procedures on the bus, and so forth.

Emotional Intelligence

The ability to perceive accurately, appraise, and express emotion; to access and/or generate feelings in an effort to think better; to understand emotion and emotional knowledge; and to reflect on, manage, and regulate emotions in ways that encourage emotional and intellectual growth.

Example:

An angry parent arrives at the kindergarten class demanding to know why his son earned a low score on number knowledge when he can count up to 100. The teacher realizes that the parent is afraid that his child is failing. Rather than arguing with him, the teacher takes a "we're in this together" approach. She shares her plans for math instruction, arranges for a volunteer tutor at school, and provides the boy's father with practical activities they can practice with at home.

(Glickman & Alridge, 2001; Taggart & Wilson, 2005). "Rather than behaving purely according to impulse, tradition, and authority, teachers can be reflective—they can deliberate on their actions with open-mindedness, wholeheartedness, and intellectual responsibility" (Cruickshank, 1987, p. 8).

Principles of Reflective Practice and Professional Dispositions

Becoming a reflective practitioner relies on dispositions. A **disposition** refers to your inwardly motivated habits of mind and characteristic ways of approaching a situation. To illustrate, suppose that you made a mistake and do not have a major assignment ready on the day it is due. Some college students would be unethical and resort to plagiarizing.

Reflective practitioners think about teaching before, during, and after their interactions with children.

Some would try to invent excuses or place the blame elsewhere. Still others would admit their mistake and try to deal as best they could with the consequences of their actions. Each of these responses reflects a disposition to be honest and accept responsibility for your own actions—or not. Clearly, the last response is the mature, professional one. A **professional disposition** is a commitment to act in consistently responsible and ethical ways. Becoming a reflective practitioner involves professional dispositions; Figure 1.4 explains them further. Cultivating these dispositions is the surest way to become a reflective, responsible, and effective teacher of young children.

Competence as a teacher does not necessarily occur with additional experience; in fact, it is possible to repeat mistakes rather than learn from them. However, if the same unsuccessful strategies are implemented, no significant growth takes place and teachers' competence degrades rather than improves over time. In order to improve, an experiential learning cycle for the teacher must be set in motion. Reflection is the power source for that cycle (see Figure 1.5).

The cumulative effect of this learning cycle, applied day after day, is what transforms teachers from novices who question the purpose of reflection to master teachers who are reflective practitioners. The following excerpt from the journal of Jane Mize, a student teacher, shows how she confronted her misconceptions and used reflection to improve her teaching.

Figure 1.4 The Basic Dispositions for Reflection

Open-mindedness which includes:	Responsibility which includes:	Wholeheartedness which includes:	Ways to move forward: "mindful, relationship-based practice":
Analyzing beliefs and assumptions; not just those of others, but also your own	Accepting responsiblity for your beliefs and their consequences	Approaching teaching with enthusiasm, energy, and dedication	Attending to the present rather than dwelling on the past or future
Listening to others' points to view and interacting in productive ways	Having social awarness and regard for moral, political, and ethical issues	Posing meaningful questions that frame and reframe thinking	Respecting the individual knowledge, strengths, and needs of everyone with whom you work
Responding to suprises and unexpected outcomes in ways that improve the situation for learners	Accepting responsibility for yourself while remaining committed to the common good	Accepting that there are few easy answers in teaching and persisting at finding appropriate solutions	Learning to consider, plan, observe, and access all of your actions and behaviors as a teacher—before, during, and after teaching
Revising options based on data and being willing to admit you may be wrong	Testing out new thinking and seeking alternatives	Expecting teaching to be unpredictable and challenging	Understanding how your values and beliefs affect your practices and everyone with whom you interact
			Learning to listen carefully, observe thoughtfully, and ask questions that promote understanding
			Fostering positive relationships between and among all of the stakeholders in the child's education

Sources: Bolton, 2001; Chilvers, 2005; Dewey, 1909, 1933; Grant & Zeichner, 1984; McMullen & Dixon, 2006; Schon, 1987; Stronge, 2002.

Figure 1.5 The Experiential Learning Cycle and Teacher Reflection

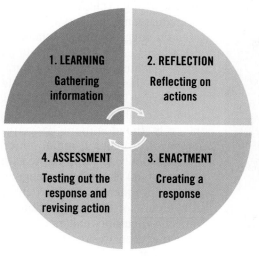

Sources: Kolb & Kolb, 2001; Snow et al., 2005; Zull, 2006.

I had a lot of information I needed to "teach" to the children. I envisioned them, eyes glued, listening to me intently. In reality, I kept having to stop during the lesson to refocus the children or attend to behavioral problems, sometimes losing my calm demeanor. After one particular lesson that had not gone well, I just stopped and sent the children back to their seats early. I realized that I was getting more and more frustrated. At first, I thought it was the children. The more I thought about it and analyzed my teaching methods, the more I realized that I had to make some changes in my approach.

Within the next several days I had my "pet invention lesson" (where the children were to create imaginary pets out of cloth and other materials). I kept my focus on the children's literature that I selected to go along with the lesson and tried to concentrate on giving clear instructions to the children about the accompanying activities. Then off the children went, and for the rest of the morning I helped with the materials, observed children eagerly learning, and listened to them tell me excitedly about what they had made. This lesson was the beginning of the change in my approach to teaching. I realized that I had been keeping the children in their seats too long and doing most of the talking instead of engaging them in good dialogue, not only with me, but also with each other. Also, I realized that in my old approach I was getting responses from the same children while others were sitting there squirming or tuning me out. I was not using the time I had with the children to the best advantage.

I decided to try to revise my approach. We still came together as a group, but not as often and not as long. I tried doing more in small groups or pairs, having the children share information with each other. I hoped that this would encourage some of the more reticent children to become involved and gain confidence with their ideas. When we did come together as a group, I read good literature. I also attempted to improve my divergent questions and tried to encourage more children to participate. (Jalongo & Isenberg, 1995, pp. 192–193)

To fully appreciate the power of reflection, consider what might have happened if Jane had not thought about this and made no intentional effort to improve. She might have become increasingly frustrated and concluded that the children were at fault. But, because she critically examined behavior and entered into an experiential learning cycle, she learned from her mistakes.

Of course, maturing as a professional occurs over time. Research suggests that teachers' reflection often begins with a focus on themselves, then moves to a focus on the task of teaching, and finally progresses to a focus on the impact of their teaching on students (Fuller & Bown, 1975; Taggart & Wilson, 2005). This does not mean that all concerns about self or task disappear with experience, only that the dominant concerns tend to follow this sequence. In general, initial concerns tend to focus on personal ability to fulfill the teaching role (self), then to pedagogy and classroom management (task), and finally to the consequences for learners (impact). Figure 1.6 is an overview of this progression. The goal is to become "reflective decision makers who can carefully observe, inquire, diagnose, design, and evaluate learning and teaching so that it is continually revised to become more effective" (Darling-Hammond, 2006, pp. 82–83).

Children's first teachers often leave an indelible impression.

Figure 1.6 Stages in Teacher Concerns

<u>Self</u> Inexperienced / Preservice Teacher	<u>Task</u> New / Inservice Teacher	<u>Impact</u> Experienced / Master Teacher
• Preoccupied with personal ability to fulfill the teaching role • Usually has a limited repertoire of teaching strategies • Tends to seek immediate, definitive answers and be impatient with theory or history • Relies on firsthand experiences and memories of childhood rather than training (Whitbeck, 2000)	• Focused on the "how to" of teaching • Begins to see how the success of lessons depends on knowing the students, understanding the content, and planning efficiently • Learns to consider the specifics of the learning situation, anticipate the difficulties children might have, and use resources more effectively • Considers various approaches, makes content and strategy choices, and adapts to the context and student needs	• Focused on enduring consequences of teaching/learning for children • Strives for continuous improvements as a professional • Analyzes experiences from multiple perspectives • Appreciates the profound influence teachers exert over students' values/behaviors/achievements • Becomes more involved with and committed to the school and community

Sources: Ball, 2000; Birmingham, 2003; Buchanan, Baldwin, & Rudisill, 2002; Carpenter-LaGattuta, 2002; Darling-Hammond & Baratz-Snowden, 2005; Fuller & Bown, 1975; Lee, 2005; Many, Howard, & Hoge, 2002; Taggart & Wilson, 2005; Whitbeck, 2000).

CONCERNS ABOUT SELF AS TEACHER

A preservice teacher wrote the following reflection in her journal:

> A group of children in my neighborhood were gathered for Scotty's third birthday party. The parents had made a videotape of the birthday boy at various ages. One of the things that he did when he was about 11 months old was to lie down on his stomach and slide quickly down five padded, carpeted stairs. One child begged to see the entire film run backwards, and the father obliged while the children laughed and squealed at all the funny situations, such as a bite of birthday cake jumping out of a person's mouth and back onto the fork. When the film segment that showed

Pause and
Reflect

About Caregivers of Young Children

Imagine that you had to trust someone else to help you care for and educate your sibling, your own child, or another child you love. What concerns would you have? What characteristics would you look for in the person responsible for the young child's care and education?

Scotty shooting down the steps was run backwards, it looked like he was being propelled up the stairs. About half an hour later, a one-year-old who had watched the film was observed stretched out on the same stairs that were in the video. Suddenly I realized that he was trying to launch himself up the stairs, just as he had seen in the video run backwards! When I said this to my neighbors, then they saw it too. This is an example of my being curious about why children do what they do. I was pleased that I was able to notice more than the average person and make sense out of a child's behavior when no other adult at the party had; I am starting to feel like I "get it" and my training as a teacher was showing.

This student has started thinking about her assets and how they will enable her to fulfill the role of a professional early childhood educator. She is, in effect, asking herself: Do I see myself as a learner? Where does my learning take place? How? What happens to me when something is hard or when I make a mistake? Do I learn from other teachers? Do I learn from children? (Gordon & Browne, 2007). On page 14, the Ask the Expert with Marilou Hyson discusses the importance of professional preparation for those who work with young children.

CONCERNS ABOUT THE TASK

The difficulty with changing behavior is that we feel unsure of ourselves, uncertain about whether we are acting appropriately. A good example is writing a lesson plan for the first time. Students typically say such things as, "I never wrote a lesson plan before," "I'm so confused," or "I have no idea what to do." In other words, these students are being asked to change their behavior and they are afraid of taking a risk. Yet real learning is, by definition, risky—no risk of mistake, no learning. When you are confronted with new challenges and unfamiliar tasks such as lesson planning, it is helpful to take stock of what you do know, based upon your experiences as a student. You probably know quite a few things about planning activities that are simply common sense, such as the need to teach something significant (a concept), the need to specify your goals (the objective), the need to capture children's attention at the beginning of the lesson (an introduction or motivation), the need to identify what resources are necessary to teach the lesson (materials), the need to think through your lesson in a logical sequence (the procedure), and the need to make certain that your information is current and accurate (resources or references).

The following is a dialogue about using academic standards between a sophomore, Miranda, who has just taught her first lesson in preschool, and two junior-level students in the same program. Notice how the juniors are able to give her advice; they are at the "concerns about task" phase in their professional development and are starting to move into the next phase, "concerns about impact."

Rachael: This is the first time you've used the Early Learning Standards, right? What did you think about that?

Miranda: Actually, as I was searching through the packet to determine which standards I felt were appropriate, I really enjoyed it and read through—even the ones that didn't apply. I think they're the basis for a lot of things in education. It was interesting to see, on that level—a preschool level—what would be expected.

Kaylee: Did the standards help to guide the lesson?

Miranda: Yes, they did. . . . I found that one lesson could cover so many standards. I probably could've listed more.

Kaylee: Our professors want us to list all of them too.

Rachael: You get used to reading through page upon page [of standards]! For closure to the story, you might complete an activity like using the song again with finger puppets and having them do the motions with you.

Miranda: Right.

Kaylee: I know you said in your reflection paper some children were doing the motions. You could teach the motions first and encourage everyone to participate.

Miranda: I sort of struggled with that. It's something you sort of go with while you're there. . . . Toward the end I just wasn't sure how to close it. That would be a good idea.

Kaylee: Even when I write lessons and someone else reads over them, they think of tons of ideas. And it's not that any of your ideas are wrong. You could bring in . . . something that they can touch, that could be a manipulative.

Rachael: Every time you write a lesson you need to think, "What will the children be doing?" Every activity we do, "What will their behavior be like?" And think, "If I were a 3-year-old, what would I be doing while waiting?" It's definitely something good to remember as you write more lessons. Always have something for them to do. (Jalongo, Rieg, & Helterbran, 2006)

Now review the Characteristics of Effective Early Childhood Educators in Figure 1.7. How does the preceding dialogue reveal that these preservice teachers are acquiring these skills?

Figure 1.7 Characteristics of Effective Early Childhood Educators

Effective teachers of young children . . .

Are open minded, flexible, culturally responsive, and committed to the principles of social justice

Regard themselves as learners and sustain an interest in learning throughout their careers

Exercise sound judgment and apply ethical principles in their decision making

Are dedicated to principles of inclusion and fairness in all of their dealings with children, families, and colleagues

Have a passion for teaching and pursue continuous improvement in their teaching effectiveness

Are capable of creating an orderly and productive learning environment

Believe that all children can learn and strive to maximize potential of each and every one of their students

Understand how young children learn and are keen and thoughtful observers of the learning process

Analyze the results of student assessment and use it as the basis for curriculum planning

Can plan and teach in ways that support all young children's attainment of high academic standards

Can adjust their teaching and adapt the curriculum to children's special needs

Pose intriguing questions and design activities that motivate children to achieve at higher levels

Work collaboratively with administrators, colleagues, professionals in other fields, families, and communities

Learn to take constructive criticism and use it to improve as professionals

Are willing to take an unpopular stand in order to advocate for the needs and rights of others

Marilou Hyson

Importance of Professional Preparation

Q: How important are degrees for early childhood teachers?

A: Many national reports and professional organizations have recommended that teachers of young children have college degrees, preferably bachelor's degrees, with specialization in child development and early childhood education. Yet some recent studies show that young children whose teachers who have college degrees, even in early childhood education, do not necessarily develop better academic abilities. Can someone be a good teacher without having gone to college? Of course. But formal, specialized education can contribute to most teachers' abilities to provide good educational experiences for children. This can only happen, though, if the college degree meets high standards of quality (NAEYC sets standards for and participates in accrediting high-quality college and university programs, including associate's degree programs).

Q: Why do babies and toddlers need caregivers who have education and training? Isn't it enough to love the children?

A: Love is the foundation, but love alone is not enough. The first 3 years of life provide incredible opportunities to build children's language, emotional competence, and cognitive and social skills. This doesn't happen by accident—research indicates that adults hold the keys. Professional development helps caregivers learn more about how to talk with infants, how to develop the kind of secure relationships that predict better development, and how to use everyday routines and active play to teach toddlers essential concepts (even in math and science!). It's not surprising that a number of states are creating specialized positions and training for infant and toddler teachers: This is truly one of the most important and challenging jobs in the early childhood field.

Q: If more education is required for early childhood teachers, won't some good people get left behind?

A: This is indeed a major concern for the early childhood field, which has prided itself on supporting diversity and open access. Many current and future teachers of young children are not well paid and may have difficulty financing further education. Educational opportunities may be more limited in communities of color, or for teachers whose home language is not English. Fortunately, many promising efforts are under way to ensure that all committed and capable educators have access to high-quality professional development. For example, the T.E.A.C.H. program provides scholarships to child-care workers in more than 20 states. Several projects have concentrated on building the capacity of college faculty to help all students succeed, including adult learners, many of whom may have been out of school for years, but who can be among the best and most dedicated students.

Q: Are there some basic things that everyone who works with children should know?

A: Absolutely! Most states, and several professional organizations such as NAEYC and the Council for Professional Recognition, have described what have been called *core competencies, competency standards,* or *professional preparation standards.* NAEYC, for example, identifies six areas in its standards for early childhood professional preparation programs: (1) Promoting Child Development and Learning; (2) Building Family and Community Relationships; (3) Observing, Documenting, and Assessing to Support Young Children and Families; (4) Using Developmentally Effective Approaches to Connect with Children and Families; (5) Using Content Knowledge to Build Meaningful Curriculum; and (6) Becoming a Professional—each with key elements or components. In this and other descriptions of core competencies, the idea is that everyone should have some level of knowledge and skill in these areas, but that the knowledge and skill should deepen and become more enriched at different steps on the early childhood career ladder—as someone moves, for example, from an entry-level assistant to a degreed lead teacher, or as someone takes on a specialized role such as a home visitor, a director, or a child advocate.

Marilou Hyson is senior consultant with NAEYC and affiliate faculty in applied developmental psychology at George Mason University.

REFLECTING ON IMPACT

Without a doubt, teaching young children involves a special type of responsibility. You have no doubt heard the expression that "First impressions are lasting ones," and this certainly applies to education. If you talk with teachers, they will tell you that at parent–teacher conference time, it is the kindergartners' parents and family members who attend in the greatest numbers. Evidently, families feel that getting children off to a good start is important. They want their children's first impressions of education to be positive ones. If you talk with adults, most of them can remember their first teacher even if it is difficult to recall the names of other teachers in their lives. As teachers gain confidence and skill, they focus less on worries about whether they can fulfill the teaching role adequately or work out pedagogical challenges. For master teachers, the emphasis is on enduring, positive outcomes for children and families. The Ask the Expert by Frances Rust on page 16 explains the concept of **intentional teaching,** which is a key outcome of reflective practice.

Your Role as a Reflective Practitioner

Here are the characteristics of a reflective practitioner that you will want to cultivate (Eby, Herrell, & Jordan, 2006):

- Reflective practitioners are **active,** meaning that they search energetically for information that affects the quality of life in their classrooms. An example of taking action is preparing to work with a child who is capable of speaking but chooses not to talk, a condition called selective mutism. Reflective practitioners would launch an effort to learn more about the condition, the particular child and family, and seek out authoritative advice.
- Reflective practitioners are **persistent,** meaning that they think through difficult issues and persist even though it may be difficult or tiring. For example, helping young children master the classroom routines necessary to work at learning centers requires patience and persistence.
- Reflective practitioners are **caring,** meaning that they have genuine concern for others, respect students as human beings, and try to create a positive, nurturing classroom. An example of behavior that demonstrates an early childhood educator's care and concern is taking the time to greet and say goodbye to every child every day.
- Reflective practitioners are **skeptical.** They realize that there are few absolutes and maintain a healthy skepticism about educational theories and practices. An example of skepticism is asking to see evidence and raising questions when someone makes the claim that an educational program is highly effective.
- Reflective practitioners are **rational.** They do not blindly follow trends, act on impulse, or do whatever is most expedient. Examples of rational behavior are gathering data in order to make a well-informed decision about the kind and amount of early intervention services a child and family need or deciding to rely on the research on best practices in early literacy instruction to guide instructional decisions.
- Reflective practitioners are **proactive,** meaning that they anticipate questions and address issues before problems mount, such as explaining the rationale behind a new math curriculum to parents and families as a way to allay their concerns.

Figure 1.8 is the inner dialogue of a teacher as she encounters a behavior problem with a student while she is being observed by her university supervisor. Because she takes the time to consider the consequences of her actions and the implications of her behavior for the child, she succeeds in improving the outcomes for all concerned.

Frances Rust

Intentional Teaching

Q: What is intentional teaching?

A: When we are learning to teach, we are often told to plan a lesson or a unit using big ideas like "transformation" and core values like "equity" to guide our work, but when we actually get into the teaching of the lesson or unit, those big ideas and core values seem to vanish. Often, this happens because we are so focused on getting through the steps of the lesson or the parts of the unit that we designed that we forget the big idea and values behind it. Intentional teaching is about making both big ideas and core values fully present in our interactions with learners. Intentional teaching requires awareness and presence: awareness of how an idea and a set of values can shape our actions; presence to the moment of interaction with a learner, for it is here, in the exchange, that we determine if and how well the learner has understood what we are trying to teach, how well we have taught.

Q: What does intentional teaching look like?

A: Let's take what seems like a relatively simple teaching moment such as helping a young child begin to work with jigsaw puzzles. Among the first moments will be looking at the picture on the box, then looking at the puzzle pieces to see how they relate to the picture, learning the concept of a "straight edge" so as to create the frame of the puzzle, finding visual "clues" about how pieces relate to one another and fit together, and, of course, building the puzzle. When I have taught 4-year-olds to work with jigsaw puzzles, we have followed this basic protocol. One always-fascinating step is teaching the concept of a "straight edge." I usually invite the child to feel for the straight edge. Together we evaluate piece after piece of the puzzle, feeling pieces that are bumpy all around and comparing them with ones that have an edge that is smooth and straight until it seems clear that the child has "got it"— the concept of a straight edge. I claim to know

this because the child consistently picks these pieces and lays them out to build the frame.

Q: How is this an example of intentional teaching?

A: With the task of beginning to build a jigsaw puzzle, what I am going after are a number of big ideas: the concepts of visual representation and duplication, of interlocking units or parts fitting together into a whole, of geometric relationships, and on and on. And then there are the values implicit in taking on the teaching of this task. Critical to my work as an early childhood educator is finding ways to support children's innate drive toward competence. I know that the eye–hand coordination required here will be valuable to the child in her movement toward reading and writing. I know that the conversation that we may have can expand her vocabulary—again supportive of literacy but also of mathematical thinking as well as of social interaction and of "school talk." All are skills that are essential to her developing competence as a learner.

Q: How can I learn to do intentional teaching?

A: One learns to work this way by taking time to reflect alone and in a community of learners. As a means of focusing thinking, writing is very helpful. Try writing for 10 minutes a day, every day and use this time to mull on a moment of teaching. Ask yourself, what was the big idea behind that lesson? How are my lessons moving my students toward that big idea? And how do my efforts toward realization of that big idea among my students fit with my core values? With whom do I do such teaching: Do I work most often with boys, girls, native English speakers, White children, Black children, brown children, and so on? Am I building on what I have learned about a child's strengths? Answering questions like these will help you to move your practice into the realm of intentional teaching. Keep track of your jottings. They are a record of your own growth as a professional!

Frances Rust is a Visiting Professor and Director of Teacher Education, Graduate School of Education, University of Pennsylvania, Philadelphia, PA.

Figure 1.8 Teacher Reflection on a Behavior Issue with a Child

SCENARIO:

You are going to read a picture book aloud to a small group of kindergarten children as one of your first practicum experiences; your university supervisor is observing you. The book that you selected is suitable for the grade level; it is about a bear that wakes up from hibernating and is very hungry (Wilson & Chapman, 2003). You have planned for it to be an interactive story reading in which you will ask children to chime in on the phrase that is the title of the book; Bear Wants More. *Now you invite the students over to a carpeted area of the classroom to sit and listen. One child begins to race around the room, singing loudly.*

Thinking about myself—"What am I supposed to do?"

At this stage teachers often revert to what our teachers or parents might have done or yell or threaten.

Teacher Reflection:

"I really prepared and it's not working. I even have a big bear puppet that I borrowed and a shopping bag 'cave' that I made to focus the children's attention. I'm being evaluated! He's ruining my lesson. I want him to sit down and be quiet. Should I just tell him to stop it? What if I do and he ignores me?"

Seeing the child—"I notice that . . ."

Focus is on immediate impressions and impulses.

At this stage, the focus begins to shift to an examination of the context as you search for explanations.

"We didn't have outdoor recess today because it has been pouring down rain so he might be full of energy. He isn't going to tire out—if anything, he is running faster. I now notice that he is singing some of the words from the song 'The Bear Went over the Mountain.'"

Hypothesizing—"Maybe it's . . ."

Focus is on generating ideas about what might be causing or contributing to the behavior and formulating a strategy for how to address it effectively.

Teacher Reflection:

"It might be the bear puppet that got him all excited. I think I'll go over to him, kneel down and speak quietly to him, and then lead him over to the circle with the group, but I'd better remind the rest of the students to stay on the carpet."

Questioning—"I wonder . . ."

Focus is on weighing the outcomes of your actions.

Teacher Reflection:

"I could just say 'Justin! Sit down!' but knowing him, his feelings would be hurt. I wonder what he is thinking and if what I have planned will stop the behavior. Should I leave the rest of the group for a moment or will that spell disaster?"

Trying out—"I've decided to . . ."

Focus is on taking action and implementing your decision.

Teacher Reflection:

"I'm going to say, 'We are going to hear a funny story about a bear. Before we begin, I want you to close your eyes and try to think of all the things you know about bears. Think about where bears live and what they do in the winter time.' Then I'm going over to Justin and quietly but firmly say 'I noticed that you are excited about the bear story and the puppet. You need to come with me and sit on the carpet so that you can see the puppet, a pretend cave, and the funny pictures in the book.'"

Reflecting afterward—"From this incident, I've learned . . ."

Focus is on evaluating the course of action.

Teacher Reflection:

"Justin *did* come along to the circle. My professor had cautioned us about shouting out orders to children from across the room so I decided not to do that, although it is what I recall most of my teachers doing. I did manage to get everyone settled down and ready to listen. My mentor teacher was impressed with the strategy that I used. Justin did cooperate and was not embarrassed because I spoke softly to him and did not make it into a battle of wills. My approach also did not label him as a troublemaker with his peers."

COLLABORATING WITH
Families

Reflecting on Home Visits with Diverse Families

Home visits are a way to build rapport. Here is one example of a form you might use or adapt when conducting home visits.

Interviewer: CK
Date: Oct. 7
Child's name: Jesus Martinez
Grade: 2nd
Parents' names: Miguel and Yolanda Guiterrez
Siblings: 1 younger sister, 1 older sister
Language(s) used: English and Spanish
Address: 1 Herringbone Lane, Phoenix, AZ
Telephone: 555-501-1212
E-mail: m-yguiterrez@hotmail.com

1. What are your child's interests (e.g., art, sports, hobbies, activities)?

   J. likes animals, computers, numbers—can do math in his head. Reads to younger sister. Likes stepfather to read to him. Watches "Wheel of Fortune." Saving his money for a cat. Rides bike and swims. Loves Net surfing.

2. How does your child seem to feel about going to school?

   Moved in July and does not know many neighborhood kids. Wants to make friends and exchange phone numbers and e-mail addresses. Does not want to go to school because of "homework he doesn't know."

3. What do you expect your child to accomplish this year?

   Oral language in English needs improvement. He's more fluent in Spanish.

4. What signs of progress were you pleased to see over the summer?

   More confident with numbers, can figure out calorie and cholesterol counts in his head to help stepfather with a special diet! Started to play word games and use rhyming words.

5. Are there any concerns that you have about your child?

   May not be challenged in math at school. Expressed concern about husband's new job and the long hours worked—J. is very close to stepfather.

6. What have you discovered about your child's particular ways of learning?

   Looks for patterns in numbers and can do some of this with letters and words.

7. What is the most important thing your child could learn this year?

   To build his confidence in speaking English. (But he wants to learn to play soccer.)

8. What hopes and dreams do you have for your child in the future?

   Has a head for numbers and math—maybe an accountant or an engineer? Dream of him working at NASA—very good at problem solving.

9. Is there anything else that I should know as I work with your child?

   J. is very sensitive and feelings are hurt easily. Has a food allergy to seafood and is allergic to bee stings.

Thank you for your time and for inviting me to your home.

One question often raised is, *"What* do I reflect on?" In this era of teacher account-ability, the focus of a teacher reflection generally falls into three categories:

1. **academic concerns,** such as the learning standards, subject matter, and student understanding of content;
2. matters of **teaching effectiveness,** which include how teachers integrate research-based practices into their teaching and use student work to make data-driven decisions; and
3. **developmental considerations,** which examine the learners' needs and motiva-tions and match them to teaching strategies (Nagle, 2009).

Another common question is, *"When* am I supposed to reflect?" Teacher reflection occurs before teaching, during teaching, and after teaching. Now read the following brief reflection written by a teacher as he viewed a video of his lesson.

Teacher's Words	Teacher's Thoughts
"Let's look at these plants I brought today. What are some of the parts of plants that you know about?"	*Using real objects to introduce this lesson on plants has captured their attention. . . . Elisa seems very quiet today.* *Wow, it's hot in here with these warm fall days and all of these windows.*
"Tell me and I'll make a list. Cara says that she sees leaves. Cara, can you come up and point to some of the different kinds of leaves you see? . . ."	*Taylor and Jason are lying down. Should I say something or ignore it?*
"I want to see everyone sitting up. That way you can all see all of the plants."	*I have to remember that Jaime's mom is picking him up for a doctor's appointment.*
"How about another part that is below the ground and that you can't see unless you pull the plant out of the soil? Ritchie? Yes, roots. I'll put that word up here on our list."	*Maria really seems to be into the lesson today. . . . When we have our student teaching seminar, I want to be sure to share the flannel board cutouts I got from a book to show the parts of a plant and how flowers grow.*

Without a doubt, teachers of young children have a special obligation. Educational experiences during early childhood are particularly significant because they:

• **Take place during a critical and rapid period of development.** It is estimated that al-most 90% of brain growth occurs before age 5 (Poppe & Clothier, 2007). Gabriela Mistral, a poet from Chile, beautifully explains why enriched early childhood experiences are so essential: "Many things we need can wait. The child cannot. Now is the time his bones are being formed, his blood is being made, his mind is being developed. To him we cannot say tomorrow, his name is today" (quoted in Boyer, 1995, p. 12).
• **Define the young child's perceptions of education.** Young children have limited ex-perience and little basis for comparison. Teaching young children is an awesome responsibility because your actions form the child's whole concept of child care, preschool, or school.

Effective teachers are cognizant of ways to engage their students.

- **Affect later experience and self-concept as a learner.** It is a basic developmental principle that early experiences affect later experiences. Early childhood is undeniably an important time for forming children's ideas about whether they are capable as learners and whether they like or dislike school.

Summary

- Pedagogy refers to the teaching of children and the specific types of knowledge required to do this successfully. Reflection refers to closely examining one's own beliefs, values, ideas, experiences, assumptions, behaviors, and biases as an educator. The practice of reflection—of thinking about teaching—is a major mechanism for building professional expertise and acquiring wisdom.

- Teachers' ability to reflect on teaching typically progresses through a process in which their initial concern is about their personal ability to fulfill the teaching role (self) and their next level of concern is with teaching and child guidance strategies (task). After teachers have attained more confidence and a higher level of skill, their concerns typically shift to the long-term consequences of their efforts to support all children's learning (impact).

- When novice teachers discuss vignettes, case studies, and insights about their own teaching with other preservice teachers, master teachers, and teacher educators, this offers a valuable opportunity to learn more about themselves as professionals.

- Fulfilling the role of a reflective practitioner requires teachers to be active (fully engaged in the teaching/learning process), persistent (willing to continue to work on challenging issues), careful (mindful of their responsibilities to others), skeptical (not easily persuaded), rational (making evidence-based decisions), and proactive (taking action before problems spin out of control).

Applying Your Knowledge of Teacher Reflection

In Assessment Activity 1, you will apply your knowledge of reflective practice to consider what you would do in the situation with Kiernan. Then, in Assessment Activity 2, you will use your knowledge of reflective practice to compose a teaching vignette.

Assessment ACTIVITY ① SHOULD KIERNAN BE HELD BACK IN KINDERGARTEN?

It is April and Kiernan's parents have been called into school to discuss his progress during the academic year. Although the parents are aware that their 6-year-old son has been "progressing, but not as fast as the school would like, particularly when it comes to words and numbers," they are stunned by the teacher's comment that he is "right on the line" of being held back for another year in kindergarten. After the meeting, Kiernan's mother e-mails a professor they know about the situation to get "any advice, insights, or help." She explains that Kiernan's brother is 1 year younger and that he would be "devastated" if he "flunked kindergarten" and both boys were in the same grade. The professor replies that "the research on retention is not at all encouraging" and suggests that they read the National Association of School Psychologist's statement posted at www.nasponline.org/information for a summary of the findings. The professor further suggests, "Might there be an alternative, such as an intensive summer program, a tutor throughout the summer, a support program during first grade, or even a year in a private kindergarten?"

When the parents meet with the school personnel a second time, they discuss some of these options. They hear about a first-grade teacher from the school who does individual tutoring in math during the summer and learn that the elementary school offers a 5-week Summer Reading Program. In addition, a nearby university has a program staffed by teachers studying to become reading specialists that provides individual help, and the local library offers a Reading Education Assistance Dogs (R.E.A.D.®) program on Saturday mornings at which the children get to read with a literacy mentor and a trained, registered, and insured dog—something that will really motivate Kiernan because he loves animals. The school personnel were not aware of the issue with Kiernan and his brother being in the same grade if Kiernan were to be held back. At the meeting, the principal says, "we all want the best for Kiernan, and if everyone commits to following through with these plans, I am in support of moving him on to first grade."

REACT	With whom do you identify most strongly in this case, and why?
RESEARCH	What issues are represented by this situation?
REFLECT	How did research and community support influence the course of action? If Kiernan's parents had not had the resources to support him over the summer, how might this have affected the outcome?

Assessment ACTIVITY ②   GETTING STARTED WITH REFLECTION: TEACHING VIGNETTES

Teachers can develop professional expertise and acquire practical wisdom by studying cases, writing vignettes, and maintaining a journal of teaching experiences and discussing these situations with fellow professionals (Epstein, 2008; Mastrilli & Sardo-Brown, 2002; McGlamery & Harrington, 2007; Tegano & Moran, 2005).

Writing a Teaching Vignette

A vignette is a short description of an incident or episode about teaching and learning. A teaching vignette includes the following elements:

- **Setting:** Describe the who, what, when, and where of the situation. Include only those things that are essential to understanding the point of the story.
- **Beginning:** Start with something that will get the reader interested in reading your story. It is not necessary to arrange things chronologically; you can begin with the most interesting part.
- **Account:** Do more than summarize the event. Carefully select some details that made the incident memorable, such as a verbatim comment, nonverbal behavior, etc.
- **Reflection:** Reflect on the adult's role in the situation.
- **Outcome:** Describe the consequences of the incident for the learner.
- **Ending:** Every story needs to build to a satisfying conclusion. Give the reader a sense of completion, as sense that the story has been "wrapped up."

You should choose a situation to write about that has powerful emotions associated with it, because these are the kinds of experiences that exert the greatest influence on behavior. Some ideas to get you started are:

- **Role Models and Mentors:** Write a vignette about an educator who had a positive influence on your decision to become a teacher. What, exactly, did that person do for you? Why did it matter so much?
- **Echoes of Childhood:** Write about a particular incident from your childhood, or that of a family member or a friend. How will you use that experience, good or bad, to be a more compassionate and responsible teacher?
- **Best and Worst Learning Experiences:** Write about a particular situation in which you felt very successful or unsuccessful as a learner or teacher. Why did this occur? What did you do about it?

ONLINE RESOURCES FOR REFLECTIVE TEACHING

Blog on Reflective Practice: Read quotations about reflective practice and join this blog.
 http://earlychildhoodstudies.blogspot.com/.../reflective-practice.html

Reflective Practice Cycle: This website contains dozens of graphic organizers that show how the reflective practice cycle works. Browse through them to find one that is a good match for *your* particular ways of thinking about teaching; just type in "Images for Reflective Practice Cycle" in the Google toolbar.
 www.google.com

Reggio Schools and Reflection: Find out more about the role of teacher reflection in these exemplary programs in Italy. www.artistsatthecentre.ca/docs/NurturingEnthusiasm.pdf

"The Getting of Wisdom: What Critically Reflective Teaching Is and Why It's Important." This chapter from Stephen Brookfield's book defines, describes, and provides a rationale for critically reflective teaching. Numerous examples are provided. See also **The Critical Incident Questionnaire** (www.ntlf.com/html/pi/9601/article3.htm) for five questions to guide reflection.
www.nl.edu/academics/cas/ace/facultypapers/StephenBrookfield_Wisdom.cfm

---

myeducationlab

Go to Topic 12 (Professionalism/Ethics) in the MyEducationLab
(**www.myeducationlab.com**) for your course, where you can:

- Find learning outcomes for professionalism/ethics along with the national standards that connect to these outcomes.
- Complete Assignments and Activities that can help you more deeply understand the chapter content.
- Apply and practice your understanding of the core teaching skills identified in the chapter with the Building Teaching Skills and Dispositions learning units.
- Access video clips of Council of Chief State School Officers (CCSSO) National Teachers of the Year award winners responding to the question, "Why Do I Teach?" in the Teacher Talk section.
- Hear viewpoints of experts in the field in Professional Perspectives.

CHAPTER 2

CHAPTER 2

Exploring History, Philosophy, and Advocacy

 Children are constantly on our minds. They are convenient symbols for our better selves, and we use them to make points, make laws, win elections. . . . For most of our history, until the twentieth century, the social worth of children was understood primarily in terms of economic rather than emotional value. . . . By the age of twelve or so most children were treated as adult producers. . . . Childhood as we have come to know it in modern times did not exist.

Paula S. Fass & Mary Ann Mason, 2000, p. 1

Meet the TEACHERS

MARISSA has been a parent volunteer in a county-sponsored child-care program for the past 3 years while she has earned her Child Development Associate (CDA) credential. Today is the day of her interview for a position as a family child-care provider. As she scans the faces of the interviewers seated at the conference table, she worries that she will have difficulty putting her ideas into words. When she is asked about her approaches to working with toddlers, she replies, "The ideal way to offer care and education to toddlers is in a setting that is natural, warm, and homelike. Although learning in the early years is playful, this is also a time of life when a firm foundation for later learning is built."

BRIAN is a private nursery-school teacher in Miami, Florida. When parents visit the school, Brian knows that families need to make informed decisions about whether or not his program is right for their children. At the meeting, Brian says, "Children need real-world experiences and meaningful learning activities, not mindless paper shuffling. The early childhood years are formative, so children need a balanced approach that includes experiences to support their development physically, socially, intellectually, emotionally, and artistically."

CYBIL teaches in the federally funded Head Start program in Detroit, Michigan. In order to qualify for the program, families have to meet the federal standards for low income (using 2010 criteria, a household income of no more than $14,570 for a family of two or $22,050 for a family of four). When a neighbor comments, "I don't see why my taxes have to pay for things like kids' meals—that's their parents' job," Cybil replies, "Children do not get to choose their financial circumstances. As a democratic society, we have an obligation to give everyone a fair chance at success. Many of the small things that we do in Head Start will prevent bigger problems later on. According to three studies described at the Early Childhood Learning and Knowledge Center, every $1.00 invested in Head Start saves $7.00 later on in services. I just wish that we had government-supported, high-quality preschool programs for all children, as they do in many other countries."

LEARNING Outcomes

In this chapter, you will learn to:

→ Become familiar with national standards and guidelines governing teachers' professional ethics (NAEYC #5, ACEI #3b, INTASC #9)

→ Define history, philosophy, and advocacy

→ Gain a historical perspective on leaders and trends in early childhood education

→ Apply your knowledge of history and philosophy to contemporary child advocacy activities

Compare

What are some commonalities among these three teachers' beliefs?

Contrast

In what ways are the teachers' points of view distinctive?

Connect

How might history—both the history of the field and their personal histories—have shaped their beliefs? In what ways are their views similar to or different from your own?

Now that you have reflected on the three teachers' perspectives and noted the learning outcomes, we preview the knowledge, skills, and dispositions you will need to acquire in order to fulfill your role in understanding history, philosophy, and advocacy.

Defining History, Philosophy, and Advocacy

History is the story of what preceded us. Throughout history, people who were ahead of their time have taken a leadership role and caused others to rethink prevailing assumptions. A knowledge of where we have been as a profession enables us to simultaneously capitalize on the wisdom of those who came before us and to avoid repeating some of the same mistakes. In 2010, *Young Children*, the professional journal of NAEYC, announced that it will feature a new column called "Our Proud Heritage" published every March, July, and November. This decision to continually publish historical perspectives illustrates the enduring influence of the past on the present.

A **teaching philosophy** is a concise statement about the beliefs, values, and attitudes that influence a teacher's thoughts, actions, and interactions. A personal teaching philosophy is not static; rather, it evolves over time as educators gain additional training and experience (Mueller, 2003). For a person who is just entering the field of early childhood education, it might begin with questions about why you want to become a teacher of young children and then become more specific by using guiding questions such as:

- How do you view young children? What is the child's role in his or her education? What do you believe about how young children learn?
- How do you view the role of the teacher? How will your views influence your teaching?
- What kind of environment do you hope to create in your future classroom? How does this relate to your basic beliefs about young children and learning?
- What do you hope young children will become? What do you want them to achieve, accomplish, learn, feel, and so on?
- What kind of feedback will you offer your students as they work? What kind of assessment will you use to be sure that students have met objectives?
- Looking back at the history of early childhood education, who or what approaches have the greatest impression on you, and why? (Chen, 2010)

Figure 2.1 highlights some of the components of a personal teaching philosophy.

Your teaching philosophy is shaped by history on many different levels—the history of the field, your personal history or autobiography, your experiential history as a professional, and contemporary events and issues, as portrayed in Figure 2.2.

DID YOU Know ?

- The history of the early childhood field reflects society's struggle to become more humane, decent, and nurturing (Osborn, 1980; Swick & Brown, 1999).

- Prior to the mid-1800s, the word "child" was synonymous with the word "offspring"—it merely referred to a biological relationship (Postman, 1982). A Swiss educator named Jean Jacques Rousseau is considered to be the architect of a concept of childhood that defined it as an important phase of human development dramatically different from adulthood (May, 2006).

- Teachers' beliefs are a powerful influence on student learning. If teachers fail to understand diversity in their students, teachers can have lowered expectations for some groups or individuals that exert a negative effect on student achievement and alter the way that they conduct their lessons (Burt, Ortlieb, & Cheek Jr., 2009; Nieto & Bode, 2008; Sadker, Sadker, & Zittleman, 2008).

Figure 2.1 Elements of a Personal Teaching Philosophy

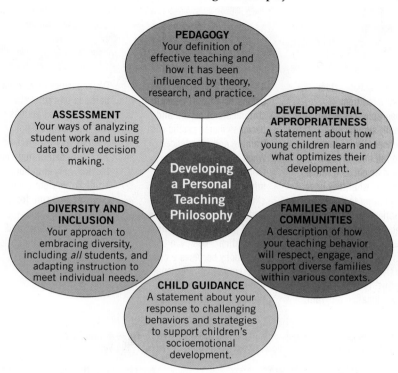

Your teaching philosophy is important for several reasons. First of all, it makes your intentions public and clear to others; second, it encourages you to reflect on guiding principles that will direct your teaching behavior into the future; and third, it prepares you to rehearse answers to some of the most common questions asked during interviews for teaching jobs.

In the field of early childhood education, **child advocacy** refers to taking action on behalf of children, supporting families, and arguing for the cause of high-quality programs. **Child advocates** are willing to do more—to go beyond common decency or expectations in their defense of children, families, and the profession (Robinson & Stark, 2002). Throughout history, individuals have used their intelligence, influence, powers of persuasion, and monetary resources in the service of children and families; in other words, they have become child advocates.

In 1997, the world mourned the loss of two prominent child advocates, Mother Teresa and Princess Diana. Mother Teresa used her unselfish commitment to humanitarian goals and the Catholic nuns who joined her order to help children around the world. In a very different way, England's Princess Diana used her access to power, wealth, and influence to

Pause and Reflect

About Your Personal History

Think about these questions in preparation for a class discussion:

1. Try to recall a particularly memorable experience or family story about you as a young child.
2. Who was your favorite teacher and why?
3. When and how did you decide to become an early childhood educator? Who or what influenced you?
4. If you were forced to choose a career other than teaching, what would it be? Why?

Figure 2.2 The Influence of History on Teachers' Beliefs

History of the Field	Personal History	Professional History	Conflicts between Philosophy and Contemporary Events/Issues
Beliefs about how children learn and develop are drawn from the history of the profession, general knowledge, experience, and reflection. Teachers may be only vaguely aware of the historical origins of some of their beliefs, yet many of their ideas have existed for decades—even centuries.	A teacher's belief system is constructed from autobiography, his or her personally significant experiences. Novice teachers tend to fall back on their own lives as children rather than rely on what they have learned during teacher preparation. Consequently, the belief systems of many entry-level early childhood majors are outdated—even before they begin—and may conflict with those of their teacher education program.	A teaching philosophy often begins as a list of general statements of beliefs and becomes more specific with training and experience. When an individual teacher's philosophy is infused with the code of ethics endorsed by the profession, it evolves into a set of professional habits, or dispositions. Finally, a philosophy becomes a code for exemplary professional conduct that governs a teacher's words and actions.	Discrepancies often exist between teachers' stated philosophy and actions in the classroom. Some reasons why teachers do not act upon their stated beliefs include: concern about students' performance on tests, pressure from administrators and parents, class size, and time or resource limitations.

Sources: Anderson, 1997; Brown & Rose, 1995; Buchanan, Burts, Bidner, White, & Charlesworth, 1998; Bullough & Gitlin, 2001; Cassidy & Lawrence, 2000; Hatch & Freeman, 1988; Kowalski, Pretti-Frontczak, & Johnson, 2001; Pajares, 1992; Vartulli, 1999.

raise money for various charities, particularly her goal of disarming land mines and bombs so that horrible injuries to children worldwide could be averted. To consider the contributions of well-known people such as Mother Teresa and Princess Diana can be rather daunting to a person who is just entering the early childhood field, but the thing to remember is that functioning as an advocate begins with awareness, can be supported by the small contributions of many individuals, and builds over time as educators gain confidence and skills (Liebovich & Adler, 2009). The great humanitarian, Mahatma Gandhi, captured the sequence of advocacy this way: "First they ignore you, then they ridicule you, then they fight you. Then you win" (Quote DB, 2010). The Ask the Expert by Blythe Hinitz on pages 30 and 31 explains the connections among multicultural education, history, and advocacy.

Leaders and Trends in the History of Early Childhood Education

The field of early childhood owes much to the early leaders—philosophers, scholars, educators, theorists, religious leaders, physicians, and scientists—who have made significant contributions to contemporary thinking about young children. In the section that follows, the dominant perspectives on children in different historical eras of Western culture are examined.

ANCIENT TIMES: THE CHILD AS UNLIKELY TO SURVIVE

When we hear about child abandonment, neglect, and exploitation and abuse of young children today, it is common to assume that children are worse off than they were in previous eras, but this is not the case. Actually, the further one goes back in history, the greater the likelihood that young children—particularly young children living in poverty—were mistreated and exploited by adults (DeMause, 1974). By today's standards of treatment, the vast majority of children in previous eras would have been categorized as abused. This is not to say that adults who cared about children did not exist previously, only that prevailing views of children were far from positive in previous eras. In ancient times, the maltreatment of children was commonplace and generally accepted as a prerogative of adults.

Survival was the focal point and few children survived due to inadequate nutrition, disease, and injury; occasional infanticide was socially acceptable because there was no birth control and many children were not wanted (Aries, 1962; Bloch & Price, 1994; Cleverley & Phillips, 1986; Osborn, 1980). In ancient times, infants were left to die from exposure to the elements as a way of controlling family size and overpopulation. Nearly all children with physical defects were left outside to die of exposure in the Greek city-states. Grain allocations were limited to one female child per family (boys were more valued for their potential as warriors) and firstborn girls were often the only ones saved. In ancient Rome, "potting" children was common: babies were abandoned by the roadside in clay pots or in the river in baskets and adorned with ornaments to invite others to take the children in if they wished.

Early childhood educators often participate in supporting families through community service activities.

Throughout history, the experience of the children of privilege was very different from that of children of the poor. Children from wealthy families were far more likely to be educated and valued, primarily in terms of their potential as adults. Two philosophers from ancient Greece, Plato (427–347 B.C.) and his student Aristotle (394–322 B.C.), both believed that a child's education should begin well before age 6 and both discussed individual differences in children's learning and personalities.

By 318 A.D., so many children were being discarded and disposed of that Roman Emperor Constantine made killing a child a crime and Emperor Augustus offered stipends to families who would raise foundlings. It was not until 400 A.D. that the first orphanages were established. Although laws against infanticide existed at that time, they were not enforced consistently and smothering or drowning infants continued because comparatively few parents were attached to their children emotionally. Even in contemporary times, when survival is at issue, children can be perceived as a drain on scant resources. Many countries continue to treat the children of the poor or children with disabilities as unwanted. For example, even today the Roma (Gypsy) children of Europe live in deplorable conditions, their parents often are banned from entering the schools, and few of the children stay in school beyond first grade.

MIDDLE AGES: THE CHILD AS MINIATURE ADULT

During the Dark Ages, poverty and high mortality rates contributed to indifference toward and abandonment of children. Approximately 40% of children did not survive to age 5 (Fass & Mason, 2000). Children were frequently viewed as just another mouth

Blythe Hinitz

Our Multicultural History as a Profession

Q: **How does the study of early childhood education history relate to what is happening in early education classrooms today?**

A: In order to fully understand what is occurring in early childhood programs today, we must be aware of the paths that the field has traveled up to this time. We need to know about our diverse multicultural history so that we can ascertain the roots of our foundational principles. We should become aware of how others have built upon these foundations to create program models, educational methodologies, curriculum, and teaching strategies. We then can draw from this rich array of ideas the theories and practices that best fit us as individuals, and those ideas that will benefit the children, families, and programs with which we work. For example: "Tools of the Mind" is a Vygotskian theoretical paradigm, with many current practical applications, developed in Colorado by Elena Bodrova and Deborah Leong. It has its roots in the 1960s "New Nursery School" of Nimnicht, McAfee, and Meier. The published writings of these five educators include detailed primary source documents, such as anecdotal logs, lesson plans, activity guides, and children's play and learning plans that are useful resources for today's teachers. We can survey the literature, build on the strengths we find, and scrutinize the problems to develop solutions and avoid as many of the pitfalls as possible. Analysis of the programs and models that have had a long life and those that fell into disuse after just a few years, using primary and secondary sources, can provide us with valuable lessons. We can learn why various methods of putting theory into practice worked and why others failed. For example: Elisabeth Irwin, Harriet Johnson, and Lucy Sprague Mitchell, Margaret Naumburg, and Caroline Pratt opened schools for young children in New York City in the early 1920s. Little Red School House/Elisabeth Irwin High School and City and Country School survive as thriving educational endeavors today. Walden School (The Children's School) and the Harriet Johnson Nursery School (Bureau of Educational Experiments Nursery School) did not survive into the new century (beginning in the year 2000) in their original form; however, their legacy continues in the literature about the Progressive Movement, and in the work of Bank Street College of Education today.

Q: **Why have you focused your attention on early childhood education history?**

A: I have always had a deep and abiding love for history and a passion for early childhood education. I discovered, as have a number of my undergraduate research students, that an effective way to combine these two interests is to study the history of early childhood education. Some examples of the topics these early childhood majors chose to study are: A History and Current Analysis of Issues in Early Childhood Education Affecting American Indian Children; Native American Mathematics: Striving to Find Success in Early Childhood Education; and Research on the Crisis in Boys' Education. Their work has been shared at national professional conferences and two students' work appears in current (2010–2011) professional books. Knowledge of our multifaceted history as a profession in the United States, with its struggles and triumphs, helps us to see our connections with the founders of our field, and with the hundreds of thousands of teachers of young children who have led the way for us. When we reach back to the past, we acknowledge the influence of our roots—from around the world and across the street; from the fields of psychology, home economics, sociology, economics, political science, women's studies, civil and human rights, multicultural and linguistic studies, immigration studies, peace education, pediatric medicine, and education.

Q: What are the key issues in history of early childhood education in the United States?

A: From a historical perspective, most of the curriculum and classroom practices in the United States originated from sources outside the country. The kindergarten was begun by Friedrich Froebel in Germany, the nursery school by the McMillan sisters in England, and the "Children's House" by Dr. Maria Montessori in Italy. The original day nurseries and infant schools in the United States were modeled after the French crèche and Robert Owen's Infant School for mill workers in Scotland. In each case, early childhood educators in the United States adapted the model to fit the country and its population. Two-way collaboration between early childhood educators in the United States and those in other countries has existed from the founding of our country and continues to the present day. Elizabeth Peabody mentored early kindergartens in Italy, while Arnold Gesell was influential in English early education. Patty Smith Hill traveled to England and Russia to speak to and meet with professional colleagues. There was a Japanese representative at the 1919 White House Conference on Children, and John Dewey's "activity school" model influenced educators around the world, including those in Soviet Russia. The history of early childhood education in the United States is a multicultural and gendered history. Our educational forbearers were female and male, spoke a variety of languages, practiced a multiplicity of religions, represented a variety of cultural and economic backgrounds, and resided in urban, suburban, and rural settings. In recent years some of the "hidden history" of the early education programs begun by specific groups of people in the United States has come to light. Jean Simpson's doctoral dissertation and NAEYC History Seminar presentations highlight some of the contributions made by Black Americans to our field, and Eugene Garcia's publications review the early education history of the Hispanic American community. James A. and Cherry A. McGee Banks engage us in a dialogue about the history of multicultural education, while David Sadker and Karen Zittleman, Dorothy Hewes, and I address gender issues.

The history of early childhood education carries many relevant messages. Let each of us discover the gems from the past that can provide helpful guidance for today and for the future.

Blythe F. Hinitz is a Professor of Early Childhood and Elementary Education at the College of New Jersey, Ewing, New Jersey.

to feed rather than a privilege or a treasure. Particularly for those living in poverty, pregnancy often was an undesirable state. Most adults lacked the ability to identify and empathize with children or to regard the early years of life as a distinctive phase in human beings' lives (Postman, 1982; Tuchman, 1978). During the Middle Ages, an adult's life expectancy was about 30 years of age and the majority of people were peasants who spent their short lives working for the aristocracy and wealthy landowners. There was no real concept of childhood as we know it; no sense that children needed to be shielded from the harsh realities of life. Children did whatever the adults did, such as witnessing public executions or working in the fields, commencing at about age 7 (Fass & Mason, 2000, p. 283).

If you examine the artwork from this era, you will notice three things. First, children are seldom depicted (other than in a few pieces of sculpture), presumably because they were not considered worthwhile subjects. Second, any child portrayed in art probably was from a wealthy, titled family and was dressed exactly like the adult he or she was expected to become someday. Finally, you will notice that typical childish facial features (e.g., turned-up nose), body configuration (e.g., large head in proportion to the body), and interests (e.g., play) are rarely represented. Mainly, children were valued for their potential as adults and were therefore portrayed as miniature adults. During the Middle Ages, a distinction was made between willful disposal of children and other causes of death, so parents who killed a child claimed to have "overlayed" the child (accidentally smothered it). Even if a parent was convicted of willfully disposing of a child, the punishment for infanticide was just a year of penance.

During this time, the concept of beginning moral and religious training early was promoted by Martin Luther (1483–1546), a religious leader from Germany. Luther believed that the family was the most important educational institution and advocated teaching all children to read so that they could access the scriptures for themselves rather than relying on the clergy to interpret (as was the case for Catholics whose religious material was written in Latin).

Children—particularly those living in poverty—continued to be exploited throughout the Middle Ages. In 1535, during the Tudor King Henry VIII's reign in England, a law was enacted to apprentice children so that they could begin working, usually beginning at age 6 or 7. Beginning in 1618 and for many years thereafter, children as young as 10 years of age were shipped from London to work as indentured servants in colonial America. A child's natural playfulness and toddlers' willfulness were seen as the work of the devil, which had to be beaten out of them. During the 1600s, children in America were expected to obey their parents without question and to address them as "honored sir" or "esteemed parent." In colonial America, parents were advised to dress up as ghosts and enter a disobedient child's room at night to frighten the child into obedience (Osborn, 1980). In 1619, the first African children landed in America and became slaves (Fass & Mason, 2000, p. 67).

THE RENAISSANCE AND VICTORIAN ERA: CONFLICTING VIEWS OF THE CHILD

Although high infant mortality continued, moral and religious agendas for children began to expand. In 1658, John Amos Comenius (1592–1671), an educator and bishop from what is now the Czech Republic, wrote the first known picture book, *Orbis Pictus* (*World of Pictures*). The work of John Locke (1632–1714)—a British doctor, philosopher, and political theorist—popularized three concepts: that the best way of teaching was by example, that education had a profound influence on the promise of education to improve children's lives, and that harsh, physical discipline would not shape character.

Children were valued for their potential as laborers; industrialization led to use of children as workers in factories, farms, mills, and mines. By the 1700s, opiates, starvation, dunking babies in cold water, and leaving them on doorsteps or at the hospital were ways to dispose of unwanted children. Throughout history, children have been exploited for their potential as workers in factories and on farms. When the War for Independence began in 1776, about one in five American children were slaves. The first factory to employ children opened in England in 1719, and it was not until the Factory Act was passed in 1833 that children under age 9 were prohibited from working in mines. Because it was the father who was the breadwinner, children became orphans when their fathers died or abandoned them. It was customary for children from poor families to be "trained for service," meaning that they were taught to become servants.

At about the same time that children were being forced to work long and hard, two influential radicals and early leaders in early childhood education emerged: a French writer named Jean-Jacques Rousseau (1712–1788) and a Swiss educator named Johann Heinrich Pestalozzi (1746–1827). Rousseau wrote a novel about a fictitious child named *Emile* (1760) that addressed the rights of the child and ultimately affected Western views of childhood (Fass & Mason, 2000). Pestalozzi advocated that the child learn at "the school of the mother's knee" until 6 years of age in his work of fiction, *How Gertrude Teaches Her Children*. Unlike most of his contemporaries, Pestalozzi argued that play was the child's way of learning, that firsthand experiences and children's interests were the way to teach, and that the young were more flexible in their thinking, making the early years the opportune time to shape character.

One of Pestalozzi's former students, Friedrich Froebel (1782–1852) transformed the philosophy into a program. The dream of Froebel's kindergarten—literally, a garden of children—was to fill the child's life with playful "occupations" that would rescue children, address social ills, reduce crime, and, ultimately, produce good citizens (May, 2006). In the 1880s, the kindergartens were equipped with materials (e.g., wooden balls, cylinders, cubes, and other shapes) that were used for instruction (Lascarides & Hinitz, 2000).

In Scotland, a religious leader named Robert Owen (1771–1858) applied Rousseau's and Froebel's ideas to a school for working-class children. In 1816, Owen campaigned against child labor and created the first factory day nursery for children 18 months to 10 years so that children could be cared for and supervised while their parents worked in his mill. Owen's program emphasized dance, song, and outdoor play. Owen also rejected harsh punishment and fear as ways to control children's behavior and endorsed more humane treatment of children.

In Prussia (now Germany), Froebel's relaxed attitude toward religion was branded as a threat to order and faith; many of Froebel's followers left Germany in search of greater political freedom and took the kindergarten concept to their respective countries. In the United States, the kindergarten movement was led by "dauntless women" who went against the prevailing opinions of their day (Snyder, 1972; Wortham, 1992; Wyman, 1995). An overview of the kindergarten movement from the 1800s up to the current day is shown in Figure 2.3.

In the late 1800s, children were not considered to be worthy of serious study. One of the first published attempts at child study was written by physiologist William Preyer in 1881. His book *The Mind of the Child* was a 3-year diary about his son's behavior, which he studied from the normative perspective of when and in what order the child would display certain adult characteristics (Cleverley & Phillips, 1986). His work inspired the evolutionist Charles Darwin and novelist Louis May Alcott to produce baby biographies of their own infants; only the children of famous individuals were considered to be of interest. A survey of major research journals found only 35 empirical studies of children in the 9-year period from 1890 to 1899 (Cleverley & Phillips, 1986).

Horace Mann (1796–1859), a teacher, lawyer, senator, and secretary of the Massachusetts Board of Education, promoted two important ideas: (1) that education should be free, universal, and available to all irrespective of economic status and (2) that religious training and school should be distinct (separation of church and state). In contrast to many educators of his day, Mann advocated a bond of mutual trust, respect, and rapport between teachers and children. To address the issue of staffing for the public schools, he advocated the preparation of female teachers to work with younger students—an idea unheard of in his day. He also instituted the normal schools—short, intensive training programs for educators that gave them supervised experiences working with children. Many of the modern-day universities that prepare teachers today began as normal schools, evolved into teachers' colleges, and expanded into universities.

Throughout the mid- to late-1800s, attitudes toward children gradually began to shift. Rather than being regarded as basically evil (due to original sin), children—at least those

Figure 2.3 Kindergarten Timeline

1837

- Friedrich Froebel established the first kindergarten for 4- to 6-year-olds. Children were viewed as innately good, innocent, and filled with potential for creative expression. With the gentle guidance of a teacher, the very young child's mental, physical, and social capabilities could be cultivated and unfold naturally.

1856

- After being trained by Froebel, Margaret Meyer Schurz opened the first kindergarten in the United States in Wisconsin; German was the primary language for instruction.

1860

- The first kindergarten in which the language of instruction was English opened in Boston and the kindergarten program was gradually adapted to the local context.

1870s

- Kindergartens were regarded as a way to support the children of immigrants and other children living in poverty, primarily in urban areas. Many of the kindergartens were privately funded by charitable organizations. The first public school, half-day kindergarten in the United States was instituted in St. Louis, Missouri.

Late-1800s

- Educator and philosopher John Dewey operated a kindergarten in his laboratory school from 1896 to 1903. He replaced Froebel's free play with practical tasks that would prepare children for the adult world, such as washing clothes, weaving rugs, and preparing food.

Early 1900s

- Kindergartens became part of the public school system as a large influx of immigrants occurred during and after World War I. These kindergartens emphasized learning the English language and inculcating American culture in the newcomers. In Italy, Maria Montessori's work with children from the slums of Rome gained international attention as a practical life skills curriculum for the very young.

Mid-1900s

- Half-day kindergartens were the most common due in part to limited funds and an inadequate supply of kindergarten teachers. National concerns about global competitiveness and the "cold war" against Communism pushed for academic skills to be taught earlier. The concept of school "readiness" gained popularity.

1960s and 1970s

- Significant expansion of state- and community-funded kindergartens occurred. Kindergartens became more oriented toward preparation for first grade, academic skills, direct instruction, and coverage of the major subject areas. Tests were used not only to determine eligibility for kindergarten placement but also to assess learning attained during the kindergarten year.

1990s

- In recognition of the importance of the early years for learning as well as the growing number of women in the workforce, more full-day kindergarten programs were established. With federal funding support, some public schools began to institute prekindergarten programs for 4-year-olds and even 3-year-olds, mainly for children "at risk."

Early 2000s

- Kindergarten generally is defined as a 1-year, formal program offered in a school or school-like setting during the year prior to first grade. In the push for accountability and cost-effectiveness, the "value-added" benefit of full-day kindergarten is investigated and results are mixed. Full-day compared to half-day appears to offer some academic benefits; however, they tend to disappear by third grade, according to one meta-analysis of 40 published studies (Cooper, Allen, Patall & Dent, 2010).

Sources: Beaty, 1995; Brosterman, 1997; Cooper, Allen, Patall, & Dent, 2010; Shapiro, 1983; Weber, 1984.

of the privileged classes—were seen as basically good and innocent. High infant mortality rates persisted nevertheless. In 1880, 288 of every 1,000 live-born infants in New York City died. As late as 1912, more than 1 in 10 New York children died during infancy (Fass & Mason, 2000, p. 427). Infants and young children were susceptible to early diseases that are now controlled by vaccination, immunization, or drug therapies—diphtheria, scarlet fever, whooping cough, tuberculosis, measles, cholera, and many others. The fates of both women and children were largely determined by the father because both were treated by law as his "chattel," or property.

In 1875, the New York Society for the Prevention of Cruelty to Children (NYSPCC) was formed. One of its first challenges was to enact legislation against the "padrone" system. In this international human trafficking scheme, recruiters (padrones) would hire the children of the poorest peasants in Italy with the promise of giving them a better life, learning a trade, and returning home. None of these promises was fulfilled, however. The money was not paid, the children were put to work on the streets as musicians, salespeople, beggars, or thieves; and the children never returned to Italy. Most of them lived on the streets or in the most deplorable conditions, a situation that prompted *The New York Times* to publish a series of articles about the "little Italian slaves" (Jalongo, 2009). Through the efforts of the NYSPCC, legislation was enacted to prohibit this practice. To see photographs from this era and learn more about the history of this group, visit The NYSPCC Story at www.nyspcc.org/nyspcc/history/the_story/.

In the past, ideas about child sexual abuse were very different. There were no child pornography laws until 1887 and children were not prohibited from living in houses of prostitution until 1889. Up until the 1860s in the United States, it was legal for a girl of 10 years of age to be married and give her "consent"—a practice that continues in many countries throughout the world today.

In the past, young children often were expected to work and contribute to the family's income.

THE 20TH CENTURY: THE CHILD AS A PSYCHOLOGICAL BEING

In the early 1900s, Italian Maria Montessori (1870–1952) pursued training as a medical doctor. At that time it was considered improper for a woman to study human anatomy, so she was not permitted to practice medicine and was given a post working with unsupervised, neglected children living in the slums of Rome. Montessori believed that children needed order and structure and should be taught practical, sensory, and formal skills, such as reading, writing, mathematics, and motor coordination. Her school, the Casa dei Bambini ("Children's House"), opened in 1908 and attracted attention because it taught academic skills, manners, and cleanliness to children younger than age 5; many of these children had special needs. Montessori methods advocated a carefully prepared environment, the teacher as directress, and offered highly detailed instructions on how to teach. Montessori believed that the major outcome of a quality education was the ability to focus and concentrate. The program was unique in that it was child centered rather than group centered and children were encouraged to expand on their interests. Over 100 years later, Montessori programs continue to flourish.

Pause and Reflect

About Early Leaders and Prevailing Views of Childhood

- What echoes of the past do you see in your ideas about teaching?
- Which of these notable individuals whose commitment to the very young has made an indelible impression on your field made the greatest impression on you? Why?
- Did you encounter any ideas that contradicted your beliefs or surprised you?

During the 1800s through the mid-1900s in America, children were valued primarily in economic terms because they contributed to the family income through their work on farms, in factories, in mines, and at various trades. The idea that adults need to identify with children, nurture their development, and try to understand them as psychological beings is mainly a 20th-century phenomenon (Fass & Mason, 2000; May, 2006). In 1911, Arnold Gesell established the Child Development Clinic at Yale University, where he studied infants and identified general and predictable markers of development. Based on these studies, Gesell concluded that development was controlled by an inner timetable of growth, or maturation. Gessell's work legitimized the study of children as a scholarly endeavor.

In 1913, Carolyn Pratt founded the City and Country School in New York (now the Bank Street School). Her curriculum included field trips and child-run enterprises, such as a school store and post office. She is credited with designing what are called unit blocks because they are standard sizes and teach basic fractions; she also added wooden figures to the blocks to encourage social play (Hewett, 2001).

In 1922, Abigail Adams Eliot founded the Ruggles Street Nursery School in Boston. Her program was based on the work of the McMillan sisters in England. An early effort to involve parents meaningfully in programs for young children was the Parent Cooperative Nursery (a program in which parents volunteered to work in the classroom), which was established by wives of faculty members at the University of Chicago in 1915.

In 1926, Jean Piaget, who had completed advanced study in biology, pursued a degree in epistemology (the study of knowledge). As a graduate student, Piaget administered intelligence tests to young children and became fascinated by the children's *incorrect* answers on the test and the reasoning behind their responses. Piaget studied his own children's intellectual development intensively and published *Language and Thought of the Child*, in which he set forth a proposal that was surprising for his day. Unlike his contemporaries, he did not argue that nature (heredity) was the most important influence on children's development, nor did he argue that nurture (environment) was the most important influence. Rather, he described a dynamic interaction between the child's heredity and environment and proposed a theory of cognitive (knowledge) development that included stages of reasoning through which children progress. Piaget also emphasized a concept called constructivism, or the belief that children actively build their own understandings about the world rather than merely soaking up information and experiences. This too was a departure from the thinking of the day.

John Dewey established the Dewey Laboratory School at the University of Chicago as a way of studying curriculum (Tanner, 1997). Considered to be the father of Progressive Education, Dewey's primary concern was the preparation of citizens for a democratic society, as described in his major work *Democracy and Education* (1916). He believed that curriculum should be child centered and include topics of study that would enable children to understand social purposes and community life. Topics of study began with the family and led out to the community rather than emanating from the teachers. Dewey's emphasis on active learning in which children used open-ended materials to understand problems, questions, relationships, and connections resulted in the Progressive Education Movement.

In contrast to Dewey's child-centered philosophy, the field of psychology was conducting studies that used patterns of reward and punishment to shape human behavior. Behaviorists, such as John B. Watson (1928), wrote about the dangers of "too much mother love" and advised parents to avoid "spoiling" their babies by being responsive to their cries.

Although the Child Study Movement had begun, during 1950 to 1958, only 362 studies of children were published (Cleverley & Phillips, 1986). Jean Piaget (1954) published his theories on children's cognitive development in a highly influential work, *The*

Construction of Reality in the Child, that stimulated more research designed to test his theories. Psychology also took a popular-press turn when Dr. Benjamin Spock's manual on baby and child care was first published in 1945 and became a best seller.

An important trend in the field during this time was the establishment of professional organizations to function as support systems for educators acting upon their commitment to nurture the young. Patty Smith Hill (1868–1946), a professor at Teachers College, Columbia University, was the founder of two major professional organizations that play a vital role in professional development today. She worked with the International Kindergarten Union, now the Association for Childhood Education International (ACEI), and in 1929, she called a meeting of the National Association for Nursery Education, which changed its name to the National Association for the Education of Young Children in 1964 and includes over 100,000 members today.

In terms of children's health care, 57,626 cases of polio were reported in 1952. Most of those afflicted were children. Parents lived in constant fear that their child would contract this devastating disease and be crippled for life. Medical researcher Dr. Jonas Salk became a national hero when he invented the polio vaccine in 1952.

In 1957 two events occurred that would dramatically change American education: (1) Russia launched the *Sputnik* satellite, beginning both a space and education race in the United States, and (2) the Supreme Court ended legal segregation in schools through its unanimous decision in the *Brown vs. Board of Education of Topeka* case. In the 1950s, there was a tacit assumption that everyone subscribed to the same basic values in the United States (Wiles & Bondi, 2007). Commencing in the mid-1960s, groups that were marginalized by the male-dominated, White, Anglo-Saxon, Protestant power group— females, Blacks, Hispanics, emigrants, gays and lesbians, persons with disabilities, those opposed to the war in Vietnam, and others—used their political power to make changes. A period of legislation to protect human rights began with the Civil Rights Act of 1964; in 1972, Title IX outlawed discrimination on the basis of gender, and in 1975, Public Law 94-142 guaranteed the rights of children with handicaps to free and appropriate educational experiences in the public schools. In the 1960s the media (e.g., Jerry Lewis telethons) and direct mail campaigns (e.g., Easter Seals) raised public awaremess of children with disabilities. Figure 2.4 is a summary of key events that have addressed poverty, parenting, and child protection policies in the United States, from the 1800s up to and including the present day.

THE LATE 1900S AND EARLY 2000S: THE CHILD AS AN ENDURING EMOTIONAL TIE

The perception of children shifted from being valued for their work to being valued as the source of emotional bonds. Experts in child development, such as Jerome Kagan, helped to usher in this era of emotional investment in children by emphasizing the effects of human interaction on children's development. As women entered the workforce in much larger numbers to seek fulfillment and to improve the standard of living for their families, Harvard pediatrician T. Berry Brazelton reassured mothers that it was possible to have both a career and a family; he also endorsed more father/male involvement in raising children. As large numbers of women entered the workforce during this era of women's liberation and the feminist movement, the demand for various child care and education options increased. Political efforts to enact a federally funded, national, universally available childcare system failed, and in-home care, licensed babysitters, family child-care homes, faith-affiliated early childhood programs, commercial child-care franchises, and a variety of other programs emerged to meet the growing demand for out-of-home care.

Figure 2.4 Poverty, Parent Education, and Child Protection in the United States

Early 1800s

- Throughout the 19th century, between 20% and 30% of children became orphans before age 15 (O'Connor, 2001). On average, four infants a day were abandoned at the Bellevue Foundling Hospital in New York City; a white-curtained bassinet in the entryway allowed mothers to leave their infants to be raised by the nuns (O'Connor, 2001). In 1825, the state of New York had just four orphan asylums (Holt, 1992).

Mid-1800s

- In 1852, over 175,000 immigrants arrived in America; by 1854, over 250,000 arrived. In 1853, a minister named Charles Loring Brace founded the Children's Aid Society (CAS) to offer temporary shelter and training opportunities for city children. In 1854, over 30,000 children were abandoned on doorsteps, in churches, and at hospitals in New York City. As a result of the Civil War, many families lost their sole sources of income and by 1866, the state of New York had 60 orphanages.

1874

- Although laws existed to protect children, they were rarely enforced. Mary Ellen Wilson, a child who suffered horrible physical abuse, set the precedent of removing a child from the custodial parents. In 1866, Henry Bergh, the founder of the American Society for the Prevention of Cruelty to Animals (ASPCA), collaborated with missionary/social worker Etta Wheeler to successfully prosecute the first case of child abuse. The New York Society for the Prevention of Cruelty to Children was founded in 1874 and investigated 200 cases of child abuse in its first year; the group also lobbied for child labor laws.

Late 1800s

- Reporter/author/photographer Jacob A. Riis raised public awareness of the deplorable conditions under which many urban children lived. Children without financial support often were sent to almshouses where they became indentured servants. Between 1854 and 1929, the Children's Aid Society placed more than 100,000 city children in new homes in rural America through the "orphan trains." Farming families—mainly in the Midwest and western states—took the children in as workers and, in some instances, into their family rather than institutionalizing them or leaving them to live on the streets of New York.

Early 1900s

- In 1909, the federal government formed the Children's Bureau to protect children. In 1911, the state of Illinois approved the first state assistance program—mothers' aid—which usually was given to women who had been widowed.

- In 1911, rural Kentucky educator Cora Wilson Stewart initiated the adult literacy movement when more than 1,200 adults enrolled in evening classes to learn to read and write. Her work inspired a wide array of adult literacy programs for those who had been denied educational opportunities, including African Americans and Native Americans.

- Social reformers and philanthropic organizations began the "free kindergarten movement." Teachers spent half of the day teaching and the rest of the day doing home visits and parent education programs. In 1912, day nurseries were established so that working mothers living in poverty had child care. Mothers' clubs and medical information were provided. Kindergartens (usually half day) were absorbed into the public school systems but were not mandatory.

- By 1919, funds for dependent children in their own homes had been provided by 39 states and the territories of Alaska and Hawaii.

Figure 2.4 continued

Mid-1900s

- After the Great Depression, federally funded nursery schools become part of the Works Progress Administration (WPA); these schools were mainly for children whose parent(s) were on relief. The WPA programs offered nutritious meals and medical care at 1,900 schools for nearly 75,000 children.

- In 1930, the Children's Charter to protect the rights of children was passed. Jane Addams earned the Nobel Peace Prize in 1931 for her work at Chicago's Hull House to support children living in poverty.

- In 1943 the Lanham Act established child care centers throughout the United States so that women could work in various industries that supported the war effort during World War II.

1965

- As part of the "war on poverty," the federal government drew on preschool intervention research, public health data, and the field of psychology to improve the development of "disadvantaged" young children. Project Head Start, begun in 1965, addressed the child's cognitive, social, and physical growth. It provided not only an educational program but also health care and nutritious meals. Parents were encouraged to participate, volunteer in the classroom, help to govern the program, and become active in the community.

Late 1900s–Early 2000s

- The Women, Infants, and Children (WIC) program was established in 1969 to provide "supplemental foods, health care referrals, and nutrition education for low-income pregnant, breastfeeding, and non-breastfeeding postpartum women, and to infants and children up to age five who are found to be at nutritional risk."

- The issue of children's rights was internationalized by the United Nations' Convention on the Rights on the Child (1989). The document was signed by all Western powers except the United States.

- Federal funding for family literacy programs promoted the idea of improving literacy levels for all family members as a way to improve the quality of children's lives.

Sources: Addams, 1910; DeMause, 1974; Fass & Mason, 2000; Free the Slaves and Human Rights Center, 2004; Holt, 1992; Hunter, 1905; Jalongo, 2005, 2006, 2008, 2010; Lascarides & Hinitz, 2000; O'Connor, 2001; Osborn, 1980; Patrick & Trickel, 1997; Riis, 2000; Rose, 2009.

21ST CENTURY: THE STANDARDS MOVEMENT

A Nation at Risk, a report published in 1983, criticized the quality of the U.S. educational system and eroded trust in public education. The reaction was an emphasis on nationwide achievement testing and comparisons of students in the United States with other children in industrialized nations. Political leaders called for "back to basics" and holding educators accountable for children's performance on tests. In 1989, President George H. Bush met with the 30 state governors to establish a list of six learning goals for all children; the goal that affected early childhood education most directly was, "By the year 2000, all children in America will start school ready to learn." Since the 1990s, governments have been concerned about global competitiveness and have sought to measure the investment in early childhood in relation to their overall economic goals (May, 2006). By 1998, the District of Columbia and 48 states had instituted mandatory testing for schoolchildren, and many of those states had adopted a standards-based curriculum. By 2000, more than 20 states had developed progression testing around

Ask the EXPERT

J. Amos Hatch

Traditions and History of Our Field

Q: Why should I care about the traditions and history of early childhood education?

A: Every profession has a knowledge base on which its members draw when they make decisions about their practice. If early childhood education is truly a profession, then those who practice it must make decisions based on the best information available. This includes the latest research findings on how young children learn and develop, how instructional experiences ought to be organized, and how teachers should teach; but the traditions and history of early childhood education are also part of the professional knowledge base in our field. What makes professionals different from laypersons is the special expertise they bring to the decisions they make about other people's lives. Individuals who make decisions that have a direct impact on the lives of young children should be drawing on a professional knowledge base that includes the rich traditions and history of early childhood education. One reason to care is that we want to be perceived by others as professionals; another, more important, reason is we want to provide the best experience possible for the young children we teach.

Q: What are ways the field's traditions and history might limit early childhood education today?

A: Using the same logic we want to make professional decisions based on the best information at hand. If new information becomes available that challenges what we previously believed to be best practices, we have an obligation to reconsider what we have been doing in light of that new information. As in any professional field, this means that the knowledge base that guides our practice is constantly changing. Think about the field of medicine. Advances in the knowledge base in medicine force medical professionals to constantly reevaluate how they treat patients, even when the new information might contradict what had been previously considered best practice. Advances in our knowledge base may not seem as dramatic as new treatments for disease; but we have the same obligation to constantly reconsider what we do when we are confronted with new knowledge, even when it challenges the field's traditions and history. When we stop doing that, we stop growing as a profession.

Amos Hatch is a Professor of Theory and Practice in Teacher Education at the University of Tennessee.

grades 4, 8, and 10 and an assessment of competency to graduate from high school. Today, the push for earlier and higher academic achievement is causing "Many early childhood educators to feel that they must implement programs that conflict with their understanding of best practice" (Meyer, 2005, p. 28).

Although conditions for children generally have improved across history there is still much work to be done. Fortunately, enlightened views on children's early years have existed alongside the more repressive views throughout history, and these ideas form the foundation for your role as a contemporary early childhood educator. To illustrate these effects in a very concrete way, consider the instructional materials that commonly are found in early childhood settings. Children have been playing with blocks, for example, for centuries (Anderson, 2010). Many of the learning materials that we take for granted today originated centuries ago, as depicted in Figure 2.5.

Figure 2.5 Where Did It Come From?

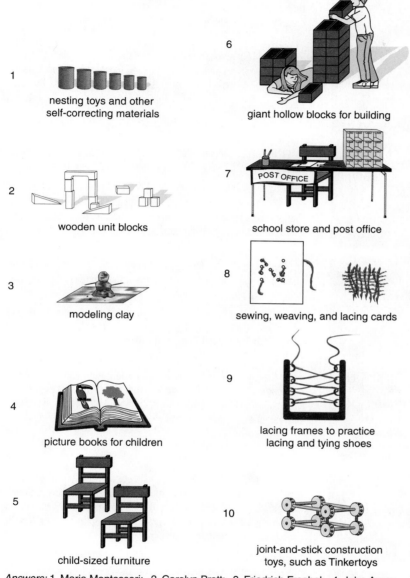

1 — nesting toys and other self-correcting materials

2 — wooden unit blocks

3 — modeling clay

4 — picture books for children

5 — child-sized furniture

6 — giant hollow blocks for building

7 — school store and post office

8 — sewing, weaving, and lacing cards

9 — lacing frames to practice lacing and tying shoes

10 — joint-and-stick construction toys, such as Tinkertoys

Answers: 1. Maria Montessori; 2. Carolyn Pratt; 3. Friedrich Froebel; 4. John Amos Comenius; 5. Maria Montessori; 6. Patty Smith Hill; 7. Carolyn Pratt; 8. Friedrich Froebel; 9. Maria Montessori; 10. Friedrich Froebel (who used toothpicks and peas).

Understanding where society has been in its views of children, provisions for their needs, and advocacy efforts broadens and deepens your understanding of history, philosophy, and advocacy. Many of the practices that originated long ago are in keeping with the latest research on the brain and are consistent with current understandings from the field of neuroscience, as described in Figure 2.6.

In the Ask the Expert feature on page 40, Amos Hatch explains how studying history can contribute to contemporary early childhood education.

Figure 2.6 Links between Neuroscience and the Traditions of Early Childhood

1. Attentional Mind-set

Children need to focus. If the learner's mind wanders, the changes required by learning will diminish.

- In the mid-1800s, Froebel's kindergarten presented children with learning materials and tasks designed to capture their interest.
- In the late 1800s, Maria Montessori promoted a "prepared environment" that coached children in basic life skills tasks; she contended that the last outgrowth of a great education is the ability to concentrate.

2. Low to Moderate Stress

In order to maximize learning, the child needs to have choices and to exercise some control over the learning conditions.

- In the mid 1800s, Johann Pestalozzi challenged Calvinism (the idea that children were tainted by original sin and required harsh punishment); he advocated instead "the school of the mother's knee" in *How Gertrude Teaches Her Children*.
- Beginning in the 1970s, David Welkart advocated child-directed, child-initiated activity.

3. Coherent, Meaningful Tasks

Learners will invest effort when they see value in what they are asked to learn and a logical progression for achieving learning goals.

- In 1918, William Killpatrick originated the project approach that involved children in in-depth study; John Dewey implemented this strategy in his laboratory school.
- In post–World War II, the schools of Reggio Emilia, Italy, emphasized a curriculum that is based on projects identified by the children.
- The project approach was popularized in the United States during the late 1900s and beyond by Lilian Katz and Sylvia Chard.

4. Massed Practice

Several times a day for several days a week usually is necessary to make enduring changes in thinking.

- In the one-room schoolhouses that dominated rural America during the 1800s, there were few materials, so recitation/repetition was the major instructional approach to provide practice.
- In contemporary early childhood in the United States, entire programs are based on the importance of mass practice prior to the start of formal schooling (e.g., Head Start, Even Start, and Follow Through).

5. Learner-controlled Feedback

Mistakes are part of learning. If the corrective feedback is distressing, success drops. The best situation is for learners to adjust the level and type of feedback.

- From the gifts of Frederich Froebel's kindergarten and Maria Montessori's self-correcting materials to the computer software that provides feedback on children's choices, early childhood education has emphasized the provision of appropriate, learner-controlled feedback.

6. Repetition of Task

Connections in the brain occur when there is new learning, but these connections have to be reinforced or they deteriorate, such as when a student forgets much of the material on a test shortly afterwards.

- Routines and repetition are a mainstay of early childhood education. Whether it is learning a self-help skills such as tying shoes, a physical skill such as swinging on a swing, a social skill such as sharing toys, or a cognitive skill such as reading a big book in unison, repetition and routines are used to bolster the confidence and learning of the very young.

7. Overnight Rest Between Learning Sessions

"Sleeping on it" is not just an expression; it is true that when the brain is at rest, "learning is consolidated, organized, and distributed to various areas of the brain for long-term storage" (Jensen, 2005, p. 73).

- Early childhood educators have a long history of endorsing adequate rest, providing for it on site, and alternating active and quiet times throughout the day.

Sources: Jalongo, 2008; Jensen, 2005, 2008.

COLLABORATING WITH
Families

Ethical Issues with Families

One of the key ethical issues for educators is confidentiality. Many times, inexperienced teachers are not clear on what types of information are protected by confidentiality. The answer is that anything that would divulge information about the child's progress in school or interactions at school is covered by the ethic of confidentiality. One way to think about it is, how would you feel if this were your child and these issues, behaviors, or work were being discussed with others? Read the following scenario concerning confidentiality issues, and then reflect on the questions that follow.

Scenario

A kindergarten student teacher was acquainted with Byron's maternal grandmother, who often picked the child up after school. When the grandmother inquired about the child's progress, the student teacher said, "he's doing very well but he might need more practice with his numbers and letters." The next morning, the student teacher was surprised to be called to a meeting with her mentor teacher and the principal. Byron's mother was furious that assessment information had been shared with the grandparent and had made an angry telephone call to the principal. The student teacher felt blindsided by this criticism; it had seemed like a very innocent remark. Based on the fact that the grandmother was a frequent visitor to the school, it was obvious that she was very involved in Byron's life. Nevertheless, the principal reminded her that *only* parents and legal guardians are permitted to get progress reports on the child's school work and, as a student teacher, she should not have attempted to answer that question herself; rather, she should have referred the grandmother and her question to the regular classroom teacher.

- Did this situation surprise you? Why or why not?
- What might have prevented this incident from happening?
- What obligation do student teachers have to be familiar with the policies of the schools where they work?
- How will thinking about this scenario affect your teaching behavior?

Summary

- The history of early childhood education includes many examples of adults who went against prevailing opinions about the meaning of childhood, generally accepted practices, and customary ways of educating or disciplining young children. A personal teaching philosophy is a concise statement about a teacher's beliefs, values, attitudes, and practices. Your philosophy is affected by your personal history (autobiography), professional history (training and teaching experience), and the history of the field.

- Although most people assume that the condition of children is far worse today than it was in the past,

generally speaking, the circumstances under which children lived are worse the further one goes back in history. Yet throughout history, there have been adults who have advocated for children's basic needs and recommended educational programs for them, even when these adults were at odds with their contemporaries.

- At various times, different concepts of childhood have predominated, such as physical survival, religious training and character development, social and emotional growth, and intellectual growth (Osborn, 1980). The field of early childhood education represents a rich tradition of care, concern, and education for the very young. Teachers, researchers, and theorists in the field and in related fields have paved the way for contemporary ideas.

■ Adults who take a stand to protect young children, defend families, and argue for high-quality programs are referred to as child advocates, and their behavior is termed child advocacy.

Applying Your Knowledge of History, Philosophy, and Advocacy

In Assessment Activity 1, you apply your historical knowledge of child advocacy to consider one teacher's response to suspected child neglect/abuse. Then, in Assessment Activity 2, you will begin thinking about your role as an advocate for young children.

Assessment ACTIVITY 1   REPORTING SUSPECTED CHILD ABUSE

Maureen works in a federally subsidized public school prekindergarten program in a region that has never recovered economically from the exit of the steel and coal industry. She is very concerned about one of her students, 4-year-old Gretchen. The most striking thing about Gretchen is that she does not smile or play; she appears to be worried and somber.

Maureen requests a meeting with principal and the school psychologist and says, "A disturbing incident occurred when Gretchen's mother and sister dropped her off at school. Her sister was dressed from head to toe in a fancy pink ski outfit and her blonde hair had been set in curlers; Gretchen is the complete opposite of this. She wears worn out t-shirts that don't fit and her hair is badly matted. I know that Gretchen is the child from a previous marriage and that her sister is the product of this new relationship. My heart ached to see one daughter so obviously favored over the other. Recently, Gretchen has become more and more withdrawn. She barely speaks and it's almost as if she were sleepwalking; there is no joy or playfulness that you typically see in a 4-year-old." The psychologist replies, "You were right to report this and I share your concerns." The building principal says, "We have mandatory reporting guidelines in this state for suspected child abuse and will follow them to the letter. I will call in the parents to talk with them and begin working with Child and Family Services. We will do what we can to help, but realize that these situations are complicated and what is decided may not mesh with what we had hoped for."

Although child neglect/abuse is suspected, the process takes months and it is difficult to make a case. The social worker says, "It is common for a first reaction to be 'remove the child from the family,' but that only puts the child into the foster care system, which isn't necessarily the best solution. We are trying to work *with* the family to make positive changes for everyone involved."

REACT	With whom do you identify most strongly in this case, and why?
RESEARCH	Investigate the laws concerning teachers' obligation to report suspected child abuse.
REFLECT	What guidance does NAEYC Code of Professional Ethics offer in situations such as this that depend on the teacher to be an advocate for the child?

Assessment ACTIVITY ② GETTING STARTED WITH ADVOCACY

Within your group, work through this plan for getting started with child advocacy that is based on the recommendations of Goffin and Lombardi (1988) and Meyer (2005).

1. **Arrive at a Definition of Advocacy.** Learn from the history that you studied in this chapter. Think about what you can do, both subtle and bold, that would put children and families first. Check out the Advocacy Toolkit of NAEYC at www.naeyc.org/files/naeyc/file/policy/toolkit.pdf.

2. **Observe and Begin Participating in Advocacy.** Look for evidence of a professional commitment in others. Get involved in group activities such as the NAEYC Stand for Children, fundraisers, letter-writing campaigns, and so forth. Explore advocacy groups and their agendas, such as the World Schooling Consortium, FairTest, and The Rouge Forum.

3. **Reflect, Share, and Discuss.** Identify a time when you stood up for a child; it need not be a big, dramatic event. Here is an example of one college student's reflection:

   > This may be a small thing but I think it shows that I am willing to stick up for kids. There is a trailer park not far from the dollar store I go to. The children gather up their pennies—often collecting bottles and turning them in for the deposit—and then they go there to buy the candy. I've noticed that the one cashier, in particular, will keep going to the next adult in line and will ignore the children until they either give up or no one else is left at the counter. This happened while I was waiting in line. When she turned to me, I said, "I think that these children were in line ahead of me so please wait on them first." The children just beamed when I said that! At least this forced the cashier to think about her behavior, if only for a few seconds. I can tell by the look on her face that she considers these children without much money to be a nuisance. The manager has used his "No shirt, no shoes, no service" sign to keep them out and people in my town call them "trailer trash," thinking that it is so funny. I think it is cruel.

4. **Strive to Understand the Community Better and Develop Leadership Qualities.** Start small and gradually increase the challenge to build your confidence with advocacy activities. Match your style with the population served and the gatekeepers of resources and power. Get involved.

5. **Develop a Plan and Take Action.** This process typically involves a needs assessment, mobilizing support for pursuing change, prioritizing advocacy issues and concerns, making a plan, implementing the plan, assessing the outcomes of the plan, and revising as necessary. Some ideas include seeking out opportunities to: learn more about an issue, donate to charities, join a professional association (and bring along a friend), collaborate with fellow professionals from other fields, co-present with a faculty member at a local conference, volunteer in the community, share children's work with families, complete a college assignment that will develop advocacy skills, speak with your neighbors and community members about the challenges that today's children and families confront, work toward accreditation and licensure for yourself and/or your program, and read all about a topic of concern and gather authoritative evidence to support your arguments.

ONLINE RESOURCES FOR HISTORY AND ADVOCACY

American Humane Association (AHA): This organization lobbies to protect children and its website has many resources on preventing child neglect and abuse and family violence. www.americanhumane.org/

Annie E. Casey Foundation: This organization produces an annual *Kids Count* report that provides state-by-state data on indicators of children's well-being. www.aecf.org/kidscount/kc2010/

Children's Defense Fund: This organization produces annual reports about the needs of children and families in the United States. www.childrensdefense.org

Federal Interagency Forum on Child and Family Statistics: This organization releases an annual report entitled *America's Children: Key National Indicators of Well-Being.* www.childstats.gov

National Association for the Education of Young Children: NAEYC offers an Advocacy Toolkit for early childhood educators.

National Child Care Information Center: This organization supplies state-by-state information about children and child care as well as links to research. http://nccic.org

New York Society for the Prevention of Cruelty to Children (NYSPCC): This nonprofit organization is dedicated to child advocacy, and its site contains many historical documents about the NYSPCC's work since it began in 1875. www.nyspcc.org/nyspcc/

The History Place: This website chronicles U.S. history from the colonial period to the present day and includes timelines, photographs, and original source material on child labor in America from 1908 to 1912.
www.historyplace.com/unitedstates/childlabor/
www.historyplace.com/unitedstates/childlabor/about.htm

PEARSON myeducationlab

Go to Topics 1 (History) and 12 (Professionalism/Ethics) in the MyEducationLab (**www.myeducationlab.com**) for your course, where you can:

- Find learning outcomes for history and professionalism/ethics along with the national standards that connect to these outcomes.
- Complete Assignments and Activities that can help you more deeply understand the chapter content.
- Apply and practice your understanding of the core teaching skills identified in the chapter with the Building Teaching Skills and Dispositions learning units.
- Access video clips of CCSSO National Teachers of the Year award winners responding to the question, "Why Do I Teach?" in the Teacher Talk section.
- Hear viewpoints of experts in the field in Professional Perspectives.

CHAPTER 3
Delivering High-Quality Early Childhood Programs

with Michelle Amodei

> . . . early childhood programs [have] a complicated and distinctive character, one filled with various strains and tensions. Some of these derive from questions about the relationship or balance to be achieved between families and society, and parents and teachers. Other tensions and strains derive from such things as the competing demands that are made on teachers of the very young because they must provide both education and physical care, while still others arise from contradictory conceptions of development that pit nature versus nurture. Early education has also been tugged and pulled by differing theories and beliefs about the origins of poverty and how people escape it; by differing conceptions of play and the proper balance to be struck between play and work; and by clashing beliefs about the benefits of didactic and holistic methods of instruction.
>
> Judith Schickendanz, 1995, p. 7

Meet the TEACHERS

MISS LINDA is a teacher in a 2-year-old toddler room at a child-care center in a small, rural community. The region has suffered severe economic hardships due to the "rust bowl"—the loss of manufacturing jobs—and many families now have a long commute to the city for their jobs. Most children in her group spend 10 or more hours in group care each day. Miss Linda empathizes with the stress placed on these families. Although she doesn't make a lot of money working in a child-care center, she loves her job and takes her responsibility to care for these toddlers very seriously. When asked about Miss Linda, a parent says; "She is like another member of our family. I don't know how I could go to work every day if it wasn't for knowing that Miss Linda is there taking such excellent care of my child. We depend on her and trust her."

MRS. SHAW teaches preschool in a Head Start classroom in an urban area. Her classroom is located within a public elementary school, which affords her class the opportunity to eat lunch in the cafeteria, play on the school playground, and use the gymnasium at regularly scheduled times for large motor activities. Mrs. Shaw says, "The opportunity for the children to attend preschool here is invaluable. Next year, when they begin kindergarten, most of them will be right in this same building and families will be familiar with the facility. We instituted a 'buddy program' so that children and families can meet the kindergarten teachers and find out what to expect. I am proud to be part of an early educational experience that makes a difference and sets the children and their families up for success."

MR. MITCHELL works with first- and second-grade children in a private Montessori school in an affluent suburban community. Today Mr. Mitchell is demonstrating a practical life skill—how to properly use a knife to slice a hard-boiled egg. Before this activity is available for the children he shows them the entire process, beginning with hand-washing. He then peels the egg, rinses off the peeled egg, pats it dry, lays it on the cutting board, holds the knife properly, and carefully slices through the egg horizontally. Afterward, Mr. Mitchell observes the children carefully as they opt to come over and practice this new skill. He remarks; "I love the multi-age grouping in Montessori and I have seen firsthand how well the structured environment enables children to select activities and learn independently. I'm sure that some people would question the value of a demonstration on how to prepare an egg, but one of the things I appreciate the most about Montessori is that the children work with real materials they will be expected to use outside of the classroom. It is a huge mistake to underestimate what children are capable of accomplishing."

LEARNING Outcomes

In this chapter, you will learn to:

→ **Understand early childhood programs and curriculum models** (NAEYC #4, ACEI #1, INTASC #1)

→ **List and describe six well-known early childhood programs/models**

→ **Explore your role in delivering high-quality programs for young children**

→ **Apply your knowledge to analyze an early childhood program**

Compare
What commonalities do you see in how these teachers define their role?

Contrast
What makes each of these programs distinctive?

Connect
In which type of program would you prefer to work? Why?

Now that you have reflected on the three teachers' perspectives and noted the learning outcomes, we preview the knowledge, skills, and dispositions you will need to acquire in order to fulfill your role in providing high-quality learning experiences for young children.

Defining Early Childhood Programs, Standards, and Models

An **early childhood program** is a planned way of supporting the care and education of young children between the ages of birth and 8 years; it includes attention to all of the domains of development—physical, cognitive, emotional, and social. What are some distinctive characteristics of early childhood programs? Early childhood programs may be federally funded, such as Head Start, may reside within public school systems, or may operate through nonprofit or for-profit agencies that charge tuition. In many other countries throughout the world—such as Great Britain, Sweden, and Australia—the government offers care and/or education programs for preschoolers that are free and available to everyone, a practice referred to as **universal prekindergarten** (Swiniarski, 2006). In contrast to these practices, the care and education of young children in the United States is a "patchwork" of different arrangements (Scott, London, & Hurst, 2005). Although a range of different early childhood programs exists in practically all U.S. communities, the types of programs, delivery models, eligibility for the programs, and overall quality vary considerably. Figure 3.1 is an overview of the main categories of early childhood programs offered in the United States, the young children for whom the programs are intended, and the teacher qualifications that typically are required.

Standards are benchmarks that are used to guide curriculum development and plan for instruction; these standards may be identified at the national, state, or local levels. At the national level, the National Association for the Education of Young Children (NAEYC) and the National Association of Early Childhood Specialists in State Departments of Education (NAECS/SDE) have issued Early Learning Standards (2002). At the state level, state departments of education typically have standards for early learning and standards that are used to determine if various types of child care can be licensed by the state. A 2010 report indicates that 48 states and the District of Columbia offer standards for assessment in literacy and in math and that nearly 40 states also provide curriculum guides and sample lesson plans matched to the standards (Sawchuck, 2010). There are also program-specific standards, often stated more globally as part of a mission statement, program goals,

DID YOU Know ?

- The National Center for Education Statistics (NCES, 2009) reports that, in 2008, 39.4% of 3-year-olds, 66.1% of 4-year-olds, and 83.9% of 5-year-olds were enrolled in early childhood programs.

- During 2008, 71.2% of 3- to 5-year-olds were enrolled in public nursery school and 74.7% were enrolled in public kindergarten; 58.2% of these programs were full-day programs (NCES, 2009).

- For children birth through age 5, 38.9% are in parental care only, 36.0% in center-based care, 15.4% in the care of relatives, 8.3% in family child care in another home, 5.1% in Head Start, 2.3% in the care of a babysitter in the child's home, and 1.7% in multiple care arrangements (NCES, 2009).

- According to data from the Center for the Child Care Workforce (2008), early childhood professionals employed in child-care programs earn an average of $9.73 per hour compared to elementary school teachers who earn an average of $36.30 per hour. In addition, other benefits such as insurance, paid vacations, and training opportunities are extremely limited for child-care providers (Hale-Jinks, Knopf, & Kemple, 2006).

Figure 3.1 Categories of Early Childhood Programs

Family Child Care	Group Child Care	Preschool or Nursery School Programs	Drop-in Child Care	Public School Kindergarten and Elementary School
• **Setting:** The family child-care provider's home.	• **Setting:** Classrooms designed for infants, toddlers, preschoolers, and school-age children that may be located a child-care facility, at the parent's/families' place of work, in churches or synagogues, etc.	• **Settings:** Programs for preschoolers may be housed in many different locations: at community centers, in churches/synagogues, in buildings provided by commercial chains, in private homes or special facilities built near private residences, and so forth.	• **Setting:** These child-care programs are located on-site to provide child care on an as-needed basis.	• **Setting:** These programs are supported by tax dollars and are typically housed in public school buildings or in a space rented by the public schools for that purpose. Most states have prekindergarten programs, often for children from low-income backgrounds.
• **Examples:** County child-care programs, home-based intervention programs.	• **Examples:** Private child-care and preschool programs, Montessori schools, child-care franchises such as Kindercare, campus child-care centers, before- and after-school care for children in elementary school, corporate child care.	• **Examples:** Child care at community centers such as YMCA, Kindercare, Montessori schools.	• **Examples:** Child care at health-care facilities such as the family member's employer, Ronald McDonald House, exercise studios, airports, shopping malls.	• **Examples:** Head Start classes for 3- and 4-year-olds housed in the public schools, early intervention programs for young children with special needs, prekindergarten through third-grade classes.
• **Children/Families Served:** The appeal of these programs is that young children are cared for in a very home- and family-like setting. Children from 6 weeks to kindergarten-entry age may be enrolled in family child care. The number of children served is smaller than in group care and the children are often of different ages, as they would be in a family. These programs may be less formal arrangements or they may be licensed or accredited.	• **Children/Families Served:** These programs typically offer extended hours that would accommodate to the needs of working parents/families. The adult-to-child ratios and other program elements are governed by state regulations.	• **Children/Families Served:** Preschool is generally defined as the 3- to 5-year-old age group. Preschool programs may be half day, full day, alternating days (e.g., T/R or M/W/F), combined with other programs (e.g., child care before and after regular preschool program hours), or some combination of these options.	• **Children/Families Served:** The purpose of these child-care arrangements is to provide temporary care for young children. Rather than attending on a regular basis, children participate in the center on an as-needed basis. They may require 24-hour care if a parent needs to leave town for a family emergency, or just a few hours of care if a single parent needs to run errands and shop, for instance.	• **Children/Families Served:** Kindergarten is generally for 5- and 6-year-olds and the primary grades in an elementary school are grades 1 through 3, serving children from approximately age 6 or 7 up to and including age 8 or 9.
• **Typical Funding Source:** Local, county, or state taxes, United Way, tuition on a sliding scale, or some combination thereof.	• **Typical Funding Source:** Tuition paid by parents and/or donations.	• **Typical Funding Source:** Grant funded, privately funded, supported by tuition or a combination thereof.	• **Typical Funding Source:** Grant funded, privately funded, supported by tuition, or a combination thereof.	• **Typical Funding Source:** Federal, state, and local taxes.
• **Family Eligibility:** Usually based on parent's proximity to home, ability to pay tuition, and eligibility criteria of specific programs.	• **Family Eligibility:** Generally based on parent's ability to pay tuition and fees.	• **Family Eligibility:** Usually determined by the parent/family members' place of residence and/or ability to pay for the services.	• **Family Eligibility:** Usually determined by the parent's participation in the business or services of an organization.	• **Family Eligibility:** Some of these programs are reserved for families with low incomes but others are open to any child who resides in the school district and meets the age requirements.
• **Teacher's Title and Credentials:** Child-care giver or family child-care provider, at least a high school diploma and often state license or Child Development Associate (CDA) is required.	• **Teacher's Title and Credentials:** Child care provider, usually requires at least a high school diploma and a state license. CDA, or other teaching credentials.	• **Teacher's Title and Credentials:** Child-care provider; usually requires at least a high school diploma and a state license. CDA, or other teaching credentials.	• **Teacher's Title and Credentials:** At least a high school diploma; may be a licensed babysitter or have a credential as a nanny; possibly an associate's degree.	• **Teacher's Title and Credentials:** A certificate or license awarded by the state is required—usually an early childhood or elementary endorsement. A 4-year baccalaureate degree from an accredited institution is mandatory.

Figure 3.2 National, State, and Program-Specific Standards for Early Childhood Programs

- **Early Learning Standards**—National Association for the Education of Young Children and the National Association of Early Childhood Specialists in State Departments of Education (2002)
- **The Head Start Outcomes Framework**—Head Start Bureau (2003)
  http://www.hsnrc.org/CDI/pdfs/UGCOF.pdf

National Standards

State Standards

- **State Examples of Program Standards**—National Early Childhood Technical Assistance Center (NECTAC)
  http://www.nectac.org/topics/quality/progstd.asp
- **State Departments of Education**—Conduct a search on any state using the state abbreviation (e.g., early childhood standards PA or child care standards TX)
- **National Association of Child Care Resources and Referral Agencies**—Evaluates state standards for child care (NACCRRA, 2010)
  http://www.naccrra.org/publications/

- **Program-Specific Standards**—Check the mission and goals statements, description of the curriculum, accreditation/licensure status, and evaluation procedures

Local Standards

or outcomes. Figure 3.2 illustrates the linkages among the national, state, and program-specific standards.

A **program model** is a detailed approach to providing a high-quality program for young children that is supported by theory and research collected over an extended period of time. Program models are viewed as "tried and true," have gained positive recognition from experts in the field, and are considered to be exemplary in some way. Program models offer detailed guidance to others who want to replicate the program or to establish programs with a similar philosophy and goals. On page 53, the Ask the Experts by Olivia Saracho and Bernard Spodek discusses the origins of early childhood programs in the United States.

Indicators of High-Quality Early Childhood Programs

A common thread among all early childhood programs is that they have evolved as a result of societal needs and political persuasions. Those needs and persuasions are complex and comprised of a multitude of factors that propel early childhood programs to new levels with each challenge that is faced. Early childhood programs simultaneously

Ask the EXPERTS

Olivia Saracho

Bernard Spodek

Origins of Early Childhood Programs

Q: When did early childhood education begin in the United States?

A: Many educators identify the introduction of the kindergarten into America as the beginning of early childhood education here. Charles E. Strickland identified three models of early childhood education that predated the kindergarten. One model was sending young children to the common school (the local primary school). Children as young as 3 were enrolled in these schools as early as the colonial period.

Another model was the infant school, created by Robert Owen in New Lanark, Scotland, in 1816. The idea came to the United States as Owen's books became available here and when Owen visited the United States and founded a community in southern Indiana. Infant schools were opened in the New England and east central sections of the United States in the 1820s and 1830s. Bronson Alcott, the father of Louisa May Alcott, who wrote *Little Women*, was probably one of the best known founders of an infant school in America.

A third model was characterized by Strickland as "Fireside Education." In this approach, young children were to be educated by their mothers in the home. Children's moral development was more important than intellectual development in this approach to early childhood education.

Q: Was there any approach to early childhood education that was native to the United States?

A: The original kindergarten came from Germany. The Montessori program came from Italy. The nursery school came from Britain. All of these programs were imported into the United States and, over time, were modified to become more American. It was the reform kindergarten—the approach to kindergarten education that took over from the Froebelian kindergarten—that was a truly American approach. These programs were inspired by the work of John Dewey and other Progressive educators as well as by child development experts. The pioneers of this approach included Patty Hill Smith, Alice Temple, and others. The reform kindergarten did away with many of the prescribed exercises of the Froebelian kindergarten and substituted more childlike activities. Play and especially dramatic play became an important part of the kindergarten program. This approach to kindergarten education was not only popular in the United States, but it influenced early childhood education throughout the world, including Europe and Asia.

Q: When did the U.S. federal government first sponsor early childhood programs?

A: Head Start is the largest program of early childhood education ever sponsored by the U.S. federal government. However, it was not the first early childhood education program sponsored by the U.S. federal government. During the Great Depression of the 1930s, the Works Progress Administration (WPA) set up emergency nursery schools to provide work for unemployed teachers. Many young children from low-income backgrounds were cared for in WPA nursery schools. Meals were provided, play activities were offered, children were provided with rest periods, and health services were offered. In addition to unemployed teachers, other professionals such as nurses, nutritionists, cooks, clerical workers, and janitors were also hired. Many of the teachers employed did not have a background in early childhood education.

WPA nursery funding ended in 1942. That year the Lanham Act set up about 2,000 day-care centers to enable mothers to enter the workforce to support the war effort. Both programs required rapid and large-scale training, often of teachers without experience with young children. Following World War II, the Lanham Act day-care centers closed down.

continued

continued

Q: **When Head Start was started in 1965 it created major changes in the early childhood education field. Were there precursors to Head Start?**

A: The WPA nursery schools that were established in the 1930s had some of the same elements as Head Start. These nursery schools were designed for children from low-income backgrounds and provided meals, play activities, rest periods, and health services.

An earlier approach to early childhood education had characteristics that were even closer to those of Head Start. The original nursery school was developed by Rachel and Margaret MacMillan in 1911. The nursery school that was created in Depthford, a slum section of London at the time, still exists and functions today. The concept of supporting the total development of the child was labeled by Margaret MacMillan as nurture. Today we would call it dealing with the whole child. She saw expressive activity, play, art, and movement as essential parts of the education of young children. Children's health also needed to be considered. Physical examinations, medical care, cleanliness, proper exercise, and living in a healthy environment were emphasized. Most important, parent involvement was an essential element of the nursery program, as it is in Head Start. While Margaret MacMillan was most interested in the education of the imagination, she also fostered literacy development in young children.

Olivia Saracho is a Professor at the University of Maryland, College Park, Maryland; and Bernard Spodek is Professor Emeritus of Early Childhood Education at the University of Illinois at Urbana-Champaign.

Many children are enrolled in multiple programs such as before- and after-school care.

preserve culture and respond to societal changes (Yeh & Barton, 2005). Figure 3.3 describes some of the influences that shape early childhood programs.

An extensive body of research documents that high-quality programs have enduring, positive consequences for young children and that they are well worth the money invested (American Educational Research Association, 2005; Frede, Jung, Barnett, & Figueras, 2009; Lynch, 2004; National Governors Association, 2005; Pianta & Howes, 2009; Wong, Cook, Barnett, & Jung, 2008). In 2010, the American Academy of Pediatrics asserted that: "High-quality early education and child care for young children improves their health and promotes their development and learning" (p. 1). Research has attempted to quantify some of the quality indicators for early childhood programs. For example, the National Institute for Early Education Research (NIEER, 2009) at Rutgers University publishes an annual report that looks at the following eight indicators of quality in early childhood programs:

1. Teacher has a bachelor's degree and specialized training in early childhood education

2. Assistant holds a Child Development Associate credential or higher

3. Staff receive at least 15 hours of in-service training per year

4. The curriculum conforms to the early learning standards set by each state

Figure 3.3 Influences on Early Childhood Program Models

Societal Trends
- Such as economic conditions, local, state, national, and world events, political policies, and advances in technology

Theory, Research, and Philosophy
- Such as theories Piaget and Vygotsky, advances in technology that make it possible to identify which areas of the brain are stimulated during different activities, and philosophical influences, such as the schools of Reggio Emilia

Knowledge of Children and Their Development
- Such as studies of children's physical growth, multiple intelligences theory, advances in neuroscience

Curriculum Standards
- Such as NAEYC's Early Learning Standards state academic standards, local policies, and school traditions

Community Expectations
- Such as public opinion, state or regional trends, and local issues

Evaluation Criteria
- Such as accreditation standards, large-scale testing programs, child assessment, and program assessment

Human Resources
- Include teachers, administrators, support staff, and the type of learning climate they create—or fail to offer—in their programs

Material Resources
- Such as funding, grants, equipment, and curriculum materials

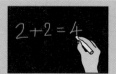
Pedagogy
- Such as research-based recommendations for best practices, efforts to integrate subject areas, and a teacher's interpretation/implementation of a program

Sources: Ball & Cohen, 1996; Brandes, Ormsbee, & Haring, 2007.

5. Class size is set at 20 or lower with a teacher-to-child ratio of 1:10 or better
6. Screenings and referrals are made for intervention services
7. At least one meal is served during the program
8. On-site visits are used to evaluate the program

As this list suggests, even though early childhood education is exceptionally diverse, high-quality programs are dependent upon factors that include: quality staff, suitable environment, appropriate grouping practices, consistent schedules, and parent/family involvement (National Central Regional Laboratory, 2010). In the sections that follow, several attributes of high-quality early childhood programs are presented and explained.

ARTICULATED PHILOSOPHY AND GOALS

In any excellent program, everyone clearly knows about the goals of the program, their specific roles, and the early childhood principles and practices that will support the program's purpose. A curricular philosophy is not a written statement of lofty ideals without much connection to classroom practices. Rather, the program's philosophy should be apparent in the daily experiences of children, families, and educators. A clearly articulated curricular philosophy is translated into goals and is evident to those who observe the program in action. Above all, the emphasis of a good early childhood program is on being of service to children and families.

CURRICULUM THAT MEETS THE STANDARDS

The standards movement has swept the nation, and as a result teachers "are encountering unprecedented demands. . . . The public now expects schools to teach all students so that they achieve high standards—rich and poor, immigrant and native-born, white and minority, special needs and mainstream—and to take on new functions beyond the traditional scope of schools' responsibility" (Johnson, 2006, p. 7).

With the public demand for **accountability**—defined as requiring evidence from teachers and schools that the benefits of education are well worth the money invested—more testing is required. Because very young children are not appropriately assessed through traditional, paper-and-pencil, group-administered tests, many states do not begin these formal assessments required by the state until third or fourth grade; however,

> all states now have instituted standardized tests to monitor students' academic progress. Some of these assessments carry "high stakes" because they determine which students will be promoted to the next grade. . . . Schools that fall below the established performance standards can be taken over by state officials or closed down altogether, and parents have the right to remove their children from low-performing schools. Faced with exams that carry such far-reaching consequences, teachers experience increased pressure to deliver high test scores for the sake of their students, their schools, and themselves. (Johnson, 2006, p. 73)

Figure 3.4 highlights the consequences of and appropriate responses to the standards movement in early childhood education.

Figure 3.4 Contributions and Limitations of Standards

Positives and Negatives

Standards can be a positive influence when they . . .

- Enhance educators' conversations about children's growth and learning as well as set higher expectations for children

- Foster communication across the grades and among various stakeholders—with families, colleagues, and the general public

- Support what teachers are already doing and serve to further professionalize the field

- Provide continuity as preschool standards are linked to primary standards

- Help to identify appropriate next steps in curriculum

- Make the connection between curriculum and assessment more explicit, thereby supporting accountability

Standards can be detrimental if they . . .

- Lead to teaching to the standards only and an inflexible curriculum

- Result in undue pressure of accountability on educators

- Push the type of curriculum suitable for more mature learners on less mature students

- Lead to a mistrust of self-directed, exploratory ways of learning and treat direct instruction as the only way to guarantee that standards are addressed

- Cause a rift between teachers/families and early childhood/elementary teachers in which each ascribes blame to the other for low performance

- Reduce the amount of time for teachers to reflect, interact, and institute best practices

- Result in the inappropriate use of testing and other assessment

- Neglect the need for teachers to have specific training and support in implementing standards

WHAT CANNOT ACCOMPLISH HIGH STANDARDS: FAILED SOLUTIONS

- **Raise the Kindergarten Entrance Age**
  Some educators may argue that a child needs "a year to grow" while, at the same time, suggest that the home environment is not sufficiently enriching from an educational standpoint. If the child is kept out of school for another year, who benefits from such a decision?

  It does not help to postpone education.

- **More Screening and Testing**
  Tests are like taking a patient's temperature repeatedly—they are an indicator but do not suggest an underlying cause.

  It does not help children achieve high learning standards to employ screening and/or readiness testing in connection with kindergarten entrance.

- **Add a Year**
  Provide a year of school between kindergarten and first grade (i.e., "junior" first grade) or retain children at the same grade level for another year. The research on holding children back or "flunking" them is very clear: it lowers expectations from parents/families and damages children's self-esteem.

  It does not help children achieve high standards to reinstate extra-year programs or to increase grade retention at the primary level.

WHAT CAN ACCOMPLISH HIGH STANDARDS

- **Direct Interaction with Materials**
  Young children's learning is enhanced through direct interaction with materials, adults, and other children.

- **Rich Verbal Environment**
  Children show growth when classrooms are "literacy rich" and include high-quality children's literature, opportunities to talk and/or write about their experiences, and many examples of print.

- **Choice Among Learning Activities**
  Effective classrooms are arranged so that children are able to make choices about what materials they will use and how to work with them.

- **Open-Ended Learning Materials**
  Broad curriculum goals are implemented through careful preparation of the physical environment.

- **Heterogeneous Groups**
  Children are assigned to heterogeneous groups rather than being "tracked" and continually grouped into "high," "medium," and "low" groups.

- **Varied Instructional Approaches**
  Teachers regularly employ a variety of instructional approaches to assure that children learn both the skills they need and challenging, worthwhile content.

Sources: Bowman, 2006; Cassidy, Mims, Rucker, & Boone, 2003; Egertson, 2004; Estok, 2006; Gronlund, 2006; Helm & Beneke, 2003; Puckett & Black, 2007.

APPROPRIATE ORGANIZATION AND STRUCTURE

A well-run program is organized so that it can make the most of team members' strengths and use available resources efficiently. Both short-term and long-term planning and agreed-upon schedules are essential. Programs that are well organized have leaders who contribute to a sense of cohesiveness through their ability to administer the program properly with a cooperative and democratic spirit. High-quality programs have structure yet sufficient flexibility to adapt to individual needs, choices, and preferences of children, families, and educators. Evaluation plays a major role in the structure and organization of programs as well. There is an ongoing system of evaluation that guides improvement, acknowledges effort, and celebrates successes.

EMPHASIS ON CONCEPT DEVELOPMENT

Every early childhood curriculum should challenge young children's intellects by raising questions that intrigue young minds and encourage the very young to explore answers in their own ways. In high-quality programs you will find teachers carefully considering what is worthwhile for children to learn, identifying the relevant skills, and promoting the dispositions that enable students to succeed. To accomplish this, early childhood teachers review the national, state, and local learning standards, identify appropriate concepts to teach, determine the best ways to develop children's understandings, and closely monitor children's progress. Exemplary programs recognize that teaching is more than telling, and that children are not merely passive recipients of someone else's ready-made knowledge. Admirable programs in the early childhood field fully appreciate that children play an active role in the construction of their own understandings within each context. Moving beyond memorization of bits of information to wider and deeper understandings is a hallmark of quality programs for the very young. Perhaps the best indicator that meaningful concepts are being developed is the quality of children's work. If children's responses all look alike, there is little chance that real thinking is taking place, because the lesson was simply an exercise in following directions.

On page 59, the Ask the Expert by Doug Clements discusses the importance of concept development in mathematics instruction for young children.

INTENTIONAL TEACHING

Effective teachers are **intentional;** this means that they not do not stand on the sidelines and wait for development to occur spontaneously; rather, they engage student interest, build motivation, and encourage each child to become fully engaged in learning activities. Instead of taking the deficit view that some children are simply lagging "behind" others, intentional teachers fully appreciate that *learning leads development*. In other words, it is through intellectually challenging activities and inviting opportunities to learn that children make strides forward. To illustrate, suppose that a child arrives in kindergarten with very little experience with books. A teacher with a deficit view would attribute the child's struggles to other things, such as socioeconomic status or lack of parental involvement, and assume that the child lacks potential. An intentional teacher would set about the task of providing more opportunities for the child to enjoy picture books, such as sharing books with peers or adult volunteers, starting a "bookpack" program (in which a collection of carefully selected books and activities can be borrowed), informing the family about free programs at the public library, and so forth. Intentional teaching takes positive action to optimize every child's full potential.

Douglas H. Clements

Early Math Education

Q: Isn't it inappropriate to sit young children down to do math sheets?

A: Usually, yes. However, just as inappropriate, or inaccurate, is assuming that this is the best or only way young children can learn mathematics. Our memories may be filled with years of doing workbooks and worksheets ourselves. But good mathematics is about *engagement*, not drudgery.

High-quality early mathematics education includes helping children decide which building is bigger (and bigger in what way) or completing a shape puzzle. It includes playing simple card and "race" games. Good mathematics education includes marching around the room while counting and counting how many steps it is to the playground. Teachers can use both planned, sequential activities and spontaneous experiences to develop their children's mathematical knowledge (neglecting either one is mis-education).

Q: Don't children need to learn a lot of skills before they can solve problems?

A: It seems silly to think that young children can solve math problems. It makes sense to ensure that children *first* learn math skills and concepts and *later* use them to solve problems. Certainly, *some* skills and knowledge are helpful. For example, a child may have four plates, and want to figure out how many more plates he needs so that each of seven dolls involved in the "tea party" on his front porch has a plate. It certainly helps that the child can count. However, the child does not need to know addition or subtraction facts to solve this problem. He may instead use

his knowledge of numbers, counting, and "keeping track." Even more striking, he can martial those ideas and combine them to *create* a way to solve the problem. "I have foooooouuur, I need *five, six, seven* [pumping his fist three times]. Three more." He has, not unlike a mathematician, *modeled* the problem and used what he knows to solve it. Teachers can invite children to solve real problems and fun, "made-up" number problems of all types.

Q: If I spend time on math, won't that hurt children's literacy and social-emotional experiences?

A: This is a reasonable concern—there is only so much time in the day, and every minute is valuable. The good news is that *children's social-emotional development benefits from high-quality mathematics activities*. Children learn sharing, taking the perspective of others, and self-regulation skills as they engage in math activities. *Time spent on math also contributes to literacy.* For example, working on shapes, puzzles, and other geometric skills builds a "visual literacy" that contributes to better writing, or composition, and even IQ scores years later. In another study, a preschool mathematics curriculum promoted children's literacy development as much as literacy curricula. In our latest study, oral language grew substantially *more* in math classrooms than in those that concentrated only on literacy.

Educators should worry about math. However, the main concern should be that many children are not engaging in *enough* high-quality mathematics activities in their early years.

Douglas H. Clements is SUNY Distinguished Professor, University at Buffalo, The State University of New York.

POSITIVE INTERPERSONAL RELATIONSHIPS

Learning is fundamentally social; therefore, children's development and learning rely on positive interactions. In fact, most of the skills that teachers identify as crucial for success in kindergarten are social rather than academic—such things as following simple directions, communicating needs, and avoiding disruptive behaviors (Lin, Lawrence, & Gorell, 2003). Close human relationships and mutual understandings facilitate learning. Warm and responsive interpersonal dynamics between children, peers, and adults promote learning and development, while cold and detached interactions retard learning because they do not nurture children's emotional and social well-being. Young children need opportunities to interact, understand, and cooperate in groups. The best early childhood programs strive to prepare young children by encouraging their growth in social skills. In order to promote positive interpersonal relationships, teachers go beyond the dominant culture or their own cultural backgrounds to value *all* children and families.

DIFFERENTIATION TO ACCOMMODATE TO INDIVIDUAL NEEDS

Instead of teaching to the "average" student and hoping for the best, early childhood educators in exemplary programs address the entire spectrum of learning needs, ranging from children who need additional support with a task to those who have already mastered the task and need something more difficult. Teachers in these programs provide the right kind, amount, and blend of challenge and support so that all students are progressing to the best of their abilities; in other words, they differentiate. **Differentiation** is the practice of skillfully adapting curriculum to the needs of individual children. It is a core value in quality early childhood programs.

INTERDISCIPLINARY APPROACHES TO SUBJECT-MATTER TEACHING

In a high-quality early education program, teachers emphasize the importance of **interdisciplinary approaches,** defined as emphasizing the connections that exist between and among different subject areas. Today it is common—but not acceptable—for

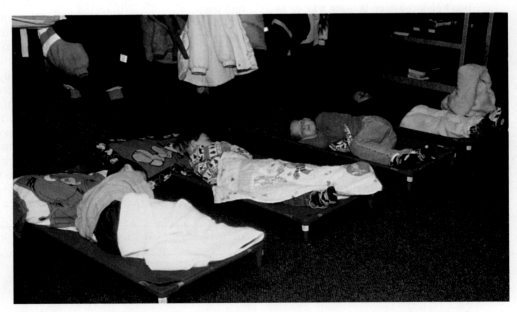

When very young children are cared for in groups for long periods of time, they need some quiet time.

art, music, science, social studies, health/safety, and physical education to be given less time, temporarily suspended, or discontinued so that young children can "cram" for tests in reading and mathematics. In effective programs, early childhood educators find ways to ensure that children experience a full spectrum of learning activities that support physical, cognitive, social, emotional, and artistic growth. They integrate content and show children the connections between and among the concepts and processes of various disciplines.

Your Role in Understanding Early Childhood Programs and Models

Throughout history, early childhood educators have been striving to develop high-quality programs for young children. Some of these programs have existed for centuries, such as the kindergarten concept that was begun by Friedrich Froebel in the 1800s. There are at least six program models that have been in existence for many years and are widely recognized in the field: (1) Montessori, (2) Reggio Emilia, (3) Bank Street, (4) High/Scope, (5) Direct Instruction, and (6) Head Start (Walsh & Petty, 2007). Two programs that originated in Italy are Montessori, which has over 100 years of history, and Reggio Emilia, which began much more recently in post–World War II during the 1940s. Four gained recognition during the 1960s in the United States: Bank Street (also known as the Developmental Interaction Approach), High/Scope, Direct Instruction, and Head Start (Roopnarine & Johnson, 2005). The paragraphs that follow provide a brief history of each approach, a synopsis of its theoretical roots, a description of the teacher's role in each, and an explanation of how each model is implemented.

MONTESSORI

Maria Montessori (1870–1952) was born in Ancona, Italy, and was one of the first women to become a physician, specializing in pediatrics and psychiatry. She worked primarily with underprivileged children and concluded that young children possessed a great deal of intelligence that would never be fully realized without an appropriate education and opportunities to develop life skills. She was inspired by the research journals of Jean Marc-Gaspard Itard, a French doctor known for his "wild boy experiment" in which he attempted to socialize a young boy who had been discovered living on his own in the forests of France. Maria Montessori studied his journals meticulously and began to develop her theoretical convictions about how best to facilitate learning for young children—particularly those living in poverty with special needs. Montessori believed that with a carefully structured environment, minimal interruptions, and time to explore freely, children could maximize their potential.

The **Montessori** Method contends that there are four important aspects to understanding how children learn:

1. The **absorbent mind,** meaning that children are capable of retaining information long before it is formally "taught" to them.

2. The **prepared environment** that was carefully structured, in advance, by the teacher as a way to foster greater independence and encourage children's exploration.

3. **Autoeducation,** meaning that learning activities are chosen by the children and that materials are self-correcting (e.g., assembled in a particular way) so that children will know when a task has been completed correctly.

4. A belief in **sensitive periods** or times in a child's growth when certain concepts could be more readily learned and nurtured.

Some of the key components of a Montessori classroom include:

- The teacher is called a "directress" and demonstrates use of materials before children are permitted to use them.
- All furniture and equipment is child-sized.
- There are three main areas in the classroom environment: practical life, sensorial area, and academic.
- Prescribed ways of completing life skills tasks, such as washing hands or cleaning the table, are taught.
- Sociodramatic play materials typically found in early childhood classrooms, such as dress-up clothes, baby dolls, and so forth, are usually not incorporated into a Montessori classroom.

Many of the Montessori schools in operation today in the United States are modified versions of Maria Montessori's original methods and curriculum.

BANK STREET

Bank Street, also referred to as the Developmental Interaction Approach, is a model with a distinguished history. It emerged in 1916 led by Lucy Sprague Mitchell, Barbara Bidin, and Ellen Shapiro and was part of a study called the Bureau of Educational Experiments in New York City. Their research was greatly influenced by the Progressive Education philosophies of John Dewey. At that time, the prevailing view was that children learned by sitting obediently and quietly at their desks as the teacher called upon them to listen, recite, or reply in unison. In contrast, Dewey believed that children would best learn through direct experiences that connected the outside world to the classroom and that society would benefit by producing citizens who were rational, thoughtful individuals. The Bank Street approach emulated this progressive philosophy and added an emphasis on respecting, understanding, and furthering young children's development.

Six guiding principles direct the development of the Bank Street program:

- Development involves shifting from simple to more complex ways of thinking, processing the world, and responding to the world in a more integrated fashion.
- Individuals develop on a continuum at different rates.
- To progress developmentally, humans must continuously work through cycles of instability and stability. Teachers work with students to enable them to proceed through those phases successfully.
- Children are naturally curious and motivated to learn about the world around them. As they gain experience and mature, their interactions will evolve from a concrete to more symbolic process.
- Children gain a sense of self from their experiences in the world. They must have opportunities to gain awareness through repeated interactions.
- Conflict is an important component of development. It is through conflict that humans learn to resolve issues and learn about social, familial, and cultural expectations.

To download a copy of the Bank Street curriculum guide, see the School for Children website at www.bnkst.edu/sfc/curriculum.html.

REGGIO EMILIA

In the 1940s, post–World War II, a small village named Villa Cella, near a region called Reggio Emilia, Italy, witnessed the beginning of an educational phenomenon. With the proceeds from selling a war tank, scavenged materials, and the volunteer services of parents, a school for young children was built. Loris Malaguzzi, having heard about the efforts of these parents, rode his bike to the village to observe for himself and ended up becoming the founder of the **Reggio Emilia** schools. The program philosophy is that "things about children and for children are only learned from children" (Malaguzzi, 1995, pp. 43–44). For the first several years of these schools' existence, they were run by parents. This was a first-of-its-kind approach to education that is now available to children ages birth through 6 years and has become highly respected worldwide.

Principles and features that guide the efforts of the Reggio Emilia approach include:

1. An *emergent curriculum* that evolves from the interests of children rather than pre-packaged unit plans and teacher-written lesson plans based on what the adults believe children need to learn.

2. *Projects* determined by children's interests that enable children to study topics more in depth over longer periods of time.

3. The "**hundred languages of children**"—a belief that children represent their knowledge in many, many different ways; children are encouraged to use art, music, puppetry, drama, writing, and other forms of expression to explore their interests and document learning. A full-time art expert, the atelerista, facilitates the impressive artwork that children produce in Reggio schools.

4. *Collaboration among home, school, and community* is integral to the Reggio Emilia philosophy. Teachers view themselves as lifelong learners, and view the process of learning as occurring not only for the children but also for teachers and parents as well. Family involvement is extensive and community members are called upon frequently to share their areas of expertise with the children.

5. *Teacher as researcher/facilitator.* Teachers guide the development of the classroom curriculum by responding to children's interests, posing good questions, and providing the resources necessary for children to pursue topics of their choice in depth.

6. *Making learning visible.* Children and teachers alike spend a great deal of time gathering data, charting their progress, and documenting learning outcomes. Teachers spend many hours observing, taking anecdotal notes, and documenting children's work through photos and videos.

7. *An aesthetically pleasing environment.* Reggio schools take the approach that schools should be beautiful and functional. Buildings are light-filled, spacious, and carefully appointed and arranged. Children's work is displayed in ways that show it is valued and treated with the same respect given to art produced by adults (e.g., drawings on a lightboard, sculptures in a display case).

Many of the Reggio-inspired programs in the United States do not follow this program entirely and are referred to as "emergent curriculum" and the "project approach."

The Ask the Expert with Jim Hoot on page 64 highlights the contributions that international perspectives can make to early childhood programs in the United States.

Ask the EXPERT

James L. Hoot

Early Childhood Programs Outside the United States

Q: **Why should prospective teachers in the United States be interested in early education in other countries?**

A: Over the next decade, those of Anglo-Saxon ancestry will be minorities in most American schools. Further, while minorities in the past were composed primarily of Blacks and Hispanics, today's growing minorities include children of Vietnamese, Hmong, Cantonese, Cambodian, Korean, Arabic, Eastern European, and other ancestries. Along with this diversity of students is a concomitant diversity of languages and values. Greatly increasing diversity presents unique challenges to teachers who remain primarily Anglo and monolingual.

Q: **Why should we study what early childhood educators in other countries are doing?**

A: Our abundance in the United States in terms of wealth often creates the misleading notion that we are the best in everything we do. As it relates to children, this fallacy was recently well expressed by an American teacher attending a conference presentation on the topic "Excellence in Teaching Young Children—A World Perspective." After teachers from Australia, Finland, and Hungary made short presentations regarding child care in their respective countries, I overheard a stunned American teacher sheepishly whisper to her colleague, "My God! We're a third-world country when it comes to child care."

Clearly, the foundations of our field were laid by thinkers from abroad. Global ideas provides us with an opportunity to benchmark current practices and assess what we might do in the future to improve programming for children. While it would be a mistake to flit from one new international (or national) model to another for the sake of change, thoughtful consideration of the world of ideas for improving the lives of children can move us toward better educational practices for all children.

Q: **How can we learn more about what is going on in other countries?**

A: One of the best ways to learn about (and from) other nations is to travel. In Europe, preservice teachers frequently study in other countries as part of their teacher education programs. In recent years, several universities in the United States have developed such reciprocal relationships as well. In addition, increasing numbers of universities now have year-long international student exchange programs. If such travel is not possible, preservice professionals can also join global professional organizations for early childhood teachers such as the World Organization of Early Childhood Education (OMEP) and the Association for Childhood Education International (ACEI).

Nations of the world are becoming increasingly interdependent. By working together with international colleagues, we become more likely to respond more appropriately to the unique needs of the world's children.

James A. Hoot is a Professor of Early Childhood Education at SUNY, Buffalo, New York, and Past President of the ACEI.

HIGH/SCOPE

In 1962, David Weikart started the Perry Preschool Project in Ypsilanti, Michigan, to address schools' concerns about students who were at high risk of academic failure. The program was based on the cognitive-developmental theories of Jean Piaget. Piaget believed that rather than merely soaking up information, children needed to actively build their own understandings through hands-on activities. This concept, called constructivism, formed the cornerstone of the Perry Preschool Project that evolved into the **High/Scope** curriculum model. A significant achievement of Weikart's model was his longitudinal study that tracked individuals who attended the preschool program and those who did not up through adulthood. The study found that on various indicators of the quality of life (e.g., marital status, educational attainment, occupation), those who participated in preschool had, as a group, much more positive outcomes. This was and is still today considered a landmark study in early childhood research.

Many of the tenets of High/Scope are similar to any early childhood curriculum that implements developmentally appropriate practice. One feature that sets High/Scope apart, however, is the *plan-do-review* sequence that is an integral part of the daily routine. Children convene to *plan* and each child decides and announces what he or she will work on that day. Next, children work, usually at learning centers, and *do* the activities that they selected. During this work time, teachers monitor the children's work, use questions and comments to stimulate children's thinking, and teach conflict resolution skills in context. After their work has been completed, the children reconvene to *review* what they have accomplished by discussing what they have achieved.

Some of the most common features of a High/Scope program include:

- Key developmental indicators (KDIs)—58 criteria that guide curriculum development
- An assessment tool called the *Child Observation Record*, which is designed to monitor each child's progress toward the 58 KDIs
- *Plan-do-review*, in which children choose a learning center, complete activities there, and assess what they accomplished
- Active, hands-on approach to learning
- Teaching of conflict resolution skills in context
- Provision of materials that represent the diversity of the children
- Integration of the arts throughout the curriculum

For more on the contributions of the High/Scope program, see Schweinhart (2005).

DIRECT INSTRUCTION

Direct Instruction is based on the behaviorist theories of B. F. Skinner. The assumptions underlying the program are that children will progress more rapidly if teachers follow a predetermined, sequenced pattern of instruction and that repetition, correction of errors, and praise for the right answers and behaviors are beneficial for children with learning challenges. In the 1960s, Carl Bereiter and Sigfried Englemann developed an early education program called the Direct Instruction System for Teaching Arithmetic and Reading (DISTAR) to use with children who were experiencing difficulties in achieving academically (Kuder, 2001; Sexton, 2001). Today, there are a variety of programs that use Direct Instruction methods.

Some features of Direct Instruction include:

- Behavioral objectives and teacher-directed lessons
- Repetition and drill for students
- Total group response to questions (children often call out answers loudly in unison)
- Highly structured teaching materials (lessons often are scripted for the teacher)
- Immediate feedback and error correction
- Frequent assessment and testing with instruments matched to the curriculum goals

Contemporary versions of Direct Instruction in reading for prekindergarten are *Language for Learning* and the *Reading Mastery* series that includes *Funnix* (a computer-based version for individual children or small groups); in mathematics, DISTAR Arithmetic is in use for high-performing prekindergarten students. To learn more about Direct Instruction, consult the National Institute for Direct Instruction (www.nifdi.org) or the Association for Direct Instruction (www.adihome.org).

HEAD START

Head Start is the only federally funded early childhood program in the United States. Developed in the 1960s as part of President Lyndon B. Johnson's "war on poverty," Head Start sought to serve children from low-income backgrounds by providing comprehensive early childhood education, health and nutrition services, and parent education programs. The program was officially launched in 1965 and serves over 1 million children in approximately 2,600 Head Start programs across the United States (National Head Start Association, 2010). Unlike some of the programs discussed here, Head Start does not use one curriculum; different approaches are used within the program. Two commonly used curricula in Head Start are the commercially available curriculum guide by Diane Trister Dodge titled the Creative Curriculum (www.teachingstrategies.org) and the High/Scope curriculum.

One of the identifying components of Head Start is the emphasis on family involvement. As a condition for their child's participation in the program, parents are required to become involved as part of the program's policies. There are many opportunities for parents to become involved through classroom volunteering, attendance at parent education workshops, and serving as a member of their Head Start's parent advisory board.

For the children, Head Start emphasizes growth in all developmental domains and strives to prepare children both socially and academically for entrance into formal schooling systems. Because Head Start has demonstrated success in its efforts, newer programs such as Early Head Start began in the 1990s to serve children from birth to 3 years of age and their families. Key components of a Head Start classroom include:

- Serves children from families with low incomes
- Provides comprehensive services, including education, health, nutrition, and parent education
- Requires parent participation
- Focuses on physical, emotional, and intellectual development

For more information on all of these early childhood curriculum models and programs, consult the Online Resources at the end of this chapter.

COLLABORATING WITH
Families

A Checklist to Guide Parents in Selecting an Early Childhood Program

Parents choose a program for their children for a variety of reasons. According to the research (Fuller, Holloway, & Bozzi, 1997), the major considerations are as follows:

- convenience and affordability (Evans, 2006)
- supportive relationships with teachers and providers
- caregivers and teachers with positive affect (e.g., warm, sensitive, caring)
- cognitive stimulation that will lead to children's success in school

The following checklist describes features of high-quality early childhood settings that parents should consider when they are seeking an early childhood program for their children.

The Teacher

- ☐ is warm, friendly, and supportive
- ☐ treats each child as a special person
- ☐ has training and experience working with children
- ☐ respects and accepts different races, cultures, religions, and ethnic groups
- ☐ listens to children intently
- ☐ interacts with children in positive ways, nonverbally and verbally
- ☐ clearly states a personal philosophy of education

The School, Center, or Family Child-Care Setting

- ☐ is pleasant, comfortable, and clean
- ☐ has disease-prevention policies and first-aid procedures in place
- ☐ has space for both active and quiet play
- ☐ has appropriate light, heat, and ventilation
- ☐ is regulated and approved by a state and/or federal agency
- ☐ provides a safe outdoor play area
- ☐ is supplied with appropriate learning materials and equipment, indoors and out
- ☐ informs families about policies for release of students and emergency procedures

The Family Support System

- ☐ encourages family participation in the program
- ☐ provides information to families about the program and the child's progress on a regular basis
- ☐ offers scheduled opportunities for conferencing as well as informal opportunities for parents, families, and teachers to interact
- ☐ uses community resources to support families and children

The Program

- ☐ gives every child a sense of belonging
- ☐ guides children in dealing with powerful emotions
- ☐ encourages self-help skills and builds independence
- ☐ prevents behavior problems and resolves conflicts in ways that respect children

Time Is Planned for

- ☐ active and quiet play
- ☐ indoor and outdoor activities
- ☐ trips, excursions, and special events
- ☐ health and safety routines
- ☐ creative expression and the arts
- ☐ language and literacy development activities
- ☐ concrete early math and problem-solving activities

Opportunities Are Provided to

- ☐ learn to get along, to share, and to respect differences
- ☐ learn about own and others' cultural and ethnic backgrounds
- ☐ speak English as well as to speak each family's native language
- ☐ develop each child's unique talents
- ☐ establish healthy self-esteem
- ☐ develop good health habits

Toys and Equipment You Should See Include For Infants

- ☐ cribs, mobiles, soft toys, and blankets
- ☐ rocking chairs, lullaby tapes, and soft lighting
- ☐ safe places to crawl and explore

continued

continued

For 1- and 2-Year-Olds

- ☐ cloth, cardboard, and plastic books
- ☐ items to sort by shape and color, and large hollow blocks
- ☐ baby dolls, beds, bottles, and other related materials
- ☐ toys with which to practice filling and emptying, and pushing and pulling
- ☐ low climbing equipment with padding underneath
- ☐ simple equipment for practicing motor skills (e.g., rocking boat, large wooden toys with wheels)

For Preschoolers

- ☐ clay, paint, books, puzzles, games, and blocks
- ☐ tapes or CDs and simple musical instruments
- ☐ computers and software
- ☐ dress-up clothes, small toys (e.g., miniature farm or house setup), house area (with toy refrigerator, stove, etc.)
- ☐ tricycles, wagons, and climbing equipment
- ☐ sensory materials such as water and sand
- ☐ variety of paper and writing utensils for drawing, writing, and bookmaking
- ☐ labeled objects and areas to help children develop independence

Summary

■ An *early childhood program* is a planned way of supporting the care and education of young children between the ages of birth and 8 years; it includes attention to all of the domains of development—physical, cognitive, emotional, and social. Some types of programs in which early childhood educators are employed include family child care, center-based child care, preschool/nursery school, drop-in child care, and public school-based programs (prekindergarten, kindergarten, grades 1 through 3). *Standards* are benchmarks that are used to guide curriculum development and plan for instruction; these standards may be identified at the national, state, or local levels.

■ Characteristics of high-quality programs include: articulated philosophy and goals, curriculum to meet the standards, appropriate structure and organization, emphasis on concept development, intentional teaching, positive interpersonal relationships, differentiation to accommodate to learners, and interdisciplinary approaches to subject matter.

■ Early childhood educators should be familiar with at least six different widely known approaches to working with young children: Montessori, Bank Street, Reggio Emilia, High/Scope, direct instruction, and Head Start.

■ Programs for young children can be analyzed along several dimensions, including: cultural context, goals and mission, need for the program, type of program, children served by the program, professionals in the program, funding support, and approaches to working with families/communities.

Applying Your Knowledge of High-Quality Programs

In Assessment Activity 1, you will draw upon your knowledge of exemplary early childhood programs to discuss a difficult situation involving after-school care. Then, in Assessment Activity 2, you will analyze a program in your community using a series of questions.

GISELLE'S AFTER-SCHOOL CARE

Giselle is an 8-year-old who lives in an upper-middle-class suburban neighborhood with her father, mother, and 4-year-old brother. Every day after school, she goes out into the yard with her brother and calls out to the retired woman who lives next door, "Hi Anna! Is it okay if we jump the fence?" Then the two young children climb over the fence that separates the two yards and spend the next hour or two on the patio with their neighbors. About this, Giselle says matter-of-factly, "My mom said that after-school care costs too much and that we can just play or watch TV until she gets home from work. This house cost *a lot* of money." The neighbor who unofficially watches Giselle and her brother says, "They are a nice family but I worry about those young children being by themselves. Giselle is really mature for her age, but she wouldn't know what to do in an emergency. My husband and I just try to arrange to be home every weekday afternoon. It's only for about an hour, and then their mom is home from her shift at the hospital."

Anna's granddaughter, who is an undergraduate early childhood major, visits her grandparents in the summer and she says, "I know you both love children and all, but have you considered the legal implications? You don't really have any agreement with this neighbor about responsibility for care. If something happens to those children, they could sue you even though you are trying to do them a favor. I think that they should be reported for child neglect."

Giselle's mother says, "I don't know what I would do if we couldn't rely on Anna. It doesn't help me much to have my children in after-school care because I have to leave work on my break to take them there, take a chance on being late getting back to work, and then go through rush-hour traffic to pick them up after my shift. I think that after-school programs should be right in the school building and supported by the community like they were when we lived in Los Angeles. We were totally unprepared for the lack of services here."

REACT	What is your initial response to Giselle's situation? What would you like to say to each of the adults in this scenario? How has program quality affected the lives of these children and adults?
RESEARCH	Read a recent, authoritative article about after-school programs, policies, curricula, or philosophies. What are some of the issues and trends?
REFLECT	Discuss what you and your classmates found in your readings. How has this discussion influenced your thinking about after-school care?

ANALYZING EARLY CHILDHOOD PROGRAMS

Locate a brochure or online description of a local early childhood program. As you review the material about the program, use the following questioning framework to analyze it (from Kamerman & Kahn, 1994).

Program Analysis Criteria

Type of Program

- What category of program is it (e.g., family child care, center-based child care, preschool, pre-K, kindergarden, public school, private school)?
- On what hours, schedules, and calendar does it typically operate?

Cultural Context of the Program

- What uniquenesses does this early childhood program appear to have?
- How has the culture and the society in which the program operates influenced standard practices?

Goals and Mission

- What is the program's primary focus and purpose?
- What type of curriculum does it offer and what outcomes does it claim?

Need for the Program

- What is the apparent demand for this type of program in the community?
- What does the program report as its achievements?

Children Served by the Program

- What is the program's basic view of the child?
- Who is eligible for and served by the program?

Families and Communities

- How are the roles of parents, families, and community defined in the program?
- Are there affiliations or linkages with other community groups (e.g., church or synagogue, intervention services, social agencies, etc.)?

Professionals in the Program

- What qualifications are necessary to work in the program?
- How are the staff members trained, compensated, and retained?

Funding Sources

- How is the program funded—single or multiple sources?
- Does it charge tuition? If so, how is the rate determined? Is it a sliding scale?

Physical Environment

- Does the indoor environment or facility appear to be adequate in terms of the building, classroom layout, materials/equipments, and access for children with special needs?
- What about the outdoor facility? Does it appear to be appropriate, safe, well-equipped, and accessible to children with special needs?

Evaluation/Accreditation

- Is the program accredited? If so, by whom?
- How is quality monitored each year (e.g., by the state, county, national organization)?

ONLINE RESOURCES FOR EARLY CHILDHOOD PROGRAMS AND PROGRAM STANDARDS

American Montessori Society: Includes the history, mission, and a variety of resources. www.americanmontessorisociety.org

Abecedarian Project: A NIEER program started in 1972 to support children from low-income backgrounds, this project has conducted longitudinal research on the benefit-cost ratio of early education. http://nieer.org/resources/research/AbecedarianStudy.pdf

Bank Street: View the philosophy, structure, and curriculum guide for this program model with a long and distinguished history. www.bankstreet.edu/sfc/curriculum.html

The Creative Curriculum: Designed by Diane Trister Dodge in 1988, this program is in wide use in Head Start and other early childhood programs. www.teachingstrategies.com

Direct Instruction: This approach is based on behavioral theory and uses repetition, carefully sequenced drill, and reinforcement to teach content. View the Institute of Education Sciences Report at: http://ies.ed.gov/ncee/wwc/pdf/WWC_ReadingMastery_081208.pdf

Inclusive Early Childhood Programs: Visit this University of Kansas site to get information about the program models, how they practice inclusion, and links to programs that have put the models to use. www.circleofinclusion.org/

High/Scope: Based on the research of the Perry Preschool Project, this curriculum is an application of Piagetian principles. www.highscope.org/

Head Start: This federally funded program began in the 1960s as a way to support young children and families living in poverty. The National Head Start Association (NHSA) is a private not-for-profit membership organization representing the many participants. www.nhsa.org/

Reggio Emilia: Visit this site to learn more about Reggio schools in the United States, see the traveling exhibit of the children's work, and watch a video of the program in action, North American Reggio Emilia Alliances (NAREA): www.reggioalliance.org/

PEARSON myeducationlab

Go to Topic 5 (Program Models) in the MyEducationLab (**www.myeducationlab.com**) for your course, where you can:

- Find learning outcomes for program models along with the national standards that connect to these outcomes.
- Complete Assignments and Activities that can help you more deeply understand the chapter content.
- Apply and practice your understanding of the core teaching skills identified in the chapter with the Building Teaching Skills and Dispositions learning units.

CHAPTER 4

Understanding Diversity and Inclusion

 Most learning in most settings is a communal activity, a sharing of cultures.

Jerome Bruner, 1987, p. 127

Meet the TEACHERS

MS. PEARLSTEIN is a teacher from a low-income background who works in a very wealthy community where most of the parents are international business leaders, doctors, and lawyers. Ms. Pearlstein observes that "Many of the parents attribute their financial success entirely to work ethic; they seem unaware of the many advantages they had growing up. One afternoon, the program director stayed after school to 'fix up' the children's work before it went home; she said 'Parents will not pay tuition unless they see evidence that the program is accelerating their child's growth.' I think that this creates a false impression of what the children can do independently."

MR. McCABE is a kindergarten teacher in a city that once was a major U.S. auto manufacturing site. Many factories have closed, leaving few employment options. The principal approaches Mr. McCabe about identifying children who are struggling academically; there is a plan for a "junior" first grade, a year in between kindergarten, and "regular" first grade. Although Mr. McCabe does not feel that it is an appropriate placement for any of his students, the principal says, "I'm going to need a few names by the end of the week in order to have a class-size group and take advantage of this funding opportunity; try to choose families that won't protest too much, if you know what I mean."

MRS. HERNANDEZ teaches third grade in a public school that has failed to make AYP—adequate yearly progress. In accordance with the No Child Left Behind legislation, the school has been put on notice that students' scores on state-mandated reading tests must improve significantly over the next three years; otherwise, the school can be closed and the teachers and administrators can be replaced. The principal calls an "emergency meeting" and recommends that all "nonessential" activities (she mentions recess, art, music, physical education, science, social studies) be suspended so that the teachers and children can cram for the tests. Mrs. Hernandez later remarks to a colleague, "I don't agree. Brain research suggests that physical activity and pursuing interests in the arts and sciences are important ways of supporting children's overall development and learning."

LEARNING Outcomes

In this chapter, you will learn to:

→ Understand the concepts of diversity and inclusion and the teacher's responsibility to develop competence in them in order to reach and teach young children (NAEYC #1, INTASC #3, ACEI #3b)

→ Define diversity and inclusion

→ Explain principles of inclusion and fairness

→ Explore your role in becoming a culturally competent teacher

→ Apply your knowledge of diversity, inclusion, and cultural competence

---

Compare

What are the ethical dilemmas in each of these situations?

Contrast

How might variables (e.g., race, income, language) be involved in these decisions?

Connect

How would you respond in each of these circumstances? Would you "go along" or would you resist in some way, publicly or privately?

Now that you have reflected on the three teachers' perspectives and noted the learning outcomes, we preview the knowledge, skills, and dispositions you will need to acquire in order to work with diverse children and families.

Defining Diversity and Inclusion

Imagine that you were transported to a completely different context where the customs, language, traditions, beliefs, and values differed dramatically from your own. Now imagine that, while you were there, no one bothered to ask about nor showed the slightest interest in your ways; in fact, they assumed that your customs, language, traditions, beliefs, values, and life practices were inferior and ought to be abandoned in favor of theirs. The United States has a long history with this practice. Referred to as the "melting pot," the assumption was that the dominant culture's way was better and that everyone else should reject what they held dear in the interest of unification. During the 1960s, people began to question this false sense of unity that attempted to gloss over differences. The multicultural era began with a "salad bowl" concept in which each culture retained its distinctive flavor yet co-existed harmoniously—a "we are all alike, we are all different" approach. Key pieces of legislation, such as the *Brown vs. the Board of Education* decision that mandated desegregation of schools and the Individuals with Disabilities Education Act (IDEA) that required accommodations for persons with disabilities, have served to expand perspectives and increase respect for others.

Diversity refers to the important differences between and among individuals that contribute to their definition of self. Figure 4.1 is an overview of just some areas of diversity you will encounter in your work with children, families, colleagues, and community members.

Understanding diversity is important for early childhood educators because it constitutes a set of knowledge and skills that will

DID YOU Know ?

- When people hear the word *diversity*, it is common for them to assume that it is in reference to racial and ethnic differences; however, race and ethnicity are only one type of diversity; Americans are also diverse in terms of language, religion, culture, ideology, disability/ability, socioeconomic status, gender, sexual orientation, and many other attributes (Bowman, 2010).

- Several states already contain a majority of people of color, and children of color are expected to compose the *majority* of Americans younger than 18 years old within the next 15 years (U.S. Census Bureau, 2008a, 2008b).

- The largest proportion of English language learners in the U.S. population is in the under-age-5 group (Garcia & Frede, 2010).

- It is common to think of urban settings when the term *poverty* is used; however, two-thirds of the people living in poverty in the United States are White and live in towns. Fifty percent of children from families with low-income backgrounds live in a household headed by a woman age 25 years or younger (U.S. Census Bureau, 2008a, 2008b).

- While the student population has grown more diverse, the teaching population is more White, middle class, and female (Achinstein, Ogawa, & Sexton, 2010; Nieto & Bode, 2008). Not only are there few teachers of color, they also exit the teaching profession in larger numbers, with up to 50% turnover within 5 years (Ingersoll & Conner, 2009).

Figure 4.1 **Areas of Diversity**

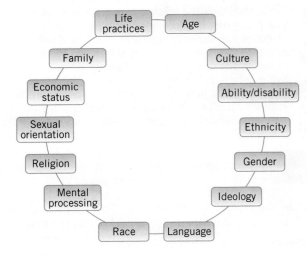

Sources: Bowman, 2010; Keengwe, 2010; Madrazo & Motz, 2005.

enable them to work more successfully with children and families from different backgrounds (Banks, 2006; Cushner, McClelland, & Safford, 2009; Nieto & Bode, 2008). As Hanson and Lynch (2010) point out,

> Like snowflakes, no two people are alike. Even identical twins learn, grow, and develop personalities that make each one unique. In spite of the many characteristics that all people share, each person differs from all the others in multiple ways. The same is true of families. All families are diverse, and diversity is one of the most intriguing parts of being human. (p. 147)

Few preservice teachers have much experience interacting with children and families that do not have similar income and social class backgrounds. As a result, they may (1) overgeneralize and assume that they understand family needs, priorities, values, and beliefs when they do not (Xu, 2007); (2) hold misconceptions or stereotypes that bias them against individuals or groups (Vaughn, 2005); (3) lack confidence in their ability to say and do the right things; and (4) tend to avoid interactions with children and families that differ significantly from their own background (Hollins & Guzman, 2005; Ray, Bowman, & Robbins, 2006). All of these things will seriously impair a teacher's overall effectiveness because "each school, each community, each culture that a teacher faces call for different understandings and different responses" (Birmingham, 2003, p. 1).

Families can be distinctive in many different ways. In order to interact successfully with families, we first need to consider what makes each one unique:

> How families are structured and who is considered to be a family member are dimensions of diversity that might be the starting point for learning more about each family. For instance, is the family comprised of a mother, a father, and children, or does the family consist of a large number of individuals who are related as a tribe or a clan? Sociocultural factors too, such as socioeconomic status, education, and family members' feelings of self-efficacy, provide information about family members' experiences and views of the world. In addition, the many components of culture and cultural identity such as primary language, race, ethnicity, religion or spiritual practices, values and beliefs related to child rearing, gender roles, traditions, aspirations, and family organization are additional dimensions that define each family's diversity. (Hanson & Lynch, 2010, p. 148)

Figure 4.2 is a sampling of some of the different ideas that families might have on early childhood education, their child's performance at school, approaches to teaching/learning, and the role of the family in supporting education. An important companion concept to diversity is inclusion.

Inclusion, as it applies to teaching, refers to the idea that, in a democratic society, *every* child merits—and gets—education, opportunities, and experiences that

Pause and
Reflect

On Your Diversity

Using the Areas of Diversity in Figure 4.1, reflect on the ways in which you may differ from a few, most, or all of your classmates. How do these differences contribute to your sense of who you are? How might your own characteristics affect your ideas about what is "normal" in families?

Teachers must demonstrate a commitment to equity and fairness.

Figure 4.2 Families' Differing Perspectives on Early Education

Perspectives on Education

Some families may:

- View schooling as a very serious endeavor and may not see a need for "fun" at school
- Expect close teacher–student relationships
- Believe that young children should be cared for at home
- Value academic skills over music, the arts, and sports
- Prefer to see lots of paperwork coming home
- Expect teachers to be authority figures/taskmasters
- Value oral traditions (e.g., recitation, debate, traditional stories) over print materials

Ideas About Performance in Class

Some families may:

- Expect teachers to uncover children's abilities
- Prefer to see their child master a skill in private before attempting it in public
- Value cooperation over individual achievement
- Expect assignments that require students to follow directions rather than creative responses
- Value politeness and humility in their child
- Be less concerned about punctuality
- Believe that collaborative learning will hamper their child's success

Preferred Teaching/Learning Mode

Some families may:

- Favor physical movement and kinesthetic approaches
- Believe in apprenticeship models of learning where children imitate adults
- Request that teachers use specific methods
- Expect warm, friendly, nurturing classrooms
- Prefer competition and extrinsic motivation
- Value concrete presentations over the abstract
- Want to see repetition and drill of basic facts

Ideas About Family's Role

Some families may:

- Assume they have no responsibility for teaching
- Demonstrate a strong work ethic
- Punish children's misbehavior at school at home
- Prefer to be contacted frequently about the child's progress
- Regard obedience as the most important trait in children
- See their role as negotiating with the school so that their child's particular needs are met
- Think it is best for children to be silent and respectful
- Ask to see lots of homework
- Believe that the school has no role in teaching values

other children get. At first, this may seem obvious—if children are in class together, they get the same things, right? According to the research, the answer is no (Banks, 2006; Hollins & Guzman, 2005; Nieto, 2009). In the same way that it is possible for children to live in the same family and have very different childhoods, children in the same class can have dramatically different experiences. A given classroom may provide high-quality experiences for some or even most children while other children do not get the same level of support (McClean, Wolery, & Bailey, 2004). Although the overall quality of a program "determines the highest level of quality experiences a child has in that setting, there is no assurance that every child in the classroom is participating in the good-quality interactions and activities that may be available. It is important to examine individual children's experiences in early care and education settings, as well as whether and how those experiences may differ from global classroom quality" (Clawson & Luze, 2008, p. 147).

To illustrate just a few common inequities in the classroom, a teacher may call on boys more than girls, give the family "on welfare" little consideration, dismiss children's bullying with "children can be cruel," or assume that the child from a low-income background is less capable academically (Delpit, 2006; Sadker, Sadker, & Zittleman, 2008).

Outside the classroom, the inequities are even more pronounced. The opportunities, resources, and access to them can be very different, even for families living in the same community (Wiseman, 2009). Early childhood educators have a professional obligation to work effectively with *all* children and families.

An important companion concept to diversity is cultural competence. **Cultural competence** refers to a person's ability to work effectively with people whose beliefs, traditions, worldviews, language, and physical characteristics differ from their own (Hanson & Lynch, 2010; Herrera, 2010; Lynch, 2004). It goes beyond knowing about others and even beyond respecting differences. Cultural competence emphasizes positive, action-driven possibilities in student–teacher relationships and requires every teacher, irrespective of his or her group membership, to have the "courage, competence, and confidence" to teach in a culturally relevant manner (Gay, 2010). Becoming a **culturally responsive** teacher requires three levels of work: self-awareness, seeking to understand, and taking action. These levels are explained in Figure 4.3. In the Ask the Expert feature on page 78, Dr. Linda Espinosa explains how early childhood educators can take actions that demonstrate cultural competence and improve outcomes for children.

Figure 4.3 Steps in Acquiring Cultural Competence

Step One: Self-Awareness

Strive to understand how your background has shaped beliefs, values, and attitudes. Challenge some of your own assumptions.

Realize that everyone has some biases. Think about what happens when you encounter differences—the comments you make, the jokes at others' expense, and the thoughts that flash through your mind but that you would not admit.

Consider how your fear of doing or saying the wrong thing can inhibit your interactions with diverse populations, which will only decrease your cultural competence over time.

Step Two: Seeking to Understand

Learn more about others' cultural and sociocultural perspectives.

Recognize that cultures differ in terms of such things as: concepts of time, ideas about personal space, physical touch, eye contact, ways of listening, patience and persistence, and so forth.

Learn about the values, beliefs, and behaviors of various ethnic and cultural groups, and assess the impact of culture on individual behavior and family or societal interactions.

Step Three: Put What Was Learned into Practice

Honor other cultures in daily practice.

Cast yourself in the role of the learner.

Realize that the curriculum is not "neutral"; it is part of the power structures of the larger society.

Sources: Hanson & Lynch, 2010; Keengwe, 2010; Larrivee, 2008; Lynch, 2004; Nieto & Bode, 2008; Xu, 2007.

Principles of Inclusion and Fairness

Throughout the world, it often is the case that "Children are not counted because they are not expected to have a stake in the present social, economic, or political arrangements . . . They do not vote and cannot claim an income and are judged not to play any recognized formative role within school or home" (Wyness, 2000, p. 25). Organizations such as the United Nations have made continuing efforts to improve the conditions of children worldwide. In 2009, the world marked the 20th anniversary of the United Nations Convention on the Rights of the Child. This statement includes 54 articles that include a definition of childhood, the child's right to play, child labor

Ask the EXPERT — Linda M. Espinosa

Working with Children from Diverse Backgrounds

Q: What types of diversity are teachers likely to see?

A: Children who enter group early care and educational programs from families with low incomes; who speak a language other than English; who represent an ethnic group that is non-White, such as Latino/Hispanic, African American, or American Indian; or who are recent immigrants to the United States are at a higher risk for school failure. Those children from non-White cultures, low-income households, or who enter school programs speaking little or no English are highly vulnerable to chronic academic underachievement and eventual school failure. There are dramatic differences in young children's achievement in mathematics and literacy by race, ethnicity, and socioeconomic status (SES) at school entry that persist throughout their schooling.

Q: Do these children struggle in school because they come from poor families, because they don't speak English, or because they are unfamiliar with school expectations?

A: Children from nonmainstream backgrounds often experience "double jeopardy." They frequently live in households that have few economic, educational, and social resources and they are more likely to attend schools that have fewer resources, which magnifies any existing educational inequalities. Children who enter school not speaking English must also face the increased demand of learning a new language while also learning academic subject matter. Children whose home culture is substantially different from that of the school culture also face sociocultural discontinuity; this disharmony can create school adjustment difficulties. The family economic, social, cultural, health, and educational conditions interact with the school characteristics and result in early inequities that often persist throughout a child's schooling.

Q: How can early childhood professionals improve the educational success of children from diverse backgrounds?

A: Early childhood educators can improve the educational outcomes for children from diverse backgrounds by:

- providing a culturally responsive curriculum that integrates features of the child's family practices into the classroom.
- providing continuous support for home-language development as the child is acquiring English.
- hiring qualified bilingual and bicultural teachers and staff.
- individualizing curriculum, interactions, learning opportunities, and assessment approaches.
- conducting continuous assessment to identify children's individual preferences, interests, and abilities in their home language and English.
- engaging families as true partners.
- recognizing and embracing the belief that diversity is a strength and bilingualism is an asset.
- recognizing that children from diverse backgrounds and non-English-speaking homes can become fully bilingual and biliterate and achieve to high standards when provided with high-quality early education combined with effective family partnership programs.

Linda Espinosa is a retired Professor of Early Childhood Education in the College of Education at the University of Missouri–Columbia. She also is the author of Getting It RIGHT for Young Children from Diverse Backgrounds: Applying Research to Improve Practice.

issues, respect for the views of the child, protection from violence and exploitation, and many more. Article 2, Nondiscrimination, is particularly relevant to any discussion of diversity. It states that all children have all of the rights spelled out in the document:

> **Article 2 (Nondiscrimination):** The Convention applies to all children, whatever their race, religion or abilities; whatever they think or say, whatever type of family they come from. It doesn't matter where children live, what language they speak, what their parents do, whether they are boys or girls, what their culture is, whether they have a disability or whether they are rich or poor. No child should be treated unfairly on any basis.

Thus, the **universal rights of children** are:

> not about what *children* do, they are about what *governments* agree to do for children when they commit to treaties and laws. Rights inform what governments do and, transform acts of benevolence—like whether or not to fund primary education for every child, and whether or not to ensure every child has a legal identity—into duties and obligations that must be honoured. (Guthrie, 2009, p. 10)

Children also have rights within an early childhood setting, things that teachers are obligated to do or provide for them so that every child is respected and all children are included (Loreman, 2009). Figure 4.4 is an overview of some of these unalienable rights of young children in educational contexts.

Respecting children and embracing diversity are essential teaching behaviors.

Figure 4.4 Children's Rights in the Early Childhood Classroom

Children have a right to . . .

- Be greeted warmly every day
- Be noticed in positive ways
- Exercise choices throughout the school day
- Enjoy their educational experiences
- Be heard and responded to by adults and peers
- Be allowed to converse with their peers
- Gain competencies, skills, and confidence
- Have their abilities recognized and regarded
- Think about and solve problems
- Explore their world
- Expect daily and weekly routines
- Learn the skills of independence
- Give and receive compliments

- Establish warm and supportive relationships with adults
- Have adventures that involve new challenges or risks
- Expect fairness in class rules, policies, and procedures
- Give and get help
- Learn to resolve conflicts
- Understand how to make, keep, and be a friend
- Be accepted Into the classroom community and make contributions to it
- Be able to make mistakes, break a rule, or act wrongfully and then make amends, repair, and recover their place in the group

Sources: Charney, 2002; Strachota, 1996.

Pause and
Reflect

About Your Cultural Competence

Go to http://gucchd.georgetown.edu/products/ NCCC_EIECChecklist.pdf and review the items on the questionnaire "Promoting Cultural and Linguistic Competency" (Goode, 2005). What new insights do you have about diversity in early childhood and the things that teachers can do to demonstrate cultural competence?

The Code of Ethics of the Division for Early Childhood (DEC) of the Council for Exceptional Children (2009) includes the following statements under the topic "Enhancement of Children's and Families' Quality of Lives:"

1. We shall demonstrate our respect and concern for children, families, colleagues, and others with whom we work, honoring their beliefs, values, customs, languages, and culture.

2. We shall recognize our responsibility to improve the developmental outcomes of children and to provide services and supports in a fair and equitable manner to all families and children.

3. We shall recognize and respect the dignity, diversity, and autonomy of the families and children we serve.

4. We shall advocate for equal access to high quality services and supports for all children and families to enhance their quality of lives.

Anti-bias education respects the right of all children to reach their full potential as they are learning to be contributing members of a democratic society (Copple & Bredekamp, 2009; Derman-Sparks & Edwards, 2010). It also challenges teachers to examine beliefs, attitudes, and actions that might deny any child that unconditional respect. An anti-bias approach to education actively teaches children to think about and make sense of information about those who are different from them (Derman-Sparks & Edwards, 2010). Anti-bias education is not a curriculum but rather a framework of four goals through which to teach children to respect themselves and others. The four anti-bias goals state that each child will:

1. demonstrate self-awareness, confidence, family pride, and positive social identities;

2. express comfort and joy with human diversity, accurate language for human differences, and deep, caring human connections;

3. increasingly recognize unfairness, have language to describe unfairness, and understand that unfairness hurts; and

4. demonstrate empowerment and the skills to act, with others, against prejudice and/or discriminatory actions. (Derman-Sparks & Edwards, 2010, pp. 4–5)

Your Role in Becoming Culturally Competent

In order to become a culturally competent teacher, at least seven roles have to be fulfilled: (1) engaging in ethical reasoning; (2) challenging assumptions; (3) mastering skilled dialogue; (4) understanding the hidden curriculum; (5) promoting diversity, inclusion, and cultural competence in the classroom; (6) integrating diversity across the curriculum; and (7) implementing strategies that honor diversity.

ENGAGING IN ETHICAL REASONING

Ethical teachers use moral principles to guide behavior (e.g., equity, freedom, respect), and identify and empathize with the welfare of others beyond duty or common decency (Tennyson & Strom, 1988). Suppose that a child in your class is being seriously neglected and arrives at school tired, hungry, unwashed, and dressed in clothes that will not protect her against the weather. Some teachers would complain bitterly about the family. Many would contact local social services agencies for support. Some would try to arrange a meeting at school with the family. Others would make a visit to the home. Still others would intervene directly and see to it that the child was fed, clothed, and bathed. At one time or another, most teachers have tried several of these strategies. Unlike situations in some other occupations, no one told these teachers precisely what to do or when to act. Rather, they relied upon their general care and concern for children and families, the input of colleagues and other professionals, their familiarity with the particular child's situation, and knowledge of school policies and state regulations and laws affecting schools. When a teacher is solving a complex (yet common) problem such as helping a neglected child, breaking it down into smaller steps and proceeding confidently toward a solution seldom occurs. More often than not, teachers have to feel their way through many possible courses of action and proceed cautiously, guided by their "ethic of caring" (Noddings, 1984). Figure 4.5 provides a series of questions that can be used as a tool in ethical reasoning.

When teachers interact with other respected professionals—particularly those who have more experience—this interaction exerts a powerful, positive influence on the ability to reflect on ethical dilemmas (Harle & Trudeau, 2006). When you think about dilemmas and challenging situations, your initial reaction might be to consider what is right and wrong—ideas that have been shaped by your family, community, culture, faith, and so forth. Each of us also has values—behaviors that we prize in ourselves and in others, such as honesty, compassion, or loyalty. Although such beliefs are obviously important and affect behavior, becoming a professional requires something more; it requires a code of ethical conduct. **Professional teacher ethics** call upon early childhood educators to move beyond personal beliefs and act upon our collective obligation to what is fair and just for all children, families, and colleagues—even for us (Feeney & Pizzolongo, 2010). As early childhood educators, we have a **code of ethics,** a statement that is based on the core values of our profession that we must adhere to in our work (Feeney, 2010; Feeney, Freeman, & Moravcik, 2008). Stephanie Feeney's Ask the Expert feature on page 83 offers additional information on the ethical code.

CHALLENGING ASSUMPTIONS

To reach and teach children, early childhood teachers must acquire insight into their students' lives outside of school. There is evidence that many teachers struggle to teach students with backgrounds different from their own (Sadker et al., 2008). "A student's unique needs could be attributed to learning styles, developmental levels, and social economic status, learning experiences, religion, social class, race, and ethnicity, sexual orientation, and physical and mental abilities. As a result, it is critical that teachers understand these attributes and respond with skill and sensitivity to help support each student to attain their full social and academic potential" (Keengwe, 2010).

Some groups of children tend to perform less well on standardized achievement tests than others. For example, in international comparisons, U.S. students do not achieve the highest scores in mathematics and science. How would a typical person on the street explain this discrepancy? They

Pause and Reflect

On the NAEYC Code of Ethical Conduct

Go to the NAEYC website at www.naeyc.org/positionstatements/ethical_conduct to view the Code of Ethical Conduct in English and Spanish. What contributions can this document make to: Protecting young children and families? Offering guidance to early childhood professionals? Unifying the profession? Communicating the profession's values to others?

Figure 4.5 Ethical Reasoning Processes

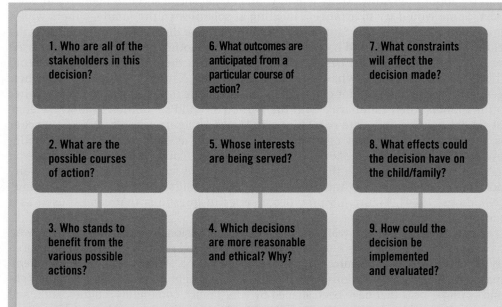

1. Who are all of the stakeholders in this decision?

2. What are the possible courses of action?

3. Who stands to benefit from the various possible actions?

4. Which decisions are more reasonable and ethical? Why?

5. Whose interests are being served?

6. What outcomes are anticipated from a particular course of action?

7. What constraints will affect the decision made?

8. What effects could the decision have on the child/family?

9. How could the decision be implemented and evaluated?

Try applying this ethical reasoning process and your knowledge of diversity, anti-bias, and cultural competence to the following scenarios.

Scenario 1: Gender Issues

"A Japanese father stopped by the preschool and was horrified to see his son in a dress, high heels, and an apron standing at the toy stove and pretending to cook. I tried to explain that it was just pretending but the father disagreed and repeated, several times, 'Don't want no gay boy!' Now what do I do? Should I restrict the boy's play choices or should I continue to allow the boy to pursue his play interests and run the risk of another confrontation with the father?"

Scenario 2: Memories of Curriculum

A teacher said, "A very vocal group among the parents pressures us to offer the curriculum that they experienced as children, one that celebrates Halloween, Thanksgiving, Christmas, Valentine's Day, and so forth or, as one parent stated, 'The way *we* remember school.' If teachers resist, parents are disappointed, suspicious, or angry with us for not responding to their wishes. I wonder if we should just give in and give up on a multicultural approach."

Scenario 3: A Misunderstanding

"One day my daughter came home and said that the school was having a food festival and that we were to bring one food item from our native country. We went to the Indian food store to get all of the ingredients so that she could share a traditional Indian sweet. When school was over, my daughter went directly to her room; this is what she does when she is upset; and didn't want to talk about it. Finally, later that evening, she told me what was wrong. She was crying and said, 'The children wouldn't eat our food and the teacher threw it in the garbage can.' I was so upset. I spoke with the head teacher about it but it may have made things worse for my daughter. I don't think the teacher likes her now."

Sources: Jalongo, 2007; Tennyson & Strom, 1988.

NAEYC Code of Ethics

Q: **Why do early childhood educators need to be concerned about ethics?**

A: Morality is based on values and refers to deeply held beliefs about right and wrong that guide people's behavior. Ethics involves making choices between values and thinking about duties and obligations to others. Professional ethics involves reflection on values and morality relating to the work that is done by the members of a profession. Early childhood educators need to be concerned with professional ethics because we work with children at a time in their lives when they are very young and therefore vulnerable. Because young children are so defenseless, it is important that those who work with them be aware of the tremendous power that they have over children's lives. They need to be aware of their obligation to do what is right and to be certain that nothing they do is harmful to children.

Another reason that professional ethics is important is that early childhood educators often find themselves in situations where they have conflicting responsibilities. They have obligations to children, families, the agencies they work for, and their communities. Each of these has needs and makes demands. Knowing about professional ethics helps educators to weigh and balance the demands of each of these groups in ways that help them put the best interests of children first.

Q: **What is a code of ethics, and why is it an important part of a profession?**

A: The goal of a profession is to contribute to society and to meet the needs of the people it serves. A code of ethics reflects the wisdom and commitments of a profession and describes its responsibilities. A code assures society that the people who do an important job will have high standards and conduct themselves in a moral way. One way to determine if an occupation is a profession is to ask if it has a code of ethics.

A code of ethics is based on the moral reflection of the profession and addresses the obligations that each practitioner shares in meeting its responsibilities. It is not a legal or regulatory document. A code supports professionals in choosing to do what is right, not what is easiest, most comfortable, or will make them most popular. It gives professionals guidance as they seek to understand and resolve moral dilemmas they encounter in their work.

Q: **How can knowing about the NAEYC Code of Ethics help teachers of young children?**

A: A commitment to ethical behavior is an essential part of every profession. Because early childhood educators make a significant contribution to young children in our society, it is important that they commit themselves to behaving ethically. For this reason, NAEYC has developed a Code of Ethical Conduct. The NAEYC Code was first published in l989 and was updated in 1992, 1997, and 2005. This Code is part of the identity of the field of early childhood care and education. It identifies the issues the profession cares about and wants new members to care about, communicates with those outside the profession about what they can expect from its members, and provides guidelines for ethical conduct. It identifies the field's core values, identifies relationships that are fundamental to members' work (children, families, colleagues, and community and society), spells out ethical responsibilities, and guides in the resolution of ethical dilemmas.

The Code is based on core values that reflect members' central beliefs, history, commitment to society, and common purpose embraced by the early childhood field. These core values are the foundation that makes it possible for early childhood educators to move from personal values and beliefs to a shared understanding of the professional values held by everyone in the field.

Stephanie Feeney is Professor Emerita of Education at the University of Hawaii. She is co-author of the NAEYC Code of Ethical Conduct and of two books on professional ethics in early care and education published by NAEYC.

Young children with special needs are included in most early childhood settings.

might say that the teachers in the United States don't work hard enough or that some students aren't motivated or come from poor families. As an educator you need to have a more informed perspective on such matters and explore some rival explanations that are based on research. In the case of international comparisons, one issue to consider is who takes the tests. In some countries, children exit the school system rather early and do not go on to high school, while some—particularly those with special needs—may not attend at all. "Poverty limits both educational opportunity and social experience. It also affects all aspects of daily life, as families try to exist in an expensive, competitive, and material world" (Hanson & Lynch, 2010, p. 151), but poverty alone is not to blame (Ladson-Billings, 2006). If teachers ignore or reject different cultural expressions of development, opportunities to learn are diminished, students can grow discouraged, and this can lead to academic failure (Nieto & Bode, 2008). In other words, a deficit view of children and families can influence teachers' principles and practices and undermine student success (Bishop, Berryman, Tiakiwai, & Richardson, 2003; Fennimore & Goodwin, 2011, in press; Genishi & Dyson, 2009).

MASTERING SKILLED DIALOGUE

Fear of saying the wrong thing and offending someone frequently is a barrier to communication across cultures. The solution is to acquire the ability to apply the **skilled dialogue** that embraces respect, reciprocity, and responsiveness when interacting with children and families from diverse cultural and linguistic backgrounds (Barrera & Corso, 2002). A simple thing such as learning a few basic words in the child's first language—hello, goodbye, please, and thank you—can demonstrate a willingness to learn more about the child and family. We can build our confidence in speaking with diverse children and families by choosing our words carefully. Even if we are unsure about which terminology to use, we can ask (Keengwe, 2010; Nieto & Bode, 2008). For instance, when a group of teachers became pen pals with a group of children from the Upper Peninsula of Michigan, they found that the children did not want to be called Indian or Native Americans; rather, they wanted the teachers to know them by the name of their tribe, the Potawatomi. By learning this, the preservice teachers were able to use the terminology that was most welcomed by that group of kindergartners.

Another way to support skilled dialogue is to place yourself in the role of the learner. For example, a teacher from a city background was responsible for a unit on farm animals, so she invited the families in the school's rural community to share their knowledge. She was delighted when a father volunteered to bring a sheep to the playground and demonstrate how the wool is sheared while the child's aunt demonstrated the process of making the wool into yarn and knitting it into clothing. Likewise, during their unit on the food pyramid, a grandfather with a large assortment of metal farm equipment toys explained how each one was used to plant and harvest; he also allowed the children to use them at one of the learning centers. When educators show interest in and an appreciation for what families know and can do—for their "funds of knowledge"—this can go a long way in promoting mutual respect (Han & Thomas, 2010; Moll, Amanti, Nett, & Gonzalez, 1992).

UNDERSTANDING THE HIDDEN CURRICULUM

Early childhood educators need to consider not just the common, public practices of school—such as waves of innovation—but also the powerful undertow beneath. The **hidden curriculum** refers to habitual ways of doing things, the taken-for-granted procedures, and the automatic responses that may reflect biases; hidden or private curriculum also includes the lessons that are learned but not written down anywhere. For example, many people assume that school curriculum is "neutral," in other words, just a body of information children are expected to learn, but there are many other things that children learn by being in school that are not part of any public document. For example, a child may learn that teachers want a particular answer to a question that they have in mind rather than an original response, or that some teachers favor certain students over others. Thus, schools can give the *appearance* of being fair yet not truly do this in daily practice. The reality is that the power group, usually those with more money and influence, decides what is included/excluded from the curriculum, what "counts" as evidence of success, and who has access to support services. In many instances, the power group will choose those things that preserve their own privileged place in society. Take, for example, the school music program. Usually, instruments are in short supply, so the school decides to concentrate on those who show promise instead of giving every child a fair chance at education in music. A school might use a test intended to determine which children have the most potential in music, but, in reality, it is a test of experience because, time after time, children whose families can afford musical training outside of school will be identified as the talented ones.

The hidden curriculum is evident when children and families are referred to in derogatory ways: "families who live in the projects," "the slow students," "poor families," "the kids who just don't get it," and so forth. All of these comments reflect a negative judgment, a tendency to look less favorably upon certain children as a group, and hint at an unwillingness to offer additional support. Chak (2006) suggests that reflective practice in which a teacher looks within offers the best opportunity for every child to achieve.

Pause and Reflect

On Your Expectations for Children

Which of the following characteristics do you think are particularly important for children: creative, obedient, assertive, confident, smart, compassionate, independent, quiet, cooperative, and respectful of adults? How might cultural background affect ideas about what we hope children will become?

PROMOTING DIVERSITY, INCLUSION, AND CULTURAL COMPETENCE IN THE CLASSROOM

The United States includes an enormous array of people from different cultures, classes, and types of families, each with various abilities and disabilities. It is thus highly likely that you will be teaching a mix of children. Some may not speak English as their first language, some may have a physical disability, or some may have two parents of the same sex—just to name a few of the differences you are likely to encounter. Your attitudes and values toward all types of diversity affect the ways that children learn and develop as well as how they learn to relate to one another.

Guidelines from NAEYC's Developmentally Appropriate Practice (DAP) in Early Childhood Programs address a child's culture as part of appropriate practice. These guidelines make it clear to teachers "to pay attention to the social and cultural contexts in which their children live and to take these into account when shaping the learning environment and their interactions with children and families" (Copple & Bredekamp, 2009, p. 331). Likewise, three of NAEYC's (2005) program accreditation criteria include diversity standards that address (1) nurturing relationships that treat all children with respect, (2) providing materials that reflect the diversity in the classroom and the community, and (3) using teaching strategies that account for differences among children. Children are so strongly influenced by what adults say and do that the attitudes children develop can be both positive and negative. To meet the needs of the children who will comprise their classrooms, all early childhood educators need to integrate diversity best practices into the classroom.

INTEGRATING DIVERSITY ACROSS THE CURRICULUM

Honoring diversity and promoting democratic values is a time-honored tradition of early education, yet it often causes teachers the greatest challenges. The most appropriate way to teach children to value diversity is for them to "live it" in the classroom. Teachers

Effective teachers try not to let a child's appearance influence expectations for achievement.

sometimes think that diversity is "just for urban schools" where the student population is more **heterogeneous,** or different in background and abilities. For instance, a preschool teacher in a suburban preschool may fail to appreciate the importance of respect for diversity because she or he assumes that the class is **homogeneous,** or similar in backgrounds and abilities. This is a common misconception. First of all, children are going to differ in significant ways, even if they all live in the same neighborhood. Second, these children may need—as much (or perhaps more) than children who are in the company of children with dramatic racial, ethnic, and economic differences—to learn to avoid stereotyping and discrimination. Respect for diversity can and should be integrated across your curriculum. Even though each of us has unique needs, we still all have the same physical needs for food and shelter, the same social and emotional needs to be with caring adults and peers who do not discriminate, and the same cognitive needs to communicate our thoughts and feelings and to engage in constructive problem solving. When you teach using broad concepts that meet everyone's needs, such as those of self, others, and the community, you meet the needs of all cultural groups. For example, children at every age need to be in classrooms that develop social skills to deepen their **self-concept,** their beliefs and feelings about themselves that influence their learning and their interactions with others. They also need to develop **prosocial skills,** the ability to cooperate and share in order to form and maintain healthy relationships with others, which includes the ability to make and keep friends by knowing how to communicate, share, and cooperate with others (Seefeldt, Castle, & Falconer, 2010). Early childhood classrooms need to be places that help children learn to value and respect themselves and others.

IMPLEMENTING STRATEGIES THAT HONOR DIVERSITY

Recognizing your own history and the histories of the children in your classroom honors diversity. The following suggestions will help you effectively teach children to develop an appropriate understanding of themselves and of others:

1. **Be open to new ideas and to learning how different people view the world.** Use differences as opportunities to learn more about yourself, others, and the world. Make the effort to see children and families, whose backgrounds differ from yours, through different lenses that will increase your knowledge about others.

2. **Use a variety of materials that reflect the children's homes, classroom, school, and community.** Materials should reflect the children in your classroom. Art materials should include a range of human skin colors in paint, crayons, paper, and dough; the aesthetic environment should include art from all of the children's home and community cultures; and displays should include photos of the children and their families.

3. **Ensure that all children have a chance to participate.** Every child needs opportunities to speak, share, and be recognized. Children learn to develop acceptance, understanding, and respect as they are more fully integrated into the life of the classroom.

4. **Use a variety of teaching strategies.** Teachers can honor different ways of learning by focusing on children's learning strengths. Strategies such as cooperative learning, brain-compatible teaching, questioning and guided discussion, role playing, and inquiry-based learning focus on different strengths.

5. **Involve children's families.** The best way for you to learn about different cultures is from the families themselves. Some teachers use questionnaires inviting families to share a child's home language and information about their particular culture and ethnic background. It is important to be sensitive in this respect because some families eagerly share such information while others are reluctant to do so. If this is the case, see if you can find other ways to learn about each child's background.

COLLABORATING WITH *Families*

Ways of Responding to Diversity in Families

Teachers' ways of responding to families who are very different from their own often range from inappropriate to appropriate. Consider what happens, for example, if a child is not achieving academically. Some teachers have negative attitudes in which they judge the family as deficient because it differs from their own family structure. It is unhelpful to blame the family for the child's problem by saying, for instance, that "they don't help to practice math facts at home" or "won't help with homework." Such attitudes fail to recognize that families may want to help very much but may not be familiar with the ways in which the subject of math is taught; parents also may be working at multiple jobs to try to provide for their children and simply lack the time and energy to invest in homework. When teachers are urged to be more considerate and understanding, they sometimes resort to feeling sorry for families and assume that they are to be pitied. Ironically, efforts at parent education frequently fail because those who offer them assume that they have all the answers and that families need to be told the "right" way to do things. The truth is that most successful efforts to collaborate with families are founded on mutual respect and a sincere desire to help in ways that are carefully matched to the individual family's strengths, interests, and needs.

Take a look at some of these very common comments from educators. Which of the attitudes about working with families that were just discussed best describe each statement? What sort of reactions would the attitudes conveyed by these statements be likely to get from parents/families? What consequences might you expect for home–school collaboration if teachers express these attitudes? Why?

- "These poor kids who live in the projects don't have a chance."
- "We discovered that the Spanish-speaking families in our neighborhood have a real networking system. Now, whenever we need to get the word out on something, we collaborate with the churches, employers, and store owners. For us, it has proven to be a much more efficient system than sending home notes with the children."
- "I think that we should sponsor some training sessions for parents to teach them how to help with homework."
- "Well, neither one of his parents graduated high school—what can you expect?"
- "We worked with the local merchants to make sure that all the children started school with the basic supplies that they needed."
- "Many of the parents indicated that they would be more likely to meet with teachers if we offered a Saturday open house. We did and it worked!"
- "It's the same old story—the parents you really need to talk to at conferences never show up."

Summary

■ Diversity refers to the many ways in which one person is distinctive from another. Demographic data suggest that the children and families with whom early childhood educators work will become increasingly diverse in the future. An important companion concept to diversity is inclusion; inclusion means that all children are accepted, get to participate, and are supported.

■ Cultural competence means that teachers are expected to make a concerted effort to know, respect, and communicate effectively with all children and families. Anti-bias education seeks to eliminate prejudice and stereotyping so that all children are given a fair chance to succeed.

- ■ In order to put principles of diversity and inclusion into practice, teachers must first understand and provide for children's rights and strive to build a genuine community of learners in the classroom.

- ■ Teachers demonstrate their cultural competence through ethical reasoning, challenging assumptions,

mastering skilled dialogue, and understanding the hidden curriculum. They need to critically examine the ideas that they take for granted, strive to expand their understandings about other cultures, and put what they have learned into practice in ways that welcome and support all children and their families.

Applying Your Knowledge of Diversity, Inclusion, and Cultural Competence

In Assessment Activity 1, you will apply your knowledge of culturally responsive teaching to a child named Autumn whose home is infested with parasites. Assessment Activity 2 offers examples of skillful ways of conversing with individuals whose cultural backgrounds differ from your own and coaches you in how to do this.

 1 **AUTUMN IS SENT HOME BY THE SCHOOL NURSE**

When children are in desperate circumstances as a result of neglect, it is sometimes tempting to blame the victims rather than taking action. Ms. Ditka, an intern teacher, was surprised to learn from the school nurse that Autumn, an 8-year-old in her class, had head lice and fleas. Although it is common for head lice to appear at school and possible for anyone to get them, Autumn's situation was extreme. When an outbreak of head lice occurred in her classroom, many of the parents were angry with the teachers for not noticing it sooner, and some blamed the school for unsanitary conditions. Soon, everyone was blaming Autumn and her family and treating them like outcasts. Ms. Ditka had to overcome her own fears about getting lice and fleas. She did this by getting accurate medical information about how to halt the transmission of these insects from one child to another and by working with the custodians to kill the insects that had infested her classroom. When Health Department officials first went to Autumn's house to fumigate, they were met on the porch by her grandfather, his shotgun, and his hunting dogs; the next time, the sheriff accompanied them and the house was fumigated. Throughout this time, Autumn was kept out of school for over a week. When she returned, Ms. Ditka had to confront her own uneasiness about physical contact with Autumn. She also found it necessary to intercede on Autumn's behalf with the class because so many of the children had been cautioned to "stay away from that dirty girl." Ms. Ditka knew that her response when Autumn walked into the room would speak volumes, so when Autumn stood hesitantly in the doorway, she welcomed her warmly and gave her a hug. What prevented Ms. Ditka from resenting Autumn, as many of her coworkers did, was simply her remembering that Autumn had no choices in or control over her physical environment. Without Ms. Ditka's advocacy, Autumn's second-grade year would have been a story of alienation from peers and damaged self-esteem. But because a caring teacher stood up for Autumn, calmed others, and controlled her own fears, Autumn was able to succeed academically and socially. She succeeded because her teacher approached the situation from the perspective of a child advocate rather than rushing to judge Autumn and her family.

REACT	With whom do you identify most strongly in this case, and why?
RESEARCH	What forms of anti-bias are represented by this situation?
REFLECT	What makes this a complex situation and an ethical dilemma in the school community?

Assessment ACTIVITY ② TALKING WITH FAMILIES FROM DIVERSE BACKGROUNDS

If they are completely candid, many new teachers—particularly if they are not married and/or do not have children—admit to feeling a bit awkward interacting with a child's adult family members. New teachers sometimes worry that families see them as having "book knowledge only" or being so inexperienced that their child will not have a highly effective teacher. How can this concern be addressed?

Research with families shows that they respect teachers who sincerely care about their child, will treat their child with compassion, see their child as an individual, recognize the child's potential, motivate their child to learn, and commit to promoting the child's development (Blue-Banning, Summers, Frankland, Nelson, & Beegle, 2004); therefore, the way to win over families is to demonstrate that you are doing all of these things. Interpersonal communication—"what is said, what is not said, and how and when such messages are exchanged"—exerts a powerful influence on your relationships with children's families (McWilliam, 2010, p. 127). Each suggestion (adapted from McWilliam, 2010) has some examples. Work in your group to generate more.

Making Families Feel Welcome
Schedule activities that leave you freer to talk with families at the start and end of the day (e.g., outdoor play, centers, or a circle time).

> "Please come in and join us—we are singing our end-of-the-day song."

> "The children are working at their centers—would you like to see how they're doing?'

Capitalize on Opportunities for Informal Conversation

> "Would it be okay if we talk while I walk you out to the car?"

> "How is your schedule this week—is there a time you could give me a call?"

Compliments About the Child

> "She is just so joyful that it is a pleasure to be around her."

> "I can tell you've been practicing the sight words—it really shows."

Compliments to the Family

> "He *loves* this book. What a great find! Where did you get it?"

> "Our behavior plan must be working; there were no problems with tantrums at all this week."

Acknowledging Feelings

> "It sounds as though this is something you really want to change."

> "It must be such a worry for you when. . ."

Clarifying Feelings

"You selected this as one of your major goals and I'm wondering if you can tell me a little bit about why it is important for you and your family."

"What changes are you hoping for? Can you describe what you are hoping to see?"

Supportive Comments

"What have you tried thus far? How has that been working for you?"

"What problems do you foresee in making this plan work for you and your family?"

ONLINE RESOURCES FOR MULTICULTURAL EDUCATION AND DIVERSITY

ACEI Diversity Standards: The ACEI Diversity Committee's (2008) guidelines for promoting diversity. www.acei.org/diversityed_84_3_158f.htm

EverythingESL.net: A comprehensive resource for working with speakers of other languages. http://everythingesl.net/

Children in Peril: Read this *New York Times* column by Bob Herbert about the effects of the economy on children and families. www.nytimes.com/2009/04/21/opinion/21herbert.htm

Instant Multilanguage Translator: This free translator can convert the texts of original books produced by children or other print materials into other languages. www.freetranslation.com

National Center for Learning Disabilities: Children with disabilities are entitled to a free and appropriate education. This site supplies the standards that guide teachers' practice. http://ncld.org/content/view/1181/456185

National Professional Development Center on Inclusion (NPDCI): Provides data on each state's progress in educating young children with special needs with their peers. Various resources, including *Fact Sheets,* provide helpful information on inclusion. http://community.fpg.unc.edu/npdci

National Association for Multicultural Education (NAME): This organization advocates for educational equity and social justice; its site contains a variety of resources and information about conferences. http://nameorg.org/

U.S. Census Bureau: Find out more about U.S. demographics in the 2009 press release *Characteristics of the U.S. Foreign-Born Population.* www.census.gov

PEARSON myeducationlab

Go to Topic 10 (Cultural and Linguistic Diversity) in the MyEducationLab (www.myeducationlab.com) for your course, where you can:

- Find learning outcomes for cultural and linguistic diversity along with the national standards that connect to these outcomes.
- Complete Assignments and Activities that can help you more deeply understand the chapter content.
- Apply and practice your understanding of the core teaching skills identified in the chapter with the Building Teaching Skills and Dispositions learning units.
- Access video clips of CCSSO National Teachers of the Year award winners responding to the question, "Why Do I Teach?" in the Teacher Talk section.
- Hear viewpoints of experts in the field in Professional Perspectives.

CHAPTER 5

Promoting Children's Development

Because of the need to solve everyday problems concerning children, researchers from psychology, sociology, anthropology, biology, and neuroscience have joined forces with professionals from education, family studies, medicine, public health, and social service—to name just a few. The field of child development is a monument to the contributions of these many disciplines.

Laura Berk, 2008, p. 4

Meet the TEACHERS

MRS. DELGADO cares for infants and toddlers in her home and knows that infants and toddlers need lots of sensory stimulation to help their brains grow. So, in her home, you might see bright objects and mirrors on the wall, colorful toys, and large picture books to stimulate the children's visual development. While feeding or diapering the children, Ms. Delgado talks in a soft, sing-song way to "bathe the children in language from the earliest days to encourage them to explore and experiment with sounds."

MS. WU teaches in a public preschool program for children with special needs. If you visit Ms. Wu's class, you will notice 3-year-old Morgan, a child with Down syndrome who does not yet talk. During her weekly visits to Morgan's home, Ms. Wu uses pictures, picture books, props, gestures, and concrete experiences to help Morgan communicate with others about her world. During Ms. Wu's visits, she keeps the conversation focused on the best ways to meet Morgan's developmental needs. Ms. Wu says, "I am here to help Morgan grow and develop, but I also realize I must consider her mother's needs and education as well. This is challenging for me."

MR. GUTHRIE teaches third grade in a school where children speak 17 languages and uses class meetings as a way to meet both individual and group needs. His September focus is teaching children how to give and receive compliments; his October focus is helping children identify and solve real classroom problems. This year, for example, during reading workshop time, children often argued about who could use the couch in the classroom. Once the children identified the problem and placed it in the problem box for discussion, Mr. Guthrie put it on the agenda for the next class meeting. After suggesting several possible solutions, the third graders decided to add a different-colored set of cards to the book check-out pocket chart and rotate them daily to give everybody a turn using the couch. Mr. Guthrie says, "children come up with great suggestions for solving their own problems."

LEARNING Outcomes

In this chapter you will learn to:

→ **Understand young children's developmental characteristics and needs** (NAEYC #1)

→ **Explore your role in promoting children's development**

→ **Explain the multiple influences on children's development** (NAEYC #1)

→ **Meet the developmental needs of learners with exceptionalities** (NAEYC #1, ACEI #1, INTASC #2)

→ **Describe the major child development theorists influencing early childhood education**

→ **Apply knowledge of child development in early childhood classrooms**

Compare

What are some similarities in the ways these three teachers support children's development?

Contrast

What differences do you notice about the ways these teachers facilitate children's development?

Connect

What impressed you about how these teachers meet children's developmental needs? How could you incorporate some of their ideas in your own teaching?

Now that you have reflected on the three teachers' perspectives and noted the learning outcomes, you are ready to begin exploring your role in promoting children's development. Because children's development is foundational to teaching and learning, we preview the knowledge, skills, and dispositions you will need in order to fulfill your role in promoting the healthy development of every child.

Children's Developmental Characteristics and Needs

Consider the remarkable changes that have occurred in your body as you developed from a newborn infant to a mature adult. Your development depended on the important interaction between **biological** and **environmental influences,** sometimes referred to as nature and nurture factors. As you come to understand the influences of typical development, you will see how virtually any biological or environmental condition can contribute to or impair healthy development.

When we refer to **development** we mean the complex and dynamic cognitive, language, physical, motor, social, emotional, and moral processes that change over one's lifetime (Berk, 2008). Because each of these areas develops independently while also being inextricably intertwined with one another, we refer to the **"whole child"** when we look at children's development. Consider, for example, physical/motor development. You began your life by not even being able to hold your head up. As your muscle development matured, you were able to eventually roll over, sit, crawl, stand, walk, run, and perhaps engage in even more complex physical skills. These changes over time also depended on your cognitive, social, and emotional development, and are what make each person unique.

Although there are some predictable patterns of development, a number of variables affect children's development. Some variables are related to age and are influenced by children's family and cultural backgrounds, individual **temperament** (a person's way of responding), and biological makeup. Knowing what young children are like is the first step toward making good child development decisions. Essentially, three primary characteristics contribute to what young children are like: (a) principles of development, (b) essential needs, and (c) developmental milestones.

PRINCIPLES OF DEVELOPMENT

Every child has a unique pattern of development. The following five principles of development will help you understand these patterns and provide guidelines for your work with all children in early childhood settings (Copple & Bredekamp, 2009; Erikson, 1993; Piaget, 1992; Santrock, 2009; Vygotsky, 1978):

1. **Development in each domain—physical, motor, social, emotional, and cognitive—influences and is influenced by development in other**

DID YOU Know ?

Key Facts About Children's Development

- Children in America lag behind those of almost all industrialized nations on key child indicators, including child poverty, child health and health coverage, and child welfare. In the United States, 13.5 million children live in poverty, almost 9 million children lack health care, 22% of children have not completed their needed vaccinations, and almost 3 million children are reported as suspected victims of child abuse and neglect and referred for investigation (Annie E. Casey Foundation, 2009; National Center for Health Statistics, 2009).

- Of children ages 3 to 17, 20% have one or more developmental, learning, or behavioral exceptionalities (National Scientific Council on the Developing Child, 2007).

- Until recently, scientists thought that a person's genes determined what the brain can and cannot do. We now know that the brain has considerable **plasticity**, the ability to change, and its development depends upon experience (deHann & Martinos, 2008).

domains. When children master any physical skill, such as climbing on a jungle gym, riding a bicycle, or kicking a soccer ball, their self-confidence usually increases. However, if children cannot reach, grasp, crawl, or walk, they are limited in how they explore their world, which influences their cognitive development. The interrelatedness of each domain is an important principle of development.

2. **Development occurs in an orderly and predictable sequence.** Development occurs from the top of the body to the bottom (cephalocaudal) and from the center of the body outwards (proximodistal). **Cephalocaudal development** works its way down, from the head to the neck, trunk, and so forth. That is why an infant's head is proportionately so much larger than the rest of his or her body; the greatest growth in size, weight, and other features first occurs at the top of the body. **Proximodistal development** begins with the large trunk and arm muscles and works its way out to the smaller muscles in children's hands and fingers. That is why preschool children need lots of opportunities for large-muscle activities such as jumping, climbing, and running before they are expected to do activities that require control of the small muscles in their hands and fingers, such as writing and coloring in small spaces.

3. **Development proceeds at different rates in each individual and in each developmental area.** There is a wide range of individual variation in the timing of developmental changes that are influenced by biological, environmental, and **sociocultural factors** such as family, temperament (emotional responses such as shyness or distractibility), learning style, and experience. Children first sit up, roll over, take first steps, lose a tooth, or learn to read at different rates. Only when children deviate considerably from the average ages for these developmental milestones is there cause to consider their development exceptional, either delayed or advanced.

4. **Development is greatly affected by the kinds of experiences children have.** Experiences are cumulative; therefore, they can either positively or negatively affect children's developing knowledge, skills, and attitudes. Experiences that occur regularly have more powerful, lasting effects than those that occur rarely. For example, children who hear a great deal of spoken language in the home and use books early and consistently are more likely to develop an understanding of the different functions of language, which is a clear advantage for later reading and writing. Conversely, young children who do not hear spoken language or have no experiences with books are often at a disadvantage for later literacy development.

5. **Development results from the interaction of each child's biological, environmental, and cultural influences.** No single theory adequately explains the complex course of children's development. Today, it is widely accepted that three major factors—biological, environmental, and cultural—are so intertwined that their combination makes each person unique. **Biological influences** originate in the genes, which determine such characteristics as height, weight, and brain development; **environmental influences** are external and include such environmental experiences as language, nutrition, and health care; and **cultural influences** come from family, peers, community, and the media. If, for example, your genetic makeup predisposes you to healthy development but you have inadequate nutrition and medical care in your early years, your development will be adversely affected.

Note the Figure 5.1 graphic that illustrates the interconnections and the complexity of each child's development. Taken together, these principles form the foundation for knowing and understanding the whole child—both the mind and the body.

Figure 5.1 Interconnectedness of Principles of Development

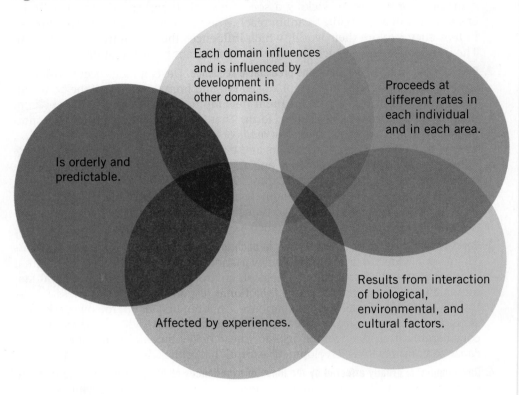

Each domain influences and is influenced by development in other domains.

Proceeds at different rates in each individual and in each area.

Is orderly and predictable.

Affected by experiences.

Results from interaction of biological, environmental, and cultural factors.

ESSENTIAL NEEDS

Just as there are universal principles of development, there are universal basic needs that affect children's well-being. *All children* have the same basic physical, social, emotional, and cognitive needs that contribute to their long-term healthy well-being and ability to thrive (Brazleton & Greenspan, 2001; Maslow, 1987).

Minimal *physical needs* include food, clothing, shelter, and medical care. Basic *social and emotional needs* include a consistent and predictable relationship with an attentive, caring adult, strong peer acceptance, and freedom from abuse and discrimination (Maslow, 1987). Minimal *cognitive needs* include the ability to communicate thoughts and feelings, to process information in a meaningful way, to engage in constructive problem solving, and to experience success both at school and in the community (White & Isenberg, 2003). How well early childhood professionals meet the following essential needs of children strongly influences what children will be like.

NEED FOR SECURITY AND SAFETY

Children need to feel safe and valued. Their world must be predictable and include at least one adult upon whom they can depend. Feelings of security influence children's ability to take risks, explore, and establish a positive sense of self (Maslow, 1987). They also need to live in an environment that protects them from physical and psychological harm and exposure to violence.

These children are the same chronological age; they show variation in the normal range of development.

NEED FOR LOVE, UNDERSTANDING, AND ACCEPTANCE

Children of all ages need love and affection from the significant adults in their lives to thrive and feel supported. They also need adults in their lives who understand and accept them unconditionally as unique individuals throughout life. Young children need these nurturing relationships for most of their waking hours.

NEED FOR COMPETENCY, RESPONSIBILITY, AND INDEPENDENCE

From the earliest years, children gradually need to learn to become competent and responsible for themselves and their own actions. Infants have a need to feed themselves, toddlers have a need to dress themselves, and school-age children have a need to use the tools of reading and writing that will help them be competent students. All children need to feel competent.

NEED FOR SUCCESS, GUIDANCE, AND RESPECT

Closely related to children's need for competency is their need for success. Being successful in much of what they undertake helps children develop self-esteem, confidence, and motivation to learn. All children need reasonable limits, suitable to their level of understanding and development, that allow them to maintain their dignity and self-respect. And, in order for children to show respect for others, the adults who care for them must treat them with respect.

DEVELOPMENTAL MILESTONES

All children develop in a universal sequence that is often referred to as *periods of development.* Approximate age ranges that depict typical behaviors and abilities of children characterize each of these periods. As children develop, they face new and different demands and challenges. Knowing what children are like at these times will help you better use best practices to help them learn and develop. The following sections describe

Pause and
Reflect

About Children's Development

List the biological, environmental, and cultural factors (e.g., height, nutrition, family) that you needed to develop into a healthy adult. What observations can you make about the necessary resources and supports that promote healthy development? Refer back to the "Did You Know" facts in this chapter and identify some current conditions that affect children's development.

the developmental milestones of infants, toddlers, preschoolers and kindergartners, and school-age children.

WHAT ARE INFANTS LIKE?

Infancy, the first 12 months of life, is a time of total dependency on adults; it also is a time of the most rapid changes in development. By their first birthdays, infants can often walk and feed themselves. Their well-being very much depends upon the nature of their early care and experiences. Infants vary in the rates at which they develop.

PHYSICAL/MOTOR DEVELOPMENT

Physical development in infants is rapid and dramatic. Some important milestones in infants' physical development are (a) increases in height and weight; (b) growth of the brain, bones, and muscles; and (c) a maturing central nervous system. During the first year, infants learn to sit up and move from place to place, hold and use objects, and increase their coordination. By 4 to 5 months of age, for example, an infant's birth weight will have doubled, and by 12 months, it will have tripled.

SOCIAL/EMOTIONAL DEVELOPMENT

Healthy social and emotional development begins at birth. During infancy, children need to learn that they can trust and depend on those who care for them. Trust develops from consistency in the love, physical care, daily routines, and other experiences adults provide. Infants also must develop good feelings about themselves. They accomplish this by forming close attachments to loving, understanding caregivers who consistently meet their needs. By 6 months of age, infants need to have established one or more emotional ties to another human being—a process referred to as **attachment.** These early attachments have an enduring effect on later social and emotional development and behavior.

COGNITIVE DEVELOPMENT

Infants' cognitive development begins with reflexes (e.g., eye blinking, grasping), moves to simple motor movements centered on their own bodies and then to repeated actions, and eventually shows the beginnings of goal-directed behavior that makes things happen (Piaget, 1992). In just a few short months, infants' rapid cognitive development helps them to move from making things happen accidentally (e.g., making sounds by dropping a rattle) to deliberately making things happen by thinking about their actions (e.g., purposefully dropping a rattle to hear the sounds it makes).

LANGUAGE DEVELOPMENT

Learning to speak and understand others begins when infants' parents or adult caretakers talk and respond to them. Babies listen to the words of their caregivers, begin to experiment with sounds, and try to repeat words they hear by cooing and babbling. Between 6 and 9 months of age, infants begin to name objects and imitate what they hear. Table 5.1 summarizes the major developmental milestones of infants.

APPLYING DEVELOPMENTAL KNOWLEDGE TO INFANTS

As an infant caregiver, you can provide regular and responsive care so that infants develop trusting relationships. You can nurture infants' development by (1) preparing a rich, sensory, and safe environment in which infants are comfortable exploring new

Table 5.1 Developmental Milestones of Infants

AGE	PHYSICAL/MOTOR	SOCIAL/EMOTIONAL	COGNITIVE	LANGUAGE
1–3 months	• hold head up • hold rattle briefly • glance from one object to another • reach toward object	• begin to smile • use smiles and gurgles to get responses • prefer people to objects	• look at colorful objects and faces • practice sucking, looking, grasping, and crying • accidentally discover what body can do (e.g., sucking thumb)	• calmed by familiar voices • cry when uncomfortable • listen to voices and sounds • coo and babble • show startle response
6–9 months	• sit unassisted • crawl • pull string to obtain object • use pincer grasp • stand with help • need help to sit down again • show hand preference	• play social games (e.g., peek-a-boo) • react to strangers • approach new people with caution • consistently show emotions • shout for attention • display shame and shyness	• intentionally try to make things happen (e.g., splashing water) • notice that objects can be used to cause things to happen (e.g., banging pot lids together to make noise)	• understand first words • begin to say words like *mama* or *dada* • look at familiar objects when named • listen to own voice • respond to requests (e.g., "Give me your rattle")
9–12 months	• push car along • pull up to stand beside furniture • take some steps • hold object with thumb and two fingers • triple birth weight	• show possessiveness by clinging or pushing others away • communicate feelings • offer or take a toy from another child • show affection • obey simple commands	• anticipate events (e.g., when mother gets the car keys, she is leaving) • look, reach for, grasp, and put object in mouth • search for hidden objects (e.g., look for a toy under a blanket)	• babble • look at person talking • understand 12 words (receptive vocabulary) • understand instructions (e.g., "Wave bye-bye") • speak first word

things; (2) engaging in close personal contact, such as cuddling and using a positive, soft voice during feeding; and (3) responding quickly to their cries of distress.

WHAT ARE TODDLERS LIKE?

The period of development from ages 1 to 3 can be somewhat challenging for toddlers and the adults caring for them. Toddlers are inquisitive, very active, and determined to be independent and to make things happen. In addition, they tend to have frequent changes in mood. Because toddlers are into everything, they need constant supervision for their own safety. During toddlerhood, children begin to become more competent and independent.

PHYSICAL/MOTOR DEVELOPMENT

Even though physical growth slows during this period, toddlers' *large muscles* develop rapidly. Improved motor control, coordination, and balance keep toddlers constantly on the move, running, climbing, and jumping. As toddlers' *small muscles* develop, they become more skillful in using their hands; they can hold a cup with one hand, string beads, and stack objects. Although they are not skilled at dressing, they are quite skilled at undressing, particularly at undoing their shoes and taking off their socks. Toddlers use their new control over their bodies to express their feelings by jumping and chuckling when they are happy, and kicking and screaming when they are unhappy. Because their rate of growth has slowed, they need less food, often become fussy eaters, and may prefer to play with their food rather than eat it. They also begin to use the toilet alone, and they continue to need periods of rest and quiet during the day.

SOCIAL/EMOTIONAL DEVELOPMENT

Toddlers seek independence from adults and show interest in children their own ages. They demand to do things for themselves and typically respond to requests with a resounding "No" or "Me do it!" These responses are helping them figure out who they are as they try to become more competent and independent. Toddlers also are meeting new expectations from adults. When they were infants, the adults in their lives promptly and patiently responded to their needs and adjusted their own schedules to accommodate them. Now, these same adults often ask toddlers to wait and say "no" to them. Suddenly, toddlers' needs are not being met as promptly as they were during infancy, and conflicts arise. They often respond by crying or having temper tantrums.

COGNITIVE DEVELOPMENT

Toddlers can recall and anticipate certain events they have experienced. For example, they not only ask for juice but also can remember where the juice is kept. This skill marks the beginning of memory. Toddlers also engage in imaginative play during which they act out their own ideas about objects and events without much regard for reality. What they think about their world depends upon the experiences they have. These early concepts about their world are the basis upon which later concepts are formed.

LANGUAGE DEVELOPMENT

Most toddlers understand about 300 spoken words. From ages 2 to 3, toddlers quickly learn new words and grammatical forms. Their first words name familiar people (e.g., *dada, mama*), animals (e.g., *kitty, doggie*), and objects they see in pictures (e.g., *car, ball*); they also include social interaction terms (e.g., *bye bye, up*). Toddlers' speaking vocabulary includes single words that stand for a whole thought and averages 200 to 275 words by age 2 (Santrock, 2009). They enjoy language for its rhythm and like to hear the same stories over and over again, more for the rhythm than the content. Looking at books and magazines and naming familiar objects they see in pictures intrigues them. Table 5.2 lists some developmental milestones for toddlers.

APPLYING DEVELOPMENTAL KNOWLEDGE TO TODDLERS

In your work with toddlers, you need to be protective, reassuring, and confident as they assume self-care responsibilities of feeding, toileting, and dressing. You can also provide toddlers with opportunities to develop *initiative, autonomy,* and *self-reliance*

Table 5.2 Developmental Milestones of Toddlers

AGE	PHYSICAL/MOTOR	SOCIAL/EMOTIONAL	COGNITIVE	LANGUAGE
12–18 months	**Gross Motor** • stand and walk • climb onto chair • push and pull toys • roll ball • squat to get toy • move to music **Fine motor** • scribble on paper • pick up small objects • feed self • pour and stack • take off shoes and socks	• are deeply attached to adult who provides regular care • explore surroundings • can give and receive toys • enjoy chasing, hiding, and other games • play beside, but not with, other children • take turn rolling a ball	• try new ways to do things • imitate behavior of others • use trial-and-error method to learn • look at picture books	• say 2 words at 12 months, 4–5 words at 15 months, and 15–20 words by 18 months • use gestures, tone, and context • understand simple directions • repeat syllables • wave bye-bye • use words to make needs known
24–36 months	**Gross Motor** • walk on toes • kick large ball • imitate animal movements • walk up and down stairs with alternating feet • ride tricycle • hang by hands from a support (e.g., jungle gym bar) • jump in place **Fine Motor** • build towers • string 3–4 beads • manage spoon and fork • snip with scissors • hold crayon with thumb and forefinger • show a preference for right or left hand • control grasp and release	• watch other children • make a choice between two alternatives • use simple role play to play house • participate in small-group activities for 5–10 minutes • know gender identity • insist on doing things independently • take turns when reminded • play alone for 15 minutes • express a range of motions through actions, words, or facial expressions	• respond to simple directions • select and look at picture books, and identify several objects within one picture • touch and count 1–3 objects • match 4 colors • attempt to play with unfamiliar toys	• understand prepositions and pronouns • say "no" • use words to ask for things • make sounds for p, m, n, w, and h at the beginning of words • use question words (e.g., why, when) • use past tense and plurals • speak in 2- to 5-word sentences • understand negatives • enjoy simple storybooks for 10–15 minutes • pretend to read familiar book to self

through the routines, schedules, simple choices, and clear limits that they need. To enhance toddlers' language development, (1) teach them the names of familiar objects and people, such as *cup* and *baby*; (2) support their efforts at saying new words; (3) look at toddlers while talking with them; (4) talk about what you are doing; and (5) describe or narrate what they are doing.

WHAT ARE PRESCHOOLERS AND KINDERGARTNERS LIKE?

The preschool and kindergarten period of development extends from 3 to 6 years. During this time, children are usually very active and energetic, show improved motor skills, and make great strides in language development. Preschool and kindergarten children become more self-sufficient in caring for themselves and begin to show less attachment to their parents. They engage in more complex play activities, are very curious, and want to explore the world outside their familiar surroundings. While older preschoolers and kindergartners show significant variation in aspects of their development, they typically have increased their ability to work cooperatively with others, to reason differently, to control their emotions, and to use verbal and written communication more skillfully.

PHYSICAL/MOTOR DEVELOPMENT

Physical development during the preschool years is steady. **Gross motor** (i.e., large muscle) skills are rapidly expanding, and children show increased facility with their arms, hands, and legs. They enjoy practicing their newly learned hopping, throwing, catching, and jumping skills. **Fine motor** (i.e., small muscle) skills become more refined, thus enabling children to perform such self-help skills as buckling, snapping, buttoning, and zipping. Mastering these skills involves a great deal of work and practice, but children enjoy the challenge. Older preschoolers and kindergarten children become even more agile; they show interest in sports, noncompetitive games, and physical fitness (Puckett & Black, 2009). Because of their increased fine motor skills, they communicate more in writing and can print recognizable letters and numbers. They do, however, often make letter reversals and write mirror images of letters.

SOCIAL/EMOTIONAL DEVELOPMENT

Preschool and kindergarten children begin to spend more time with people outside their family. They like to be with and accepted by other children of similar ages, and are generally happy, imaginative, and pleased with their own ability to plan and complete projects. New experiences interest them and they want to know more about other people, what other people do, and what they themselves can do. They spend much time experimenting with adult roles they have observed, which are primarily carried out in imaginative play activities. While preschoolers show increased autonomy, they still move back and forth between their need to be independent and their need to be dependent. Although their ability to delay gratification of their needs and wants has increased, they still become easily frustrated and frequently cry when things do not go their way. Many children also experience an expanding range of emotions and learn how to express these emotions in socially acceptable ways. Fear and anxiety are common emotions during these years. Many preschoolers typically fear the dark, unfamiliar animals, and potentially dangerous situations such as fire or deep water. By the end of this period of development, most children outgrow these fears.

COGNITIVE DEVELOPMENT

From the ages of 3 to 6, children's thinking is a combination of fantasy and reality, and their understanding is based upon their own limited experiences. Young preschoolers' thinking is focused on the "here and now." They have difficulty with concepts related to the past and the future, and they are able to think aloud about only one idea at a time. As they mature and have more experiences, preschoolers' thinking becomes more objective and realistic. Older preschoolers and kindergartners, for example, can sort objects by more than one attribute (e.g., color, size, shape), but their thinking is not systematic and they often stop in the middle of what they are doing and go on to something else. Children between the ages of 3 and 6 ask many "why" questions. Although they sometimes do this to get attention, generally their questions stem from their strong need to find out about their world, which is how they learn.

LANGUAGE DEVELOPMENT

Children's vocabularies increase rapidly during this period. Usually, 3-year-olds have vocabularies of 200 to 250 words, 5-year-olds have vocabularies of about 2,500 words, and the vocabularies of 6-year-olds consist of about 20,000 words. Preschoolers usually understand more words than they actually speak. Most preschoolers love to talk and are curious about words. Sometimes, however, they use words that they do not understand merely for the practice and pleasure that new words bring. In doing this, they give the impression that they understand what they are saying. Adults, therefore, must be careful not to assume that young children understand all of the words they use. Table 5.3 describes the major developmental milestones of preschool and kindergarten children.

APPLYING DEVELOPMENTAL KNOWLEDGE TO PRESCHOOLERS AND KINDERGARTNERS

Adults who work with preschoolers and kindergartners should provide a wide variety of interesting materials that encourage children to make and act on their choices

Table 5.3 Developmental Milestones of Preschoolers/Kindergartners

AGE	PHYSICAL/MOTOR	SOCIAL/EMOTIONAL	COGNITIVE	LANGUAGE
3 years	**Gross Motor** • stand on one foot briefly • kick and throw ball • ride tricycles • use swings, slides, and climbers; walk on tiptoes • do forward somersault **Fine Motor** • make simple drawings • dress and undress self and still ask for help • cut paper • paste with forefinger • build 8-block towers	• like to please adults • have occasional, short temper tantrums • look to adults for security, recognition, and encouragement • take turns, share, and use language to settle disputes • try to follow directions • show interest in family activities • may act like a baby • accept suggestions • test limits	• stack objects by size • understand simple questions, statements, and directions • ask many questions and understand more words than they use • count by rote and recognize some letter names • like rhythm, repetition, and humor • put simple geometric shapes into correct slots	• use familiar words and longer sentences with plurals and past tense • talk out loud to self • play with language for fun and practice • name objects, people, and events in a picture • recite nursery rhymes and poems

continued

Table 5.3 continued

AGE	PHYSICAL/MOTOR	SOCIAL/EMOTIONAL	COGNITIVE	LANGUAGE
4 years	**Gross Motor** • balance self • run, jump, climb, and hop in place skillfully • bounce and catch ball • build bridges with blocks • walk backward **Fine Motor** • copy *O* and *X* • use fork and safe knife • follow lines when cutting paper • use zippers and buttons • print letters • draw simple figures	• are proud of what they can do • prefer playmates of their own age • seek attention by showing off, making up stories, and being silly • express displeasure loudly and through aggression • tolerate some frustration • are developing a sense of humor • like nonsense words • show a balance between dependence and independence	• know own sex, age, and last name • point to six basic colors when asked • give long answers to questions • draw what they know • have limitless imagination • see differences among some shapes and colors • show interest in books and printed words • count objects while pointing or touching each one	• answer out loud to "Hi" and "How are you?" • speak clearly in sentences • make up words • ask many "how" and "why" questions • speak of imaginary conditions • tell tall tales • use adverbs and 5-word sentences • like repetition of sounds, words, and rhymes
5 years	**Gross Motor** • run on tiptoe • skip, jump rope, and walk a straight line • roll ball to hit objects • ride two-wheeled bicycle with training wheels • dribble and bounce ball **Fine Motor** • copy designs, letters, and numbers • cut, paste, and fold paper • grip pencil correctly • show handedness • copy numerals 1–10 and a triangle	• play together with others • enjoy visiting friends alone • cooperate with adults and peers • recognize the rights of others • try to conform to rules • generally feel good about themselves and their world	• understand yesterday, today, and tomorrow • know difference between reality and fantasy • can remember more than two ideas for a short time • have keen interest in numbers and counting • remember own address • identify pennies, nickels, and dimes • ask for information and facts • hear differences and similarities in letter sounds • remember number, letter, and counting sequences	• use sentences with correct grammar • talk to others with poise • ask direct questions and want real answers • use longer sentences with connectors (e.g., *but, because*) • are interested in word meanings • try out new words and can define some simple words • like stories • understand nouns and verbs

of activities and offer opportunities for children to experience success. They (1) are tolerant of children's mistakes, (2) encourage children's independence, (3) set reasonable expectations for each child's skill and ability levels, and (4) make available a variety of authentic, real-life experiences.

WHAT ARE SCHOOL-AGE CHILDREN LIKE?

School-age children, ages 6 to 8, show dramatic changes in development. They are losing temporary teeth and gaining permanent teeth, their motor coordination continues to be refined, and they work hard at mastering the basic skills of reading, writing, and mathematics. School-age children's thinking becomes more orderly and logical. Friends are important in their lives, and school-age children become increasingly aware of how they look to others (Berk, 2008; Wood, 2007). Older school-age children prefer to work with same-sex peers. Most school-age children enjoy group projects and activities, have a delightful sense of humor, and respond to adults with beaming smiles when praised and sad looks when they are criticized.

PHYSICAL/MOTOR DEVELOPMENT

During this period, school-aged children's vision becomes sharper, they may have frequent illnesses, and they tire easily. Gross motor development includes such fundamental movements as running, kicking, and reaching, which prepare children for the more complex coordination needed to play organized sports. Playground games such as tag and hopscotch are very popular and important for school-age children. Fine motor development is evident in greater dexterity and control over drawing and writing, which makes copying from the chalkboard easier (Puckett & Black, 2009; Wood, 2007). Older school-age children produce smaller and more detailed pieces of art.

SOCIAL/EMOTIONAL DEVELOPMENT

School-age children are now more responsible and independent, are more prosocial in their peer interactions, work harder at making friends, and are more self-critical. Younger school-age children still seek adult approval and tend to tattle, whereas older school-age children are more interested in forming clubs and selected groups. Older children also have fears and worries that they carefully mask; these may take the form of nail biting, inattention, or changed eating and sleeping patterns.

COGNITIVE DEVELOPMENT

School-age children are eager, curious, and delightful learners who thrive on opportunities to discover and invent. They learn through such forms of play as puppet shows, story retellings, games, and secret codes. Younger school-age children's thinking is intuitive and based on concrete, active experiences. Older school-age children think more logically. They can now plan and reflect on what they are learning but their thinking still needs to be related to familiar experiences. Older school-age children have a more focused attention span that enables them to assess their accomplishments; they also have more permanently stored information in the brain's memory that allows them to access information to facilitate learning. These abilities enable them to begin to understand differences, cause and effect, and multiple perspectives (Gallagher, 2005).

The school-age child is learning to use symbols and understand detailed information.

Pause and
Reflect

About Characteristics of Young Children

Think about a child you know very well. Use at least two of the developmental domains just discussed (i.e., physical/motor, social/emotional, cognitive, and language) to list the three most important age-related characteristics of that child. What do you think a teacher ought to know to optimize the child's development?

LANGUAGE DEVELOPMENT

School-age children have a good understanding of both oral and written language. Their oral language is quite like that of an adult, and they tend to dominate conversations. Their talk gleefully includes metaphors, jokes, puns, and riddles, because they now understand multiple meanings. They also use language to communicate their feelings and understand and use more appropriate grammatical structures such as plurals, possessives, and past tense in their oral and written language. Their vocabularies continue to expand, and they show a new interest in the meanings of words. The written language of school-age children typically includes invented spellings, which are evidence of their understanding of the connection between letters and sounds. Table 5.4 describes the major developmental milestones of school-age children.

APPLYING DEVELOPMENTAL KNOWLEDGE TO SCHOOL-AGE CHILDREN

In your work with school-age children, you will need to provide developmentally appropriate materials and resources—such as projects, hands-on activities, and other concrete, investigative activities—that offer opportunities for school-age children to set and achieve realistic goals. You will also want to (1) communicate to all children that they can master the basic knowledge and skills in academic subjects by focusing their attention on the progress they are making rather than stressing the deficits in their learning, (2) ensure flexibility in the curriculum, (3) respond to individual differences, and (4) take advantage of these children's emerging ability to teach each other.

The miniportraits provided in Tables 5.1 through 5.4 of common developmental milestones of children from birth through age 8 can be a powerful tool for you. They can help you know what to expect, understand what challenges children may face at different periods of development, and provide a framework for understanding how to meet the needs of all children.

Your Role in Promoting Children's Development

As a teacher, you will be making *intentional, purposeful decisions* about children that are based, in part, on their development. Knowing how to translate your knowledge of children's development into high-quality practice is important. A good example of intentional decision making based on child development knowledge comes from Ms. Cochran, a first-grade teacher:

One of Ms. Cochran's first graders, Vu, is a 6-year-old bilingual child who reads fluently. During free choice time, children select from a variety of concrete materials and usually interact in small groups or pairs. Vu chooses to work alone and seldom speaks with his classmates. During these times, Ms. Cochran talks with Vu about what he is doing. While he does answer her, the conversation is very one-sided—initiated by Ms.Cochran and finished when she no longer asks questions or makes comments. Ms.Cochran has observed that Vu also needs help taking turns, sharing, cleaning up, using words to ask for something or to respond to a question or request, and during transitions. Based on her observations of Vu and what she knows about 6-year-olds, Ms.Cochran spoke with other specialists and Vu's parents to see how to best meet Vu's developmental needs.

Table 5.4 Developmental Milestones of School-Age Children

AGE	PHYSICAL/MOTOR	SOCIAL/EMOTIONAL	COGNITIVE	LANGUAGE
6 years	**Gross Motor** • enjoy challenging acrobatics and outdoor activities • ride a bicycle • can do standing long jumps • begin to use a bat **Fine Motor** • have good visual tracking • make simple figures with clay • sew basic stitches • use table knife for spreading food	• are competitive and enthusiastic • test boundaries • can be bossy and critical of others • get upset easily when hurt • believe in rules for others but not self • have pride in work • like surprises • enjoy routines and have difficulty with transitions	• use symbols • work in spurts • begin using logic • can put stories and events in sequence • sort and classify information, sets, and objects	• explain things in detail • use enthusiastic language • have some speech irregularities
7 years	**Gross Motor** • balance on one foot • walk on balance beam • hop and jump in small spaces • do jumping jacks **Fine Motor** • brush hair • use table knife for cutting	• are sometimes moody and shy • rely on adult help • are afraid to make mistakes • are sensitive to others' feelings • have strong likes and dislikes • draw and write about same theme repeatedly • are eager for adult acceptance	• use abstract thinking • like maps and detailed information	• talk with precision • converse easily with others • are curious about word meanings • send notes and use secret codes
8 years	**Gross Motor** • are highly energetic and agile • alternate hopping to a beat • enjoy rough-and-tumble play • have coordinated skills for sports **Fine Motor** • use common household tools (i.e., hammer, screwdriver)	• have keen awareness of adult and child worlds • show disappointment when things do not go their way • crave acceptance from peers and adults • may worry about academic performance	• classify and sort spontaneously • discover, invent, and take things apart to investigate how they work • want perfection and erase constantly • work slowly	• explain things in detail • use enthusiastic language • have some speech irregularities

Ms. Cochran is demonstrating her role in *intentionally promoting* children's development. Although child development knowledge is essential for all early childhood professionals, it alone is not sufficient. Your role in promoting children's development can be guided as follows:

1. **Possess a thorough knowledge of child development.** Early childhood educators rank knowledge of child development as the number one competency they need. Ms. Cochran knows that 6-year-olds typically talk to other children and the teacher in one-to-one, small-group, and large-group interactions. Vu was not using oral language in these ways. Using this knowledge, Ms. Cochran developed strategies to help Vu acquire the social skills he needs to become a more integral part of the group. She spoke with Vu's parents and encouraged them to establish a playtime for Vu each week with children his own age and to spend time talking with him at home.

2. **Be a keen observer of children.** Observation is essential for understanding and responding to children. It is your basic tool—your eyes and ears—and gives you important information about children's needs, interests, and strengths. Knowing typical behavior at certain ages enables you to observe and compare against expected behavior. When children's development is not typical, your documented observations provide the evidence needed to identify a child who may require additional services from other professionals such as a pediatrician, counselor, speech and language specialist, or social worker. In the preceding scenario, Ms. Cochran was aware that Vu's social development and oral language development were not typical of 6-year-olds and sought early support for him.

3. **Create safe, caring, and appropriate environments for all children.** All children need supportive environments for their optimal development. They also need adults who view them as unique, who know as much as they can about them, and who will adjust their goals based on each child's strengths, culture, interests, and abilities. Through her commitment to creating a supportive environment, Ms.Cochran enlisted lots of support for Vu. She knew that Vu needed to develop social skills, so she began asking him questions that could not be answered with a simple "yes" or "no." She also knew that children from Vu's culture often speak only when spoken to. Thus, Ms. Cochran arranged for other student helpers that Vu could contact if he needed something, and she chose children to be helpers who already had established a trusting relationship with Vu. Ms. Cochran's practices illustrate the importance of using child development knowledge to provide children with the high-quality experiences they need to develop the necessary knowledge, skills, and abilities to be successful learners (Santrock, 2009).

4. **Develop children's social and emotional competence.** We know that teachers who establish firm boundaries, foster warm personal relationships in the classroom, and give students a say about their learning strengthen students' attachments to school, their interest in learning, their ability to refrain from self-destructive behaviors, and their positive behaviors (Goleman, 1998). Ms. Cochran's concern for Vu's well-being and social competence clearly will help Vu to become part of the classroom community where his emotional and social competence is valued and cultivated.

Promoting children's development also includes knowing the major influences on every child's development.

Influences on Children's Development

Children develop faster during the first 5 years than at any other stage of their lives. In these years, they are not only establishing the basic foundations for physical, cognitive, and social/emotional development, but also are forming beliefs, attitudes, and behavior patterns that influence how they view themselves and the world in which they live. As a teacher, the more you know about the influences on children's development, the more appropriate your teaching will be. Making good professional decisions considers children's brain development, cultural and social backgrounds, and exceptionalities. We will discuss each of these important influences on child development separately.

THE BRAIN AND CHILDREN'S DEVELOPMENT

The human brain, the mind's organ, is deeply affected and shaped by its experiences. In fact, the same stimulus processes that shape the developing brain are also responsible for storing information and developing new skills throughout one's life. Thus, we can say that the brain mediates everything we were, are, and will be. Brain development is best understood when considered in relation to other areas of development because those developmental areas help us understand what is happening within the brain. Children's capabilities in each area of development mirror their brain development at any given time. For example, we know what is happening within children's brains as we see evidence of their developing visual skills, language capacity, or motor abilities.

Brain development continues through one's life and is consistent with the lifelong capacities for thinking, feeling, and adapting. Young children's brains are more plastic (impressionable) than those of older children and adults. On one hand, this means that young children's brains are more likely to develop typically and be open to learning from the enriching influences in their lives; on the other hand, this means that young children are also more vulnerable to atypical development should the learning and environmental influences in their lives be impoverished. Recent research on brain development provides you with knowledge of the positive and negative influences on healthy brain development (Diamond, Casey, & Munkata, 2010; Gallagher, 2005; Shonkoff & Phillips, 2001). Figure 5.2 identifies the key facts on brain development as well as the positive and negative influences.

SOCIAL AND CULTURAL INFLUENCES

Although children all over the world have universal developmental characteristics, the social and cultural settings in which children live significantly shape their development and contribute to each child's uniqueness. By **social setting** we mean the significant people in children's lives who influence their development; by **cultural setting** we mean the values, behaviors, languages, dialects, and feelings about being part of a particular group that all children possess. Knowledge about these is critical to ensure that learning experiences are meaningful, relevant, and respectful for the participating children and their families (Copple & Bredekamp, 2009).

Since the civil rights movement of the 1960s, educators have become increasingly informed and sensitized to how deeply children's development is influenced by their social and cultural worlds. Just as you and I want to be accepted for who we are, so too do children from diverse backgrounds want the same full acceptance. Being aware of different cultures will help you be more open and accepting of children from cultures with which you may not be familiar and help all children learn to respect and care for one another and their world.

Figure 5.2 Facts About Brain Development

Prenatal Brain Development

- Brain growth begins shortly after conception and develops rapidly during the prenatal period. The brain develops more quickly than the other organs or limbs.

- By the 6th prenatal month, the brain contains nearly all of the billions of **neurons** of a mature brain. The brain creates about 250,000 new neurons every minute. New neurons migrate to the areas of the brain where they will function.

Brain Development After Birth

- Infants' brains are not fully formed at birth. Brain growth reaches 70% of its adult weight by age 2, 90% by age 6, and full weight by puberty.

- Neurons have specialized functions and form connection (**synapses**) with other neurons that enable them to store information.

- The brains of young children generate more synapses than the mature brain needs to function efficiently. Thus, the brain *prunes* unused synapses to make it operate more efficiently and *retains* synapses that are used often.

- Individual experiences foster new brain growth and refine existing brain structures that make each individual brain unique.

IMPLICATIONS FOR HEALTHY BRAIN DEVELOPMENT

Healthy brain development requires stimulation in all domains. The following effective practices contribute to healthy brain development:

- Talking, singing, reading, and playing with children.

- Protecting children from environmental hazards, such as alcohol and household chemicals.

- Receiving proper prenatal and postnatal care, such as nutrients for expectant mothers and immunizations for infants.

- Creating age-appropriate rich and varied experiences and expectations.

Sources: Data based on Berk, 2008; Diamond et al., 2010; Gallagher, 2005.

America has always been characterized by the blending of many cultures, which has shaped this country into what it is today. Yet, its basic values still reflect a Western European tradition. European American characteristics, such as individual responsibility for one's own actions, a strong work ethic, and a focus on the individual rather than the group, dominate American culture (Banks, 2006; Berns, 2010).

NAEYC's position statements on linguistic and cultural diversity (2009) and developmentally appropriate practice (DAP; Copple & Bredekamp, 2009) strongly affirm children's linguistic and cultural diversity as critical influences in children's optimal development and learning. These statements recognize the early childhood teacher's responsibility to create experiences that appreciate children's home language and culture in addition to supporting their learning of English as a second language, to value the families and communities of all children, and to honor diversity as a strength and not a deficit.

It is beyond the scope of this book to provide selected characteristics from each cultural group that you might encounter. The very best way for you to learn about the diversity of the children in your classroom is from their families. They will help you better understand the children's values, behaviors, language, and traditions. Because each child will bring many different needs, you will be learning ways to affirm each one's diversity. Knowing that children's development is shaped within their social and cultural worlds makes it imperative that you appreciate, honor, and accept children's rich, diverse backgrounds in making the best educational decisions for them. In addition to the brain and social and cultural influences on children's development, children's exceptionalities greatly influence their development. We discuss next those influences and how to best meet the needs of learners with exceptionalities.

Healthy brain development requires stimulation in all domains.

Meeting the Developmental Needs of Learners with Exceptionalities

By now you are probably aware that there will be all kinds of learners in your classroom. Though learners with exceptionalities need individualized supports and services to help them develop, learn, and be successful in school, they also need to have their *abilities* recognized and nurtured. As an early childhood professional you will interact with these children in the same positive manner as you would with every other child, because children with **exceptionalities** are more similar to than they are different from other children. They have the same basic needs to be cared for adequately, be treated fairly, and be successful. The term **exceptional learner** refers either to children with disabilities or children with gifts and talents. Each of these will be discussed next.

CHILDREN WITH DISABILITIES

A **disability** is defined as "an inability to do something or a diminished capacity to perform in a specific way" (Hallahan, Kauffman, & Pullen, 2008, p. 7). Although you are not expected to have in-depth knowledge of every disability, you do need to learn about specific needs of the children in your setting. While it is beyond the scope of this book to discuss each category of special needs, we do want to introduce you to relevant legislation, categories of exceptionality, and the notion of inclusion, which are important influences on children's development.

LEGISLATION

Since the mid-1960s, various federal laws have been enacted to ensure that educational needs are met for children with exceptionalities and that their abilities are recognized. These laws provide funding and guidelines to educate eligible children with disabilities

Table 5.5 Landmark Legislation Affecting Children with Exceptionalities

LAW	YEAR	MAJOR HIGHLIGHTS
Public Law 106-402, Developmental Disabilities Act (DDA), Section 504 of the Rehabilitation Act of 1973	1973, reauthorized 2000	• Requires states that offer preschool services to children with disabilities to offer comparable services to children with disabilities who do not qualify for special education, such as children with attention deficit disorder (ADD) or sensory integration (SI) issues.
Public Law 101-476, Individuals with Disabilities Education Act (IDEA) (Amended with same name 1997)	1990	• Reauthorizes and extends PL 94-142 (1975) and PL 99-457 (1986). • Changes language from "handicapped children" to "children with disabilities" and adds autism and traumatic brain injury to eligible categories for services.
Reauthorized as PL 108-446, Individuals with Disabilities Education Improvement Act (IDEIA), also known as IDEA-04	2004	• Lists 11 disabilities and discusses developmental delays that qualify for services.
Public Law 101-336, Americans with Disabilities Act (ADA)	1990	• Provides civil rights protection for individuals with disabilities in the workplace and in all public facilities. For young children, ensures access to all early childhood programs with reasonable accommodations.

from birth through age 21 in the most effective settings. In addition, the laws require that classroom aides or resources, specialized training for classroom teachers, therapy services, family training and counseling, and home visits be made available when needed. Table 5.5 lists four pieces of landmark legislation, and their highlights that impact children directly.

CATEGORIES OF EXCEPTIONALITY

The **Individuals with Disabilities Education Improvement Act (IDEIA)** was amended in 2004 from the 1990 Individuals with Disabilities Education Act (IDEA) and lists 11 different disabilities that qualify children for special education services. Identifying these disabilities, their basic characteristics, and the services available for children with such disabilities is essential to fulfilling your role in promoting the development of learners with exceptionalities in a regular education setting. These 11 categories are:

1. **Autism:** a disorder that affects verbal and nonverbal communication and social interactions; may be mild to severe; sometimes called *autism spectrum*.
2. **Emotional disturbance:** social/emotional disorder that interfere with a child's daily adaptation and learning.

3. **Hearing impairment:** a temporary or permanent partial or complete hearing loss.

4. **Mental retardation:** a cognitive delay in which children consistently function below the level of the average population.

5. **Multiple disabilities:** two or more equal disabilities; no primary disability can be identified.

6. **Orthopedic impairment:** a motor skill impairment that impedes the ability to move; also called *physical disability*.

7. **Other health impairment:** ongoing medical attention is necessary for health problems that can negatively affect children's ability to learn.

8. **Specific learning disability:** a processing disorder in children with normal intelligence that often leads to difficulty in learning to read, write, or do math.

9. **Speech or language impairment:** a communication disorder that includes stuttering, impaired articulation, or an inability to gain meaning from language that is basic to many of the other disabilities, especially hearing impairment and specific learning disability.

10. **Traumatic brain injury:** a temporary or permanent brain injury caused by an outside influence that may affect one or more areas of development.

11. **Visual impairment, including blindness:** a temporary or permanent loss of vision.

In addition to these 11 legal categories, the term **developmental delay** is often used to describe a nonspecific disability that affects children's learning. Being knowledgeable about the different categories of exceptionality that qualify for services is an important first step for all adults in regular early childhood settings. It will help your ability to support children and family members who need comprehensive services, which can positively affect development. Read what Richard Gargiulo, noted early childhood special educator, says about teaching young children with exceptional needs in the Ask the Expert feature on page 114.

INCLUSION

Inclusion is a way of educating all children with exceptionalities in the most natural settings within their community, particularly in the early years. Early childhood teachers are increasingly expected to teach in inclusive settings. Thus, a common definition of what inclusion means is essential for determining best inclusive practices. The joint position statement that was developed by the Division for Early Childhood (DEC) of the Council for Exceptional Children and NAEYC "serves as a blueprint for identifying the key components of high quality inclusion programs" (2009, p. 1). Inclusive practices are also supported by NAEYC's position statement on developmentally appropriate practice (Copple & Bredekamp, 2009).

Read the boxed feature on page 115 that defines early childhood inclusion and its three main characteristics to help you (a) explore the ideas behind inclusion, (b) examine your own attitudes toward children with special needs, and (c) think about your beliefs about the capacity of children with special needs to learn in regular early childhood settings. Then respond to the questions at the end.

Richard M. Gargiulo

Young Children with Exceptional Needs

Q: Why are so many early childhood teachers afraid or reluctant to teach young children with exceptional needs?

A: This perception is unfounded. Young children with disabilities are more like their typically developing classmates than they are different. I strongly encourage teachers to remember that a child with exceptionalities is first and foremost a child. Just because a child has exceptional needs should never prohibit professionals from realizing just how typical he or she is in many other ways. Good teachers look for similarities between all children and their peers, not differences. It is vitally important that early childhood teachers focus on the child, not the impairment; separate the abilities from the disability; and see the child's strengths, not the weaknesses.

Q: In what kind of environment should I teach young children with exceptional needs?

A: Contemporary thinking suggests that *all* young children with exceptional needs should receive intervention and educational services in settings designed for children without those needs, that is, in typical environments such as child-care centers, Head Start programs, or regular classrooms. Known as *full inclusion*, this concept has evolved into one of the most controversial and complex practices in the field of early childhood education. Some early childhood educators mistakenly believe that federal laws require us to educate children with exceptional needs only in general education classrooms. This simply is not true. Where appropriate, we need to educate young children with exceptional needs in the least restrictive environment, that is, with their typically developing peers. This, of course, implies the need for a continuum of placement options. To illustrate, some children with exceptionalities need a more restrictive setting, such as a preschool program for children with disabilities or for children with multiple impairments, which is a more appropriate environment than a private preschool or a public school kindergarten.

Q: If children with disabilities are so much like their typical counterparts and there is a push for full inclusion, why are early childhood teachers in the field of special education prepared differently from their classmates?

A: This is a perfectly valid question. I wonder the same thing. In fact, I believe the time is right for a collaborative preparation program. Support for this proposal is growing both in early childhood circles and in the field of special education. I believe we need to develop a seamless or inclusive model for preparing teachers of young children so that all are prepared to teach all children regardless of the type of setting they work in. We teach children, not disability labels. A unified model of preparation makes good sense. Preservice teachers could draw upon effective practices from both fields and thus provide services that are age and developmentally appropriate while also being responsive to the individual needs of each learner. I am convinced that young children need teachers with multiple competencies capable of providing effective instruction in a variety of settings. Such professionals will be well suited to meet the challenges of today's workplace.

Richard M. Gargiulo is a Professor of Education at the University of Alabama at Birmingham.

EARLY CHILDHOOD INCLUSION

"Early childhood inclusion embodies the values, policies, and practices that support the right of every infant and young child and his or her family, regardless of ability, to participate in a broad range of activities and contexts as full members of families, communities, and society. The desired results of inclusive experiences for children with and without disabilities and their families include a sense of belonging and membership, positive social relationships and friendships, and development and learning to reach their full potential. The defining features of inclusions that can be used to identify high quality early childhood programs and services are access, participation, and supports" (DEC/NAEYC, 2009, p. 2).

ACCESS: "Providing access to a wide range of learning opportunities, activities, settings, and environments is a defining feature of high quality early childhood inclusion" (DEC/NAEYC, 2009, p. 2). Access can include *structural modifications* such as a ramp, *instructional modifications* such as extra time or small-group work, and *technological modifications* such as a larger computer screen.

PARTICIPATION: "Some children will need additional accommodations and supports to participate fully in play and learning activities with peers and adults" (DEC/NAEYC, 2009, p. 2). A range of approaches, from "embedded, routines-based teaching to more explicit interventions—to scaffold learning and participation for all children" is needed.

SUPPORTS: A system of "supports must be in place to undergird the efforts of individuals and organizations providing inclusive services to children and families" (DEC/NAEYC, 2009, p. 2), such as ongoing professional development for family members, teachers, and administrators to acquire the knowledge, skills, and dispositions required to implement effective inclusive practices.

1. What do you think about these ideas? Do any concern you? If so, explain which ones and why.

2. What questions do these ideas raise for you?

3. How do the ideas presented here relate to those that Richard Gargiulo shared in the Ask the Expert feature on page 114? Share one of your ideas with the whole group.

Source: From A Joint Position Statement of the Division for Early Childhood of the Council for Exceptional Children and the National Association for the Education of Young Children, April 2009, Chapel Hill, NC.

It is important that teachers of young children create experiences that maximize learning for *all* children, adapt instruction and materials to meet individual needs, assess children's performance accurately, know when and if to refer a child, and actively participate in team planning in eligibility and individualized education plan (IEP) conferences. NAEYC's position statement on DAP supports inclusion and the need for all teachers to be prepared to meet the needs of children with exceptionalities.

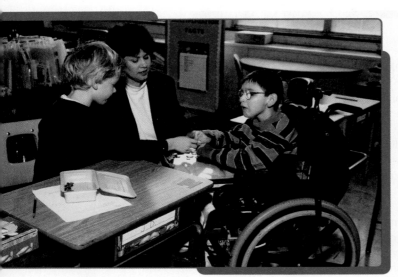

Young children with disabilities are more like their typically developing classmates than they are different.

CHILDREN WITH SPECIAL GIFTS AND TALENTS

Gifted children have high academic ability; talented children show excellence in such areas as art, music, drama, or sports. A talent can occur in one or more areas of development. In early childhood classrooms, children with special gifts and talents need to be challenged and stimulated just as every other child. Intellectually gifted children progress faster than their peers academically and often have a deep interest in books and reading, large vocabularies, a wide range of interests, and a desire to learn. To maintain their motivation they need a nurturing classroom social climate; learning that is challenging, relevant to their personal interests, and sometimes individualized; and teaching methods that match their learning styles (Hallahan et al., 2008).

Children with exceptional needs often experience academic and social challenges in school. Knowing this will increase your sensitivity to all children. It will also help you to explore new ways of educating children with disabilities and children with gifts and talents. All early childhood professionals must accommodate individual differences and develop the skills necessary to work with the entire professional support team to maximize the potential of every child. This process necessitates a more inclusive interpretation of developmentally effective practices (NAEYC, 2009; Puckett & Black, 2009).

Major Child Development Theories

WHAT IS A THEORY?

Pause and Reflect

About Children with Exceptional Needs

Think about a child who has a disability, special gift, or talent. Describe the child's characteristics and what you think the child's teacher did or did not do to support his or her development. What are your concerns about teaching children with exceptionalities?

A **theory** is an organized system of knowledge that describes, explains, and predicts behavior. Theories "guide and give meaning to what we see [and] . . . theories that are verified by research often serve as a sound basis for practical action" (Berk, 2008, p. 7). As noted in the opening quotation from Laura Berk, noted expert on children's development, the field of child development consists of many theories that are not only scientifically important but also are very useful to early childhood professionals.

Effective early childhood professionals use their knowledge of child development in their practice. The theories that follow are often used to explain what children are like. We discuss four theories from the fields of psychology and anthropology to portray different views of children's development. For each theory, we describe development from that theoretical perspective, identify how each theorist's key ideas have most influenced our views on development, and apply the theory to best practices.

PSYCHOSOCIAL THEORY OF ERIK ERIKSON (1902–1994)

Erikson's (1993, originally published in 1963) psychosocial theory emphasizes that development occurs throughout the lifespan in a series of stages, with each stage contributing to and being influenced by the one preceding and following it. He proposed eight psychosocial stages, four of which are crucial to development in the years between birth and age 12. Each stage is characterized by a conflict or crisis that influences one's social development and reflects the particular culture unique to each individual (Erikson, 1993). Erikson suggests that healthy social interactions come from the successful resolution of the unique developmental tasks that one faces. How individuals resolve the social conflicts at each stage influences their attitudes and skills. Erikson reinterpreted Freud's psychosexual stages and gave more emphasis to the interactive nature of development and less emphasis to biological factors. Consequently, Erikson believed that children play an active role in shaping their development through the kinds of experiences they have. He emphasized the role of developmental needs as a way to understand what age-appropriate social and emotional behavior should be. Erikson's theory is the most widely read and influential of the psychoanalytic theorists. Erikson was a German psychoanalyst who was strongly influenced by his studies with Sigmund Freud, the father of psychoanalysis. Table 5.6 summarizes the first four of Erikson's eight psychosocial stages, including the key characteristics, major outcomes, and significant persons.

APPLYING ERIKSON'S PSYCHOSOCIAL THEORY IN THE CLASSROOM

Fostering Trust and Autonomy in Infants and Toddlers Infants and toddlers need warm, loving, caring adults who understand their social needs during each period of development. Adults are their social and emotional models and can use the following best practices to help infants and toddlers develop *trust and autonomy*.

- Ensure that infants have adults who consistently meet their needs, who talk with them calmly, and who nurture their feelings of trust. In this way, infants develop a sense of a safety, security, and confidence in the people in their world and come to see their world as predictable.
- Provide opportunities for toddlers to engage in self-help routines such as feeding, dressing, and toileting. It is important to maintain a reassuring, confident attitude to support toddlers' basic attempts at mastering motor and cognitive skills.
- Select literature that fosters trust and autonomy, such as the lift-the-flap book *Baby Danced the Polka* (Beaumont, 2004) or *Llama, Llama Red Pajama* (Dewdney, 2005), which addresses bedtime and separation anxiety.

Fostering Initiative in Preschool Children Preschoolers like trying new tasks, assuming responsibility for themselves and materials, playing with others, and discovering what they can do with the help of adults. They use pretend play as one way to make choices and decisions that increase their sense of autonomy and competence, and to master the social and cultural world in which they live. Teachers can foster initiative in preschool children by using the following best practices.

- Provide children with many opportunities for selecting and using materials in a variety of ways, allowing children long, uninterrupted periods for play.
- Encourage children to engage in all forms of play. Children practice appropriate social skills and develop feelings of competence through play.
- Use unbreakable cups and pitchers that are easy to pour, grasp, and balance.
- Show children how to clean up or revise a product that is not quite right.

Table 5.6 Erikson's Four Psychosocial Stages Related to Early Childhood Development

PSYCHOSOCIAL CONFLICT/AGES	KEY CHARACTERISTICS	MAJOR OUTCOMES	SIGNIFICANT PERSONS
Trust versus mistrust Infancy (0–12 months)	• Infants' conflict centers on care and nurturance. • Their needs must be satisfied.	• If needs are met consistently, infants develop trust in others and a hopeful, confident outlook. • If needs are met inconsistently, infants do not develop the hope that they will receive the care they need.	• Responsive, sensitive, and consistent caregiver
Autonomy versus shame and doubt Toddlerhood (1–3 years)	• Toddlers' conflict centers on their ability to exert ownership over their bodies and actions after they develop trust and good feelings about themselves and their environment.	• If toddlers have the opportunity to manage themselves and their environments appropriately, they develop autonomy, a sense of an emerging separate self, and will. • If the environment is so rigid that children feel overcontrolled by others, they resist such control and may become filled with doubt about their ability to control themselves successfully.	• Significant, consistent adult
Initiative versus guilt Preschool years (3–5 years)	• Preschoolers struggle between their ability to undertake and complete tasks and their fear of failing at those tasks and feeling guilty. They go back and forth between the wish to be big and independent and also to be helpless like a baby. • They generally will take responsibility for self-care, want to belong to a group, and begin to play together cooperatively.	• Preschoolers who show initiative have a sense of direction and purpose to their work and play. • Preschoolers who cannot test their independence and are punished too quickly may feel unnecessarily guilty.	• Basic family • Preschool teachers
Industry versus inferiority (6–12 years)	• Elementary children become increasingly focused on doing and making things. • They want to master intellectual and social tasks, do things well, and be competent.	• Elementary children who show a sense of industry demonstrate feelings of competence by a "can-do" attitude toward school tasks. • Elementary children who do not feel industrious feel incompetent, and often demonstrate a "can't do" attitude toward school tasks.	• Neighborhood, peers, and those at school

Source: Data based on Erikson, 1993 (originally published in 1963).

- Acknowledge children's attempts at independence and make sure that each child has a chance to experience successes rather than failures by providing developmentally appropriate tasks.
- Select literature that fosters initiative, such as *Where the Wild Things Are* (Sendak, 1964), *Moss Gown* (Hooks, 1987), or *Min-Yo and the Moon Dragon* (Hillman, 1992).

Fostering Industry in Elementary-Age Children A healthy sense of industry includes a positive but realistic self-concept, pride in accomplishment, moral responsibility, and cooperative participation with age-mates. During the elementary years, children continue to refine their sense of self. Teachers of elementary-age children should use the following best practices to support children's developing sense of *industry*.

- Select literature that can help children with the struggles they face. For example, a sense of industry or task orientation can be understood through *Island of the Blue Dolphins* (O'Dell, 1960) for older children or *Daniel's Story* (Matas, 1993) for younger children.
- Make sure students have opportunities to set and achieve realistic and achievable school and personal goals, through challenging but not overwhelming assignments that are short at first and lengthened as appropriate, monitoring their own progress through a journal, and engaging their curiosity and motivation to master tasks.
- Provide students with opportunities to demonstrate responsibility, such as caring for living things, being accountable for their own belongings and homework, and using technology appropriately.
- Support students who feel discouraged through individual contracts that show student progress or portfolios that show work samples over time.

COGNITIVE-DEVELOPMENTAL THEORY OF JEAN PIAGET (1896–1980)

Piaget's theory of the stages of children's intellectual development focuses on how children's thinking, reasoning, and perception differ from those of adults. Piaget's cognitive-developmental theory is based upon the in-depth, observational studies of his own children. These studies were used to figure out how children think about their world. Piaget's background as a biologist, with its emphasis on adaptation, strongly influenced his theory of cognitive development. The theory is based upon the following four assumptions about cognitive development (Piaget, 1992):

1. Biological and environmental influences interact continuously to develop an individual's thinking, reasoning, and perceptual ability.
2. Cognitive development is initially the result of direct experience in an environment; eventually children become capable of transforming their experience mentally through internal reflection.
3. The pace of an individual's development is influenced by the social context.
4. Cognitive development involves major qualitative changes in one's thinking.

Piaget hypothesized that the development of all children's thinking moves through a series of four cognitive stages. The rate of progress through these stages varies from individual to individual, but each stage has unique characteristics. The first three stages occur during the early childhood years; these include (a) the **sensorimotor stage** (0–2 years), during which infants and toddlers use their senses and reflexes to respond to their immediate world but do not think conceptually; (b) the **preoperational stage** (2–7 years), during which children have an increased ability to think symbolically and conceptually about objects and people outside of their immediate environment, which is evident through children's increasing use of language and imaginative play; and (c) the **concrete operational** stage (7–12 years), which is characterized by the ability to use logical thought to solve concrete problems related to concepts of space, time, causality, and number. The fourth stage, **formal operations** (ages 12 and on), marks the beginning of logical and scientific thinking and is characterized by the ability to make predictions, think hypothetically, and think about thinking. Table 5.7 summarizes Piaget's first three stages of cognitive development and lists the major characteristics of each.

Table 5.7 Piaget's Stages of Cognitive Development

COGNITIVE STAGE	APPROXIMATE AGE RANGE	KEY BEHAVIORAL CHARACTERISTICS	PRACTICAL APPLICATIONS
Sensorimotor	Birth–2 years	• react to stimuli with simple reflexes, such as rooting and sucking • develop first habits, such as sucking when shown a bottle • accidentally reproduce interesting events, such as kicking a mobile and hearing music (which is called primary circular reaction) • focus on the world outside of self, such as imitating sounds of others (which is called secondary circular reaction) • are curious about what objects can do, and what they can do with objects, such as rolling a ball to knock an object (which is called tertiary circular reaction) • develop the concept of object permanence: the understanding that objects exist even when they cannot be seen	• provide stimulating, colorful, safe objects for infants and toddlers to reach for, grasp, and explore • encourage sounds and responses to stimuli such as clapping, singing, and cooing
Preoperational thinking	2–7 years	• have the ability to mentally represent an object that is not present, as in pretending to drive a car while playing (symbolic function) • are egocentric, able to focus only on own perspective, not on those of others • project animism, giving life to inanimate objects, as in thinking that clouds cry • show *centration* in thinking, focusing attention on one characteristic of an object or event, such as color, shape, or size, to the exclusion of others • display a rapid increase in language • use fantasy and imaginative play as natural modes of thinking	• provide props to represent images in children's environment • talk about how certain behaviors (e.g., pushing, grabbing) make others feel to reduce egocentrism • encourage classification of objects by shape, size, weight, or color • provide rhymes, songs, and poems that play with the English language • provide opportunities to work in groups of two or three

continued

Table 5.7 continued

COGNITIVE STAGE	APPROXIMATE AGE RANGE	KEY BEHAVIORAL CHARACTERISTICS	PRACTICAL APPLICATIONS
			• encourage new gross motor activities that stretch children's comfort zones • provide open-ended activities (e.g., blocks, art, writing, pretend play) • provide sensory experiences
Concrete operations	7–11 years	• can think through series of steps, then mentally reverse the steps and go back to the starting point • can classify and divide sets and subsets and consider their relationships (e.g., understanding that one's mother can also be somebody else's sister and daughter at the same time) • become more analytical and logical in their approach to words and grammar	• use concrete, manipulative objects and materials to help children draw conclusions • provide concrete materials as a bridge to representational thought • provide opportunities to make decisions and exchange points of view

Sources: Data based on Piaget, 1992; Santrock, 2009; Woolfolk, 2010.

APPLYING PIAGET'S COGNITIVE-DEVELOPMENTAL THEORY IN THE CLASSROOM

Piaget's theory has greatly influenced our thinking about how to promote children's intellectual development. His ideas have implications for how we prepare early childhood environments and how adults interact with the children they teach. In fact, several different early childhood programs and practices have been designed explicitly using Piagetian principles, particularly concerning the interaction patterns between the adult and the child. One such program is "Educating the Young Thinker," an inquiry approach aimed at promoting the development of representational competence by using language to provoke cognitive disequilibrium (Copple, Sigel, & Saunders, 1984). A second approach uses group games to promote the development of children's logic and social and moral values (Kamii & DeVries, 1980). From Piaget's theory, we use the following best practices.

- Prepare early childhood classrooms that encourage exploration and discovery. Include a wide variety of interesting materials and experiences for all children. Because young children's thinking is based on motor experiences, the best learning environment has interesting materials available to children at different levels of development. Such materials might include colorful stacking toys for *infants*, ample puzzles and construction materials for *preschoolers* and kindergartners, and board games and manipulative materials for *elementary children*. These materials must be worthy of children's attention to develop their thinking through exploration, experimentation, hypothesis testing, and reflection (Copple & Bredekamp, 2009).
- Provide a variety of opportunities for play to enhance children's practice with symbols. During play, you will notice that children practice what they know and use

important thinking abilities, such as problem solving, negotiation, and decision making. Practicing new skills in play is inherently satisfying to children. Such repetition may be as simple as infants grasping and dropping an object or preschoolers repeatedly working the same puzzle, in and out of the frame, until all variations have been mastered. From Piaget we learn that as children develop, they practice different and more varied skills, and thus become more effective with them.

- Understand that *preoperational children* (ages 2–7) think concretely. Guiding preoperational thinking should include using concrete materials, such as chips or cubes, whenever possible; keeping instructions as brief as possible and using actions as well as words; and providing a wide range of experiences, such as field trips, cooking, and learning about community workers, in order to build a foundation for concept learning and language.

- Understand that the *concrete operational* (ages 7–11) child thinks concretely. Guiding concrete operational thinking should include the continual use of concrete materials and visual aids such as graphic organizers, diagrams, and timelines; keeping demonstrations and readings short and focused; and using familiar examples to explain difficult concepts, such as measuring two different rooms to understand the concept of area.

- Select literature that capitalizes on preoperational children's growing intellectual capacity to enjoy fantasy and humor through books such as *Kitten's First Full Moon* (Henkes, 2004) and concrete operational children's growing intellectual capacity to use problem solving and perspective taking through books such as *The Cats in Krasinki Square* (Hesse, 2004) or *Hot Dog with Abbot Avenue* (English, 2004).

Opportunities for children to practice new skills help them gain confidence.

ECOLOGICAL SYSTEMS THEORY OF URIE BRONFENBRENNER (1917–2005)

Bronfenbrenner, an American developmental psychologist and co-founder of the Head Start program, emphasizes the critical importance of social and cultural influences on development (Bronfenbrenner, 2004). Though Bronfenbrenner acknowledges the biological influences on development, his theory emphasizes the **ecological** (environmental) **contexts** that influence development. For Bronfenbrenner, children are shaped by the social and cultural world in which they live but they also shape their worlds and the people in them. These **bi-directional social and cultural contexts**—the family, educational setting, community, and broader society—are interrelated, influence the others, and all impact the developing child. Each system is in constant interaction with another and influences the others; together they are like a set of nested blocks— each embedded inside one another, acting separately but functioning as a unit when put together. Bronfenbrenner's nested model includes the following five different social systems, each of which influences the other and affects the developing child. These systems are illustrated in Figure 5.3.

1. The **microsystem** is where the child lives and experiences most of his or her activities and relationships, such as in the home, school, neighborhood, and with friends. If, for example, a new baby is born, the baby influences the parents and the other members of the family just as much as they influence the baby.

Figure 5.3 Bronfenbrenner's Ecological Systems Theory

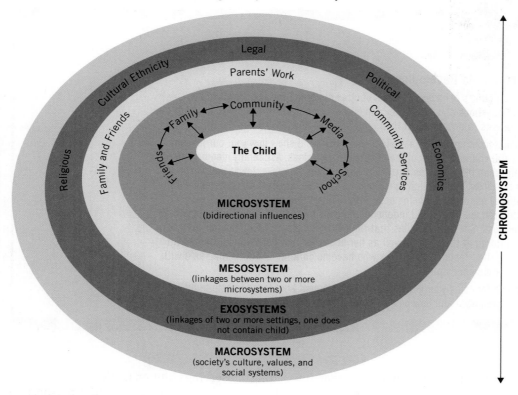

2. The **mesosystem** links two or more of the child's microsystems, such as the connections between the family and school and the relationship between the family and neighborhood. Conferences between the teacher and the parent are a good example of linkages in the mesosystem.

3. The **exosystem** links two or more social settings, one of which does not include the child but indirectly influences the child—for example, the parents' workplace and the educational system. If, for example, a parent is highly stressed in the work environment, that parent's stress may influence how the parent relates to the child after work.

4. The **macrosystem** includes the values, beliefs, laws, and customs of a child's culture and ethnicity that are transmitted from generation to generation and affect the interactions among the family, school, and community in the child's immediate world.

5. The **chronosystem** includes the dimensions of time with ever-changing life events as they affect the child. This influence can be external, such as a divorce or death, or internal, such as a child's growth process.

APPLYING BRONFENBRENNER'S ECOLOGICAL THEORY IN THE CLASSROOM
Bronfenbrenner's theory significantly guides interactions with children and their families. The most important impact occurs at the microsystem and mesosytem levels. Use the following best practices to provide consistent support for children and their families.

COLLABORATING WITH
Families

Is This Typical? Insights into Child Development

Many parents want to know if their child's behavior is typical of other children that age. They usually follow that question with further questions about how they can encourage proper development. Here are two suggestions that address parents' concerns about their child's development:

1. Have a family informational meeting on typical child development and show how your curriculum relates to the developmental characteristics of the children in your class. Ask family members to bring in a picture of them when they were the age of the children in your class. Invite them to share a memory of something they liked to do at that age. Compare their memories to the developmental levels and discuss what they remember as being easy or difficult at that particular age.

2. A teacher whose own children are grown and independent keeps pictures of them when they were her students' age on her desk. She tells families that the pictures help her to remember the needs and interests of children at that age as well as her hopes for how her own children would be taught and cared for by their teachers. Teachers who have no children could do the same with their own or another family member's picture.

These suggestions are a beginning for using your growing child development knowledge to help families better understand what their children need and how best to support them.

• Know children in more than one setting. Observing children in different social settings (e.g., the school, home) and inviting families to provide their perspective and knowledge is essential for obtaining the most complete picture of individual development.

Children's basic and growth needs must be met if they are to be successful in school.

• Study children in a variety of settings over a period of time. This helps early childhood educators see common as well as individual characteristics of children.

• Create and maintain an environment that invites good communication between home and school. Involve families in learning activities at home, welcome parents in your classroom in a variety of roles, and learn about the child's community and culture.

HIERARCHY OF NEEDS THEORY OF ABRAHAM MASLOW (1908–1970)

Humanistic psychologist Abraham Maslow (1987) formulated a theory of human motivation based upon a hierarchy of universal basic and growth needs. **Basic needs** include physiological needs (e.g., food and drink) and safety and survival needs (e.g., physical and psychological security). *Growth needs* emerge as children's basic needs are being met. Growth needs include the need for *love and belonging* (e.g., being accepted and belonging to a group both in the family and in the school). They also include the need for *esteem* that comes from recognition, approval, and achievement from both peers and adults and leads to a sense of competence and can-do feelings. Such feelings of self-worth are derived from authentic, not trivialized, accomplishments. Maslow suggests that these needs motivate individual behavior and lead to healthy development, when satisfied. For Maslow, healthy development is a continual series of choices that each person makes throughout a lifetime in which he or she must choose between satisfying basic or growth needs. He also believed that as needs are met individuals naturally tend to seek higher needs, the highest of which is **self-actualization,** the desire to use one's abilities and talents to the fullest. Motivation to satisfy growth needs increases when they are being met and decreases when they are not being met. For Maslow, children whose basic safety needs are clearly being met will naturally seek stronger needs for love, belonging, and so forth, up the hierarchy of needs.

APPLYING MASLOW'S THEORY IN THE CLASSROOM

Maslow's theory provides a window into the development of the whole child—the interconnectedness of a child's physical, social, emotional, and cognitive needs. Early childhood educators must know which of children's basic and growth needs are or are not being met if they are to help them develop in healthy ways. From Maslow, we implement the following best practices.

- Provide predictable routines in the daily schedule to help children feel secure in their setting.
- Ensure adequate health, safety, and nutrition, but also know how to access other services, such as physical, dental, or social services.
- Help children feel like a part of the family or school group to satisfy the need for belonging and love.
- Provide opportunities for making choices or solving interesting problems so children can learn to trust their own ideas.
- Facilitate children's investigative capacity by accepting a range of solutions to problems, and encourage children to express a range of feelings and ideas to satisfy the need for esteem.

From these theorists, we learn that there are many approaches to understanding children's development. We also learn that no single theoretical perspective tells us all we would like to know. Knowing about multiple approaches to child development enables you to select and use whatever is best for each child at a given time. That is called an *eclectic approach* to development. At this point, it is time to summarize the key ideas from this chapter and extend your thinking about child development with some assessment activities.

Summary

■ Development refers to the complex and dynamic cognitive, language, physical, motor, social, emotional, and moral processes that change over one's lifetime. While each area develops independently, it is also inextricably intertwined with the other areas, which is why we refer to the *whole child* when we look at children's development. Typical development follows a predictable overall sequence of milestones that are affected by the child's age, individual temperament, and biological makeup and influenced both by the child's family and cultural background.

■ Teachers must make *intentional, purposeful decisions* about children that are based, in part, on each child's particular patterns of development.

■ Children develop faster during the first 5 years than at any other stage of their lives. Their development is influenced by many factors, including their brain development and cultural and social background.

■ Though learners with exceptionalities need individualized supports and services to help them develop, learn, and be successful in school, they also need to have their *abilities* recognized and nurtured. Children with exceptionalities are more similar to than they are different from other children. They have the same basic needs to be cared for adequately, be treated fairly, and be successful. The term *exceptional learner* can refer to children with disabilities, children with gifts and talents, or children from diverse backgrounds.

■ The theories of Erikson, Piaget, Bronfenbrenner, and Maslow are regularly used to explain what children are like and portray different influences on children's development.

Applying Your Knowledge of Child Development

In Assessment Activity 1, apply your knowledge of child development to what would you do as Angelica's teacher. Then, in Assessment Activity 2, apply your understanding of inclusion by comparing what inclusion means and does not mean.

 **ANGELICA'S BABY PICTURES**

Four-year-old Angelica was adopted from South America at age 2. Angelica lives with her single-parent mother in a diverse community near a major city.

Angelica's preschool class was studying about how living things grow and change. One day, Angelica came home from school crying because she couldn't do her homework. Angelica's teacher, Ms. Kane, had sent home a piece of adding machine tape with the following directions: "Cut the paper to the length you were when you were born, and please bring a photo of you when you were a baby, so we can see how much bigger you are now, and how different you look now that you are older."

For the first 2 years of her life, Angelica lived with a foster family in South America and came to this country with only the clothes on her body. There were no photos, so Angelica's mother would never know what Angelica looked like when she was a baby, when she said her first word, or when she took her first step.

Because Angelica was so sad, her mother made an appointment to speak with Ms. Kane. Ms. Kane explained that she was having her class make books about themselves, including special information about when they were babies. Ms. Kane seemed to think this was a perfectly appropriate activity for preschoolers and could not understand why Angelica was so upset.

During the course of the conversation between Angelica's mother and Ms. Kane, Angelica's mother shared how this seemingly harmless activity created a series of painful questions between Angelica and her mother about Angelica's past. She could not be told who her birth parents were, why they didn't want to keep her, whether there were pictures of her when she was a baby, what she looked like, or who her friends were. Angelica's mother reminded Ms. Kane that she had filled out the family questionnaire at the start of the school year and reported that Angelica was adopted; she was surprised that Ms. Kane had selected an adoption-insensitive assignment for Angelica and her classmates.

To find out more information about adoption-sensitive assignments, Ms. Kane talked with the community social worker who served the preschool. Ms. Kane learned that certain typical school projects, such as finding baby pictures, making family trees, exploring family heritage, and making Mother's Day presents, may upset children who are adopted. The social worker told Ms. Kane how important it was for her to be sensitive to the needs of adopted children because even though they don't appear to be different, their needs are somewhat unique, and to never dismiss an issue as insignificant because, to adopted children, it is not. She also reminded Ms. Kane that children do not like to feel different and that anything teachers of young children can do to affirm who they are contributes to their sense of self. The social worker invited Ms. Kane to talk with the other preschool staff and determine their interest in a staff development seminar entitled "Adoption Awareness in the Schools," which she would be happy to conduct.

REACT	Think about how the perspectives of Angelica's mother, Ms. Kane, and the social worker are alike and different. What might be some reasons?
RESEARCH	Visit the websites of several adoption agencies and search the Internet for authoritative information that will help you learn more about the characteristics and needs of adopted children. A good resource is the Center for Adoptive Families at www.adoptionstogether.org. What key characteristics of adopted children did you find that apply to child development?
REFLECT	What assumptions about adopted children do Ms. Kane, the social worker, and Angelica's mother hold? List some ways you can be adoption-sensitive in your setting, such as having children make gifts for other family members on Mother's Day or Father's Day if children have only one or no parents.

Assessment ACTIVITY ② UNDERSTANDING INCLUSION

There are many reasons to include young children with exceptionalities in the regular early childhood classroom. Inclusion can benefit children with and without disabilities, teachers, and families of all of the children. Based upon your answers to the questions in the following boxed feature, brainstorm statements that describe what early childhood inclusion means and what it does not mean. Use the following example as a starting point to complete your own comparison chart.

Once you have completed your chart, think about why inclusion is or is not needed for children with exceptional needs.

INCLUSION MEANS	INCLUSION DOES NOT MEAN
Having children with a disability attend regular early childhood classes.	Placing children with disabilities in regular classrooms without the access, participation, and supports they need to be successful.
Regular education teachers use appropriate strategies for the varied needs of children in the class.	Having separate pull-out programs for children according to disability.

ONLINE RESOURCES FOR PROMOTING CHILDREN'S DEVELOPMENT

American Academy of Pediatrics: Read the report "The Importance of Play in Promoting Healthy Child Development and Maintaining Strong Parent-Child Bonds." It offers guidelines on how pediatricians can advocate for children by helping families, school systems, and communities consider how best to ensure that play is protected as they seek the balance in children's lives to create the optimal developmental milieu. www.aap.org/pressroom/playfinal.pdf

ASCD Whole Child Initiative: Offers resources and practical tips on how to ensure that each child is healthy, safe, engaged, supported, and challenged. You can also watch a video on healthy school communities showcasing an elementary school in Iowa. www.wholechildeducation.org

Child Development Theories: Provides brief overviews of child development theories for those theorists discussed in this chapter. http://psychology.about.com

National Dairy Council/Nutrition Education: Provides nutrition education information and resources for teachers, parents, and children. www.nutritionexplorations.org

Zero to Three: This organization provides information for professionals and parents on the growth and development of infants and toddlers. http://zerotothree.org/

PEARSON myeducationlab

Go to Topic 2 (Child Development/Theories) in the MyEducationLab (www.myeducationlab.com) for your course, where you can:

- Find learning outcomes for child development/theories along with the national standards that connect to these outcomes.
- Complete Assignments and Activities that can help you more deeply understand the chapter content.
- Apply and practice your understanding of the core teaching skills identified in the chapter with the Building Teaching Skills and Dispositions learning units.

CHAPTER 6

Fostering Children's Engagement in Learning

Properly organized learning results in mental development and sets in motion a variety of developmental processes that would be impossible apart from learning.

Lev Vygotsky, 1978, p. 90

Meet the TEACHERS

MRS. SUAREZ teaches toddlers in a child-care setting. If you visit her class, you will see Mrs. Suarez sitting on an oversized pillow on the floor while reading books to a few children, one of whom is sitting on her lap. She is talking to them about the characters they see in their books. Mrs. Suarez believes it is important to talk with and read to children regularly and she helps the children's parents do the same in their homes. She suggests that the parents use short, simple sentences to talk with their children, and helps them find good books to read to their infants and toddlers because, as she says, "Children's brains are being wired for learning from birth."

MS. BURKE teaches in an inclusive, public preschool. As she plans for instruction, she wonders how to respond to the children's interests and incorporate academic standards. At the same time Ms. Burke was trying to reconcile these questions, the children expressed interests about the school renovation—the trucks, the heavy equipment, and the demolition that was happening in and around the school. She and the children toured the construction site, photographed the workers and the machinery, and created a pictorial timeline that documented the transformation of the building. Ms. Burke then gathered a variety of picture books about construction, and read *The Three Little Pigs* to help children extend their concept of building. She noticed the children's rich conversations, their complex play, and detailed drawings about the school construction and now considers children's needs and interests as "essential to how children learn."

MS. DOMBROWSKI uses math journals in her first grade as one way to integrate the national mathematical standards in her curriculum and assess children's mathematical understandings. She uses that knowledge to introduce math journals to her first graders because, she says, "Communication in mathematics helps the children clarify their ideas and helps me to understand what mathematical knowledge and concepts they possess, and how they express that knowledge." Ms. Dombrowski's first graders write and draw about word problems, counting sequences, and patterns for such mathematical concepts as missing addends, counting money, telling time, and identifying place value. Ms. Dombrowski believes "that true understanding of mathematics comes from representing and explaining their ideas in different ways."

LEARNING Outcomes

In this chapter you will learn to:

→ Define learning and identify five features of authentic learning (NAEYC #1 and #4, ACEI #1, INTASC #1)

→ Use learning principles to guide your role as a facilitator of learning

→ Describe the importance of learner-centered experiences

→ Consider the central role of play in children's learning (NAEYC #4)

→ Explain how to foster learning through technology

→ Describe five major learning theories and discuss their implications for young children

→ Apply knowledge of learning theory in early childhood classrooms

Compare
What are some similarities in how these three teachers help children learn?

Contrast
Do you notice any differences in the methods they have used to foster children's learning?

Connect
What impressed you most about these teachers' views of learning? How do you think you will incorporate these ideas with children?

Now that you have reflected on the three teachers' perspectives and noted the learning outcomes, we preview the knowledge, skills, and dispositions you will need to fulfill your role in fostering children's engagement in learning.

A Definition of Learning

Picture the difference in yourself when you are learning something new and when you are doing something that you have already learned. In which situation do you feel more confident about demonstrating what you know? Though there are many different theories about what learning is, most agree that **learning** is the natural process of making sense of information and experience that is fostered through interactions with others. According to Santrock (2009), learning is "a relatively permanent influence on behavior, knowledge, and thinking skills, which comes about through experience" (p. 231). To illustrate, recall what it was like when you first learned to drive a car. You knew it was a natural activity for most teenagers and adults, but you first needed to figure out how to shift gears, reverse, park, brake, and so forth. The more practice you had behind the wheel with a more experienced driver, the more your experience helped your driving improve. Now, years later, you can see a permanent change in your driving behavior from the first day you took the wheel.

Research in cognitive neurosciences (Sawyer, 2006), multiple intelligences (Gardner, 1993, 2000), and multicultural education (Banks, 2008) has deepened our understanding of how all people learn. This research has clear implications for early childhood educators because it provides evidence that every child can learn.

Features of Authentic Learning Experiences

People learn best when they believe in themselves and are confident that they can learn (Bandura, 1997, 2001). Authentic learning experiences resemble situations that people naturally encounter outside the classroom and that make sense to them in their interactions with people, materials, and/or ideas (Jacobsen, Eggen, & Kauchak, 2009). Before we discuss the features of an authentic learning experience, consider the following scenario involving preschoolers Danielle and Maria:

> Danielle and Maria were building with large, hollow blocks. Together, they decided to build a maze for their animal figures so they could have an animal relay race. They collected blocks; built large enclosed spaces with side openings and lanes to connect each space; wrote signs that said Start, Stop, and Tickets; and gathered a variety of animal figures from the box of accessories nearby. While the girls were concentrating on their building and deciding which animals were going to participate in the relay race, their teacher passed by the block building area. Here is what she noticed: Danielle and Maria were (a) measuring space, (b) writing their signs, (c) selecting the correct number of blocks to build each side of their enclosures, (d) using two small blocks to equal one long block (which demonstrated an understanding of equivalency), and (e) classifying as they sorted the blocks by shape to put them away.

Danielle and Maria are naturally making sense out of their block play. They are demonstrating what they know about measurement, spatial relations, and early literacy through authentic learning. **Authentic learning** involves comprehension and develops learners who see possibilities, want to know about things, and use what they are learning; nonauthentic or **rote learning** involves memorization and develops learners who focus on correct answers and passive responses (Jacobsen et al., 2009; Pica, 2008; Woolfolk, 2010). Authentic learning experiences share the following five features:

1. **Authentic learning experiences use children's prior knowledge to spark their interest in meaningful, purposeful activities.** All children learn best when teaching begins with what they know or think they know. Take, for example, one of the most well-known authentic learning projects, the 1994 building of the Amusement Park for Birds, found in the La Villette School in Reggio Emilia, Italy. The school site attracts lots of birds, which capture children's interest, spark questions, and encourage talk about birds. Children throughout the years have explored the grounds from a "bird's eye view," built interesting birdhouses, and created unusual drinking fountains for the birds in their midst. While the children's interests were sparked by the birds, the teachers' awareness of how to deepen children's curiosity, provide opportunities to choose how to follow their interests in birds, and allow children to work at their own pace provide the cornerstone for authentic learning experiences. Notice also that Danielle and Maria used their knowledge of relay races to construct their racetrack.

2. **Authentic learning experiences promote strategic thinking. Strategic thinking** teaches specific skills in contexts that the learners need to use. To become better readers, for example, all children need command of how and when to use a variety of strategies. Using picture cues, making predictions, and asking questions for advance organizers all help children apply the skills they need as readers. Strategic thinking allows children to discover new meanings and understandings and to develop the reflective skills to make them independent learners (American Psychological Association, 2005; Jacobsen et al., 2009).

3. **Authentic learning experiences involve some social interactions.** Vygotsky (1978) believes that learning is a social process and that children first learn new knowledge through social relations with others, which they later internalize. Starting from birth, children's communication with others is essentially social. They use language for different purposes: to ask for something they need, to get things done, to find out information, or to maintain relations with another (Vygotsky, 1978). Communicating ideas with others promotes improved collective understanding and promotes appropriate higher-level thinking skills.

DID YOU Know?

Key Facts About Children's Learning

- Movement is a child's preferred mode of learning, and physical activity activates the brain more so than doing seatwork. While sitting increases fatigue and reduces concentration, movement feeds oxygen, water, and glucose to the brain, optimizing its performance. Learning by doing creates more neural networks in the brain and throughout the body, making the entire body a tool for learning (Hannaford, 2005).

- Children lack knowledge and experience, but not reasoning ability. Although young children are inexperienced, they reason with the knowledge they have (Donovan & Bransford, 2005).

- By the time a student graduates from high school, he or she will have watched 20,000 hours of television, more than the number of hours spent in the classroom (Lynch, 2005).

- Only half of 3-, 4-, and 5-year-olds are enrolled in public or private preschool programs, including Head Start (Jensen, 2008).

Pause and Reflect

About Learning

Think about one of your most successful learning experiences. What made it meaningful, memorable, and enjoyable? Now think about one of your least successful learning experiences. What made it uninteresting, irrelevant, and discouraging? List the characteristics of each and compare and contrast them.

What makes this an authentic learning experience?

4. **Authentic learning experiences are based on each child's ways of learning and displaying knowledge.** Not all children learn in the same way, at the same rate, or have the same interests. Howard Gardner (1993, 2000) suggests that we all learn skills, concepts, and strategies through at least eight different intelligences, which provide multiple ways of learning. (See Table 6.3 and Assessment Activity 2 of this chapter for a description of Gardner's eight intelligences.) Similarly, we demonstrate what we know in different ways. A good example of this is a study of the rain forest by a second-grade class. The children read books about the rain forest, such as *Save My Rain Forest* (Zak, 1992), learned specific vocabulary words related to the rain forest, and wrote stories about tropical evergreens and endangered species. Some children counted and graphed a vast array of evergreens and endangered species, and some made a class mural depicting the different species of plant and animal life. Throughout their study, the second graders transformed their classroom into a rain forest and invited their families to come and experience all that they had learned. Some children read and told stories about the lives of specific organisms in the rain forest; others provided their parents with headphones to listen to their tape-recorded information about life and life cycles. What did the children learn? Aside from vocabulary words, they practiced the reading, writing, oral language, and mathematical and science skills that were expected at the second-grade level in their school district. When you consider children's multiple ways of learning, children at any age can approach almost any topic from a variety of perspectives.

5. **Authentic learning experiences help children apply their learning to other situations.** Research from cognitive neurosciences suggests that most learners have difficulty with *transfer,* defined as appropriately applying knowledge learned in one setting to a different setting (Bransford, Brown, & Cocking, 2000; Jensen, 2008; Shonkoff & Phillips, 2001). Being able to transfer knowledge, skills, concepts, and strategies from one situation to another is an essential aspect of learning. When younger children learn to use picture cues to "read" a story from one book, they use that strategy over and over again in "reading" other books. When older children learn to read to the end of the sentence to get its meaning before sounding out an unfamiliar word, they are using the context of the sentence to increase their reading comprehension and then use that strategy in other reading situations.

These five features of authentic learning highlight how central learners are to the learning process. Because teachers are expected to reach all learners, you will need to understand your role as a facilitator of children's learning.

Your Role as a Facilitator of Learning

Being a **facilitator of learning**—one who is a partner with children in the learning process—is a significant way to influence children's learning. As a facilitator, you view learners as active participants in the learning process (Epstein, 2007; Henniger, 2009), and you view your role as engaging children in learning and promoting their understanding rather than simply transmitting knowledge by providing both **adult-guided** and **child-guided experiences.** *Adult-guided experiences* reflect both the teacher's goal and the children's engagement; *child-guided experiences* reflect both the children's interests and behaviors and the teacher's support (Epstein, 2007). Your commitment to both types of experiences helps children value learning—a message that is as critical as the content you teach. It also honors the reciprocity between you and the learner, and exemplifies the simple but powerful words of Robert Fulghum (1986), in the book, *All I Really Need to Know I Learned in Kindergarten.* Your role in fostering children's learning includes (a) being aware of your beliefs about learning, (b) creating opportunities for co-learning, (c) encouraging social interaction and sharing, and (d) modeling and teaching lifelong learning skills.

Adult-guided experiences reflect both the teacher's goal and the children's engagement.

1. **Beliefs about learning affect children and their families.** Your beliefs about how children learn guide your relationships with children and their families, your daily schedule, your room arrangement, and the experiences that you plan. Sometimes you may use open-ended questions to probe children's thinking; at other times you may use closed-ended questions that focus on factual information. These decisions reflect your beliefs of how children learn. Your personal belief system greatly influences what you do, constitutes a large part of your teaching, and impacts your ability to promote children's learning (Gallagher & Mayer, 2008; McCombs & Whisler, 1997).

2. **Create opportunities for co-learning.** As a partner in learning, you must select materials that will help children move from learning with assistance to learning independently. For example, when young children can consistently solve a particular kind of math problem using manipulatives, they next need to try to solve it using pictures, and then finally solve it more abstractly, using their minds. These different levels of learning indicate the type of support children need to internalize the concepts that lead them toward independence. As a co-learner, planning how and when to support children's learning at different levels is one of the most challenging tasks you will encounter, because as children see their success, they gain confidence in their own capacity to learn (Bodrova & Leong, 1996, 2005; Copple & Bredekamp, 2009).

3. **Encourage social interaction and shared experiences.** Because social interaction is central to learning (Vygotsky, 1978), children need many opportunities to share and compare their thinking with that of others. The others can be peers or adults who provide the opportunity to refine and develop thinking. As a facilitator, you can increase children's learning with some of the following strategies that rely on social interactions: cooperative learning, peer tutoring, cross-age tutoring, group investigations, sociodramatic play, and sociodramatic play centers. Each of these strategies respects children as resources in constructing their own learning (Copple & Bredekamp, 2009; Gallagher & Mayer, 2008).

4. **Model and teach lifelong learning skills.** Lifelong learning skills enable you to engage in continuous learning that can be applied to new situations. The following skills are

needed to be a lifelong learner (Berns, 2010): confidence ("I can do it"), motivation ("I want to do it"), effort ("I am willing to try"), responsibility ("I follow through on commitments"), initiative ("I am a self-starter"), perseverance ("I finish what I start"), caring ("I show concern for others"), teamwork ("I work cooperatively with others"), common sense ("I use good judgment"), and problem solving ("I use my knowledge and experience effectively"). To facilitate children's learning, you need to be knowledgeable about learner-centered experiences.

The Importance of Learner-Centered Experiences

Think back to the way you learned in school. Were you mostly concerned with memorizing facts and reciting correct answers to your teachers' questions? Or do you remember having opportunities to ask questions and become involved in answering many of your own questions? Both of these ways of learning are common in schools. While you probably remember what you learned in school, do you also remember how you felt while learning, and how your teachers kept you interested in learning? Based on advances in the study of learning, educators are changing their understanding of learning from a passive view of learners who accumulate information through a series of reinforcement techniques to an active view of learners who utilize learning strategies to construct knowledge (American Psychological Association, 2005; Copple & Bredekamp, 2009; Daniels, Kalkman, & McCombs, 2001; Hyson, 2008; Stipek, 2002).

A **learner-centered** focus looks at how learners come to understand their world (McCombs & Whisler, 1997). This focus takes into account (a) the learning needs of diverse learners, (b) the impact of brain research on learning, (c) lifelong learning, (d) social and emotional learning as well as intellectual learning, and (e) child-guided learning. These five principles are described in the following paragraphs.

LEARNER-CENTERED EXPERIENCES MEET THE NEEDS OF DIVERSE LEARNERS

All early childhood classrooms have children who differ in how they learn. Yet, many teachers feel uncomfortable with learners from different cultural, language, and economic backgrounds. Regardless of background, all children bring talent with them that influences their learning. To meet children's diverse learning needs requires your insight about a child's individual abilities, knowledge of the child's cultural background, and skill in creating a responsive learning environment in the classroom (Banks, 2008; Espinosa, 2010). Knowledge and skill in using a variety of learning models, such as **learning styles** (i.e., how individuals process thoughts and feelings) and **multiple intelligences** (i.e., how individuals come to learn content), is essential for addressing children's diverse learning needs. Notice how Carol Brunson Day's Ask the Expert feature on page 137 answers teachers' concerns about the influence of culture on children's learning, the focus of multicultural education on children's learning, and anti-bias education.

LEARNER-CENTERED EXPERIENCES ARE BASED ON BRAIN RESEARCH

The explosion of research in the cognitive neurosciences on the brain's role in learning confirms what early childhood educators have always known—that the early years are critical for building a strong foundation for learning. Brain research also illustrates

Ask the EXPERT

Carol Brunson Day

Cultural Influences on Learning

Q: How does culture influence how children learn?

A: Culture operates as a set of rules for behavior, shaping values, beliefs, and ways of being in the world. Every child grows up in an environment governed by cultural rules and learns them in the socialization process. At birth, cultural rules start to shape such things as the ways children express themselves, determining what language they speak and understand; what they regard as important and how they prioritize what they pay attention to—the meanings that are in words or the context that surrounds them. When children enter school—even infant programs—they are already empowered to participate in their own development and learning, through the ways cultural rules have shaped their behavior and expectations. When there is continuity between home and school, their power to develop is enhanced and their development continues to build. But when what they have learned to do and say no longer works, their development is disrupted.

Q: In multicultural education, isn't it better to focus on sameness and not difference?

A: Developmental theory tells us that children are *simultaneously* human beings, individual personalities, and cultural beings. As human beings, children share some sameness with all other children, as individuals every child is unique, and as cultural beings children share characteristics with members of the group to which they belong—all at the same time. In early childhood education, it is easy for us to talk about meeting children's needs as individuals—in fact we are quite proud of that. Yet cultural differences make us uneasy, not because children are cultural beings, but because in this society racial and cultural bias attach negative value to certain groups. So it is the response to culture that is the problem and thus our multicultural education should have as its goals unlearning negative responses to the differences that culture creates. That won't happen if we only focus on sameness.

Q: If young children are not exposed to bias, doesn't anti-bias education unnecessarily raise negative issues?

A: It is a mistake to assume that young children either don't notice or aren't exposed to bias. Studies have shown that by age 3 children notice difference in skin color and are learning to attach value to those differences. In fact, children at this age can demonstrate a preference for White images and negative attitudes toward dark-skinned people and objects. Families cannot fully shield children from general societal attitudes. So teachers and parents together must work to introduce nonbiased messages to counteract these influences. Unless there is a deliberate plan to teach positive views about difference, children will absorb society's prevailing attitudes and beliefs.

Carol Brunson Day is President of the National Black Child Development Institute, Washington, DC.

the importance of the first 3 years of life for "wiring" pathways in the brain for a lifetime of learning. These pathways develop from children's positive stimulation with adults, events, and objects. They also affect how children learn, their interactions with others, and their beliefs about themselves, all of which they carry throughout life (Commission on Behavioral and Social Sciences and Education, 2001; Gallagher, 2005). Figure 6.1 lists four major principles of how the brain affects learning.

Figure 6.1 How the Brain Affects Learning

1. **Functioning.** The brain operates both consciously and subconsciously and in different ways simultaneously. These functions include physiology, thoughts, emotions, imagination, and predispositions.
2. **Feelings.** The brain is fundamentally social. Human relationships and emotions profoundly influence the ways in which the brain processes information.
3. **Patterning.** The brain searches for meaning through patterns. It identifies the familiar, responds to new stimuli, and perceives parts and wholes.
4. **Learning.** The brain's tendency to seek greater complexity is enhanced by encouragement and inhibited by threat.

Sources: Bransford et al., 2000; Halfon, Shulman, & Hochstein, 2001.

LEARNER-CENTERED EXPERIENCES FOCUS ON LIFELONG LEARNING

An essential outcome of school for all children is **lifelong learning**—the disposition to become knowledgeable, responsible, and contributing adults. Learner-centered experiences help children become *knowledgeable* because they naturally motivate children to learn and use new information in their lives. They help children become *responsible* by offering them opportunities to make decisions that affect others as well as themselves, and they encourage contributing behavior by experiencing concern about others as well as themselves.

Learning occurs from birth through old age. In conceptualizing how we learn new knowledge, skills, attitudes, or dispositions, Bredekamp and Rosegrant (1992) propose a cycle of learning. They describe a four-step recursive **learning cycle** that begins with awareness, moves to exploration, then to inquiry, and finally to utilization. Think about yourself now as you begin to learn to teach young children. You are at the beginning of a new learning cycle about learning to teach. Suppose, for example, that you have observed a smoothly operating early childhood classroom where children work at centers, and now you are trying to learn how to manage several small groups of children engaged in different learning tasks at the same time. Your *awareness* might consist of paying closer attention to how experienced teachers orchestrate several groups; your *exploration* might consist of trying it yourself and noticing what happens when you work with several small groups simultaneously; and your *inquiry* might involve further application of what you are learning as well as a comparison with what others are doing with the same skill. At this stage, you adapt your practice based upon what you know about the process and what you have experienced. Last, you

The brain is impacted by human relationships and emotions.

utilize this skill in a way that enhances children's learning and allows you to monitor their learning levels and tasks simultaneously. This cycle repeats itself many times over, because once you utilize your knowledge of managing small groups, you develop new awareness about the gaps in what you know or do not know about managing small groups. The more you revisit the learning cycle, the deeper your knowledge or skill becomes.

LEARNER-CENTERED EXPERIENCES ARE CHILD-GUIDED

As noted, experiences that help children to assume some responsibility for their own learning are referred to as *child-guided*, those experiences that capture children's interests, engage their minds and bodies, and also have teacher support (Copple & Bredekamp, 2009). Recall your positive memories about learning. You probably remember being able to pursue ideas that interested you, being given reasons for why you were being asked to learn something, or being trusted to make other good learning choices. These attributes help children learn because they foster intrinsic motivation by sparking children's curiosity and interests (American Psychological Association, 2005; Bodrova & Leong, 2005; Denton, 2005; McCombs & Miller, 2007). Early childhood teachers who use child-guided learning experiences are reflecting Dewey's (1916) theory of **Progressive Education,** in which the overarching purpose of schooling is to prepare students for the realities of today's and tomorrow's world. Educators assume that children can make good learning choices, that the process of learning is just as important as the products children make, and that learning to make decisions is an important skill and a fundamental right in a democratic society. Although child-guided learning is an important part of learner-centered experiences, children need to experience a balance between child-guided and adult-guided learning in order to succeed in this complex world. To be considered a learner-centered experience, children must be deeply engaged in the activity.

As teachers, these five principles remind us of our students' central role in learning both content and process. In the next section we focus on the role of play as one of the primary ways young children learn.

The Central Role of Play in Children's Learning

You might have overheard conversations with parents of young children who say, "But all my child does is play," or ask, "When is my child going to learn something?" How will you respond when you are the child's teacher? Knowing why and how play contributes to children's learning will help you answer these questions. It will also help you understand that the absence of play in young children often impedes their capacity for learning.

A DEFINITION OF PLAY

Think about the following scenario in a kindergarten classroom where three children are preparing a pretend birthday celebration for the child who plays the role of the aunt. When they realize they need a present, one of the children says, "We can make a birthday basket." This is a reference to the book, *A Birthday Basket for Tia,* by Pat Mora (1992), in which Little Cecelia and her cat Chica plan a surprise birthday party to celebrate her Tia's 90th birthday. While Mama is cooking, Cecelia and Chica put together a birthday basket containing a favorite book, a mixing bowl, a flowerpot, and other objects that represent activities that Cecelia and her Tia like to share. Cecelia then surprises Tia with a basket full of special objects. After the children locate the book in their library center, they take on the roles of Cecelia and her cat—as they search for a birthday present for their "Tia." When they finish the celebration for Cecelia's "Tia," they plan another celebration for their pretend Mama. The book has become the content for role playing, trying out different intonations that might sound like Cecelia, her Tia, and Mama, and deciding how to enact their pretend birthday celebration. This particular scenario illustrates the definition of **play** as any activity that is freely chosen, meaningful, active, enjoyable, and open-ended (Fromberg & Bergen, 2006; Frost, Wortham, & Reifel, 2008). Play benefits every child's learning and demonstrates the following characteristics.

- Play is symbolic and allows children to demonstrate what they know. Symbolic play enables children to represent reality as they mentally think through solutions to problems (a "what if" attitude) and deepen their thinking (an "as if" attitude). For the two kindergartners, the "what if" thinking occurred when they imagined the roles of Cecelia and the great aunt. The "as if" behavior occurred when the children actually created a pretend birthday basket filled with favorite items.

- Play is meaningful and helps children make sense out of their experiences. In the preceding scenario, the children were relating what they knew about birthdays to the content of the book they had heard, *A Birthday Basket for Tia.*

- Play is active and is a natural process of mentally and physically doing something. The children's reenactment of the familiar story demonstrates how they "learned by doing" by exploring the roles of Cecelia and her great aunt and inventing their own version of a birthday celebration.

- Play is pleasurable and supports children's different ways of learning even when the activity is serious. The idea that children's enjoyment can actually enhance their learning is often difficult to understand and accept, yet we know that the two children are enjoying their reenactment and at the same time seriously preparing a birthday celebration for the child who plays the role of the great aunt.

- Play is voluntary and intrinsically motivating, and capitalizes on children's curiosity. The children's initiative in locating the book and establishing the scenario to enact is a good illustration of this characteristic.

- Play is rule-governed, whether the rules are implied or expressed, and allows children to apply rules to different settings. In play, children establish and sometimes change the rules; nevertheless, there are rules for appropriate role behavior and the responsibilities of the players. These rules organize children's play, as is evident in the roles taken on in the preceding scenario.

- Play is episodic, as there are emerging and shifting goals throughout the experience. In the *A Birthday Basket for Tia* play scenario described earlier, the children completed their enactment of the birthday party for the child playing the role of the great aunt and then immediately began to plan another birthday party for their Mama, shifting the focus of the play.

In play, children make sense of their world, become empowered to do things for themselves, and experience social competence. In addition, the play context contributes to children's learning across all of the learning domains.

THE IMPORTANCE OF PLAY

Most educators do not understand how play or playful ways of knowing benefit learning for children through the primary grades. If you ask teachers what play is, they might say, "It is when children are dressing up and pretending, or using games, or going outside during recess." These views of play are limited mostly to physical activity and do not represent how play contributes to all aspects of children's development and learning.

Early childhood educators have long respected play as the primary way children learn. Indeed, in NAEYC's 2009 position statement on developmentally appropriate practice (Copple & Bredekamp, 2009), one of the 12 principles states that "play is an important vehicle for developing self-regulation as well as for promoting language, cognition, and social competence" (p. 14) across ages. The work of Vygotsky (1978) and Piaget also illustrates the important role of play. For Vygotsky, play leads development; for Piaget (1980), play "fosters the social life and constructive activity of the child" (p. viii). Through play, children discover what they can do, test their physical and mental abilities, and compare these with those of their peers.

For primary children, play is equally important. First, engaging in playful language activities enables children to experiment and practice the new vocabulary and language skills they need to become proficient readers and writers. Second, playful learning activities help children better understand abstract mathematical and scientific concepts so necessary to success in school and in life (Elkind, 2007). And third, through play, primary-grade children acquire stronger social-emotional skills by interacting in a variety of social situations and adopting appropriate social behaviors (Riley & Jones, 2010). Doris Pronin Fromberg, noted expert on play, answers some commonly asked questions about play in the Ask the Expert feature on page 142.

PLAY AND CHILDREN WITH EXCEPTIONALITIES

All children, regardless of their exceptional needs, play. Yet, depending on their **exceptionality** (e.g., delays in motor skills, speech and language, or social development), some children may play differently and less effectively than their peers without exceptionalities because they may have less opportunity for social play, or are unable to think symbolically or use language like their peers without exceptionalities (Allen & Cowdery, 2009; Frost et al., 2008). Your role in helping children with exceptional needs learn through play is to intervene and support their development of play skills. You can support children's learning by providing opportunities for them to practice specific skills, adapting the play setting to accommodate their needs, and helping them enter a play situation once they have mastered specific skills. The more opportunity for social interaction, the more likely children with exceptionalities will increase the complexity of their play.

PLAY AND CHILDREN FROM DIVERSE BACKGROUNDS

The increasingly diverse population of children mandates that early childhood teachers provide opportunities that encourage understanding of others. Young children's play provides adults with important information about children's cultural experiences. You can learn about special traditions, celebrations, and family values by watching and listening to children at play. One appropriate way to do this is to provide culturally relevant toys

Ask the EXPERT

Doris Pronin Fromberg

The Value of Play

Q: What are the differences among work, exploration, and play?

A: Children usually define a particular activity as *play* if they choose to do it; they might define the same activity as *work* if the teacher asks them to do it. Philosopher John Dewey suggested a continuum of drudgery—work, play, fooling—and proposed that a balance between work and play is appropriate for schools. *Exploration* is when we find out what something or someone can do, and *play* is when we see what we can do with it or another. Work, exploration, and play can be satisfying or challenging, but exploration and play are typically self-motivated and pleasurable, even when serious.

Q: If children play, how will teachers have time to cover the curriculum?

A: When children play, they are engaged in what they are doing. At the same time they are learning concepts, skills, and attitudes through the tasks and experiences in which they engage and organize if you provide the settings, props, and opportunities. Children's thinking develops in many ways, but their awareness of their own ideas as compared with those of others takes place particularly during sociodramatic play. For example, they learn an enormous amount about how to create collaborative oral playwriting as they negotiate sociodramatic play episodes with other children. The feedback that they receive from playing with one another helps them to understand how effectively they communicate their child-to-world thoughts, a precursor to writing and comprehending stories.

Q: If children play, will the families complain that they are not learning in school?

A: We need to help families see that extensive research indicates that children who engage in pretend and sociodramatic play increase their literacy skills; cognitive development, particularly problem solving; social competence; and capacity to generate new connections in a creative way. Some ways to let parents know what children are learning in a class are the following: (a) save children's drawing and writing samples to show progress over time; (b) with digital photographs and video, document learning experiences that are active and show the uses of different materials and thematic props for use at parent meetings; (c) save shared writing charts for display; (d) four-for-the-day: send four one- or two-line notes each day to four different parents informing them of something that their children learned that day and how their children participated; and (e) consider creating a collaborative newsletter with other teachers that records children's comments about their school activities.

Doris Pronin Fromberg is a Professor of Education and Past Chairperson, Department of Curriculum and Teaching, Hofstra University, New York.

and materials for children's play (Frost et al., 2008). Toys such as dolls, games, puppets, puzzles, and motor toys are common to children worldwide and are differentiated only by their decoration or presentation. Through the use of culturally appropriate materials and toys, children have the opportunity to learn about others, practice newly acquired skills, take on new social roles, and "play out" what is already familiar to them.

Recall that earlier in this section we defined play as a condition for learning that has unique characteristics. Children learn best when play is linked with other conditions, such as social interaction, concrete experiences, and a sense of competence. The characteristics of play (e.g., that it is active, voluntary, and symbolic) support children's learning of specific content knowledge and skills and growth in each developmental domain. Table 6.1 illustrates the connections between play and learning.

Table 6.1 Play and Learning

LEARNING DOMAIN	PLAY EXPERIENCES	SKILLS AND CONCEPTS LEARNED
Cognitive	• sorting objects • playing school	• solving problems, testing hypotheses • planning ahead, evaluating oneself
Language	• repeating rhymes, using nonsense words, telling jokes and riddles, and chanting jump-rope songs • role playing a trip to the hospital and maintaining a complex play theme	• using language to organize and maintain their play; understanding multiple meanings; understanding words, sounds, and grammatical structure; exploring the phonological, syntactic, and semantic rules of language • using purposeful language with explanations, discussions, negotiations, and commands; exploring the forms and functions of language
Literacy	• pretending to read a book, write a shopping list, read environmental print, and reenact stories	• developing interest in stories and books, comprehending stories and story structure; understanding fantasy in books; and symbolically representing the world
Social/ emotional development	• engaging in dramatic and sociodramatic play, reenacting stories, working through conflicts, learning how to enter an ongoing play event, and creating a puppet show	• seeing other perspectives; taking turns; sharing roles, materials, and responsibilities; communicating both verbally and nonverbally for needs and wants; waiting for a turn • developing empathy for others' feelings; expressing one's own feelings and coping with them
Physical	• writing and drawing with different tools (e.g., markers, paintbrushes, pencils) • running and climbing activities and games	• developing and refining fine motor skills, gross motor skills, and body awareness and fitness
Creative	• pretending to go on vacation; using scraps of material and paper for creating art products; and interpreting familiar roles in new ways	• solving problems, using imagery, flexible thinking, and alternative responses to situations

Source: Information from Isenberg & Jalongo, 2010.

Play is an important vehicle for helping all children develop self-regulation, language, cognition, and social competence.

TYPES OF PLAY

Children's play develops in a sequence that parallels their cognitive and social development. **Cognitive play** reflects children's ages, understandings, and experiences. It includes sensorimotor play, symbolic play, constructive play, and games with rules (Piaget, 1970; Smilansky & Shefatya, 1990). **Social play** describes children's interactions with their peers. It includes onlooker, solitary, parallel, associative, and cooperative play (Parten, 1932). While both cognitive and social play develop sequentially over time, some types of play are more typical of particular periods of children's development. Nonetheless, all types of play occur in different forms throughout one's life. Table 6.2 lists the types of cognitive and social play, provides a definition of each, and supplies age-appropriate examples.

Fostering Learning Through Technology

Today's children live in a rapidly growing technological world. Infants use books and other toys that are computer based and contain synthetic voice output, toddlers manipulate computer software programs using touchscreens and large trackballs, preschoolers and kindergartners use computer art programs, and school-age children learn through the Internet. Technology has a more central role than in the past in the early childhood classroom, requiring the need to teach such technological skills as **digital literacy,** effective communication, and **higher-order thinking skills** (Swaminathan & Wright, 2003). The technology revolution also challenges teachers to find technologically appropriate ways to foster children's thinking and problem solving (Clements & Sarama, 2003; Copple & Bredekamp, 2009). NAEYC's "Position Statement: Technology and Young Children—Ages Three Through Eight" (NAEYC, 1996) and the 2007 standards established by the International Society for Technology in Education (ISTE; www.iste.org) encourage teachers to promote learning by using classroom technology effectively, selecting appropriate software and websites, and using assistive technology for children with disabilities.

USING CLASSROOM TECHNOLOGIES EFFECTIVELY

Consider the following scenario in a second-grade classroom. Pairs of children are using the software program Kidspiration (2000) as part of their study of the cycle of plant life. The children chose pictures from a "library" of pictures created by scanning in photos they selected of the different stages of a plant's life cycle, placed them in correct order in the cycle, and then wrote about what each stage represented. During this process, the children shared using the mouse and doing the typing, but consulted one another about which picture came

Pause and Reflect

About Play

Think back to some of your most pleasant moments when you were invited to "come and play." How do you think these experiences helped you learn? Relate your experiences to what Doris Pronin Fromberg says about how play fosters learning in the Ask the Expert feature on page 142.

Table 6.2 Types of Children's Play

TYPE OF PLAY	DEFINITION	AGE-APPROPRIATE EXAMPLE
Cognitive Play Sensorimotor	Repeated movements with or without materials—sensorimotor play is the primary type of play for infants and toddlers.	Infants and toddlers: stacking and unstacking rings on a pole Preschool and kindergartners: repeating a pattern while stringing beads School-age children: practicing jump-rope skills and rhymes
Symbolic	Transforming one object into another and later transforming self and object to satisfy needs in dramatic play. Symbolic play emerges around age 2 and dominates in the years between ages 2 and 7.	Infants and toddlers: pretending to drink from a toy cup Preschoolers and kindergartners: pretending to rescue people from a burning building School-age children: using secret codes or made-up languages to communicate
Constructive	Making things from a preconceived plan—constructive play combines sensorimotor and symbolic play.	Preschoolers and kindergartners: constructing a plane from a building set School-age children: creating sets for a story reenactment
Games with rules	Using predetermined rules to guide acceptable behavior—games with rules emerge in simple form in infancy but predominate in the school-age years and beyond.	Infants and toddlers: playing peek-a-boo Preschoolers and kindergartners: playing simple singing and circle games School-age children: playing card games, board games, group games
Social Play Onlooker	Observing what others are doing, not joining in the play but involved as a spectator. Toddlers engage in a great deal of onlooker play.	Infants and toddlers: watching another child paint at an easel Preschoolers and kindergartners: watching an ongoing play group before deciding to enter School-age children: watching a group game before participating
Solitary	Playing alone, child concentrates on the activity rather than on other children. Solitary play is typical of infants and toddlers and young preschool children, but may be seen in older children as well.	Infants and toddlers: playing alone and showing no interest in others Preschoolers and kindergartners: playing with own toys School-age children: choosing to play alone for privacy or to think about how to elaborate a play theme

continued

Table 6.2 continued

TYPE OF PLAY	DEFINITION	AGE-APPROPRIATE EXAMPLE
Parallel	Playing side by side but not with others, using toys similar to others, and may imitate the behavior of other playing children. Parallel play is typical of toddlers and young preschool children.	Infants and toddlers: playing nearby others with little or no interaction Preschoolers and kindergartners: using shared toys but not sharing toys School-age children: using own materials but aware of others using the same materials
Associative	Playing with others with an interest in being with each other rather than the play itself. Associative play first appears in young preschool children and is often the first attempt at group play.	Preschoolers, kindergartners, and school-age children: playing in the same area with the same materials but for different purposes and different ends
Cooperative	Play with shared goals and social interaction. Uses negotiation, differentiated roles, and division of labor to create, coordinate, and enact a play theme. Cooperative play is most typical of older preschoolers and school-age children.	Older preschoolers and school-age children: building an airport and deciding how to get there, what to see, and how to build a lounge, air-traffic control tower, hangar, and parking lot

next. In one conversation, one child said to the teacher: "I'm doing the odd-number stages, and she's doing the even-number stages."

In this scenario, the teacher demonstrates the following effective uses of technology:

1. Use technology as a tool that gives children the opportunity to "seek information, solve problems, understand concepts, and move at their own pace" (Copple & Bredekamp, 2009, p. 315).

2. Apply a range of skills and encourage social interaction. Computers encourage social interaction among children, who willingly seek other children's involvement if the software is engaging and interactive (National Research Council, 2009).

3. Provide both children and teachers access to limitless knowledge and information that invite many ways of expressing ideas, of communicating, creating, and controlling their own worlds, and that enable them to be active, engaged participants in their own learning.

4. Integrate the computer into learning that connects to children's units of study, makes learning meaningful, and builds concepts and big ideas.

5. Provide equal access for boys and girls.

SELECTING APPROPRIATE SOFTWARE

Teachers can facilitate children's learning by selecting appropriate **software,** the instructions that make the computer do something specific, and integrating it appropriately in the curriculum. Appropriate software should be *interactive, appeal to a wide range of children's interests, abilities, and learning styles, and support the ongoing learning in the classroom.* It should also include a *simple design* that has many possibilities; provide *clear instructions* so that children can use the program with little adult involvement; have *high-quality technical features*, such as color and clarity; and have *easy access to* and *exit from* the program (NAEYC, 1996; ISTE, 2007).

Computer drawing programs, such as Delta Draw, Color Me, and Thinkin' Things Collection 3, encourage discovery and the invention of stories. **Open-ended software,** such as Millie's Math House, Bailey's Book House, Kidspiration, Pixie, and KidPix, encourages children to work together to create a quality product. **Problem-solving and inquiry-oriented software,** such as Destination: Neighborhood, Destination: Time Trip USA, Create Your Own Adventure with Zeke, and Oregon Trail, provides children with possibilities to gather information, make decisions, and test their solutions. Computer materials such as Ani's Rocket Ride and Ani's Playground reflect the Reggio Emilia approach to learning and encourage children's intellect, curiosity, social interaction, and interests. Before using any software, review it for quality and for an appropriate match to the outcomes for children in your classroom. (See the websites www.netc.org and http://childrenandcomputers.com for more resources and information on selecting appropriate software.)

Appropriate software should be interactive; capture children's interests, abilities, and learning styles; and support classroom instruction.

THE INTERNET

Selecting appropriate websites is a second consideration. **E-learning,** acquiring knowledge and skills using electronic technologies such as the Internet, is common in today's classrooms. The following three types of websites are available for children:

1. An *information site* that is used to help children gain new knowledge and answer questions, such as that of the National Zoo (www.si.edu/national zoo).

2. A *communication site,* which puts children in touch with one another in the classroom, center, school, community, nation, or world, such as **WebQuests,** an inquiry-oriented activity in which some or all of the information comes from resources on the Internet. For extensive examples, go to http://webquest.sdsu.edu/materials .htm and click on "Find WebQuests."

3. A *publication site* that provides a place to post children's products, such as Kid Pub (www.kidpub.org/kidpub).

While there are many Internet sites, they are far less researched than software, and will need to be evaluated before use. You will want to ensure that the websites are developmentally appropriate and that children "can find information, think about it critically, and develop self-protection skills and a sense of efficacy"(NAEYC Technology and Young Children Interest Forum, 2008, p. 50).

ASSISTIVE TECHNOLOGY FOR CHILDREN WITH DISABILITIES

Assistive technology refers to any item or device that improves the mobility and communication of those with disabilities. It includes a wide range of applications that can be used with children of all ages and enables them to have access to people and information that might not otherwise be accessible to them. Some examples of assistive technology devices include touchscreens, voice-activated software, communication boards, talking word processors, specialized keyboards, communication devices, arm and wrist supports, amplified telephone handsets, screen magnifiers, and environmental controls (Alliance for Technology Access, 2004).

In the next section, we conclude this chapter with five theories that underlie learning.

Major Learning Theories

How you think children learn strongly influences what and how you teach them. Many scientifically tested theories of learning have endured and are used widely. But because learning is so complex, early childhood educators use multiple theories to understand how children learn. In the paragraphs that follow, we explore the maturation, behavioral, social learning, constructivist, and multiple intelligences theories of learning. For each theory, we describe learning from that theoretical perspective, identify its theorists who have most influenced the field of early childhood, and apply the theory to best practices in the classroom.

MATURATION THEORY OF LEARNING

Maturation theory regards development as a genetically determined process that naturally unfolds through a predetermined sequence under the proper conditions. It focuses on predictable patterns that are the result of a biological, genetic plan and assumes that efforts to teach behaviors before they naturally occur are unnecessary and may indeed be harmful to children's learning (Gesell, 1933). To illustrate, most children begin to sit, walk, talk, play, and read at about the same ages. These early developmental milestones set the stage for learning more complex skills throughout one's life. Even though all children progress through typical sequences of development, they do so at different rates. Consequently, maturation theorists assume that children who are not ready to learn a skill do not benefit from intervention.

   Maturation theorists who have influenced our view of early learning are Arnold Gesell, Jean-Jacques Rousseau, and Noam Chomsky.

ARNOLD GESELL (1890–1961). Arnold Gesell was a physician at the Yale University Clinic for Child Development who studied the process of maturation. Gesell was the first theorist to provide systematic, **normative descriptions** of children's development in all domains—physical, language, intellectual, and social—through detailed descriptions of children from birth through age 10. His research, commonly referred to as "ages and stages," provides typical characteristics of children by ages that represent a predictable sequence of development for all children, regardless of race, culture, or economic status.

   Other maturation theorists who have influenced our thinking about learning include Jean-Jacques Rousseau and Noam Chomsky. Rousseau (1712–1778), a French philosopher and author of Émile, believed that children are inherently good and should be left to develop naturally so their inherent goodness can develop. Rousseau was the first to identify "childhood" as a stage of life. Chomsky (1928–), a noted linguist, emphasizes the important role of maturation in learning language. He suggests that children are "prewired," or biologically endowed, to learn language at a particular time and in a particular way, thus explaining the differences in the capacity for children's language to develop (Woolfolk, 2010).

APPLYING MATURATION THEORY IN THE CLASSROOM

Maturation theory has helped parents, pediatricians, and teachers clarify expected behaviors for children at particular ages and provide age-appropriate learning experiences. The following best practices have their roots in maturation theory.

1. **Use developmental milestones as the basis for your teaching.** Assess children's progress and plan experiences based on what they can do today and what is anticipated

that children will next be able to accomplish. However, be careful not to label children as delayed rather than identifying their strengths as individual learners as the starting point for learning.

2. **Rely on your own ability to monitor each child's acquisition of knowledge and skills.** Children develop at different rates in one or more areas. Because there are no fixed criteria for what constitutes delayed development, early childhood teachers must have a clear understanding of how children learn.

3. **Provide learning experiences at each child's present level of ability.** The notion of readiness has its roots in maturation theory. This concept can sometimes be counterproductive by maintaining children's current level of learning rather than providing them with appropriate levels of challenging learning opportunities. Decisions about the appropriate time to enter kindergarten based solely on age is still evident today.

BEHAVIORAL THEORY OF LEARNING

Behavioral theory identifies all learning in terms of behavior that can be observed, measured, and recorded. Although behaviorists acknowledge that heredity somewhat limits what people can learn, they view the environment as the most influential element on learning. For behaviorists, learning is the accumulation of knowledge and responses through selective reinforcement; it occurs when one reacts to aspects of the environment that are pleasurable or painful. From the behaviorist perspective, learning occurs in three different ways: *through association* (**classical conditioning**), *through reinforcement* (**operant conditioning**), and *through observation and imitation* (**observational learning**). Learning through **association** occurs when a person generalizes between events. When a young child says "bird" for all things that fly, adults provide reinforcing responses, such as, "We call that an airplane." Eventually, the child distinguishes birds from other flying things. Learning through **reinforcement** happens when adults try to stop an inappropriate behavior by ignoring it or praise a behavior to keep it. Learning through **observation** occurs when children watch the behaviors of peers and adults, form mental pictures of them, and later try to imitate those behaviors. Because behaviorists consider learners to be passive recipients of stimuli from the environment, they believe that learning results from the adults' shaping and changing of children's behavior through the use of cues and reinforcement techniques in a carefully designed external environment.

Behavioral theorists who have impacted our view of learning include B. F. Skinner, John Locke, Edward Thorndike, and John Watson.

B. F. SKINNER (1904–1990). B. F. Skinner theorized that all behavior can be modified and that the basic principles of learning apply to all learners, regardless of age. He assumed that specific behaviors can be increased through a range of **reinforcers** such as smiles and praise, and decreased through **punishment,** such as withdrawal of special privileges.

John Locke (1632–1704), a prominent English philosopher, theorized that environment and experience determine learning. He proposed that environment is the primary factor in shaping individual development and learning. Locke's ideas paved the way for future behaviorists.

Edward Thorndike (1874–1949) studied learning through association and suggested the stimulus-response method. From his research on animals, Thorndike concluded that learning depends on associations, which in turn form learned habits. Complex learning is the result of combined associations.

John Watson (1878–1958), an American psychologist influenced by Russian psychologist Ivan Pavlov, is known for his ideas about classical conditioning. In his view, learning depends only on observable behaviors. Watson claimed he could shape the entirety of a person's learning by taking full control of all events of a child's first year of life and by discouraging emotional and social connections between parents and their children.

APPLYING BEHAVIORAL THEORY IN THE CLASSROOM

Behavioral learning theory is among the most influential views of learning today. It has given rise to practices that are orderly, carefully sequenced, and demonstrate change in observable behavior. Behavioral learning principles employ the following best practices.

1. Associate positive, pleasant events with learning, such as cooperative learning and group activities versus individual competition.

2. Use praise appropriately, such as making sure the child understands the specific action or accomplishment being praised, acknowledging a child's progress in relation to that child's past efforts, or appreciating the attainment of a specific goal.

3. Encourage positive behaviors by having positive consequences for following class rules, noting something right for every student, and supporting children who encourage one another.

SOCIAL LEARNING THEORY

Social learning theory suggests that children learn social behaviors by observing and imitating models, especially those of their parents. It accepts the key behavioral learning principles of conditioning and reinforcement but has expanded them to include how children learn social skills. Social learning theorists view learners as being active in shaping their own learning and believe that observational learning, a cognitive influence on learning, is central to how children learn. They also acknowledge the central role of children's identification with key family members in influencing their learning of language, dealing with aggression, developing a moral sense, and learning socially acceptable behaviors (Bandura, 1997, 2001). Today, social learning theory is more influential than behavioral learning theory in considering how children learn.

ALBERT BANDURA (1925–). The leading social learning theorist is Albert Bandura, a contemporary behaviorist, who expanded the principles of behaviorism and conceived the theory of social learning. He recognized that children learn much of their social behavior from imitating or watching others. As a result, modeling became a major principle of learning that has prompted parents and teachers to explicitly demonstrate expected forms of behavior. Bandura's work adds cognitive aspects of thinking—that what children think and believe about themselves, and how they judge their own expectations about learning strongly influences their behavior and their beliefs about their own abilities to learn.

APPLYING SOCIAL LEARNING THEORY IN THE CLASSROOM

Social learning practices are widely used to help children develop appropriate behaviors, skills, and approaches to learning. They bridge behavioral theories with cognitive theories by acknowledging the active role children play in their own learning and the cognitive influences on learning (Bandura, 1997, 2001). Among the applications of social learning theory that will influence learning in your classrooms are the following best practices.

1. **Model appropriate skills and behavior.** When young children have difficulty in getting along with other children, for example, you can model appropriate ways of

getting along in the following three ways. *First*, if a preschooler wants a toy from another child and grabs rather than asks for it, you can model appropriate behavior by encouraging the child to use words to ask for what he or she needs. *Second*, use peers in group work so others can see different behaviors and attitudes, or as "teachers" or "leaders" in welcoming a new child or a child who has returned from an extended illness. *Third*, model the skills you teach through "think-alouds," such as helping children see how you read to the end of a sentence to get the meaning of a sentence even if you cannot read all of the words.

2. **Promote self-efficacy.** Hearing adults' comments about children's efforts (e.g., "I'm pleased that you didn't give up on that task even though it was hard and frustrating" or "I know you can figure that problem out") helps children view themselves as can-do rather than can't-do learners. Such comments also promote interest in learning through self-efficacy and the development of personal standards and expectations.

3. **View children as active learners.** Children play an active role in their own learning, particularly in choosing whose behavior to imitate. These models may be significant adults such as parents or teachers, or they may be television heroes. When children spend many hours watching cartoons or adult television programs, for example, they often adopt the behaviors of those characters as their own.

4. **Promote opportunities for self-regulation.** Children can participate in appropriately setting their own learning goals, monitoring their progress, and assessing the effectiveness of their efforts with the help of supportive adults. Checklists, choice charts, and conferences can be used to help children develop self-regulation.

CONSTRUCTIVIST THEORY OF LEARNING

Constructivist theory focuses on how people make meaning both on their own and in interaction with others. Influenced by research in the cognitive, computer, and social sciences, constructivism emphasizes the active roles of the learner, prior knowledge, social interactions, and authentic tasks in constructing understanding rather than imposing knowledge (Woolfolk, 2010). Constructivism is rooted in the works of Jean Piaget, Jerome Bruner, and Lev Vygotsky and can be viewed from the perspectives of both *cognitive developmental* and *sociocultural theory*.

Two leading **cognitive developmental theorists** who have given us new ways of thinking about learning are Jean Piaget and Jerome Bruner.

JEAN PIAGET (1896–1980), a Swiss biologist and theorist, studied how children acquire knowledge and how thinking and learning develop in children. Piaget assisted in standardizing the first intelligence test at the Binet Laboratory in Paris. While assessing the intelligence of French schoolchildren with this test, he became intrigued with children's incorrect answers to questions. Simultaneously, he noted that children's responses appeared to be age related.

Central to Piaget's cognitive theory is the concept of adaptation. **Adaptation,** which begins in infancy and continues over a lifetime, is how the mind develops cognitive structures to make sense of the outside world. According to Piaget, learning is the active **construction of knowledge** through interactions with people and their environment that takes place in stages. It results from the interactions among the reciprocal processes of *assimilation, accommodation,* and *equilibration.* From children's interactions with their environment, they organize mental structures that become the foundation for more complex thinking and learning. They do this by taking in new information into existing structures **(assimilation)** or by changing existing structures to accommodate the new information **(accommodation),** therefore creating a balance between the new and the old information that makes sense to them (**equilibration**). Imagine yourself arriving for your first class at your current college or university. You first had to figure out certain features of the building, such as where your room was, how you got from the classroom to the restroom, and perhaps how you could get a snack during a break (*assimilation*). Familiarizing yourself with the building enabled you to routinely enter the building and find essential places in the future so that you would not have to think each time about how to find your classroom. You changed your mental structures and used *accommodation* to learn your way around the building. Learning your way around the building illustrates *equilibration*, the mental need to find ways to maneuver in a new environment. For Piaget, the changes in behavior reflect changes in thinking occurring in distinct stages with unique features that correlate with specific ages of development.

In Piaget's theory, children's minds develop in a series of four stages, each of which is characterized by distinct ways of thinking. Each stage builds upon the preceding one, which becomes the foundation for new ways of thinking about and responding to the world. From birth through age 2, children are in the **sensorimotor stage.** Infants learn about their world by using their senses to solve sensorimotor problems, such as shaking a rattle to hear noise or finding hidden objects. This sensorimotor thinking evolves into the **preoperational stage,** which lasts from ages 2 to 7. During this stage, children use symbolic thinking to show what they know, especially through pretend play and language. Preoperational thinking lacks the logical qualities that are characteristic of the thinking of older children and adults. In the next stage, the **concrete operational stage,** children ages 7 to 11 build upon preoperational thinking and think in more logical ways, but their thinking and learning are tied to concrete objects. Though children organize objects into various categories and hierarchies at this stage, they are not yet ready to think abstractly. From about age 11 on, children in the **formal operational stage** are able to think and reason abstractly in ways that are similar to those of mature adolescents and adults (Piaget, 1970).

JEROME BRUNER (1915–), influenced by the work of Piaget, promoted the idea of **discovery learning** and individual concept learning through the study of the thought processes of perception, memory, strategic thinking, and classification. He described a **spiral curriculum,** one that introduces children to "big ideas" or concepts in all subjects in the early childhood years and continues to revisit them more deeply in subsequent years (Bruner, 1966). Unlike Piaget, Bruner does not propose stages of these thinking capacities; rather, he theorizes that they are simply less well developed in children. Bruner likens learning to a computer, because learning occurs as much from the outside in as from the inside out. Thus, the mind actively codes, transforms, and organizes information as it takes it in. Bruner views children as active learners who organize information into higher and more complex categories and modify their own thinking as it makes sense to them in their environments.

APPLYING COGNITIVE DEVELOPMENTAL THEORY IN THE CLASSROOM

Cognitive developmental theory has fundamentally changed the way we view teaching and learning. It has been applied using the following best practices.

1. **Stimulate children's curiosity** through the use of concrete inquiries, experiments, and discovery learning that involve hands-on and minds-on use of open-ended materials. In a science study of shadows, for example, younger children might investigate how to make long and short shadows using flashlights and paper; older children might use shadows to determine the size of objects. Both of these experiences enable children to construct knowledge about sources of light at different levels of complexity.

2. **Facilitate, rather than direct, learning.** Provide meaningful activities and ask questions that promote children's thinking, decision making, and the exchange of viewpoints. Encouraging children to explain their answers and reasons stimulates their thinking.

3. **Foster exploration, discovery, big ideas, and investigation.** Early childhood classrooms must include a variety of equipment and materials for children to use each day. Having time to explore and think about materials helps children to build conceptual understanding. To understand the concept that mixing different proportions of colors produces new colors, for example, children need time to experiment with mixing colors, observe the changes that occur, and infer how to match someone else's color mixture rather than having an adult tell them what will happen during this process.

4. **Connect content to the real world.** Children construct more meaningful understanding when they make connections to their own world and their own experience. Always ask children what they already know about a topic so that you can provide appropriate learning activities that build upon their current understandings. For example, when *preschool and kindergarten children* study living things, provide a variety of experiences and activities for them to make connections to what is familiar. In the dramatic play center, add farmer and chef clothes and props and related books so that children can create their own market and act out stories. Or in the construction area, have them use pots, pans, empty seed packs, and rulers to design their own gardens. *Primary children* may germinate seeds to gain firsthand knowledge of the life cycle of plants or care for animals at home and in the classroom to develop foundational concepts of the basic needs of all living things.

Children need time to think and experiment.

SOCIOCULTURAL THEORY

LEV SEMENOVICH VYGOTSKY (1896–1934), a Russian psychologist, asserted that culture and social interactions shape what children learn about their world. Sociocultural theory is an outgrowth of Vygotsky's studies of educational practices with Russian children with disabilities. Many of these disabilities were caused by years of war, famine, and poverty that beset the Soviet Union early in the 20th century, suggesting that cultural influences strongly impact children's learning.

According to Vygotsky (1978), children learn primarily through their relationships with other people, particularly in dialogue between each child and a more knowledgeable person. These social relationships form the basis for later communication and thinking. Vygotsky emphasizes the importance of family, social interaction, adults and more capable peers, and play as primary influences on learning, and believed that, as a result, learning occurs first on the social level and then on an individual level.

Three major concepts about learning permeate Vygotsky's sociocultural theory: the zone of proximal development, scaffolding, and the role of the adult. First, Vygotsky theorized that a child has an actual and a potential level of learning. The distance between what a child can do independently (*actual level*) and what that child can do with assistance (*potential level*) is called the **zone of proximal development** (ZPD) and substantially influences children's learning when they encounter a problem to solve (Vygotsky, 1978). When children work at their *potential* level, they experience what is possible to do independently before they can actually do it.

Vygotsky's second major concept is **scaffolding,** a support system that enables children to move along the learning continuum by building new competencies. For scaffolding to take place between an adult and a child, the child must be engaged in meaningful, problem-solving situations with mutual give-and-take between the learner and the adult.

Last, Vygotsky ascribed major importance to the *role of the adult* in children's learning. Through the use of the zone of proximal development, supportive adults can guide children's learning in many areas. Vygotsky viewed learning as a socially mediated process—as dependent upon the support that adults and more mature peers provide as children try new tasks. If you return to the chapter-opening quote by Vygotsky, you can better reflect on what Vygotsky means by *organized learning*.

APPLYING SOCIOCULTURAL CONSTRUCTIVIST THEORY IN THE CLASSROOM

Vygotsky's emphasis on the relationship between culture and learning has given rise to the following best early childhood practices.

1. **Teach to a child's zone of proximal development.** Adults must provide learning experiences that are slightly above the children's level of functioning and assist children's inquiry and investigations in reaching toward the child's upper limit of understanding with assistance. You can support children's self-initiated learning by asking if there is anything you can do to help or by encouraging a child to keep practicing a skill.

2. **Use more capable peers, where appropriate, to guide learning.** Strategies such as **cooperative learning** activities (e.g., think, pair, share; cooperative learning groups) with a mix of ability levels provide important opportunities for children to learn. Classroom practices, such as multi-student projects and center-based learning, offer children opportunities to solve problems together through verbal exchanges and negotiation. Imaginative play, small-group activities, and mixed-age grouping offer additional valuable learning experiences that capitalize on the social aspects of learning.

3. **Scaffold children's learning.** When children are learning a new skill or concept, provide models, prompts, sentence starters, coaching, and feedback. As the children become more capable, they can have more opportunities for independent practice. Allow children choice in choosing projects and encourage them to seek help when and if they really need it.

MULTIPLE INTELLIGENCES THEORY OF LEARNING

HOWARD GARDNER (1943–), a psychologist at Harvard University, is best known for identifying eight different frames of mind, or intelligences: linguistic, logical/mathematical, musical, visual/spatial, bodily/kinesthetic, interpersonal, intrapersonal, and naturalist. Gardner (1993) views intelligence as more than a single ability that can be enhanced, taught, and changed. For Gardner, each form of intelligence involves unique cognitive skills that can be demonstrated through solving problems and creating products that are culturally valued. Problem solving enables learners to figure out how to reach a stated goal; creating products allows learners to display their knowledge, feelings, and understandings of their world. Gardner suggests that while each of us has certain intelligences that dominate, all of the intelligences work together to help individuals solve problems and accomplish a task, an idea grounded in brain research (see Figure 6.1). This inclusive view of intelligence differs from the narrower, traditional view that intelligence can be measured as a single entity that is demonstrated outside of one's natural learning environment through standardized testing. Table 6.3 describes each of Gardner's intelligences, and suggests possible applications for best practice.

APPLYING MULTIPLE INTELLIGENCES THEORY IN THE CLASSROOM

If you consider for a moment the strengths in learning that your friends or family members have, you might notice that some are especially good at getting along with others. According to Gardner's theory, these individuals would have high interpersonal intelligence. Others you know may be especially capable of using language to express their knowledge and understand their world. In this case, they would be high in verbal/linguistic intelligence. Knowing these different capacities helps you to reach all types of learners when teaching skills and concepts so that children have an opportunity to show what they know and understand. Although Gardner's research is still new, it provides insights into the many ways children learn. Multiple intelligences (MI) theory asks the question, "In which ways is this child smart?" The following best practices represent this theory.

Table 6.3 Applying Gardner's Eight Intelligences

INTELLIGENCE	DESCRIPTION	APPLICATIONS
Verbal/ linguistic	using language to express ideas and to understand others	writing in a journal, reading a book, listening to a story, telling about an experience
Logical/ mathematical	using reasoning to discern numbers, quantities, and abstract patterns (sometimes called scientific thinking)	making projects following a plan, comparing and contrasting objects, graphic organizers, performing calculations
Visual/spatial	forming images in the mind	expressing ideas and feelings with no words (e.g., drawing, making posters, inventing an imaginary character), engaging in pretend play
Bodily/ kinesthetic	using all or part of your body to make something or solve a problem	dancing, using movement, enacting a play, dramatic play, pantomime, noncompetitive games
Musical	thinking in music by hearing, recognizing, and remembering tonal patterns; sensitivity to rhythm and beat; humming	creating raps and songs, playing musical instruments, appreciating different kinds of music (e.g., folk and classical)
Interpersonal	understanding, getting along, and working well with others; relies on all other intelligences	teams, projects, cooperative group learning, verbal and nonverbal communication
Intrapersonal	having insight into personal assets, challenges, and conditions necessary for growth	reflecting on own actions, metacognitive activities (e.g., thinking strategies used in reading), writing about self
Naturalist	discriminating among living things (e.g., plants and animals) and developing sensitivity to the rest of the natural world	environmental units, caring for pets and plants, observing and touching real plants and animals outside, asking questions about similarities and differences in plants and animals, categorizing natural materials

Sources: Armstrong, 2000; Campbell, Campbell, & Dickinson, 2004.

1. **Incorporate curriculum approaches that tap into different intelligences**, such as journaling, playing games of logic, having children make up songs, encouraging children's imagination and work in groups, and creating a naturalist learning center in the classroom. Differentiating teaching in this way acknowledges the different talents that children possess.

2. **Use assessment strategies that help students show what they know** in a variety of ways. Authentic assessments such as portfolios and projects give children choices of how to display their learning (e.g., a play, a graph, a song). These strategies are consistent with a multiple intelligences view of learning.

3. **Personalize teaching to meet children's cultural and learning needs.** Linking learning to children's real-life experiences and their cultural backgrounds maximizes learning potential. Knowing, for example, that some children often learn best through interpersonal relations, a teacher might tap into this intelligence through cooperative projects that include experimentation and improvisation. Knowing that others may prefer holistic, concrete, and social approaches to learning, a teacher might provide them with opportunities to express their knowledge through art, music, drama, and dance in addition to verbal and linguistic forms to affirm their dominant intelligences (Berns, 2010). Table 6.4 compares the key theoretical perspectives on how children learn.

Given the array of theories on how children learn, you must understand your own view of learning as well as that of the learner. The Pause and Reflect About Theories of Learning feature provides a good opportunity for you to think about what it means to learn.

Pause and Reflect

About Theories of Learning

Think of something you taught to a younger person. What theoretical perspectives were you using? How would these theories inform your own philosophy of learning? Compare and share your responses with a peer.

Table 6.4 A Comparison of Theoretical Perspectives on How Children Learn

THEORY	THEORIST	VIEW OF LEARNING	VIEW OF LEARNER	ROLE OF ADULT	PRACTICAL APPLICATIONS
Maturation	Gesell (1890–1961) Rousseau (1712–1778) Chomsky (1928–)	• develops naturally by age-related stages • maturation is the key factor in learning; occurs when children are ready	• passive • emphasis on nature	• nonintervening; allow child's learning to unfold	• readiness—waiting for readiness skills to appear before beginning formal instruction
Behavioral	Skinner (1904–1990) Locke (1632–1704) Thorndike (1874–1949) Watson (1878–1958)	• behavior can be observed, measured, and recorded • quantitative increase in learned behavior as children grow older • modeling and conditioning are primary principles of learning	• passive recipient of stimuli in environment	• shapes and changes behavior through cues and reinforcement techniques by direct intervention	• behavior modification • time out • stickers and rewards • behavioral charts • direct instruction

continued

Table 6.4 continued

THEORY	THEORIST	VIEW OF LEARNING	VIEW OF LEARNER	ROLE OF ADULT	PRACTICAL APPLICATIONS
Social Learning	Bandura (1925–)	• results from observation and imitation of significant role models, especially parents • cognition is a strong influence on learning	• active in shaping own learning • how one thinks about one's own experiences influences beliefs about self-efficacy	• models expected behaviors and skills	• modeling • direct instruction
Constructivist: Cognitive Developmental	Piaget (1896–1980)	• mental structures determine how children understand their world • stages distinctly different from one another • new learning depends on prior understanding	• active, not reactive • individual makes sense of world by actively constructing knowledge	• presents useful problems to solve that challenge and support children's innate drive to seek solutions to problems • prepares an environment with hands-on learning materials that challenge students' thinking while doing	• discovery and inquiry learning • concrete objects to teach concepts (e.g., manipulatives in mathematics)
Constructivism: Cognitive Developmental (*continued*)	Bruner (1915–)	• active processing of experiences • quantitative increase in perception, attention, memory, and problem-solving skills with age • occurs from the interaction of nature and nurture • cultural context impacts learning	• actively processes experiences		

continued

Table 6.4 continued

THEORY	THEORIST	VIEW OF LEARNING	VIEW OF LEARNER	ROLE OF ADULT	PRACTICAL APPLICATIONS
		• imaginative play helps children separate thought from action, influences learning			
Constructivist: Sociocultural	Vygotsky (1896–1934)	• occurs first on a cultural level and then on an individual level • dialogue and language are critical to learning; self-talk provides guidance and direction to learning	• focus on the social context mediated by dialogue with others • more capable peers and adults influence learning • children internalize the essential social and cultural values, beliefs, and attitudes that guide their behavior	• does not assume a direct teaching role • provides variety of materials to be used in different ways • scaffolds learning to continue to build new competencies when learner is working at the edge of ability • teacher as a partner • asks questions that require investigative thinking and abilities	• cooperative learning • play leads learning activities • assisted learning and performance • shared activities • think-alouds and talk-alouds • discovery learning • children's interests
Multiple Intelligences	Gardner (1943–)	• intelligence has more than one dimension	• active in seeking more than one way of knowing	• provides learning opportunities that use different intelligences in the teaching/ learning process	• teaching concepts through different intelligences • learners choose ways to learn • learners choose how to demonstrate knowledge • interdisciplinary curriculum • projects • authentic assessment

COLLABORATING WITH *Families*

What Is a Good Learning Experience?

Children's interests are important sources of good learning experiences; these interests provide opportunities for developing and expanding knowledge and skills. The following example shows one way that you can help families use children's interests as an important part of their learning.

Ms. Davis sent the following letter to the families of the children in her class. The letter was translated into the different languages the families spoke.

Dear _____ ;

Please take a few minutes to watch your child's activities at home. Then, answer the two questions and return this paper in your child's Friday folder.

    1. What activity does your child **spend the most time** doing?

    2. What activity does your child **not seem to want to do at all?**

This information will help me get to know your child better, so I can provide learning experiences that will interest him or her. In a few weeks, I will share our activity calendar for next month and will send home an activity that is special for you and your child.

Thank you for your support.

Beth Davis: _____

Child's Name :_____

Adult's signature

As a follow-up, Ms. Davis sent home the following activity to one family:

Dear _____ :

Thank you for letting me know what Antonio likes to do at home. You said that he likes number games and to go on scavenger hunts. So, I am sending some home learning packets that might interest Antonio and that support what he is learning in school.

Home Learning Packet:

Number activity: Included are a deck of cards and a pair of dice. Have two or more people roll the dice or choose a card to see who has the highest or lowest number. This develops number awareness.

Scavenger hunt: List objects related to the color blue. Have your child record, draw, or check the blue objects:

What can you find that is blue?

    __ ball   __ shirts

    __ blocks   __ other things

    __ shoes

Summary

■ Learning is a relatively permanent influence on a person's behavior, knowledge, and thinking ability that occurs through experience and practice. Authentic learning experiences make sense to children and involve prior knowledge, promote strategic thinking, involve some social interaction, are based on children's ways of learning, and enable children to apply learning to other situations.

■ A facilitator of learning—one who partners with children as they learn—provides both child-guided and adult-guided experiences. Teachers who facilitate learning provide good models for learning, opportunities for co-learning and social interaction, and are aware of how their beliefs about learning influence children and their families.

■ A learner-centered focus takes into account (a) the learning needs of diverse learners, (b) the impact of brain research on learning, (c) lifelong learning, (d) social and emotional learning as well as intellectual learning, and (e) child-guided learning experiences.

■ Play has long been respected as the primary way children learn. Indeed, in NAEYC's 2009 position statement on developmentally appropriate practice (Copple & Bredekamp, 2009), one of the 12 principles states that "play is an important vehicle for developing self-regulation as well as for promoting language, cognition, and social competence" (p. 14).

■ Teachers foster learning through technology by using technological tools that give children the opportunity to find information and solve problems at their own pace, that apply a range of skills and encourage social interaction, and that invite many ways of expressing ideas, of communicating, creating, and controlling their own worlds. Teachers must integrate technology in ways that connect to children's units of study, make learning meaningful, build concepts and big ideas, and provide equal access for boys and girls.

■ Early childhood educators use multiple theories to understand how children learn. Five theories that help us understand learning are the maturation, behavioral, social learning, constructivist, and multiple intelligences theories of learning.

Applying Your Knowledge of Learning

In Assessment Activity 1, apply your knowledge of learning to what would you do as Alexander's teacher. Then, in Assessment Activity 2, apply your understanding of multiple intelligences by answering the questions about the implications of a multiple intelligences approach to learning listed at the end of the learning experiences.

 **1 ALEXANDER'S STRUGGLE TO LEARN TO READ AS AN ENGLISH LANGUAGE LEARNER**

Alexander is in the third grade. In Russia, where he came from, Alexander was reading at grade level in Russian, his first language.

In Alexander's school, there are many children whose first language is not English. They are called English language learners. On the school support staff there is an English-as-a second-language (ESL) teacher and an ESL specialist who assesses children's literacy levels and provides support for both second-language learners and their teachers. Alexander's teacher, Ms. Myers, referred Alexander to

the ESL assessment specialist with the following note: "Alexander lacks comprehension in content-area reading. He does not pay attention in reading group, nor
does he show word recognition, or answer questions at the end of a reading
assignment. Alexander cannot sit still during reading time, and is often excluded
from the group. He has difficulty writing in English in his journal, completing long-
term projects, and he is frustrated in his ability to read and write even in his first
language."

In Alexander's ESL class, the ESL teacher approaches reading and writing in
English in a different way. Before beginning to read the text, his teacher formulates
questions about the topic, finds out what Alexander knows about it, and uses picture
clues and other supports to assist Alexander through the text. For content reading,
the ESL teacher teaches Alexander strategies for gathering and recalling information. According to his ESL teacher, Alexander is making steady progress in English
as a second language and is very attentive to the task of learning to read under her
tutelage.

Soon after Alexander began having difficulty with reading and was becoming a behavior problem in her class, Ms. Myers called Alexander's parents, who are fluent in
English, for a meeting with the ESL team and herself. Alexander's parents expressed
surprise when Ms. Myers reported Alexander's lack of progress in learning to read and
his lack of interest in school. At home, Alexander reads a variety of things in Russian,
his first language, and shows none of the behaviors Ms. Myers reports. Ms. Myers suggests that Alexander's parents stop using Russian at home. The ESL specialist suggests
that he spend more time in her class using her ESL strategies. Alexander's parents do
not want him to stop using his Russian. They end the meeting without arriving at an
agreement on what to do for Alexander.

REACT	Think about how the perspectives of Ms. Myers, the ESL teacher, and Alexander's parents are alike and different. What might be some reasons?
RESEARCH	Search the ERIC website for articles on teaching reading to young English language learners. What are the key learning principles?
REFLECT	What assumptions about learning do Ms. Myers, the ESL teacher, and Alexander's parents make? Generate some key strategies for teaching reading to English language learners.

Assessment
ACTIVITY (2) **LEARNING THROUGH MULTIPLE INTELLIGENCES**

When you think about fostering learning for every child, you surely want to consider
Howard Gardner's theory of multiple intelligences (MI) discussed earlier in this chapter. MI theory suggests that people have many forms of intelligence that are unevenly
distributed and developed and can be improved through practice. One way to do this
is to create a balance of learning experiences that tap all of children's intelligences.

This approach to teaching helps children to form and express their conceptual understanding and make personal connections to their learning in all areas of the curriculum. It also provides opportunities to develop their untapped talents.

Using Gardner's theory of multiple intelligences, two first-grade teachers designed and implemented a mental health unit. They used the following three concepts to guide their unit: (a) physical affection can be an expression of friendship, celebration, or a loving family; (b) there is a difference between stressful and relaxing situations; and (c) both individuals and the community need to be sensitive to persons with disabilities. Here is how they used all eight intelligences to design the learning experiences to reach all learners (Liess & Ritchie, 1995):

INTELLIGENCE	LEARNING EXPERIENCES
Bodily/Kinesthetic	write in Braille by hole punching or gluing peas on a card; assist blindfolded friends around the school
Visual/Spatial	draw pictures of sounds you would miss if you could not hear or sights you would miss if you could not see
Musical/Rhythmic	write songs and raps about disabilities
Verbal/Linguistic	read stories about disabilities; decode sign language and Braille riddles
Interpersonal	select pictures from magazines of people helping each other
Intrapersonal	reflect on learning in journals on the computer or by drawing
Logical/Mathematical	measure areas of the school for wheelchair use; examine the building to identify what needs to be done for people with disabilities
Naturalist	look for animals with a physical disability and discuss what accommodations are necessary

Now, think about the implications of providing a balance of learning experiences that tap into children's intelligences by considering carefully the following questions.

- How does a multiple intelligences approach to teaching foster children's learning?
- In what ways does it set the stage for further learning?
- What kinds of planning do teachers need to use this approach?

Source: Adapted from "Using Multiple Intelligence Theory to Transform a First-Grade Health Curriculum," by E. Liess & G. Ritchie, 1995, *Early Childhood Education Journal, 23*(2), 71–79.

ONLINE RESOURCES FOR LEARNING

Alliance for Childhood: Provides links and articles on play and other learning issues.
www.allianceforchildhood.net

To read "Crisis in the Kindergarten: Why Children Need to Play in School," go to
www.allianceforchildhood.org/sites/allianceforchildhood.org/files/file/kindergarten_report.pdf.

To read "Fools Gold: A Critical Look at Computers in Childhood" (in English and Spanish), go to
http://drupal6.allianceforchildhood.org/fools_gold.

American Speech/Hearing/Language Association: Reports the latest research findings on applications
of technology for individuals with hearing impairments or deafness. www.asha.org

Assistive Technology Guidelines

Able Net: Suggests ideas that make teaching students with disabilities easy, fun, and fulfilling.
www.ablenetinc.com

Brain-Based Learning

Provides links and practical classroom applications based on current brain research.
www.Brains.org

Multiple Intelligences Activities

Today's Teacher: Lists learning activities in each area of Gardner's multiple intelligences.
www.todaysteacher.com/MILearningActivities.htm

PEARSON
myeducationlab

Go to Topic 8 (DAP/Teaching Strategies) in the MyEducationLab
(www.myeducationlab.com) for your course, where you can:

- Find learning outcomes for DAP/teaching strategies along with the national standards that connect to these outcomes.
- Complete Assignments and Activities that can help you more deeply understand
  the chapter content.
- Apply and practice your understanding of the core teaching skills identified in
  the chapter with the Building Teaching Skills and Dispositions learning units.
- Hear viewpoints of experts in the field in Professional Perspectives.

CHAPTER 7

Creating High-Quality Learning Environments

The environment teaches us about ourselves—as teachers, children, and families. It regulates our feelings and behaviors, and shapes a significant part of our identity.

Margie Carter, 2006, p. 18

Meet the TEACHERS

MS. KOEN teaches 3-year-olds and was frustrated by their behavior. She says, "My classroom is small and everything winds up on the floor. The children argue over materials, and often wander aimlessly from activity to activity." After reading about good environments, talking with her colleagues, and reflecting on her classroom organization, Ms. Koen redesigned her classroom space starting with the housekeeping area. She created a corner by placing the sink, stove, and refrigerator catty-corner to each other, and she placed the dolls and dress-up materials in separate containers so the children could more easily locate and put away the items. Next, she enlarged the block center to facilitate building, added figures and other materials to extend the children's play, and moved the sand table to a location where it could be easily wheeled onto a drop cloth. Almost immediately, Ms. Koen noticed a change in the children's behavior from aimless wandering to longer, more engaged play.

MS. ENDO'S kindergarten classroom includes a child who is confined to a wheelchair and a child with a visual impairment. After consulting with other members of the school team (the nurse, social worker, speech-language therapist, and psychologist) as well as the children's families, Ms. Endo modified parts of the physical environment. She put adhesive-backed Velcro on the bottom of some fine motor materials to help the child in the wheelchair attach items to the lap tray. She also cleared the pathways to accommodate the wheelchair and increase mobility for the child with low vision. Next, Ms. Endo adapted her classroom to help children process visual information. For example, she painted brightly colored letters on some wooden blocks to make them easier for the child with visual impairment to see and used lots of big books with enlarged type and pictures, a molded plastic globe, an abacus, and a clock with a raised face. Ms. Endo also marked the child's name on his cubby with a textured sign that he could feel and taped small objects or toys on the outside of bins so that children knew where materials belonged.

MS. DIAZ teaches third grade in an urban school. Each fall, she organizes her classroom space in **cluster style** (arranging desks and tables so that small numbers of children can work face to face in small groups). She does this because she believes that "The relationships children have with one another deeply affect what and how they learn. Children need to be able to interact, express their ideas clearly, and ask for what they need to live harmoniously in their world." Ms. Diaz uses this arrangement because it supports her use of **cooperative learning,** in which students help each other learn. Ms. Diaz expects individuals in her cooperative learning groups to work on a part of a large topic and then teach that part to others, thereby deepening their own knowledge.

LEARNING Outcomes

In this chapter, you will learn to:

→ **Define and discuss the essential principles of high-quality learning environments** (NAEYC #1c, ACEI #5, INTASC #3)

→ **Explore your role in creating respectful and challenging learning environments**

→ **Organize high-quality indoor learning environments** (NAEYC #5b)

→ **Organize high-quality outdoor learning environments** (NAEYC #5b)

→ **Adapt environments for children with exceptionalities**

→ **Apply your knowledge of learning environments to early childhood classrooms**

Compare

What are some similarities in the ways these three teachers create their learning environments?

Contrast

What messages do these environments give to children about learning, about using materials, and about a sense of belonging?

Connect

What impressed you most about these teachers' learning environments? How could you incorporate some of these ideas in your own teaching?

Now that you have reflected on the three teachers' perspectives and noted the learning outcomes, we preview the knowledge, skills, and dispositions you will need in order to fulfill your role in creating high-quality learning environments.

A Definition of Environment

Imagine entering someone's home and immediately sensing that you are in a special place. There is music playing in the background; the smell of favorite foods is in the air; there are comfortable places to sit, beautiful wall decorations and plants to admire, and light permeates through the house. Your host and hostess are interested in who you are and engage you easily in conversation. You feel welcome and valued. The attributes that convey this comfortable, homey feeling are the same ones that characterize good early childhood environments. High-quality learning environments invite children into a community that is healthy, caring, respectful, and supportive.

By **learning environment,** we mean all the influences that affect children and adults in early childhood classrooms (Bullard, 2010; Copple & Bredekamp, 2009; NAEYC, 2005b). These include the planned arrangement of physical space, the relationships between and among the people, and the content, values, and goals of a particular classroom. Although each environment is unique because of how these influences interact, they are all interrelated. One useful way to think about the learning environment is to consider its physical and social parts. The **physical environment** includes such elements as the space, room arrangement, schedule, equipment, and materials; the **social environment** comprises the interactions between and among children and adults that include content experiences, values, goals, and daily organization. Although both parts must be considered in every environment, together they make up the total learning environment that is based on the following five principles.

PRINCIPLES OF HIGH-QUALITY LEARNING ENVIRONMENTS

Creating a high-quality learning environment is based on what we know about children's growth, development, and learning. The differences in environments can be found in children's opportunities to become a member of a community of learners, the classroom organization, the attention to goals and outcomes, the protection of children's health and safety, and children's access to age-appropriate materials and learning experiences. Each of these research-based principles is discussed next.

HIGH-QUALITY LEARNING ENVIRONMENTS HAVE A CARING COMMUNITY OF LEARNERS

The first guideline for developmentally appropriate practice (Copple & Bredekamp, 2009) is to create a caring **community of learners**—one "in which all participants consider and contribute to one another's well-being and learning" (p. 35). Being part of such a community contributes to children's school success because children gain a sense of acceptance and belonging, two essential

DID YOU Know?

- Depending on how it is arranged, the physical environment can elicit either negative or positive social behavior. The classroom physical environment can contribute to preschool children's social interactions by providing "safe havens" for play (Copple & Bredekamp, 2009).

- Preschool children typically spend more than a third of their time in transitions and routines, such as standing in line, cleaning up, washing hands, and eating, rather than in other learning activities (Early et al., 2005).

- Warm, caring relationships between children and adults and between children and their peers in classrooms improve their attitudes toward schools and learning (Martinez-Beck & Zaslow, 2006).

- For most children, outdoor play offers the only opportunity to engage in aerobic activities that enhance fitness—strength, flexibility, and endurance—and help compensate for faulty diets. Children who take time for physical education do at least as well academically as children who devote all of their time to academic tasks (Frost, Wortham, & Reifel, 2008).

needs that affect learning and development. High-quality learning environments must support children's positive relationships in a respectful setting to develop healthy relationships with others, and to learn about themselves and their world (Copple & Bredekamp, 2006, 2009). These conditions help children feel like part of their community, where all children are included in all aspects of classroom life. It also enables children to appreciate individual differences and value the concept that each child is unique and has something to offer. Cultivating a sense of belonging wherever possible is an essential principle of the social environment.

HIGH-QUALITY LEARNING ENVIRONMENTS ARE ORGANIZED, CHALLENGING, AND AESTHETICALLY PLEASING

For children to respond favorably to an environment, it must be predictable, stable, and comprehensible to them (Copple & Bredekamp, 2009; Hendrick & Weissman, 2006; NAEYC, 2005b). **Predictable environments** have simple routines and rituals that help children to feel secure and safe, and to understand what behaviors are expected of them; predictable environments also have flexible structures that make it easy for everyone to work and be productive. Think back to Ms. Koen, the teacher of 3-year-olds whom you met in the opening scenario. Initially, her environment was not orderly or predictable—indeed, it was quite chaotic! After Ms. Koen reorganized her space, the children knew where to find what they needed and how to maintain a sense of order. She had provided *predictability*. Moreover, Ms. Koen made clear her behavioral expectations about the use of materials. How you organize your physical environment reflects the needs and developmental levels of the children you teach, your beliefs about teaching and learning, and the goals and values of the community in which you teach (Edwards, Gandini, & Forman, 1998). High-quality learning environments are also pleasant places to be. They often have living green plants, attractive colors, comfortable furniture, soft lighting and colors, open spaces, and a clean fragrance. A pleasant environment for living and learning invites both adults' and children's learning and is an essential element of the physical environment.

HIGH-QUALITY LEARNING ENVIRONMENTS REFLECT CLEAR GOALS

The goals of every classroom are expressed directly in the arrangement and relationships of the environment. How you relate to children and families, how you arrange physical space and select materials, and how you use space and time reflect your goals. While these goals vary widely because of age, community, culture, and experience, your environment reflects your goals. If, for example, one of your goals is to nurture children's curiosity and disposition to learn, your environment would likely include regular opportunities for children to engage in individual, small-group, and large-group problem solving and social interactions that offer multiple ways of learning and showing what they know (Fraser & Gestwicki, 2002; Harms, Clifford, & Cryer,

Ideas about high-quality learning environments have changed through the years.

2004). In contrast, consider the American classrooms last century that had students' desks bolted to wooden floors: Clearly the goal was to have all the children learn the same knowledge and set of skills at the same time and at the same rate. The focus in these classrooms was on whole-group activities during which children were doing the same tasks. Goals are an essential element of the social environment.

HIGH-QUALITY LEARNING ENVIRONMENTS PROTECT CHILDREN'S HEALTH AND SAFETY

All learning environments affect children's brain growth, their relationships, and their attitude toward learning. At a minimum, **physical health and safety needs** include adequate space and appropriate entrances and exits. Physical health and safety needs also include food, clothing, shelter, rest, medical care, and a balance between active, sensory stimulation and quiet opportunities for reflection. **Psychological health and safety needs** include a consistent, predictable relationship with a caring adult who has high, positive expectations, strong peer acceptance, and respect for children as they are. *Psychologically safe classrooms* encourage children to take risks, invite them to express their feelings and ideas without fear of ridicule, and value all children's voices (Pecaski-McLennan, 2009). Children know they are in a safe place when they feel welcome and relaxed. Children who grow up with their basic physical and psychological needs met are likely to trust themselves and others and rely on inner resources for coping with difficulties. On the other hand, children who grow up without having their basic physical and psychological needs met are at a clear disadvantage for becoming successful learners (Carnegie Task Force, 1994; Hyson, 2008; Maslow, 1987). Feeling safe and secure is an essential element of the *social environment*.

HIGH-QUALITY LEARNING ENVIRONMENTS PROVIDE AGE-APPROPRIATE MATERIALS AND EQUIPMENT

Materials and equipment are learning tools that suggest what children can do. They also support children's physical, intellectual, social, and emotional development. **Materials** are classroom items, such as crayons, paints, and paper, that are regularly replaced or replenished; **equipment** refers to the large, more costly items such as furniture and outdoor structures. The best materials for all children are attractive, have strong sensory appeal, invite children to imagine and create their own ideas and interpretations, are culturally relevant, and allow for active exploration. These materials are:

- developmentally appropriate and match children's abilities and interests.
- open-ended—they offer flexibility, variety, and multiple uses for children of different ages and abilities.
- culturally appropriate and reflect the children's families and community, and promote equality and tolerance rather than perpetuating stereotypes.
- safe, durable, nontoxic, well designed, and have good workmanship. (Bullard, 2010; Isenberg & Jalongo, 2010)

Having access to age-approriate materials and equipment supports the physical environment.

Figure 7.1 illustrates the interaction of these principles to advance children's learning and development.

Pause and
Reflect

About Principles of Learning Environments

Think about your current college classroom where you are now studying to become a teacher. What environmental principles are evident or not evident, and how do they affect your learning? What changes could you realistically make for your classroom to be more conducive to learning?

Figure 7.1 Essential Features of High-Quality Learning Environments That Interact to Advance Children's Learning and Development

Appendix A at the end of this book suggests basic materials and equipment by age group, including those for infants and toddlers, preschoolers and kindergartners, and school-age children.

High-quality learning environments promote children's learning and development. If you follow these principles, you will become a teacher who can engage children in their learning and make good learning choices (Isenberg & Jalongo, 2010).

Your Role in Creating the Learning Environment

Creating learning environments is an important skill for early childhood educators. Consider the following example of a second-grade teacher, Ms. Schutta, as you think about your role in creating high-quality learning environments for all children.

Ms. Schutta's second-grade classroom is divided into specific activity areas. There are clear entrances and exits to these areas, pathways within the classroom for the children to move about safely, and tables clustered together where children do their work. Ms. Schutta's classroom is full of plants and has displays of children's work, comfortable and cozy areas, and a few aesthetically pleasing prints and posters on clean, painted walls. The daily schedule begins first thing in the morning with a large block of time (45 minutes) called "breathing out" time, during which children transition from home to school and have time to settle into the school routines (Wassermann, 2000). During "breathing out" time, Ms. Schutta observes from the sidelines and then works one-on-one with children who need specific instruction on a skill or concept. There is also a 2-hour language arts block, during which children pursue individual projects, including a variety of hands-on, small-group experiences, followed by a sharing and debriefing time. During this time, the children choose from among three or four centers. Each center is clearly labeled; materials are accessible and inviting. Some of the centers in this class are a class library that contains collections of books of many different sizes and genres; an art center that has an easel stand with tempera paints and watercolors; a wikki center with a board for wikki sticks (i.e., wax-covered, bendable sticks the size of pipe cleaners that are used for construction and can stick to different surfaces); a game-and-puzzle center where children together or independently work wooden puzzles, Lego blocks, pattern blocks, or unifix cubes or play checkers, dominoes, or board games; and a magnet center filled with a variety of magnetic letters that children put together to make sounds and words that they know. The content taught through Ms. Schutta's centers is based upon county and state standards of learning. One of the first things Ms. Schutta's second graders do upon arrival at school is to select an area for work by hanging a tag on a choice board, allowing them to occupy a space at a particular center. The morning block ends with a sharing time, during which children share meaningful aspects of their projects.

One of Ms. Schutta's second graders, Jon, a child with learning disabilities, has difficulty with writing. When the class was studying the life cycle of the pumpkin, Jon drew pictures to tell the story of the pumpkin's stages of growth. He explained each stage of his drawing to Ms. Schutta, who wrote down his words so he could share them with his classmates. Chad, however, is receiving services for being gifted and talented in math and reading, but he does not like to write. Ms. Schutta noticed how he loves baseball and provided him with trade books and research formats to learn more about the sport. Chad used the long time blocks to illustrate and write about a baseball book he was reading. He created a baseball diamond, listed baseball facts, and used his love for baseball to develop his writing skills.

Ms. Schutta's classroom is a high-quality learning environment. Educational researchers have identified the following six guidelines for establishing such environments.

ARRANGE SPACE TO MEET THE NEEDS OF ALL LEARNERS

One of the very first decisions you will make when you have your own classroom is to determine how to use the space you have. How and where you place the furniture, arrange the materials, and organize the space will affect the children's behavior and learning (Clayton, 2001; Curtis & Carter, 2005; Kritchevsky, Prescott, & Walling, 1977; Read, 2007). Space must be arranged to accommodate a variety of learning experiences occurring in different-sized groupings and to meet the children's different developmental needs and physical sizes. Finding the right use of space is a challenge for all teachers, both experienced and new; somehow, classrooms never seem to have enough of it. Notice that Ms. Schutta arranged her space into centers, or areas, where children work together on projects in small groups, in pairs, or individually. She labeled each area clearly, and arranged the materials so that the children can access them easily and independently. Figure 7.2 shows Ms. Schutta's room arrangement for school-age children. Figure 7.3 shows a room arrangement for infants and toddlers. Figure 7.4 provides a sample room arrangement for preschoolers and kindergartners.

Figure 7.2 Room Arrangement for School-Age Children

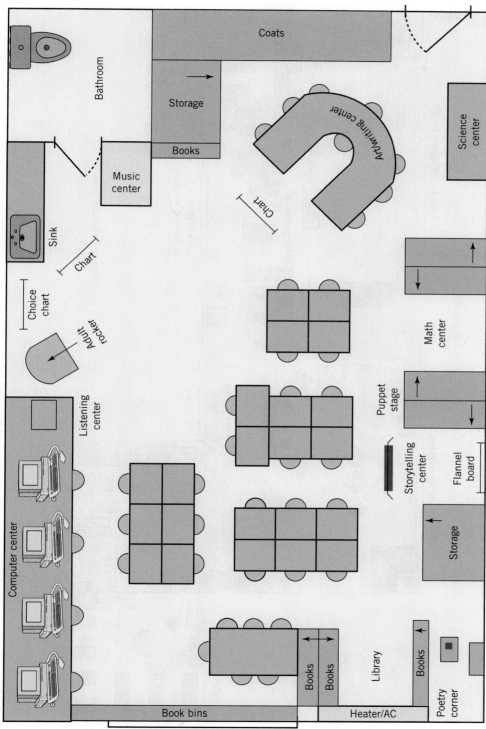

Source: Courtesy of Mary Schutta and Robyn Cochran, Deer Park Elementary School, Fairfax, VA.

Figure 7.3 Room Arrangement for Infants and Toddlers

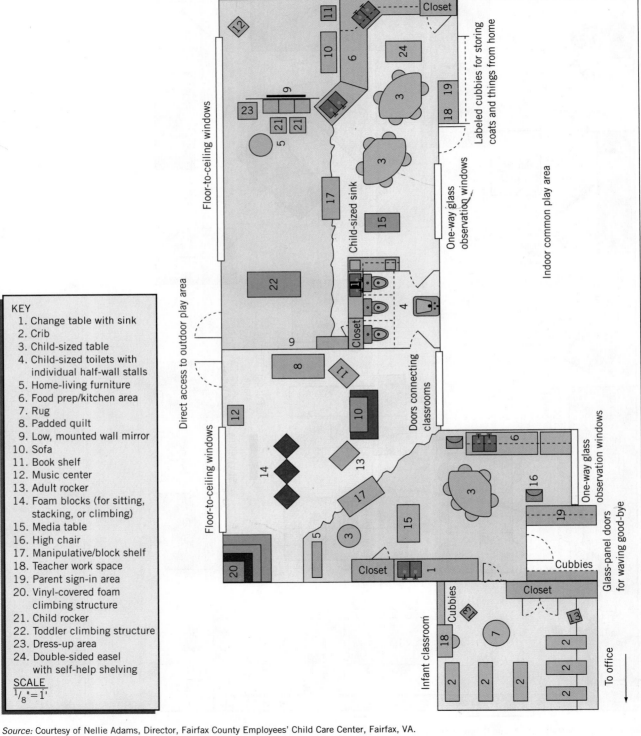

KEY
1. Change table with sink
2. Crib
3. Child-sized table
4. Child-sized toilets with individual half-wall stalls
5. Home-living furniture
6. Food prep/kitchen area
7. Rug
8. Padded quilt
9. Low, mounted wall mirror
10. Sofa
11. Book shelf
12. Music center
13. Adult rocker
14. Foam blocks (for sitting, stacking, or climbing)
15. Media table
16. High chair
17. Manipulative/block shelf
18. Teacher work space
19. Parent sign-in area
20. Vinyl-covered foam climbing structure
21. Child rocker
22. Toddler climbing structure
23. Dress-up area
24. Double-sided easel with self-help shelving

SCALE
$1/_8" = 1'$

Source: Courtesy of Nellie Adams, Director, Fairfax County Employees' Child Care Center, Fairfax, VA.

Figure 7.4 Room Arrangement for Preschoolers and Kindergartners

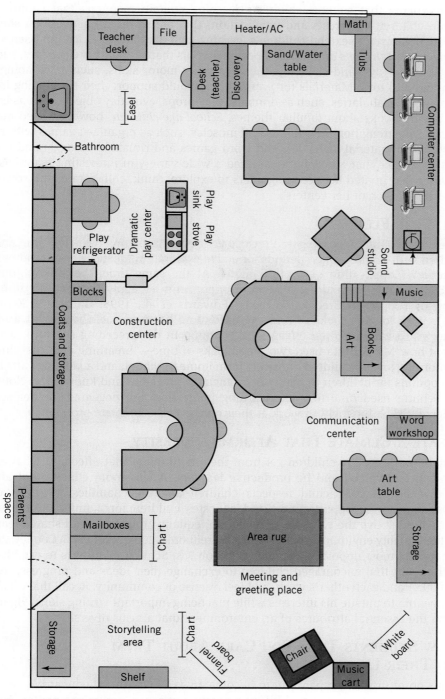

Source: Courtesy of Gall Ritchie, Kings Park Elementary School, Fairfax, VA.

SELECT APPROPRIATE MATERIALS

Environments that support children's learning contain materials that capture and sustain children's interests and imagination, that are stored attractively on shelves, that are organized to extend children's learning, and that facilitate cleanup (Isenberg & Jalongo, 2010). *Infants and toddlers* need materials that stimulate their senses, such as soft, textured toys, and challenge their emerging motor skills, such as climbing and push-and-pull toys. Materials for *preschoolers* should support their developing imagination and vocabularies, such as dramatic-play props, everyday objects such as boxes, and picture books about familiar themes. *School-age children*, however, need materials that will strengthen their minds and muscles, such as organized games with rules, construction materials, puzzles, and word games and rituals like Boggle and tongue twisters. Notice that Ms. Schutta selected a wide variety of interesting materials and activities that invited her second graders to explore, think, collaborate, and solve real problems in each of her centers.

USE TIME FLEXIBLY

Time affects student learning and reveals your priorities. Long blocks of time provide children with uninterrupted periods for active exploration, deeper understanding, and higher-level application of subject matter. At the same time, they allow you, the teacher, to provide children with more opportunity to apply concepts to authentic problems (Copple & Bredekamp, 2009; Edwards et al., 1998; Garreau & Kennedy, 1991). With longer blocks of time, you are more likely to use a variety of teaching strategies to keep children engaged in learning. In the preceding scenario, we witnessed how Ms. Schutta used two long blocks of time—"breathing out" first thing in the morning to help children transition from home to school, and a language arts block with options for children to apply their language arts skills and knowledge. Note that Ms. Schutta used *time* to make learning interesting and engaging for her second graders by allowing them to work at their own pace to complete projects.

CREATE A CLIMATE THAT AFFIRMS DIVERSITY

Climate is the feeling children get from the environment that affects to what extent they will feel valued and be productive learners. A classroom climate that affirms the diversity of each child respects children and their families, provides equal access to learning opportunities, and educates children for a multicultural world. Children must live the values of cooperation, equality, tolerance, and shared learning in a high-quality environment (Swiniarski & Breitborde, 2003; Williams & Cooney, 2006). Perhaps the most important teaching decision Ms. Schutta made was to establish an environment that encouraged children to exchange their ideas and progress, respect each other and each other's work, and feel a sense of community. Recall that Chad had the freedom to pursue his interests while practicing important writing skills. Figure 7.5 shows the essential attributes of an environment that affirms diversity.

SHOW STUDENTS THAT YOU CARE ABOUT THEM AND THEIR LEARNING

At this point in your preparation to become an early childhood educator, you might feel uncertain about your ability to create appropriate environments. As you gain confidence in doing so, be certain to show children that you care about them and their learning. A true spirit of caring is at the heart of high-quality environments. You show caring when you find out about children's interests, and

Figure 7.5 Essential Attributes of an Environment That Affirms Diversity

Security
- Each child must feel safe enough to take risks.

Identity
- Each child must feel valued and appreciated as an individual with unique needs and abilities.

Responsibility
- Each child must feel a sense of belonging to the group.

Dignity
- Each child should have self-respect and respect for the thoughts and actions of others.

Community
- Each child should have a sense of trust that is created and supported by the children, families, and teachers in the environment.

Sources: Association for Supervision and Curriculum Development, 1997; Swiniarski & Breitborde, 2003.

offer them just enough support, structure, and expectation to be self-directed, responsible learners. The **ethic of care** is aptly discussed by Nel Noddings (1992), who states that "caring for students is fundamental in teaching and . . . developing people with a strong capacity for care is a major objective of responsible education" (p. 678). Ms. Schutta exhibited an *ethic of care* with both Jon and Chad. She cared about their individuality (e.g., Chad's love of baseball) to teach them skills in a supportive way through what is important to them (e.g., taking dictation from Jon about a pumpkin's life cycle so he could share his ideas). She provided appropriate support to each child to increase his or her participation, achieve a sense of belonging, and help make learning meaningful.

CONNECT WITH THE CHILDREN'S FAMILIES

It is well known that strong families make strong schools. As a teacher of young children, you will want to find many ways to connect with the children's families. Involving families sends the message that you value their children and want to build respectful, two-way communication about their children's learning (Copple & Bredekamp, 2006, 2009; NAEYC, 2005b). For example, send home positive notes—you can always find something positive to say about every child. Such notes let parents know that you have a vested interest in their children's learning and that you care about their children's progress.

The classroom environment directly affects how children behave, develop, learn, and form values. Many behavior problems in classrooms can be reduced or eliminated by creating healthy conditions for learning. These conditions make learning safe and supportive, and they encourage all children to develop confidence, take risks, work independently, and strengthen their social skills.

Organizing Indoor Learning Environments

The indoor learning environment is the place in which children acquire skills, concepts, attitudes, and values about the world. It is, in fact, the children's home for learning that they visit each day, and it has a crucial impact on the way the brain develops (Strong-Wilson & Ellis, 2007). Effective early childhood teachers design opportunities for children to develop self-help skills, make good learning choices, become self-directed, and feel competent and confident.

Think back now to the teachers you met in the Meet the Teachers opening section of this chapter. Recall how Ms. Koen rearranged the space to encourage more appropriate play, Ms. Endo adapted her environment so all children could participate, and how Ms. Diaz used a cluster-style arrangement to encourage peer relationships in learning. Reread that section and think about those teachers as you explore how to design the physical and social learning environments.

THE PHYSICAL LEARNING ENVIRONMENT

The physical learning environment is the most visible. A well-organized physical environment provides a safe, supportive place for children to live, learn, and grow; provides a balance of teacher-guided and child-guided activities; and invites children to learn in purposeful and meaningful ways (Copple & Bredekamp, 2009; Kontos & Wilcox-Herzog, 1997; Wortham, 2010). Think about the essential features of high-quality indoor learning environments—space, room arrangement, schedule and routines, materials and equipment—as you read the next section.

SPACE

How classroom space is used can critically affect children's learning and development (Bullard, 2010; Clayton, 2001; Firlik, 2006; Frye & Mumpower, 2001). When teachers divide space into defined interest and learning areas, they protect children from distractions and promote a more intimate setting for learning. Separating the active from the quiet and the messy from nonmessy areas also organizes space in a way that can enhance children's persistence at tasks and improve the quality of their social interactions. Moreover, the versatility of organizing space into learning centers makes such an arrangement an essential part of early childhood classrooms. Two other spatial considerations include attention to **ambiance,** the light, color, texture, and noise, and access to **privacy** if needed. These three spatial features, *learning centers, ambiance,* and *privacy,* will be discussed next.

Learning Centers **Learning centers** are well-defined, organized areas of the classroom set aside for specific learning purposes without the teacher's constant presence and direction. They enable teachers to integrate the curriculum, develop cultural awareness, address multiple intelligences, and nurture children's spontaneity and originality (Bullard, 2010; Isbell & Exelby, 2001; Isenberg & Jalongo, 2010). A center arrangement enables children to interact more frequently than they can in large groups. In centers, children are more likely to get immediate responses to their ideas, communication, and work. Centers allow for self-directed activity with opportunities to work individually or with a partner, thereby helping the child to become more independent or learn to work cooperatively.

Some possible learning outcomes for children in center-based learning environments include the following:

- problem-solving ability, by making good learning choices that determine the direction of their play and their work
- responsibility, by selecting, using, and caring for their materials

- persistence, by carrying out plans to completion (Isbell & Exelby, 2001; Isenberg & Jalongo, 2010; Sanoff, 1995)
- learning by working at their own pace and ability level to meet appropriately individualized goals and objectives (Tiedt & Tiedt, 2010)

Ambiance **Ambiance** refers to sensory information that increases comfort, understanding, and learning. The sights, sounds, smells, and textures in every environment bring it to life for the present but also become part of long-term memory to be recalled long after one has left that setting (Crumpacker, 1995; Curtis & Carter, 2005). *Light* is one important aspect of ambiance. The environment should have as much natural light as possible through windows and doors. Hanging things in windows and mirrors on the walls creates a spacious feeling. Where this is not possible, a variety of soft lighting, such as desk and floor lamps instead of glaring fluorescent lighting, should be used for a softer effect. *Color* also contributes to the feeling of an environment. High-quality environments for children have enough color to stimulate but not overwhelm the senses. *Texture* stimulates tactile learning, which is important for all children, especially those with special needs. High-quality early childhood environments have many materials with soft textures, such as finger-paints, modeling dough, and cozy furnishings, such as beanbag chairs, carpeting, and pillows (Jones & Prescott, 1978); soft and cozy items make children feel safe and secure. *Noise* that comes from children's natural interactions in active learning environments is healthy. However, excessive noise is uncomfortable and can negatively affect children's ability to communicate, interact, concentrate, and learn (Readdick, 2006). In many early childhood classrooms, you will find special spaces designed for children to seek privacy by being able to escape from the bustling activity of a classroom filled with engaged learners.

Privacy Children have different needs for levels of interaction. Some children need time alone and enjoy silent periods; others do not. For children who easily become overstimulated, tired, or upset, places to be alone are important, because they respect children's need to enjoy quiet moments to regain control of their ability to focus on learning. You can create private spaces in safe alcoves that contain soft features such as carpeting and pillows or as part of a loft where children can be quiet but still see the rest of the classroom. Quiet spaces set off by themselves and stocked with some books and perhaps a few floor cushions send the message, "Here is a place where I can think, watch, and collect myself in a safe way." There should be space for children to play alone or with a friend, protected in some way from other children, in every classroom (Cryer & Phillipsen, 1997).

ROOM ARRANGEMENT
Your classroom can be arranged in two different ways. The space can be arranged according to children's developmental areas, such as physical, social, or cognitive development, or by curriculum areas, such as writing, reading, science, and art. Regardless of how you arrange it, space should facilitate, not hinder, learning. Your *room arrangement* should include the following:

- a large area to hold group demonstrations, meetings, and discussions
- small areas for work in small groups, in pairs, and alone
- individual areas to facilitate independent work on projects

- displays that invite children to look, touch, and converse about instructional materials, reference materials, or their own work
- clearly labeled work areas and easy access to engaging materials to encourage independence (Clayton, 2001; Frye & Mumpower, 2001; Harms et al., 2004)

Large Area Some teachers locate a large area in the center of the room and have smaller areas around the room; others arrange a quiet corner of the classroom for it; and still others use a large classroom library for this purpose. In the large area of your classroom, you will need an easel for group work such as class news and charts. Within easy reach, you will also want an organized supply of materials, such as markers of various colors, chart paper, scissors, a magnetic board, or a cookie sheet with an assortment of magnetic letters and shapes, sentence strips, and masking tape or other tape.

Small Areas Teachers often use low bookshelves, tables, and other furniture to create centers or areas where groups of children can work together. Using these as dividers gives the room an open, uncluttered look and gives you an unobstructed view. Dividers can double as a display for instructions, examples of children's work, or storage for reference materials. Small work areas should have enough space, materials, and chairs for the number of children who will typically be working there. Crowded areas frustrate children and make it difficult for them to work together productively. If you have desks in your classroom, you might want to cluster some together to form a worktable. Research shows that small-group interactions improve children's attitudes, achievement, social skills, and voluntary participation (Moore & Lackney, 1995).

Individual Areas Every classroom needs space for individual projects. Even though children can work independently at a common table, they need enough space for their own materials. Moreover, some individual areas should be quiet places where individuals can work without distraction, thereby providing more psychological than actual separation.

Displays Classroom displays should encourage children to observe, question, and investigate, so be especially mindful of how you use them. The best displays are inviting and should reflect what you want the children to notice (Bullard, 2010). Crowded walls that are overstimulating *discourage rather than encourage* learning (Curtis & Carter, 2005; Frye & Mumpower, 2001). Displays should be at the children's eye level so they can revisit their work and use reference materials easily. A large display space is best used for a piece of well-loved writing that becomes shared reading the children go back to again and again, or for a classroom mural that many children had a hand in creating. Teachers use displays to allow children to discuss their own work and the work of their classmates, and they point out the positive qualities of all pieces. When walls and dividers are covered with children's work, appropriate posters, and aesthetically appealing art that reflects the cultures of the children, they send the message that the children and families in the group are valued and valuable. However, when walls and dividers are covered with cartoonlike materials or oversized management tools, such as classroom rules, they can be visually noisy and stressful for children and offer little or no connection between past and future learning opportunities (Pecaski-McLennon, 2009).

Clearly Labeled Work Areas and Easy Access to Materials Most classrooms include a number of learning areas. Some may be permanent centers, such as those for art and writing; others may be changed according to children's interests, needs, and the particular topic under study. These work areas, or centers, have clear pathways so children can safely move in and out, are labeled clearly so the children and teachers know what to do at each center and how many children can be in there at one time, and contain materials that facilitate children's thinking and exploration. The following are suggestions for making centers work:

- Identify the center with print or an appropriate picture.
- Arrange commonly used materials in clearly labeled containers that are accessible from where the children are working independently. Children should know how the materials are used and stored.
- Introduce centers one at a time, explicitly demonstrating and practicing the routines for using each one with the children.
- Have an adequate supply of materials.
- Use a work board to establish routines for participating in centers. The work board can be on an eye-level easel or can lean against a wall. Children can choose and monitor center use through this tool. Figures 7.6 and 7.7 show work boards used by Mary Kleinpaste in her inclusive preschool classroom. Notice how she uses her boards to give children responsibility for developing independent and self-help skills and choosing centers with the aid of pictorial representations.

Storage You will need storage for materials and for children's daily work. Children need space to keep work-in-progress, finished work that will be used to assess their progress,

Figure 7.6 **Example of Work Board for Self-Help Skills**

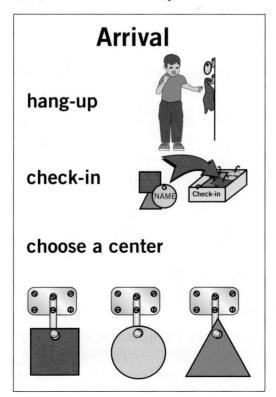

Source: Courtesy of Mary Kleinpaste.

Figure 7.7 Example of Work Board for Choosing Centers

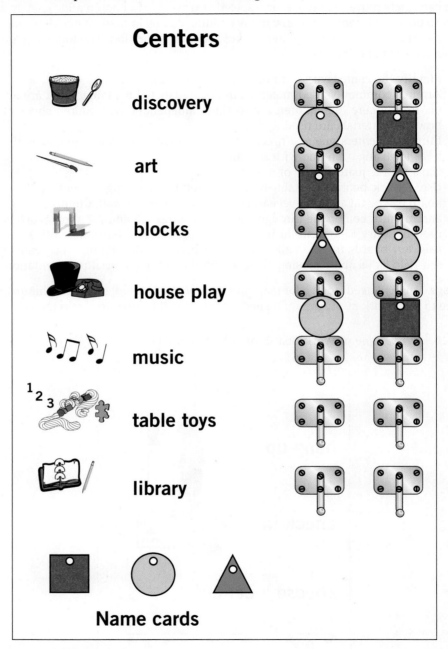

Source: Courtesy of Mary Kleinpaste.

and personal belongings. Materials, supplies, and work can be stored in a variety of ways but should be orderly and aesthetically pleasing. Here are some suggestions:

- Use easy-to-find storage containers that have different and interesting textures, such as berry baskets or decorated boxes.
- Consider balance and design when arranging materials, displays, and furniture.

- Store daily work in a labeled, clear plastic tub or box.
- Use a plastic crate with hanging files for finished writing.
- Try a drying rack for drying paintings.
- Use a plastic shoe rack for storing puppets.
- Cut cereal boxes in half, cover them with contact paper, and have students store their materials in them. These boxes can easily be placed in the center of worktables to designate particular children who should work there.

SCHEDULE AND ROUTINES

The **schedule** is a way to organize who does what and when throughout the day and is important for the children, teacher, and families. The schedule must be thoughtfully planned. Each day, you need to provide enough time for a balance of large-group, small-group, and individual activities. Your *schedule* provides consistency for learners so they know what to expect; this gives children control over their day, and conveys a clear message about what you think is important. Your schedule also documents how you are going to use the time each day and provides a way for families to understand what is happening on a given day or in a given week, or longer. For example, we know that long blocks of uninterrupted time help children to be more productive, self-directed, and self-expressive, and they send the message that their work is important (Garreau & Kennedy, 1991; Tegano, Moran, DeLong, Brickman, & Ramsisini, 1996). A good place to keep your daily schedule is in your meeting area, where you and the children can review it each morning. Other places could be on a white board at the entrance to your classroom and sending a hard copy or e-mail attachment to families so that all families have access to learning experiences their children are having throughout the day.

Which features of high-quality learning environments are apparent in this classroom?

Routines are the regular and predictable activities that form the basis of the daily schedule and ensure effective use of time and space. They help children sense the passage of time (e.g., snack follows cleanup) and help them to anticipate events (e.g., a musical selection marks the end of the day). A consistent but flexible schedule and regular routines provide a strong foundation for high-quality indoor environments. They set the stage for learning and can create an atmosphere that makes your classroom special for every child.

Figure 7.8 provides sample schedules for half-day preschool, full-day kindergarten, and second grade that can guide your planning. One note of caution: Adhering to a rigid schedule can impede children's thinking just as much as not having any schedule at all.

MATERIALS AND EQUIPMENT

Materials are the tools children use to learn. Developmentally appropriate materials are concrete, real, and meaningful to children (Copple & Bredekamp, 2009). They allow children to investigate, explore, and experiment. Teachers choose materials that can be used by children with a wide range of abilities, are easily manipulated and safe, and meet the needs of the children in the group. All children are responsible for the care and cleanup of the materials. The following are some things to think about when providing good learning tools for children:

- Have plenty of materials available.
- Include adequate props and materials for play.

Figure 7.8 Sample Schedules

Half-Day Preschool

8:45–9:00	Arrival and Greeting
9:00–9:15	Class Meeting
9:15–10:15	Choice and Centers
10:15–10:30	Cleanup
10:30–10:50	Sharing and Snack
10:50–11:20	Outdoor Play
11:20–11:45	Story and Preparation for Home

Full-Day Kindergarten

8:50	Arrival, Greeting, Group Time
9:25	Centers and Work Time
10:45	Whole-Group Sharing and Debriefing
11:00	Gross Motor Activity (indoors or out)
11:30	Lunch
12:00	Whole-Group Story and Discussion
12:30	Integrated Language Arts, Science, Math
2:30	Group Share, Story, Music
3:00	Preparation for Home

Second Grade

8:15	Free Choice
8:30	Investigative Centers
10:00	Cleanup
10:15	Class Meeting
10:30	Outdoors
10:45	Integrated Science and Math
12:15	Lunch and Story
12:45	Integrated Language Arts/Social Studies/Arts
2:45	Music and Preparation for Home

- Model the appropriate use of materials when necessary.
- Find resources for your classroom, such as using recycled materials, asking parents to provide and construct items, and beginning your own collection of scraps and inexpensive items.

It goes without saying that an important aspect of the learning environment has to do with the materials available for children's use. Table 7.1 provides guidelines for safe and appropriate materials for children of all ages.

In the following section, we explore how to design the social learning environment.

THE SOCIAL LEARNING ENVIRONMENT

The **social learning environment,** the relationships that affect how children think, feel, and act, needs the same attention as the physical environment. The social environment impacts children's social skills, academic success, and brain development. It also dictates how safe children feel to take risks and express their ideas, how valued children feel, and how engaged they can be as learners (National Scientific Council on the Developing Child, 2004; Hyson, 2008; Jacobs & Crowley, 2010). Children of all ages need a safe, secure, and welcoming environment in order to learn. Appropriate social learning environments include a **caring community of learners** and are **culturally responsive.**

A CARING COMMUNITY OF LEARNERS

At the beginning of this chapter (see pp. 166–167), we noted the importance of a caring community of learners as an essential part of the *social environment*. You might want to re-read that section now as we elaborate on those ideas here. A community

Table 7.1 Guidelines for Selecting Appropriate Materials for Children of All Ages

AGE	GUIDELINES	APPROPRIATE MATERIALS
Infants (0–1 year)	• equipment should be sized appropriately • too large to swallow • washable • brightly colored • free of small or removable parts • free of sharp edges and toxic material • nonelectric and durable • soft and varied textures • rounded and smooth edges on furnishings	• soft cloth and thick cardboard books, musical toys • push-pull toys, infant bouncers • simple rattles, teethers, sturdy cloth toys, squeeze-and-squeak toys, colorful mobiles, activity boxes for the crib • soft rubber blocks, dolls, animals • soft hand puppets • tactile toys
Toddlers (1–3 years)	• nonelectric • painted with lead-free paint • easily cleaned • cannot pinch or catch hair • too large to swallow • no glass or brittle plastic • suited to child's skills, and the right size and weight • helps child learn new skills and practice learned skills	• simple picture books and poems about familiar places and people • toys to push and pull such as wagons, doll buggies • ride-on toys • low slides and climbers, tunnels for crawling, variety of balls • dressing dolls, activity boxes, simple puzzles with large knobs • stacking toys, sandbox toys, finger-paints
Preschoolers and Kindergartners (3–5 years)	• durable, nontoxic, flame retardant • designed to promote children's large and small muscle development • designed to foster children's interest and skills in literacy • nonelectric • designed to enhance children's interest in adult roles, growing imaginations, and increasing motor skills	• props for imaginative play (e.g., old clothes, hats, cookware) • puzzles • art materials and media • simple board games • wheeled vehicles • woodworking sets (hammer, preschool nails) • sewing materials • bead-stringing materials
School-Age Children (6–8 years)	• require involvement and concentration • expand children's school experiences (e.g., computers, planting) • suited to individual's skill level to promote interest	• simple card games • simple board and table games (e.g., Bingo) • collector's items (e.g., shells, rocks) • sports equipment (e.g., for baseball, hockey)

Sources: Data from Copple & Bredekamp, 2009; Isenberg & Jalongo, 2010.

Brain research confirms that relationships can either support or hinder children's sense of well-being.

of caring teaches the *whole child* through the messages the learning environment sends, through *caring adults* who create a trusting community with the words and actions they intentionally use, and through *caring children* who respect themselves, their peers, their learning, and their learning environment (Falk, 2009; Noddings, 1992, 2002). The environment sends the message, "This is how we do things here." Caring adults are intentionally mindful of the *language* they use and the *relationships* they foster so children believe in their abilities to succeed. They are mindful of the impact of their *language*—their tone of voice, the words they use, and nonverbal language, such as facial expressions or other body language that conveys respect. They are equally mindful of the quality of *relationships* because brain research confirms that relationships can either support or negate children's sense of well-being (Bransford, Brown, & Cocking, 1999; Shonkoff & Phillips, 2000). Adults can teach care through modeling, practice, dialogue, confirmation, and, most of all, knowing children well (Noddings, 2002). Holding class meetings, acknowledging each child every day, and speaking with genuine respect are some examples of how to create caring communities of learners. In the words of Nel Noddings, "The time spent on learning to care . . . is not time taken away from academic instruction. Kids who are friendly, happy, and cooperative tackle their academic work with more confidence, and both teachers and students enjoy greater success" (2002, p. 2).

A CULTURALLY RESPONSIVE ENVIRONMENT

A *culturally responsive* social learning environment helps children understand and appreciate their own backgrounds as well as the backgrounds of others. It reflects both the home culture and group culture of the families of the children and acknowledges the need for culturally diverse students to find meaningful connections between themselves, their learning tasks, and their learning environment (Gay, 2000; Montgomery, 2001; Villegas & Lucas, 2002). Culturally responsive classrooms invite children into the learning process, use the strengths the children bring with them, and improve children's ability to be successful in school.

Children begin to notice differences early; therefore, the classroom environment should reflect the lives of its children and families. Just as your lifestyle and home suit your needs, culture, and community, so, too, should the setting in which children learn. What would a culturally responsive environment look like? It might include posters on the walls that represent the cultures of the children in the room; a dramatic play center with dolls, toys, and books from a variety of cultures; and a classroom library containing a rich selection of books and music from many cultures (Harms et al., 2004; Jalongo, 2007; Montgomery, 2001; Wortham, 2010). It would also ensure that each child shows a sense of family pride, expresses understanding of human differences, recognizes and describes unfairness, and develops the ability to denounce prejudice and discrimination

Pause and
Reflect

About the Indoor Environment

Consider one of the floor plans shown in Figures 7.2, 7.3, or 7.4. Describe at least three features of high-quality indoor learning environments that you notice. What message does the room convey about the teacher's values? What changes could you suggest to make it more inviting and appropriate for young children?

Figure 7.9 What to Look for in a Culturally Responsive Environment

Classroom Climate
- Children's artwork is visually present and displayed.
- Centers and play areas have ethnically diverse materials.
- Classroom displays represent the families of the children.
- Displays acknowledge and celebrate every child's efforts.

Materials
- Books explore a variety of cultural traditions and a range of culturally diverse literature.
- Toys and materials reflect the cultural backgrounds of the children.
- Content area materials represent the cultural and linguistic backgrounds of the children in your classroom and of other major cultures.
- Learning materials depict a variety of cultures, roles, family lifestyles, and disabilities.

Activities
- Children have rich oral language experiences in their home language.
- Experiences reflect family traditions, such as family recipes, family photo collages, and class books about weekend routines.
- Children are encouraged to learn about others' cultures through such activities as family-facts games, family cookbooks, and video exchanges.
- Children use the Internet to communicate in their native language with children from similar linguistic and cultural backgrounds.

Teacher's Role
- Teachers support children's home language and many different ways to communicate.
- Teachers provide a range of books and songs that represent the children's home language.
- Teachers invite families to share traditions and stories of their home cultures.
- Teachers take time to understand cultures other than their own and plan a variety of multicultural experiences.

Sources: Data from Corson, 2001; Montgomery, 2001; NAEYC, 2005a, 2005b.

(Derman-Sparks & Edwards, 2010). Figure 7.9 lists tips to enhance positive classroom climate, materials, activities, and teachers' roles.

In addition to creating appropriate physical and social environments, a high-quality environment also includes your ability to create environments that build children's healthy bodies and healthy minds. To help you in this area, in the following section, we discuss the important role of nutrition and fitness in your classroom.

Nutrition and Fitness A major objective of Goal 1 of the *Goals 2000: Educate America Act* (U.S. Department of Education, 1994) is to ensure that all children receive the nutrition and care they need to build healthy bodies and healthy minds. The relation between nutrition and development (i.e., how nutrition contributes to children's development and learning) is clear; thus, in early childhood classrooms, building healthy nutrition and fitness habits is essential to children's optimal learning (NAEYC, 2006). In contrast, poor nutrition and fitness habits place children at serious risk for suboptimal learning. Standards and appropriate learning experiences for healthy nutrition and fitness are available in *Make Early Learning Standards Come Alive* (Gronlund, 2006). Two websites that offer appropriate lesson planning and assessment resources are www.mypyramid.gov, supported by the USDA, for resources for children in prekindergarten through fourth grade, and www.PEcentral.com. In addition, NAEYC (2006) and the American Alliance for Health, Physical Education, Recreation, and Dance (AAHPERD, 2006a, 2006b) recommend the following hands-on nutrition and fitness activities that support successful learning:

- **Integrate learning activities about nutrition and fitness.** Use seed catalogues and real vegetables to explore, taste, and talk about the nutritional value of different vegetables. The class might also want to make vegetable soup. Incorporate health-related fitness activities across the curriculum, such as movement both indoors and outdoors and "brain breaks," to ensure good physical fitness in your classroom (Picar, 2006).
- **Learn about diverse cultures.** Use the cultural backgrounds of children in your classroom as a theme for the day's snacks, meals, or cooking experiences. Explore the different cultural influences on food. At the same time, engage children in movement and dance activities that also support children's cultural backgrounds.
- **Plan a balance of indoor and outdoor physical activities.** Activities such as jumping, pulling, walking at different paces, playing tag, stretching, reaching, or hanging support children's control, balance, strength, and coordination.
- **Visit local markets.** Help children become aware of how food is grown and sold in places other than a supermarket.
- **Use replicas of healthy food.** Place pictures and models of fruits, vegetables, cheeses, and bread in the dramatic play area that serve as good examples for play related to foods.
- **Serve nutritious snacks and meals** in an atmosphere that encourages social or self-help skills (Colker, 2005). Children enjoy sandwiches cut into shapes and finger foods such as apple slices, orange and grapefruit sections, dried fruit, cheese sticks, or celery and green bean slices.
- **Engage in pleasant interactions during snack and mealtimes.** These times encourage children to accept new foods and develop healthy eating habits. They are more pleasurable when food is served on a predictable but flexible schedule, when there are small portions of food and drink so children can ask for more, and when the conversation focuses on the children, not the food.

High-quality learning environments are safe, welcoming, and respectful. They include adults who acknowledge and understand children and who can meet their needs. These learning environments also are characterized by consistent, responsive adults and by children who feel assured that they will be secure and protected. In the next section we provide guidance on how to ensure these kinds of learning environments by regularly evaluating your indoor environment.

Evaluating the Indoor Environment

Periodic evaluation of your indoor environment helps you meet your learning outcomes. Some early childhood teachers use one of the many observational instruments (Harms et al., 2004; NICHD Early Child Care Research Network, 2002; Pianta, LaParo, & Hamre, 2005) to assess the quality of their environments as related to child outcomes. Whatever criteria you use, when assessing your environment, consider the *physical*

Figure 7.10 Checklist for Evaluating Your Indoor Environment

Does the Physical Environment   Yes   No

✓ Have large spaces for the whole group to meet comfortably?

✓ Provide medium spaces for small-group instruction that are
   far enough apart to reduce interference?

✓ Have small spaces where two or three children can work together?

✓ Offer quiet spaces for individual tasks and privacy?

✓ Provide soft spaces with rugs, pillows, or cushions that
   make the room warm and inviting?

✓ Provide materials that are easily accessible, aesthetically
   pleasing, and organized, and that invite exploration?

✓ Have an ample supply of open-ended materials to
   challenge thinking and prevent frustration?

✓ Have a range of culturally sensitive materials?

✓ Consider safety in available materials, supplies, and equipment?

✓ Use moveable walls, furniture, or bookcases to divide centers?

✓ Label interest areas clearly?

Does the Social Environment   Yes   No

✓ Display children's work attractively at eye level throughout the room?

✓ Display positively worded signs and messages?

✓ Represent the children's lives and interests throughout the room
   with work samples, photographs, sketches, and cultural artifacts?

✓ Use language that is welcoming, accepting, and responsive
   to all children, families, and adults?

✓ Encourage children to work together?

✓ Demonstrate warm, positive relationships and support children's
   friendships?

✓ Invite the participation of all children?

---

characteristics, such as room arrangement, light, and time; the *social characteristics*, such as the cultural backgrounds and needs of the children; and the *unique qualities of the local community*, such as neighborhood safety, that affect the children. Noted expert Thelma Harms discusses the importance of assessing environments in the Ask the Expert piece on page 188, and Figure 7.10 is a checklist to evaluate your indoor environment.

Organizing Outdoor Learning Environments

Organizing the outdoor environment is as essential as organizing the indoor environment, yet it is often neglected. Outdoor environments stimulate children's thinking and ability to solve problems, make decisions, socialize, and try new ideas in ways

Ask the EXPERT — *Thelma Harms*

Assessing Learning Environments

Q: Why should I devote so much time to planning my environment?

A: The learning environment significantly influences all aspects of children's development. Quality environments must meet all three basic needs of children: protection of their health and safety, emotional and social support, and meaningful opportunities for learning. Yet many programs focus on only one of these needs and largely ignore the other two. For example, offering exciting hands-on activities is part of a high-quality program for children, but it cannot by itself meet children's equally important needs for warm nurturance or protection from illness and injury. That is why the four widely used classroom assessment instruments my colleagues and I have developed contain items to cover all three basic components of quality: protection, emotional support, and opportunities for learning. These scales, the Early Childhood Environment Rating Scale Revised (ECERS-R), the Infant/Toddler Environment Rating Scale Revised (ITERS-R), the Family Child Care Environment Rating Scale Revised (FCCERS-R), and the School Age Care Environment Rating Scale (SACERS), are comprehensive process quality assessments.

Q: Do I need to use a comprehensive assessment instrument to evaluate my own classroom environment?

A: Educators get a more objective picture of the actual quality of their classroom by using a comprehensive assessment instrument with proven reliability and validity. There are now a number of classroom observation instruments that teachers can use as *self-assessment guides*. For example, national quality recognition programs such as NAEYC Center Accreditation and the National Association for Family Child Care (NAFCC) Accreditation, as well as the Child Development Associate (CDA) Credentialing, all include classroom observation instruments.

An observation with any assessment instrument must be accurate and objective to be helpful. Therefore, in order to get the greatest benefit from a classroom self-assessment, teachers should:

- Be trained on the instrument to understand and use the scoring system accurately.
- Read the instrument thoroughly and make sure they understand all the requirements.
- Get someone else, preferably an outsider who knows the instrument well, to observe the classroom at about the same time as the self-assessment is done.
- Compare and discuss their scores and insights with those of the outside observer.

Q: If I use an environment assessment tool, will it help me be a better teacher?

A: To improve the daily practices in the classroom, information observed during assessment of the environment provides a good basis for planning and implementing change. Research has shown that high-quality learning environments result in children's better social and intellectual development. Since an accurate observation based assessment provides specific information about actual practices, it can serve as a good baseline from which to plan for improvement. Making significant changes in a classroom environment requires the active involvement of both teachers and administrators. Schedules may need to be modified, new materials purchased, and additional training provided. By getting the whole team working together to reach more immediate short-term goals, an ongoing improvement process is initiated that can result in achieving more challenging long-term goals.

Thelma Harms is Research Professor Emerita and Director of Curriculum Development, Frank Porter Graham Child Development Institute, University of North Carolina, Chapel Hill, and President of the Environment Rating Scales Institute, Inc.

that are often different from those in indoor environments. To maximize children's learning outdoors, the outdoor environment must be as enriching as the indoor environment. High-quality outdoor environments focus on equipment and materials that hold children's interest over time to promote their motor development, cardiovascular endurance, enjoyment of the outdoors, and their thinking; are safe in their design, construction, and supervision to minimize accidents yet also offer motor challenges; and house materials that are easily accessible to children and easily stored for teachers to facilitate their activity. The outdoor environment should provide children with the following:

- a wide range of activities, such as gross motor activities, pretend play, and group games
- plenty of well-organized space, such as sand and water areas, natural gardens, and pathways for wheeled vehicles
- easy access from the indoor environment and a secure enclosure for outdoor space
- adult supervision from many vantage points
- unstructured, movable equipment and materials for use in different areas
- aesthetic surroundings, including plants and well-cared-for equipment
- defined areas for different activities and easy movement between play areas, such as digging and constructing, role playing and enactment, mixing and pouring, and painting and splashing (Frost et al., 2008; Rivkin, 2002; Wellhousen, 2002)

All children need outdoor time every day, weather permitting (Copple & Bredekamp, 2009; Frost et al., 2008; Gronlund, 2006). Outdoor play is beneficial for children's brain development through frequent opportunities to move (Frost et al., 2008). It also benefits children's physical development through physical exercise and play that helps children enjoy vigorous and healthy movement activity.

For young children, carefully planned and supervised daily outdoor activities are important for their total development. Older children usually have scheduled recess for an entire grade or grade level, and many primary-grade teachers use the outdoors to teach specific lessons in social studies and science. The rules of a caring classroom community also apply outdoors.

Research on children's health and fitness identifies a decline in children's physical fitness, an increase in childhood obesity and related diseases, more sedentary activity, and a decrease in recess and physical education (Frost et al., 2008). Read the Ask the Expert feature on page 190, which recounts Joe Frost's views on children's play and playgrounds and why children need a well-planned outdoor play environment. Notice his mention of playground design, safety, and the appropriate role of the adult in the outdoor environment.

Physical motor play is important for children at every age.

Ask the EXPERT — Joe Frost

Outdoor Environments

Q: Do children need adult-designed playgrounds?

A: Today's children do need planned playgrounds to compensate for crowded conditions in urban areas, to provide reasonably safe play areas, and to help ensure that children play. Children reared in rural areas have ample places and opportunities to play in rich natural environments filled with hills, streams, vegetation, and animals. In these environments, there is less threat from the hazards of cities—crime, traffic, and drugs. In urban areas, however, natural play spaces are limited or nonexistent. We must create spaces for urban children, including well-designed environments at schools, in public parks, and in children's museums. *Well-designed* means incorporating many of the advantages of the countryside into these built environments.

Q: Must national playground safety standards result in boring playgrounds?

A: The growing emphasis on national safety guidelines and standards for playground equipment *can* contribute to "cookie-cutter," boring playgrounds, which were the norm throughout the last half of the 20th century. The mentality that focused on limited conceptions of play in earlier periods unfortunately is alive and well today, but a growing number of contemporary playgrounds are light years ahead of those of even a decade ago. The most authoritative national play equipment guidelines and standards apply to standard equipment, for example, climbers, slides, and swings. The elements that most influence creative play—nature areas, gardens, storage facilities, building materials, pets, and water and sand areas—are virtually untouched by playground standards. Continuing revision of national safety standards and state regulations is resulting in inconsistencies between national and state requirements, growing complications in interpretation and litigation, and is contributing to the decline of school recess. Playground safety standards at all levels sorely need reexamination, simplification, and clarity.

Q: What is the appropriate role of adults in children's play?

A: Several European countries, notably England, Sweden, and Denmark, surpass the United States in understanding how adults can best contribute to children's play. Over the past decade, they moved from the concept of "play leader" (one who leads children in play) to the present conception of "play worker" (one who interacts with children in a play atmosphere of cooperation and respect). The basic premise for play work is that children's play is free—freely chosen by the child, yet supported by adults who ensure that children have many opportunities for play in rich, reasonably safe environments. Adults provide the materials and places for play, allow ample time for play, and interact cooperatively about play, leaving the lead in play roles to children. Perhaps the most fundamental requirement for adults in enhancing children's play is that they value and understand play and allow children freedom to shape their own play worlds.

Joe Frost is the Parker Centennial Professor Emeritus, University of Texas, Austin, TX.

Figure 7.11 Checklist for Evaluating Your Outdoor Environment

Questions to Consider: Does the Outdoor Environment	Yes	No
✓ Provide appropriate spaces for individuals and small groups of children according to their ages, physical sizes, interests, and abilities?		
✓ Have places for games and paths for wheeled toys?		
✓ Contain interesting and challenging play spaces for climbing, swinging, and balancing?		
✓ Offer a pleasant area to enjoy the natural elements and a visually appealing look?		
✓ Provide varied ground surfaces such as hardtop for games and vehicles, grass, soft mulch, or sand?		
✓ Offer easy access to coats, toilets, and drinking fountains?		
✓ Have shaded areas, benches, tables, and support materials for group activities?		
✓ Promote independent and creative use of flexible materials such as sand and water?		
✓ Provide materials for gross motor and fine motor development?		
✓ Provide for children's interactions with materials, peers, and adults?		
✓ Have adults actively supervising?		
✓ Have accessibility, materials, and equipment for children of all abilities and disabilities?		
✓ Meet the physical and neurological needs of all children?		

EVALUATING THE OUTDOOR ENVIRONMENT

As with indoor environments, evaluating your outdoor environment will help you meet your learning outcomes. You will want to consider the *space*, such as play areas, groupings, surfacing, and shade; *materials*, such as active, quiet, flexible usage, and variety; *experiences*, such as interactions, gross motor, fine motor, and cardiovascular; and *safety*, such as supervision, materials in good repair, cushioning materials, and no litter. Figure 7.11 is a checklist to evaluate high-quality outdoor learning environments.

The Inclusive Environment

Today, children with exceptionalities have the same access to public education as all other children. It is likely that you will have an **inclusive environment,** one that will have children with exceptionalities learning alongside their typically developing peers. Children with exceptionalities need the same type of learning environments as other children, even though they may have different developmental needs (Division for Early Childhood and NAEYC, 2009; Gargiulo & Metcalf, 2010). They may, however, need changes in the amount or arrangement of *space* and *materials*, or require a different kind of *access* to areas in the classroom. For example, lofts may not be appropriate for a child with a physical disability, and using a pictured schedule may help a child with autism negotiate the day more successfully (McWilliams, Wolery, & Odom, 2001).

In adapting the inclusive learning environment, you may either add something that is not there, use something that is already there in a different way, modify the schedule so that all children can participate, or adjust adults' usual roles and routines. Before making any modifications, be sure to contact the families about the child, the special need, or the special equipment (Copple & Bredekamp, 2009; Gargiulo & Metcalf, 2010, Harms et al., 2004). Following are some suggestions for adapting the environment for children with particular special needs.

ADAPTING ENVIRONMENTS FOR CHILDREN WITH LIMITED MOTOR ABILITIES

Limited motor ability applies to children whose ability to move negatively affects that child's participation in an activity. This could be the result of cerebral palsy, spina bifida, or a child in a wheelchair either temporarily or permanently. These children need access in the classroom. The following are suggestions for adapting the environment for children with limited motor abilities (Allen & Cowdery, 2009; Diener, 2010; Gargiulo & Metcalf, 2010):

- **Access.** Be sure children can enter the building and classroom through wide paths, doorways, and walkways. Have low sinks, water fountains, and table surfaces for a child in a wheelchair. Put lever-style handles on faucets and doors for simpler operating movements than those required by traditional knobs and faucets.
- **Circle time.** Children with limited motor abilities often have difficulty finding a place to sit and see. You can have all children sit on chairs at circle time, keeping everybody's eye level the same and making the child in a wheelchair feel "less different."
- **Art.** Coloring, drawing, and illustrating are difficult skills for these children because of poor fine motor skills or inability to reach the materials and equipment. You might provide a variety of more-accessible areas and surfaces for children to paint on, such as a window, a wall, or the back of a divider.
- **Books.** Many children have difficulty turning the pages or cannot reach the books from the bookshelves. You can arrange shelves at different levels so the books are accessible to everybody; provide headphones and tapes so children can listen to the stories; or provide books in several areas of the classroom, especially if your regular classroom library is in a loft or other inaccessible place.
- **Computers and technology.** Technology for children with limited motor abilities is often easily adaptable. Try touch-sensitive computer screens, hand-held devices, and voice-input computers; place stickers on keyboard keys for a particular program to help children locate keys more easily, or set a template over the keyboard so only certain keys show. Be sure that the input speed allows plenty of time for children to respond to the software programs.
- **Space.** Entrances to centers need to be wide and free from materials for children who are in wheelchairs or who need a walker. Table height can be adjusted so a wheelchair can fit underneath. Adjusting legs on large pieces of equipment, such as an easel, will make activities accessible to more children.

ADAPTING ENVIRONMENTS FOR CHILDREN WITH SENSORY IMPAIRMENTS

Children with sensory impairments need multisensory experiences to feel like a part of the learning environment. Allen and Cowdery (2009) and Diener (2010) suggest the following adaptations for a more inclusive environment:

- **Vision.** Use brightly colored boxes to hold objects for discussion. Illustrate main events of the day on your daily schedule. Use tactile and auditory cues for children to find their way around the room.

COLLABORATING WITH
Families

Why Use Learning Centers?

Ms. Davis uses centers as an important part of her learning environment. Because family members are often unfamiliar with centers, at the first open house for families Ms. Davis plans a "mini" center time for the adults. Participating in a center activity helps family members get a flavor of what and how their children learn at school. The adults use the posted center directions that are translated into the home languages of the children to complete the center activities. Here is what the sign in the **Science Center** said:

Materials:

> **Electricity Box:** an open box with batteries, wires, switches, small light bulbs, and magnets; a small basket with a variety of familiar objects; an old radio and tools to take it apart

> **Discovery Area:** assorted leaves, pods and cones, twigs, acorns, tree barks and pieces of wood from trees, magnifying glasses of different sizes, balance scale, clipboards, markers, pencils, books about trees and leaves

Purpose: The more young children know about and understand their world, the more they become independent, confident learners. The *Science Center* is designed to encourage children to ask questions, to look for answers, to experiment, and to engage in the scientific method of learning. It sends a message to children that thinking about new ideas is important. When children finish their investigations in the center, they show what they are learning in pictures, words, writing, or constructions with others.

> **Task 1:** Use the materials in the Electricity Box to figure out more than one way to make the light bulb shine.

> **Task 2:** Observe the natural found objects using the magnifying glass. What similarities and differences do you notice? Compare the appearances of the objects by using words to describe the color, shape, texture, or size of the objects. Record your observations in the journal. What questions do you have? Look in some of the books to find your answers.

Conclusion: What did you notice about your experience? What do you want to know more about?

> **Note:** We also have sample activity kits for the natural found objects that your child can bring home. Each kit includes:
>
> > An assortment of small tree parts in a ziplock bag
> >
> > A picture or a photo story on DVD of related classroom activity
> >
> > Picture book, *Leaf Man* (Ehlert, 2005) and poem about trees
> >
> > Journal or observation log to record or draw about experience at home
> >
> > Directions that include some activities to do at home such as making a leaf man or a leaf collage; sorting, counting, and weighing objects; or drawing pictures of what the children see with their eyes and with a magnifying glass.

Encourage your child to bring one home!

- **Hearing.** Vary the tone of your voice and the pace of your talk. Make sure you have audiotapes of sounds in children's natural environments such as the cafeteria or the school bus. Check for a blinking light on the fire alarm in case of emergency.
- **Touch.** Use a "talking wand," a small tube held by the child who is speaking and then passed on to others so that the speaker is clearly identifiable. Make sure you introduce all new materials before adding them to the centers for children's exploration and use.
- **Smell.** Add scented items to containers with perforated tops and have a "smell and tell" instead of "show and tell" on some days.

ADAPTING ENVIRONMENTS FOR CHILDREN WITH DIVERSE ACADEMIC NEEDS

Every early childhood classroom has children with a range of academic abilities. Following are some suggestions for meeting the diverse academic needs of each child:

- **Space.** Have a quiet place for children who are easily distracted, need to calm themselves down, or work on a task independently.
- **Time.** Allow sufficient time for all children to process and complete their play and work. Some may need more time to clean up, finish a project, or move from one activity to another before beginning preparation for the next activity.
- **Transitions.** Moving from one activity to another or from one space to another creates difficulty for some children. Some may need specific instructions and practice with transition behaviors, such as where to put away materials and how to move quietly from one area to the next. Others may need you to reiterate what the next activity will be. You may need to give several notices that the activity will soon end before using an abrupt transition warning such as a light or bell. The efforts you make to modify your environment to include all children can result in a new level of learning for all children and adults in the environment.

Summary

- The learning environment includes the organization of physical space, the relationships between and among the people, and the content, values, and goals of a particular classroom. High-quality learning environments have a variety of opportunities for children to become part of a caring community of learners; have an organized, challenging, and aesthetically pleasing classroom; reflect clear goals and outcomes; protect children's health and safety; and provide age appropriate materials and equipment.

- Your role as an early childhood teacher is to create a respectful and challenging learning environment by arranging space to meet the needs of all learners, selecting appropriate materials, using time flexibly, affirming diversity, caring about students and their learning, and connecting with children's families.

- The indoor learning environment is the place in which children acquire skills, concepts, attitudes, and values about the world and contains both the physical and social learning environment. The *physical learning environment* includes the use of space, the room arrangement, the schedule and routines, and the materials and equipment. An appropriate *social learning environment*—the relationships that affect how children think, feel, and act—has a caring community of learners and is culturally responsive.

- High-quality outdoor learning environments have equipment and materials that hold children's interest over time to promote their motor development, cardiovascular endurance, enjoyment of the outdoors, and their thinking; are safe in their design, construction, and supervision to minimize accidents yet also offer motor challenges; and house materials that are easily accessible to children and easily stored for teachers to facilitate their activity. Outdoor environments stimulate children's thinking and ability to solve problems, make decisions, socialize, and try new ideas in ways that are often different from those in indoor environments.

- Adapting the learning environment for children with exceptionalities may mean changes in the amount or arrangement of *space* and *materials*, or may require a different kind of *access* to areas in the classroom. In planning inclusive learning environments, you will want to make some adaptations by either adding something that is not there, using something that is already there in a different way, modifying the schedule so that all children can participate, or adjusting adults' usual roles and routines.

Applying Your Knowledge of Environments

In Assessment Activity 1, apply your knowledge of high-quality learning environments to what you would do as Robert's teacher. Then, in Assessment Activity 2, apply your understanding of learning environments by re-reading Thelma Harms's Ask the Expert feature on early childhood environments (page 188) and responding to the two questions.

Assessment ACTIVITY (1) CREATING A SENSORY-RICH ENVIRONMENT FOR ROBERT

Four-year-old Robert goes willingly to preschool, usually plays by himself, and does not often participate in group activities. At a conference with Robert's mother, Ms. Green, Robert's teacher shared her concerns about Robert's difficulty in paying attention, calming down, and approaching his peers to play. She also mentioned his underdeveloped fine motor coordination that makes his handwriting look very immature. Ms. Green suggested that Robert's mother arrange some play dates to help his social development and work on some fine motor tasks at home.

Robert's mother knew some of her son's behaviors were unusual, but she did not know how to help him. She knew that Robert played alone often at preschool, and rarely liked to go home after school in anyone else's car. Robert still sucked his fingers, walked on his toes, and did not speak clearly.

Meanwhile, Robert's pediatrician referred him to an occupational therapist (OT), who identified Robert as having a sensory processing disorder (SPD), a complex disorder of the brain that makes children misinterpret everyday sensory information, such as touch, sound, stringing beads, and movement. This can lead to behavioral issues and difficulties with coordination.

Robert began weekly occupational therapy sessions during which he engaged in sensory-rich activities involving touch, pressure, and movement in a safe and comfortable environment to help his body properly learn how to "read" sensory information. The OT also suggested that Robert's mother schedule an evaluation with the county Child Find office. Following a comprehensive assessment, here is what Robert's mother learned.

The Child Find team noted that Robert's s delayed social and emotional development clearly is interfering with his ability to interact with his peers and his ability to feel confident in himself. His difficulty in attending to tasks makes it appear as though he is not cooperating or not understanding, when in reality, he just needs assistance in organizing or planning his task. Personal or small-group instruction where each step of the expected task is clearly stated and demonstrated, if possible, will keep Robert from becoming overwhelmed and allow him to learn the components of the project, which he can then internalize and draw on for future use. The Child Find team and the private OT recommended a balance of sensory activities, such as a variety of tactile experiences like using small table blocks and eating foods with different textures; motor experiences such as climbing and crawling through tunnels; spatial awareness experiences such as playing catch, or hammering golf tees into thick Styrofoam; visual experiences such as playing flashlight tag, and playing board games; and auditory experiences such as drawing to music, or humming.

As a result of the consultations with Robert's mother, Ms. Green realized that her environment needed to better support Robert's attempts to interact with others and to be successful with academic tasks. Ms. Green first lowered the noise level in the classroom to keep background noise from interfering with instruction. She also read books to the class about how to be a good friend, and during stations, Ms. Green created small groups instead of letting the children divide themselves into groups. She noted that her discussion of friendships and grouping children with peers they may not have chosen to play with greatly reduced the "cliques" in class and enriched the experience of many other children as well. While Ms. Green made sure that either she or her assistant was available to help Robert get started on a new task or activity, she also wanted to work on purposeful play and planning with the entire class. She used the plan-do-review method (Hohman & Weikart, 1995), which involved having the whole class talk about the next activity, such as going to a learning station, *plan* what they wanted to do, *do* the activity, and then *review* it as a class to see if they really did what they had planned to do.

REACT	Think about how the perspectives of Ms. Green, Robert's mother, and the occupational therapist are alike and different. What might be some reasons? With whom do you most identify?
RESEARCH	Interview two teachers about their learning environments. Find out how they 1. encourage children's social interactions with one another; 2. organize a challenging and pleasing classroom that meets the needs of all learners; 3. arrange space and select materials; and 4. respond to children who appear not to focus and attend to directions. Compare the teachers' responses with the essential features of high-quality environments described in Figure 7.1. What conclusion can you draw from your interviews?
REFLECT	What assumptions about children who need support in making friends and initiating and maintaining peer interactions do Ms. Green, Robert's mother, and the occupational therapist make? Using the data gathered from your interviews, generate some ways you can more appropriately respond to children like Robert in your class.

Assessment ACTIVITY 2   CREATING A HIGH-QUALITY LEARNING ENVIRONMENT

Read the Ask the Expert feature by Thelma Harms, Assessing Learning Environments, presented earlier in this chapter. Respond to the following points that Harms makes about high-quality environments by answering the two questions that follow. Then, share your responses with a partner.

- High-quality environments meet three basic needs of children: health and safety protection, emotional and social support protection, and meaningful opportunities for learning.
- Early childhood educators can get a more objective picture of the actual quality of their classroom by using a comprehensive assessment instrument, with proven reliability and validity, to guide their classroom. To improve daily practices in the classroom, information observed during assessments provides a good basis for planning and implementing change.

1. What do you think of these ideas?
2. Do you think you could implement them? Discuss why or why not.

ONLINE RESOURCES FOR HIGH-QUALITY LEARNING ENVIRONMENTS

Children's Health and Safety: Provides resources and ideas for children's health and fitness in the classroom. www.kidshealth.org

To download or listen to resources on playground safety in Spanish and English, go to http://kidshealth.org/parent/fitness/safety/playground.html.

Design Share: An international site that provides access to a variety of ideas for improving space for all learners and descriptions of award-winning early learning environments. www.designshare.com

To download a fact sheet on 12 design principles based on brain-based learning research, go to www.designshare.com/Research/BrainBasedLearn98.htm.

Learning Centers

Busy Teachers Café: Provides ideas and resources for content and activities for learning centers. www.busyteacherscafe.com/

National Network for Child Care: Provides extensive resources and publications for child care and early childhood development. www.nncc.org/

PreK Now: Provides access to information on high-quality preschools and has state-by-state information on high-quality prekindergarten programs. www.preknow.org

To take a virtual tour showing the important features of high-quality learning environments, go to www.preknow.org/resource/classroomtour.cfm.

Quiet Classrooms: Provides information on reducing noise levels in schools and classrooms. www.quietclassrooms.org/

PEARSON
myeducationlab

Go to Topic 7 (Curriculum/Content Areas) in the MyEducationLab (**www.myeducationlab.com**) for your course, where you can:

- Find learning outcomes for curriculum/content areas along with the national standards that connect to these outcomes.
- Complete Assignments and Activities that can help you more deeply understand the chapter content.
- Apply and practice your understanding of the core teaching skills identified in the chapter with the Building Teaching Skills and Dispositions learning units.
- Examine challenging situations and cases presented in the IRIS Center Resources.

CHAPTER 8

Developing Curriculum

 Teachers are the agents through which knowledge and skills are
communicated and rules of conduct enforced.

John Dewey, 1938, p. 18

YVETTE EAGLE is the new director of a rural child-care center. At a recent conference, Yvette was sharing her new role with her colleagues: "At this point, I must implement a curriculum with an existing staff that is not used to viewing curriculum as a plan to guide children's learning rather than a series of unrelated, cute activities." Yvette believes that curriculum should reflect children's physical, social, emotional, language, and cognitive needs. Her biggest challenge is convincing her teachers that curriculum development is an important responsibility.

MS. ORNSTEIN teaches a full-day kindergarten class. An important part of Ms. Ornstein's curriculum is having her kindergartners record and chart their completed work to share with the group each day. On one particular day, Lukas was constructing a plane from his woodworking plan, Juan was recording his favorite part of *Peter Rabbit* after listening to the story on audiotape, and Elena drew a picture of the solar system that looked like a puzzle she had just completed and recorded the names of the people who helped her. Having children record and chart their work each day "offers children an important way to communicate their ideas to others and to make sense of their experiences to themselves."

MS. BLACKER is a third-grade teacher who uses "lots of whole-group teaching for basic-skills instruction." While taking a graduate class on curriculum in early childhood, she learned that teaching mathematical skills in isolation can be confusing to many children and that children need to apply mathematical operations to real-life situations. So, Ms. Blacker provided experiences for children to learn math by doing math. She developed small-group activities with pattern blocks and invited children to observe, experiment, and discover answers to questions about particular characteristics of the pattern blocks. They shared their findings with their peers and reused the pattern blocks in different ways after listening to classmates' ideas. The more Ms. Blacker used authentic situations to teach math concepts, the clearer she saw how each student made better connections to larger mathematical concepts.

LEARNING Outcomes

In this chapter, you will learn to:

→ **Define curriculum and tell why it is important**

→ **Explore your role in developing curriculum** (NAEYC #5, INTASC #1, ACEI #2)

→ **Explain approaches to the written curriculum**

→ **Describe different ways to approach the taught curriculum** (NAEYC #5b)

→ **Understand curriculum theory and theorists**

→ **Apply your knowledge of curriculum to early childhood classrooms** (NAEYC #5c)

Compare
What do these teachers know about children that guides their curriculum decisions?

Contrast
How do these teachers differ in their ideas about the curriculum?

Connect
What aspects of curriculum do you think you will look for when you begin observing teachers of young children?

Now that you have reflected on the three teachers' perspectives and noted the learning outcomes, we preview the knowledge, skills, and dispositions you will need in order to fulfill your role in developing curriculum.

A Definition of Curriculum

The **curriculum** is the pathway of education; it is what children actually experience in schools from arrival to departure and reflects the philosophy, goals, objectives, and child outcomes of the program, classroom, or school district. According to Copple and Bredekamp (2009), curriculum "consists of the knowledge, skills, abilities, and understandings children are to acquire and the plans for the learning experiences through which those gains will occur" (p. 20). The curriculum includes what children are expected to learn **(content)**, how children will learn it **(instruction)**, when the material is best learned **(timing)**, and documentation that children have learned the stated objectives **(assessment)** (Bredekamp, 2009; Copple & Bredekamp, 2009; Henson, 2010). In other words, a curriculum is a plan for what children need to learn in schools, how and when they will learn it, and ways to teach it.

In its written form, the curriculum sets the goals and objectives, defines the content, identifies learning experiences and teaching strategies, and chooses assessment methods that support children's learning. In its taught form, the curriculum is what you see the teacher doing to make the written curriculum come alive. Simply stated, what we teach differs from how we teach it and how children experience it. Early childhood professionals incorporate research and theory about children's development and learning, best practices, different program models, and standards in their definition of curriculum. Ultimately, however, the curriculum should help children develop the knowledge, skills, values, and dispositions they will need to become productive members of society.

The Importance of the Curriculum

It is common to think of curriculum only as standards and academic content, but there are other important dimensions. Although there are some local, state, and national curriculum standards that teachers are expected to follow, differences in teaching practices, differences in implementing legislated policies, and differences in testing emphasis lead to great variations in the quality of curriculum for children. A visitor could observe several early childhood professionals teaching the same lesson and notice very different ways of teaching as well as clear variations in what and how children are learning. What makes the difference is not the required content, but how each teacher plans and implements the curriculum. To develop a comprehensive and effective curriculum (Copple & Bredekamp, 2009), a teacher needs to consider not only the curriculum standards and content, but also the intent of all of the experiences children have while they are in school. In other words, there is a **written curriculum** (documents and standards) and a **taught curriculum** (the teacher's practices and tested curriculum).

Teachers develop curriculum according to their beliefs about children, teaching, and learning. Thus, your knowledge of the children and the content you will teach, your ability to provide for children's strengths and interests, and your attention to what is worth knowing are important criteria to consider in your curriculum. And the key ingredient for any curriculum is always the learner. Early childhood professionals can look to NAEYC's position paper *Developmentally Appropriate Practice in Early Childhood Programs* (Copple & Bredekamp, 2009) for guidance on making informed curriculum decisions for young children.

DEVELOPMENTALLY APPROPRIATE PRACTICE AND THE CURRICULUM

Developmentally appropriate practice is *not* a curriculum. Rather, it is a set of principles that center on what children know and can do. The core of developmentally appropriate practice is **intentionality,** the decisions that adults make on children's behalf that add up to "practice that promotes young children's optimal learning and development" (Copple & Bredekamp, 2009, p. 16). To make good decisions, teachers must consider what they know about (1) child development and learning, (2) each child as an individual, and (3) the social and cultural contexts in which each child lives.

Adults who work with children take into account children's needs and characteristics to set challenging and achievable goals for them (Copple & Bredekamp, 2009). First, adults make decisions based on what is known about how children typically develop and learn within a general age range as well as decisions about the environment, materials, activities, and interactions. Next, they consider each individual child by developing learning experiences that take into account children's strengths, interests, and needs and recognize that children learn in different ways and at different rates. And third, adults incorporate family needs, values, and cultural backgrounds. Treating children and families with respect is essential to making learning relevant to all learners (Copple & Bredekamp, 2006, 2009).

A curriculum based on these three elements of developmentally appropriate practice is likely to lead to an effective curriculum that early childhood teachers intentionally plan and that guides each child's learning. Note what Sue Bredekamp says about developmentally appropriate practice in the Ask the Expert feature on page 202.

WHAT DOES RESEARCH SAY ABOUT EFFECTIVE EARLY CHILDHOOD CURRICULA?

Studies of programs and practices that produce successful outcomes for all children suggest the following agreed-upon principles for effective curricula (Center on the Developing Child, 2007; Copple & Bredekamp, 2006, 2009; Landry, 2005; NAEYC,

DID YOU Know (?)

- Qualified teachers produce better student achievement, regardless of which curriculum materials, pedagogical approach, or reading program they use (Allington, 2002; National Center for Education Statistics, 2009).

- From research on the brain, we know that the curriculum must be meaningful to children so that children truly understand the content they are learning (Jensen, 2005).

- Teacher language—what we say to children and how we say it—is one of the most powerful aspects of the curriculum. It shapes children's understanding of content and also shapes their relationships, sense of responsibility, and ability to reason (Denton, 2007; Sternberg, 2008).

In a developmentally appropriate classroom, adults make decisions based on child development, individual development, and family and cultural backgrounds.

Sue Bredekamp

Developmentally Appropriate Practice

Q: What is developmentally appropriate practice?

A: *Developmentally appropriate practice* means teaching in ways that vary for and adapt to the age, experience, interests, and abilities of individual children within the age range for which they are intended. Accomplishing this goal requires that teachers: (1) meet children where they are, (2) help them reach challenging and achievable goals, and (3) draw on a wide repertoire of teaching strategies to help each child continue to make learning and developmental progress.

Q: Does developmentally appropriate practice mean watering down or oversimplifying what is taught to young children?

A: NAEYC continues to be concerned about the trend in schools toward "push-down curriculum," in which next-grade expectations are routinely pushed down to younger children. But this does not mean that they oppose rigorous, challenging curriculum content. To be developmentally appropriate, a curriculum must be not only achievable but also intellectually challenging and engaging, because the foundations for all later learning are laid during the early years of life. For example, later mathematics ability doesn't just build on earlier understandings, it depends on them. We now know that young children are capable of more sophisticated mathematics than we assumed in the past and that they enjoy mastering math. We also know that a mathematics achievement gap is present as early as preschool, and we therefore have an obligation to provide high-quality, developmentally appropriate mathematics as well as all other areas of the curriculum in early childhood programs. In addition, young children are naturally curious and eager to learn just about everything there is to know about their worlds.

Q: Can I use direct instruction in developmentally appropriate practice?

A: To help children achieve challenging learning and developmental goals, teachers must be intentional in everything they do, whether setting up the environment, planning curriculum, using a variety of learning contexts and grouping configurations, adapting teaching, or interacting with children. Effective teaching strategies include acknowledging and encouraging, modeling and demonstrating, supporting and facilitating, and providing specific information and directions. All of these strategies can be effective in either child-guided or teacher-guided learning experiences, as long as the teacher is intentional about the scaffolding provided.

Q: Does developmentally appropriate practice apply to children with exceptional needs?

A: One of the most well-known principles of human development is that there is a wide range of individual variation on every dimension; therefore, it is impossible to be developmentally appropriate without also being individually appropriate. Because each child in a developmentally appropriate program must be viewed as an individual for whom teachers assess, plan, and adapt the curriculum and teaching, developmentally appropriate programs are ideal environments in which to include children with disabilities or special learning needs. However, many children with exceptional needs will need more specialized instruction to achieve their individual goals.

Q: Is developmentally appropriate practice responsive to cultural and linguistic diversity of children and families?

A: The very idea that any set of practices could be called developmentally appropriate for all children is criticized because it assumes that there are universals of development irrespective of cultures. Because all development occurs in and is influenced by social and cultural contexts, early childhood programs cannot be developmentally appropriate unless they are also culturally appropriate.

Sue Bredekamp is an Early Childhood Education Consultant and Author, Washington, DC.

2003, 2009). These principles of practice apply to early childhood curricula for children from birth through age 8.

Effective curricula provide for all areas of a child's development. Early childhood curriculum focuses on the "whole child" (Barnett, 2008; Copple & Bredekamp, 2006, 2009; NAEYC, 2003, 2009). For example, the curriculum supports children's *physical development* through movement or small motor experiences; *social and emotional development* through working cooperatively in groups, and caring for each other and for materials; and *cognitive development* through acquiring the skills of reading, writing, and numeracy, and posing and answering questions about their world. Children's early learning experiences affect their performance in school and beyond. Research on brain development, indicates that during the first 10 years of life, a child's brain has already formed most of its lifetime connections (Commission on Behavioral and Social Sciences and Education, 2001; Shonkoff & Phillips, 2000; Wolfe, 2001).

Effective curricula include content that is worth knowing and meaningful. Content that is worth knowing builds on big ideas and fosters deep understanding. While some early childhood teachers would shudder at the thought of teaching physics to young children, in fact, the content of physics, which includes the study of motion, can be made appropriate. At the simplest level, children can explore how objects move and what makes them move. When *preschool children* experiment with the effect that changing the incline has on a ball, they are doing physics on a level that they understand. The same is true of *primary-grade children* who put drops of colored water and oil in a pan and carefully tip the pan at different angles, speeds, and directions to observe differences in the moving circles. Both of these activities help children discover worthwhile content about their physical world by conceptualizing how objects move (Chaille & Britain, 2003; NAEYC, 2003, 2009).

Effective curricula are culturally relevant. Culturally relevant curricula support children's home culture and language while also developing each child's abilities to participate in the shared school culture. Children's first languages and their cultural values are essential to a good early childhood curriculum. When teachers use stories written in a child's home language and then retell them in English, they convey an important message about the value of another language. Moreover, early childhood classrooms that display signs and labels in other languages, display children's writing, and incorporate culturally appropriate songs, dances, and drama affirm children's culture and language (Espinosa, 2009; Gay, 2004; Tiedt & Tiedt, 2010).

Effective curricula have clearly stated outcomes. Outcome-based curricula expect all learners to show improved short-term and long-term results. Studies show that children from low-income families who participated in such programs were less likely to drop out of school, be placed in special classrooms, or engage in criminal activity (Barnett, 2008; Lazar & Darlington, 1982; National Study Group for the Affirmative Development of Academic Ability, 2004; Schweinhart & Weikart, 1996). Moreover, an extensive body of research concludes that it is important for teachers to expect that every child can learn. Rosenthal and Jacobson's (1968) classic study on teacher expectations, as well as many that followed it, demonstrated that children rise or fall to the level of their teachers' expectations (ASCD Advisory Panel on Improving Student Achievement, 1995; NAEYC, 2009). If, for example, teachers expected you to read well, you probably did. If, however, teachers thought you would not learn to read well, you probably did not.

Effective curricula are developed by teachers who believe in themselves and their practice. Over and over again, research has indicated that the best teachers believe in their power to influence children's lives for the better (Bandura, 1997; Copple & Bredekamp, 2009; Raines & Johnston, 2003). They believe that they can exert a positive influence on children's lives despite the complex challenges that characterize teaching today. Confident teachers do not blame the school, the family, or the child when learning is difficult. Instead, they do everything in their power to improve the situation so that all children can reach their full potential.

These five research-based principles form the foundation of the early childhood curriculum. They make clear why curriculum must be challenging and achievable for every child.

Your Role in Developing Curriculum

Your role in developing curriculum shapes what children should learn and how they should learn it. Simply stated, you are the link between the child and the content. As a teacher, you will offer children experiences that help them develop knowledge, skills, cultural values, and appropriate behaviors. Today's early childhood teachers often feel pressured to add more rigorous content from later grades; as noted in the Ask the Expert feature on page 202, this is sometimes referred to as the "push-down" curriculum. The expectations for such a curriculum are often unattainable because they include excessive amounts of paper-and-pencil lessons, whole-class instruction, and abstract experiences for children (Copple & Bredekamp, 2006, 2009; Miller & Almon, 2009).

The best curriculum for children relies as much on your own personal experiences and beliefs as on your subject-matter knowledge and methodology. To create an effective curriculum with challenging and achievable child outcomes, you need to use your understanding and skill in the following five areas:

1. **Understand and use knowledge of children's development to plan curriculum.** A primary principle of curriculum development is teaching the *whole child*. This means using your knowledge of children's typical developmental patterns, their needs and interests at different ages, and their different ways of learning so that each child can learn optimally. We know, for instance, that preschool children have high energy levels, so teachers plan short group times that offer children many opportunities to talk and move. Likewise, we know that peer relationships are very important to children in second or third grade, so teachers provide many opportunities for children to learn with and from each other (Hendrick & Weissman, 2011; Jackman, 2009; Wortham, 2010).

2. **Understand and use the content you teach to create a curriculum worth teaching.** All early childhood teachers must have specialized knowledge in the subject areas they teach in order for content to have integrity. Thus, you must know the key concepts, facts, principles, and processes for each discipline, because they provide a coherent means of organization. In addition, you want to make sure that the subject matter represents authentic, real-life experiences so that children have a way to solve problems. To illustrate, suppose you were teaching key concepts about measurement to young children. You might have *preschool children* pour and measure

Pause and Reflect

About Effective Curriculum

In your own words, how would you define an effective curriculum? Include what kinds of activities you might see that would be appropriate and what kinds of activities would concern you. Now, compare your responses to the five principles of practice just described and tell which principle of practice each response met.

sand and water, but *primary-grade children* might weigh the containers to see which weighs the most (NAEYC, 2001; Wortham, 2010). In this way, you tailor a key concept from mathematics to the children's age and experience level while teaching them concepts with enduring value.

3. **Understand and use teaching strategies that help children become successful learners.** Knowing content is different from knowing **strategies** (how to teach the content). Teaching strategies simply are how teachers present content to children so they can use it. Knowledge of a wide range of teaching strategies helps teachers pace instruction to maximize each child's learning. Some appropriate strategies you might use are hands-on learning, investigations, units and projects, choice of learning experiences, coaching or guiding children with skill acquisition and use of reference materials, demonstrations, modeling, role play, and problem solving. Your knowledge of how and when to use different strategies also includes what misunderstandings, challenges, and prior knowledge children bring to their learning (Copple & Bredekamp 2009; Jackman, 2009). You put your own imprint on curriculum by selecting illustrative examples, explaining how to accomplish tasks, monitoring children's activities, and revisiting topics to ensure children's understanding.

Teachers use a wide range of strategies to maximize children's learning.

4. **Understand and use curriculum that reflects the diverse populations in your class.** When studying a topic, be sure to include the cultures of the children in your class. Be certain also to be sensitive to every family. Pay attention to the strategies you use with diverse populations. If, for example, you use mostly methods that rely heavily on memorizing verbal material, you will meet with limited success when working with diverse groups of children. A heavy reliance on words and recall inhibits positive teacher–child communication, particularly when the child's ethnic background or first language differs from the teacher's or when the child has a language delay or disorder. If, however, you use methods that utilize direct involvement with real materials, you have a much better chance of helping children make sense of their experiences because children learn best with concrete, real experiences that involve direct participation rather than through abstract ideas.

5. **Realize that your curriculum reflects your own personal experiences, as much as your knowledge of content and pedagogy.** Your experiences with schools, teachers, and learning up to this point affect how you view curriculum. These experiences are what will make you a unique teacher of children and at the same time will influence how you implement the what, how, and why of your curriculum. One of the first steps you might take is to reflect on your own background and begin to explore the way you feel about children and families who differ from you. This personal journey will help you support the children and families through your curriculum because teachers teach who they are (Palmer, 1998).

While your role in developing curriculum is focused on planning effective learning experiences for children, you must also focus on how you will teach them to maximize children's learning. In the next section, we explore two different types of curricula—the *written curriculum* and the *taught curriculum*—and what each one means.

Understanding the Written Curriculum

The **written curriculum** is a comprehensive document for each grade level that contains the general goals, objects, or outcomes that every child should meet, a sequence of study for selected topics, and suggested learning activities. The written curriculum can be *general,* usually developed by a state curriculum office for use across that state, or *specific,* usually developed by a local school district or provider, a specific school, or a particular program. The purpose of the written curriculum is to standardize the learning expectations using local, state, or national standards to determine what children should know and be able to do at a particular grade level. Most early childhood educators believe that high academic standards and high teacher expectations lead to higher achievement when the curriculum is personally relevant, meaningful, and interesting.

STANDARDS-BASED CURRICULUM

How do we know what children are supposed to learn at different grade levels? A **standards-based curriculum** specifies what children should learn, focuses on practices that meet those standards, and continually assesses children to see if they have met the standards. It is one way to ensure that each child has the same opportunity to achieve excellence and equity. To meet this new demand, most states have adopted state standards that define what children should know and be able to do in each subject area. Additionally, almost all states have identified early learning standards for preschool children below kindergarten age (Gronlund, 2006). **Early learning standards,** the expectations for children's learning and development in all domains and developmental stages, provide the foundation for later learning. And Head Start has developed a Child Outcomes Framework. Curriculum standards enable teachers to know what to teach and how to assess what is being taught. When we talk about curriculum standards, we mean both *content standards* and *performance standards* (Bowman, 2006; Bredekamp, 2009; Gronlund, 2006; NAEYC, 2003, 2009; Seefeldt, 2005b).

CONTENT STANDARDS

Content standards, what learners should know and be able to do in the subject areas at specific grade levels, include the knowledge, skills, and dispositions toward learning that children need to develop. For example, in a science study of plants, children at different levels might know the following: names of plants, different parts of plants (e.g., leaves, stems, blossoms, and roots), how plants grow, and the particular botanical techniques that keep plants healthy and alive. Children would also need to know and use some of the scientific processes, such as inquiry, observation, systematic description, and hypothesis testing, to gather and evaluate information and to communicate that information to others. The depth of this knowledge would differ for children according to their age, experience, and interest level (Bowman, 2006; Squires, 2005).

All teachers need to be able to answer positively the following curriculum content questions in order to realize positive child outcomes.

- Is the content meaningful and relevant to the children I am teaching?
- Is the content accurate according to the standards of the subject area?
- Is it reasonable to teach specific skills and knowledge at this time or would children benefit from learning it at a later time?
- Does the content build on and extend what children already know and can do?

These questions are typical for each subject area.

PERFORMANCE STANDARDS

Performance standards show what children can do in a particular subject area or a particular developmental domain, such as using age-appropriate social skills. For example, in evaluating the writing of kindergarten children, teachers need to know what constitutes mastery along the literacy learning continuum. One child might be using drawings for writing; another might be stringing letters together; yet another might be writing conventionally. These indicators are essential in determining what children can do in particular content areas (Bowman, 2006; NAEYC, 2003, 2009; Squires, 2005).

Early childhood professionals are very much a part of the standards movement. While high *content and performance standards* are necessary, they are not sufficient by themselves. Standards set the direction for the teacher. But, it is the way the teacher implements the curriculum—the quality of teaching—that in the end actually makes the difference in children's learning (Copple & Bredekamp, 2009; NAEYC, 2003, 2009; National Board for Professional Teaching Standards, 2001; Wortham, 2010).

CONTENT AREAS OF THE EARLY CHILDHOOD CURRICULUM

What, then, is appropriate content for young children? By *curriculum content,* we mean those key concepts, ideas, skills, and processes that are unique to the subjects of language and literacy, mathematics, science, social studies, technology, the arts, health, and physical education. For example, some key concepts in *mathematics* include number sense, estimation, and geometry; some key concepts in *social studies* include time, the environment, and consumption. Having a deep understanding of this content as well as knowledge of what discipline concepts are appropriate for children at different ages to learn is essential because content makes up a large part of the early childhood curriculum. Table 8.1 lists and defines the content areas of the early childhood curriculum, and identifies key national content area standards that have been developed by each specialty association.

For a complete list of content standards and benchmarks for prekindergarten through grade 4 in both searchable and browseable formats, go to the website for the Mid-Continent Regional Education Laboratories (McREL) www.mcrel.org/standards-benchmarks/.

All teachers must know the content that they teach and appreciate the unique concepts, processes, inquiry tools, and applications to real-world settings of the knowledge in those areas to develop effective curriculum for children. Table 8.2 suggests age-appropriate learning experiences for five different content areas.

APPROACHES TO ORGANIZING THE WRITTEN CURRICULUM

Once you understand the content of the written curriculum, you can use different approaches to organize it. You may organize your curriculum by developmental domains or by content area. Or, you may implement it as integrated, emergent, or culturally responsive. A description of each of these five approaches follows.

Table 8.1 Overview of Early Childhood Curriculum
Content-Area Standards

CONTENT AREA	DEFINITION AND GOAL	NATIONAL STANDARDS	PROFESSIONAL ASSOCIATION
Language and Literacy	The ability to be active, critical users of not only print and spoken language but also of the visual language of film and television, commercials, political advertisements, and photography **Goal:** To communicate using both oral and written language	**Reading Standards:** 1. Print–sound code 2. Getting meaning 3. Reading habits **Writing Standards:** 1. Writing in diverse forms and content 2. Writing for different audiences and for diverse purposes 3. Language use and conventions **Listening Standards:** 1. Active listening to recall, interpret, evaluate, and respond to information from a variety of sources **Speaking Standards:** 1. Communicating for varied purposes and to varied audiences in a variety of contexts **Viewing and Representing Standards:** 1. Viewing, understanding, and using nontechnical visual information and representations for critical comparison, analysis, and evaluation	International Reading Association (IRA) www.ira.org National Council of Teachers of English (NCTE) www.ncte.org
Mathematics	The search for sense and meaning, patterns and relationships, and order and predictability **Goal:** To develop conceptual understanding of quantitative, logical, and spatial reasoning	**Process Areas:** 1. Problem solving 2. Communication 3. Reasoning and proof 4. Connections 5. Representation **Content Areas:** 1. Number operations 2. Algebra 3. Geometry and spatial sense 4. Measurement 5. Data analysis and probability	National Council of Teachers of Mathematics (NCTM) www.nctm.org
Science	The application of science to problems of human adaptation to the environment	1. Unifying concepts and processes 2. Science as inquiry 3. Physical science	National Science Teachers Association (NSTA) www.nsta.org/standards

Table 8.1 continued

CONTENT AREA	DEFINITION AND GOAL	NATIONAL STANDARDS	PROFESSIONAL ASSOCIATION
	Goal: Science literacy	4. Life science 5. Earth and space science 6. Science and technology 7. Science in personal and social perspectives 8. History and nature of science	
Social Studies	The development of knowledge, attitudes, values, and skills believed necessary for citizens to participate, continually improve, and perfect society Goal: To help children become effective participants in a democratic society	Geography Standards: 1. The earth is the place we live 2. Direction and location 3. Relationships within places 4. Spatial interactions 5. Regions History Standards: 1. Time 2. Change 3. The continuity of human life 4. The past 5. The methods of the historian Economics Standards: 1. Scarcity: The awareness of difference between needs and wants 2. Understanding contributions of those who produce goods and services 3. Career choices and roles 4. Decision making about resources Social Relations/Civics Standards: 1. Participate as members of a group 2. Recognize similarities among people of many cultures 3. Learn principles of democracy 4. Learn respect for all others	National Geographic Society www.nationalgeographic.com/education/xpeditios/standards/matrix.html The National Council for Social Studies (NCSS) www.ncss.org
Technology	A tool to help children live, learn, and work successfully in an increasingly complex and information-rich society Goal: Technological literacy	1. Basic operations and concepts 2. Social, ethical, and human issues 3. Technology productivity tools 4. Technology communications tools 5. Technology research tools 6. Technology problem-solving and decision-making tools	International Society for Technology in Education (ISTE) www.cnets.iste.org

continued

Table 8.1 continued

CONTENT AREA	DEFINITION AND GOAL	NATIONAL STANDARDS	PROFESSIONAL ASSOCIATION
Health	The capacity of individuals to obtain, interpret, and understand basic health information and services and the competence to use such information and services in ways that enhance health **Goal:** To develop lifelong healthy skills and attitudes toward nutrition, safety, personal hygiene, and exercise	1. Concepts related to health promotion and disease prevention 2. Health information and health-promoting products and services 3. Health-enhancing behaviors that reduce health risks (most applicable for preschool health education) 4. Influence of culture, media, technology, and other factors on health 5. Personal, family, and community health 6. Interpersonal communication skills to enhance health	National Health Education Standards with Association for the Advancement of Health Education (AAHE) and American Public Health Association (www.apha.org) Alliance for Health, Physical Education, Recreation, and Dance (AAHPERD) www.aahperd.org
Physical Education	The acquisition of sequential movement skills and increased competency based on the unique development level of the individual **Goal:** To develop lifelong, positive habits of fitness	1. Movement forms 2. Physically active lifestyle 3. Physical fitness 4. Responsible personal and social behavior in physically active settings 5. Respects self and others in physically active settings 6. Physical activity for health, enjoyment, challenge, self-expression, or social interaction	National Association for Sport and Physical Education (NASPE) www.naspe.org Alliance for Health, Physical Education, Recreation, and Dance (AAHPERD) www.aahperd.org
Music	The acquisition of song and melodic understanding **Goal:** Musical literacy	**For Preschool Children:** 1. Singing and playing instruments 2. Creating music 3. Responding to music 4. Understanding music **For Kindergartners and School-Age Children:** 1. Singing alone and with others; a varied repertoire of music 2. Listening to, analyzing, and describing music 3. Performing on instruments, alone and with others, a varied repertoire of music 4. Reading and noting music	The National Association for Music Education (MENC) www.menc.org

Table 8.1 continued

CONTENT AREA	DEFINITION AND GOAL	NATIONAL STANDARDS	PROFESSIONAL ASSOCIATION
Visual Arts	The ability to create visual images and interpret images that others have made **Goal:** Arts literacy	1. Media techniques and processes 2. Choosing and evaluating a range of subject matter 3. Knowledge of structures and functions 4. Visual arts in relation to history and cultures 5. Characteristics and merits of own works and works of others 6. Connections between visual arts and other disciplines	Consortium of National Arts Education Associations (NAEA) www.org/compendium/standard.asf

Table 8.2 Examples of Age-Appropriate Learning Experiences

CONTENT AREA	AGE-APPROPRIATE EXPERIENCES
Mathematics	**Topic: Classification** **Toddlers:** Sort blocks by shape in a sorting box **Preschoolers and kindergartners:** Sort objects that are alike (e.g., in shape, color, size) in one place **School-age children:** Sort objects into two or more groups (e.g., by color and size)
Language and Literacy	**Topic: Writing** **Toddlers:** Provide opportunities to make random marks on paper, chalkboard, and other surfaces **Preschoolers and kindergartners:** Provide a print-rich environment, including class lists, murals, group stories, song charts, and children's labeling of their own work using sound spelling **School-age children:** Utilize different forms of writing, such as diaries, editorials, journals, and stories
Social Studies	**Topic: Families** **Toddlers:** Look at pictures of own family; identify people **Preschoolers and kindergartners:** Explore roles and functions of family members (e.g., provides basic shelter and food); illustrate family roles and functions through pictures, class poster, or class mural

continued

Table 8.2 continued

CONTENT AREA	AGE-APPROPRIATE EXPERIENCES
	School-age children: Gather and organize data to create a timeline of family celebrations represented in the class; invite children and their families to share special celebrations with the class
Visual Arts	**Topic: Making Art** **Toddlers:** Make marks on large paper using large, sturdy markers, crayons, or fingerpaint; use soft play dough for rolling **Preschoolers and kindergartners:** Use brushes of various widths and markers of different styles (e.g., chisel, fine point); experiment with making different kinds of lines (e.g., wavy, curly, zigzag) **School-age children:** Draw or paint on different textures and surfaces (e.g., transparencies, fabrics, wallpaper); use different tools (e.g., yarn, tubes, marbles) to create different results
Health	**Topic: Nutrition** **Toddlers:** Taste and name healthy snacks, such as fruits and vegetables **Preschoolers and kindergartners:** Provide healthy cooking activities such as making stuffed celery or fruit salad or spreading cheese on a cracker **School-age children:** Categorize food by food pyramid through class and individual books, displays, food carts; identify source of food product

DEVELOPMENTAL DOMAINS

Kostelnik, Soderman, and Whiren (2011) suggest using **developmental domains,** areas of children's development, to organize curriculum. This approach is truly learner centered; teaches the whole child; and allows children to integrate their developing knowledge, skills, abilities, and dispositions as the teacher decides what, how, and when to teach certain concepts and skills. Developmental domains provide a broad view of curriculum, a balanced view of the whole child, and help teachers match content to each child's abilities to achieve positive outcomes. Figure 8.1 lists each of the six domains and provides the purpose of each.

CONTENT AREAS

A second way to approach your curriculum is by **content areas.** Because a large portion of the curriculum comes from the specialized knowledge of each content area, this approach to the curriculum makes sense to many teachers, school boards, and curriculum developers. To guide content learning, early childhood teachers "use their knowledge of academic disciplines to design, implement, and evaluate experiences that promote positive development and learning for each and every child" (NAEYC, 2009, p. 15). We will now describe four of the content areas—literacy, mathematics,

Figure 8.1 Developmental Domains as a Curriculum Organizer

Aesthetic Domain
- Builds appreciation for and participation in the expressive arts and other sensory experiences

Affective Domain
- Develops self-awareness and self-esteem and learns to handle emotions

Cognitive Domain
- Acquires knowledge, skills, and dispositions in content areas
- Builds understanding of complex concepts; develops information-processing and problem-solving skills

Language Domain
- Develops listening, speaking, reading, and writing abilities
- Fosters positive responses to high-quality children's literature

Physical Domain
- Builds gross and fine motor skills
- Fosters care, respect, and nutrition for the body
- Encourages positive attitude toward physical health and activity

Social Domain
- Develops social attitudes
- Learns social interaction skills, as well as respect for cultural and individual differences
- Enhances social studies content

Source: Information from Kostelnik et al., 2011.

science, and social studies—and see what a content approach looks like for young children.

The Literacy Curriculum In *literacy,* children develop basic concepts of print and then begin to experiment with reading and writing. Very young children become aware that print carries a message; *preschoolers and kindergartners* develop the basic concept that books contain stories and information that can be retold; and *primary-grade children* develop the understanding that print can be read and written as they gain skill with reading and writing simple stories with increased fluency and independence (Morrow, 2005).

The Mathematics Curriculum In *mathematics,* children develop basic concepts of number, counting, geometry, and measurement through active physical and mental interaction with materials, peers, and supportive adults in order to make sense out of ideas (Charlesworth & Lind, 2007). In geometry, for example, *preschool and kindergarten children* can build their concepts of shape and size by drawing and cutting shapes; by reading books about shapes, such as *Shapes, Shapes, Shapes* (Hoban, 1986); by positioning their bodies into various shapes; and by experimenting

Children learn mathematics concepts through authentic and concrete experiences.

with shapes from different materials. *Primary-grade children build spatial understandings through making symmetrical designs, reading books such as *Rosie's Walk* (Hutchins, 1968), constructing figures, and making body movements to show positional words such as *in, on, over,* and *under* (Charlesworth & Lind, 2007).

The Science Curriculum In *science,* children learn scientific concepts through problem solving and inquiry, with topics such as "Change is all around us" and "Things that move in different ways." They also learn to use **science process skills** to test hypotheses through observing, comparing, classifying, and communicating—skills that lead to the development of knowledge and concept development in science. All children develop scientific understanding through teacher-developed and child-generated problems and investigations (Charlesworth & Lind, 2007).

The Social Studies Curriculum In *social studies,* children at all ages learn history concepts, such as the concept of time. Young children's concepts of time are more intuitive than conventional, but their intuitive knowledge is necessary to understand the concept. All children enjoy learning about their own lives, which helps them gain understanding of the passage of time. A personal history book with pictures, stories, notes, and growth chart records helps them understand time concepts. Through active questioning, experiences, and conversations that describe events and routines in a sequence, they use methods of the historian, such as cause-and-effect relationships, analyzing records of the past, and drawing conclusions (Seefeldt, 2005a).

A content approach to the curriculum, however, causes some concerns for early childhood educators. Because it is expert based, much of the content is difficult for children to understand. Making specialized knowledge accessible to children at their varying levels of understanding often leads to a watered-down, inaccurate, or confusing curriculum and places primary responsibility on the learner to make connections within and across the content areas. Moreover, content by itself is not adequate enough because it often leads to "fragmented, isolated skill development or the exclusion of other kinds of knowledge and skills essential to children's ultimate success in society" (Kostelnik et al., 2011). Early childhood teachers need the knowledge, skill, and understanding to teach subject matter in age-appropriate ways to each child.

INTEGRATED CURRICULUM

A third approach to curriculum development is an *integrated* one. The word *integrated* means "joining all parts of something together to make a whole." Thus, an **integrated curriculum** joins learning in more than one developmental domain, more than one content area, or across domains and content areas. The linkage is based on the study of a broad concept or theme, and on the developmental needs of the learners. An *integrated curriculum* promotes children's learning by:

- Helping children connect their past experiences to their current learning by focusing on processes and concepts in each content area and connecting them to the other content areas.
- Emphasizing children's actual experiences or interests and their interactions with each other, with materials, and with ideas, and promoting active learning through hands-on and minds-on experiences with materials and people.

- Providing ample time for children to experiment with and explore ideas that promote all aspects of children's development as well as their developing knowledge, skills, and dispositions. (Fleener & Bucher, 2003/2004; Wortham, 2010)

Think about Ms. Curtis's second-grade class that is studying trees. Ms. Curtis began the children's study of trees by reading the book *Tell Me Tree: All About Trees for Kids* (Gibbons, 2002) and then guided the children's creation of a graphic organizer to help them make connections with the text and learn about the types of trees, the parts of trees, and characteristics of trees. As the children read or heard the story, they completed sections of the graphic organizer. Figure 8.2 shows how to use children's literature as a starting point for integrating the curriculum.

In this case, children were answering their own questions, such as "What do trees need to live?" "What kinds of food come from trees?" or "Why do people and animals need trees?" In *art*, the children explored the large watercolor pictures in the book and made collages of leaf patterns; in *science*, they charted the types of trees and animals they learned about or perhaps planted a tree for their class; in *language and literacy*, they created a tree identification book, or developed a word wall list of tree words. Some children chose to illustrate other stories or poems about trees; others read other literature about trees (such as *Trees, Leaves, and Bark* [Burns, 1995]); still others created advertisements for their favorite tree. Through a

Figure 8.2 Integrated Curriculum Graphic Organizer for Study of Trees Using Gail Gibbons's Book *Tell Me Tree: All About Trees for Kids*

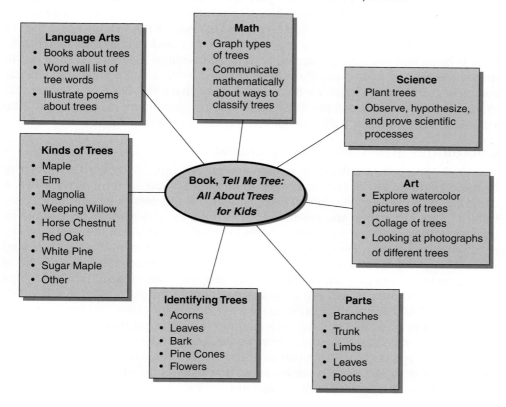

variety of learning experiences related to the topic of trees, Ms. Curtis linked different subject areas and developmental domains to deepen children's knowledge and skills.

The idea of integrated curriculum is not new; it has its origins in the ideas of John Dewey (1938), William Kilpatrick (1936), and Jean Piaget (1965). These respected thinkers suggested that curriculum for children should be holistic, that knowledge should be integrated and include some child-directed activity, that children and teachers should decide together what to learn, and that content should be learned through the study of themes and big ideas. Curriculum is most meaningful for children when they make connections among concepts, experiences, and school to what they know.

EMERGENT CURRICULUM

A fourth approach, **emergent curriculum,** considers children's interests, needs, prior knowledge, cultural backgrounds, and questions as the core of the curriculum (Lewin-Benham, 2006; Jones & Nimmo, 1994; Stacey, 2009). Children learn best when what they are learning interests them, means something in their personal lives, builds on what they already know, and answers their questions about the world. Emergent curriculum responds to children's needs and interests, involves children and teachers in planning and evaluating projects and learning activities, has general learning objectives, and documents children's learning. While emergent curriculum emphasizes children's interests, it does not ignore intentionally deepening children's understanding. Teachers, who are keen observers of children and listen carefully to them, capitalize on children's interests from many sources (Jones & Nimmo, 1994). They note what occurs in children's play and conversation, such as going to the beach; use the interests and passions of teachers and other adults in the environment, such as weaving or studying medicine; respond to children's questions about the environment, such as protecting the water and the earth; and use developmental tasks such as being part of a caring community. When curriculum is developed around children's interests, they are more likely to be engaged in the content to be studied. The emergent curriculum is based on the belief that the characteristics of the learner and the way children learn are the most important considerations in curriculum. The schools in Reggio Emilia, Italy, provide the model for emergent curriculum.

CULTURALLY RESPONSIVE CURRICULUM

The final approach, a **culturally responsive curriculum,** acknowledges diversity in the classroom and accommodates it in the curriculum in three ways. First, a culturally responsive curriculum accepts and affirms differences by communicating to all children that they are welcomed and valued by giving them time, showing interest in their families, and finding ways to involve all of them in quality experiences (Banks & Banks, 2005). Second, it accommodates different learning styles by using a variety of effective approaches, cultural practices of the children in the classroom, teaching strategies, and tools that "develop positive, respectful relationships with children whose cultures and language may differ [from the teacher's]" (NAEYC, 2009, p. 15). And third, a culturally responsive curriculum uses children's cultural backgrounds to promote personal pride and motivation in children, to build a more positive sense of self-esteem, and to develop respect for others (Tiedt & Tiedt, 2010).

Whichever approach or combination of approaches you use to develop your curriculum, it must reflect what is known about how children learn and develop. If your school system or program typically approaches curriculum by content areas, you might try to match some of its goals, outcomes, and activities to the domain areas. You may also integrate two or more subject areas, use children's interests, and capitalize on the children's cultures as you prepare to teach your curriculum.

Understanding the Taught Curriculum

The **taught curriculum** is *what* someone sees the teacher and children doing in the classroom. It is *how* you make the written curriculum meaningful to a particular group of children. **Meaningful curriculum** is relevant to that particular group of children and considers their developmental needs and interests and the environment and culture in which they live. Meaningful curriculum also promotes active learning of age-appropriate, subject-area knowledge for every child (Copple & Bredekamp, 2009; NAEYC, 2009; Wortham, 2010). Take a moment now to refer to the opening quote by John Dewey. What do you think he meant when he said that teachers are the agents through which knowledge and skills are communicated and rules of conduct enforced? In the next section we will look at how you can become the agent for meaningful curriculum.

CHARACTERISTICS OF MEANINGFUL CURRICULUM

Standard 5 of NAEYC's Standards for Professional Preparation Programs (2009) and the curriculum recommendations by NAEYC and the National Association of Early Childhood Specialists in State Departments of Education (2003) address the critical curriculum questions for children from birth through age 8. As discussed in an earlier section of this chapter, the five research-based principles of good curriculum—content worth knowing, cultural relevance, clear outcomes, all areas of development, and teachers who believe in themselves and their practice—are most likely to lead to meaningful curriculum. These principles are used and restated as distinguishing characteristics of *meaningful curriculum*, as follows.

1. **A meaningful curriculum is comprehensive.** A comprehensive curriculum teaches the whole child. That is, it addresses both developmental domains and content areas. Meaningful curriculum focuses on key concepts and relevant ideas that link children's learning to their real-life experiences, interests, knowledge, and development. Consider, for example, a first-grade class studying homes. A meaningful *literacy curriculum* might have children reading books about homes, such as *A House Is a House for Me* (Hoberman, 1978) or *The Village of Round and Square Houses* (Grifalconi, 1986); writing stories and drawing pictures about their own homes; or taking inventories of what is in each room of their own homes. In *social studies*, children might investigate houses that people lived in long ago, and in *math*, they might make blueprints of houses and then construct them from blocks using different shapes. In *science*, they might explore homes for different animals, such as turtles and hermit crabs. If done in pairs or small groups, these learning activities also address social skill development and self-regulation. They are *meaningful* because they build on and extend what children already know and develop both developmental domains and content (Copple & Bredekamp, 2009; NAEYC, 2009).

2. **A meaningful curriculum is active and engaging.** Children learn when they are actively involved in experiences that help them connect the information and skills they are learning to their own lives. For example, if a second-grade class is studying living things, children may choose to read books on a topic that interests them or take a

walking field trip through the neighborhood to identify living things unique to their community; they practice literacy skills as they read, write, and draw about what they are learning. Engaging learning experiences actively encourage children to demonstrate true understanding by explaining, finding evidence, generalizing, applying, and representing the topic in a new way (Piaget, 1965; Vygotsky, 1978). Teachers create engaging learning environments by respecting children's ideas, modeling strategies such as thinking aloud, problem solving, and problem posing, and helping them see familiar ideas in new ways (Hyson, 2008; NAEYC, 2001).

3. **A meaningful curriculum is culturally relevant and inclusive.** Curricula that capitalize on the diverse backgrounds of each child in the classroom use a variety of culturally sensitive resources, such as pictures, books, music, technology, and language, that represent the different cultures in the classroom. For example, you might want to include different cooking materials, such as a wok or tortilla press, in the home living center. Or you might find out about the children's after-school activities and their holiday customs so that children's families can be resources in celebrating the cultural practices of the children in your class. You may also want to emphasize values, such as courtesy and respect, that cross all cultures so that each child notices different yet acceptable ways of demonstrating these cross-cultural values in school. Creating a literacy corner with books and writing materials that appeal to every child and introduce children to other cultural practices and backgrounds is a powerful way to build a meaningful curriculum that is sensitive to diversity. See the References and the Appendices at the end of this text for further recommendations of appropriate resources for creating a culturally responsive curriculum. Additionally, an inclusive curriculum promotes feelings of belonging for all learners. The benefits of such a curriculum are increased opportunities to interact with typically developing peers, to participate in experiences that enable children with disabilities to use their skills in typical early childhood activities, and to interact with competent peer models to build new social and communication skills. Children without exceptionalities also benefit from increased opportunities to develop

Curriculum is meaningful for children when they make connections between concepts and experiences to what they know.

positive attitudes about children with exceptionalities and to develop caring and unselfish behaviors (Allen & Cowdery, 2009; Diener, 2010).

4. **A meaningful curriculum is aligned with standards.** Knowing the early learning standards (Gronlund, 2006) and the standards for each content area is essential to implement curriculum that is meaningful to children. Such standards provide guidance as to what each child should know and be able to do at different ages and in different content areas that lead to greater possibility for positive learning and development. Both sets of standards can be incorporated into all areas of your curriculum and all curricular approaches. Figure 8.3 visually depicts the overlapping relationship of how these four characteristics contribute to a meaningful curriculum.

Notice how Diane Trister Dodge answers important curriculum questions about young children in the Ask the Expert feature on page 220.

Pause and Reflect

About Meaningful Curriculum

In today's schools, some school districts and programs expect teachers to teach the curriculum exactly as it is written or in a prescribed way. Others expect teachers to have more input in implementing the curriculum as long as they teach the key concepts and skills that have been prescribed. Whichever situation you are in, list three different ways you could make teaching a prescribed concept meaningful to the children in your classroom.

Figure 8.3 Characteristics of Meaningful Curriculum

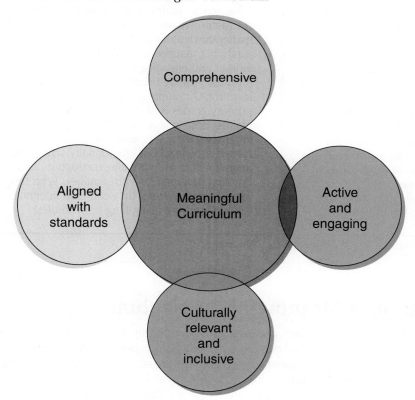

Sources: NAEYC, 2009; NAEYC & NAECS/SDE, 2003.

Ask the EXPERT   *Diane Trister Dodge*

Early Childhood Curriculum

Q: What does curriculum mean in early childhood education?

A: An early childhood curriculum should be comprehensive, addressing all aspects of children's development and learning. It must explain *why* particular practices are effective as well as provide guidance about *what* and *how* to teach young children. It must be grounded in child development theory and based on current research on how children learn best. Recognizing that the most important factor in children's learning is the quality of teacher–child interactions, the curriculum should show teachers how to create an engaging learning environment, structure the day, use a range of teaching strategies to guide children's learning and development intentionally, and develop partnerships with families.

Q: Is a preschool curriculum also appropriate for kindergarten?

A: As children's social–emotional, physical, language, and cognitive skills develop, the environment, experiences, and instructional strategies must change to promote further learning. Children become increasingly able to assume more responsibilities, and the kindergarten classroom should also recognize that the children are making the transition from concrete to symbolic thinking. Some aspects of a preschool curriculum still apply to kindergarten, for example, offering children daily opportunities for hands-on investigations and tasks that encourage them to explore, share and try their ideas, and create representations of what they have learned. Long-term studies provide a way for teachers to engage children in these kinds of experiences and to integrate content learning.

Q: Why talk about curriculum in the primary grades when teachers are required to follow subject-matter curriculum guides adopted by their schools?

A: In the primary grades, we want children to develop a passion for learning about engaging topics and to see themselves as competent learners. Subject-matter curriculum guides tell teachers what to teach, but teachers must find ways to create vibrant and engaging classroom environments that promote positive behavior and collaborative, active learning. Our approach to curriculum in the primary grades is to give teachers a framework for making decisions about setting up the classroom, organizing the day, creating a classroom community, teaching intentionally, using ongoing assessment to individualize instruction, and building partnerships with families. With this management system, they can then integrate content learning using long-term studies.

Diane Trister Dodge is Founder and President, Teaching Strategies, Inc., Washington, DC

Teaching a Meaningful Curriculum

There are many ways to teach a meaningful curriculum. However, the best curriculum for children focuses on broad concepts that reflect the content and standards you need to teach, the processes unique to those content areas, the appropriate strategies, and the thoughtful consideration of the children's development, families, and community. Two primary approaches typically used by early childhood teachers to teach meaningful curriculum are *thematic units* and *projects,* as described next.

THEMATIC UNITS

Thematic units are a curriculum approach that relates learning experiences to key concepts or ideas about a particular topic of study and last over a period of time. They use a variety of relevant experiences in more than one content area and are interesting to children. Thematic units help children link their learning from many different subject areas, generalize knowledge and skills from one experience to another, and connect what they are learning to real life.

Thematic units take different forms. Some center on a certain type of literature, such as the study of fairy tales. In this type of unit, the children may read and listen to different fairy tales, talk about their characteristics (e.g., royalty, magic, a setting in a faraway time and place, and commoners finding great riches and power), and perhaps write or enact fairy tales using those characteristics. Others focus on a topic that links several content areas, including music, art, play, mathematics, social studies, and science. For example, with the topic of farms, children might ask questions about what they wanted to find out about farms, and then read, write, and illustrate their findings. Skills would be taught where appropriate. Suppose, for example, in studying farms, the children decide to plant individual and classroom vegetable gardens. They may make a classroom bar graph on the growth of the seedlings (*mathematics*), write or draw about the progress of the seedlings in journals (*literacy*), and illustrate and categorize the different plants in a class mural (*art*). Still other units may be organized around multiple intelligences.

Whatever form you use, thematic units must include children's ideas and interests, their previous experiences, and knowledge that is worth knowing (Katz & Chard, 2000). Figure 8.4 provides a list of commonly used early childhood thematic units.

Approaching a meaningful curriculum through *thematic units* helps teachers make decisions that support guideline 3D of NAEYC guidelines for developmentally appropriate practice (Copple & Bredekamp, 2009). This guideline states "teachers make meaningful connections a priority in the learning experiences they provide children, to reflect that all learners and certainly young children learn best when the concepts, language, and skills they encounter are related to something they know and care about, and when the new learnings are themselves interconnected in meaningful, coherent

Figure 8.4 Commonly Used Early Childhood Thematic Units

Notice that many thematic unit topics for these thematic units fit into multiple categories, making it important to integrate your curriculum so it is engaging, relevant, and interesting.

Social Studies

My Family and Me; My Neighborhood; Jobs and Work; Wants and Needs; Family Traditions; Children Now and Long Ago; People, Places, and Events; Beginnings; Caring for our Earth

Science

Environmental Studies; Caring for Pets; Endangered Species; Living Things; Light and Shadows; Water; Physical World; Natural World; Sea Life; Mysteries and Secrets; Change

Mathematics

Patterns; Opposites; Colors and Shapes; Numbers; Time; Measurement; Stores; Space

Literacy

Fairy Tales; Fables; Folk Tales; Author Study; Chants and Rhymes; Chapter Books

Interdisciplinary Study

Transformations; Old and New; Near and Far; Above and Below; Containers; Ways of Communicating; Cycles and Systems; Clothing; Health and Wellness; Relationships; Public Service; Offices and Factories; Similarities and Differences

ways" (Copple & Bredekamp, 2009, p. 21). Effective thematic curriculum should enable children to:

1. build on what they already know, stimulate questions they want to answer, capitalize on interests, and relate information to their lives.

2. understand basic concepts and processes from the subject areas rather than focusing on isolated facts.

3. learn accurate facts and information related to the unit study.

4. integrate content and processes from all the subject areas by using content in more than one way and at more than one time.

5. engage in hands-on activities as they inquire about the topic.

6. grow in each of their developmental domains.

To illustrate, consider an example of a *third-grade study* of outer space during which children learn concepts and facts about the planets, sun, moon, and space exploration. In *math*, the children compare temperatures of the planets or measure distances between the sun and other planets; in *social studies*, they relate life on other planets to their own lives or illustrate life in a spacecraft; in *science* they study different moon and cloud formations or explore what life might be like on other planets; and in *language arts*, they write about their knowledge of space or learn phonics skills from the books they are reading on space; this helps children to integrate the content and processes from all subject areas, participate in hands-on activities to inquire about the topic, and use the same content in more than one way and at more than one time. Effective thematic units engage each child in the curriculum.

PROJECTS

Projects are focused, in-depth studies of something that children, in collaboration with teachers, initiate, direct, organize, and develop. These deep investigations can take different forms, such as the project approach (Katz & Chard, 2000), emergent curriculum (Edwards, Gandini, & Forman, 1998), and long-term studies (Dodge, Colker, & Heroman, 2002). *Projects* support children's natural ways of learning, promote their thinking by making learning meaningful, and spark their curiosity by challenging their abilities. Teachers who approach curriculum through projects facilitate and document children's progress while ensuring their learning of skills, content, and processes in different subject areas. Projects have their roots in Dewey's (1938) and Kilpatrick's (1936) ideas that experience-based learning forms the foundation of education. More recently, the schools in Reggio Emilia, Italy, have used the project approach successfully with the entire preschool community.

Projects can last for a day, a week, a month, or even a year and are characterized by five features: individual and group discussion, field trips, representations of children's knowledge, investigations, and displays of learning. The following example of a pet store project created by kindergartners illustrates some of the key principles of projects.

Ms. Puhl's kindergartners engaged in extensive group and individual discussion about their pets, what they knew about them, and questions they had about caring for pets. From this expressed interest, Ms. Puhl added books and pictures about pets to her classroom library. The children's questions sparked an interest in further studying their own pets. Ms. Puhl then created a large word-and-picture chart for children that asked the question, "What do you think we will find out about our own pets?"

The kindergartners used a checklist to record which animals and pet toys they expected to find and then compared those data to what they actually discovered after their study. Planning the project sparked children's investigations of their pet study. They generated lists of what they already knew about pets and what they needed to know, read several more books about all kinds of pets, and planned specific questions about pets to ask one another, their parents, and their teachers. The children represented what they already knew and what they were learning about pets by creating fact folders, drawing what they saw during their virtual online explorations of caring for pets illustrating stories they read and stories they wrote, and making diagrams and sketches of the block and dramatic play area

Learning allows children to study topics in depth and learn from one another.

where they had created their own "Caring for pets" area. They also learned the basic economics of buying and selling through enactment of different pet scenarios. Small groups, planned and developed other experiences such as a final sale of pet goods including food, toys, specially constructed name plates, and other pet care items for the other kindergarten and first-grade classes in the school and an open house for the parents and families to celebrate the children's accomplishments. Some children confidently explained the key aspects of their pet study while others shared their writings, labeling, and artwork. In this project, the kindergartners demonstrated *math skills* by classifying pets; *science processes* by using charts, graphs, and written reports to record scientific data; *art skills* by sketching, drawing, and painting pictures of real and imaginary pets; and *writing skills* by labeling, copying, and making signs for the displays.

Whatever approach to curriculum you use, your curriculum should be informed by one or more theoretical frameworks. Such an orientation can help enhance your students' ways of learning, guide your daily practice, and explain why your curriculum is the way it is. In the next section, we examine five major curriculum theories.

Curriculum Theories

Have you ever wondered about the behavior of certain animals, the nature of rainstorms, or why some things are easy for you to learn and others are not? These speculations are based on certain assumptions you make about those things and are called theories. A theory is knowledge that is systematically organized, applies to a wide variety of circumstances, and can explain or predict a set of phenomena. You can prove or disprove a theory as you deepen your knowledge about it.

The idea that curriculum theories reflect different assumptions about children, teaching, and learning is important for all teachers. The theory or theories that inform your curriculum provide a window into what you think about how children learn, what knowledge is worth knowing, how content should be taught, and how learning should be evaluated (Copple & Bredekamp, 2009; Henson, 2010; Posner, 2004). Differing assumptions have spawned many theories about what and how children should learn. While each theory offers its own perspective about curriculum, together, they serve us well in providing the most effective curriculum for children.

How you view curriculum theory influences the way you develop curriculum. Table 8.3 lists the key theorists, the teacher's role in each theory, and illustrative methods of each theory.

Table 8.3 Key Curriculum Theorists and Theoretical Perspectives

THEORIST AND PERSPECTIVE	GOAL	SOURCE OF KNOWLEDGE	TEACHER'S ROLE	METHODS
Traditional, E. D. Hirsch	intelligent citizens teaching the same core body of knowledge to all children	specialized facts and vocabulary of each academic discipline	teach factual information and basic skills through direct instruction	worksheets, workbooks, seatwork, drill and practice, isolated teaching
Knowledge-Centered, Jerome Bruner	each child learns at his or her level of understanding in all subject areas that fit the child's cognitive abilities	using objects, ideas, and information with both intuitive and analytical thinking skills	develop children's critical and creative thinking through solving problems	experiences using Bloom's taxonomy of thinking skills: knowledge, comprehension, application, analysis, synthesis, evaluation
Experiential (Learned), John Dewey	experience is the source of the curriculum; knowledge is constantly changing	children's real-life experiences, needs, and interests; child development; cultural values of individuals and groups	connect children's learning with past experiences; stimulate interests and ideas to increase their understanding and learning	self-directed learning; learning contracts; problem-solving experiences; experience-based, child-centered practice
Behavioral, B. F. Skinner	student achievement for clearly specified, observable, and measurable objectives mastery learning	predetermined standards and goals; precise objectives; carefully sequenced objectives in the content areas	efficient and effective means to achieve specific ends	scope and sequence of learning tasks; reinforce correct responses; modeling; guided practice; independent practice
Constructivist, Jean Piaget	development of cognition	meaning and understanding in learning content and in learning to think about their world	facilitate children's thinking and concept development in learning to make sense of their world; focus on child outcomes	group experiences and projects using real, active, and purposeful learning experiences related to thinking, reasoning, and problem solving

Sources: Based on data from Eggen & Kauchak, 2010; Henson, 2010; Posner, 2004.

Building Connections with Families About the Curriculum

Ms. Davis's children have been studying about plants. Each week, she invites a child to select a take-home pack (PAK) that contains a related activity to be completed by the child and an adult in the home. Families with limited English literacy skills may complete the activity and the feedback form verbally on a cassette tape. Following is an example of a PAK for *Growing Vegetable Soup* by Lois Ehlert.

Materials Needed

One-gallon plastic bag, canvas bag, or small knapsack

A copy of *Growing Vegetable Soup* with cassette tape

A recipe for vegetable soup taken from the back flap of the book

An Activity Card

A Feedback Form

Activity Card

Name of Activity

Cooking Activity

What the Child Will Learn

Measuring skills (math, science)

Using the senses of smell, taste, touch, seeing, and hearing (sensory/physical skills)

Observing how vegetables change when baked (science)

Using fine motor skills (physical skills)

Counting ingredients as added (math)

Describing steps taken to make the soup (language)

What to Do

- Gather the ingredients, directions, and utensils necessary to make the soup.
- Read *Growing Vegetable Soup* with your child (or listen to the cassette tape and follow along with the book).
- Suggest that, together, you make some vegetable soup and talk more about the story. Follow the directions by allowing your child to "read" the pictures on the recipe, Wash and cut up vegetables, make the soup, and then enjoy!
- Clean up supplies and answer the questions on the Feedback Form.
- Send the PAK back to school.

Feedback Form

☐ Did you complete the activity with your child?		Yes	No
☐ Did your child "read" the recipe?		Yes	No
☐ Did your child talk about measuring ingredients?		Yes	No
☐ Did your child taste the soup?		Yes	No

What did your child like best about the activity? _____

_____

What did you like best? _____

_____

Signature _____ Date _____

Summary

- The curriculum is what children actually experience in schools from arrival to departure and reflects the philosophy, goals, objectives, and child outcomes of the school. Curriculum includes content, instruction, timing, and assessment.

- Your role in developing curriculum includes your ability to use your knowledge of child development, the content you are teaching, the strategies you incorporate to teach the content, the diverse population represented in your classroom, and your own values, beliefs, and expectations.

- You may develop the written curriculum through many different approaches, including developmental domains, content areas, integrated curriculum, emergent curriculum, and culturally responsive curriculum.

- The taught curriculum is what someone sees the teacher and children doing in the classroom. A taught curriculum that is meaningful is comprehensive, active, engaging, culturally relevant and inclusive, and aligned with standards.

- Curriculum reflects different theories that shape what and how we teach. These are traditional, knowledge-centered, experiential, behavioral, and constructivist theories. Each has a particular perspective of children, learning, and teaching.

Applying Your Knowledge of Curriculum

In Assessment Activity 1, apply what you know about developing curriculum by answering three questions about Benjamin's kindergarten play. Then in Assessment Activity 2, use your knowledge of curriculum by brainstorming with curriculum webs.

Assessment ACTIVITY 1 ① **BENJAMIN'S KINDERGARTEN PLAY**

Each year, Benjamin's kindergarten teachers plan an elaborate annual play. In this year's performance, *About the Presidents*, each child was assigned the part of a U.S. president. Benjamin was assigned the 31st president, Herbert Hoover.

The teachers asked parents to help their child find three or four interesting facts about the presidents their children were studying. They also asked the parents to try to dress their children for the performance in clothing that represented their president's time period. In school, the children practiced their parts, which consisted of facts they researched and memorized with the help of their parents, and sang songs about George Washington and Abraham Lincoln. Benjamin's teachers believed that having parents help their child research interesting facts, practice their parts, and prepare special clothing was a worthwhile way to involve them in their children's learning.

Benjamin's mother, a single, working parent, first heard of her son's kindergarten play through a written notice from the teachers. When she learned that she had to help her son research facts, Benjamin's mother was excited. But she soon discovered that Benjamin had little or no understanding of Herbert Hoover, of what a president is or does, of wars, or of what it means to be a humanitarian. The more Benjamin's mother explained to Benjamin about Herbert Hoover, the more frustrated she became, because Benjamin was not interested in this president. He only wanted to be "George Washington," a name that had some familiarity to him. Thus, preparing Benjamin for his part in the school play became his mother's project.

On the day of the performance, children spoke so softly they could hardly be heard; others looked frightened and stiff but said their parts. Three months later, Benjamin cannot recall any of the facts about Herbert Hoover, but he can tell you which of his friends played certain presidents.

This profile of Benjamin, his mother, and the kindergarten teachers raises a number of issues about developing curriculum. What is appropriate content for children? How can teachers make that content accessible to young children? How should children represent that content to each other and to their families?

REACT	Think about how the perspectives of Benjamin, Benjamin's teachers, and Benjamin's mother are alike and different. What might be the underlying reasons? Why should the lives of children's family members influence teachers' expectations for their involvement?
RESEARCH	Read about the appropriate roles of social studies in the early childhood curriculum. Go to the website for the National Council on Social Studies (www.ncss.org) and look at its standards for all of the social studies. Read and discuss these with your classmates. Which of these ideas will affect the kinds of social studies experiences you develop for children?
REFLECT	What values, attitudes, and dispositions about living in a diverse and democratic world does each child gain from using drama to teach social studies? Generate a portrait of what appropriate drama for kindergarten children should look like in order to develop such values and attitudes.

Assessment ACTIVITY 2 ② **BRAINSTORMING WITH CURRICULUM WEBS**

Curriculum webs are tools that help develop a curriculum that is most relevant to the children whom you are teaching. Brainstorming, a method of problem solving in which all members of the group spontaneously contribute ideas, is useful because it allows many ways to develop your curriculum.

Using the ideas discussed in Ask the Expert: Sue Bredekamp on Developmentally Appropriate Practice, which was presented on page 202, brainstorm an appropriate topic of study for a particular age group. Follow these steps while brainstorming:

1. Choose a topic to explore by examining your grade-level curriculum.
2. Brainstorm with the children about what they already know about the topic and what they want to know about the topic.
3. Brainstorm with your colleagues about the concepts or big ideas to be learned, the topics to be covered, and the activities and lessons to be integrated into each curriculum area or domain.
4. Organize your ideas into the form of a web. Figure 8.5 provides an example of a brainstorming web for a kindergarten study of animals, and Figure 8.6 illustrates a third-grade brainstorming web for a study of Greece.
5. Select resources and a means of assessment.

Figure 8.5 Brainstorming Web for Kindergarten About the Study of Animals

LANGUAGE ARTS

Listening
- Retell or act out
- Literature experiences: read *Q Is for Duck* (early finishers)
- Animal guessing game: clues
- Following directions for class book:
  - Cut out shape of animal's head
  - Cut clothes from magazine and paste

Reading
- *Make Way for Ducklings*, R. McCloskey
- *Find Demi's Sea Creatures*, Demi
- *Louis the Fish*, A. Yorinks
- *Big Red Barn*, M. W. Brown
- *Animal, Animal Where Is Your Home?*, J. B. Moncure
- *Visit to the Aquarium*, Aliki
- *Q Is for Duck*, M. Elting and M. Folsom
- *Animals Should Definitely Not Wear Clothing*, J. Barrett
- *Whose Baby?*, M. Yabunchi
- Big Books: *Sea Life* and *Wild Animals*, Educational Insights

Writing
- Journals: animals in unexpected places
- Rewrite *Q Is for Duck*
- Make animal counting book (1 bear, 2 birds,)
- Zoo books: writing animal names
- Language experience chart to summarize unit

Social Studies
- Where do animals live?: house, farm, desert, mountain *(Animal, Animal, Where Do You Live?)*
- Animal habitats: aquarium, zoo, farm. What is the difference in animals?

ANIMALS
1. water   2. land/air

Science
- Different animals in different homes: land, air, water
- Fish aquariums: different sea life
- Water/land/air murals
- Discuss similarities and differences between animals and humans (Venn diagram)
- Compare animal and human coverings (skin, fur, feathers)

Math
- How many fish in your aquarium?
- Count how many different underwater animals we can think of
- Compare sizes of land animals
- Estimate weights of animals
- Animal counting books
- Animal pictures: sorting, counting, graphing
- Count number of animals on farm mural and write numbers
- Graph animals according to special homes (zoo, farm, and aquarium)

Art/Music
- "Old MacDonald Had a Farm"
- Torn-paper animals to make into book
- Fish aquariums
- Water/land/air mural
- Farm mural
- Make class books:
  1. *Animals Should Definitely Not Wear Clothing*
  2. *On the Farm* (Big Book)

Special Activities
- Pet day
- Second-graders share zoo books
- Animal videos: National Geographic Society
- Movement: follow the leader or act out animals
- Guess Zoo?, an animal matching memory game

Source: Courtesy of George Mason University interns.

228

Figure 8.6 Brainstorming Web for Third Grade About the Study of Greece

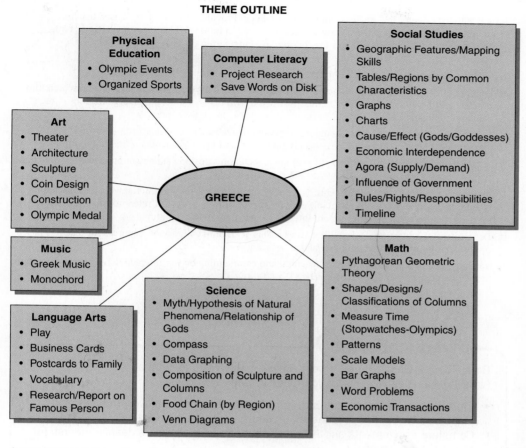

THEME OUTLINE

Physical Education
- Olympic Events
- Organized Sports

Computer Literacy
- Project Research
- Save Words on Disk

Social Studies
- Geographic Features/Mapping Skills
- Tables/Regions by Common Characteristics
- Graphs
- Charts
- Cause/Effect (Gods/Goddesses)
- Economic Interdependence
- Agora (Supply/Demand)
- Influence of Government
- Rules/Rights/Responsibilities
- Timeline

Art
- Theater
- Architecture
- Sculpture
- Coin Design
- Construction
- Olympic Medal

GREECE

Music
- Greek Music
- Monochord

Math
- Pythagorean Geometric Theory
- Shapes/Designs/Classifications of Columns
- Measure Time (Stopwatches-Olympics)
- Patterns
- Scale Models
- Bar Graphs
- Word Problems
- Economic Transactions

Language Arts
- Play
- Business Cards
- Postcards to Family
- Vocabulary
- Research/Report on Famous Person

Science
- Myth/Hypothesis of Natural Phenomena/Relationship of Gods
- Compass
- Data Graphing
- Composition of Sculpture and Columns
- Food Chain (by Region)
- Venn Diagrams

Source: Courtesy of George Mason University interns.

Then, construct a curriculum web by doing the following:

1. Brainstorm the possibilities related to an appropriate topic for the age level you are teaching (see Figure 8.5 for a list of suggestions).
2. Think of key words or terms and appropriate activities associated with your topic.
3. Group some of the ideas together by a common category to form a few broad categories.
4. Search for information, resources, and reference materials to support the categories.
5. Select the major concepts to be learned and identify connections among the web strands.

Finally, ask yourself, "How does this web compare to the characteristics of effective curriculum?

ONLINE RESOURCES FOR DEVELOPING CURRICULUM

John F. Kennedy Center for the Performing Arts ArtsEdge: Provides free standards-based teaching materials for arts-integrated teaching, as well as access to integrated lessons organized by both arts subjects and all other subjects for children in kindergarten through grade 4. http://artsedge.kennedy-center.org/

To see integrated lesson plans, go to http://artsedge.kennedy-center.org/teach/les.cfm.

Mid-continent Research for Education and Learning (McREL): This organization translates research into practice and provides a variety of standards-based lesson plans and activities, organized by content area and topic and linked to McREL's standards by grade level. www.mcrel.org

National Council of Teachers of Mathematics: Explore this website to find math standards and expectations, lessons and resources, weekly problems, and tips for teachers. http://nctm.org

National Science Teachers Association: To read the association's position statement on elementary science, go to www.nsta.org/about/positions/elementary.aspx?lid=ele

Thinkfinity: This site promotes 21st-century skills by providing a variety of interactive, cross-disciplinary, standards-based lesson plans, printable activity sheets, videos, podcasts, reference materials for teachers and parents, and after-school interactive resources. www.Thinkfinity.org

US Department of Education, Doing What Works: This is an online library of resources for teachers based on research-informed instructional practice. www.ed.gov

To watch a video of a preschool teacher teaching and commenting on her interactive reading lesson, go to http://dww.ed.gov/see/?T_ID=15&P_ID=31

PEARSON myeducationlab

Go to Topic 7 (Curriculum/Content Areas) in the MyEducationLab (www.myeducationlab.com) for your course, where you can:

- Find learning outcomes for curriculum/content areas along with the national standards that connect to these outcomes.
- Complete Assignments and Activities that can help you more deeply understand the chapter content.
- Apply and practice your understanding of the core teaching skills identified in the chapter with the Building Teaching Skills and Dispositions learning units.
- Examine challenging situations and cases presented in the IRIS Center Resources.

CHAPTER 9

CHAPTER 9

Planning for Children's Learning

 Teacher planning is the thread that weaves the curriculum, the 'what' of teaching, with the instruction, the 'how' of teaching. Planning provides for some measure of order in an uncertain and changing environment.

Jerome Freiberg & Amy Driscoll, 2005, p. 22

MS. OLIVERA teaches preschoolers with special needs and responds to children's interests when she plans. She says, "Finding out about children's interests is a key tool for the way I plan. I know children stay engaged in activities when they interest them. In many ways, using children's interests in planning my curriculum allows children to operate on many different developmental levels and at their own pace. Many teachers I know think that brainstorming ideas around a seasonal theme or a topic that they choose is the best way to inspire learning. I say, 'The theme is just the big umbrella under which different types of learning occur.'"

MS. KIM is a beginning first-grade teacher who has a daily read-aloud time. But many of her children do not seem interested in the books she is reading. She concluded that, "First graders have short attention spans." After talking with a colleague about her situation, Ms. Kim realized she was not planning her read-aloud time in the same way she was planning in other areas. She was reading whatever books were available. So, Ms. Kim started to plan for her read-aloud time by first reviewing *The Read Aloud Handbook* (Trelease, 2006). Next, she carefully selected picture books, informational books, and poetry and invited children's comments as she read to them. Finally, Ms. Kim placed each read-aloud book in the classroom library so that children could reread it alone or look at it with others. Ms. Kim says, "By planning my read-aloud time, I am providing a meaningful reading experience that increases the children's appreciation of literature. Planning has also boosted my confidence as a teacher."

MR. PERLMAN just completed student teaching in a third-grade classroom. In his final journal, he wrote, "I learned that I can plan in advance, although what I plan may not be what I do. I love to research—to look for activities—to create my own lessons because I think I can better meet specific needs of the children. This takes so much time, and requires so many modifications, that I learned I couldn't do it constantly. I was surprised by how much time planning consumed." Mr. Perlman simplified his plans well in advance of actually teaching them, "tried them on" in his imagination as he watched his cooperating teacher teach, and then talked through his ideas with her. That strategy led directly to better planning, better teaching, and better learning outcomes for children.

LEARNING
Outcomes

In this chapter, you will learn to

→ **Define and describe planning** (NAEYC #4, INTASC #7, ACEI #3.1 and #3.2)

→ **Identify principles of effective planning**

→ **Investigate five components of planning**

→ **Explore your role as a planner**

→ **Understand the different types of planning and approaches to long-term planning**

→ **Apply your knowledge of planning to early childhood classrooms**

Compare

What are some similarities in the ways these teachers plan for children's learning?

Contrast

What differences do you notice in how these teachers plan?

Connect

What surprises you about how these teachers plan for children's learning?

Now that you have reflected on the three teachers' perspectives and noted the learning outcomes, we preview the knowledge, skills, and dispositions you will need to acquire in order to fulfill your role in planning for each child's learning.

A Definition of Planning

Think about the best parties you have ever attended. Before those parties, your hosts or hostesses needed to think about whom to invite, what kind of party to have (e.g., barbecue, birthday, fiesta), when to have it, how long it should be, and any special items that were needed (e.g., paper plates, hats, gifts, games). During those parties, the hosts or hostesses made sure the food was ready, the guests were comfortable, and the gifts were opened at the appropriate time and place. And after the parties were over, the hosts or hostesses probably thought about what they might do or might not do again for another party. To have a successful party, then, there has to be planning.

Planning is the ability to think ahead and anticipate what is likely to make an event run smoothly. Just as there is a need to plan for social events, so too there is a need to plan for children's learning. Planning involves making decisions about the content you will teach, the experiences you will prepare, the ways you will engage children in the learning process, how to group children for learning, what materials you will need, and how you will assess and manage children's learning. Because planning involves creating and arranging teaching events in your mind, it helps you manage time and make instructional decisions that will benefit each child. It also includes troubleshooting, the ability to predict what might be confusing or require additional time or practice (Arends, 2009).

To facilitate children's learning, you need to think about planning *before*, *during*, and *after* each lesson or activity. Figure 9.1, Questions to Ask for Effective Planning, lists questions for each of these three planning stages.

Teachers need to plan for the following: curriculum in the content areas and developmental domains; the environment; the routines, procedures, and transitions that provide the predictability of the day; and for children's interests and special needs. Otherwise, learning is left to chance.

Good planning at every level is the roadmap that connects meaningful curriculum to the overall goals and outcomes of the program or school district. The planning decisions you make will affect what your students will know and be able to do. In the next section, we describe four principles of effective planning that influence teaching and learning.

DID YOU Know (?)

- New teachers plan differently from experienced teachers. They spend more time writing down specific details of their lesson plans to help them understand the complexity and demands of daily teaching. Planning helps new teachers begin to reflect on what it means to teach and apply what they have learned in their teacher education programs, such as having a classroom management plan, planning for transitions between lessons, and pacing activities (Shambaugh & Magliaro, 2006).

- Research shows that children's brains actually change with their experiences, which influences how they are prepared for future learning opportunities (Bowman, 2010).

- Teachers' plans reduce—but do not eliminate—the uncertainty in teaching. When teachers' plans are flexible, students learn more than when teachers teach to their plans regardless of what is happening with the students (Morine-Dershimer, 2009; Woolfolk, 2010).

Figure 9.1 Questions to Ask for Effective Planning

Before Teaching
- What do I want children to know and be able to do?
- How can I meet the needs of both individual children and the group and provide for active involvement?
- What background knowledge will the children bring to this learning experience?
- How will I assess children's learning?

During Teaching
- Is what I planned really engaging the children?
- Am I using the children's prior knowledge to capture their interest and engage them?
- Do the children understand the content and concepts?
- Do I need to make any adaptations or adjustments to my plan?

After Teaching
- What parts of the plan worked and what parts need to change?
- How intentional was my planning?
- How well did I assess what the children learned?
- What will I do differently if I teach a similar lesson?

Principles of Effective Planning

There is considerable evidence that effective planning is essential to good teaching. In your career as an early childhood teacher, you will be engaged almost continually in some kind of planning and will also be developing your own style of planning. It will occur in *each phase of the teaching process—before teaching* (e.g., making decisions about the purpose for learning, identifying child outcomes, and writing down the steps to take through the teaching-learning activity), *during teaching* (e.g., making necessary changes with your procedures, materials, and the content as you are teaching and noticing children's responses and level of engagement), and *after teaching* (e.g., assessing your teaching in terms of its outcomes, thinking about what will affect your teaching for the next day or week, and noting changes you want to make). In each planning phase you will be making decisions about what to teach and how to teach it. The best planning is characterized by: (1) accountability to local, state, and national

Time spent in planning is essential to a well-run early childhood classroom.

standards; (2) grouping patterns that meet the needs of all learners; (3) a way for every child to be successful in school; and (4) best practices based on research. These principles of effective planning are discussed next.

PLANNING FOR ACCOUNTABILITY TO STANDARDS

Teacher accountability to standards means that you know and use your local, state, and national standards in your plans. Your plans will also include assessment of each child's progress toward meeting standards. Most states have standards that clearly state what children should know and be able to do in kindergarten through third grade. Moreover, most states have developed standards for preschool children. Head Start has adopted specific learning outcomes for children to reach by the end of preschool. In addition to state standards, professional organizations have also identified outcomes in content areas that children should achieve at particular grade levels (Copple & Bredekamp, 2009; Gronlund, 2006).

In many schools and programs today, you probably will be asked to teach topics and will most likely be given standards and benchmarks, goals, objectives, and a prepared curriculum guide to follow. It is likely that you will be given one or more of the following: a list of competencies that students are expected to achieve, specific textbooks to use to teach certain subjects, and perhaps some curriculum kits. You can best incorporate these standards and materials into your curriculum when you are clear about how your own goals and outcomes for children mesh with other mandates such as local and state curriculum standards. In this way, you will have control over what you plan and how you teach (Arends, 2009; Gordon & Williams-Browne, 2011; Price & Nelson, 2011; Woolfolk, 2010).

PLANNING FOR INDIVIDUAL AND GROUP LEARNING

When you appreciate students' unique needs, you take into account what each child brings to your classroom. You also recognize that no two children and no two groups of children come into the classroom in quite the same way. Children bring their own experiences, attitudes, skills, interests, questions, and problems with them to school. Only the teacher—knowing the children, their families, and the school environment—makes a deliberate effort to plan a curriculum that meets individual children's needs (Kostelnik, Soderman, & Whiren, 2011; Silver, Strong, & Perini, 2000; Woolfolk, 2010). When you are responsive to the wide range of abilities and learning styles of the children in your classroom, you demonstrate that no one particular teaching method effectively meets every child's individual needs.

One way to facilitate individual learning is to use a variety of grouping practices. Basically, there are four types of groups that you will regularly use: *large groups* for such activities as class meetings, demonstrations, or sharing common experiences; *small groups* for peer teaching or tutoring, centers, skill building, and interest groups; *one-on-one interactions* for observation, assessment, or adaptive teaching; and *individualization* for choices, projects, or contracts. Grouping should be flexible and vary in size consistent with the learning activity, allow for child-guided and teacher-guided activities, foster social and emotional learning, and have appropriately paced activities to enhance learning.

PLANNING FOR EACH CHILD'S SUCCESS

Teachers have a responsibility to optimize each child's chance to be successful in school. That responsibility carries with it the need to plan with **intentionality,** which is thoughtful and purposeful planning (Epstein, 2007). When teachers plan intentionally, they plan specific objectives in all learning domains, use child development knowledge and a repertoire of teaching strategies that accommodate all types of learners, and deliberately decide "which materials, interactions, and learning experiences are likely to be most effective for the group and for each individual child in it" (Copple & Bredekamp, 2009, p. 36). Planning for each child's success depends largely on the outcomes that you select, the strategies that you use to reach those outcomes, your interactions with individuals and groups of children, and your decisions during unplanned moments (Jacobsen, Kauchak, & Eggen, 2009). Consider how the three teachers you met in the chapter opener try to ensure success for each learner: Ms. Olivera said, "Teachers need to know that finding out about children's interests is a key tool for planning"; Ms. Kim now uses a variety of age-appropriate books and read-aloud strategies to better engage the children; and Mr. Perlman talked through his mental and written plans with his classroom teacher to better meet the needs of his students.

Teachers who plan with intentionality are thoughtful and purposeful.

Building a planning repertoire of appropriate instructional strategies is important for teachers who want to improve their teaching and facilitate children's learning. While it is beyond the scope of this book to present in-depth instructional strategies to address students' diverse needs, we offer some general guidelines in Figure 9.2.

Planning Based on Research

Research on teachers' planning supports what most experienced teachers have concluded: that planning is critical to teaching and learning. We know from research (Arends, 2009; Berliner, 1986; Borko, Bellamy, & Sanders, 1992; Clark & Dunn, 1991; Clark & Peterson, 1986; Jacobsen et al., 2009; Lawler-Prince & Jones, 1997; Price & Nelson, 2011) that there are major differences in the planning process between new teachers and their more experienced counterparts. For example, experienced teachers have more pedagogical and subject-matter knowledge than new teachers; they also have more highly developed mental systems for organizing and storing this knowledge and use different strategies for solving problems. Finally, they are more adept at adapting lessons before they teach them and reflecting on what worked and what did not work after the lesson has ended. Consequently, in each of the three phases of teaching, experienced teachers process information more efficiently than do new teachers.

Experienced teachers are better able than new teachers to use their knowledge of children, content, and pedagogy to plan in their heads, making mental maps to guide their teaching and support children's learning. Their plans are more detailed and more richly connected to learning than those of novices. Experienced teachers include a greater number of student actions, teacher instructional moves, and routines for common classroom activities (Borko et al., 1992). Figure 9.3 compares and contrasts the differences between experienced and new teachers' planning.

Good planning also has other benefits, ranging from providing a snapshot picture for a day, week, month, or quarter, to making content accessible to each child, to using time wisely and productively, to being flexible and creative, and to asking higher-level questions. No matter what kind of planning you do you must have a learning goal and outcome in mind. We discuss the essential components of planning in the next section.

Figure 9.2 Strategies to Meet Learners' Diverse Needs

Strategies for Cultural and Ethnic Diversity
1. Incorporate the home culture into the classroom and activities.
2. Encourage active participation from families.
3. Use culturally relevant curriculum materials across all curriculum areas.
4. Identify and dispel myths.
5. Demonstrate concepts, use manipulatives, and show the correct way to do something.
6. Create culturally appropriate learning environments.
7. Use various grouping patterns and provide opportunities for children to work together.
8. Model respect by listening and accepting children's ideas and feelings.

Strategies for English Language Learners
1. Connect experiences to what children already know.
2. Use multi-age and peer tutoring to enhance communication.
3. Use language that invites children's participation so they can understand.
4. Simplify your language.
5. Bring the child's home language and culture into the classroom.
6. Provide books written in the various languages.
7. Use picture books, photo albums, and personal histories to develop children's pride and a positive view of literacy.

Strategies for Children with Exceptionalities
1. Provide the consistency and structure that children with special needs require to thrive.
2. Use audiotape materials for children who cannot read successfully.
3. Provide visual reminders (e.g., pictures, graphs, charts) for children who have difficulty attending.
4. Give directions in small steps.
5. Capitalize on children's interests and strengths.
6. Provide a circle-time space for every child, such as a small rug or mat.
7. Demonstrate new materials, equipment, and activities.
8. Be sensitive to what prevents children from learning.

Sources: Copple & Bredekamp, 2009; Epstein, 2007; Espinosa, 2010; Salend, 2010.

Essential Components of Planning

A beginning teacher recently said to us, "Planning is the hardest thing I do. Be sure your preservice teachers learn how to plan well so they can have more control over their teaching in their own classrooms and with their planning teams." This teacher has a good insight into an important aspect of teaching: being able to articulate what she wants to do and how she will accomplish it.

Figure 9.3 Planning Characteristics of Experienced and New Teachers

Experienced Teacher	New Teacher
Before Teaching	
1. Has system for teaching effective lessons matched to unit and lesson topics previously used and modified (e.g., folders, files, Internet lessons)	1. Focuses on detailed, written lesson plans and gathering resources
2. Uses extensive pedagogical and content knowledge and conceptual organizers	2. Has limited mental plans and experiences to draw upon
3. Attends to lesson flow	3. Tries to stay with plan "no matter what"
During Teaching	
1. Uses an extensive array of teaching strategies to teach activities and lessons	1. Uses a limited repertoire of teaching strategies
2. Has well-defined beliefs about student learning and child outcomes	2. Has untested and undefined pedagogical beliefs about student learning and content
3. Uses a variety of instructional and management routines and procedures, leading to more effective responses	3. Uses a limited number of routines and procedures and tends to focus on surface features of events
After Teaching	
1. Reflects on learning experiences and revises lessons based on an extensive array of teaching strategies to make content more accessible to each learner	1. Reflects on lessons and makes revisions based on a limited number of teaching strategies to make content more accessible to each child
2. Attends to children's performance and interests	2. Attends primarily to children's interests

All planning includes the following five important components: goals and objectives, processes and procedures, activities and lessons, assessment and evaluation, and differentiation (Arends, 2009; Morine-Dershimer, 2009; Price & Nelson, 2011; Schoenfeldt & Salsbury, 2009). Each will be discussed in the following paragraphs.

1. **Goals and objectives. Goals** are broad purposes for learning (e.g., in science, a goal is to build on children's natural interest with water), whereas **objectives** define the specific behavior, skill, or concept you wish the child to attain (e.g., to create a model of the water cycle). *Goals* take into account learners' needs, the content to be learned, and the community values and interests. Whatever your goal, clearly identifying the purpose of a lesson or activity is necessary so you think about what children will learn. *Objectives* are specific behaviors that

Pause and Reflect

About Effective Planning

Reread the opening section, Meet the Teachers, about the importance of planning. Now, discuss how these teachers might have planned differently to meet standards, to group children differently, or to ensure children's learning.

children will show as a result of their learning. Benjamin Bloom and his associates (Anderson & Krathwol, 2001) categorized educational objectives into three domains—cognitive, affective, and psychomotor. **Cognitive domain objectives** concern thinking and reasoning abilities, such as recalling or applying information. An objective in the cognitive domain might be "The child will identify a noun and verb in a sentence." **Affective domain objectives** address attitudes, emotions, and values that you want children to learn. An objective in the affective domain might be, "The child will share ideas as part of a group." **Psychomotor domain objectives** relate to learning physical skills, such as holding a pencil or using science equipment appropriately. Whatever the domain, all objectives should answer the question, "What should children know and be able to do when this lesson, activity, or project is finished?" When writing instructional objectives, keep the focus on specific changes that will occur in children's knowledge, skills, attitudes, or values. Be certain that your activity or lesson plan matches the objective you hope to achieve (Arends, 2009; Morine-Dershimer, 2009; Price & Nelson, 2011; Schoenfeldt & Salsbury, 2009).

2. **Processes and procedures. Processes** are ways of thinking about and making sense of information. For example, children use the scientific processes of observing and classifying and the mathematical processes of measuring and counting to understand information; they use the reading processes of predicting and inferring to gain meaning from text. These basic process skills are necessary for conceptual understandings. **Procedures** are the steps you plan to take to teach a lesson. They include how you will introduce the lesson to access children's prior knowledge and gain their interest, how you will develop a lesson including the strategies you will use to teach the content in an age-appropriate way, how you will group children, how you will individual children's needs, and how you will assess children's learning. Procedures should also include a way to help children transition to the next experience.

3. **Activities and lessons. Activities and lessons** are specific learning experiences, designed by the teacher or together with a child or children, to meet the intended outcomes, goals, and objectives. The term *activity plan* is most commonly used at the prekindergarten level; the term *lesson plan* is most commonly used in the elementary grades. Whatever term is used, the activity or lesson should be worth doing and meet a particular outcome. For example, writing responses to literature in language arts, graphing family members in mathematics, and formulating hypotheses about plants in science are typical lessons and activities in early childhood. Effective planning requires that activities and lessons are age appropriate and match the abilities and skills of individual children in a group. It also requires identifying resources and materials needed and deciding which procedures and methods will be used (Copple & Bredekamp, 2009; Kostelnik et al., 2011).

4. **Assessment and evaluation.** These are methods and criteria you will use (e.g., rubrics, observation checklists, anecdotal records) to assess your stated objective(s). The methods used should provide a way to determine what children know and can do following the lesson or activity. The results of your assessment will help you to determine the next steps you will take and how to revise your instruction based on children's performance and responses.

5. **Differentiation. Differentiation** is the way you adapt an activity or lesson for individual learners based on assessment data that you have collected. Teachers accommodate children's levels of interest, ability, and learning style by differentiating: (1) the content and skills for children to learn, (2) the processes or learning experiences that

help children make sense of what they are being taught, (3) the products or culminating projects that show what children have learned, and (4) the learning environment. For example, differentiation may include using flexible groups (processes), finding out what children already know before teaching a particular skill (content), or offering options in a final project so children can show what they know in different ways. To keep children engaged in learning, you will also want to be responsive to their needs for more practice, more challenge, more independence, or a more active approach to learning (Tomlinson & Cunningham-Eidson, 2003).

Planning that includes these five components helps you think and act like a professional. To make your plans come alive for every child, you will need to explore other aspects of your role as a planner.

Your Role as a Planner

Planning is one of the most important skills of effective early childhood teachers. Consider the following example of five student teachers planning an integrated social studies unit on Families for primary-grade children. It included the mandated state and local social studies standards and goals and the required content to be taught. As you follow these student teachers' planning process, think about what planning roles they assumed.

The student teachers began their collaborative planning for the Families unit by first reviewing the information about their schools and students. After examining the national, state, and local standards, they created a general statement about how to make the topic of families relevant to the lives of their students. They stated that studying about families was important because all children build a strong sense of self and others through their experiences with their own families. Families also provide an important context for children to understand themselves in terms of how they might experience the social studies themes of time, continuity, and change (National Council for the Social Studies, 1994). Through discussions, the student teachers agreed on three major goals for the social studies unit: students would be able to (a) appreciate historic events that happened while a family member was living, (b) experience a family member's work, and (c) understand where they live in relation to the school and their classmates. The student teachers identified the school district goals in each of the content areas (e.g., language arts, math, science, social studies, and the arts) that would guide their choice of activities. To decide what learning experiences to prepare, the group also used the key concepts of self, others, needs, family, and responsibility to understand the past, as described in their school district's curriculum guide.

Guided by the content goals and standards, the student teachers located books, poetry, multimedia, and websites appropriate for their particular student population. They chose nonfiction books such as *I Love My Family* (Beal, 1991) and *Papa Do You Love Me* (Jossee, 2005); picture books such as *Tell Me Again About the Night I Was Born* (Curtis, 1996) and *The Keeping Quilt* (Polacco, 1988); poetry books such as *Me I Am* (Prelutsky, 2007) and *Gracias, Thanks* (Mora, 2010); and professional resources such as *Social Studies for the Preschool/Primary Child* (Seefeldt, Castle, & Falconer, 2010) and *Active Experiences for Active Children: Social Studies* (Seefeldt & Galper, 2006). They also examined numerous websites for teaching and learning about social studies, such as NAEYC's website at www.naeyc.org/files/yc/file/200509/ResourcesBTJ905.pdf, to learn about available multimedia and online resources for teaching and learning about social studies. The student teachers noticed that many of the resources they located

Figure 9.4 Concept Web for Standards-Based Primary Unit on Families

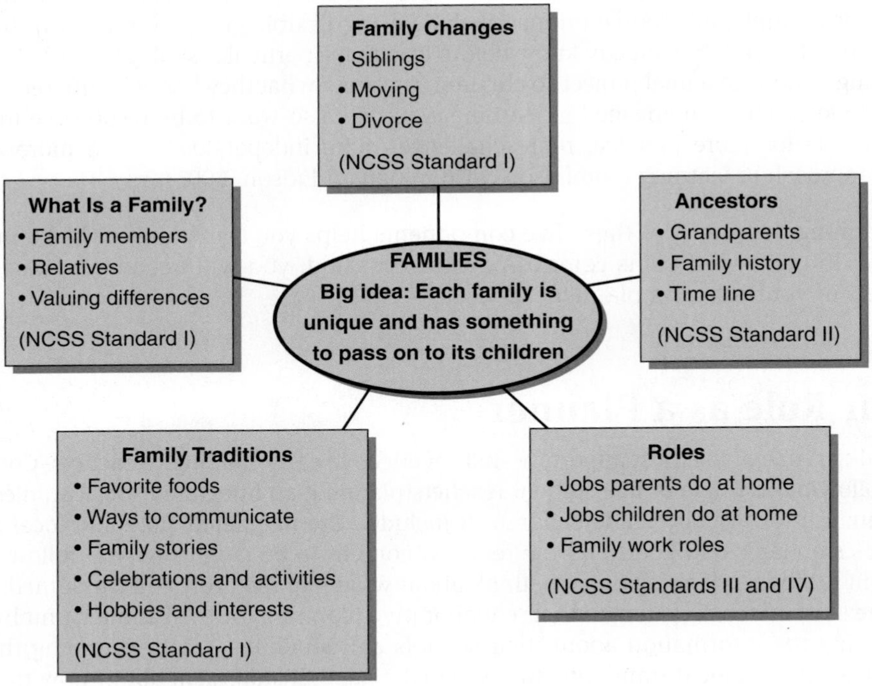

Family Changes
- Siblings
- Moving
- Divorce

(NCSS Standard I)

What Is a Family?
- Family members
- Relatives
- Valuing differences

(NCSS Standard I)

FAMILIES
Big idea: Each family is unique and has something to pass on to its children

Ancestors
- Grandparents
- Family history
- Time line

(NCSS Standard II)

Family Traditions
- Favorite foods
- Ways to communicate
- Family stories
- Celebrations and activities
- Hobbies and interests

(NCSS Standard I)

Roles
- Jobs parents do at home
- Jobs children do at home
- Family work roles

(NCSS Standards III and IV)

naturally formed categories such as What Is a Family? Family Traditions, Family Changes, Where Families Live, and Family Roles and Responsibilities. These categories helped them brainstorm topics, which led to their **concept web,** a planning tool to organize the curriculum content they hoped to use. Figure 9.4 shows the concept web linked to national social studies standards that they used for planning their Families unit.

With their web created, the student teachers next planned to find out what the children already knew about families as a starting point for their unit. They decided to use a **K-W-L** inquiry strategy (Ogle, 1986) to build on children's backgrounds as a way to engage children in new learning, gain their input into the learning, and provide the teachers with a starting place for new learning. During a class meeting on the first day of the unit, they would ask the children, "What do you already know about families?" (**K**) and "What do you want to know about families?" (**W**). And after the unit was finished, they will ask the children, "What did you learn?" (**L**). The student teachers planned a variety of teacher-guided and child-guided experiences to meet their goals, enhance the children's sense of self, and build respect and understanding for others and their families. For example, in *language arts*, the children would read and write stories about their own families and homes; in *math*, they might create a class graph about family members and class pets; and in *science*, they might identify special sounds in their homes. The student teachers also *learning centers* focusing on family-centered activities, such as creating family history books and making a multi-generational timeline; a library center with special books on the topic, including books children would and career roles of the family members in the class. To do this, they also planned for appropriate room arrangement to accommodate centers and the diverse needs of the learners.

After the topics were selected and organized, the student teachers turned their attention to developing meaningful activities. They identified *special vocabulary* terms (e.g., adoption, divorce, single-parent, and two moms) associated with the study of families that characterized some of the children in their classes. They talked about these terms' meanings to develop sensitivity for children who are members of these kinds of families. This helped them anticipate some questions children might ask about families. Look at Figure 9.5 and notice how the student teachers planned *developmentally appropriate* experiences and assessments in each content area to meet the standards. These student teachers have demonstrated the essential components of their role in planning for children's learning that are now described in the following paragraphs (Copple & Bredekamp, 2009; Freiberg & Driscoll, 2005; Price & Nelson, 2011; Seefeldt et al., 2010).

A unit on families needs to show sensitivity to nontraditional family groups.

PLAN FOR CHILDREN'S NEEDS

Good planning begins with the children themselves. **Developmentally appropriate practice (DAP)** requires that teachers make decisions based on three important kinds of knowledge: (a) child development and learning; (b) individual needs, abilities, and interests; and (c) social and cultural contexts in which children live (Copple & Bredekamp, 2006, 2009). Considering children's ages, developmental levels, uniqueness, and social and cultural backgrounds greatly enhances planning. Younger children need large blocks of time for play and spontaneous exploration; older children do more project-oriented and structured planning to more accurately represent their learning. Notice how the student teachers took into account the characteristics of primary-grade children by providing many meaningful activities for them to work in small groups and expand their academic skills across the subject areas. Notice also how they addressed the children's cultural backgrounds through the resources identified, the connection with the children's families, and the activities planned.

PLAN THE CONTENT THAT CHILDREN NEED TO LEARN

Content refers to the concepts, information, facts, and vocabulary contained in each area of learning (Epstein, 2007). **Concepts** are the "big ideas" that help us organize similar events, ideas, objects, or people (Woolfolk, 2010). Each professional subject-area organization for teachers, as well as state and local school districts, has identified key standards, content, and concepts considered essential to learn at different ages. One of the first sets of questions you will ask yourself is "What content and concepts will I be teaching? What do the children already know and how can I build on that? What are the most effective age-appropriate ways to teach this content?" This kind of planning focuses on results and positive child outcomes. You will want to plan experiences that are meaningful, challenging, and will extend children's thinking, but that also help them to be successful learners. Whatever *content and concepts* you teach must have integrity and be worthy of children's time (Katz & Chard, 2000). In the unit on families previously described, we saw how the student teachers selected books on topics

Figure 9.5 Developmentally Appropriate Experiences for Standards-Based, Integrated Primary Unit on Families

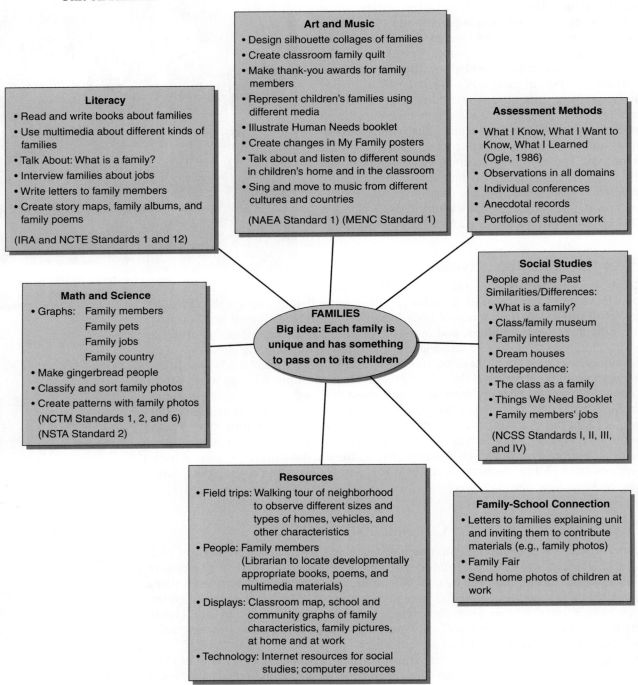

Art and Music
- Design silhouette collages of families
- Create classroom family quilt
- Make thank-you awards for family members
- Represent children's families using different media
- Illustrate Human Needs booklet
- Create changes in My Family posters
- Talk about and listen to different sounds in children's home and in the classroom
- Sing and move to music from different cultures and countries

(NAEA Standard 1) (MENC Standard 1)

Literacy
- Read and write books about families
- Use multimedia about different kinds of families
- Talk About: What is a family?
- Interview families about jobs
- Write letters to family members
- Create story maps, family albums, and family poems

(IRA and NCTE Standards 1 and 12)

Assessment Methods
- What I Know, What I Want to Know, What I Learned (Ogle, 1986)
- Observations in all domains
- Individual conferences
- Anecdotal records
- Portfolios of student work

Math and Science
- Graphs: Family members
          Family pets
          Family jobs
          Family country
- Make gingerbread people
- Classify and sort family photos
- Create patterns with family photos
(NCTM Standards 1, 2, and 6)
(NSTA Standard 2)

FAMILIES
Big idea: Each family is unique and has something to pass on to its children

Social Studies
People and the Past
Similarities/Differences:
- What is a family?
- Class/family museum
- Family interests
- Dream houses
Interdependence:
- The class as a family
- Things We Need Booklet
- Family members' jobs

(NCSS Standards I, II, III, and IV)

Resources
- Field trips: Walking tour of neighborhood to observe different sizes and types of homes, vehicles, and other characteristics
- People: Family members (Librarian to locate developmentally appropriate books, poems, and multimedia materials)
- Displays: Classroom map, school and community graphs of family characteristics, family pictures, at home and at work
- Technology: Internet resources for social studies; computer resources

Family-School Connection
- Letters to families explaining unit and inviting them to contribute materials (e.g., family photos)
- Family Fair
- Send home photos of children at work

directly relevant to primary children and planned graphing activities using children's family members and pets to teach math concepts. Notice, too, that the activities they planned were worth doing.

PLAN A VARIETY OF EXPERIENCES TO MEET THE NEEDS OF DIVERSE LEARNERS

Good planning consists of varied experiences that maximize all children's learning. Planning for children from diverse cultural and linguistic backgrounds, children who are "at risk" for school failure, and children with exceptionalities is important because not all children learn in the same manner (Price & Nelson, 2011). The abilities, interests, and backgrounds of children even of the same age vary, so activities must be open-ended and flexible enough to be used by a number of children Instead of working with one set plan for all children, stretch yourself to incorporate the different types of intelligences into your planning (Gardner, 1993; Silver et al., 2000). This effort recognizes that students learn differently and allows them to express themselves in their own ways. In the Families unit, you can see that the student teachers planned a variety of authentic activities, which met different learning styles. They included graphing for those who prefer patterns, writing stories for those who prefer words, cooking and carpentry for those who like spatial activities, and individual activities for children to do alone as well as activities to be done in a group. In this way, their plan was to work from children's strengths and to choose teaching strategies that use multiple modes of representation of performance (Price & Nelson, 2011; Silver et al., 2000; Tiedt & Tiedt, 2010).

Planning a variety of experiences also takes into account children's interests and strengths. Most children have particular interests and enjoy pursuing them. That usually leads them to find out more about their interest and to gain skill and expertise in it—sometimes lasting a lifetime. This can also lead to children being exposed to other interests, which in turn leads to other competencies. For example, exposing kindergarten children to different family occupations may spark an interest in a particular career option in one or more children in the class.

PLAN APPROPRIATE METHODS OF ASSESSING CHILDREN'S LEARNING

How will you know what children have learned? Planned, ongoing assessment of children's learning leads to better knowledge of what individual children know and can do as well as how the group as a whole is progressing. This knowledge leads to better planning. Note that the methods of assessment planned by the student teachers who developed the unit on families show evidence of good planning. They planned to assess children's prior knowledge through the K-W-L strategy (Ogle, 1986) and to start the unit by building on children's prior knowledge and increasing their understanding from that point. Teaching for understanding means children can do "a variety of thought demanding activities with a topic—like

Know the children and families for whom you are planning.

Pause and
Reflect

About Your Role
as a Planner

Think about your role as a planner in relation to the integrated social studies unit on families. What did you realize about planning when you read about these student teachers' plans? What questions do you have from reading this description? Think of ways to connect these ideas with ways to communicate with families.

explaining, finding evidence and examples, generalizing, applying, and representing the topic in a new way" (Perkins & Blythe, 1994, pp. 5–6). The student teachers also planned for ongoing observations in all domains, using work samples for portfolios, and conducting individual conferences. Each of these assessment strategies is tied to the unit goals and reflects the importance of unifying goals and assessment from the outset.

PLAN TO REFLECT ON YOUR TEACHING

Reflection is an essential part of your role as a planner. It allows you to become more thoughtful in your decision making for future planning, to evaluate an experience, to repeat successful strategies, and to learn from your teaching. As you plan, you make decisions about what to teach, how to teach it, and the environmental conditions in which the children will learn. After teaching, thoughtful teachers reflect on questions about student learning and their own teaching methods. Ask yourself: "What have my students learned?" "What evidence do I have that shows they are learning?" This is the reflective aspect of planning. As you think about the outcome of your planning, identify the aspects of your teaching that worked and those that did not and why that was so. Look at the part of the lesson or activity that did not work as well as you would have liked. What can you change about it to improve it? You will need to think about your teaching every day to improve it in order to optimize children's learning (Hiebert, Morris, Berk, & Jansen, 2007). In essence, reflecting on your planning helps you know how good your decisions were. Only you can best answer these questions (Jacobsen et al., 2009).

PLAN AHEAD

Your best teaching will occur when you plan well in advance of the teaching day so you have enough time to think through how standards and practices fit together. You will want to find a regular planning time for yourself, and with your teaching team, to ensure the best planning. Writing down your daily, weekly, and monthly plans gives you the flexibility you need to implement them. You might also consider planning extra or optional activities to make you feel more confident in case your planned activities take less time than expected or are just not engaging the children as you had hoped.

Effective planning is an important part of your role as an early childhood professional. In the next section, we discuss two different types of planning—long-term planning and short-term planning. We also show you some models of different planning tools so that you have an idea of what different plans look like.

Types of Planning

Teachers engage in two basic types of planning: **long term** and **short term.** Most future teachers cannot wait to start planning lessons and activities for children. What they sometimes fail to realize is that they will be teaching in a program or school district that has predetermined objectives and outcomes for the children to meet. Even though there may be specific content and skills to teach, as a teacher, you are continually shaping and reshaping lessons and activities based on your knowledge of both child development and curriculum.

LONG-TERM PLANNING

Long-term planning serves as a framework for later planning efforts. It includes yearly, semester, or quarterly planning, and thematic unit or project planning. While each has its own purpose, each is connected to the other. **Yearly plans** are very general and should contain the overall knowledge, skills, and attitudes to be taught (e.g., caring, tolerance, respect), topics of study (e.g., understanding self and others, literary genres, change), and cycles of the school year (e.g., grading periods, holidays, best times to introduce new topics) that will influence your planning over the course of the year (Arends, 2009). *Semester, quarterly, thematic unit,* and *project plans* contain more specific goals, objectives, concepts, and skills that you hope children achieve during that particular period of time. Long-term planning helps you decide the content and topics to teach (the *what* and *why* of planning), the sequence in which those topics will be taught (the *how* and *where* of planning), the amount of time to spend on each topic (the *when* of planning), and the assessment of child outcomes (the *how, what, why, when,* and *where* of planning) (Jacobsen et al., 2009).

Long-term planning gives you a general idea of what you are going to teach so you can begin to gather materials and plan experiences that will enhance children's learning. You will also be able to share your plans with families so that they have advance notice of events that call for participation and a better understanding of what their children will be learning. Long-term plans should be flexible to meet the changing needs, interests, and abilities of your children. Flexibility enables you to capitalize on unanticipated learning opportunities or "teachable moments," align your planning with state standards, develop achievable goals for each child, determine the extent to which each child will be expected to achieve those goals, and implement meaningful ways to assess student learning (Freiberg & Driscoll, 2005; Henson, 2010). Figure 9.6 provides long-range plans, organized by topic, for first grade.

WEBBING

Many teachers like to begin their planning by brainstorming possibilities using a web as a planning tool. **Webbing** is a way to brainstorm possible key concepts, ideas, and learning experiences and then connect them through a pictorial or graphic. You may create a web around a topic (e.g., plants), subject areas (e.g., language arts, science), or program or school district goals (e.g., multicultural education, critical thinking). Figure 9.7 illustrates a curriculum web organized around "The Self" for preschool and kindergarten children. Note that web is organized around concepts and subject areas.

APPROACHES TO LONG-TERM PLANNING

There are primarily two kinds of long-term plans: the thematic unit approach and the project approach. The following paragraphs describe each of these planning approaches.

The **thematic unit approach** involves a variety of planned, integrated learning experiences around a big idea, question, or problem that helps children make connections and further their understanding of the world around them. It has intellectual integrity, is relevant and meaningful, and represents in-depth thinking and problem solving that can be studied at different age or grade levels (Chaille, 2008). Examples of big ideas include human relationships, patterns, changes, traditions and celebrations, and communities. How children study a big idea changes with their age, interests, background, and grade level.

When planning with *thematic unit approach*, you want to consider topics that can meet each of the following five elements (Kostelnik et al., 2011):

Relevance: the big ideas or concepts to be taught are directly related to children's experiences and build on what they know. Universal themes such as family, self,

Figure 9.6 Long-Range Plans for First Grade

Subject	September	October	November	December	January
Social Studies	Families Everyone is Special All About Me Rules Citizenship	Families I Am Part of a Family Christopher Columbus	Families Thanksgiving Veteran's Day Children of long ago	Families Traditions and celebrations Needs and wants	Families People of the World Martin Luther King Jr.
Reading	Reading Assessment Text levels Letter identification	Shared language: pumpkins, fall, trees	Shared language: families, homes	Shared language: *Too Many Tamales* Celebrations	Shared language: winter, snow
Writing	Writing assessment	Ongoing assessment is used to determine the needs of individual students and plan instruction accordingly. Scope of instructional emphasis includes •Using multiple strategies to attach meaning to print •Sentence structure •Word usage •Capitalization •Punctuation •Spelling •Structural analysis •Letters and sounds			
Math*	Investigating numbers: patterns, comparing number relationships	Addition sentences Counting on Measurement: nonstandard units	Numbers 11–15 Shapes Subtraction	Numbers 16–19 Measurement: weights (nonstandard), money	Equal groups problems Solving with + Combinations Facts: zeroes, doubles
Science	Five senses	Leaves Adopt a tree The Harvest	Parts of a Tree Leaves	Evergreens	Seeds Recording plant growth Winter
Health	School safety Bus safety Emergency Procedures and 911	Fire safety Police officer	Poison Prevention Pharmacist	Medicines Flu Prevention	Nutrition
Handwriting	Formation of letters Fine motor skills	Formation of letters Fine motor skills	Formation of letters Fine motor skills	Formation of letters Fine motor skills	Formation of letters

*Graphing Calendar Activities integrated throughout the year.

Source: Courtesy of Diana Sparrgrove, Parklawn Elementary School, Fairfax, Virginia.

Figure 9.6 continued

February	March	April	May	June

Families
The World:
    different types
    of families
Chinese New Year
	Families
	How the
	    environment
	    affects how we live
	Maps/Geography
		Families
		Local community
			Families
			Community
			Economics
				Families
				Review

Shared language:
    national
    celebrations
Plants
	Shared language:
	    plants, weather
		Shared language:
		    weather, flowers
			Shared language:
			    seasons
				Shared language:
				    summer

•Building vocabulary •Story structure •Author's craft •Writing in different forms •Using informational sources in the classroom •Planning before writing •Self-monitoring strategies •Initiating writing •Revising to help clarify or expand meaning •Developing oral language •Collaborating with others for the purpose of writing

February	March	April	May	June

10's and 1's
Place value
Time duration
On the hour
	Measurement:
	    length
	Solid shapes
	Subtraction
	    sentences
		Relating addition
		    and subtraction
		Counting forward
		    counting backward
		Money
			Measurement:
			    capacity, weight
			2-digit numbers
				Area
				Fractions
				Multiplication
				Division

Propagation:
    growth without
    seeds
	Clouds
	Tree growth
		Flowers	Grass
			Plants
			Flowers
				Flowers

Nutrition Dental health Personal Hygiene	Nutrition Physical Activity	Emergencies	Strangers Safety procedures	Playground and pool safety
Formation of letters	Formation of letters	Formation of letters	Formation of letters	Formation of letters

Figure 9.7 Concept Web and Standards-Based Subject-Area Web for Preschool and Kindergarten Children

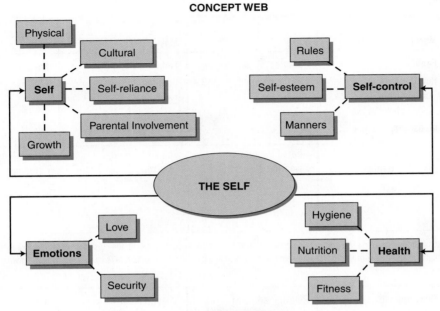

CONCEPT WEB

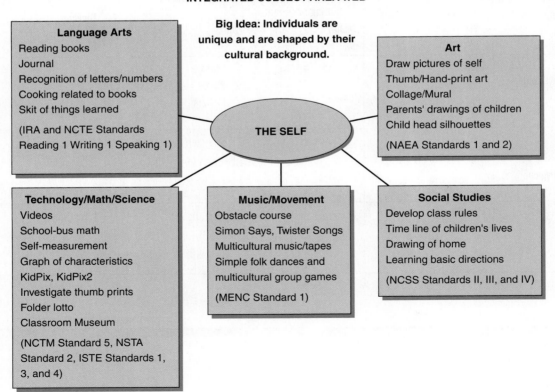

STANDARDS-BASED INTEGRATED SUBJECT-AREA WEB

Big Idea: Individuals are unique and are shaped by their cultural background.

THE SELF

Language Arts
Reading books
Journal
Recognition of letters/numbers
Cooking related to books
Skit of things learned

(IRA and NCTE Standards
Reading 1 Writing 1 Speaking 1)

Art
Draw pictures of self
Thumb/Hand-print art
Collage/Mural
Parents' drawings of children
Child head silhouettes

(NAEA Standards 1 and 2)

Technology/Math/Science
Videos
School-bus math
Self-measurement
Graph of characteristics
KidPix, KidPix2
Investigate thumb prints
Folder lotto
Classroom Museum

(NCTM Standard 5, NSTA
Standard 2, ISTE Standards 1,
3, and 4)

Music/Movement
Obstacle course
Simon Says, Twister Songs
Multicultural music/tapes
Simple folk dances and
multicultural group games

(MENC Standard 1)

Social Studies
Develop class rules
Time line of children's lives
Drawing of home
Learning basic directions

(NCSS Standards II, III, and IV)

Source: Courtesy of George Mason interns.

and transportation all have relevance to young children and help them understand themselves and the world around them.

Hands-on activities: activities that allow children to experience content being studied through *firsthand experiences* with objects or phenomena through exploratory play, guided discovery, and inquiry. Firsthand experiences, such as caring for living things in the classroom or visiting a local garden shop, are rich examples of real-life experiences. If children have no experience with the theme under consideration or firsthand experiences cannot be provided, consider another theme.

Diversity and balance across the curriculum: a variety of themes that explore the content areas and/or developmental areas should be available to children over the school year. Many topics, such as the study of homes, can include more than one content area (e.g., literacy, social studies, math, and science) as well as developmental areas (social skills and cooperation).

Resources and materials: real materials need to be accessible to support children's meaningful learning. Carefully consider and select **open-ended materials** to support the content and big ideas, strengthen children's understanding, and foster independence, motivation, and interest—all essential components of learning.

Project potential: this refers to open-ended activities that emerge from the children's deepening understanding. In a study of homes, for example, the potential to learn facts about different kinds of homes, jobs needed to build homes, to make visits, both virtual and real, to different homes, to construct and equip real and imaginary homes in the classroom, and to read books and use technology about homes is vast. The potential of a thematic approach can motivate children to ask questions and learn more facts and increase their conceptual understanding around the big ideas while integrating multiple subject areas and other learning domains.

A word of caution is needed about using holidays as a basis for planning thematic units. First, holiday themes are often limited to making cute decorations or crafts that do little, if anything, to deepen children's conceptual understanding about the holiday or develop new skills in different areas of the curriculum. Second, children have ample opportunities to learn about their holiday lore at home and through the community, which is not true for engaging in more meaningful, worthwhile topics such as spiders, homes, friends, or storytelling, where early childhood teachers can add richness, variety, and experiences not so easily obtained elsewhere. Third, the significance of certain holidays may be reduced to simplistic activities that unintentionally promote stereotypes while assuming that every family celebrates particular holidays similarly. None of these assumptions is in keeping with the cultural and religious sensitivity that early childhood professionals strive to achieve. To be inclusive, holiday activities may appropriately comprise some of the non-theme-related concepts in a given unit, such as family traditions or people living together. These topics support children's growing awareness of the similarities as well as differences among people (Derman-Sparks & Edwards, 2010; Kostelnik, 2008).

Thematic units should include both teachers and children in the planning. You will be using your knowledge of children (e.g., their interests, their prior knowledge, and their learning styles); you will also be utilizing your knowledge of curriculum (e.g., choosing content and learning experiences; selecting appropriate products) as well as your knowledge of teaching (e.g., using a variety of teaching strategies). Inviting children into the planning can lead to more meaningful activities, to the formation of a healthy learning environment, and to more active learning (Keefe & Jenkins, 2002; Kostelnik et al., 2011; Seefeldt et al., 2010). Figure 9.8 is an overview of a social studies thematic unit for primary grades.

COLLABORATING WITH
Families

Communicating with Families About Meaningful Activities at Home

Each month, Ms. Davis sends home a calendar of activities for children and families to do that are related to what the children are learning at school. Following is a *portion* of one of her February calendars. Suggest some other activities that would be appropriate for families to do with their children.

February Home Activities

Monday	Tuesday	Wednesday	Thursday	Friday
2 Ask your child what *communicate* means.	3 Read with your child the picture message or rebus chart brought home today.	4 Write a rebus message about what you did after supper tonight.	5 Sing "Little Cabin in the Woods" with and without words—just hand signs!	6 Select and make a recipe from the *Home-to-School Cookbook.*
9 Collect 20 old envelopes with stamps on them— 15 for home and 5 to take to school.	10 Have your child sort the 15 envelopes. How many ways did your child sort the envelopes?	11 Make a valentine to send to someone special. Address and stamp the envelope.	12 Deliver the valentine in person or through the postal system.	13 Read *A Letter for Amy* by Ezra Jack Keats.
16 Finish the picture phone book with your child. Call a friend in the new phone book.	17 Take turns acting out activities you do during the day. Can you guess the activities?	18 Select four or five pictures of your child at various ages. See if your child can arrange the photos in order from babyhood to present.	19 Give your child a hug and say "I love you." How many ways can you tell each other "I love you"?	20 On a piece of paper write the word *communicate*, then find pictures in magazines that show ways to communicate. Make a collage.

Pause and
Reflect

About Long-Term Planning

Search the Internet for suggestions for long-term plans. What did you find that would be useful to you? How will you judge the worthiness of those plans located on the Internet? What questions do you still have?

The **project approach** is planned, in-depth investigations of a topic worth learning about. The investigations are usually undertaken by a small group of children within a class, sometimes by a whole class, and occasionally by an individual child, about a topic posed either by the children, the teacher, or the teacher working with the children (Katz & Chard, 2000). The goal of a project is to learn more about the topic by applying higher-level thinking skills rather than to seek right answers to questions posed by the teacher. It epitomizes the collaborative nature of teaching, during which teachers and children think, plan, and evaluate together.

The project approach has three basic phases. *Phase 1, getting started or beginning the project,* involves the selection and refinement of topics that must be closely related to the children's experience and have enough depth to be explored for an extended time period. *Phase 2, field work or developing the project,* is when the

Figure 9.8 Overview of Social Studies Unit for Primary Grades

TOPIC: Where we are in place and time
UNIT TITLE: *Schools—Past and Present*
FOCUS SUBJECT: Social Studies
LEVEL: Primary
BIG IDEA: People, places, and things change over time.
UNIT OBJECTIVE: SWBAT* demonstrate knowledge that people, places, and things change over time.
UNIT STANDARDS: VA History Standard 1.1 and NCCS II.a

CULMINATING ASSESSMENT: Venn Diagram Quilt

	Day 1	Day 2	Day 3	Day 4	Day 5
Daily Topic, Theme, or Question	What is a school?	Why do we go to school?	Who makes our school work?	Old Fashioned School Day	School Architecture
Daily Objective	Students will be able to illustrate and label the elements that make up a school.	SWBAT attribute skills needed in society to skills they learn in school.	SWBAT explain the roles of the different people who make up our school.	SWBAT will describe elements in the past classroom that differ from their current classroom.	SWBAT produce representations of past and present school buildings.
Instructional Activity and SS Materials	Introduce Word Wall Picture sort—example and nonexample	Whole-class discussion and review of jobs in the community Think-Pair-Share of skills learned in school needed for jobs in the community.	Brainstorm with the class who makes up a school (must include students and teachers). Interview people around the school (head of school or principal, nurse, custodian, lunchroom staff, office staff).	Simulation of a penmanship lesson incorporating classroom practices including seating.	MM presentation on school buildings then and now. Picture sort of school buildings then and now.
Daily Assessment	Draw and label a school and at least 3 of its elements.	Oral presentation on at least 3 skills learned in school needed for jobs in the community.	Jigsaw interview findings and use anecdotal notes to record.	A *reflective* journal entry on 3 things students experienced that are different from the present classroom.	Create 2 quilt squares representing past (blue) and present (yellow) school buildings.

*Students Will Be Able To

continued

Figure 9.8 continued

	Day 6	Day 7	Day 8	Day 9	Day 10
Daily Topic, Theme, or Question	Field Trip: Historical Schoolhouse	Artifacts	Schoolyard Games	Schools in Time	Wrap-Up and Reflection
Daily Objective	SWBAT identify features of school buildings in the past.	SWBAT locate and describe pictures of school artifacts.	Content: SWBAT differentiate between games children played in the past, games they play now, and games played in both eras. Process: SWBAT demonstrate the ability to participate in several schoolyard games.	SWBAT group people, places, and things on a timeline. SWBAT demonstrate an understanding of the past and present by reflecting on and choosing what would go into a time capsule.	SWBAT create a quilt that represents how people, places, and things change over time.
Instructional Activity and SS Materials	Photo scavenger hunt.	Opening of old time capsule. Read: *A Country Schoolhouse.* Locating pictures of old artifacts in the classroom library.	Large-group game (Simon Says). Game centers (marbles, jacks, hopscotch).	Sort pictures and create a timeline. Students will *choose* 3 items to draw and drop in the time capsule.	Create and assemble quilt.
Daily Assessment	Photo display of features of school buildings in the past.	Present and describe findings to class or download online from collections from Children's Museums.	Content: Worksheet that distinguishes between past, present, and games common to both. Process: Participation in the games.	Create a timeline showing past and present, including at least 1 person, place, or thing. Write a sentence describing each part of the timeline. Score time capsule item on appropriateness using checklist.	Quilt squares and teacher checklist.

*Students Will Be Able To

Source: Courtesy of George Mason University Fast Train students.

children are engaged in direct investigation of the topic through field trips to places, observing, constructing models, recording findings, predicting, discussing, and dramatizing their new understandings (Katz & Chard, 2000). And **Phase 3, culminating and debriefing or concluding the project,** focuses on children and their teacher(s) presenting the results of their investigations in the form of displays of findings, artifacts, and talks about their project.

The following boxed feature uses the voices of kindergarten teachers Marilyn Ornstein and Susan McClanahan of Duke School in Durham, North Carolina, to describe the three phases of a chair project using the project approach that their kindergartners engaged in for 12 weeks. As you read each phase of the project, think about how it meets both content and performance standards.

CHAIR PROJECT

Phase 1	**Beginning the Project** Our chair project grew out of our beginning-of-the-year study about ourselves. After exploring our names, birthdays, families, and friends, we made a web with ourselves in the middle. In several brainstorming sessions, the children generated many topics for our web, including homes. When we webbed further under the homes idea, the children were interested in exploring items found in their homes, including furniture and machines. Later we listed furniture items that were of interest, with chairs fascinating teachers and children alike. Little did we know how far the children's interest would carry us! We generated questions about chairs that included types (e.g., lawn chairs, high chairs, wheelchairs, easy chairs), materials from which chairs are made, sizes, and more. We solicited "chair stories" from the children and involved the parents by asking for photos of favorite chairs. With the help of parents, friends, and colleagues, our investigations began.
Phase 2	**Developing the Project** Wanting to stay close to home for field work, our study began with the chairs in our school environment. Each child chose a classroom and specific chair to explore. They made observational drawings, recorded chair measurements, and took photos, then returned to class to discuss and compare the results with classmates. After exploring the variety of chairs in our school, we invited parents and colleagues to be guest experts and share chairs of interest with us and talk about their importance and "history." We had an overwhelming response. A teacher's friend donated an old swivel easy chair that remained in the classroom all year. Some children were fascinated with the swivel mechanism, and explored springs and how they worked. Others wanted to know about the fabric and elements in upholstering chairs. A group even re-upholstered a teacher desk chair! A local medical supply store lent us a wheelchair for an entire week free of charge. A parent, who had spent several weeks of her pregnancy in a wheelchair, talked to us about her experience. We took the wheelchair out to our playground so each child could maneuver it. Another parent arranged a visit by a young man who

continued

demonstrated his electric wheelchair and the van that helps transport him places. We explored an antique wooden highchair that converted into a child glider. The gear mechanism became intriguing and a small group of children studied about the gears and how they worked in this chair. We created a gear center so that children could learn about gears through manipulative play. The drama center was transformed into a chair factory where the children used big blocks, cushions, fabric, and other materials to create chairs to sell. Other props included a cash register, computer, charge cards, and student-made money and sales slips.

As each chair remained in our room, children used a variety of media to represent the chairs. Working with useful junk, model magic, wood, paint, and fabric, the children constructed their favorite chairs for our parent display.

Phase 3

Concluding the Project

Parents were invited to our "Chair Museum." They circulated the room and discussed the different chairs with child experts at each station. The children answered questions and demonstrated their knowledge during this period of time. In addition, parents were treated to the array of representations that filled our room. Comments: When we started this project, we had some misgivings about the topic and how interested the children would remain as we expanded the idea with them. We could not have been more wrong! We were amazed at the depth of attachment that the children expressed in the stories they told. Parents were intrigued by the importance of these objects in their child's life. This project has wonderful potential for those teachers who have difficulty leaving the premises for field work—so much of what we did took place in our own surroundings with the "work" coming to us.

The project approach encourages children's direct investigations through constructing models, observations, and conversations.

In the Ask the Expert feature on page 257, noted project-approach expert Sylvia Chard answers questions about the difference between thematic units and projects, how the project approach demonstrates essential principles of planning, and how it addresses the needs of diverse learners.

Sylvia Chard

The Project Approach

Q: What are the differences between the project approach and thematic units?

A: Thematic units are sequences of lessons, activities, and experiences planned by the teacher to enable a class of children to learn about a theme. A project is an in-depth collaborative study undertaken by a class or group of children. The topic of study for a project is usually selected from the everyday world of the children and is something worth knowing more about. A thematic unit may be completed in 1 or 2 weeks, whereas a project usually lasts for 6 to 9 weeks. In a thematic unit the children complete the same activities, whereas in a project different children are usually working on the different aspects of the study according to their interests. Like a jigsaw puzzle, the whole study is made up of parts through different children sharing their work.

As distinct from a thematic unit, a project has a narrative quality to it. The progress of the study can be described in story form from the children sharing experiences and understanding they have at the outset, through developing questions to investigate, visiting field sites, interviewing local experts, consulting secondary sources of information, representing new knowledge in a variety of ways, and, finally, presenting their new understandings to other children and/or parents in class or evening meetings.

Q: How does the project approach demonstrate essential principles of planning?

A: Planning for a project involves selecting a topic, deciding the scope of the study, determining field sites and visiting experts, developing a variety of investigations and representations, and deciding on how to share new knowledge at the conclusion of the study. The topic is selected by the teacher, who takes account of the likely scope of the investigation, the science or social studies curriculum, the availability of local resources, and the interest of the children. The likely scope of the study can be mapped out in advance in a *topic web*, a categorized collection of words that will be used in discussion of the topic. An additional web, a *curriculum web*, can help the teacher see the relationship of the topic to the subjects of science, social studies, language, and math, as well as to other learning goals.

The first phase of the project offers the children opportunities to share personal experiences related to the topic and to develop their curiosity and interest in it. A list of questions can launch the second phase of the project in which the topic can be investigated at field sites, by interviewing expert visitors to the classroom, and through the use of secondary sources of information in books, videos, and on the Internet. As children form interest groups they can share the results of their investigations and develop individual and group representations to demonstrate what they have learned.

During the processes of representation students can share their strengths in math, writing, reading, or in drawing, drama, or music. In the third phase of the project each child can apply his or her preferred representational skills in helping the group members to present what they have learned about the topic through the research they have carried out. Project work allows for a wide range of individual talents to be applied for the good of others. The teacher's role in planning can be to anticipate the most successful outcome for each child by assessing his or her prior knowledge, individual learning strengths, and level of interest in the topic. The teacher then plans to guide children's individual and group work throughout the project based on this information. NOTE: Planning in project work is not all done in advance. Teachers respond daily to the individual and group learning needs and

continued

Ask the Expert continued

interests and change direction of the study, as these new directions may become fruitful.

Q: **How does planning for the project approach address diverse learners?**

A: Planning a project addresses the needs and abilities of diverse learners in at least four important ways. *First*, in selecting the topic, the teacher has the children in mind with a good sense of their learning needs and interests. In thinking through the potential scope of the project, the teacher has in mind what all children could learn, what most could learn, and what a few children and/or particular individual children could learn. This is done with a brainstorming of vocabulary that the study might use and making notes of the possibilities for the particular children in the class. *Second*, the teacher attends to diversity is in the first phase of the project. Collectively, a class of children knows a lot already, but each child individually may have quite limited experience and understanding. The teacher assesses this prior knowledge and helps the children to formulate questions for investigation that will particularly address these learning

needs. By the end of the first phase the children will have shared their stories of experience and have a common baseline of knowledge from which to continue the study. *Third*, teachers encourage children's engagement in investigations that address their strengths and interests. They share the results of their investigations so that everyone in the class can follow the progress being made by different groups of children or individuals. Children undertake representational activities that are appropriate for the information to be shared and in which they can apply their strengths. Children work together in pairs or groups and learn how other children think and apply their representational skills. Teachers initiate, monitor, and manage a variety of activities, encouraging children to work together or alone with particular reference to their diverse learning needs and abilities. *Fourth*, teachers ensure that documentation of the progress of the project through careful display of the children's work enables every child to follow the development of knowledge about the topic of study. The work of individual children addresses their personal needs and interests in the way it is documented and displayed.

Sylvia Chard is Professor Emeritus, University of Alberta, Edmonton, Alberta, Canada.

SHORT-TERM PLANNING

Planning for daily or weekly learning experiences called short-term planning. Short-term planning is more specific and detailed than long-term planning because it addresses the day-to-day decisions that you will make as a teacher. It includes weekly and daily plans that identify the activities, experiences, and lessons to be used in the classroom. **Weekly plans** identify the activities and lessons for each day of the week. Some teachers write weekly plans in a brief calendar format; other teachers like to be very specific and detailed about each activity or lesson in their weekly plans; and still others like to include adaptations for certain children each week. **Daily plans** include the schedule and activities for each day. Some schools require teachers to write daily plans and follow a prescribed format; others allow teachers more flexibility in their planning. Regardless, *weekly and daily planning* take a variety of forms and contain a variety of detail. Whatever form your plans take, they often contain key concepts, specific objectives or anticipated child outcomes of lessons and activities that are related to long-term goals, and a way to assess your lessons and activities. As you prepare your daily plans, consider which knowledge, skills, concepts, and attitudes children need to develop throughout the days and weeks ahead. Your planning will also include ways to organize your learning environment and your time, how best to integrate the subject areas (e.g., math, literacy)

Figure 9.9 Daily Plan for Full-Day Child Care for 4- and 5-Year-Olds

Time	Activity
7:15	Arrival: Quiet Area choices (manipulatives, books, art/tactile media available) and/or dramatic play and block areas are prepared and available
8:15	Breakfast offered, children use the bathroom as needed. Set timer/clean-up
8:40	Early morning storytime
8:45	Gross motor play (playground/multipurpose room)
9:40	Circle: group gathering for music, movement, and/or language arts activities
9:55	Small-group activity/children plan
10:15	Choice time: all areas open/snack offered
11:20	Set timer/clean-up/recall time in small group
11:30	Storytime
11:40	Lunch Children: bathroom, brush teeth, and choose a book
12:20	Book and stories on cots
12:30	Soft music and lights off for rest time
2:30	Children begin to awaken; bathroom Afternoon choice time/snack offered (continuation of earlier projects and new activities)
3:30	Set timer/clean-up
3:45	Circle: group gathering—music/science
4:00	Playground or other gross motor activity (Multipurpose Room available 4:30–5:00)
5:00	Activities—games/stories/exploration
5:45	Departure/Staff prepare for next days events

Source: Courtesy of Nellie Adams, Fairfax County Employees' Child Care Center, Fairfax, VA.

across thematic units and projects, how to best meet individual children's needs, and how best to sequence and assess children's learning. Short-term planning also includes detailed lesson planning for particular parts of each day, such as transition times and opening and closing the day (Arends, 2009; Henson, 2010). Figure 9.9 provides a sample daily plan for full-day child care for 4- and 5-year-olds, and Figure 9.10 provides a sample daily plan for first grade. Notice the different planning formats that teachers use.

PLANNING FOR ACTIVITIES AND LESSONS
Activity and lesson plans provide the working documents of a program or classroom. Activity or lesson plans focus on a single teaching episode. In most preschool programs, the term activity is used for planning; in most primary and elementary grades, the term lesson is used. Both, however, have similar components.

Figure 9.10 Daily Plan for First Grade

Tuesday

Date: _____

Special Information for today: _____

9:00–9:30   Morning Choice Time/Announcements/Attendance
- hang up backpacks and check job chart
- each child chooses an activity (read books; play games on rug; computer; explore manipulatives from math center; use writing center, art center, or listening center)
- morning announcements and pledge—about 9:15 A.M.
- take attendance after announcements; messengers take it to office

9:30–10:00   Morning Meeting
- children are on the rug, calendar helper fills in and reads calendar, schedule; does weather chart, number of days in school, ABC chart
- read poem: _____ *October* _____;
- choose two children to share news; write news on white board
- Focus Lesson: *Interactive writing—What we will learn later about October*

10:00–10:45   Writing Workshop   Program of Study Link: _____
- Fill out individual calendars and weather graphs
- Writing activity: _____or journals
- Group 1: _____ *Kitty and the Birds and Tom Is Brave* _____
  _____
- Group 2: _____ *Uncle Bundle and Our Granny* _____
  _____
- Group 3: *Ali's Little Brother and Me Magnetic Letters. Practice names.* _____

10:45–11:30   Reading Workshop
- Shared Reading: _____ *Health-Fire Safety* _____
- Reading Response: _____ *Stop-Drop-Roll* _____
- Small Group _____
- Quiet Reading from Book Boxes
- Sharing Circle

11:30–11:50   Outdoor break, then bathroom break before lunch

11:50–12:20   Lunch (pick up children at door by main stairs)

12:20–12:30   Bathroom break

12:30–12:50   **Storytime and Discussion Sharing**

Figure 9.10 continued

Book: <u>Finish Picking Apples and Pumpkins</u>

12:50–1:40 **Math**

Program of Study Link: _____

Developing Number Sense: _____ *Math Happening** _____

Concept Lesson: _____ *Addition/Problem solving* _____

Activity: __ *Ways to make 5—use cut-paper squares to record, in groups of three* __

Small Groups: _____

_____

_____

1:40–2:00 Free choice or outdoor break and snack

2:00–2:30 **Library**

2:30–3:15 Mrs. Prince every other week/Science (2:30–3:15 or 3:00–3:30)

Concept Lesson: _____

Activity: _____

_____

_____

3:15–3:30 **DEAR Time** (Drop Everything and Read) (independent reading or buddy reading) after science ends at 3:15

3:30–3:45 **Prepare for Dismissal**
- stack chairs, pick up things off floor, tidy centers
- check cubbies and pack bags

3:45 **Dismissal** (children gather by door and sit on the floor)

*A Math Happening is an authentic math problem that occurs in children's natural daily activities (e.g., How many snacks are needed for the children after counting those who are absent and subtracting that number from the number of children in the class?).
Source: Courtesy of Diana Sparrgrove, Parklawn Elementary School, Fairfax, Virginia.

The term activity is preferred for younger children because it implies a less formal and rigid approach to learning. In this text, we make the distinction by age only. At a minimum, the activity and lesson plans describe what is planned for that day, including the goals and objectives for the activities, the time frame within which they are to be carried out, and a means of assessment and evaluation. In addition, activity and lesson plans provide information about which teacher will be in charge of the activity, in what part of the classroom each activity is to be carried out, and what materials are needed. Although activity and lesson plans can take many forms, they should be complete enough so that any teacher can pick one up and know for any given day what is planned and why it is planned. Figure 9.11 shows two lesson planning forms. The first

Figure 9.11 Short and Long Forms of Activity or Lesson Plans

Short Form for a Lesson or Activity Plan

I. Activity or Lesson Plan — (What is the name of what you will teach?)

II. Lesson Overview — (What are the standards, goals, concepts, or skills you will teach?)

III. Teaching Procedures — (What will you do before, during, and after teaching?)

IV. Materials — (What materials, resources, and space do you need?)

V. Assessment — (How will you know what the children learned? How will you evaluate your own teaching?)

VI. Other Comments — (Is there anything specific you need to do for this lesson or activity?)

Long Form for a Completed Lesson or Activity Plan

I. Lesson Topic: — This completed plan is based on the overview of the Social Studies unit described in Figure 9.8 on pp. 253–254 of this chapter.

II. Lesson Overview — Social Studies, Time and Place

   A. *Concept:* People, places, and things change over time.

   B. *Objectives:* The student will:
   - identify elements of learning materials as past or present
   - categorize learning materials as past or present

   C. *Standards:*
   - **VA history 1.1** . . . compare everyday life in different places and times, and recognize that people, places, and things change over time.
   - **NCSS Standard II. a** . . . use correct vocabulary associated with time such as past, present, future, and long ago; identify examples of change.

III. Materials
   - Photographs of learning materials past and present, cut in half
   - PowerPoint presentation with different types of learning materials past and present (downloaded from Internet)

IV. Procedures

   Introduction (15 minutes)
   - Gather students to review yesterday's lesson.
   - Access prior knowledge about classroom practices in the past and how they differ from the present.

Figure 9.11 continued

- Introduce topic of learning materials.
- Talk about learning materials, focusing on features of present and past materials and their similarities or differences.

Instructional Strategies

Activity 1 (8–10 minutes):

- Show PowerPoint presentation of past and present learning materials. Invite students to identify some elements of past learning materials (e.g., slate and chalk vs. computer; pen and inkwell vs. markers; black and white vs. color illustrations; school bell vs. loud speaker) through questions about the features of these materials in the past/present.

Activity 2 (8–10 minutes):

- Provide each child with half a picture of one of these materials and have them find the person with the other half of their picture. Each pair must talk about and be prepared to tell the class why they believe that the particular item belongs to the past or present and describe at least two elements of what they see.
- Post their composite picture on the appropriate area of the board (past or present).
- Evaluate each other's work by deciding if the materials have been categorized correctly.

Summary:

- Have children imagine past life learning with those materials.
- Compare that with their experiences with their current learning materials. Use that experience for introduction during tomorrow's lesson.

Extensions:

- Categorize pictures of learning materials into past and present.
- Use Venn diagrams to organize similarities and differences between past and present materials. Use the classroom library to do research.

V. Assessment (15–20 minutes)

- Note children's knowledge of elements of past and present using anecdotal records.
- Note children's use of correct vocabulary related to time and understanding of changes over time.

VI. Differentiation

Students with more advanced writing skills can write sentences describing their materials. Students with less advanced writing skills can orally describe their materials and the teacher can scribe for them.

Source: Courtesy of Anna Eileen Gomez, George Mason University, Fast Train Program, Fairfax, VA.

is a very short form providing the basic information; the second is a longer, standards-based form that contains all elements of effective planning. The completed long planning form illustrates how to build an effective lesson plan based on the overview of a Social Studies Thematic Unit described in Figure 9.8 on pp. 253–254.

One final word is needed about planning. Good planning includes a variety of carefully prepared self-selected activities that are related to the needs, interests, and cultural backgrounds of particular children. Being too rigid about continuing on with a plan regardless of children's engagement in it limits learning. Planning begins before the school year and continues until the children leave at the end of it. The decisions you make when you plan will greatly affect child outcomes. Keeping these strategies in mind will increase your success as a planner. You will have the opportunity to examine some types of planning in the Assessment Activity 2 at the end of this chapter.

Summary

■ Planning is the ability to think ahead. Planning for children's learning involves making decisions about the content you will teach, the experiences you will prepare, the ways you will engage children in the learning process, how to group children for learning, what materials you will need, how you will assess children's learning, and how you will manage the learning process. To maximize positive outcomes you need to think about planning *before, during,* and *after* each lesson or activity.

■ Effective planning is characterized by four essential principles: (1) accountability to local, state, and national standards; (2) grouping patterns that meet the needs of all learners; (3) a way for every child to be successful in school; and (4) best practices based on research.

■ All planning includes five key components: goals and objectives, processes and procedures, activities and lessons, assessment and evaluation, and differentiation. Each is important to the total planning process.

■ Your role as an effective early childhood professional involves the important skill of planning. It includes planning to meet children's needs, planning the content children need to learn, planning a variety of experiences to meet the needs of diverse learners, planning appropriate assessment methods, planning to reflect on your teaching, and planning ahead.

■ Long-term planning is very general and serves as a framework for later planning efforts. It includes yearly, semester, and quarterly planning, and thematic unit or project planning. Short-term planning is for daily or weekly learning experiences.

Applying Your Knowledge of Planning

In Assessment Activity 1, apply what you know about effective planning by answering three questions about Shayna's kindergarten teacher. Then in Assessment Activity 2, apply your knowledge of planning for diverse learners.

 Assessment ACTIVITY 1 ① **SHAYNA GOES TO KINDERGARTEN**

Shayna was a curious kindergartner who was quick to learn but had difficulty adjusting to large groups of children and large-group activities. Shayna's teacher believed in teaching a rigorous, skills-based class with lots of group work. Each day, the children completed many papers. According to Shayna's teacher, the more papers they completed, the more it meant that everything was running smoothly. Shayna, who was already reading and speaking two languages, was spending her days coloring pictures and circling pictured objects beginning with the same letter.

One day, as usual, Shayna's teacher gave the children ditto sheets to complete and she insisted that the children remain quiet while they worked on them. Suddenly, Shayna started to chant softly, *"Boring, boring, boring"* and one of her classmates began to tap in rhythm to the words with a fat crayon. Soon, every child took up the chant, and, like penitentiary prisoners, "BORING, BORING, BORING" grew louder and louder. The teacher was incensed! She marched Shayna to the principal's office and called her parents because Shayna had "started a kindergarten revolt"!

Although Shayna's parents took the incident seriously, they did not see the humor in the situation. They wondered how things might be different if Shayna's teacher had planned her curriculum with Shayna's needs, interests, and abilities in mind. Before each activity, she should have considered what Shayna brought with her to school—her culture, her family background, the influences of her community, and her prior experiences—and what kind of grouping pattern would work best for Shayna. During each activity, Shayna's teacher should have noticed Shayna's reactions and interactions with the work and with her peers. After the lessons, Shayna's teacher should have evaluated Shayna's intellectual, behavioral, and attitudinal outcomes, as well as unintended effects.

REACT	Think about how the perspectives of Shayna, her parents, and Shayna's teacher are alike and different. What might be some reasons? With whom do you most closely identify?
RESEARCH	Shayna's teacher is using the direct instruction model of teaching. Compare this way of teaching with the strategies for meeting children's diverse learning needs through using the project approach as described by Sylvia Chard in the Ask the Expert feature on pages 257–258 and Marilyn Ornstein's and Susan McClanahan's kindergarten chair project on pages 255–256. How could Shayna's teacher have planned to better meet Shayna's needs and still hold true to her beliefs that she was covering the material and getting Shayna ready for first grade? Search the Internet and find support for your rationale.
REFLECT	What alternatives does Shayna's teacher have in planning to meet Shayna's needs and keep her engaged in learning?

Assessment ACTIVITY 2 ② **PLANNING FOR DIVERSE LEARNERS**

Planning for diverse learners requires the teacher's thoughtful attention to expected outcomes for each child. All teachers must be able to adapt their instruction to accommodate the needs of diverse learners, such as attending to children's cultural and linguistic backgrounds; children's special gifts, talents, and exceptionalities; and children who are at risk of school failure. Thus, a "one size fits all" approach to teaching will clearly be ineffective, as will writing individual learning plans for each child. What, then, does a teacher do to plan for diverse learners?

Think about an activity or lesson you have taught or have seen taught as part of a larger project or thematic unit and complete a planning matrix for that lesson. Divide a sheet of paper into two columns. Label the left-hand column "What was done well" and the right-hand column "What can be done more effectively to meet diverse learning needs." Now, use the guidelines discussed in the section "Your Role as a Planner" on page 241 of this chapter and the strategies for meeting needs of diverse learners in Figure 9.2 to examine the following elements of effective planning and discuss each of the categories. In small groups, discuss (a) the strategies you used in initial planning, (b) strategies designed to meet the needs of specific diverse learners (e.g., children who have difficulty maintaining attention, children who are English language learners, children who are academically gifted, or children who are academically challenged), and (c) any information that you have that does not fit on the chart. Finally, discuss the strategies you might use to compile your planning matrix into a classroom chart that allows for easy access to implementation. How do you think a planning matrix contributes to improving the learning of all children? Explain why you believe your adaptations are likely to be helpful to the learners.

ONLINE RESOURCES FOR PLANNING

A to Z Teacher Stuff: Offers ideas on thematic units and lesson plans created by teachers. www.atozteacherstuff.com

Differentiation Strategies and Applications: Provides lesson plans, videos, and other strategies for differentiation. www.differentiationcentral.com

Mid-continent Research for Education and Learning (McREL): Provides lesson plans on a variety of topics in various subject areas. http://mcrel.org/standards-benchmarks

Scholastic Teachers: Has lesson plans, activities, and thematic units as well as other teacher tips. http://teacher.scholastic.com

The George Lucas Educational Foundation: Provides differentiated instruction lesson plans, unit plans, and weekly plans from Lake Forest Elementary School teachers in Columbia, South Carolina. Also offers free resources, reading lists, web tools, and other resources for differentiated instruction. Watch video of kindergarten children at Auburn Early Learning Center in Auburn, Alabama, engaged in long-term projects. www.edutopia.org

The Project Approach: Learn more about the project approach and see sample projects submitted by teachers and organized by grade level at this site. www.project-approach.com

Teaching PreK–8: Offers ideas for classroom activities in every subject area as well as technology integration suggestions. www.TeachingK-8.com

---

PEARSON myeducationlab

Go to Topic 6 (Curriculum Planning) in the MyEducationLab (www.myeducationlab.com) for your course, where you can:

- Find learning outcomes for curriculum planning along with the national standards that connect to these outcomes.
- Complete Assignments and Activities that can help you more deeply understand the chapter content.
- Apply and practice your understanding of the core teaching skills identified in the chapter with the Building Teaching Skills and Dispositions learning units.
- Hear viewpoints of experts in the field in Professional Perspectives.

CHAPTER 10

Assessing Children's Learning and Documenting Progress

It is widely believed that academic careers are made or broken in the early grades. . . . The standards movement has resulted in a barrage of testing; millions of teacher-hours spent aligning curriculum to standards and tests, and a huge range of remediation packages in both traditional and online formats.

Linda Tolbert & Paul Theobald, 2006, p. 271

Meet the TEACHERS

MRS. YU operates a state-licensed facility in her home and she is responsible for the toddlers. "For most of the families, this is a first experience; some have heard it's best to 'just leave them and let them cry' but my experience and reading (Lee, 2010) suggests that it is better if the family member spends a little time doing something familiar with their child in the unfamiliar environment, such as looking at a book. If the child gets more relaxed and becomes interested in something else, there are fewer tears from children and less guilt from parents about leaving their young one at child care."

MR. McCAUGHLIN works at a private preschool that is seeking accreditation from the National Association for the Education of Young Children. He attended a full day of training on the process at the national conference and is now reporting back to all of his colleagues: "The good news is that we are, overall, in compliance with the standards. Now we need to gather the evidence, shore up any weaknesses, and present a convincing argument that we have a high-quality program. You may be wondering, 'Why do all of this work if we already know our program is good?' The answer is that having the endorsement of a respected national organization definitely is worth it for the children, for us, and for the families and community."

SELENA is a student teacher in an urban first-grade classroom. After co-teaching a math lesson on one-to-one correspondence with her mentor teacher, they gather up the children's papers, a worksheet that required them to match various sets of equal numbers (e.g., 5 dogs to 5 bowls, 3 cats to 3 toys, etc.). Selena's mentor teacher asks her to analyze the children's work and determine what to teach next. Selena reports back, "I noticed that some children drew a line from each set to the matching set without any difficulty; for them, the task should be more challenging, so we could introduce the concept of unequal sets. On other papers, the children did not match the items consistently, so something more concrete, such as having them match sets of clip art with lengths of yarn could help. For the children who drew lines without demonstrating any understanding of the concept, we might make it more concrete, so I collected some small stuffed bean bag toys and a set of plastic bracelets to put around each toy's neck." Selena's mentor teacher is very impressed by her ability to make data-driven curriculum decisions.

LEARNING Outcomes

In this chapter, you will learn to:

→ Become familiar with national standards and guidelines governing the early childhood educator's role in assessment of children's learning and program effectiveness (NAEYC #3, ACEI #4, INTASC #8)

→ Define *assessment*, identify its purposes, and understand its implications for young children, their families, early childhood educators, and programs

→ Develop knowledge and skill in observing, recording, analyzing, and reporting information about children's progress to parents/families

→ Apply knowledge of observational skills and understand the role of assessment in teachers' professional development

---

Compare

What are some commonalities among the assessment practices of these three educators?

Contrast

How do these educators think about assessment? How would you characterize the outlook of each one?

Connect

In these scenarios, what made the greatest impression on you, and how will you incorporate this into your teaching?

Now that you have reflected on the three teachers' perspectives and noted the learning outcomes, we preview the knowledge, skills, and dispositions you will need to acquire in order to fulfill your role in assessing children's learning and documenting their progress.

A Definition of Assessment

When young children enter school, parents/families wonder, "How is my child doing in comparison to other children? Will the teacher evaluate my child fairly? What types of information and work samples will be used to assess my child's performance? If my child is experiencing difficulty, what assistance is available? How will I be kept informed about my child's progress?" These concerns of parents and families not only have educational implications, they also have social and ethical consequences for the child. That is why assessment is such an important issue for you as an early childhood educator (Snow & Van Hemel, 2008).

"Effective assessment provides teachers with important knowledge of students and their growth as learners, informs ongoing curricular and pedagogical practice, is a basis for helping students reflect on their own learning, and serves as a window for parents into the power of the teaching-learning exchange that involves their sons and daughters" (Perrone, 1997, p. 305). The National Association for the Education of Young Children defines **assessment in early childhood** as "the process of observing, recording, and otherwise documenting the work children do and how they do it, as a basis for a variety of educational decisions that affect the child" (Bredekamp & Rosegrant, 1992, p. 22). In other words, there is assessment *of* learning (evaluating what was learned) and assessment *for* learning (using data to determine what to teach next and how best to teach it) (Sheets, 2005; Wiggins & McTighe, 2005).

The four main purposes for assessment in early childhood are: (1) to plan instruction for individuals and groups of children, (2) to communicate with parents and families about the progress of individual children, (3) to identify children and families who need specialized programs and support services, and (4) to evaluate the effectiveness and quality of early childhood programs and services. Early childhood assessment fulfills these purposes only if:

- the assessment tools are well designed;
- the assessment tasks take children's linguistic and cultural differences into account;
- the content and the means of data collection are matched to young children's developmental levels;
- the results are used to benefit children rather than label them or deprive them of opportunity; and
- the assessment process values families and effectively communicates assessment data to children's parents/legal guardians (Gullo, 2006a, 2006b).

DID YOU Know ?

- According to a national poll, over 80% of parents believe that students achieve only a small part of their potential (Rose & Gallup, 2007).

- Most state departments of education require diagnostic/developmental tests throughout the early childhood years and most have a set of learning standards all young children are expected to attain (National Early Childhood Accountability Task Force [NECATF], 2008; Scott-Little, Kagan, & Frelow, 2006).

- The diversity in early childhood programs presents particularly difficult assessment challenges. Ideally, early childhood assessments should be based on research, examine different developmental domains (and the interactions among them), and enable early childhood educators to use the data to inform planning and instruction (Bowman, Donovan, & Burns, 2004; Hirsh-Pasek, Kochanoff, Newcombe, & de Villiers, 2005; NECATF, 2008).

Figure 10.1 Purposes of Assessment

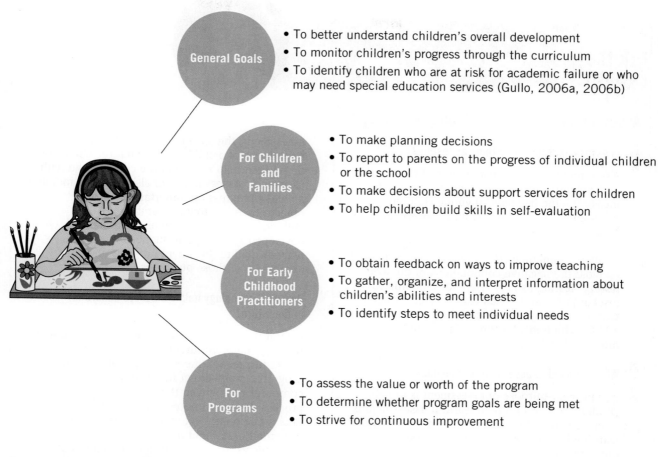

General Goals
- To better understand children's overall development
- To monitor children's progress through the curriculum
- To identify children who are at risk for academic failure or who may need special education services (Gullo, 2006a, 2006b)

For Children and Families
- To make planning decisions
- To report to parents on the progress of individual children or the school
- To make decisions about support services for children
- To help children build skills in self-evaluation

For Early Childhood Practitioners
- To obtain feedback on ways to improve teaching
- To gather, organize, and interpret information about children's abilities and interests
- To identify steps to meet individual needs

For Programs
- To assess the value or worth of the program
- To determine whether program goals are being met
- To strive for continuous improvement

Sources: Gullo, 2006a, 2006b; McAfee & Leong, 2011.

Figure 10.1 describes the purposes of assessment in greater detail. On page 272, the Ask the Expert by Deborah Leong provides answers to various questions about appropriate ways of assessing young children's development.

Principles of Assessment

The major types of assessment are observation, tests, and performance assessment.

OBSERVATION

The basic question answered by **observation** of individual children is, "How is this child doing?" "Observing students in diverse contexts across the curriculum calls on teachers to take a closer look at themselves, their practices, their students, and their students' learning. In doing so, the details of the learning process are revealed, clarifying the kinds of environments and practices that support different learners to learn in different ways. Rather than 'teaching to the test,' teachers are supported to 'teach to

Deborah Leong

Assessment, Development, and Technology

Q: Is assessment the same thing as testing?

A: Assessment is more broadly defined than testing and encompasses many different ways of measuring the behavior of young children. Assessment may include testing, observations of children, samples of their work, interviews, and the performance of a skill or the solving of a problem. Sometimes the term *assessment* is used to avoid the negative connotations of the word *testing*. Testing usually refers to standardized tests or paper-and-pencil tests through which teachers elicit specific responses from children and the children's responses are scored in a numerical fashion.

Q: Why do I need to assess more than once?

A: The primary purpose of assessment is to help children in their efforts to learn. If assessment is to be used to help teachers make decisions about learning in the classroom, then assessing a child only once a year or even twice a year is not enough. The purpose of beginning and end-of-year assessment is to sum up the child's performance. However, the real strength of good assessment information is that it helps the teacher really decide what will be the optimum steps in the teaching-learning exchange.

Q: How can assessment help me teach?

A: Assessment can help the teacher identify a child's zone of proximal development (ZPD). The ZPD is the area that encompasses the skills that are just on the edge of emergence. Thus, scaffolding or supporting learning within the ZPD is most beneficial for later development. Through assessment, the teacher can discover the boundaries of a child's ZPD, what the child can do without help and what the child can do with assistance. Assessment can also help you monitor a child's progress on important goals and objectives. As a growing number of early childhood programs, such as Head Start, developed specific performance outcomes, teachers had to document progress and attainment of those outcomes.

Q: How will technology help me assess children in the future?

A: One of the most exciting developments today is the way that computers will support assessment in the future. Scanners and optical recognition programs make direct input of data into the computer possible so that teachers can easily process their own notes, which they ordinarily take while observing students. Many teachers use small hand-held devices, such as iPods and Blackberrys, to record child assessment data. Children can take some assessments on the computer. The computer can keep records straight and track progress on skills as diverse as math facts and literacy. Computers can make the saving of images of children's work easy and can help teachers weave these together with coherent parent reports of child progress. With the advent of artificial intelligence, computers can spot error patterns, provide profiles of individuals, and provide alternative means of analysis of information. Computers will never be able to replace the experience and knowledge of an expert teacher, but they can make the management of assessment information easier.

Deborah Leong is a Professor of Psychology, Metropolitan State College of Denver, Denver, Colorado.

Teacher observation is a major method of assessment.

the child'" (Falk, 2000, p. 126). Figure 10.2 identifies major errors that are commonly made when teachers first begin observing young children. Be certain to study this information carefully before you begin gathering observational data.

The five most commonly used types of observation are (1) anecdotal records, (2) checklists, (3) rating scales, (4) interviews, and (5) surveys and questionnaires. Figure 10.3 defines each type and supplies a short example.

Acquiring skill in observation is particularly important for early childhood educators because children cannot always tell us what they are experiencing or thinking. As Strickland (2006) notes, effective teachers are

> keen and competent observers. They study what students do every day in various situations. They observe to determine what students can do independently with success. They note areas of growing competence and areas of difficulty. They use what they learn to inform their plans for intervention and curriculum adjustment. Teachers gather information through anecdotal records, checklists, personalized conferences, formal and informal observations, and by systematically collecting work samples. They examine the information to determine how learners are progressing. (p. 82)

One of the challenges of observation is finding the time to gather information while teaching. Figure 10.4 suggests some convenient ways of collecting and organizing observational data.

TESTS

Tests are the most familiar of assessment tools used in the United States. A **test** is defined as a sample of behavior in a particular area or domain (e.g., reading readiness,

Pause and Reflect

About Assessment Tools

Visit the site called Teacher Vision (www .teachervision.fen.com). Type the words "observation printable" in the search box. Then refine the search in the box at the right by selecting a grade level. You can print out four for free. The Circle of Inclusion website posted at www.circleofinclusion.org/ has a variety of observation forms as well; go to the website, then choose "materials," then "forms index."

Figure 10.2 Major Errors in Observation

Error: Being overly judgmental
Example: "She's probably just lazy."
Why Not? Judging children does not solve anything. If you judge them, you merely absolve yourself of responsibility for facilitating changes in behavior that will serve them better, both now and in the future.
Alternative: Be careful and actually describe behavior, saying, for instance, "Janine sometimes moves from center to center without engaging in the activities there. We have found that it is important to invite her into the ongoing activities and get her started."

Error: Overgeneralizing
Example: "He never finishes any of his work."
Why Not? It is not accurate to say that someone never finishes anything. This is clearly an overstatement.
Alternative: Be precise, saying, for instance, "At the end of the day, Xi frequently has several activities that he has begun but not finished."

Error: Labeling
Example: "He is sloppy."
Why Not? It is not fair to characterize someone's entire personality with a word.
Alternative: Describe and actual behavior; saying, for instance. "Krish has a tendency to rush through his work, particularly when it involves handwriting."

Error: Stereotyping
Example: "These children from the housing projects aren't like other children."
Why Not? It is prejudicial to categorize a group of children in this way based on family income.
Alternative: Say what needs to be addressed and be a child and family advocate, saying, for instance, "It is often the case that these toddlers arrive at school without much prior experience with lap reading of picture books. We have been collaborating with the public library to use the bookmobile as a way to offer toddler story times and to provide greater access to high-quality literature."

Error: Blaming
Example: "The way she keeps acting out, it's clear that she doesn't get any discipline at home."
Why Not? You have no basis in fact for making such an assumption. It could even be the case that the child is disciplined severely at home and that she is acting out at school as a cry for help.
Alternative: Work to find out what might be causing the behavior, for instancce, conferring with a parent or other family member and saying, "I am concerned that Sean has been giving other children karate chops and pushing them down on the playground. Can you think of any reason why he might be behaving in this way?"

Error: Making long-term predictions
Example: "He's never going to amount to anything. I wouldn't be suprised to find out he's in trouble with the law while he is still in junior high school."
Why Not? Teachers cannot see into the future, and making dire predictions only results in lowered expectations that are communicated to children and may have a self-fulfilling prophecy effect.
Alternative: Note what the child is doing right, saying, for instance. "I noticed that Lucien really helped out when Adrianna fell at the bottom of the slide by comforting her and going to get help."

Error: Comparing children to peers and adults
Example: "He's the best artist in the class. He draws even better than most adults."
Why Not? Teachers need to focus on what children can do, and it is better to encourage them than to praise them. The difference is that praise tends to say, in effect, "Just keep doing what you are doing to please me and stay ahead of the others." Encouragement, however, lets children know that their efforts are recognized and that they bear responsibilty for self-evaluation.
Alernative: "Monroe frequently chooses to go to the art table first. I have noticed that he is interested in trying different media to produce prictures, including not only crayons, but also paints, chalk, colored pencils, and a variety of materials and tools."

Figure 10.3 Observation Processes and Methods

OBSERVATION PROCESSES

Perception
What you notice, based upon sensory input, prior experience, individual ways of reacting to experience, the cultural context, teacher education, beliefs about children, educational values, personal ethics, and society.

Description
What you capture in words, on tape, or on video and use to describe the settings, events, and verbal and nonverbal behaviors based on direct observation or inferences from the data collected.

Interpretation
How you make sense of the behaviors and events you perceived. This process typically includes noting patterns, generating hypotheses, and making recommendations.

METHODS FOR OBSERVING AND RECORDING

Anecdotal Record

A narrative (storylike), factual account recorded after behavior occurs. Often used to obtain details on a child's behavior. Describes observable behavior and usually includes verbatim comments.
- Example:
  Tchr. presented a lesson on colors. Ch. mixed food coloring and water to produce diff. colors. Ch. were instructed to use all 8 colors in their crayon boxes to produce pictures. Tchr. questions/comments: "How many diff. colors did you use?" "I see words in your picture, could you read them to me?" "Did anyone experiment with mixing colors?" "I noticed that you made shapes." "Could you tell me more about your picture?" To J., tchr says, "I like those railroad tracks" and walks away. J. says to E., "The tchr. didn't even know that it's a sidewalk!"

Checklist

Indicates the presence or absence of a behavior
- Example: Checklist of a Toddler's Self-Help Skills

Child is toilet trained.	Yes	No
Child dresses her/himself.	Yes	No

Rating Scale

Rates behavior in terms of kind or amount
- Example: A Rating Scale for Home Literacy Practices

Listens to stories	Frequently	Sometimes	Seldom
Attempts to write	Frequently	Sometimes	Seldom
Pretends to read	Frequently	Sometimes	Seldom

Interview

A person-to-person meeting that asks for self-report information from the interviewee
- Example: Home Visit Interview Before Child Begins Kindergarten
  What are your child's special interests and hobbies?
  How does your child seem to feel about going to school?
  What do you expect your child to accomplish this year?
  What signs of progress were you pleased to see over the summer?
  Are there any concerns that you have about your child?
  What have you discovered about your child's particular ways of learning?
  What is the most important thing your child can learn this year?

Survey & Questionnaire

A self-report tool that uses paper-and-pencil or electronic means to gather information
- Example: Self-Evaluation of Physical Activity Skills by Third Graders
  "I already know how to ..."
  "Right now I am learning how to ..."
  "Next, I want to learn..."

Figure 10.4 Materials for Recording Observations

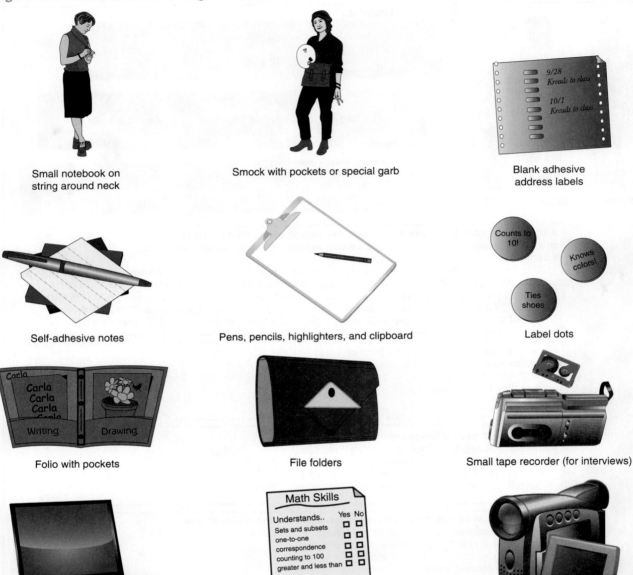

Small notebook on string around neck

Smock with pockets or special garb

Blank adhesive address labels

Self-adhesive notes

Pens, pencils, highlighters, and clipboard

Label dots

Folio with pockets

File folders

Small tape recorder (for interviews)

Netbook computer

Specially designed evaluation sheets

Video recorder

mathematics achievement). In today's educational climate, standardized test scores often are considered by policymakers to be the only thing that "counts" as evidence of children's learning (Groark, Mehaffie, McCall, & Greenberg, 2006). Test results have consequences, not only for children's learning, but also for teachers' pedagogical approaches and classroom practices (Johnston & Rogers, 2001). Most standardized tests in wide use are published tests that are administered and scored in a specified way—this is what makes them "standardized." Standardized tests are rooted in a comparative concept of assessment. The procedure is to administer the test to some groups of children; they then become the "norm" to which subsequent test takers are compared. The advantages of published, formal, norm-referenced tests are that they are efficient, inexpensive, convenient, and considered by the general public to be objective (Educational Testing Service, 2003).

The disadvantages of **testing** are numerous, however. Perhaps the most obvious failing of these tests is that they provide virtually no guidance in planning instruction. After the test scores arrive in the mail, the teacher has a number on a piece of paper for each child rather than any direction about what to teach next or how to present it. Too often, a single test score becomes the basis for making important decisions, such as deciding who will be admitted to a program (e.g., qualifying for a gifted and talented program), which programs will survive (e.g., determining how much money to allocate to Head Start), or which children will gain access to support services (e.g., deciding which infants qualify for intervention services). Very young children do not understand testing procedures and the importance of tests. Common errors of naïve test takers include not responding at all (even when they know the answer), losing their place in a test booklet (and getting most of the subsequent answers wrong), becoming distracted from completing the task, or copying from someone else's test paper. For all of these reasons, young children are notoriously poor test takers, and their test scores are not necessarily a reflection of their true abilities. Educators need to proceed cautiously when using tests with young children. Many professional organizations have issued position statements on assessment that offer clear guidance to teachers (International Reading Association/National Council of Teachers of English, 1995; NAEYC & National Association of Early Childhood Specialists in State Departments of Education, 2003). Several of these position statements are listed in the Online Resources at the end of this chapter.

Despite all of these concerns, standardized tests are very much with us in early childhood education. Four categories of standardized tests that are commonly used in early childhood are:

- A **developmental screening** is a quick procedure designed to identify children who should receive further diagnostic assessment. A screening basically answers yes or no to one question: "Does there appear to be a problem that requires more thorough evaluation?" A good example of a developmental screening is a vision or hearing test that is given to all children upon kindergarten entrance. The advantage of a developmental screening is that it is an efficient and cost-effective way to evaluate the presence or absence of a problem; the two possible outcomes are to either refer the child for more thorough evaluation or not.

- A **diagnostic assessment** is a process used to definitely identify those children with a disability or specific area of academic weakness. If, for example, a young child is being considered for early intervention services, the child would be presented with a variety of tasks to complete, and often this would take place in the child's home so that it is a more natural, relaxed environment. The advantage of diagnostic assessment is that it supplies some of the data necessary to render a decision and suggests what specific areas need support early on (Litty & Hatch, 2006).

- A **readiness test** is a brief achievement test designed to determine a child's relative preparedness to participate in a particular classroom program or area of the curriculum. Reading readiness tests often are administered at the end of prekindergarten or kindergarten to predict which children may need additional literacy support as they transition into first grade.
- An **achievement test** assesses the extent to which a child has acquired certain information or skills that are identified as curricular objectives. In compliance with the No Child Left Behind Act, each state must test the 9-year-olds in reading and math in order to qualify for federal funding. Nearly all states now have achievement tests that are used not only to assess children's academic achievement but also to rate teachers and to compare the performance of one school with others across the state.

Figure 10.5 highlights issues to be considered in test preparation and in reducing test anxiety in young children. The Ask the Expert by Sue Wortham addresses many controversial issues about testing and young children.

Figure 10.5 Test Preparation and Test Anxiety

Disadvantage of Teaching to the Test

- Test preparation can reduce instructional time with new material or other activities that benefit children (e.g., outdoor play, art, music, social studies).
- Repetition of the same work frequently results in boredom and burnout, particularly for students who have already mastered the basic material.
- Intensive preparation for the test may actually heighten students' fears and test-anxiety problems.
- Both the teacher and student can become frustrated as the classroom environment, where learning and critical thinking are supposed to take place, becomes completely focused on test taking.
- Labeling can result from in-class preparation for tests. Some children catch on quickly and are viewed as "helping" the individual teacher, the school, and the district while those who struggle are treated as a "drain" on the higher test scores that will determine funding and the reputation of a teacher, program, and school.

Way to Minimize Test Anxiety

Test anxiety refers to an array of cognitive and physical responses that are aroused when people feel that they are being personally evaluated.

- Select tests carefully and use them for their intended purpose.
- Consider the developmental appropriateness of the test.
- Avoid allowing the text to dictate the curriculum.
- Explain the nature and purpose of the tests to the students.
- Select culturally relevant tests.
- Appreciate students' cultural backgrounds.
- Be aware of infuences on student learning.
- Choose tests that correspond to curricular goals.

Ask the EXPERT

Sue Wortham

Assessment

Q: Should standardized tests be used with young children?

A: There are circumstances when standardized tests can be used appropriately with young children. Children who have developmental disabilities or a lack of experiences with concepts and language might need to be assessed using a standardized test. There are individual tests to determine if a child needs to be served in an intervention program in the preschool years. Other strategies, such as observation and parental reporting, should be part of the evaluation process. It should be remembered, however, that most children in the preschool years should not be administered standardized tests, particularly to determine if a child is accepted for a preschool program or is screened to determine if he or she can move to the next level or be retained in a prekindergarten or kindergarten program. There is national concern about the practice of placing young children in transitional or junior first-grade classes because a standardized test has determined that they are not "ready" for first grade. Preservice teachers need to remember that standardized tests can have weaknesses and cannot necessarily be relied on to measure individual student development and achievement. The younger the child, the more likelihood that results of a standardized test are inaccurate.·

Now, in the 21st century, there are new concerns about the use of standardized tests with children in the primary grades. Since the advent of the No Child Left Behind (NCLB) law in the 1990s, there has been an increased emphasis on teaching to standardized tests for accountability that has had a negative impact on teaching and testing in elementary schools, including the curriculum used for preschool children.

Q: What are some appropriate assessment strategies that can be used with young children?

A: Observation is a primary source for assessing young children. This is because watching children at play or working on classroom tasks can reveal much more about their development than a formal test. Teachers can observe all domains of development while children are engaged in daily activities. Teachers can use checklists and interviews with children to acquire information about their understanding of concepts and topics being studied in the classroom. They can also collect samples of the children's work and organize the work into portfolios. This can provide the teacher, student, and parent with a longitudinal record of a child's progress through writing samples, artwork, photographs of projects, and other examples of the child's accomplishments.

Q: What is performance assessment?

A: Performance assessment is evaluation of what a student can both understand and use. For example, if a teacher gives a student a work page on simple addition and the student answers the problems correctly, then the teacher knows the student understands how to complete addition problems. But if the student is asked to refer to a grocery ad and correctly determine how much would be spent purchasing the items on a shopping list, then the child has demonstrated both knowledge and application. There are different types of performance assessments. A student who demonstrates how to conduct a science experiment or shows a group of peers how to arrange puzzles and construction toys on a shelf correctly is demonstrating both understanding and application. With young children, observation,

continued

Ask the Expert continued

work samples, and project products are some possibilities for performance assessment. Performance assessment can also be called authentic assessment because the student is being assessed in a real-life or purposeful activity.

Q: **What is the connection between assessment and instruction?**

A: The common understanding of assessment has been as a tool to determine student achievement and progress. However, it has been perceived as a way to determine how well students have learned in order to give grades on a report card. It is sometimes not understood that the primary reason for assessment is to guide the teacher in planning for classroom activities and instruction.

All assessments, including performance and portfolio assessments, should be used to determine a child's progress and to plan experiences that will further that progress. The assessments should reflect how well instruction and classroom activities assisted the child in accomplishing learning objectives designed by the teacher. If various types of assessment have been used, the teacher, parents, and child should be able to understand and describe how the child has demonstrated development and learning. Fortunately, there has been a positive trend toward performance assessment that has given teachers more options on how to evaluate children's learning. Revision of the NCLB Act will reflect this flexibility beyond standardized tests.

Sue Wortham is Professor Emerita of Early Childhood and Elementary Education, University of Texas at San Antonio.

PERFORMANCE ASSESSMENT

In everyday use, the word *perform* refers to executing a task or process and bringing it to completion. Given this definition, in **performance assessment,** learners' abilities are assessed as they produce work of their own by drawing upon their knowledge and skills, considering the context, and responding to a task (Wiggins, 1998). One of the arguments in favor of performance assessment is that it is a more authentic, "real-world" appraisal of what children know and can do. Even though a published, standardized test that arrives in neat little plastic-wrapped stacks along with a booklet that specifies all of the administration and scoring procedures certainly seems more official and objective than one teacher's anecdotal records, it may not be an accurate depiction of children's abilities. The same child who has difficulty matching a clock face to the time written in numerals on a test might have a clear idea of his daily schedule at home and at school, including lunchtime, bedtime, and so forth. In other words, there is a difference between knowing about something and knowing how to do something. In performance assessment, children are called upon to produce something rather than merely select the correct answer from several choices. Performance assessment tasks are more relevant to what children are likely to encounter outside the classroom. Because of this emphasis on practical application of skills, performance assessment is sometimes called **authentic assessment.** It also is referred to as **alternative assessment** because it is a departure from traditional testing methods. Many educators believe that performance or alternative assessment is a better means of developing and documenting higher-level thinking skills in students (Meisels, Bickel, Nicholson, Xue, & Atkins-Burnett, 2001). Advantages of performance assessments include that they:

- Focus on the developmental and achievement changes in children over time
- Focus on the individual child rather than on groups of children
- Do not rely on a "one-chance" opportunity for the child to demonstrate competence

- Do not interrupt the process of curriculum implementation
- Help children better understand their own learning, as children reflect in conjunction with the teacher or other children
- Provide concrete information to share with families (Gullo, 2006b, p. 143)

A **student work portfolio** is an organized, purposeful compilation of evidence that shows a child's development and learning over time; portfolios reveal a child's effort, learning processes, tasks accomplished, and the progress made (Dale-Easley & Mitchell, 2003; Seitz & Bartholomew, 2008). If traditional testing is like a snapshot, then portfolio assessment is more like a photo album—a collection of pictures that reveal growth and change over time (McTighe, 1997). As a teacher, your assessment practices should be "a means to find out what children know, can do, and care about" (Smith & Goodwin, 1997, p. 117), and performance assessment plays a key role in documenting this.

Listening to a child read aloud is an example of performance assessment.

Your Role in Assessment

Effective teachers are constantly documenting how their students are doing, gathering evidence of progress, identifying problems, and adjusting instructional plans accordingly. Some key roles for early childhood educators where assessment is concerned are discussed next.

RECOGNIZING UNETHICAL, ILLEGAL, AND OTHERWISE INAPPROPRIATE ASSESSMENT

Your first and most important responsibility in assessment is to be fair and ethical. It is this conviction that forms the foundation for assessment practices. One of the worst things that anyone could say about you as a teacher is that you identify favorite children in the group who receive preferential treatment. At first, this might seem out of the question, because you imagine a blatant instance of favoritism, such as a teacher's pet. But unfair assessment practices can creep into your practice in unanticipated ways. It might be allowing a few more seconds for one child to respond to a question and jumping in sooner for another child. Or, inequity might be expressed by giving a second chance to a child whose family is very vocal and involved in the school program while immediately reprimanding a child whose family is uninvolved in school events. Effective early childhood educators have a strong commitment to equity and fairness and reflect upon their assessment practices (Jewiss & Clark-Keefe, 2007).

Pause and Reflect

On Reports About a Child's Progress

Think about a child with whom you have a close bond. Now consider how you would feel if you were called into school for a meeting because the child is "having problems with reading." What initial concerns might surface? What might cause you to feel angry or defensive? How far would you go in protesting a decision with which you disagreed?

Confidentiality is an essential aspect of assessment (Mindes, 2007). Clearly, it is entirely inappropriate for a teacher to sit in the lunchroom with colleagues and remark about a child, "What can you expect? He got the lowest score on the reading readiness test in the entire class . . . and everyone knows what his family is like." Such public pronouncements are likely to taint everyone's opinion of that child's abilities and do irreversible reputational damage to the family. When the child moves on to the next grade level, his teacher probably will recall some of these negative remarks and expect to experience difficulty with the child. If such negative remarks were overheard in conversation outside the school, it would be even worse, and it would reflect unfavorably on the teacher and on the entire school. Part of becoming a professional is knowing when to keep quiet and protect confidentiality. A useful guideline in making these decisions is to ask yourself how you would feel about a member of your family being treated in this way. If your sibling or child had scored low on a test, would you want it known by anyone who happened to

Carefully analyzing children's work enables teachers to plan effectively.

pass by in the grocery store or broadcasted to every teacher in the school? Without a doubt, professional information can be shared in unprofessional ways with colleagues and with other members of the community; you must guard against such unprofessional behavior in yourself. Remember that only the parent or legal guardian is the one who is entitled to a child's assessment information.

DOCUMENTING AND SUPPORTING CHILDREN'S LEARNING

In your assessment role with the very young, your goal is to document that significant contributions were made to children's learning. This means that what they achieved with your guidance and support was appreciably better than what one would expect from normal maturation. The most fundamental assessment question where the individual child is concerned is one of "value added"—how did the learning activities that you designed and the educational programs for which you are responsible improve each child's learning and life? Some examples of individual assessments include anecdotal records, rating scale and checklist data, parent/family questionnaire data, notes from home visits, student work portfolios, and test results. Charting progress usually necessitates establishing baseline behavior. A **baseline** provides information on the starting point for the child, before he or she begins a task, a curriculum, or the program. Having baseline data enables you to show what advances were made as a result of participation in the program. A common form of baseline assessment is a **pretest,** an assessment given before you teach a particular concept or skill. To illustrate, preschoolers may know of a few words that are colors and use them to respond to all questions about colors, irrespective of the actual color. So, a child might say "green" when asked about a favorite color, the color of the sky, and the color of the cat's fur. If you were teaching a unit on colors, you might begin by asking an aide or volunteer to use a simple performance assessment with each child. Using a box of eight crayons, the adult would ask the child to identify the crayons of the various colors (e.g., "Can you find the red crayon?") and record the results. These results would be your baseline or pretest data, and you would use them to find out which children know all, some, or none of the words for colors and can match them to the appropriate hue. Then, after a variety of learning activities about colors, this task of identifying crayons by color could be repeated for those children who were still learning the concept as a **posttest,** a test given after the instruction has been completed. When you can document that value has been added, you have fulfilled an essential dimension of your role as an early childhood educator.

ADMINISTERING, SCORING, AND INTERPRETING THE RESULTS

Teachers are notorious for carrying tote bags full of students' work back and forth between home and school. If you could look inside student teacher Tina Hidalgo's bag, you would see illustrated math problems that her first graders invented by working with a partner. They used the folktales and nursery rhymes with which they were already familiar to develop math sentences, and then they represented them pictorially. One pair of children drew three bears, three bowls of porridge, three chairs, and three beds along with the equation $3 + 3 + 3 + 3 = ?$ The partners were also responsible for figuring out the correct answer, writing it on the back of the page, signing their names, and evaluating their number sentences using a simple ☺ or ☹. As Tina analyzes these papers, she does much more than mark the answers right or wrong and hand out stickers or stars. Rather, she analyzes children's errors, makes notes about what to teach next, and plans for mini-lessons with small groups of children who share the same misunderstandings. Just think of how much more Tina knows about her students' abilities than the teacher who gives a timed test on math facts! Not only can she see their mathematical reasoning from concrete drawings to abstract equations, but she also can tell if they are learning to use mathematical symbols and even find out something about their literacy skills, because the problems are based on the class's prior knowledge of stories. Tina recognizes that gathering data on students does not accomplish much unless it is tied to instruction. When the total curriculum (written), daily learning experiences (taught), and methods of evaluation (tested) are aligned across the child's educational experiences, children are far more likely to increase their understandings and improve their skills (Kagan, Carroll, Comer, & Scott-Little, 2006).

INVOLVING CHILDREN AND FAMILIES IN ASSESSMENT

Think about your experiences with assessment as a child. Perhaps your parents or guardian met for 5 or 10 minutes with the teacher once or twice a year. They probably had to sign your report card and return it to the school. But assessment practices in some schools have changed in several significant ways.

First of all, some programs and schools conduct home visits. A **home visit** is a face-to-face personal interview with a child's family that takes place in their home. Although home visits are time consuming and require additional effort from teachers, there is a large body of research suggesting that, when properly used, home visits can provide a more holistic perspective on the child, promote home/school collaboration, help to set a course for the child's learning, and increase cultural competence (Lin & Bates, 2010).

Contemporary parents and families are likely to be directly involved in setting goals for children, particularly those with special needs. A good example of this is the individualized educational plan (IEP). Developing an IEP for a child typically includes a goal-setting meeting in which the parents/family, teachers, and various specialists all participate. For younger children, ages birth through 3 years, the plan is called the individualized family service plan (IFSP). If this team agrees upon a goal, such as

Consider using student-led conferences as part of your overall assessment plan.

supporting the ability of a child with a physical handicap to feed himself or herself, each adult at the meeting would bear responsibility for carrying out this plan. The teacher would be responsible for helping the child to become more independent during meals served at school, the physical therapist would suggest some adaptive strategies to facilitate self-help skills (e.g., a special spoon, a bowl with a suction cup on the bottom, a stainless steel wheelchair tray with high edges), and the family members would agree to reinforce this learning during meals served at home by cosigning an IEP document with school and support services personnel.

With children in kindergarten and the primary grades, **student-led conferences** may become part of the assessment process. Instead of hearing about the results of parent/teacher conferences second hand, the children are active participants in the conferences with the adults. Students are prepared for their role in the conference, first by reflecting on learning goals they had set for themselves. Some examples of kindergartners' self-selected goals include "I want to make a big book and read it to the whole class," and "I want to learn to spell all my friends' names." Next, the teachers can send home brief surveys to parents and families asking them about their goals for their child's learning. Some examples are, "I hope that he learns to like reading," "If she can learn her alphabet, we will be very pleased," and "We want him to learn to count and add." The last outgrowth of student-led conferences is an opportunity to set goals for the child's future learning. Figure 10.6 summarizes your multiple roles in early childhood assessment.

Figure 10.6 Your Multiple Assessment Roles in Early Childhood Assessment

Evaluating Children's Work
- Evaluating the progress of individual children
- Communicating assessment information to families, educators, and professionals in other fields
- Protecting children's confidentiality
- Planning for differentiation

Evaluating Program Effectiveness
- Determining the success of the lesson
- Evaluating the curriculum in various areas
- Participating in the large-scale evaluation of the total program

Evaluating the Learning Environment
- Conducting a comprehensive review (e.g., using *The Early Childhood Environment Rating Scale*)
- Noting what children accomplish at learning centers
- Observing what children learn through outdoor activities

Evaluating Professional Performance
- Documenting your progress as a skillful observer
- Providing professional feedback to colleagues
- Developing skill in self-evaluation

Your Multiple Assessment Roles

COLLABORATING WITH
Families

A Question-and-Answer Session with Parents on Portfolios

Read the following script of an actual conversation that took place between a teacher and a group of parents on Back-to-School Night, where parents had an opportunity to raise questions concerning the new school year.

Parent A: I noticed you said that you will be using portfolios to grade the children. What's wrong with tests and regular grades?

Teacher: I have used both approaches—portfolios, and tests and grades—in recent years and I have found that the children learn more about the subject matter and themselves with the use of portfolios. The problem that I see with relying exclusively on tests and grades is that children are placed in a competitive situation with their classmates. A combination of tests, grades, and work samples is the most comprehensive way of representing a child's effort, progress, and growth.

Parent B: But competition is what the real world is about. You should be preparing our children to succeed in a tough world, not babying and coddling them.

Teacher: Actually, I have wrestled with that point about helping children to develop skills that they will use throughout life. Business and industry tell us that teamwork is important. How do I reconcile teamwork and competition? I tell the children that they must compete with themselves to try to do better than they have done before. I also help them to realize that sometimes the best way to do a better job is to work with others and share ideas.

Parent A: I don't feel as though I see enough workbook pages and practice sheets coming home with grades on them. How do I or you know if she is learning anything?

Teacher: Children can show us what they know in so many ways—by telling us, by writing a story, by drawing a picture, by performing a play they have written, by building with blocks, and so many others. Portfolios give me a means to document what a child has learned in a way that is meaningful to him or her. The children and I have many opportunities to discuss their work, and they select with me what they want to include in their portfolios. Think about your jobs. If the only information that was given about your work performance was a letter grade, you would probably feel that a grade alone would not adequately describe your capabilities. The same holds true for children in school. I want your children to learn to do their best and to take more responsibility for self-evaluation. When they reflect on their accomplishments, evaluate their work, plan revisions, and set goals, they are also developing skills that will serve them well throughout their lives.

Parent C: But how do you evaluate their work?

Teacher: I use their work to assess their progress in achieving the standards of learning and the skills and knowledge within the school system's curriculum. I look for problem-solving skills and evidence that the child is really thinking. Portfolios may contain a variety of information, including such things as writing samples, a reading list, a spelling file, a video of a play, a recording of an original song, and so much more.

Parent B: What can I do to help my child?

Teacher: When you talk with your child about what he or she is learning at school, ask challenging questions, such as "Why do you think that happened?" or "What might have happened if you had. . . ?" Help your child to understand that real learning is a thinking process, not just memorization of some facts.

USING ASSESSMENT DATA FOR CONTINUOUS PROGRAM IMPROVEMENT

If you contend, "we offer high-quality care for infants at this center," "these children are learning to read," or "this is a good program," you should expect that parents, families, colleagues, community members, school administrators, and professionals in other fields will be asking, "How do you know?" "What is your evidence that these children really are learning?" Program evaluation answers the question, "Am I providing a quality program?" Of course, program evaluation depends on who is responsible for deciding about program quality. A child enrolled in a program may view it differently from how a parent views it, and a trained external evaluator might regard a program differently from how the director of the program views it. Thus, it is important to consider program quality from multiple perspectives. Katz (1993) suggests that there are five different perspectives on program quality and all must be considered in order to evaluate a program comprehensively:

- The **top-down perspective** examines easily observed and measured characteristics. Top-down program characteristics set the stage for effective instruction to occur. For example, is the classroom space adequate? Are there sufficient toys and equipment in the room? Are there enough adults to work with the number of children in the class?
- The **bottom-up perspective** focuses on the quality of the daily experience of the child in the program. It answers questions such as, Does the child feel valued, accepted, and successful? Are there interesting activities for children to pursue? Are children's special needs and circumstances addressed appropriately? Is school a place that children want to be?
- The **inside perspective** deals with the working conditions experienced by teachers. For instance, Are their basic needs being met through adequate salary and health-care benefits? Are they treated with respect by colleagues and supervisory personnel? Is there support for their ongoing professional development?
- The **outside perspective** deals with the relationships among the educational program, the community, and the larger social context in which it operates. It answers questions such as: How is the kindergarten program viewed in our community? How is the program regarded in our country? Is there a general belief among community members that the program is supporting children's development and preparing them for more productive lives?
- The **outside-inside perspective** emphasizes the relationship between early childhood educators and families. It includes considerations such as: Do parents and other family members feel welcome at school? Is there regular communication between teachers and families? Can families rely upon the educational system for support?

There is a wide array of formal assessment tools that can be used to evaluate various dimensions of early childhood programs or the entire program (La Paro, Pianta, & Stuhlman, 2004; Mathers, Linskey, Seddon, & Sylva, 2007; Myers, 2004). One comprehensive way of evaluating programs is through the process of documentation (Fleet, Patterson, & Robertson, 2006; Project Zero, 2003). Documentation is often used to make children's learning visible to others and capture the essence of a class or school-wide project (Carter & Curtis, 1996; Chard, 1996; Curtis & Carter, 2000; Gandini & Kaminsky, 2004; Helm & Helm, 2006). The schools in Reggio Emilia, Italy, are known worldwide for their documentation practices (New, 2003). In these schools and in the traveling exhibits of children's work that have come out of Reggio Emilia, you can see beautiful displays of children's work at various stages, photographs that chronicle the progress of projects, written comments about the children's work from teachers and parents, and transcripts of discussions with children about their work. Large tables, display cases, and three-dimensional bulletin boards are all ways in which the life cycle of a class project—and the learning that it produced—can be communicated to others. The features of documentation are noted in Figure 10.7.

PROVIDE EFFECTIVE ASSESSMENT

How will you know if your assessment plan is balanced and working well? One indicator is student motivation to learn. If learners understand why learning is important, know what is expected, and are confident that they will be treated fairly, they are much more likely to produce work that is of high quality. In a balanced early childhood assessment program, teachers realize that learning is far more complex than memorizing information. The connections between and among a child's knowledge, skills, attitudes, and values are recognized and respected. Children progress as learners when adults believe in their abilities, show them how something is done, provide guided practice, and set clear performance standards.

As you work with young children, adhere to the 11 indicators of effective assessment practices identified by NAEYC (2003). These principles are:

1. Ethical principles guide assessment practices.

2. Assessment instruments are used for their intended purposes.

Figure 10.7 Key Features of Documentation

It has the goal of showing others what children have learned and getting children involved in planning and evaluation processes.	It begins with a guiding question—something about which children are genuinely curious—and maintains a focus on children's ways of learning.	It uses words and pictures—different media—as a way to portray, acknowledge, and enhance children's learning.
It results in public sharing as children and adults reflect upon, revisit, and refine their work and share it with different audiences.	It approaches the topic from multiple perspectives and uses collaboration to strengthen the analysis, interpretation, and evaluation.	It shapes curriculum as teachers use children's work to guide their efforts and design future learning experiences.

Sources: Kroeger & Cardy, 2006; Rinaldi, 2004; Seidel, 2003; Vecchi, 2001.

3. Assessments are appropriate for the ages and other characteristics of the children being assessed.

4. Assessment instruments are in compliance with professional criteria for quality.

5. What is assessed is developmentally and educationally significant.

6. Assessment evidence is used to understand and improve learning.

7. Assessment evidence is gathered from realistic settings and situations that reflect children's actual performance.

8. Assessments use multiple sources of evidence gathered over time.

9. Screening is always linked to follow-up.

10. Use of individually administered, norm-referenced tests is limited.

11. Staff and families are knowledgeable about assessment.

Summary

- Assessment is the process of observing, recording, and documenting children's work in order to make decisions about instruction, curriculum, and the program. Assessment *of* learning evaluates what and how children learn, and assessment *for* learning uses data to decide what to teach next and the most effective way of guiding children's learning.

- Early childhood educators are responsible for observing, recording, and analyzing information about children's learning and development, the curriculum, and the program. The main categories of assessment used are (1) observations, (2) tests, and (3) performance assessment.

- Early childhood assessment is fulfilling its purpose when: the assessment tools used are reliable and valid, both the content and means of data collection are suited to the young child's developmental level, the tasks take children's linguistic and cultural differences into account, the results are used to benefit the child rather than to label or deprive him or her of opportunities, and the assessment process values families and effectively communicates assessment data to them (Gullo, 2006).

- Teachers need to use their knowledge of assessment to work to meet the learning needs of all students, plan for instruction, evaluate the curriculum, reflect on their teaching practices, and enhance overall program quality.

Applying Your Knowledge of Assessment

In the following two activities, you will apply your knowledge of assessment. In Assessment Activity 1, you will draw upon your knowledge of observation to reflect on the case of Damien, a drug-exposed child who is living in a crack house. Assessment Activity 2 combines your knowledge of assessment and reflection as you consider how your performance will be evaluated as you progress through your college program.

 1 **DAMIEN, A DRUG-EXPOSED CHILD**

On a tour of a program for preschoolers at-risk, the program director said to a visiting early childhood professor, "I guess we should warn you. There is a crack-exposed child in the preschool classroom we will be visiting next. I know this is terrible, but he has kicked and bitten and thrown things so often that we call him 'the attack child.' He needs a full-time aide. Fortunately, he's a lot better now than he was at the beginning of the year. Our new principal, who was just transferred here from the high school, expelled the boy for 3 days. Everyone knows that this boy lives in a crack house. How is spending more time there supposed to solve his problems?"

They entered a classroom to see and hear a first-year teacher reading Eric Carle's (1981) picture book *The Very Hungry Caterpillar* aloud. A biracial boy with light brown ringlets and hazel eyes was seated on a young woman's lap. This was Damien, the child the visitor had been forewarned about.

During her observations, the visitor noted that while the children were responding to the story and playing a game, Damien participated enthusiastically. But when they were assigned to color, he began to race around the room and scream. Then he swept a shelf of toys and a puzzle rack onto the floor with his arm while the other children watched him uneasily. His aide, a frail-looking young African American woman who appeared to be fresh out of high school, managed to catch Damien and attempted to restrain him by speaking softly, leading him to another area of the classroom, and encircling him with her arms. Damien struggled at first and then he relaxed.

It was time for free play. Damien sat down, opened up a miniature barn, and took out the toy animals, people, and farm equipment stored inside. The other children kept their distance. It was as if a magnetic field had been created, with Damien repelling every other person. All of the adults, including his aide, were positioned on the opposite side of the room.

The visitor approached Damien cautiously and knelt down on the carpet. He was making the plastic tractor and the wagon attached to it go around in a circle, over and over again. The visitor picked up a plastic spotted cow, waddled it over toward the roly-poly farmer who was positioned in the driver's seat, and said in a goofy voice, "Hi, Damien. I want to go for a ride. Can I, please? Huh? Huh? Can I please?" Damien peered at the cow intently, then at the visitor, his jaw dropping in amazement. He nodded affirmatively. The play continued in this way with different plastic toys sometimes leaping over fences, screeching into the barn, losing a passenger, or giving Damien a noisy kiss on the cheek. Some of the other children stopped by to watch and ask what Damien was doing and why he was laughing. What they were really wondering, the visitor concluded, was whether it was safe to play with Damien.

Later that day when all of the adults had an opportunity to talk, the teacher, aide, and program supervisors wanted to know what the visitor thought about Damien. "I would capitalize on the fact that Damien has the services of a full-time aide. Her time might be better spent in one-to-one playful interaction rather than in attempting to control Damien during group time. As long as everyone is wary of Damien and tends to keep away, his opportunities for social development will be limited. I think the most pressing issue is Damien's acceptance into the group. You need to give yourselves permission to treat him differently, to focus on furthering his social and emotional development, rather than being overly concerned about making sure that he covers the content." The aide shared her frustration with the situation and reported that they had been working with social services to try to have Damien removed from his mother's custody. So far, all of their efforts had been futile.

REACT	In what ways are the perspectives of the program director, the visiting professor, and the aide in the class alike?
RESEARCH	Investigate the subject of prenatal drug exposure and identify the major issues and recommendations. What beliefs did the adults in this situation seem to be acting upon? How did their responses to Damien compare with the recommendations you found?
REFLECT	How did the visitor use observation to arrive at an idea about what to do for Damien?

Assessment ACTIVITY ② EVALUATION OF PRESERVICE EARLY CHILDHOOD EDUCATORS

Colker (2008) asked 43 early childhood educators to identify the characteristics that are integral to effective teaching. They included: (1) passion about children and teaching; (2) perseverance/dedication/tenacity; (3) taking the risks necessary to advocate for children and families; (4) pragmatism/willingness to compromise; (5) patience with children, families, and colleagues; (6) flexibility in adapting to demands for change; (7) respect for others/appreciation of diversity; (8) creativity and resourcefulness when working with limited resources; (9) authenticity/integrity/commitment; (10) love of learning and ability to inspire children to learn; (11) high energy; and (12) a sense of humor.

Gather copies of the observation forms, evaluation forms, procedures, and policies that will be used to evaluate your performance during various field experiences. Consider these questions:

1. What is the purpose of the assessment? When does it occur? Who conducts the assessment? How is it shared with the preservice teacher?
2. Are there items that focus on the preservice teacher's knowledge? skills? dispositions?
3. How could the college student use the feedback from the assessment for professional growth?
4. What rights and responsibilities are outlined for the preservice teacher?
5. After reviewing these materials, what is your group's sense of the characteristics and behaviors in preservice teachers that would result in them exceeding, meeting, or failing to meet expectations?

ONLINE RESOURCES FOR ASSESSMENT AND PROGRAM EVALUATION

General Resources

Education Week: Produces statistics in an annual report called *Quality Counts;* includes a state-by-state "Report Card" and analysis of students' test performance. www.edweek.org/rc/

Fair Test: Review the National Forum on Assessment's "Principles and Indicators for Student Assessment Systems." www.fairtest.org

National Education Goals Panel: Provides *State Scorecards* of progress in achieving the eight National Education Goals; see also No Child Left Behind for Parents. www.negp.gov and www.nochildleftbehind.gov/parents/index.html

National Center for Education Statistics: Provides the most recent statistics and publishes an influential annual report, *The Condition of Education.* http://nces.ed.gov

Assessment of English Language Learners

Home Language Survey: This site offers a home language survey (2008) that has been translated into 20 languages from the Illinois State Board of Education. www.isbe.state.il.us/bilingual/htmls/tbe_tpi.htm

NAEYC: View the NAEYC's 2009 position statement "Where We Stand: On Assessing Young English Language Learners." www.naeyc.org/positionstatements

Assessment of Children with Disabilities

Division for Early Childhood (DEC) of the Council for Exceptional Children (CEC): View the DEC/CEC 2007 recommendations "Promoting Positive Outcomes for Children with Disabilities: Recommendations for Curriculum, Assessment, and Program Evaluation." www.naeyc.org/about/positions/pdf/PrmtgPositiveOutcomes.pdf

Early Childhood Intervention Clearinghouse: Provides information on assessment in early childhood, with an emphasis on early intervention efforts. www.eiclearinghouse.org/

PEARSON myeducationlab

Go to Topic 4 (Observation/Assessment) in the MyEducationLab (www.myeducationlab.com) for your course, where you can:

- Find learning outcomes for observation/assessment along with the national standards that connect to these outcomes.
- Complete Assignments and Activities that can help you more deeply understand the chapter content.
- Apply and practice your understanding of the core teaching skills identified in the chapter with the Building Teaching Skills and Dispositions learning units.
- Hear viewpoints of experts in the field in Professional Perspectives.

CHAPTER 11

Guiding Children's Behavior and Creating a Classroom Community

Our example is the most powerful teaching strategy we have in terms of influencing children and families.

T. Berry Brazelton & Stanley Greenspan, 2000, p. 99

Meet the TEACHERS

CHARLES is employed at a child-care program at the local hospital. "I work with the medical personnel to plan appropriate activities for the children in the playroom. I also work with families to help them get things back to normal as much as possible when the child is well and ready to return home. A hospital stay often intensifies the child's fear of separation and abandonment and may cause the families, who were so worried about the child, to become overly protective or permissive. A big part of my role is to help the adults consider the child's point of view, give additional support when needed, and set reasonable limits for the child's behavior."

TWYLA is an early childhood major who gains more experience with young children by working at the university-sponsored child-care center part-time. The rule at the center is that nobody owns any of the toys or materials; children are expected to share. But when a toddler brought his favorite teddy bear to school and didn't want to share, Twyla felt that he was entitled to cling to his toy and say, "It's mine!" She decided to read several children's books during the week about "attachment objects" (blankets, soft toys, and other items that young children form a connection with) and then talk with the children about their most treasured items. She was surprised by the children's idea to modify the rules about very special toys. They decided that, "Other kids can look at them, but not take them away" and that, "Sometimes, you don't have to share."

MS. PETTIT has a child in her class named Tonya who frequently arrives at school tired, hungry, and neglected. Tonya lives with her chronically ill mother and 3-year-old brother and has responsibilities far beyond her 7 years of age for cooking, cleaning, and babysitting. Ms. Pettit describes what happened during the first few weeks of school: "Other children arrived with new school supplies, and Tonya, who can be quite persuasive, started to make deals with her classmates in which they ended up with the bad end of the bargain—such as Kim's new backpack being traded for a set of markers that were going dry. Then I received an angry telephone call and a note from parents asking me what was going on. I explained to Tonya that it wasn't right for her to make unfair trades and insisted that she 'make things right' with her classmates. Then I used my $100 allocation from the local parent group to equip several backpacks with writing and drawing supplies so that Tonya has access to the materials that she wanted so desperately."

LEARNING Outcomes

In this chapter, you will learn to:

→ Become familiar with national standards and guidelines concerning the early childhood educator's role in guiding children's behavior and classroom management (NAEYC #1, ACEI #3d and #3e, INTASC #6)

→ Define *child guidance, classroom community*, and *self-regulation*

→ Understand principles of child guidance and appropriate responses to conflict in the classroom

→ Develop greater confidence in fulfilling your role in guiding children's behavior

→ Acquire more skillful ways of communicating with children and families when difficult issues arise

Compare

What are some commonalities among these three teachers?

Contrast

How do these teachers think about their roles in guiding children's behavior?

Connect

What made the greatest impression on you, and how will you incorporate this into your teaching?

Now that you have reflected on the three teachers' perspectives and noted the learning outcomes, we preview the knowledge, skills, and dispositions you will need to acquire in order to fulfill your role in guiding children's behavior.

A Definition of Child Guidance and Classroom Community

DID YOU Know ?

- Most beginning teachers report feeling inadequately prepared to handle classroom management; only 17% were confident about working with diverse groups of children (Martin, Chiodo, & Chang, 2001; Silvestri, 2001). Preservice teachers quickly discover that rather than relying on formulas for classroom management, they need to respond to concerns about specific situations on a case-by-case basis (Martin et al., 2001).

- When educators are confronted by children's challenging behavior, they tend to resort to punitive methods (e.g., losing privileges, threatening to contact parents or the principal) (Maag, 2001). Actually, the research supports more positive approaches, such as discussion of problems, rewards for good behavior, and student involvement in decision making (Kaiser & Rasminsky, 2006; Lewis, 2001).

- Boys usually have more dopamine in their bloodstream and they process more blood flow in the cerebellum, the part of the brain that controls physical action; therefore, boys often prefer to be more active. Brain scans show that when boys are at rest, their level of brain activity is less than girls'; therefore, boys may benefit from being allowed to move a little (e.g., draw, or hold a squeeze ball) as an aid to concentration and alertness (Gurian & Stevens, 2005).

- In an increasing number of cases, young children with behavioral problems are being expelled from classrooms (Gilliam, 2005; Zaslow & Martinez-Beck, 2006). Boys are five times more likely to be expelled from school than girls (Gartrell, 2006).

In early childhood education, **child guidance** refers to leading young children to more socially acceptable ways of handling powerful emotions and coping with the inevitable conflicts of interacting with others. Child guidance is founded on positive relationships with children and families and calls upon teachers to identify with children, have compassion for their circumstances, strive to understand the underlying reasons for their behavior, model appropriate behaviors for them, and coach them in socially acceptable ways to resolve conflict. Figure 11.1 compares/contrasts child guidance strategies with discipline.

Why should teachers be concerned about building relationships and helping every child to be a valued member of a **classroom community**? Children need positive relationships with peers and adults in order to flourish. In addition to the basic needs such as food, shelter, clothing, and safety, all human beings have fundamental personal and social needs, including:

- **autonomy**, the need to exert an influence on decisions and events rather than feeling powerless and the victim of circumstance;
- **relatedness**, the need for love, affirmation, and a sense of connectedness with others and belonging to a group; and
- **competence**, the need to accomplish new things, acquire new skills, and successfully put these learnings to use. (Deci & Ryan, 1985; Maslow, 1968; Rodgers, 1998)

A classroom community exists only if *all* children's needs for autonomy, relatedness, and competence are met. Strategies that promote a sense of community give children hope—a sense of moving forward, making progress, and anticipating a brighter future. Every classroom should be a community of learners with clearly understood goals, a sense of belonging to the group, effective communication, fair treatment, agreed-upon standards for behavior, opportunities to deal with ideas and feelings, care and concern for all members, and dynamic, interactive learning experiences (Boyer, 1995; Sowers, 2004). "Creating a community of learners in the classroom has a significant impact on how children work together, how they feel about school, and the relationships that are built with them as individuals and as a group" (Heroman & Copple, 2006, p. 61).

Young children feel that they are valued members of a classroom community when teachers convey the following important messages to every child:

Figure 11.1 Child Guidance versus Discipline

Contemporary Child Guidance

Child is encouraged to . . .

- Exercise self-control over emotions and override impulses
- Distinguish what is right, just, and good from what is wrong, unfair, and bad
- Internalize a code of conduct
- Recognize others' feelings and consider the consequences of behavior
- Cope with powerful emotions and act autonomously
- Engage in problem solving and consider underlying motives

"Old-Fashioned" Discipline

Child learns to . . .

- Yield to impulse in the absence of a threat of punishment
- Wait for an adult to pass judgment on behavior
- Fear punishment or negotiate for rewards, dismiss others' feelings, and focus instead on avoidance of punishment or attainment of rewards
- Repress emotions temporarily and retaliate later when authority figure is absent
- Keep score of who wins and loses

Child Guidance Versus Discipline

Encouragement

- Teaches children to evaluate their own efforts
  Examples: *"Was that fun?" "Are you glad you tried to . . . ?" "You seem pleased about . . ."*
- Does not judge children on their work
  Examples: *"I noticed that you were . . ." "Which of your paintings do you like best?"*
- Focuses on the process rather than the outcome
  Examples: *"How did you use the software to do this?" "It looks like you are working on your sign." "I see you are enjoying . . ."*
- Is a **private** event that does not embarrass children in public or compare them with each other
  Examples: *"Thanks for helping to clean up today." "I appreciate that you . . ." "Aren't you pleased that you were able to . . . ?"*

Praise

- Teacher is the judge of what is good and bad
  Examples: *"You have been very good today, so here is a sticker for you."*
- Judges children and their work
  Examples: *"What a great story!" "You had the best idea."*
- Focuses on the outcome
  Examples: *"I am putting the best papers up on the bulletin board." "Who has their work finished?"*
- Is a public announcement or event
  Examples: *"Room 5, you have been very good today." "Look at Sheri's paper, everyone. She did it correctly." "The winners of the contest are . . ."*

People like me here; I can come back.

I have my own space here; I can leave my stuff and it will be safe.

Nice things happen here; I can depend on good things happening again.

I might not get finished today, but I can work on it some more later.

There are kind people here; I can become like them.

I am getting better at this, and I can learn new things.

My behavior can change my reputation for the better; I do not have to stay the way that I am right now.

What I want and think matters; I can make responsible choices.

Even if I make a mistake, I can set things right.

I don't have to depend on others all of the time; I can do some things well all by myself.

Learning to share and take turns is essential to a classroom community.

My work matters to me and to the group; I can do outstanding work.

What I am learning at school works in other places and at other times, too.

There are so many choices, I can try and succeed at new things. (Gannon & Mncayi, 1996)

In fact, a major source of children's challenging behavior is denial of these needs. When these needs (or basic needs) are denied, children resort to antisocial behaviors such as seeking attention, exerting their power, trying to even the score through revenge, or resisting passively by ignoring adult demands (Dinkmeyer & McKay, 1989).

All of us have had experience with discipline. Usually, it consists of some combination of rewards and punishments. Punishments are unpleasant or painful experiences that are imposed upon others to "teach a lesson" and enforce compliance, as in, "Go sit by yourself in time-out. I asked you twice to clean up the toys and you did not do it." Corporal punishment is physical pain inflicted to force compliance, as in spanking. Threats are warnings about the punishments that will occur if compliance with the rules is not forthcoming, as in, "If you do not finish your work on time, you will miss recess." Rewards are pleasant experiences that are held out to recognize compliance, as in, "Those of you who did well on your papers get a sticker." Bribes are promises of future rewards, as in, "If you work quietly for the next 10 minutes, we will get to make play dough this afternoon" (Kohn, 1996; Wein, 2006). These approaches, while undeniably powerful in shaping behavior, have limitations. To illustrate, consider the case of Jason, a kindergarten boy who adjusted readily to a full-day program when school started in August. Yet later on in the school year, he started to cry, not at the start of the school day, but in the afternoons shortly before the school bus arrived. Although his teacher was sympathetic at first, she eventually lost patience with him and complained that Jason's daily crying was "driving her crazy." In desperation, she resorted to a behavioristic approach and tried to ignore the crying but as the winter began, Jason's tears and protests grew more intense.

Clues to the puzzling pattern of Jason's behavior began to emerge after a concerned neighbor reported the child's situation to Children and Youth Services. Jason's mother had abandoned the family during the summer, and his father, who had a demanding job and a long commute, suddenly had sole responsibility for the boy. Monday through Friday, 5-year-old Jason was home alone until his father arrived at the house around 7:00 P.M. When the social worker spoke with Jason, he confided that he had been frightened by the TV commercials for horror movies during Halloween and was terrified to stay by himself when it was dark outside (Isenberg & Jalongo, 2010). As this kindergartner's situation illustrates, guiding young children's behavior is a complex and challenging task, particularly when adults have different expectations and conflicting beliefs (Shore, 2003).

Pause and Reflect

About Discipline

Which of the following did you experience as a child? How did you feel about such statements?

- "All of you will sit here and miss recess until the person who broke the rules comes forward."
- "If everyone gets 100% on the spelling test on Friday, we will have a popcorn party."
- "You know the rule. Now you have to write 'I will not throw snowballs' 500 times."
- "I like the way that Heather is working. Look at Heather's picture, everyone."

On page 297, the Ask the Expert by Marjorie Fields provides an overview of key concepts in child guidance.

Ask the EXPERT   *Marjorie Fields*

Guidance and Discipline

Q: If you don't punish or reward children, how do you get them to obey?

A: Helping children to learn personal responsibility for their behavior and to judge between right and wrong is a much higher goal than teaching obedience. Many people fear that children will run wild unless adults force them to obey, but teaching children personal responsibility creates people who monitor their own behavior and don't require policing from others. If we use punishments and rewards to get desirable behavior, the only time we can count on good behavior is when someone is there to give out the punishment or reward. Asking only for obedience is asking for far too little.

Q: We are told to respond to the cause of misbehavior, but how can we figure out why children act inappropriately?

A: The best way to determine the cause of a child's behavior is to observe the child carefully and record your observations. You need to know a lot about a child to plan effective discipline. You need to note whether this is usual or unusual behavior, and also under what circumstances it occurs. What do you know about the child's home routine, health, or family situation that might provide some clues?

Never overlook the possibility that you may have caused a discipline problem. Unfortunately we often see teacher expectations and school environments that are not appropriate for children's levels of development, individual temperaments, or cultures; in these cases the teacher causes discipline problems.

Unmet needs also cause inappropriate behaviors. These may be physical needs such as hunger or tiredness or they may be emotional needs such as trust, attention, personal power, friendship, or self-esteem. Helping children get these needs met will improve their behavior much more than punishment or rewards. Missing social skills or communication skills account for much of the negative interactions between children; teaching these skills will improve the behaviors. Punishment will not.

Q: If we focus on building relationships with children, won't that get in the way of teaching them to mind?

A: Building relationships with children doesn't mean being their buddy and letting go of your adult role. It means making sure that each child knows you care about him or her. Unless a child knows you care, and unless that child is concerned about maintaining a relationship with you, there is really no reason for the child to pay attention to what you ask. If you don't have a caring relationship with a child, your only recourse is punishment or reward—with their ultimately negative impact on behavior.

Caring relationships require investing some time in listening respectfully to children and having other pleasant interactions with them. This investment will pay off during a behavior crisis.

Marjorie Fields is an Early Childhood Education Professor Emerita, University of Alaska, S.E.

Adults in crisis, such as Jason's father and teacher, can make bad decisions when they disregard the child's needs in their haste to eradicate an unwelcome behavior, so, here again, reflection is an important tool for teachers (McFarland, Saunders, & Allen, 2009). When a child is hungry, it is cruel to berate the child for not paying attention in class. When a child's father is in jail, it is inconsiderate to sponsor a father-son event. When a child has witnessed a drive-by shooting, it is disrespectful to act as if nothing has happened. As you teach, bear in mind that "Children carry their home lives to school as easily as the books and papers in their backpacks" (Krahl & Jalongo, 1998). Studies suggest that children's behavior exerts a powerful effect on their overall success in school (Bagner, Boggs, & Eyberg, 2010) and that some agreement exists on what children need for kindergarten success in the United States. In a study of an ethnically diverse group of parents, three clusters of skills were agreed upon as essential for kindergarten success: (1) listening, feeling confident, and following directions; (2) counting, reading, and writing; and (3) enthusiasm, effective communication, and appropriate behaviors (Diamond, Reagan, & Bandyk, 2000).

Principles of Child Guidance

Before you rush to change children's behavior, reflect on the following five questions.

1. **Is it necessary?** A child-care provider who works with 3-year-olds insists that every child lie down and take a nap in the afternoon. For the children who are in the habit of taking an afternoon nap, this procedure is fine. For those who are unaccustomed to naps, it is a constant struggle. She spends much of her time leading them back to their cots or saying "Shhhh!" loudly and frequently. The real question is not whether children are napping or not but whether a nap is necessary. If the nap is designed to keep children from getting overtired, and some children clearly are not tired, then why is a nap required? Wouldn't it be sufficient to have a quiet time instead of attempting to enforce a nap? Might the naptime be more for the teacher's benefit than the children's?

2. **Is it productive?** In a Head Start classroom, all of the 4-year-olds are required to assemble in a circle and seat themselves on pieces of masking tape placed on the carpet. The circle time lasts for nearly 30 minutes, and every time a child moves from the tape, the teacher sends the child to a "growing-up chair." By the time the large-group session is over, about a third of the children are in chairs as punishment because they did not sit still. In fact, by the end of this excessively long and boring circle time, it almost looks like a game of musical chairs! If you talk with the teacher, she will tell you that her students "just don't know how to behave." What she really needs to do is to rethink group time. Ironically, what she considers to be a punishment (moving to chairs) is actually more of a reward because the children get to move around and have escape from the tedious circle time the teacher conducts day after day.

3. **Is it fair?** A second-grade teacher has attended a workshop on assertive discipline, and one of the recommended strategies is to list the names of children who misbehave and place a checkmark next to the child's name with each new incident of violating classroom rules. She decides to try this. After a child accumulates three checkmarks, that child loses a privilege. A regular visitor to the classroom asks why the same names are on the board all of the time. Afterward, the teacher wonders to herself, "How can I say that this system is working if the children who need to learn self-control aren't improving? I need to reevaluate this approach."

4. Is it appropriate?   A private nursery school in a wealthy suburb has high tuition and a long waiting list. The director knows that parents and families send their children there in the hopes that their children's development will be accelerated, so she pressures the teachers to "get more out of" the children to build her program's reputation for developing precocity in children. Because the competition for the available slots in each class is keen, the director decides to institute more-stringent policies about entrance requirements and a more academic focus. When several of the toddlers do not sit quietly during stories, memorize songs and fingerplays, or paste shapes cut out by the teachers in the correct way, the director invites the parents in and asks them to remove their children from the program to make room "for those who can benefit." There is undeniable damage done by this decision—the parents/families feel as though their son or daughter has failed preschool and they begin to wonder and worry about their child's capabilities.

Guiding young children's behavior requires a strong commitment to communicating effectively.

Child guidance also has to be culturally responsive (Weinstein, Tomlinson-Clarke, & Curran, 2004). Teachers in the United States sometimes assume that children should make eye contact, be outspoken, and be competitive. In many groups throughout the world, however, these behaviors are not encouraged because the culture values deference to authority, quiet listening, and group effort. Before you expect certain behaviors from children, find out more about their families' expectations.

5. Does it respect the natural behavior of young children?   A 5-year-old boy comes running into the classroom and slides across the floor on his knees. He went to the library yesterday and was given a temporary tattoo as a prize for reading 10 books. With that, he lifts up his t-shirt to show his friends, commenting "Yeah, it makes me look tough!" When the teacher approaches, he says proudly "I'm only 5 and I already look like a man!" How would you handle such a situation as a teacher? Sadly, many teachers would take this boy aside and speak with him harshly, put him in time out, or reprimand him in front of his peers. A better approach would be to emphasize what is right and notice the rest: "Wow, Darnell! Ten books! Good for you! Yes, I see that tattoo. How long do they last?" and then, quietly, just for him to hear, "I can see why you are so are excited but don't forget about no running. I don't want you to slip on the floor and get hurt." It is possible to gently remind children of rules intended to protect them without quashing the joy a child is feeling. Realize that somber, quiet, tightly controlled environments are not suitable for the very young. As Dan Gartrell (2006) reminds us,

> energetic classrooms, rich in nurturing and encouragement, are good for all children. Let's face it: classrooms in general (particularly in light of the obesity epidemic) need to be less like Sunday school and more like summer camp—which of course would make them more developmentally appropriate and healthier . . . young people—boys and girls—learn through movement. (p. 93)

When you see a child misbehave, ask yourself what might be motivating him or her. William Glasser (1999) argues that all human beings have at least five basic needs:

(1) survival, (2) love and belonging, (3) power, (4) freedom, and (5) fun. Children behave as they do, good or bad, in response to one or more of these motivating factors. The great majority of the time, young children strive to please adults and comply with their requests. The rest of the time, you will need to dig deeper to learn what might be causing a behavior. Some underlying causes of children's behavior include:

- **Physical environment**—for instance, the child may be new to an environment and unfamiliar with procedures; there may not be enough materials to go around, and this leads to disputes; the classroom layout may be poor and fail to clearly demarcate quiet and noisy areas; the room may not be arranged in ways that encourage children to access materials and put them away independently
- **Child's basic needs are unmet**—for example, the child may be neglected, abused, ill, tired, or hungry; may feel inadequate or incompetent; may feel unaccepted by peers and/or adults
- **Curriculum issues**—for example, the academic demands may be unrealistic for the child's age or stage; an inflexible schedule might cause the child to act out; the child may be generally unchallenged and disinterested in the required activities
- **Cultural differences**—a family may feel overwhelmed by the adaptive demands of a new culture; a child may not have mastered the language well enough to make his or her needs known; a child may have suffered traumatic experiences in the process of immigrating; the family's values may conflict with certain school or class policies and procedures (Barrera & Corso, 2003; Bronson, 2006).
- **Special needs**—the child may be abused or neglected or subjected to physical harm, sexual molestation, emotional maltreatment, or a disregard of the child's basic needs; may have attention deficit disorder, characterized by the inability to concentrate on a task long enough to process information or accomplish a goal; may be autistic, a severe impairment of two-way verbal or nonverbal social interaction in which the child's activity is dominated by repetitive and ritualistic behaviors; may have a behavioral disorder, characterized by a difference from the norm in the amount and intensity of the child's reactions; may have a learning disability, a variety of problems manifested as difficulty with verbal or mathematical skills, with fine or gross motor skills, or with visual, auditory, and tactile perception.

One way to get the behavior that you hope for from children is to take a positive, school-wide approach (Elementary Educators, 2006). Focus on coaching children in how to interact more successfully rather than reprimanding and punishing (Severson & Walker, 2002; Walker, Ramsey, & Gresham, 2003/2004). Establish a few simple rules and repeat them often. Remember that in order to succeed in school, young children need to be able to follow directions, participate in group activities, express their needs and ideas, conform to classroom rules, and interact appropriately with adults and peers.

Your Role in Child Guidance

Many preservice teachers have nightmares (literally) about children's misbehavior. You may walk down the hall, see children engaged and productive, and marvel at another teacher's ability to manage the classroom. An even more eye-opening experience is to see the very children who do not listen to you listening attentively as they work with someone else. What is the secret to success? Effective teachers have learned to do the following things.

ANTICIPATE AND PREVENT PROBLEM BEHAVIORS

One of the most important things that any adult responsible for the care and education of young children can do is to try to prevent behavior problems before they occur (Dunlap et al., 2006). Figure 11.2 provides an overview of prevention strategies.

On page 304, the Ask the Expert by Wanda Boyer explains the importance of self-regulation and emotion regulation in young children.

ACTIVELY TEACH SKILLS IN SELF-REGULATION

When invited to talk about "kids who are bad," 5-year-old David said, "Kalessha is really bad. She moved away and I'm glad. 'Cause one time, I was trying to write in my journal and she was holding my arm so I couldn't even write! And Oliver, he's really bad too. One time the teacher made him go to the principal's office because he was kicking other kids." These children have gotten a bad reputation with their peers because they were continually singled out for punishment instead of being taught the skills of self-regulation. Visit Rashid's first-grade classroom on any given day, and you are likely to see him in time-out. Because Rashid is repeatedly isolated from the group, his peers treat him as untrustworthy and reject his overtures of friendship. Children like Rashid, who are less adaptable, more distractible, and more intense, really need to learn how to adjust to new circumstances, concentrate, and calm themselves. Putting him in time-out does nothing to accomplish this (Gartrell, 2006). As a result, Rashid is considered to be a troublemaker by his peers. As you interact with children, remember that it is possible to see that a child *has* a problem without seeing that child *as* the problem. A more effective approach is to clearly demonstrate what the child needs to actually do. For example, when the teacher's aide saw Rashid handling the classroom pet rabbit roughly, she intervened immediately with, "I know that you want Whiskers to like you. Let me show you how to hold him and feed him so that the two of you can be friends. Guess what?! He knows how to walk on a leash. Would you like to give it a try?" Notice how this response helps the child in choosing the right behaviors instead of harping on what he did wrong. Try to see yourself in the child and identify with him or her (Strachota, 1996). Figure 11.3 offers suggestions for promoting self-regulation and emotion regulation in young children.

Classroom organization and established procedures can prevent behavior problems.

FOCUS ON THE CHILD'S NEEDS

Put aside your worries about appearing inept and losing face. Think about the child and realize that the child's behavior may be invoking exactly the opposite of what that child truly needs from adults. Second-grader Marjorie is a good example. When the teacher directed everyone to draw pictures of their families, Marjorie grew sullen and refused to comply. The more the teacher pressed, the more adamant Marjorie became, and her teacher saw it as open defiance. What her teacher did not realize is that Marjorie's father had abandoned the family to move in with his new girlfriend. Marjorie was mourning the loss of her father and had overheard her mother talking

Figure 11.2 Preventing Behavior Problems

Focus on General Goals

- Create order so that the group can function effectively and so that all children can learn
- Teach children to take responsibility for their own actions and to acquire self-discipline
- Teach children to handle powerful emotions and express their feelings in socially appropriate ways
- Foster cooperation between and among children and adults
- Teach children the social responsibility and ethical principles necessary to function as citizens in a democratic society

Coach Children in Ways to

- Approach others positively
- Express wishes and preferences clearly
- Assert personal rights and needs appropriately
- Avoid intimidation by bullies
- Express frustration and anger appropriately
- Collaborate with peers easily
- Participate in discussion and activities
- Take turns
- Show interest in others
- Negotiate or compromise with others
- Accept and enjoy people of diverse backgrounds
- Employ appropriate nonverbal greetings and communications

Build Positive Interactions

- Treat children with dignity
- Be fair
- Engage in one-to-one interactions with children
- Communicate warmth and respect
- Get on the child's level for face-to-face interactions
- Use a pleasant, calm voice and simple language
- Follow the child's lead and interest during play
- Help children understand classroom expectations
- Provide warm, responsive physical contact
- Redirect children when they engage in challenging behavior
- Listen to children and encourage them to listen to others
- Acknowledge children for their accomplishments and effort
- Promote positive peer interactions

Know Students' Abilities and Limitations

- Try to foster independence so that children's frustrations are reduced
- Avoid rushing children, as this usually results in stress and acting out
- Avoid leaving children waiting with nothing to do; give them something to do, such as playing a game

Have a Well-Organized Classroom and Established Routines

- If everyone decides that the blocks go on the shelf this clarifies what to do during clean up
- Engage as many senses as possible when teaching routines; for example, a picture of a flowerpot, a stick-person poster near the plants to show what he or she is expected to do, and an auditory signal for helper time
- Demonstrate procedures and have children repeat the instructions before they actually perform the task

Figure 11.2 continued

Discuss Rules and Consequences

- Keep rules simple and clear, such as "No closed games in first grade."
- Make consequences clear, such as, "If you spill water on the floor, you have to mop it up."
- State the value of compliance: "If you clean out your desk, you'll be able to find things when you need them."

Teach, Model, and Review Appropriate Behaviors

- Trust children and believe them. They are not trying to make you look bad or being difficult deliberately.
- Instead of *telling* children what they should do, *show* them what they should do. If teachers do not wash their hands but require it of children, then children will wonder why they are supposed to do this.
- Use children's literature to illustrate children who engage in inappropriate behaviors, the consequences of those behaviors, and different ways of "trying on" solutions.

Learn to Be a Troubleshooter

- Be alert to signs of difficulty and anticipate situations that will require special support.
- Realize that young children often are doing something—such as cutting shapes out of the middle of a piece of paper—for the very first time.
- Let children know there is a problem. Beginning teachers sometimes smile sweetly at virtually any behavior. It is better to project a serious, concerned facial expression when difficulties arise.

Think Before You Speak or Act

- Try to see behavior through a child's eyes; if a teacher sees a child pinching another child and says, "Come and sit by me," that child might think it is a privilege.
- Do not threaten children, saying, for instance, "You will have to stay after school if you don't get your work done" when the child rides the bus and there is no way this will happen.

Sources: Ganz & Flores, 2010; Mindes, 2006; Nelsen, Erwin, & Duffy, 1995; Ostrosky & Jung, 2006; Rief, 1993.

about being without money. The second grader was terrified that they would be poverty stricken in the desperate ways she had seen portrayed in movies. Finally, Marjorie relented and drew the picture, but when she arrived at home, she cried bitterly about the fact that she "lied at school," because her picture depicted the entire family "even though I know Daddy doesn't live with us anymore."

KNOW THE POLICIES

A common concern is that the classroom will spin out of control, and that a child's behavior will "infect" the rest of the group with a spirit of rebellion when they see a classmate "getting away with" noncompliance. As an initial step in guiding children, determine the policies. Does the center, school, or district have a behavioral code? Are there classroom rules that every child is expected to follow? What is the procedure for making a referral? What about safety rules? Ignorance of the policies can cause problems for teachers.

Ask the EXPERT — Wanda Boyer

Self-Regulation and Emotion Regulation

Q: What are self-regulation and emotion regulation?

A: I can! I will! I believe! I have a dream! Yes, we can! All of these words of action and the positive attitude come from a place of self-regulation and emotion regulation. So how can we help children be a part of this positive movement? We need them to learn how to self-regulate and emotion regulate. **Self-regulation** is the ability to start, change, or stop verbal or motor behaviors in varied contexts. This allows children to put aside an object or goal in order to do what is right without anyone knowing or supervising them. **Emotion regulation** involves that same ability to start, change, or stop, but now we are thinking about internal feeling states, emotion-related physical responses, and goals that are emotionally fuelled. This allows children to learn how to understand and use their emotions to vary behavioral responses in order to achieve their goals. Self-regulation and emotion regulation are integral to our ability to have positive interactions with others while ultimately having our own needs met appropriately.

Q: Why should teachers be concerned about children's self-regulation and emotion regulation?

A: In my study of 150 children and their families and their 15 early childhood educators across varied communities and cultures, parents and educators in interviews and focus groups said that self-regulation and emotion regulation were vital to child development. Specifically, they felt working together to engage in children's acquisition of self-regulation and emotion regulation had the potential to promote social intelligence, optimism, empathy toward others, moral reasoning, mental and physical wellness, and improved linguistic and cognitive strategies for learning. Moreover, self-regulatory and emotion regulatory skills can optimize receptivity to learning experiences.

Q: What can teachers do to promote self-regulation and emotion regulation in young children?

A: From this discussion you can see that it is not easy to learn how to self-regulate or emotion regulate. Children will need our help. In a recent phenomenological research study, I investigated what 15 experienced preschool educators have come to know about children's self-regulation and emotion regulation development. Early childhood educators indicated that educators and families need to be sympathetic and recognize that children will need to learn how to practice inhibitory control, or soothability, as a means of persevering or sticking to a challenging task. Because children do not miraculously know how to comfort themselves when distressing things happen, as teachers we will need to observe and assess children's behavior, for example, in distressing and nondistressing situations. Once we have noted their responses, then we can assist them in learning what to say to themselves and others and what to do in order to practice self-soothing strategies. The early childhood educators also noted they needed to create a secure base for children and provide challenging and engaging learning events. They recommended creating a consistent schedule, setting limits and behavioral expectations in advance, and modeling appropriate behaviors. The early childhood educators also noted a sequence of four methods to support self-regulation and emotion regulation, including opportunities for (1) children to take different people's perspectives, (2) supporting social intelligence via following directions, (3) safely and appropriately modifying rules for activities, and, finally, (4) adapting activities to meet special developmental needs. Early childhood educators recommended use of modeled demonstrations where they would act as mentors to help children begin to recognize their emotions and what these emotions signal and to cultivate their ability to take the perspectives of others in order to transition from a singular awareness of self toward a more refined responsiveness to others. When we cultivate self-regulation and emotion regulation, we engage children and provide them with a connection to others and a way to discover their own abilities and strengths through our eyes.

Wanda Boyer, Ph.D., is an Associate Professor of Early Childhood and Elementary Education in the Department of Educational Psychology and Leadership Studies at the University of Victoria in Victoria, B.C., Canada.

Figure 11.3 Goals, Strategies, and Activities to Promote Self-Regulation

GOALS

Control Impulses
- demonstrate patience
- manage difficult situations
- verbalize feelings
- resist tempting objects

Follow School Routines
- learn and comply with rules
- organize school materials
- accept evaluative comments
- make classroom transitions

Manage Group Situations
- maintain composure
- appraise peer pressure
- participate in group activities
- describe effect of behavior on others

Manage Stress
- adapt to new situations
- cope with competition
- tolerate frustration
- select tension-reducing activities

Solve Social Problems
- focus on the present
- learn from the past
- anticipate consequences
- resolve conflicts

STRATEGIES TO PROMOTE SELF-REGULATION

- **Provide usual reminders,** such as social interaction rules posted in the classroom, lists of tasks to be done, or the tracking of strategies used to solve problems.

- **Focus on the process.** Pose exploratory questions to get children engaged In the task. Connect with their interests and natural curiosity.

- **Take a positive approach.** Use reinforcement and carefully planned classroom management strategies and encourage children to reflect on them.

- **Create a positive climate** that reflects the enthusiasm, enjoyment, and emotional connection that the teacher has with the children as well as the nature of peer interactions.

- **Provide choices** in activities so that children regulate where they want to go and what they want to do; supply open-ended materials.

- **Model social-emotional problem solving.** Use videos or stories and pictures; provide practice using the strategies in a variety of settings, such as class meetings.

- **Address naturally occurring disagreements** to teach about social problem solving and to model self-regulation.

- **Design appropriate activities.** Create activities that help children learn academic content and incorporate elements of self-regulation.

ACTIVITIES TO PROMOTE SELF-REGULATION

- Place sink/float experiment materials in the science area for use by two or more children. Encourage verbal discussion as well as problem solving.

- Introduce a variety of books that deal with perspective taking, feelings, and emotions in the literacy corner.

- Arrange the family living area to include a doll house with people of many cultures represented.

- Provide rainbow ribbons in the music area so children can come together in dance to express themselves.

- Place giant floor puzzles in the manipulative area so that children can work together toward a common goal.

- Play a parachute game where cooperation is necessary during large motor activities.

- Promote helping skills and acts of kindness by setting up opportunities in the dramatic play area, such as a pet hospital or baby care.

- Follow a simple recipe and share the food.

- Include open-ended materials in the block area.

- Plan for positive group experiences, such as working on a mural together.

- Have older students work together to prepare a readers' theater or puppet play.

- Supply paint, brushes, and a very large piece of paper for the whole class to make a mural in the art area.

- Display children's work in the classroom at their level.

Sources: Henley, 1996; Nissen & Hawkins, 2010; Preusse, 2006; Zaslow & Martinez-Beck, 2006.

One student teacher found this out first hand when she decided to put a star chart on each of her first graders' desks to get them to behave. As she walked around the room, she would stamp stars on the charts of children who were working quietly. After accumulating five of these stamps, a child was permitted to get a piece of candy from a jar. Stamps could also be crossed off for inappropriate behavior.

There were numerous difficulties with this practice, including:

- Distributing candy was against the new policy of the school intended to address the childhood obesity problem. It specified that no sugar-laden foods or beverages were to be distributed or consumed at school. The custodian complained that hard candy was being spit out and trampled into the carpet.
- The student teacher had to focus on surveillance of good and bad behavior and spend her money keeping the candy jar filled.
- Parents concerned about dental decay, food allergies, and diabetes complained to the principal.
- Other teachers in the building disapproved of this method because it had been tried before with the outcome that some children continued to be the "winners," while those who had difficulty complying with classroom rules continued to be "losers."
- Children started to tattle more when they were under someone else's supervision at music, art, library, physical education, recess, or on the school bus in an effort to get more stars or to get someone else's stars removed.

As this example illustrates, it is important to be familiar with the culture of the school or center and the expectations of administrators, teachers, support staff, families, and communities.

MODIFY YOUR BEHAVIOR

Some teachers rely upon tired, old approaches, saying such things as, "Shari, you aren't paying attention," "Brian, remember to raise your hand," "I'm going to have to call your mother if you don't settle down," and "One more time, Carlos, and you are going to the principal's office." Resolve to learn something new rather than falling back on what you recall others saying (Adams & Baronberg, 2005; Marion, 2007). Far too many teachers defend their practices on shaky grounds, saying, for example, "That's what my parents did to me and I turned out okay," "I always heard that you were supposed to make an example out of the ones who break the rules," or "Don't smile for the first month of school." It is the rare educator who admits that, "In the face of inappropriate behavior my job is to create a change in order to effect a change. I may change the structure of the classroom, the method of instruction, the peer interaction, my actions or thoughts or expectations, or I may simply command change in the actions of the child. Of these, the last is the least effective" (Tobin, 1991, p. 38).

REMAIN CALM, ASSERTIVE, AND REFLECTIVE

New teachers sometimes panic when a child acts out. The first thing to remember is to stay calm and assertive and take a moment to think through your actions.

Kiera, a college sophomore, was getting some initial experience in preschool. Back on campus, Kiera's professor asked them to reflect on a situation that they found difficult. Kiera answered the questions (as noted in Korthagen & Vasalos, 2005) as follows:

What was the context?

I was completing my field experience in a Head Start classroom in a class for 3- and 4-year-olds. After Ben fell on the playground and scraped his knee. Tina, one of his classmates, did what she had seen teachers do—she moistened a paper towel and placed it on his knee. But, after I praised Tina for helping Ben, Tina began to pursue him around the classroom, pressing more firmly, until he yelled, "Stop it, Tina! You're hurting me."

What did the children want?

I think that Ben wanted Tina to stop chasing him around and pressing on his knee. I think that Tina wanted to get more praise from me.

What did I want?

I always want my students to treat one another with kindness, but this situation surprised me and I wasn't sure what to do about it. I didn't want to hurt Tina's feelings but I also didn't want Ben to feel pain and get angry.

What did the children do?

Ben asked me to intervene; Tina modeled what she thought the adults would do.

What did I do?

At first, I just watched what was going on. Then I realized that I needed to put a stop to this, but I also needed Tina to understand the difference between helping and hurting. I moved her away from the group and spoke with her. I had this brainstorm and asked, "Did you ever get a really big hug from someone that felt like you were being squished?" and Tina said, "Uh-huh. My uncle gives bear hugs." So I told her that Ben was feeling that way about the help she was giving—it was too much. She had helped him and now she needed to leave his knee alone so that it could get better. Tina seemed to get what I meant.

What were the children thinking?

Ben wanted Tina to quit mothering him. Tina wanted my approval and got carried away showing what a good helper she could be.

What was I thinking?

I felt as though my attempt at praise sort of backfired and that I needed to do something fast.

How did the students feel?

They went on playing as if nothing had happened.

How did I feel?

It was good to see Ben and Tina's conflict resolved.

Kiera used this next set of questions to write a reflective essay:

What problems did I encounter or am I still encountering?

What was the ideal situation that I wanted to bring about?

Pause and Reflect

About Children's Need to Feel Significant

Now that you have examined different types of conflict that typically occur in classrooms, try to explain how each one is a child's effort to say, in effect, "I am important."

Guiding children's behavior extends beyond the classroom to other settings.

What limiting behaviors in me—actions, feelings, images, beliefs—got in the way of achieving the ideal? What core qualities do I need in order to overcome the limitations and realize the ideal situation?

How can I mobilize these core qualities and begin to experiment with new behaviors? (Korthagen & Vasalos, 2005)

As Kiera's situation illustrates, guiding young children's behavior begins by building a relationship with them and depends upon effective communication.

LEARN HOW TO TALK WITH CHILDREN ABOUT BEHAVIOR

Beginning teachers often do not know what to say in response to a child's behavior. If a child is behaving well, it is common to say "okay," "good," or something similar, over and over again. A much better approach is to show that you really *noticed* what the child did and to make a specific comment, such as, "Thanks for helping me put the puzzles away, Sean" or "It looks like you had fun playing house together, Kate and Mariposa." If a child's behavior is surprising and inappropriate, teachers need to speak with the child about it clearly and specifically. Figure 11.4 offers examples of common sources of conflict in the classroom and how to speak with children about their behavior. As you read them, notice that (1) this is not what people without early childhood training probably would say to young children, (2) the statements are respectful of the child yet make the expectations clear, and (3) the responses suggest a positive outcome for compliance or encourage the children to problem solve. Remember that you are not the judge and jury or referee; your job is to help children develop the social skills they will need for a lifetime. In fact, your intervention in children's conflicts may be thought of as a continuum, ranging from most to least invasive or direct, so you need to decide what is warranted in each situation.

Figure 11.4 Common Sources of Conflict and Skilled Ways of Responding

After reviewing these examples, try writing several of your own and sharing or role-playing them for the class.

Misunderstandings About Expectations, Procedures, or Materials

Young children are inexperienced as members of a particular classroom community; they need to be coached in order to comply with classroom rules, master the routines, and learn the appropriate uses for classroom resources.

Examples of Teacher Talk:

"On this walk, we will be looking for signs of fall. It will be very important for everyone to stay together and hold your partner's hand. That way, nobody will get lost."

"I have placed all of the materials that you need to conduct your experiments with the dry cell battery in this box. Each of you has a specific responsibility."

"Naya, wipe your brush on the side of the jar, like this. That way your paint won't run down your picture when you are at the easel."

Possession Disputes

Possession disputes occur when arguments arise over ownership; they are the number-one reason for conflict between children.

Examples of Teacher Talk:

"Remember the rule about using the slide: one person at a time gets to stand on the top step."

"Who has an idea about what to do when everyone wants to pet the guinea pig?"

"What could we do about sharing the soccer equipment?"

Attention Getting

Attention getting refers to using aggressive or inappropriate behavior to demand attention. At first, it might be difficult to imagine that inappropriate behavior would be used to gain attention, but negative responses may be preferable to no response at all to the child who is generally overlooked.

Examples of Teacher Talk:

"Trish, your friends will like it better if you walk up to them and speak softly instead of yelling."

"I know that it is hard to wait for your turn to pass out the milk, Bahar. Remember that there are lots of different jobs to do in first grade; let's look at the Helpers Chart together."

"Whoa! Slow down, Terry. Gina wants to hear the story too and she doesn't like to be pushed. Don't worry; I'll make sure that you can see the pictures."

Physical Aggression

Refers to behaviors intended to inflict injury on someone else, either directly (e.g., hitting, biting, kicking) or indirectly (e.g., destroying their materials).

Examples of Teacher Talk:

"Look at Gita's face, Charley. I don't think she likes Ultimate Fighter kickboxing, do you? Let's see if we can think of a better way to let Gita know that she is your friend."

continued

Figure 11.4 continued

"Second graders, you all know that even though we have new gravel on the playground, it is not for throwing. Why?"

"Tony, when the other third graders made their model of a zoo out of boxes and paper, they did not want anyone to ruin their work. How can you help them feel less angry with you for messing up their project?"

Power Struggles

Conflicts that result when children want to be first or to compel others to play "their way." Remember that children are inexperienced in negotiating and that part of your job is to teach them how to negotiate.

Examples of Teacher Talk:

"It looks like we have three children who want to be brides but just one veil. What could we do to solve this problem together?"

"Remember, only five people at a time in the center. You can come back to the center later when it isn't so crowded."

"I know you are upset that your diorama is falling apart. How can your group work together to solve this problem?"

Group-Entry Disputes and Boisterous Play

Group-entry disputes occur when children try to join the ongoing play of another group. Well-known kindergarten teacher, author, and researcher Vivian Paley (1992) considers "You can't say you can't play" to be the single, most important rule in her classroom.

Examples of Teacher Talk:

"Make room for Juanita! She wants to work on the adopt-a-pet posters for the animal shelter too."

"The baby carriage is not for crashing into other people. If you want to play house, you need to use it for the dolls and drive the carriage carefully, just like you would for a baby."

"Brad, I can't let you kick other people, even if you are playing. Remember our rule? It's not okay to kick. How can you still play ninjas without hurting anyone?"

Teasing and Name Calling

Teasing and name calling are disputes that result when names that are hurtful or embarrassing to one child are used by another (NAEYC, 1996). Although some insensitive teachers dismiss such behavior as an inescapable part of growing up, remember that you are a significant adult in children's lives and, as such, you can influence children for the better.

Examples of Teacher Talk:

"Yes, you can write your own name on your painting, Erica. But Kira is only 2 years old, and she needs help writing her name. That does not mean she is a baby."

"Sometimes, children tease other children or call them names. This week, all of our stories are about why we should not treat our friends in this class that way."

Sources: Beaty, 2006; Saifer, 2003.

COLLABORATING WITH
Families

Teaching the Skills of Negotiation

Read the following two responses to a common conflict scenario and think about what children might learn from each one. Consider how you would go about communicating these ideas to parents and families.

Scenario: Bill, Robbie, and Samantha are playing a board game together. The game requires children to take turns. Whoever gets to the last space on the game board first is the winner. After several turns, Robbie finds that he is falling behind the other two players. At that point, he overturns the game board and sends the pieces flying. "That's a stupid game!" he yells out. Bill and Samantha are confused and upset. As the teacher, I approach the table. What would you do?

Response 1: Robbie is told that he is not using the materials correctly and is to blame for stopping the game. He is told that his behavior is wrong and that he has to pick up the pieces and apologize to his friends.

What would this action teach? (a) Adults are in charge of all the rules, so children always need to turn to adults to be the referees; (b) feelings that caused the outburst are not discussed and therefore may be seen as unimportant; (c) saying that you are sorry settles conflict (even if you don't mean it); and (d) Robbie has lost by being declared the troublemaker, so he will probably try to find an opportunity to be the winner (for example, by tattling on someone else), or he will accept the idea that he is basically bad and make little effort to change that judgment.

Response 2: The adult approaches the children and calmly asks what has happened while she gathers them together into a small circle. Each child is given a turn to say what he or she thinks happened and how he or she felt about it. The adult summarizes the comments and states the problem, "You were all playing the game and now the game is over with all the pieces on the floor. It seems that Robbie wanted to stop the game because he decided that he didn't like it and didn't know what to do." The adult then asks if there are other ways to solve this problem. The children suggest that you could leave the game just by saying you wanted to leave, removing your game piece, and going on to another activity. That way, the other children who liked the game could continue. The children also decided to pick up the pieces and restart the game. Bill and Samantha asked Robbie if he wanted to play this time.

What would this action teach? (a) Everyone has feelings, which should be respected; (b) there are many solutions to a problem, and some are better than others; (c) adults are not the only ones who can solve problems; children can participate in and practice this process; and (d) adults can be counted on to guide children's problem solving.

Young children need to learn that feelings are okay, but that how you express your feelings is not always okay. They need to develop skill and confidence in their ability to handle their own problems in socially acceptable ways rather than being branded as "bad." They need to learn how to live with others and work things out instead of constantly running to adults to serve as judge and jury. Think about how you might apply the second type of response to some of the behaviors that you like least. Imagine a long car trip during which two siblings are fighting about space in the back seat. How might the first response actually fuel the arguments? How might the second response build a better relationship?

continued

continued

Teacher Reflection: Use a small, square cardboard box with the numerals 1 through 4 on each side. Roll the box and read the discussion question on the corresponding reflection card. Within your group, brainstorm possible solutions, share ideas, and think about new ways to approach difficult situations. Choose a recorder for your group to take notes on comments, thoughts, points, various views, and so on. Be prepared to share with the total group.

Reflection Card 1. Reflect on terminology. What words come to mind when you think about discussing children's behavior problems? What terminology would you avoid when speaking with families, and why?

Reflection Card 2. Reflect on breaking the news. What reaction do you think you'll get if you tell a parent that his or her child is experiencing difficulty with social interactions?

Reflection Card 3. Reflect on personal experience with behavior problems. Tell your group members about a time when a teacher reported something negative about you, a family member, or a child you know well. How did this affect the individual's behavior?

Reflection Card 4. Reflect on concerns. What is something you'd like to learn about or discuss when communicating with parents? Explain why this is important to you.

SET REASONABLE LIMITS ON CHILDREN'S BEHAVIOR

Beginning teachers sometimes are too permissive. This may occur because the teacher draws upon his or her knowledge of being responsible for one child, such as experience with babysitting, but interactions with children in groups have to be different. Kurt, for example, really enjoyed being in the company of children and interacted with them as he did with his young cousins. He would say, for example, "Hey, buddy! C'mon over here. Where'd you get that haircut? Are you having a bad hair day? I think so!" and then tousle the child's hair or roughhouse with the children, particularly the boys. Kurt was completely shocked when the other teachers asked to speak to him about his unsatisfactory work performance and the gender bias that was evident in his behavior. Clearly, Kurt had selected the wrong "script" for how to interact with young children in group care. He had to make significant changes in his customary way of responding to the children in order to earn the respect of his new colleagues. Kurt was able to admit that his current style was "headed for disaster," because the children had begun to test the limits of how far they could go and some had insulted and even hit him. He had to set new standards for behavior that were not so permissive and was able to do this with the support of more experienced early childhood educators.

MANAGE TRANSITIONS WELL

A common "trouble spot" in managing the classroom is when children need to switch from one activity and/or setting to another, such as coming back to the room after lunch, lining up and walking down the hall to a school-wide presentation, cleaning up after playing, or going from school to after-school child care. These changes call upon the child to make an extra effort of adaptation and young children may become distracted or unruly. Effective teachers have many different strategies for smoothing transitions. It might be a puppet that emerges only after the children are quiet, a song to sing while they work, a pantomime (e.g., "Let's pretend to be snowflakes as we go down the hall, quiet and floaty"), or a predictable set of choices of activities at centers when they arrive at after-school care.

MAKE DECISIONS AS A GROUP

When children participate in arriving at solutions they begin to see that they can exercise control over situations through consensus about what is acceptable behavior. These skills take time to develop so start small and build; use the guidelines in Figure 11.5 to teach children the group decision-making process.

Figure 11.5 Group Decisions: Keeping Children Engaged in the Process

Respect and Tolerance

- Be tuned in to children's interests and concerns. Teach them to respect others' ideas and to be considerate of others' feelings.
- Show that their ideas matter by keeping a written record of what each child contributes to the discussion. It could be a list, a web of ideas, a prioritized list of activities, or a wall chart. Try breaking the group into smaller discussion groups that meet with an aide or parent volunteer so that everyone has a chance to contribute.

Timing and Patience

- Explain what a decision is. Offer some concrete examples, such as choosing what to wear or what to eat, then ask children to give some examples. Start with simple decisions, such as where to put a poster or what song to sing. Progress to more challenging decisions in which children may need to give up something in order for things to work out, such as allocating computer time.
- Allocate time devoted to discussion based on children's developmental levels. Teach them to try to stick with a topic long enough to discuss it. For preschoolers, just 5 minutes may be long enough. For third graders, it might be as much as 15 or 20 minutes.

Imagination and Leadership

- Use props to focus children's attention and harness their imagination. Allow a child to use play binoculars to scan the room for a problem area when children have failed to clean up. Give the group leader an object to wear (e.g., a special scarf) or to hold (e.g., a yarn pompom).
- Let children implement their group decisions immediately so that they can see the positive outcomes of the group planning process.

Cooperation and Communication

- Use activities that build a sense of cooperation and group unity. Have children play a game in which everyone grasps the edge of a round plastic tablecloth or a blanket and works together to bounce a ball in the center; hold hands and sway to the music while singing a spirited song together; invite children to demonstrate a new skill (such as skipping or whistling) and clap for them.

Sources: Carlsson-Paige, 2009; Church, 1997.

Summary

- Child guidance is the process of helping children to handle powerful emotions and learn how to interact with others more humanely and effectively. It differs from "old-fashioned discipline" in that it actually coaches children in the skills of social interaction rather than pointing out wrongdoing and punishing. Learning to self-regulate—to manage emotions and behavior—is a major achievement of the early childhood years and an important life skill.

- Every early childhood educator has an obligation to help each child become a respected and valued member of the classroom community. Success in achieving this depends on fostering positive relationships between the child and his or her peers and the child and all school personnel.

- Human behavior is motivated by needs for survival, love and belongingness, power, freedom, and fun; therefore, when considering children's behavior, try to discover what the child's goal might be. Before taking action, teachers need to consider if the behavior that they expect is truly necessary, productive, developmentally and culturally appropriate, and respectful of the natural behavior of young children.

- Learning to fulfill your role in child guidance requires you to anticipate and prevent problem behaviors, modify your own behavior, remain calm and assertive, learn how to talk with children about behavior, set reasonable boundaries, manage transitions well, and make decisions as a group.

Applying Your Knowledge of Child Guidance

In the following two activities, you will put your knowledge of child guidance into practice. In Assessment Activity 1, you will meet Earl, a first grader who was taken into custody by the state police. In Assessment Activity 2, you will deal with some difficult situations using a problem-solving strategy.

Assessment ACTIVITY ① EARL'S CHALLENGING BEHAVIOR

Earl is a first grader who already has a police record. It seems that he was standing in his front yard pitching rocks as cars passed by, and one of the rocks hit a driver's windshield and broke it, causing an accident. At school, Earl is frequently in trouble despite the fact that he has the attention of the school psychologist, a foster grandparent volunteer, a social services caseworker, his teacher, and a student teacher. Within a 1-hour period, the following observational notes were taken about Earl:

> E. arrives at school in blue jeans, cowboy boots, and a house key chained to his belt. He is excited about a badge his father gave him that reads, "Kiss me if you love truckers." E. sits down at the desk, looks at the girl sitting next to him, and remarks, "Your eyes are really blue. Do you wear contacts?" The girl frowns and says, "No!" Then she turns away. E. says, "Well, I do. See?" and blinks his eyes rapidly. Then he says, "Look, I can stick this pin in my skin and not bleed—want to see me do it?" "No. That's disgusting," the girl responds. With that, E. slides the point of the pin under his skin and demonstrates that the pin is now attached to his finger. "Want to see me do it again?" E. asks.

Again, a no. At this point, the teacher takes the pin away from E. and puts it in her desk drawer.

Time for partner reading. Children go to various corners of the room, arrange plastic tub chairs side by side, or stretch out on the floor. Most settle down and begin reading. E. stacks chairs on top of a table, and just as he is ready to climb on, the student teacher stops him, reminding him that chairs stay on the floor. E. walks to the restroom and on the way sees two boys absorbed in a book. "Hey, man! Get out of my chair," E. says to the boys. The boys look at him blankly and E. continues, "If you ain't outta my chair when I come back, you and me's gonna have words." E. takes a few steps away, then walks back, saying, "I mean it, man. That's my favorite chair." When E. emerges from the restroom, he challenges the boys to a fight. The student teacher directs E. to wash his hands and sit down. E. complies, then walks up to the teacher's desk, puts on some hand lotion, and pulls the desk drawer open to look at his badge. The teacher asks what he is doing and E. replies, "Nothing."

Time for the children to write in their journals. E. stares at the paper, then begins to wail loudly that he doesn't know how to write, puts his head down on the desk, and moves his head and shoulders slightly as if sobbing. He glances around to see if anyone has taken notice. The student teacher kneels down next to E. and reminds him of some of the things that he might write, such as his name, letters of the alphabet, words such as *stop, no,* and so on. With that, E. brightens. He says, "I want to copy the words off the badge that my dad gave me. My dad is a trucker. When he's on the road, I can take care of myself."

- Earl's teacher says, "I have to watch Earl like a hawk. When he was absent for a couple of days, my classroom was peaceful. I have tried everything to get him to behave, but nothing seems to work," while Earl's student teacher says, "Based upon comments that Earl has made, he is left by himself much of the time since his mother abandoned him. I know that he is hurting and wants so much to be accepted, but he is often rejected by his peers."

- The social worker says, "We are currently investigating Earl's case, and it is clear that Earl is neglected. If this situation continues, Earl's father may lose custody."

- The foster grandparent and volunteer in the classroom says, "Earl is a very needy little boy. I hear all of these horror stories about him, but whenever I work with him individually, he never gives me any real problems. I enjoy the time we spend together."

REACT	In what ways are the perspectives of these adults alike? How do their approaches to meeting Earl's needs vary?
RESEARCH	Read several articles at the library about children who exhibit challenging behaviors. What is recommended?
REFLECT	What might be the underlying reasons for the differences in the responses to Earl's situation? Which perspective do you identify most strongly with, and why?

Assessment ACTIVITY ② DEALING WITH PROBLEM SITUATIONS

For each of the following incidents (Hewitt, 1995), consider everything that you have learned from this chapter and apply the following problem-solving strategy (from Tobin, 1991). You will begin by working independently and then join a group.

A Problem-Solving Strategy for Practitioners

- What bothers you about the behavior?
- Does it seem like typical behavior or something unusual?
- What are your hypotheses about possible reasons underlying the behavior?
- On your own, jot down some possible words and actions for each situation.
- As a group, decide what you might say and which courses of action are most appropriate.
- What might be the intended or unintended outcomes of your choice?

Situations

1. A teenage father brings his 4-year-old son to class on the first day of nursery school. When the child begins to cry, the father says, "Stop being such a wimp! You're embarrassing me. Step up and be a man."

2. A teacher is on playground duty and a child says, "Ms. B., didn't you tell us not to go in the parking lot? Look at Jason and Miguel. They are in the parking lot."

3. Cheryl is talking to her kindergarten classmates about what she did over the summer. She says, "Me and my mama went to Disneyworld and we had breakfast with the princesses, Cinderella and Snow White." "Uh-uh," says Denny, "I live on her street and she didn't go nowhere this summer. She was right here all the time."

4. Two toddlers are playing on the carpeted floor of their child-care provider's home. They both want to use the toy vacuum cleaner at the same time, and one child bites the other.

5. A group of first graders is singing together, and the teacher asks if there are any special requests. Geoff wants to teach the group a song and begins to sing "Frosty the Snowman," but he forgets the lyrics. When the other children grow restless, he becomes increasingly frustrated. He scowls, turns bright red, and then screams loudly, "Just shut up, all of you. I can't think." Then he stomps away from the group and yells over his shoulder, "Assholes!"

6. A professional couple brings their son to preschool to meet his teacher. The boy is 3½ years old but is not toilet trained. When they discuss this issue, the parents say that they do not want to toilet train him until he is ready. While they are talking, their son goes over into the corner, squats down, and has a bowel movement in his diaper. He then sticks his finger inside his diaper to show the parents that his diaper needs to be changed. Later, when the boy begins at the preschool, children begin to ridicule him for still wearing diapers.

7. Hong is a very bright third grader with high academic achievement. He is also obese. Lately, he has been tormented on the bus and arrived in the classroom crying after a bully took Hong's lunch away, saying "You don't need it anyway because you're a big fat hog."

ONLINE RESOURCES FOR CHILDREN'S BEHAVIOR

American Psychological Association (APA): Multiple articles are listed under the search "Early Childhood Behavior." http://search.apa.org/search?query=Early%20Childhood

National Association of School Psychologists (NASP): Provides resources on learning disabilities, ADHD, functional behavioral assessment, autism, parenting, psychological assessment, special education, mental retardation, mental health, and more. www.nasponline.org/ See also www.schoolpsychology.net/

PEARSON
myeducationlab

Go to Topic 9 (Guiding Children) in the MyEducationLab (**www.myeducationlab.com**) for your course, where you can:

- Find learning outcomes for guiding children along with the national standards that connect to these outcomes.
- Complete Assignments and Activities that can help you more deeply understand the chapter content.
- Apply and practice your understanding of the core teaching skills identified in the chapter with the Building Teaching Skills and Dispositions learning units.

CHAPTER 12

Building Supportive Relationships with Families and Communities

Co-authored with Laurie Nicholson,
Indiana University of Pennsylvania

 . . . excellent early childhood programs have in place a process that pulls the energies and abilities of all the members of the school community together . . . schools impact the lifepaths of children, families, educators and all else who have a stake in the life success of the children.

James P. Comer & Michael Ben-Avie, 2010, p. 87

Meet the TEACHERS

MRS. MALECKI works at a private child-care center for infants and toddlers that is housed in the local YMCA. One of the center's policies is that families need to supply diapers for the children; however, Sathya's mom, Prita, keeps forgetting to comply. When asked about it the third time, Prita's eyes fill with tears and she says, "My mother usually takes care of the shopping but she is undergoing chemotherapy for cancer." "Oh, I'm so sorry Prita," Mrs. Malecki says. "I had no idea. Let us get an extra package of diapers and you can pay us."

MR. PEYTON works in a Head Start program that is housed in the basement of a local church. The advent of huge commercial farms has hit the region hard and families find that if they leave their property, they will be unable to afford housing but if they stay, there are few jobs. Mr. Peyton observes, "These families feel embarrassed that their income levels are below the poverty line. At times, children make comments that give me a glimpse of their struggles, such as 'My dad watches TV all the time and my mom yells at him,' or 'We don't buy stuff at the store, we shop at yard sales and Goodwill'."

MRS. MOORE, a first-grade teacher from Philadelphia, collaborated with the librarian to present a Saturday workshop on the importance of reading aloud to children. As the teacher began to gather up her materials, one young mother stayed behind and said. "I see what you are saying but you gotta understand. Reading sort of falls through the cracks when you're worried about a roof over your head. That's all." Mrs. Moore felt her face flush and was at a loss for what to say. Afterward, Mrs. Moore worked to get a grant that would support families residing in the homeless shelter.

LEARNING Outcomes

In this chapter, you will learn to:

→ Become familiar with national standards and guidelines governing the early childhood educator's role in working effectively with diverse families (NAEYC #2 and #4, ACEI #5c, INTASC #10)

→ Define the terms *family, family engagement,* and *cultural capital*

→ Understand the principles of parent/family engagement and support

→ Explore your role in communication, collaboration, and support of diverse families

→ Apply knowledge of effective ways to work with parent and families

---

Compare

What are some commonalities among these teachers, even though they are working with different families and in different situations?

Contrast

How do these teachers think about families? How would you characterize the outlook of each one?

Connect

What made the greatest impression on you, and how will you incorporate this view of families into your teaching?

Now that you have reflected on the three teachers' perspectives and noted the learning outcomes, we preview the knowledge, skills, and dispositions you will need to acquire in order to fulfill your role in collaborating with families and communities.

A Definition of Family Engagement and Cultural Capital

When most Americans hear the word *family*, they think of a mother, a father, and a child or children. Most families in America, however, do not fit this pattern. Thus, as a first step in connecting with families, early childhood educators need to expand their definition of a family. A **family** is "a social system characterized by a kinship system and by certain sentiments, values, and perceptions" (Elkind, 1995, p. 11).

Many families consist of a single-parent mother with one or more children while others include extended families, such as grandparents, aunts and uncles, or adult siblings. Others live with certain family members at different times of the year and stages in their lives as result of custody arrangements. Still others reside with no biological family member, such as those in foster care or from international adoptions. In addition, there are many new lifestyle options such as blended families created by divorce and remarriage, gay couples with children, or children who are products of artificial reproductive technology. Thus, it no longer makes sense to think of families strictly in terms of traditional legal guidelines of relationships formed by blood or marriage (Barnett, 2008). Contemporary families have to contend with an ever-increasing range of pressures and stressors, as described in Figure 12.1.

Families also differ in terms of their cultural capital. **Cultural capital** refers to a person's access to relevant resources, power to affect positive change in the environment, and esteem within the community. Those with money, prestige, and respect tend to attract more of these things; those without it encounter many barriers. Within the school setting, "Families with more social and cultural capital tend to be more involved at school because these families are more comfortable with teachers and schools and are more likely to have supportive social networks" (Berthelsen & Walker, 2008, p. 36). Due in part to these inequities, different families follow different pathways in supporting their children (Lareau, 2003). Some parents may have their children scheduled into many different types of lessons, sports, and structured activities outside of school in hopes of giving their child every possible advantage, while other families keep their children at home because they live in a violent neighborhood and/or cannot afford the added expense of many out-of-school activities. Some parents/families confidently chat with a teacher because they have comparable levels of education, while others will be very ill-at-ease due to language barriers or social-class differences. Some families will invest considerable interest and energy into helping their child with homework while others will have high aspirations for their children yet lack the skills

DID YOU Know ?

- Generally speaking, parents and families decide to participate in their child's education if and when: (1) their participation is necessary or important, (2) their involvement will promote their child's academic achievement, and (3) their contributions are welcomed by educators (McDevitt & Ormrod, 2009).

- The federal poverty level is $22,050 a year for a family of four but families need twice that amount to cover basic expenses. Using this standard, 41% of U.S. children live in low-income families (National Center for Children in Poverty, 2010).

- Most children living in poverty have parents who work—6 in 10 have at least one parent who worked full-time all year, and another 1 in 10 have a parent who worked at least half-time all year. (For more facts on families, see http://newfederalism.urban.org.)

- Full-time child care for just one child can cost 50% of two parents' full-time minimum-wage salaries, forcing some families to rely on family members or multiple child-care arrangements that may compromise children's development (Ceglowski & Bacigalupa, 2002; Sachs, 2005).

Figure 12.1 Issues and Stressors Affecting Families

Different family configurations and changes in family roles that are attributable in part to the high divorce rate, artificial reproductive technologies, and gay/lesbian families.

Economic downturn, underemployment, and unemployment that create additional stress about providing adequately for children.

Threats to overall family quality of life, influenced by such things as family interactions (e.g., the capacity to handle ups and downs), parenting (e.g., knowing people in child's life), emotional well-being (e.g., having time for own interests), and physical/material well-being (e.g., feeling safe at home/school).

Greater reliance on early childhood programs for support (e.g., intervention services, child care, after-school care programs).

More transitions as children and families adjust to various child-care and education arrangements (e.g., family members, babysitters/nannies, child-care providers, prekindergarten, kindergarten, elementary school, after-school care).

Demanding/conflicting schedules in work, school, and other activities that reduce time shared with family members.

Increased family concern about protecting children (e.g., from abuse, violence, illness) and providing insurance.

Limited availability of unskilled jobs that leads to a demand for higher levels of literacy and interpersonal skills in employees.

Societal expectations for higher educational attainment, job training, and 24/7 availability via digital technologies that mean less time reserved for the family.

Medical advances and longer life spans that place many families in the position of caring for older family members.

Sources: Anderson & Sabatelli, 2007; Baum & Swick, 2008; Bronfenbrenner, 2005; Gestwicki, 2009; Griebel & Neisel, 2009; Laverick & Jalongo, 2011; Souto-Manning, 2010; Zuna, Selig, Summers, & Turnbull, 2009.

and resources to help them. These differences do not make one family "right" and another "wrong." Rather, each family has distinctive strengths and needs and relies—in different ways and to a different extent—on early childhood educators for support (Cheadle, 2008). In fact, the less cultural capital a family has, the more it is likely to need additional support from the school.

Of course, families also have commonalities. In many societies, families are expected to provide (1) love and affection, (2) daily care and health maintenance, (3) economic support, (4) identity development, (5) socialization and guidance, (6) support for educational and vocational development, and (7) recreation, rest, and recuperation (Hanson & Lynch, 2010, p. 149).

All too often, teachers define parent involvement in terms of what they recall from their school days long ago—coming to the school for conferences, events, and support of school projects. This is just one facet of family engagement in children's learning. **Family engagement** includes behavior with or on behalf of children, at home or at school, as well as the expectations that parents hold for children's behavior (Reynolds & Clements, 2005). Family engagement also includes such things as family decisions about children's care and education, sharing of information with school personnel, discussion and supervision within the home, teaching/learning activities at sites other than school, and interactions with school personnel through

Pause and Reflect

About Diversity in Family Configurations

Use squares or recycled heavy paper or index cards to quickly sketch a picture, one for each person in your family—pets can be included! Write your first name and last initial on the back of each card. Then spread the cards out on the floor and take a look at the different family groupings represented in your class. Try making a graph of different family sizes, making sets (e.g., all the grandparents), or inventing categories (e.g., family with all females). How might you use a similar activity with young children or a group of parents/guardians to send the message that different family configurations are to be celebrated (Berry & Mindes, 1993)?

American families have changed dramatically over the last half-century.

means and at places other than the school context (Copple & Bredekamp, 2009; Dimock, O'Donoghue, & Robb, 1996; Ho & Willims, 1996).

Parents and families—particularly those who have been disenfranchised from the educational system—may be at a loss when called upon to support learning at home. A Saudi Arabian father explained that, even though he was an engineer, he was unable to help his third-grade son with math homework because the symbols used and procedures being taught differed from those he had learned. Likewise, if parents/families are expected to share storybooks at home, they may not do so for many reasons, such as being barely literate themselves, having limited access to suitable books in their first language, being uninformed about the public library services, or trying to get their child to listen to a story without success. Rather than assuming that parents/families are not interested in their child's education, try to think about the many ways in which families support their children's learning that may go unrecognized. Kevin Swick's Ask the Expert feature on page 323 provides additional suggestions on working with families who are homeless.

Ask the EXPERT — Kevin Swick

Homeless Children and Families

Q: Why is homelessness such a major problem in lives of young children and their families?

A: Over the past 30 years homelessness among young children and families has increased dramatically. A conservative estimate is that 1 to 3 million children in the United States are homeless. The causes of homelessness among children and families are diverse, but major issues are: economics, illiteracy, and abuse/violence in the family. In addition, natural disasters also cause many families to be homeless. On a global scale, war, famine, and disease have affected millions of children and parents.

Q: What misconceptions persist about children and families who are homeless?

A: There are some misconceptions or "myths" about children and families who are homeless. One such myth is that homeless parents are lazy and do not work. In fact, over 65% of homeless parents work part time or full time. Many parents who are homeless ask for services such as child care so they can get training and go to work.

Another myth is that parents who are homeless do not care about their children. Nothing could be further from the truth. Research shows that homeless parents are more often involved in the care of their children than parents who are not homeless but at risk for poverty-related problems. Ellen Bassuk of Harvard University found that homeless mothers took better care of their children than peers who were living with friends or family and not technically homeless.

A myth that is especially damaging is that homeless children do not do their schoolwork. Just the opposite has been noted. Indeed, homeless students do their work quite well when they have the needed support and materials.

Q: What are the roots of homelessness among children and families?

A: The sources of homelessness in children and families are in three areas: violence, crises in the family of origin, and consistent problems with mental illness and/or drug abuse. While the situation of each homeless family is unique, in most cases violence in the family, some prior trauma in the parent's family of origin, and chronic problems in social and emotional relations prevail and negatively impact the family.

Q: What are the implications for early childhood professionals?

A: First, develop and use a holistic view of the family's situation. Take into account the many stressors that influence their lives.

Second, exhibit positive and supportive behaviors with children and families. Show parents and children some hope; show them that there are helpful and nurturing people in their lives.

Third, engage parents in being an important part of their children's lives.

Fourth, empower parents through helping them strengthen their educational competence.

By understanding the complexities of what homeless families experience, we can be more responsive to the challenges impeding their lives. For example, family literacy and adult education strategies have been successful in empowering parents, both educationally and economically. Providing basic services such as child care and transportation can make a powerful difference in how families work and interact in the world. We need to realize that we indeed are powerful people in the lives of homeless families. We do make a difference when we make it possible for them to open up to new possibilities in their lives.

Kevin Swick is a Professor of Early Childhood Education at the University of South Carolina, Columbia.

Principles of Parent/Family Engagement

Parent/family involvement in children's education is not a new strategy. Since the beginning of civilization, parents have been the first teachers and socializers of their children, passing on the skills, customs, and laws of their cultures, intentionally or unintentionally, so that their children would be able not only to meet their own basic needs but also to become productive citizens and carry on their cultural traditions (Berger, 2007). Basic principles of family engagement include (1) family-centered practices, (2) reciprocal trust and respect, and (3) a family strengths focus.

FAMILY-CENTERED PRACTICES

Parent/family involvement efforts over the past several decades have been widely criticized for being inflexible, superficial, and gender biased (Bouffard & Weiss, 2008; Lopez, Kreider, & Caspe, 2004). Parents were invited to school at the school's convenience, for example, with conferences scheduled during the day or one evening per year. Often, when parents did volunteer time, they were given menial tasks to do such as cleaning up the classroom. Moreover, the focus was on homemaker mothers who could bake cookies, plan party games, accompany children on field trips, or assist at book sales (Henderson, Marburger, & Ooms, 1992). Frequently, there were few ways for fathers to participate without feeling like outsiders (McBride & Rane, 1997).

Today, an increasing number of families need not to "help out" at school, but for the school to reach out and help *them*. **Family support** is of three broad types—informational, material, and emotional—as illustrated in Figure 12.2. So, rather than

Figure 12.2 Three Types of Family Support

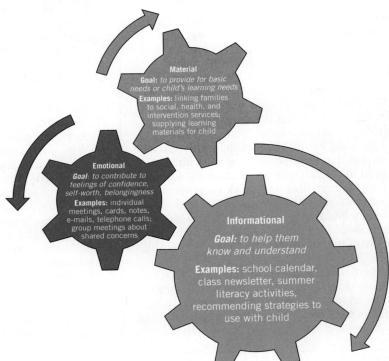

placing additional demands on parents/families, realize that they may be working at multiple jobs, may lack reliable transportation, and may not be able to afford school supplies, provide a quiet area to study, have someone to help with homework, or have computers/Internet access at home. Increasingly, parent/family engagement takes the form of family support; in other words, rather than taking a "schoolcentric view," educators need to collaborate with others in the community, get resources to where the children and families are, assist families in accessing needed support, and volunteer to show commitment to families (Lawson, 2003). As a society, we need to ask more questions about what nurtures families, what assists them most effectively in supporting their children's learning, and how satisfied they are with the level of shared communication between school and home (Lester & Sparrow, 2010).

What will you do to promote father/male involvement in young children's education?

Family-centered practices also include how you talk about and to families. Resist the tendency to make thoughtless, destructive comments such as, "Well, he comes from a broken home, you know. What can you expect?" and "That's not her husband, that's her live-in boyfriend," and "Can you imagine? Seven people in that little house!" Statements such as these reflect a bias against diverse families. Even complimentary comments, such as "They're such a nice family," can cause children who seldom hear any positive comments about their families to feel ashamed of their family situations. It is far better to make specific, nonjudgmental comments that recognize the care and attention that families give to their children, such as, "It looks like somebody braided your hair for you," or "I see that you brought in some leaves for the collection," or "Mmmm. Somebody packed a good lunch for you," or "I noticed that you are wearing your warm scarf and gloves today." Teachers need to continually examine their own attitudes and values about differences because this is the only way to recognize injustice and inequality (Kendall, 1996).

RECIPROCAL TRUST AND RESPECT

The first step in connecting with families is to build reciprocal trust and respect. We know that "Offering involvement activities without forming strong family-school partnerships is unlikely to yield increased parental participation, especially for those families that are most alienated by traditional schooling practices. . . . While the frequency of family-school contact can foster relationships, the quality of contacts makes the largest difference" (Berthelsen & Walker, 2008, p. 41). It is irrefutable that the quality of family–school relationships exerts a profound effect on children's success in school (Fantuzzo, McWayne, Perry & Childs, 2004). The child's risk is lowered if the relationships between child and family, as well as family and school, are functional and if the home and school communicate and supply consistent, congruent messages (Christenson & Sheridan, 2001). We also know that when families support learning at home by supervising activities, monitoring homework, and engaging in conversation about school tasks, their children show higher achievement in reading, mathematics, and writing, and higher grades on report cards (Fantuzzo et al., 2004; Henderson & Mapp, 2002).

Teachers build trust and respect when they reach out to families. Consider these early childhood educators' approaches to letting families know that they are a valued part of their child's education:

- A second-grade teacher realizes that the families of her second graders shop at the Muñez Market, so she asks the store owner to post signs, illustrated by the children, to remind families about parent/teacher conferences. While the teacher does not speak Spanish fluently, she used the Babel Fish Translation website (babelfish.yahoo.com/)to create a rough draft, and then had the middle school's Spanish teacher proofread before making the final copy.

- A public school teacher works near a large university. This year, he has two internationally adopted children and the children of four graduate students and faculty members who are new to the United States. At the kindergarten orientation, he noticed that these parents had concerns centering on what to expect from U.S. schools. The teacher decided to work with an intern from the Communications Media Department to develop a video that would capture the essence of kindergarten. It included a script that was translated by college student/native speakers of the various languages represented, and copies with narration in the families' first language were made for them.

Earning the trust and respect of families is the other part of building relationships. Beginning teachers may feel overwhelmed when they begin working with families. First of all, teachers enjoy the company of young children but may not be as confident or relaxed in the company of adults. Moreover, new teachers who are not parents themselves may feel that their knowledge about children is dismissed as "book learning" and lacks authority in parents' eyes. New teachers often worry that parents and families will ask them questions that they cannot answer or be disappointed that their child did not get a more experienced teacher. New teachers can address such concerns by being avid learners. They can seek authoritative information, advice from esteemed colleagues, input from professionals in other fields, and, of course, learn directly from children and families.

A Family Strengths Focus

Family members know children in ways that the school can never know them. Usually, family members have been with children over extended periods of time and have witnessed many developmental milestones. The adults in a child's family typically have been involved with the child on a one-to-one basis in a wide variety of contexts, such as in the backyard, at the grocery store, at religious ceremonies, at the shopping mall, in the swimming pool, or at family gatherings and excursions. Diverse families feel more welcomed when teachers acknowledge the many everyday things that families do outside of school that demonstrate their care, commitment, and support of their child's education. Learning activities are not necessarily "school-like" tasks; they often take place during natural, everyday activities. Figure 12.3 describes everyday learning in natural contexts.

Families' and educators' views of the same child contribute key pieces to the puzzle of who a child is, how he or she is doing, and what might be causing a particular behavior. For a true partnership to exist there must be mutual respect, shared decision making, and appreciation for the contributions made by each person. Tips for communicating more effectively with parents and families are listed in Figure 12.4.

Positive Relationships

"Healthy interactions between educators and families create the necessary conditions for the early childhood programs to (1) impact the lifepaths of the families; and, in turn, (2) to engage the families in the work of improving the early childhood program (Comer & Ben-Avie, 2010, p. 87). If parents lack confidence in the caregivers of their children, they question the quality of the care and education that their children receive and usually disenroll their children from the program (Gonzales-Mena 2006; Mensing,

Figure 12.3 Everyday Learning in Natural Contexts

Family Routines

• Grocery shopping, washing clothes, running errands, recycling, home repair/maintenance, visiting family members, interacting with neighbors, picking up siblings at school, going to the mall, going to the park or playground, caring for pets, planting flowers, keeping a garden, having a family meeting, learning another family member's hobby, listening to traditional stories, taking a walk, having a rummage sale, watching a movie together, health check-ups

Family Celebrations

• Birthday parties, picnics and cookouts, holiday gatherings (e.g., Chinese New Year, Day of the Dead, Kwanzaa), family reunions, weddings, graduations, vacations, going camping, celebrations for special achievements (e.g., getting good grades, winning a contest, or excelling in sports or the arts)

Churches/Clubs/Organizations

• Faith-affiliated meetings (e.g., Sunday school, after-synagogue gathering, choir practice), historical society celebrations, ethnic festivals, Saturday art classes, participating in a dance performance, a car wash to raise money, used book sale, food or clothing drive to help others, watching a demonstrations (e.g., of how service dogs are trained), neighborhood clean-up project

Special Excursions

• A concert in the park, visiting the zoo, an amusement park, going to the pool or beach, going to a farm or farmers' market, visiting a museum, participating in a program at the public library, nature or science center, watching a puppet show or play, going to the fair, taking a hike

Sources: Dunst, Raab, Trivette, & Swanson, 2010; Raab & Dunst, 2004.

French, Fuller, & Kagan, 2000). Parents/families are powerfully affected by how early childhood professionals relate to their children.

> When parents hear the teacher capture the child that they know, they feel reassured that their child is visible in her classroom—that the teacher actually sees and knows him or her—and they get the message that she really cares. (Lawrence-Lightfoot, 2003, p. 114)

Generally speaking, parents/families want:

• to know that the teacher knows their child as an individual and recognizes the child's strengths and talents;
• to see evidence that the teacher genuinely cares about their child and motivates him or her to learn;
• to work with competent early childhood professionals who deliver the services effectively and in ways that actually meet their needs;
• to be regarded as an effective member of their child's education team;

Figure 12.4 Tips for Communicating Effectively with Families

General Communication

- providing literature (e.g., pamphlets, newsletters, daily schedule, school calendar)
- audiovisual material (e.g., recordings of child performances, explanations of the curriculum, orientation to class students)
- computer-delivered information (e.g., lists of helpful websites, summer literacy activities, school home page)
- surveys (e.g., home literacy practices and needs, training and involvement opportunities, preferred ways of being contacted)

Group Gatherings

- small groups (8–12) with shared concerns (e.g., working with an IEP, open houses)
- focus groups to obtain feedback from families on programs, policies, and practices and to involve them in decision making
- large groups (e.g., parents with a child entering kindergarten, panel discussion by parents with successful children, guest speaker)
- school-wide gatherings (e.g., music, dance, and art performances by the children; open house for families)

Individual Communication

- written notes sent home (e.g., report cards, a "happygram" to celebrate a child's success, permission forms for a field trip)
- family journals used to gain insight into children's everyday experiences
- face-to-face meetings (e.g., conferences with family on child's progress, meetings to set goals or resolve a problem)
- home visits to learn more about the family
- technology-assisted communication (e.g., class web page, homework via e-mail, recorded telephone messages, texts translated into family's first language)

- to be heard, sought out for feedback, and take part in shaping the agenda that impacts them;
- to have their ideas recognized and used in creating quality programs; and
- to form a positive relationship with early childhood professionals that is collaborative and communicative (Boyer, 1995; Knopf & Swick, 2007; Swick, 2004a, 2004b, 2004c; Swick & Hooks, 2005).

Figure 12.5 offers practical suggestions on ways to build rapport with families.

Community action and fundraising are other ways to act upon care and concern for others.

Figure 12.5 Practical Ways to Build Rapport with Parents/Families

- **Try to ease families' concerns about children's adjustment.** Orientation days are opportunities for children to become familiar with school and school routines before officially beginning school. Many schools use a buddy system, in which, for example, current kindergartners are paired with incoming kindergartners to help ease new students' transition to school.

- **Strive to communicate by keeping professional jargon to a minimum and speak in ways that the family understands.** One way to stimulate a family's interest in and a child's answer to the age-old question "What did you learn in school today?" is an Ask-Me-About badge. These are short sentences written on paper badges that invite parents to talk with their children about particular activities or experiences that they had in school or at the center. The badges supply information to parents and also provide children with opportunities to recall and describe particular learning activities, such as having a guest storyteller or going on a walking field trip.

- **Keep it easy for the family to stay informed.** Newsletters that feature children's work and are sent to the home let parents and families know about classroom experiences, open the door to two-way communication, and invite parents into their children's learning. Newsletters can cover a variety of topics, such as an upcoming family night, special projects under study, and good books to read. Computer software makes it increasingly easy to produce a professional-looking newsletter. This is a great way to have parents help out as well. No matter how confident you are about your writing skills, however, be certain to have others help you proofread the finished product. Other possibilities for contacting parents include a homework hotline, e-mail, and a home page on the Internet.

- **Offer opportunities for families to gather informally and network.** School-sponsored family gatherings, such as a summer picnic before school begins or a noncompetitive family game night, offer opportunities to make connections. A parent who has a child with Down syndrome may feel that contacts with other families who are raising children with special needs offer a particularly beneficial type of support. When families are closely tied to the community, children's adjustment and development are enhanced. Social events enable families and educators to get to know one another as people.

- **Schedule meetings at various times so that more families can participate.** Meetings scheduled at different times and locations meet the particular needs of families and invite more participation. For example, working parents could come to see a display of the children's work and be served a light breakfast by the children. Meetings could be scheduled on an evening or a Saturday morning, with child care provided.

- **Use a variety of strategies to enhance communication with families.** Be sensitive to the fact that not all parents have English as their first language or take time to read written messages from school. Some ways to let parents know how their children are doing at school that don't depend on the family's reading skills include messages in different languages recorded on the telephone about upcoming classroom events; videotapes of school events, such as the children singing, that can be circulated or viewed at home or at the library; and audiotapes of a child reading aloud. Rinaldi (2000) reminds us that documenting children's progress is really "visible listening," a valuable component of sharing information about children.

- **Strive to identify with and meet the special concerns of families.** Each family has a unique set of circumstances that influences how parents and families respond to teachers' efforts to work with them. For example, when children have physical handicaps, families can be excessively protective, and when children are chronically ill, families sometimes fail to set reasonable limits on children's behavior. In such situations, families often appreciate an information sheet about appropriate learning games to play at home, a professional magazine article, or an informational brochure written especially for parents. Some excellent materials are those published by the Consumer Information Center in Pueblo, Colorado; professional association brochures (e.g., those published by the Association for Childhood Education International, the National Association for the Education of Young Children, and the International Reading Association); and a wide variety of literature from community and social service agencies and organizations.

- **Be sensitive to some family members' discomfort in the school setting.** Not all parents have had positive prior experience with schools or helpful interactions with teachers and administrators. Home visits or meetings held at a location other than the school, such as the public library or the neighborhood community center, are sometimes more appealing to families.

- **When difficulties arise, keep a problem-solving focus instead of blaming.** During a parent conference, it is sometimes tempting to blame the parent for a child's behavior at school. One way to bring up a difficult issue, such as a child who seldom completes activities at school, is to first ask the parent to share his or her views on the child's work habits at home. Often you will find that parents are already aware of the difficulty and are willing to collaborate on a mutually agreed-upon solution.

continued

Figure 12.5 continued

- **Focus on all families instead of being satisfied with the participation of a few with higher income levels or more leisure time.** Very often, you will hear teachers say that the parents whom they really want to see never come to school for conferences or school events. Making everyone feel welcome is the teacher's responsibility. For example, an evening when children share their accomplishments and every child has an equal opportunity to participate encourages all family members to participate (Liess, 1995).

- **Give parents the latitude to contribute in their own ways.** Some teachers develop a family questionnaire to find out about parents' jobs, hobbies, cultural specialties (e.g., songs, games, recipes), or travel pictures, or their interest in helping provide recycled materials, participating in special events such as birthdays, or volunteering in the classroom. Invite parents at various times throughout the year to demonstrate a skill, tell a story, or play a musical instrument.

- **Admit it when you need to seek outside assistance.** Part of the skill of being a teacher is to know the limits of your professional preparation. If, for example, you are faced with a child whose mother was killed in an automobile accident or a child who is having difficulty adjusting to the birth of a new sibling, seek the advice of other professionals who work with young children.

Your Role in Family Engagement

It is clear that old ways of involving families are not adequate to face today's challenges and that building positive relationships with parents and families is beneficial for children's learning. Therefore, to fulfill your role, you'll need to challenge common assumptions. Perhaps the most damaging assumption is that other families need to conform to our ideas of and experiences with family.

Put yourself in this situation: you are a public school first-grade teacher in a rural community and you decide to begin the school year with a unit on the family. You have many ideas about ways to involve the families, such as a family breakfast before school that will be prepared by the students; an open house to share the children's drawings, maps, and diagrams of their homes; and an evening musical performance by the children during National Education Week. When you ask the children to draw a picture of their families and homes, one child reveals that his mother is in jail, another depicts living in a local shelter for victims of domestic violence, two are being raised by a grandparent(s), three live in subsidized housing projects, and two live a trailer park.

When children, parents, and families depart from the teachers' expectations of what is "normal," they often are disregarded and, as a result, these families often feel disconnected or undervalued by school personnel (Powers-Costello & Swick, 2008). Perhaps you think that this classroom scenario sounds extreme, but consider this: 1.35 million U.S. children experience homelessness each year, and 40% of those living in shelters are under the age of 5; this represents a 9% increase since 2007. The most recent Census Bureau statistics note that there are 3.9 million (6%) children in the United States living in a grandparent's home, up 76% from the 2.2 million (3%) who did so in 1970. The prison population in the United States is

Pause and Reflect

About the Influence of Your Family on Your Expectations

Think about your own early years and what it meant to arrive home after a day at school. What were some of the routines that you came to expect? What opportunities were there for after-school play in your neighborhood? How was homework handled? What did your family do to support you? Now consider how such routines would be affected by inadequate housing, parents working multiple jobs to pay the bills, or a violent neighborhood. How will you take such things into consideration in your work with children?

one of the highest in the world, with approximately 1 in 100 adults incarcerated (Pew Center on the States, 2010). Incarcerated men and women are parents to 2% of the 73 million children in the United States, and nearly 1.5 million children have a parent in prison (Murray, 2007). Thus, your first role in working with families is to avoid judging them and to include all of them in your efforts to support the child's learning. What expectations will you need to change?

MEETING NATIONAL STANDARDS

A mentor teacher who works with student teachers had this sign posted on her door: "Remember . . . Teachers are NOT in private practice!" A wide array of leading professional organizations would concur with this sentiment; a summary of the national standards that guide educators' efforts in working with parents/families is provided in Figure 12.6.

Early childhood educators are in a unique position to identify the child's needs. You will lose that asset, however, if you alienate the parent and do not put the child first and remain professional, even when your first reaction is indignation. A second grader named Lizzie illustrates this point. The child's teeth were black with decay and the infection was upsetting her stomach. Lizzie needed immediate medical attention. When the teacher called the home to speak with Lizzie's mother, the grandmother answered and said that her daughter was at the beauty shop having her hair done. Lizzie's teacher hung up the telephone, bristling with anger and ready to march down to the teachers' room to tell this story to her colleagues. On further thought, however, she realized that an indictment of the second grader's family would accomplish nothing. Although the teacher confided in her husband without mentioning any names, she resolved to use her power to help the child instead of to criticize the parent. Because the teacher invested her energies in finding a dentist who would help Lizzie for a small fee and succeeded in enlisting the mother's approval, the child began to feel well again and had a good year in second grade. Lizzie's mother wanted dental care for her child but had inquired about the prices with several dentists and concluded that there was no way she could afford the extensive help required; she had just about given up when the teacher contacted her.

INVITING COMMUNICATION

In the teachers' lounge, Kira, a student teacher, is having lunch with her mentor teacher. They are delighted that 95% of the parents/families participated in the open house that was held at the school from 4 P.M. until 8 P.M. the previous day. Another teacher is complaining loudly about the parents' poor turnout for her open house and says, "It doesn't matter when we have this or how long we stay. I've said it before and I'm right! We never see the parents we really need to see!" Kira's mentor teacher has 13 years of experience in a school where over 80% of the children qualify for free lunches, yet she has maintained a positive attitude. She turns to Kira and says, "Always remember that families don't need to be 'fixed,' they need to be supported! They will pick up on negative attitudes in a heartbeat and once their feelings have been hurt, it is so hard to win them back."

Conferencing with parents and families is "one of a teacher's most important responsibilities" (Seplocha, 2004, p. 96). Conferences are an important vehicle for significant adults in children's lives to exchange information about their learning and development. Conferences provide an opportunity to support home–school partnerships through a free exchange of insights and observations about a particular child. They can be routinely scheduled (e.g., semiannually) or can be spontaneous, as when you chat with families informally while you are waiting for the bus or out in the

Figure 12.6 National Standards and Guidelines for Collaborating with Parents/Families

Federal Mandates

The federal government, professional organizations, and leading authorities have identified parent involvement as an "essential ingredient" for high-quality early childhood programs (Seplocha, 2004).

No Child Left Behind
- Calls for more structured modes of communicating children's progress, their test scores, and the performance of their school in comparison to other schools in the district and state.
- Provides parents with more flexibility in exercising choice if their child's school is not performing adequately over time. For additional information regarding No Child Left Behind, consult www.ed.gov/parents/academic/involve/nclbguide/parentsguide.html.

Goals 2000: Educate America Act, Goal 8
- Directed every school to promote partnerships that would increase parental involvement and participation in enhancing the social, emotional, and academic growth of children.
- Acknowledged that parents are partners in their children's education, and that all teachers must assume a role that facilitates such partnerships.
- Recognized the need for all early childhood settings to create family-friendly policies that truly support today's families.

Association for Childhood Education international/National Council for the Accreditation for Teacher Education
- *Standard 5.3 Collaboration with Families*—Candidates know the importance of establishing and maintaining a positive collaborative relationship with families to promote the intellectual, social, emotional, and physical growth of children. Colleges and universities that prepare early childhood educators must show evidence through students' documented class work and field experiences that students know multiple strategies for involving families that encompass a broad range of traditions, beliefs, values, and practices (www.acei.org/rubrics, 2002).

The National Parent Teacher Association (PTA)
- Standard I: Communicating—Communication between home and school is regular, two-way, and meaningful.
- Standard II: Parenting—Parenting skills are promoted and supported.
- Standard III: Student Learning—Parents play an integral role in assisting student learning.
- Standard IV: Volunteering—Parents are welcome in the school, and their support and assistance are sought.
- Standard V: School Decision Making and Advocacy—Parents are full partners in the decisions that affect children and families.
- Standard VI: Collaborating with Community—Community resources are used to strengthen schools, families, and student learning.

National Association for the Education of Young Children
- NAEYC Code of Ethical Conduct—Ideal 1–2.4 of this document states that the early childhood professional has an ethical responsibility "to respect families' childrearing values and their right to make decisions for their children."
- *Guideline Number 5*—Establishing reciprocal relationships with families.

community. In order to maximize attendance and participation at conference events, make certain that you advertise. For example, one teacher from a rural area discovered that many of the children, their parents, and families gathered on Saturday mornings at a bank parking lot where a farmers' market was held throughout late summer and early fall. She used this venue to distribute information, display children's artwork,

Community members can share their skills and talents with children.

and present musical performances by the class. In doing so, she changed the impression of many parents that school personnel had less care and concern for the children of farm laborers.

Some schools include children with their parents/families during conferences while others do not. Either way, make sure that all of the communication regarding conferences clearly outlines whether children are to be present or not. When children are included in conferences, teachers need to plan ahead with them, help them select appropriate work samples to discuss, and ensure adequate participation from them. Including children in conferences helps them take more responsibility for their own learning by enabling them to contribute insights about their progress in all developmental areas. Some teachers have students lead conferences and share their goals and accomplishments. It is equally important to prepare parents for conferences at which children are present. If you do not set their expectations, some parents may assume that the purpose of meeting with you is for them to demonstrate to you that they are strict disciplinarians who can demand obedience and get it by reprimanding their children in your presence. Even if children are not included in conferences, it is a good idea to share some things about the conferences with them after the conferences have taken place. For additional guidelines on conducting conferences, see Figure 12.7.

PRACTICING INCLUSION

Even though a classroom may, generally speaking, be of high quality, this does not mean that every child in the classroom is participating in all of the high-quality interactions and activities that are available (Clawson & Luze, 2008). Often, parents of children with disabilities need additional services and resource materials to meet the special challenges. As a future teacher, you must be sensitive to the special needs and dynamics of parents of a child with a disability. The Code of Ethics of the Division for

Figure 12.7 Your Role in Conducting a Conference

Provide a Flexible Schedule

- Offer several windows of opportunity for conferences at different times of the day. Suggest several times for the conference, let the parent select, then confirm by making sure the parent knows the time, date, place, and length of the conference.

Allocate Sufficient Time

- Be present with the parent or family member for the entire conference time. Remember to build in a few minutes between conferences so that you can bring closure to a conference, rather than just stopping the meeting because the next parent has arrived.

Involve the Child

- Ask the child what information he or she wants to share with parents or family members. If there is a particular piece of work, drawing, or favorite activity area that the child would like to have highlighted, take the time to include that information in the conference.

Create a Welcoming Atmosphere

- Treat families as honored guests. Arrange an inviting environment, and get all the children involved in preparing the classroom for visitors. Establish rapport by welcoming the parent to the room and stating your pleasure in seeing him or her. Eliminate distractions. Give the parent you are speaking with your undivided attention. Sit beside the parent, not at or behind your desk.

Be Organized and Well-Prepared

- Know what you are going to say and what evidence of the child's progress you are going to share. Have a written outline, if needed. Be as specific as possible. Have student work examples ready in a folder and be ready to explain how and what that child is learning.

Be Responsive to Different Backgrounds

- Understand that vocal tone, inflection, body posture, and eye contact are behaviors that vary with culture, ethnicity, religion, and ways of life. If you are wondering what is customary, take the time to research it online.

Open the Meeting on a Positive Note

- Begin by commenting on the child's interests, strengths, and abilities. Point out a displayed piece of work, share a story from yesterday, show a photo of a project, or a picture of the child working with others.

Encourage Family Members to Share Their Perspectives

- Listen to what the parents, grandparents, or guardians have to say. Much can be learned from their impressions of the child's experience and from the child's comments at home about school.

Exercise Restraint

- If a parent becomes hostile or confrontational, remain professional and stay calm. Tactfully end the conference and schedule another time to meet and talk.

Avoid Jargon

- Phonemic awareness, cognitive processing, and motor skills may all be terms with which you are familiar. However, remember your audience. Communicate in ways that are direct and understandable without talking down to families.

Offer Suggestions for At-Home Activities

- Make helping the child part of everyday routines—a list of activities that can be done in the car as they travel to school, shopping together in the market, or while preparing a meal at home are apt to be much more useful than drill on schoolwork.

Figure 12.7 continued

End on a Positive Note

- Thank the family member for coming and share one more strength, skill, or interest of the child as a closing remark. In this way, the conference ends on an upbeat note and encourages further communication.

Record Notes

- Make a note of important points or agreements that were reached; share them with other school personnel, if needed and appropriate.
- Summarize follow-up—who is responsible for what, and how participants will know they have fulfilled their agreed-upon obligations.
- Tell the child about the conference so that he or she will know areas in which you have reached agreement.
- Send the parent a thank-you message for participating—a note, a telephone call, e-mail, or some other sign of appreciation.

Early Childhood (DEC) of the Council for Exceptional Children (2009) includes the following statements about responsive, family-centered practices:

We shall:

1. demonstrate our respect and appreciation for all families' beliefs, values, customs, languages, and cultures relative to their nurturance and support of their children toward achieving meaningful and relevant priorities and outcomes families desire for themselves and their children.
2. provide services and supports to children and families in a fair and equitable manner while respecting families' culture, race, language, socioeconomic status, marital status, and sexual orientation.
3. respect, value, promote, and encourage the active participation of ALL families by engaging families in meaningful ways in the assessment and intervention processes.
4. empower families with information and resources so that they are informed consumers of services for their children.
5. collaborate with families and colleagues in setting meaningful and relevant goals and priorities throughout the intervention process, including the full disclosure of the nature, risk, and potential outcomes of any interventions.
6. respect families' rights to choose or refuse early childhood special education or related services.
7. be responsible for protecting the confidentiality of the children and families we serve by protecting all forms of verbal, written, and electronic communication.

STRIVING FOR CULTURAL COMPETENCE

"Culture is commonly thought of as the customs, practices, and traditions that characterize, distinguish, and give stability to a group . . . it is knowledge of shared

Pause and
Reflect

About Composing a Letter to Families

When you are teaching you will want to write to families to explain the curriculum, to inform them about a special project or field trip, and so forth. Letters home should be: (1) upbeat, positive, and relevant to families; (2) addressed to parents/families and legal guardians of the child; (3) clear, concise, and free of jargon; (4) completely free of errors and approved by colleagues/administrators; and (5) formatted as a friendly letter (e.g., date, a salutation, a closing, and a signature). In terms of content, the letter should include the purpose for the activity, what children will learn, ways that families can participate or support at home, and specific ways to get in touch with you if they have any questions. When you write to families, be considerate. Do not impose last-minute requests or assume that "everyone" has resources available. Try drafting such a letter and share it with your classmates and instructor to get their input.

norms and rules" (Bullough & Gitlin, 2001, p. 112). Having enough information and background about families increases the likelihood of establishing good rapport and a good working relationship with the child and family. Be aware that some families may not have experience with things we take for granted, such as terminology. One Turkish father, for example, was confused and upset when the teacher asked if his son was a "walker"; "Yes," he said, "my son can walk" (Isik-Ercan, 2010). What the teacher actually meant by her question was, "Does your child walk to school or ride the school bus?" Likewise, the early childhood program's structure, organization, policies, and curriculum with which we are so familiar can be mystifying to parents/families. Sometimes parents and teachers have different expectations regarding discipline, timeliness, or celebrations. Some mannerisms, such as touching, can unintentionally offend culturally diverse families. Even something seemingly innocuous, such as food, can become an issue. For example, three first-grade teachers who planned a pizza party were careful to order vegetarian pizza, but the Muslim children and mothers still refused to eat. One of the mothers explained that because the same knife had been used to cut all of the pizzas and had touched the pork, their religious beliefs prevented them from eating it.

Teachers often perceive the failure of families to participate in parent/family involvement programs or in other school functions as evidence that parents are not interested in their child's education (Lawrence-Lightfoot, 2003). The stereotype that "parents do not care" is rooted in teachers' perceptions of what "caring" parents do to support their child's education and classroom functioning. Sometimes parents do not feel welcome or comfortable in the school because of previous negative experiences or anxiety about discussing their children's progress. Some families do not know how to access resources; others fear that if they ask questions or complain, it will be "taken out on" their children later. Whenever you are tempted to say that a parent does not care, bear in mind that expressions of care and concern are most fully realized in environments that we trust and when we feel valued and empowered (Swick, 2004b).

Managing Conflict

As you work with families, realize that their attitudes toward authority figures and gender may affect their interactions with you. Many cultures see schools and teachers as authority figures and therefore unapproachable (Kendall, 1996). In some cultures, men refuse to deal with female authority figures and a father may not be willing to talk with a female teacher. There may be times when you can compromise and others when you cannot. In the case of a father who does not want to speak with a woman, the teacher might bring a male colleague to participate in the first few conversations to help the father recognize that it is in the best interest of the child for him to work with the teacher. On the other hand, if a parent directs you to use corporal punishment with his or her child, you will have to make it clear that this is not an option. You will need to explain that you cannot agree by saying, for example, "I understand what you are saying, but it is against our school rules and our laws in this country for teachers to hit a child. We will have to find another way, a way to encourage good behavior, rather than punish misbehavior."

One way to diplomatically disagree is to use "feel/felt/found" (Garmston, 2005):

- Accept the feelings expressed by the person:
  "Some people feel as you do . . ."

- Identify with the concern personally, acknowledging that you once felt this way (if that is true):
  "I used to have some of those same concerns. . ."
- Show the progression of how you changed your ideas, what you found:
  "But now that I have worked with many, many young children, I have found. . ."

When conflicts arise, try not to take it personally. Think about some underlying reasons for the family's point of view. Remember that parents love their children, and may just need to be reassured occasionally that they have chosen a high-quality program for their children (Gennarelli, 2004). For example, 6-year-old Krista had been in first grade for just 2 weeks when her mother made an appointment with the teacher and asked why her daughter was not yet reading independently. The teacher's initial reaction was to say, "Give me a chance! School just started!" Instead, she listened carefully, not only to what Krista's mother said, but also "between the lines" to her underlying concerns. It seemed that Krista's father had a reading disability, and her parents were very worried that their daughter might be affected, too. Because the teacher really heard what Krista's mother had to say, an angry confrontation was avoided and a positive plan of action was put into place. Krista's mother left with ideas and materials instead of frustration, because the teacher had sought to communicate effectively and professionally instead defending herself. Holding different expectations does not mean that there is no "common ground"; work to arrive at a meeting of the minds.

Still, there will be times when you realize that a second, third, or even more opinions from colleagues and professionals in other fields are needed. Guidelines for making referrals include:

1. Recognize when you are in over your head and need to gain additional support.
2. Look upon this need for additional support as a professional response rather than a personal defeat.
3. Know the agencies, organizations, and services in your area.
4. Identify competent people in those groups with whom you can work.
5. Make referrals to these specific individuals, not just a general referral.
6. Secure family members' agreement that they will participate.
7. Ask family members to predict what might prevent them from participating and get them to identify ways to overcome obstacles to participation.
8. Check out the family's progress on proposed solutions and have alternative resources available in case difficulties arise.
9. Plan for a follow-up meeting.

As you grow in confidence and competence in working with families, you will want to set higher standards for yourself. Figure 12.8 describes basic, intermediate, and advanced communication strategies for work with families.

COLLABORATING WITH

Families

Respecting Parents'/Families' "Funds of Knowledge"

The experience of two teachers in the following scenarios illustrates the importance of focusing on family strengths or "funds of knowledge." The term *funds of knowledge* refers to the knowledge and skills essential for household or individual functioning and well-being that have been accumulated over time and through the culture (Gonzáles, Moll, & Amanti, 2005).

Scenario 1: Inez, a third grader and a child of a migrant farm worker family, was being teased at school for "talking funny." When she met with her teacher, he was surprised to hear Inez say, "They don't know what I have. I live with my Mama, Papa, Tio, and Abuelito. We all work and we love each other. In the evenings, we look at what has been brought home from the fields, cook, and eat. We talk and tell stories in Spanish. There is much laughter. Sometimes we sing the old songs." As the teacher reflected on these comments, he realized that his assumptions about the quality of this child's life had been inaccurate and prejudicial in many ways. The teacher had assumed that because Inez was a recent immigrant from Mexico and lacked the material things that many of her classmates had in abundance, she was horribly deprived. Thinking about Inez's heartfelt remarks prompted him to consider the family's strengths.

Scenario 2: Carla is a young teacher who just graduated from a 4-year teacher preparation program. As part of that program, she participated in an urban experience and decided to pursue a teaching career in a large urban district as a kindergarten teacher. An experienced colleague tells her "not to expect too much" because these children "have so few prior literacy experiences." As evidence, the colleague shares the results of her survey sent home to parents/families, which includes items about how much time is spent reading aloud, how many children's books are in the home, and so forth. Carla questions this approach. For example, what if the parents rely more on the public library for books? Is reading aloud the only type of literacy activity that "counts"?

In conversation with her students, Carla concludes that if the definition of literacy is more expansive, children are getting quite a bit of literacy experience. They talk about reading the newspaper to see "who got in trouble," participating in events at the public library, sharing family stories, and a wide array of church-related literacy activities, such as reading the church bulletin or singing in the choir. Taking the time to find this out about her students becomes a real resource for Carla's teaching. For example, instead of just cutting things out of magazines and newspapers to make a collage, she collects the coupon section of the Sunday paper so that the children can find their family's favorite food items and clip the coupons at the same time that they are looking for particular letters of the alphabet. Because Carla has a very limited background in music, she asks the parents and families who play the piano and sing to help her with the music curriculum. Instead of focusing only on writing imaginary stories, she asks the children to share a favorite family story about a treasured object and they create a classroom museum/slide show with a photograph of the item and the child's dictated story that is run on a continuous loop during open house. By learning more about the lives of the children in her kindergarten class, Carla is seeing much more parent/family participation, and some of her colleagues are showing interest in her approach. Carla says, "I'm beginning to think of this as a campaign against the 'blame game' and the assumption that parents 'don't care'. My evidence is painting a very different picture from my experienced colleague's biased survey."

Figure 12.8 Basic, Intermediate, and Advanced Strategies for Communicating with Families

ADVANCED STRATEGIES—three-way or many-way communication
- Home visits
- Student-led conferences
- Establishing parent resource rooms
- Contacting parents/families on a regular basis to convey good news
- Functioning as a family advocate in the community
- Building a personal knowledge base of families' and community members' interests, occupations, and affiliations
- Providing opportunities for families to improve their situations
- Involving parents and families in decision making at school

INTERMEDIATE STRATEGIES—two-way communication
- IEP and IFSP meetings
- Language translators to facilitate communication
- Parent-teacher conferences
- Open houses
- Potluck dinners
- Sending children's work home and asking for comments back
- Workshops in which parents/families acquire new skills
- End-of-year celebrations

BASIC STRATEGIES—one-way communication
- Newsletters, school calendar
- Notes, tapes, and videos sent home
- Grades or progress reports sent home
- Announcements of events
- Contacting parents/families when problems arise
- Requesting parent volunteers
- Guest speakers

Summary

■ A family is a kinship system that has certain sentiments, values, and perceptions.

■ Cultural capital refers to a person's access to relevant resources, power to effect positive change in the environment, and ability to gain esteem within the community. Family engagement is parents'/families' behavior with or on behalf of children at home and school; it includes expectations that parents hold for children, decisions about children's care and education, interactions with school personnel, supervision within the home, and teaching/learning activities at nonschool sites.

■ Three broad categories of family support are: (1) informational, giving families the knowledge that they seek; (2) material, helping families to gain access to the physical resources that they need; and (3) emotional, recognizing families' affective needs and responding appropriately.

■ Principles of family engagement include: family-centered practices, reciprocal trust and respect, a family strengths focus, and relationship building.

■ Your role in promoting positive relationships with young children and families includes meeting national standards, considering families' expectations, inviting communication, practicing inclusion, responding to families' expectations, striving for cultural competence, and managing conflict.

Applying Your Knowledge of Family Engagement

In Assessment Activity 1, apply your knowledge of working effectively with families to the situation of a kindergartner being raised by his grandparents. Then, in Assessment Activity 2, apply your understanding of family engagement to design an informational brochure on a topic of interest to families.

Assessment ACTIVITY 1 ROMAN IS RAISED BY GRANDPARENTS

Five-year-old Roman is being raised by his maternal grandparents, 63-year-old Grace and 65-year-old R. J. Anderson. Grace rides the bus to attend a parent/teacher conference with Mrs. Everly, Roman's teacher at the public school kindergarten. When Grace Anderson arrives, Mrs Everly says "I'm so glad to meet you! Roman has told me so much about his 'MawMaw.'" Grace and R. J. never expected to become their grandson's primary caregivers, but his mother became addicted to painkillers after sustaining a serious injury in a car accident and his father is a Marine sergeant stationed in Iraq. Although Roman's grandparents say that he is "keeping them young," they also feel out of synch. Grace says, "Roman's classmates' parents are all young, like our daughter. They don't have things in common with us." Both of Roman's grandparents are baffled by children's fascination with technology. After R. J. attended a family workshop at school where some of the parents were discussing the video games on their children's wish lists, he admitted to feeling "entirely disconnected from the conversation," and responded by spending the next Saturday morning at WalMart, having a young saleswoman demonstrate some of the games to him. Grace confides that "There are things that kids do today that we never did with our children or cannot afford to do now—technology, sleepovers, birthday parties at restaurants, and trips to Disneyland and Sea World." As the school year progresses, Mrs. Everly says, "Grace and R. J. want so much to do everything for Roman. When he talks about things the other kids do that they have not experienced or cannot afford, they are so troubled by it. I have gained new insights into what it means for grandparents to raise a young child and have begun to re-examine some of the assumptions we make about families in our activities here at school. When I want to share resources, I print them out because they don't have a computer or Internet access; they really appreciate it. In fact, after I informed them about a grandparents-raising-children support group that meets once a month in a community just a half hour away, they joined. When I saw R. J. at the grocery store, he thanked me and said, 'It's made a huge difference to us. It's a chance for Grace and me to share our concerns, and to laugh and cry a little with others who are going through this.'"

REACT	In what ways are the perspectives of Mrs. Everly, Grace, and R. J. alike? In what ways are they different?
RESEARCH	Locate current statistics on the number of grandparents raising children. Explore the resources for grandparents at reputable websites.
REFLECT	What modifications would need to be made to family involvement activities commonly offered at schools in order to help grandparents feel included?

Assessment ACTIVITY (2) CREATING AN INFORMATIONAL BROCHURE

One way of informing parents about important ideas is to create a tri-fold brochure on a topic. Some examples of the titles for brochures that our students have developed for parents have included: How to Share a Book with a Toddler, Why Children Need to Play, Questions Parents Ask About Starting School, Free or Inexpensive Summer Activities for Preschoolers, Ten Reasons to Read to Your Child, and Services for Young Children and Families in Our Community.

To begin, fill the roles and follow the procedures outlined below.

1. Investigator

Role: Locate examples of brochures

- Collect and examine several brochures written for parents online or in print. *Be certain to use authoritative sources.* Some good sources include professional organizations (e.g., the National Association for the Education of Young Children, the International Reading Association, the National PTA, Association for Childhood Education International). Places where you can usually find print brochures include pediatricians' offices, shopping-mall displays, schools or child-care centers, mental health associations, and women's shelters.
- *First meeting with your group to select a topic and have it approved by your instructor.*

2. Researcher

Role: Gather authoriative resources on the topic selected

- Use your textbook to get started. Then consult high-quality professional journals and books. Gather sufficient information to support the points that you plan to make in your brochure. Be certain to include the complete references for all of the sources-print and URLs-so that you can list them in American Psychological Association referencing style at the end of the brochure.
- *Second meeting with your group to choose a title and outline the brochure.*

3. Author

Role: Draft a copy of the text

- Remember that your information will need to be clear, concise, and logically organized. Analyze the way that material is written for parents/families in publications such as *Our Children* (National PTA), *Parent's Magazine, Working Mother* magazine, and so forth. Include a bulleted list of important points or ideas from experts in the field. Include a few short quotations from leading experts. Type a draft of the text.
- *Share a digital copy of the draft of the brochure's text with your group.*

continued

(continued)

4. Designer

Role: Format the brochure

- Select one of the tri-fold brochure templates on Microsoft Word and experiment with different arrangements, headings, formats, and illustrative materials until you discover the best layout to get your message across. For example, you might use a question-and-answer format, a checklist format, or a SmartArt diagram from Word, or scan in examples of children's work or comments.
- *Share a digital copy of the draft brochure with your group.*

5. Editor

Role: Proofread and correct the text

- Be sure to run a spell check on the text and proofread carefully. Even after you think it was corrected, go through it again before the final copy is produced. Be sure to list the full names of all of the people who worked on the project directly on the brochure.
- *Submit the brochure to your instructor.*

Evaluation Criteria

A high-quality brochure for parents:

- Focuses on ideas that are important for parents and families to understand
- Identifies a topic and approach that would be helpful for children and families
- Effectively synthesizes and translates material from a variety of professional sources into language that is understandable to general audiences
- Offers a clear, consise explanation supported by concrete examples (e.g., children's comments, samples of children's work, common situations parents can identify with)
- Makes appropriate use of the work of leaders in the field of education (e.g., brief quotations from experts, bulleted lists of recommendations compiled from various sources, all work cited appropriately)
- Presents material in an original, engaging, and visually appealing way
- Supplies a complete list of references as well as agencies, organizations, or companies that can serve as resources.
- Has been carefully proofread and edited to make certain writing style is conversational and the text is error free
- Has an attractive and appealing design that would invite parents/familes to read the brochure

ONLINE RESOURCES FOR FAMILIES IN CRISIS AND FAMILY SUPPORT

Child Abuse

On average, four children die from child abuse in America each day, yet few people report suspected abuse. Each of the four sites below provides current facts and resources.

American Professional Society on the Abuse of Children (APSAC): http://apsac.fmhi.usf.edu/

CBS News: Watch the video "Concerns About Child Abuse." www.cbsnews.com/video/watch/?id=4477483n

National Clearinghouse on Child Abuse and Neglect Information: www.calib.com/nccanch

Child Welfare League of America: View the article "When Should Teachers Report Abuse? A Child Investigator Offers Tips for Educators." www.cwla.org/articles/cv0111teachers.htm

Resources for Grandparents

The following four reputable websites support grandparents, particularly those who have major responsibility for raising grandchildren.

American Association of Retired Persons Grandparent Information Center: www.aarp.org/families/grandparents

Generations United: www.gu.org

Grands Place: www.grandsplace.com

Kinship Information Network: www.kinsupport.org

Homelessness

Learn more about the rights and problems of children who are homeless at these three sites.

National Association for the Education of Homeless Children and Youth: www.naehcy.org/

National Center for Homeless Education: www.serve.org/nche/

National Coalition for the Homeless: www.nationalhomeless.org/

Hunger

One in four children in the United States is hungry.

CBS News: Watch "Childhood Hunger in America," a May 28, 2010, video on the effects of the recession on families. www.cbsnews.com/video/watch/?id=6500626n

Research on Families

These three sites disseminate research and national standards for working with families.

The Center for Family Policy & Research in the Department of Human Development and Family Studies at the University of Missouri http://CFPR.missouri.edu

The National Parent/Teacher Association www.ptasonline.org/kspta/national_standards.pdf

Poverty

The following three sites provide resources for professionals and families.

National Law Center on Homelessness & Poverty: www.nlchp.org/

Childhelp USA: www.childhelpusa.org

Family Support America: http://familysupportamerica.org/content/home.htm

---

PEARSON myeducationlab

Go to Topic 3 (Families/Communities) in the MyEducationLab (www.myeducationlab.com) for your course, where you can:

- Find learning outcomes for families/communities along with the national standards that connect to these outcomes.
- Complete Assignments and Activities that can help you more deeply understand the chapter content.
- Apply and practice your understanding of the core teaching skills identified in the chapter with the Building Teaching Skills and Dispositions learning units.

CHAPTER 13

CHAPTER 13

Developing as a Professional Early Childhood Educator

 Professional development is not just a matter of describing or modeling 'good practice.' There is a considerable element of trust needed before teachers are prepared to risk failure, to make significant changes, and to question their thinking.

Wendy Lee, 2008, p. 99

MS. HUONG started working with toddlers at a private child-care center and she knew that the director wanted to improve by earning NAEYC accreditation. First, Ms. Huong attended an all-day Saturday training at a conference and met others who were pursuing the same goal. Ms. Huong led her colleagues and, a year later, after the center was accredited, everyone kept saying, "We never could have done it without you!"

MRS. SOSA is teaching a child on the autism spectrum for the first time and concludes, "I have a lot to learn from Dallon. He is advanced in math but is experiencing difficulty during transitions." Mrs. Sosa begins by visiting the websites of the Autism Society of America (www.autism-society.org/) and the National Autism Association (www.nationalautismassociation.org/) to learn more. "One of my colleagues has a master's degree in special education. She suggested that I make routines more predictable and more concrete by using visual cues. I found an excellent article about using songs to smooth transitions (Kern, Wolery, & Aldridge, 2007) and, with these strategies in place, Dallon is adapting well."

MS. RENZULLI has been teaching kindergarten for 25 years and in recent years she has felt a growing dissatisfaction with her teaching. "I used to be the worksheet queen," Ms. Renzulli admitted. Now I have a poster outside my classroom door that reads, 'Real learning isn't measured by the weight of your child's backpack!' I was inspired by an excellent student teacher. I marveled at how much progress the children made from her intentional teaching strategies. So, I revolutionized my teaching, had a great burning of the busywork, and I love teaching again."

LEARNING
Outcomes

In this chapter, you will learn to:

→ Become familiar with national standards and guidelines concerning the early childhood educator's professional growth and development (NAEYC #5, ACEI #5a and #5d, INTASC #10)

→ Define *professional development*

→ Understand the influences that shape professional development and the stages through which teachers typically progress

→ Explore your role in implementing the strategies that support professional development

→ Apply knowledge of career development to different scenarios

Compare

What are some commonalities among these three teachers, even though they work in different settings and are at different stages in their careers?

Contrast

How do these teachers think about teaching? About learning? How would you characterize the outlook of each one?

Connect

What evidence do you see of a commitment to lifelong learning in these educators?

Now that you have reflected on the three teachers' perspectives and noted the learning outcomes, we preview the knowledge, skills, and dispositions you will need in order to develop as a professional early childhood educator.

A Definition of Professional Development

Professional development is the ongoing process of becoming a more competent and caring teacher; it includes all of the formal and informal learning experiences that teachers pursue as a route to career growth, beginning with preservice education and lasting all the way to retirement (Fullan, 2007). The National Association for the Education of Young Children (2004) describes early childhood professional development as:

> a continuum of learning and support opportunities designed to prepare individuals for work with and on behalf of young children and their families, as well as opportunities that provide ongoing experiences to enhance this work. These opportunities lead to improvements in the knowledge, skills, practices, and dispositions of early childhood professionals. (p. 1)

Teachers develop as professionals when they have teaching and learning experiences that support the acquisition of professional knowledge, skills, and dispositions as well as the application of this knowledge in practice (Buysee, Winton, & Rous, 2009). Professional development activities encompass "all types of facilitated learning opportunities, for example, those that result in college credit or degrees as well as those that generally are less intensive and do not yield credits or degrees, those that occur largely through formal coursework, and those that are more informal and situated in practice" (Buysee et al., 2009, p. 238). Figure 13.1 is an overview of some of the tools early childhood educators use to promote professional development.

Perhaps you have thought to yourself, "When I get my certificate/degree/first job, I will finally be ready!" The bad news is, no matter how excellent your program is, it is only the beginning. Professional development is not a project that teachers are "done with" when they exit a teacher preparation program; rather, it requires teachers to act upon a lifelong commitment to doing their best for all children, families, and colleagues. At this stage in your career, you might be dreaming about the day when you have completed your program. That hopeful dreaming might include abandoning your books, tests, and presentations, trading them for exciting lessons, and spending your time in the company of young children.

Actually, every state requires public school teachers to participate in some sort of professional development after they become employees. Many schools have **mentoring programs** in which new teachers attend workshops or are paired with more experienced, in-service educators. If you talk with teachers you will find that, in

DID YOU Know ?

- A teacher's formal education is not finished with the completion of a 2-, 4-, or even 5-year program and initial certification. Nearly every state in the United States requires public school teachers to earn additional credits in order to maintain certification; many states require training every 5 years (Editors of *Education Week*, 2002).

- In a 2010 report that rated the demand for professionals in various fields, child-care workers were ranked 2nd and teachers 14th. It is estimated that, due to growth and replacement needs, the United States will need 532,1000 child-care workers, whose average current U.S. salary is $24,354, and 2.68 million new teachers, whose current U.S. salary is $35,810 for elementary teachers (The Work Buzz, 2010).

- In a survey of 1,100 teachers, 88% reported some form of collaboration with colleagues, 90% said that they could turn to colleagues to support them in trying new ideas at least some of the time, and 93% said that they rely on fellow teachers for good advice (Little, 2001).

Effective collaboration with adults—families, colleagues, and other professionals—is essential for today's teachers.

order to move beyond initial certification or to add on a certification in another area of specialization, most states require a specified number of hours of training beyond a 4-year undergraduate degree. In fact, so many teachers in the United States return to the college classroom to maintain and enhance their credentials that about half of them have a master's degree. Becoming a master teacher is a career-long goal.

Principles of Professional Development

Three experienced teachers were having dinner together when one of them said, "I can tell that I am lacking confidence about something when I have the teaching nightmares I used to have as an undergraduate. In this dream, the children are completely unruly and I can't get them to pay any attention to me at all." Another teacher agreed, saying, "My nightmare is a little different. In it, I find out that I forgot to attend a class and now I can't graduate." A third teacher laughed and said, "Me too! Only in my nightmare, they take back my teaching degree!" As the candid thoughts of these teachers illustrate, professional development is a lifelong goal and ambition. The next three points about professional development are crucial to your fulfillment of the teaching role: (1) professional development is ongoing, (2) the context exerts a powerful influence on the course of teachers' professional development, and (3) professional development is self-directed.

PROFESSIONAL DEVELOPMENT IS CONTINUOUS

As you grow into the role of teacher, you will discover that you will progress through different stages that are related to your competence and confidence. Rather than being static, your concept of yourself as a professional is constantly shifting and evolving in

Figure 13.1 Tools for Professional Growth

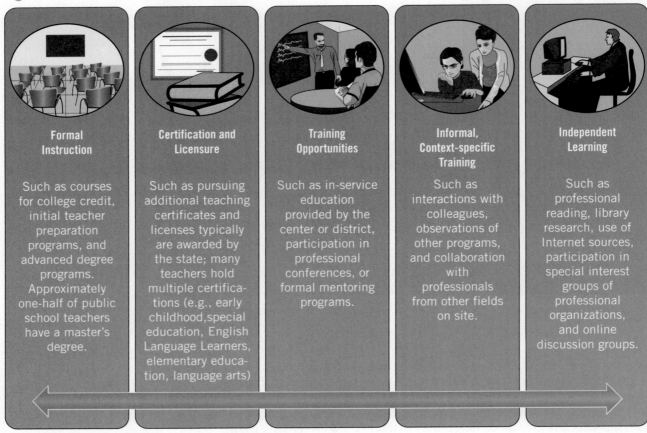

Formal Instruction	Certification and Licensure	Training Opportunities	Informal, Context-specific Training	Independent Learning
Such as courses for college credit, initial teacher preparation programs, and advanced degree programs. Approximately one-half of public school teachers have a master's degree.	Such as pursuing additional teaching certificates and licenses typically are awarded by the state; many teachers hold multiple certifica-tions (e.g., early childhood,special education, English Language Learners, elementary educa-tion, language arts)	Such as in-service education provided by the center or district, participation in professional conferences, or formal mentoring programs.	Such as interactions with colleagues, observations of other programs, and collaboration with professionals from other fields on site.	Such as professional reading, library research, use of Internet sources, participation in special interest groups of professional organizations, and online discussion groups.

Sources: Buysee et al., 2009; Zaslow & Martinez-Beck, 2005.

response to your experiences (Smith, 2007). Figure 13.2 is an overview of the stages in teachers' professional development.

It is no mistake that the first stage through which teachers progress often is referred to as "survival." Most preservice teachers are still in the process of making their career deci-sion and are worried about their ability to fulfill the role of the teacher. One common mis-take that beginners make is expecting classroom experience to resolve any problems that surface. A key understanding for preservice and beginning teachers is that "It is not just the availability of classroom experience that enables teachers to apply what they are learning . . . when teachers study and reflect on their work and connect it to research and theory, they are better able to identify areas needing improvement, consider alternative strategies for the future, and solve problems of practice" (Darling-Hammond, 2006, p. 103).

Beginning teachers understandably approach their first teaching experiences with a mixture of excitement and anxiety. Some of the most common worries of student teachers and beginning teachers include the following:

- **Relationships with children and families.** What should I expect from children of this age? What if they misbehave? How will I respond? Will my response be appropri-ate? What if children, parents, or families don't like or respect me? What if a child has a problem that I know nothing about how to handle? How will I talk with parents and families during conferences? I've never done this before!

Figure 13.2 Stages in Teachers' Development

Novice
- Theme: Survival
- Question: Am I cut out to be a teacher?
- Metaphors: "Just learning the ropes." "Barely keeing my head above water."

Advanced Beginner
- Theme: Consolidation
- Question: How can I grow in competence and confidence?
- Metaphors: "Putting it all together." "Finding my way."

Proficient
- Theme: Renewal
- Question: What can I do to improve with experience rather than lose effectiveness?"
- Metaphors: "Avoiding falling into a rut." "Seeking new challenges."

Expert
- Theme: Maturity/Generativity
- Question: What impact have I had on the lives of children and families?
- Metaphors: "Really making a difference." "Taking on the mentoring role for the next generation of teachers."

Sources: Berliner, 1994; Katz, 1977, 1995; Swick & Hanes, 1987.

- **Relationships with adults.** What if my supervisors don't like or respect me? What if I make a terrible mistake? What if I am observed on my very worst day of teaching? If my supervisors think that my teaching is bad, what will I do? Will I be encouraged and helped, or simply branded as a bad teacher? What about my grade point average or other types of evaluation? What if my supervisors don't agree on what I should be doing? I don't want to be caught in the middle!

- **Instructional approaches and learning activities.** What if the activity that I have planned turns out to be a disaster? What if children are disinterested or won't cooperate? What if I plan something for half an hour and the children are done in a few minutes? How will I ever find the time to plan adequately for everything I am expected to do? How am I going to assess children's learning? What can I do to make sure that I treat children fairly? What if the kids ask me questions and I don't know the answers?

- **Future career.** Will I be able to find a good job? How will I conduct myself during interviews? What would be a career-ruining move? How will I make sure that prospective employers know what I can do and give me a chance? (Britzman, 2003; MacDonald, 1991)

Most people don't fully appreciate the skills required to work effectively with groups of young children.

Pause and
Reflect

About Your Metaphor
for Teaching

An early childhood major who was working in a public school prekindergarten chose the metaphor of "a covered-dish dinner" because she worked on an instructional support team consisting of the classroom teacher, a special education teacher, a social worker, and various other professionals. She selected this metaphor because "everyone brings something important to the experience, and when all of those contributions are combined, the result is wonderful." What metaphors or mottos do you live by as a teacher of the very young?

Experienced and effective teachers, while well aware of the flaws and foibles of education, have a determination to work within the system as advocates for children, families, colleagues, and community—that is what "keeps them going" (Nieto, 2003). The proficient teacher is able to "draw connections to students' prior knowledge and experiences, choose appropriate starting places and sequences of activities, develop assignments and assessments to inform learning and guide future teaching, and construct scaffolding for different students depending on their needs" (Darling-Hammond & Bransford, 2005, p. 176).

CAREER GROWTH IS AFFECTED BY THE CONTEXT

Maturing into a master teacher is not easy for many reasons:

> a career dedicated to the care and education of children, while commonplace, is unique among the professions. Teaching is also characterized by complexity and challenges. Three in particular stand out. First, learning to teach requires new teachers to understand teaching in ways quite different from their own experience as students. . . . Second, learning to teach requires that new teachers not only learn to "think like a teacher" but also to "act like a teacher." . . . Teachers need to do a wide variety of things, many of them simultaneously. Finally, learning to teach requires new teachers to understand and respond to the dense and multifaceted nature of the classroom. . . . They must learn to deal with this 'problem of complexity,' which derives from the nonroutine and constantly changing nature of teaching and learning in groups. (Darling-Hammond, 2006, p. 35)

One way of promoting professional growth is to interact with colleagues.

As teachers contend with all of these demands, the circumstances in which they find themselves are important. Most early childhood educators will readily call to mind other, more experienced teachers who were willing to function as their mentors. Many teachers leave one early childhood setting for another, hoping to find more supportive administrators and colleagues, better working conditions, and more resources. The same teacher may prefer to work on some goals independently using technology and seek out peer collaboration to achieve other professional development goals. Without a doubt, professional development is affected by the people involved, the contexts in which it occurs, and the approaches that are used. Figure 13.3 highlights some of the influences on professional growth.

On page 352, the Ask the Expert by Jerlean Daniel explains the contributions that membership in a professional organization can make to ongoing professional development.

Figure 13.3 Influences on Teachers' Professional Development

People

- The establishment of friendly, supportive, and trusting relationships with teachers, student teachers, aides, administrators, families, school support personnel (e.g., clerical, janitorial, bus driver), and other professionals (e.g., nurse, counselor, psychologist, consultant, etc.) that build a sense of community

Programs and Systems

- An emphasis on personal and professional growth and a staff-development system that enables all educators to learn about the best that the field has to offer

Roles

- Clearly defined roles and policies combined with leaders who have clear expectations, plan carefully, function efficiently, and who encourage and support staff
- Fairness and equity regarding promotions, raises, and other rewards

Democracy

- Meaningful staff involvement in decision making and agreement among staff members on goals and objectives

Environments

- Physical environments that are well equipped, maintained, and organized
- Materials and resources that support effective instruction

Innovation and Improvement

- Professionals who have developed the ability to adapt flexibility to new demands and change in ways that continuously improve curriculum, teaching, and learning

Relationships with Familes and Communities

- Effective ways of working with families and educating the public to the realities of teaching and learning so that continuous improvement becomes a reality

Jerlean Daniel

National Association for the Education of Young Children (NAEYC)

Q: **What makes NAEYC unique as a large-membership organization?**

A: Founded in 1926, NAEYC has nearly 85,000 members. It is the nation's largest organization of early childhood professionals and others dedicated to improving the quality of early childhood education programs for children from birth through age 8 years. NAEYC's primary goals are to improve professional practice and working conditions and to build public understanding and support for high-quality childhood programs.

Q: **What kinds of issues does NAEYC address?**

A: NAEYC, like other large-membership organizations, faces two major tensions. The *first* pertains to the dual roles of the governing board to serve and to lead the membership. If the governing board acts only in response to the concerns and directives of the membership, then it runs the risk of failing to lead. Leadership requires vision and the ability to anticipate. But leadership without responsiveness to the membership is doomed. The *second* tension revolves around the primacy of children's needs versus the needs of the profession. The majority of NAEYC's membership affirms the primacy of children's needs. The balancing of the two major tensions, following versus leading and children versus profession, create a synergy, which represents the political realities of progress toward optimal services for children and families. I, for one, see no real competition, but rather an interdependent convergence toward mutually inclusive goals.

Q: **How does NAEYC work to increase standards in the field of early childhood?**

A: An example of the productive convergence of the two major tensions is NAEYC accreditation. In the 1980s, NAEYC accreditation was a leadership vision brought to the membership by the staff and governing board. While the membership had not specifically requested accreditation, the commitment to better standards of early care and education was why people joined NAEYC. The membership responded positively to the idea, and the organization began a process of consensus building, which created the original set of NAEYC accreditation criteria. Consensus, one of NAEYC's strengths, is the link between responsiveness and leadership.

Twenty-five years ago NAEYC accreditation criteria set a high standard for quality. In 2006, NAEYC accreditation was "reinvented" to reflect cutting-edge research across the developmental domains as well as the critical issues related to early childhood teaching and program management. The revised standards for program improvement and research-based criteria once again raised the bar that defines a high-quality early childhood program. Because NAEYC has no authority to require programs to become accredited, the process relies on *voluntary* self-study and subsequent on-site assessment of observable program practices and print documentation.

NAEYC accreditation also balances the second set of organizational tensions. The accreditation criteria set a higher standard for early care and educational programming, establishing the primacy of children's needs. The self-study process enhances professional development, thereby setting a professional standard. Self-study is a valuable, classroom-specific in-service training tool. It allows staff members to cooperatively evaluate their performance, expand their developmental knowledge, make appropriate adjustments, and achieve better-quality job performance. The innovation of NAEYC accreditation continues to generate further clarification of practice in the field in the form of developmentally appropriate practices (DAPs).

Q: **Why should I belong to NAEYC or any other professional organization?**

A: NAEYC, along with other professional associations, offers a framework for our combined talents to make a difference, to efficiently focus our passion, and to effectively use our knowledge base to advocate for what ought to be. If any reader should think that he or she is not counted among the legions of committed, knowledgeable professionals charged with the responsibility to make early care and education services what they ought to be for young children and their families, I must ask, if not us, together, now, then who, and when?

Jerlean Daniel is a Past President of NAEYC and is currently Executive Director of NAEYC.

PROFESSIONAL DEVELOPMENT IS SELF-DIRECTED

An experienced third-grade teacher had saved for many years to travel to Australia. The study of Australia was part of her social studies curriculum, and the teacher was seeking both personal and professional development through travel. She described her reason for pursuing this goal by saying, "In this job you have to take care of yourself." The idea that a teacher should be in charge of his or her own learning may be a rather startling concept. Educators are, as a group, very altruistic; most people would expect a great teacher's life to be a path of self-sacrifice rather than a plan for self-fulfillment. But becoming a masterful teacher is not a choice between attending to our professional growth and the needs of others; it is doing both. The belief that dedicated teachers deny their needs and attend exclusively to the needs of students is a destructive myth. Teachers who learn to take care of themselves professionally are smart rather than selfish. As architects of their professional growth, they recognize how their level of satisfaction with teaching influences relationships with colleagues, families, and ultimately affects children's learning. No matter how supportive the institutions in which you work may be, professional growth is not something that someone else does for you; each teacher needs to identify her or his own professional growth needs and monitor progress toward the goal of becoming a better teacher.

Pause and Reflect

About Your Own Development as a Professional

1. What have you learned thus far about yourself as a teacher? How does teaching young children differ from working with students at other levels?
2. If you were asked to draw a path or diagram of your hoped-for career, what would it look like?
3. What philosophical or theoretical orientations, powerful ideas, effective strategies, and role models do you use to guide your professional practice?

Your Role in Professional Development

Jennifer and Kelly are two college students who are required to observe and participate in a second-grade classroom. Kelly tends to stay on the sidelines, waiting for the teacher to stop and give her instructions. She is, in her own words, "totally clueless about what to do" during her field assignment, even though a detailed student handbook sits on her desk. One requirement is to write in her journal every day, but this is Friday and she has not written anything all week, so she frantically jots down a few statements during her planning period. When Kelly is confused, she panics and protests that she "wasn't prepared" for this particular situation by her teacher education program.

In contrast, Jennifer pitches in and suggests a way she might help whenever an opportunity arises in the classroom. She has entered the due dates for each assignment on her calendar and refers to it frequently to pace herself. Jennifer reads the information carefully before formulating a specific question, then she decides who would be the best person to answer that question. When a child with autism joins the class, Jennifer reads several articles about autism, attends a presentation on the topic at the local Council for Exceptional Children meeting, stops by the local mental health association to get information, and speaks with teachers and professors who have training and experience in special education. Jennifer has strategies in place to promote professional growth, is capable of self-evaluation, and is working toward reflecting upon her experiences, while Kelly has no such strategies and is not working toward these goals.

Kelly has very naïve views about teaching; she wrongly assumes that someone else should just tell her how to teach.

> Most people tend to think of the act of teaching as largely intuitive: someone knows something and then "teaches" it to others—a fairly straightforward transmission model. . . . However, as mountains of research now demonstrate, this notion of transmission teaching doesn't actually work most of the time. The reality of effective teaching is much different: successful teachers link what students already know and understand to new information, correcting misimpressions, guiding learners' understanding through a variety of activities, providing opportunities for application of knowledge, giving useful feedback that shapes performance, and individualizing for students' distinctive learning needs. They do all this while juggling the social and academic needs of the group and of individuals, the cognitive and motivational consequences of their moment-to-moment teaching decisions, the cultural and community context within which they teach, and much more. (Darling-Hammond, 2006, p. 8)

Becoming a teacher, then, is much more complicated than awaiting instructions from a supervisor or following the teacher's manual.

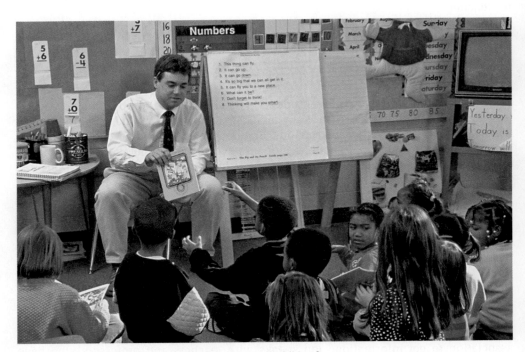

What obstacles may face men who want to teach young children?

Implement Strategies for Professional Development

Research on adults' learning confirms that adults usually approach learning as a series of self-selected projects; they want to learn now what will enable them to be more effective tomorrow, and that they prefer to go at their own pace (Drago-Severson, 2009). Look back on your life at some of the projects you eagerly pursued and how you went about this. Perhaps it was learning a physical skill, such as swimming; an arts or crafts goal, such as playing a musical instrument; work on your character, such as striving to be more patient with others; or pursuit of a particular task, such as training your dog. Chances are, you availed yourself of a wide variety of resources—print and non-print media, enrolling in a class, and talking with other, more experienced individuals. Becoming a better teacher relies on all of these approaches, and more. Sharon Lynn Kagan's Ask the Expert on page 356 discusses this process of professional growth for early childhood educators.

Acquire Skill in Self-Evaluation

It is not uncommon to feel overwhelmed by the daily demands of teaching and to feel inadequately prepared for the complexities of the teaching role. "The realization of the great responsibility they have for the group of children, as well as the discrepancy between the success they expect and the reality of the classroom, result in anxiety and feelings of inadequacy" (Essa, 2002, p. 95). The rules and regulations, stamina required of the job, the amount of paperwork, the range and intensity of students' needs, the parents who lack confidence in them, and the lack of support or recognition for their efforts often are a "reality shock" (Ryan & Cooper, 2006). As is the case in most "helping professions," such as teaching, social work, and nursing, some level of disillusionment is inescapable. Applied to teachers, **disillusionment** refers to the discrepancy between what teaching would be like in a perfect world and the day-to-day realities of the classroom. Most of those entering the early childhood field do so with a somewhat romanticized view of the career and, although a large measure of optimism and hope are assets for early childhood educators, part of the maturation process includes becoming more pragmatic and realistic.

Learning to self-evaluate is crucial to teachers for several reasons. First of all, self-evaluation is a form of reflection that deepens and widens your understandings of your role as a teacher. Second, the amount of feedback that you will get on your teaching after you exit your teacher education program is likely to be rather minimal. In public schools, for example, formal observations are infrequent—usually no more than once or twice a year for the new teachers and even fewer for experienced teachers. In fact, much of your administrators' and colleagues' determination of who is doing well and who is struggling is informal; in other words, it is noticed when they stop by your classroom briefly, walk down the hall, or see you in settings other than the classroom (e.g., on the playground, in the lunchroom, at a school-wide assembly, etc.). If you expect frequent feedback about how you are doing and rely on praise and recognition from others, you are apt to find a career in teaching to be rather disappointing. Acquiring practice in self-evaluation is therefore more important for teachers than for many other professionals. There are many different tools that the teachers who went before you have developed for use in reflection. Suppose, for example, that you want to self-evaluate your skill in

Ask the EXPERT

Sharon Lynn Kagan

Public Policy and Teachers' Professional Growth

Some Common Misconceptions About Public Policy and Teachers' Professional Growth

Misconception 1: Policy construction is expected to be rapid and predictable.

We all learn in many ways, but those of us who get to teach learn a great deal from our students and from the questions they ask and the ideas they bring to discussions. For the most part, my students are very, very bright. They have shown some interest in child development and policy because they have taken the prerequisites for the formal courses; those seeking individual guidance (via independent study or thesis advisement) are already quite advanced in their work. They ask good questions, have keen insights, and are in a policy hurry. They want to be policymakers—quickly.

I have been interested that they perceive policy construction as a linear, predictable, and fully knowable process. In their desire to "master" it—to have all the tools in hand before they plunge into the real world—they want it to be rational, to follow a formula. Often, students are mystified that policy is as much about chance, electability, and favors as it is about social justice and equity. They are stunned—and often intrigued—to hear the behind-the-scenes nuances of the policy process. Their surprise and freshness delights me and makes me realize that no work in policy can be complete without a policy practicum. Students constantly remind us, then, that the real work of teaching is to infuse reality without diminishing hope.

In their haste to make waves in the policy world, students often want to move fast. They usually feel that while it is desirable to be theoretically grounded in a discipline, it takes time—and a lot of it. Consequently, many launch into the policy world lacking any empirical understanding of young children and their development, lacking understanding of different theoretical approaches to pedagogy, and lacking any historical exposure to the complexities of the early care and education world. I lament this, because there is simply no substitute for rich empirical, theoretical, and historical understandings—they are the intellectual bedrock of policy work, providing both wisdom and credibility. Many students, therefore, need to learn that there is no substitute for academic training; simultaneously, we need to learn to help them understand the practical value of the empirical, theoretical, and historical perspectives that undergird our discipline.

Misconception 2: Real leadership is simple and effortless.

Beyond being well grounded in practice and theory, students need to realize that real leadership doesn't come easy. Leaders do tend to make leadership look simple: The President waltzes onto the podium and delivers the perfect speech effortlessly; we waltz into our classes and deliver the perfect lectures or seminars; master teachers waltz into their classrooms and seem to magically create the perfect learning environment for children. But behind all this apparent effortlessness are years of hours of work, and countless trials and errors, coupled with some dashed ideals and probably some embarrassing mistakes. We need to let our students know that it isn't all easy and without effort. They need to learn that leadership means having courage and using it; it means having integrity and using it; it means being willing to take risks; it means working hard and sticking to it; and sometimes it means lots of personal sacrifice. My biggest concern and students' most common misconception, then, is that many students perceive child-related policy work to be glamorous, effortless, and somewhat substanceless. My big job is conveying that it is precisely and fully the exact opposite.

Sharon Lynn Kagan is the Associate Dean for Policy at Teachers College, Columbia University and Leonard Marx Professor Adjunct of Early Childhood and Family Policy, Co-Director of the National Center for Children and Families, and Professor Adjunct at Yale University's Child Study Center.

conducting conferences with parents/families. You could review the questions in Figure 13.4 as a way of preparing for the conferences and revisit it later, after conducting the conferences, to assess your performance. The professional literature is full of such tools for reflection, and effective teachers use them to self-evaluate.

STRIVE FOR CONTINUOUS IMPROVEMENT

A group of elementary school principals who are earning the doctorate and the superintendent's credential were discussing their concerns about hiring new teachers. One said, "We live in constant fear of being on the six o-clock news. If a teacher uses bad judgment—or, even worse, is unethical—it all comes back on us as principals, on the school's reputation, and on the district." Another said, "Our district pays well so we get hundreds of applications for each position. What I'm looking for is someone who is willing to do more than what is required. I want to work with teachers who won't file a grievance if the after-school meeting goes past 4:00 or who always rush out the door right behind the school buses." "Our situation is different,"

Effective teachers of young children strive for continuous improvement.

Figure 13.4 Evaluating Your Role in a Conference

Use conferences as opportunities for reflecting on your role as a professional early childhood educator. Following conferences, ask yourself these questions, and try to assess honestly the areas where you have grown and where you need continued work.

- Did I share a positive anecdote about the child?
- Did I start by stating the purpose of the conference and how I planned to conduct it?
- Did I share information about the child's strengths or what the child *can* do?
- Did I share the child's work samples, to demonstrate specific points, arranged to highlight progress and effort?
- Did I encourage parental information and questions?
- Did I ask open-ended questions that invited discussion?
- Did I listen to what the parent had to say about his or her child?
- Was I alert to nonverbal cues and the way that things were said rather than focusing on the words alone? Did I "listen between the lines"?
- Did I suggest ways the home and school can collaborate? Did we agree upon a plan of action? Did we set goals together for the child?
- Did I summarize the conference and end on a positive note?

another principal added, "we are a small, rural elementary school with, on average, just one position opening up in a year. There is considerable pressure to hire a local teacher or somebody's relative or friend, but I am determined not to 'waste' that slot! If I make a mistake, I may have to live with it for a very long time and, with just 10 teachers in the building, one bad one can do a lot of damage." As these candid comments from people who make hiring decisions illustrate, expectations for new teachers are high and many schools have complex systems that they use to interview and hire new teachers. What are they looking for? Figure 13.5 is a list of some of the attributes that effective early childhood educators need to develop. Use them as a guide to reflect on your behavior now and as a set of goals for your future as a teacher of young children.

Figure 13.5 Characteristics of Outstanding Early Childhood Educators

Committed/Mission-Driven

- has a genuine calling to become a teacher and is passionate about making a contribution to the profession of early childhood education

Inclusive/Ethical

- is caring, compassionate, respectful, empathetic, and fair with everyone; has the courage to behave ethically despite difficulties

Competent/Intentional

- selects suitable approaches, applies principles of learning, bases decisions on research, communicates well with learners, and encourages children to learn

Enthusiastic/Creative

- believes she or he can make a difference in children's lives (teacher efficacy), has high energy, and aproaches professional tasks and solves problems with originality, resourcefulness, persistence, and a sense of humor

Leadership

- is authentic, pragmatic, earns others' respect, and leads through example; inspires others to do their best

Lifelong Learner

- seeks out opportunities to learn, both formal and informal; views becoming an effective teacher as a career-long project; goes beyond what is expected or required

Perceptive/Responsive

- listens, reads the context well, and is responsive to others' feelings; possesses strong interpersonal skills and builds positive relationships

Sources: Colker, 2008; Jalongo et al., 2004; Korthagen, 2004.

COLLABORATING WITH
Families

Sending Supportive Messages to Families

In your interactions with families, you often will be in the position of trying to be helpful and supportive. Research on listening processes suggests that several things need to be in place in order for a message to be received (Bodie & Burleson, 2008). First of all, you need to take the message recipient's point of view. To illustrate, suppose that a child's parent attends parent–teacher conferences and much of the focus is on the child's problems. It would not be surprising if the parent defended his or her child or even stopped attending conferences. Another key element is the environment. If parents/families are herded into a room and expected to sit at children's desks while someone talks to them, it is easy to see how that environment would interfere with effective communication—the parents/families may rightly feel as though they are being "talked down to." A third critical component in effective communication with parents/families is making sure that the message is understandable. This is particularly important for families whose first language is not English. They need comprehensible input in order to listen and communicate. Of course, communication can break down with English speakers as well if teachers use too much professional jargon. If a teacher says, "Your son is in the lower quartile in reading," for example, the parent may not understand but might not ask for clarification.

When the messages that were intended to be helpful do not communicate well, the predictable outcome is that the support attempt fails and negative attitudes toward the educator often surface. Conversely, if educators really strive to take the parent/family member's perspective, create a "family-friendly" environment, and formulate clear and concise messages that are helpful, then a meeting of the minds can occur and positive changes can be accomplished.

Read each of the examples below that is intended to be helpful. Why might it fail to have the desired effect with parents/families?

- "Crystal is having trouble learning the alphabet so I am sending home flash cards for you to practice at home."
- "Please check the homework website to see what your son missed while he was ill."
- "We will be implementing a behavior modification intervention with your son to address his socially unacceptable behaviors in the classroom."
- "Leah has been referred to the Speech/Language pathologist for services because of her stuttering problem; we need your approval and signature on this form."
- "We are recommending that your baby get special services because he appears to be developmentally delayed. We will be contacting you to set up weekly home visits."

Summary

- Professional development refers to the career-long project of becoming a more competent and caring early childhood educator. Some sources that support growth as a professional include education (both formal and informal), reflections on experience, interactions with others, participation in professional groups, and effective use of resources.

- A high-quality teacher preparation program can inaugurate a teacher's journey but can never fully prepare a person for all the realities and complexities of teaching. Even when teachers are equipped with a repertoire of effective teaching behaviors, they still have many decisions to make—which strategies to use, how to implement them effectively, and which students to use them with. Professional development for teachers is continuous and lasts throughout a career, is affected by the specific contexts in which teachers work, and is largely self-directed as educators seek out both formal and informal opportunities to become more effective and intentional teachers.

■ Although much of what teachers need to understand and do is learned through on-the-job training, training and credentials will not suffice unless early childhood educators implement strategies for professional development, acquire skill in self-evaluation, and strive for continuous improvement.

Applying Your Knowledge of Professional Development

In the following two activities, you will use your knowledge about teachers' professional development. In Assessment Activity 1, you will apply your knowledge of professionalism to the situation of a Head Start teacher who is conducting a home visit. Then, in Assessment Activity 2, you will apply your understanding of professional development to the task of becoming a valued colleague.

Assessment ACTIVITY 1   ROLANDO'S MOTHER GETS INVOLVED IN HEAD START

When Twila, a Head Start teacher, knocked on her door, Mrs. Garcia suddenly realized that she had completely forgotten about the home visit she had scheduled several weeks ago. Mrs. Garcia's infant daughter had just spit up on her, and the house was a complete mess as a result of a family visit over the weekend. As she spoke with Twila, Mrs. Garcia held her front door half-closed and tried to rush through the interaction. Sensing her discomfort, Twila said, "This doesn't seem like the best time to talk. Would you like to reschedule?" With a smile of gratitude, Mrs. Garcia agreed.

After she shut the door, Mrs. Garcia started to think about this opportunity for her son Rolando. Rolando was born with spina bifida: a place in his spine did not fuse together. He moved around by using the upper part of his body to drag his legs across the floor or by using a special wheelchair. What if the other children made fun of Rolando? If they did, then he surely would be better off at home. But the teacher had seemed very kind and had invited Mrs. Garcia and her husband to visit the classroom any time they wished. They even had a special orientation day when Rolando could attend a full day of school with a peer as his guide, and Mrs. Garcia would be permitted to be there throughout the day. She felt hopeful that Head Start would give Rolando a chance to learn and to make friends.

Mrs. Garcia later discussed this with Rolando's father but he was opposed to the whole idea. "What if Rolando picks up all those childhood illnesses? Doesn't he have enough problems to deal with? Besides, you are home all day. It's your job to take care of him."

In the car after leaving the Garcia's home, the Head Start teacher wondered whether this family would agree to participate in the program. "Why would they refuse all of this help for their son?" she thought to herself. "He needs to form good peer relationships as much as strong family ties."

REACT	In what ways are the perspectives of the three adults alike? Which perspective do you identify most strongly with, and why?
RESEARCH	Locate information about spina bifida at the library. What are some ways of helping children with this condition to be accepted by their peers and have successful learning experiences?
REFLECT	Rolando's mother, father, and the Head Start teacher have definite ideas about how to meet this young child's needs. What might be the underlying reasons for the differences in their ideas? How do their approaches compare with what you have read?

Assessment ACTIVITY 2 BECOMING A VALUED COLLEAGUE

The Code of Ethics of the Division for Early Childhood (DEC) of the Council for Exceptional Children (2009) includes the following statements about professional collaboration:

1. We shall honor and respect our responsibilities to colleagues while upholding the dignity and autonomy of colleagues and maintaining collegial interprofessional and intraprofessional relationships.

2. We shall honor and respect the rights, knowledge, and skills of the multidisciplinary colleagues with whom we work, recognizing their unique contributions to children, families, and the field of early childhood special education.

3. We shall honor and respect the diverse backgrounds of our colleagues, including such diverse characteristics as sexual orientation, race, national origin, religious beliefs, or other affiliations.

4. We shall identify and disclose to the appropriate persons using proper communication channels errors or acts of incompetence that compromise children's and families' safety and well-being when individual attempts to address concerns are unsuccessful.

Teachers are often advised to develop the skills of colleagueship. What, exactly, does this mean? A colleague may be defined as a person who accepts responsibility for her or his own actions, yet has a commitment to others and to the mission of the organization. Think about your work with others—in jobs, with your classmates, and in organizations. What makes one person a coworker whom you would seek out? Generate a list of attributes, then compare/contrast it with the one that follows.

A Valued Colleague

- Puts children's and families' needs first
- Is committed to equity and fairness
- Can be trusted with confidential and important things
- Thoughtfully considers others' points of view
- Volunteers, steps forward
- Is filled with energy
- Possesses enthusiasm for teaching
- Has a sense of humor
- Avoids blaming others
- Share success stories that reveal how teachers learn from their students
- Realizes when teaching efforts fail and strives for excellence
- Notices what you do well
- Seeks advice appropriately
- Is an avid learner
- Develops an ideological map of group members' philosophies
- Is dependable and trustworthy
- Knows you as a person, not just a coworker
- Listens and carefully considers what you have to say
- Shares books, ideas, and other resources
- Talks about interests beyond teaching
- Has a vision of where he or she is headed personally and professionally
- Is candid yet diplomatic
- Knows when to take a stand and when to go along
- Can disagree without rancor
- Dwells on solutions rather than problems
- Is willing to take the risks necessary to improve education
- Acknowledges mistakes and genuinely strives to do better

How Might You, in the Role of a Valued Colleague, Handle the Following Situations?

Situation 1:

Another student teacher has twice asked to "borrow" your lesson plans but never offers to plan with you, share plans, or develop the ones that you have given to him or her. What would you say the third time?

Situation 2:

You are sharing a ride with another teacher who has caused you to be late for school twice in the past 2 weeks because the person was not ready when you arrived. Your supervisor has told you that this is unacceptable and must be stopped immediately. What would you say to the other teacher? To your supervisor?

Situation 3:

There is a local conference being held on campus on a Saturday and student teachers are expected to attend. A friend asks you to sign in for her so that she can sleep in instead of being there at 8 A.M. How would you handle this?

Situation 4:

Two inservice teachers are in the hallways before school starts, engaging in destructive gossip about a family whose children attend the school. They seem to want you to participate and start telling you all about an arrest report that appeared in the paper last night. You are a student teacher in the building. How would you respond?

Source: Information from Graves, 2001.

ONLINE RESOURCES FOR PROFESSIONAL DEVELOPMENT

Association for Childhood Education International (ACEI): ACEI is a global community of educators and advocates who unite knowledge, experience, and perspectives in order to exchange information, explore innovation, and advocate for children. http://acei.org/

Characteristics of Effective Teachers: Read I. J. Colker's (2008) article "Twelve Characteristics of Effective Early Childhood Teachers, from *Beyond the Journal*, available online from NAEYC. http://journal.naeyc.org/btj/200803/BTJColker.asp

Division for Early Childhood (DEC): Read the Code of Ethics from the Council for Exceptional Children (CEC), updated in 2009. www.decsped.org/uploads/docs/about_dec/position_concept_papers/Code%20of%20Ethics_updated_Aug2009.pdf

National Association for the Education of Young Children: NAEYC is committed to becoming an increasingly high-performing and inclusive organization. Watch the series of videos, Parts 1–7, on this topic on YouTube. www.naeyc.org/

Neuroscience for Professional Development: Check out the latest tips from the Dana Foundation (www.dana.org/) on brain-research-based ways to improve your learning. http://yourbrainatwork.org/

National Early Childhood Teacher Assistance Center (NECTAC): Provides a database of state policies on professional development for the early childhood workforce. www.nectac.org/portal/ecdata.asp

---

PEARSON myeducationlab

Go to Topic 12 (Professionalism/Ethics) in the MyEducationLab (**www.myeducationlab.com**) for your course, where you can:

- Find learning outcomes for professionalism/ethics along with the national standards that connect to these outcomes.
- Complete Assignments and Activities that can help you more deeply understand the chapter content.
- Apply and practice your understanding of the core teaching skills identified in the chapter with the Building Teaching Skills and Dispositions learning units.
- Access video clips of CCSSO National Teachers of the Year award winners responding to the question, "Why Do I Teach?" in the Teacher Talk section.
- Hear viewpoints of experts in the field in Professional Perspectives.

LIST OF
Appendices

Note to Students

As an early childhood teacher, you will always be looking for new ideas and resources that will enhance your teaching and facilitate children's learning. As you work with children, remember the resources in the following seven appendices and use them often. These resources are found in most high-quality early childhood settings. Appendices A–G provide a starting point for you to obtain information and assistance—add to them regularly and make them work for you; they are *not intended* to be a definitive list of every resource that is available to you.

Appendix A Basic Materials to Support Development by Age Range

Appendix B Free, Inexpensive, and Recycled Materials

Appendix C Health, Nutrition, and Safety Resources

Appendix D Materials for Learning Centers

Appendix E Professional Resources for Teachers

Appendix F Organizing Professional Resources

Appendix G Internet Resources

> **Internet Disclaimer** All Internet resources are accurate at the time of publication of this edition. However, the authors and publisher cannot guarantee that these URLs and web addresses will be current for the duration of this edition.

APPENDIX A

Basic Materials to Support Development by Age Range

INFANTS AND TODDLERS (BIRTH–AGE 3) **Infants** learn by sensory exploration and social interaction. They need a variety of textured objects to view, hold, and reach for. They also need materials that make sounds, are soft and squeezable, and are simple, realistic, and safe. **Toddlers** are *actively seeking independence* and have a high energy level. They need action toys to take apart and put together and materials scaled to their size that require different kinds of manipulations, such as nesting, stacking, and bouncing. Here are some beginning suggestions:

The Arts
music (CDs of appropriate types of music, simple instruments, tape recorders), art (brushes, easel, painting surfaces, smocks), media (crayons, play dough, paper of assorted colors, nontoxic washable paints), movement and pretend play (props, hats, scarves)

Cognitive
aquarium, blocks, books, floating and sinking pieces, gear-turning toys, jumbo beads, nesting toys, number puzzles, plants, shells and rocks, stacking toys, sorting toys, texture balls

Communication
books (cloth, cardboard, picture), pictures for discussion, boxes containing materials of different textures (soft, hard, bumpy, crunchy, etc.), flannel board, language games, puppets

Gross Motor Equipment (Indoor/Outdoor)
apparatus (boxes, climbers), dramatic play (unbreakable dishes and utensils, clothes and props that reflect children's families), large-muscle toys (balls, blocks, push and pull toys), sand play (cups, spoons, buckets), water play (fill-and-empty containers, tubing)

Health and Safety Materials
child gates, emergency fire extinguisher, first aid and toilet supplies (posted emergency telephone numbers, locked cabinets), food service (bibs, bottles, flatware), resting facilities (cots, cribs with slats less than $2\frac{3}{8}$ apart), diapers, sanitation (diaper-changing pads), smocks, towelettes, washcloths

Indoor Equipment and Maintenance Supplies
adult seating for comfortable feeding, brooms (adult and child-sized), brushes (bottle, counter, hand), bulletin boards, cabinets, chairs (adult and child-sized), clothes rack, cubbies, dishpan, dishtowels, disinfectants, file cabinet, food preparation and eating area, hand-held portable vacuum, heating and serving dishes, infant stroller, safety gates, shelves (high and low), sponges, storage bins on rollers, tables (changing table at adult height, other tables at child height), toilet facilities, towels, trays, wastebaskets (covered)

Manipulatives
Infants: clutch ball, infant gyms, squeeze toys, teething toys

Toddlers: beads, large-sized stacking and locking sets, giant pegboard, plastic vehicles

Record Keeping
attendance sheets, booklets for observation notes, card file, parent forms, health sheets

Sensory Materials
listening (bells, chimes, sound games), smelling (sealed spices), tasting (foods), touching and feeling (textured materials and games), looking (color paddles, sight matching games)

PRESCHOOLERS AND KINDERGARTNERS (AGES 3–5) **Preschoolers** and **kindergartners** show increasing social ability, fascination with adult roles, growing mastery over their small and large muscles, and interest in pretend play. The materials and equipment for this age group should support their developing social skills and interest in these areas. Here are some suggestions:

The Arts
aprons (plastic or cloth), brushes and holders, chalk, collage materials, containers, crayons, easels, newspapers, nontoxic paint, washable markers (assorted), paper (assorted), play dough, printing materials, recycled materials, blunt scissors

Audiovisual Equipment
cassette recorder, cassettes, CDs and DVDs, filmstrips, record player, records, tapes

Building and Construction
blocks (assorted table, unit and hollow), boards, building sets, carpentry, sand/water play, vehicles, wheeled toys

Dramatic Play

animals, camping, child-sized table and chairs, cooking and eating equipment, doctor/nurse, doll equipment, a wide variety of dress-up clothes and props, finger puppets, furniture for housekeeping, multiracial dolls, puppets, telephones, transportation, traffic signs

Health and Safety

child-safe gates and doors, first aid supplies, flashlight, food preparation and service supplies (blender, bottle opener, can opener, flatware), health records accessible and up to date (immunizations, allergies, contact information), measures, plates, storage containers, tablecloths, trays, mops, soap, sponges, toilet paper, towels, vacuum cleaner

Indoor Equipment and Maintenance Supplies

bookcase, bookshelves, brooms (push, regular), buckets, bulletin board, cabinets (movable), chairs (adult and child), chalkboard, cleaning cloths, cleansers, cubbies, dishpan, drying rack (folding), drinking fountain (child height), electrical extension cord and plug, filing cabinet, plunger, rugs, sink, smoke alarm, tool box

Language Arts

alphabet letters, assorted books (child-authored, multiethnic and multiage characters, nonstereotyped roles, fiction, real and fantasy, poetry), audio books, camera, chart paper, computer, felt board, listening tape/book sets, puzzles, writing materials (assorted crayons, pencils, markers)

Mathematics

attribute beads or blocks, concept games and puzzles, counters, food to cut and divide, geometric figures and shapes, information books, matching sets, measuring equipment, money (play, homemade), number games, pegboards, shapes, sorting collections and containers

Music

autoharp, CD and cassette player, rhythm instruments (bells, maracas, tambourines, triangles, wooden blocks), xylophone

Office Supplies and Record Keeping

bulletin board, calendar, computer supplies, file cabinet, manila folders and envelopes, message pads, paper clips, pencils and pens, stationery, thumbtacks, yardstick

Perceptual Motor Materials

beads and laces, counting rods, dressing frames, games, linking toys, magnetic board

Psychomotor Development

balls, bars for hanging, bean bags, bowling pin sets, climbing and sliding equipment, crates, hoops, pails, pulleys, rakes, rope or tire swing, tossing games

Science/Technology

air experiments, animal foods and types, books about science concepts, food and gardening, light and heat, machines, magnets, magnifying glass, picture collections, seeds, simple interactive computer programs, water toys (sieves, tubs, funnels), sand toys (utensils, molds)

SCHOOL-AGE CHILDREN (AGES 5–8)

School-age children are refining skills and talents that they prize, are relying more and more on their peers, and are becoming more organized and logical thinkers. Materials and equipment for this age group should reflect their need for *realistic, rule-oriented, and peer activities*. Following are some suggestions:

Art

aluminum foil, brushes, chalk, containers, crayons, drying rack, glue, laundry starch, markers, needles, paint, paper, paper cutter, pens, pipe cleaners or wikki sticks, scrapbooking supplies (stickers, papers, pinking shears), sewing supplies with blunt needles, stapler, weaving looms

Health and First Aid

Items available in nurse's or director's office, fully stocked first aid cabinet, posted list of emergency contact numbers

Indoor Equipment and Maintenance Supplies

air conditioner (where appropriate), boards, book racks, brooms, brushes, buckets, cabinets, carpeting, chairs, chart holders, clock (wall), dishpan, easels, file cabinet, floor pillows, mirror, mops, sink, sponges, towels, wastebaskets

Language Arts

alphabet wall cards and sets, audio books, bookends, book holder, books (chapter, pop-up, recipe, information), chart tablets, complex board games, flash cards, letters, pocket wall chart, puzzles, recordings, rubber stamps, writing tools (assorted pencils, crayons, papers)

Mathematics

blocks, calculators, cash register, chart to 100, clock, counting frames and sticks, dice, flannel board and cutouts, floor graph, magnetic board, measures, number lines, pegs

Media/Computing

audiovisual player, AV carts, books, book racks, camera, cassette recorder, cassettes, easel for book display, headphones, listening station, VCR/DVD player, computer with simple word processing/drawing programs and Internet connection

Music

autoharp, bell sets, castanets, cymbals, drums, electronic keyboard, listening station equipment, music books, music children can move to, records, rhythm sticks, sand blocks, teaching aids, tone block, triangles, xylophone

Perceptual Motor

balance beam, balls, bean bags, climbing apparatus, cones for obstacle course, hoops, hopscotch, jacks, jump ropes, marbles, parachute, puzzles (assorted pieces and levels of difficulty), records and cassette tapes for movement, slide, tires

Science

ant farm, aquarium, bulbs (garden), cages, cooking equipment, collections, flower containers, garden equipment, magnets, magnifying glasses, microscope, prisms, pulleys, timers

Social Studies

block accessories, blocks, community resource file, construction toys, dramatic play materials, games, globe, magazines, maps and atlas, newspapers, puppets, and puppet stage

Supplies

chalk, chalkboard erasers, chart tablets, colored folders, fasteners, markers, metal rings, paper (assorted), paper clips, pencil erasers, tagboard (assorted), transparencies

Sources: From *Selecting Educational Equipment and Materials for School and Home*, by J. Moyer (Ed.), 1995, Wheaton, MD: Association for Childhood Education International; *Creative Thinking and Arts-Based Learning: Preschool Through Fourth Grade* (5th ed.), by J. Isenberg & M. R. Jalongo, 2010, Upper Saddle River, NJ: Pearson; and *Serious Players in the Primary Classroom* (2nd ed.), by S. Wassermann, 2000, New York, NY: Teachers College Press.

APPENDIX B

Free, Inexpensive, and Recycled Materials

EDUCATOR MATERIALS

Anti-Defamation League
www.adl.org/education/education_resources_prek.asp
Register for curriculum connections to receive free online educational resources for integrating multicultural, anti-bias, and social justice themes into your curriculum. Download a calendar for multi-faith observances.

Environmental Protection Agency (EPA)
www.epa.gov/teachers/
Offers a collection of lesson plans, activities, games, websites, and documents that you can use to explain environmental topics.

Free Teaching Aids
www.freeteachingaids.com
Provides printed curriculum materials, videotapes, computer resources, and mixed-media resources.

Local Retailers
Try your local retailers for discarded items, samples, and other unwanted items (carpet stores for carpet samples for group meetings; ice-cream shops for discarded displays for dramatic play; wallpaper stores for discontinued wallpaper books for book covers, bulletin boards, and collage material).

Parents' Internet Sources
Call the U.S. Department of Education's Publication Center (ED Pubs) at 1-800-4ED PUBS to request your free copy of this resource that helps parents make the best use of the online world as an educational tool.

Teaching Tolerance
www.teachingtolerance.org
Provides teachers with copies of classroom activities by grade level and subject area that promote classroom community and subscriptions to its magazine free of charge.

HOUSEHOLD, NATURAL, AND RECYCLED MATERIALS
A large variety of household, natural, and recycled materials helps children to experiment, imagine, and explore what materials can do and what they can do with materials as they make discoveries and find answers to their own questions. In this way, they learn to use the language of art (color, line, texture), scientific processes (observation, prediction, experimentation, and communication), mathematical processes (problem solving, reasoning, connections, and communication), mathematical content (numbers, operations, and geometry) and literacy (spoken, written, and visual language) to identify, classify, observe closely, make comparisons, ask questions, and describe what they discovered.

Household Materials
buttons, pots and pans, calculator, carpentry tools, plastic containers, bottle caps, cooking utensils, real objects that appeal to children's imagination, simple camera, old typewriter and/or computer, paper and pencils

Uses: SCIENCE: observations and discoveries, MATH: counting, sorting and classifying, ART: texture, line, and color, LITERACY: data gathering, language, and communication

Natural Materials
pebbles, seed pods, sticks, shells, twigs, leaves, rocks, pine cones, sand, mud, water, smooth beach glass

Uses: SCIENCE: observations and discoveries, MATH: sorting and classifying, ART: texture, LITERACY: data gathering, language, and communication

Recycled Materials
Assorted papers, such as the clean side of used paper and envelopes, catalogs, construction, gift wrap, tissue, magazines, cardboard rolls, assorted boxes of various sizes and shapes, inserts from paper packages, front and back notebook covers

Uses: various art activities and exploration of color, line, texture, balance, patterns, symmetry, sorting and classifying; ecology

Fabric scraps, such as sample swatches, old clean clothing, carpet and cloth scraps and samples, burlap, lengths of ribbon or yarn

Uses: various art activities and exploration of color, texture, symmetry

Plastic containers and lids, such as assorted plastic cartons (milk, yogurt, egg), empty washed assorted bottles, berry baskets

Uses: stacking, nesting sorting, painting, planting

Styrofoam, such as packing materials from shipments and stores

Uses: woodworking, construction, and various art projects

Recycle City, organized by geographic region, to learn about reducing waste and recycling materials for grades K–5—visit *www.epa.gov/recyclecity/se.htm*

Materials Request Form

The easiest way to build a useful collection of free, inexpensive, and recycled materials is to invite the families to contribute if they can. The requested wording shown in the next column facilitates family engagement by contributing materials for their children's learning.

Dear _____:

We are studying about _____. To do our projects, our class needs _____. If you can help us with any of these materials, please send them to school this week.

Thank you.

APPENDIX C

Health, Nutrition, and Safety Resources

Health, nutrition, and safety are traditionally parts of early childhood programs that get overlooked. Here are some useful resources.

ORGANIZATIONS AND ASSOCIATIONS

American Academy of Opthamology
www.aao.org
(Obtain a free eye chart and a variety of pamphlets on eye problems by visiting online)

American Academy of Pediatrics
www.aap.org
TIPP—The Injury Prevention Program *(Injury prevention advice is available online at www.aap.org and pamphlets are available)*

American Alliance for Health, Physical Education, Recreation, and Dance (AAPHERD)
www.aahperd.org
Head Start Body Start promotes physical activity and healthy eating for Head Start, Early Head Start, and child-care programs with a variety of tools, including a monthly activity calendar and electronic newsletter. Visit *www.aahperd.org/headstartbodystart/* for free resources.
Journal: *Journal of Health Education; Journal of Physical Education, Recreation, and Dance*

American Automobile Association
Traffic Safety Department *(Check with local branch office for address)*
Pamphlet: *Bicycling Is Great Fun*

National SAFE KIDS Campaign
www.safekids.org/educators/
Provides a variety of activities on child safety, including safety resources (fire, poison, toy), safety fact sheets, lesson plans, and position statements.

Southeastern Michigan Dietetic Association
www.semda.org
Provides food guides for different ethnic and cultural groups, and a nutrition tip of the week. Go to *www.semda.org/info/pyramid.asp* for specific food guides and *www.semda.org/info/tips.asp* for the Tip of the Week.

U.S. Department of Agriculture Food and Nutrition Information Center
Hosts a complete library of resources on food, nutrition, and safety.
For a complete list of FNIC resources go to *http://fnic.nal.usda.gov/resourcelists*
Two useful resources are:

Eat Smart Play Hard
(www.fns.usda.gov/eatsmartplayhardeducators/), which offers educators downloadable practical tools to help motivate children and caregivers to eat healthy and be physically active. Organized by topic, format, and age. In Spanish and English.

MyPyramid
(www.fns.usda.gov/tn/kids-pyramid.html), which offers downloadable materials for elementary-age children to learn about MyPyramid food guidelines. Lesson plans and activities are available for grades 1–2 and grades 3–4.

ADDITIONAL RESOURCES

www.healthychild.net
An online magazine with articles about child health and safety.

www.floridajuice.com
Download recipes and nutritional information for children.

www.kidshealth.org
Access medical information and tips from experts on such topics as first aid, food safety, immunizations, illnesses, indoor and outdoor hazards, and ADHD. For children there are games, experiments, movies, health and safety information, and much more.

www.kidsource.com
Obtain activities, information, websites, and a tip of the day on health and safety issues for teachers and parents.

http://cpsc.gov
The National Consumer Product Safety site that provides information on toy and safety-seat recalls and links to other sites.

www.scrubclub.org
Scrub Club offers the Healthy Schools, Healthy People toolkit for use in schools at *www.itsasnap.org/snap/pdfs/SNAP%20Toolkit%20FINAL%204.pdf*.

www.dole5aday.com
Provides games, comics, lesson plans, and activities and other information about why fruits and vegetables are good.

http://exhibits.pacsci.org/nutrition/
An interactive site for children that offers several nutrition games and other information.

http://eclkc.ohs.acf.hhs.gov/hslc/ecdh/Health/Nutrition/Nutrition%20Program%20Staff/IMIL/IamMovingIam.htm
The "I Am Moving I Am Learning" approach to preventing childhood obesity for Head Start children. Provides quality, planned movement activities and ideas for healthy food choices.

APPENDIX D

Materials for Learning Centers

Carefully designed centers enable teachers to integrate the curriculum, engage in natural and ongoing assessment, be culturally responsive, and teach to all of children's intelligences. Well-designed centers contain an array of materials that are concrete, durable, and interactive. The following examples are listed by center.

ART CENTER

easel	water, tempera, and finger paint	paintbrushes
paste and white glue	newsprint, tissue, construction paper	tape
chalk	markers, crayons, colored pencils	hole punches
clay and clay tools	books related to art topics	sponges
	recycled materials	scissors

BLOCK CENTER

unit blocks	hardwood hollow blocks	brick blocks
traffic signs	play people and animals	Legos and Duplos
play vehicles	architectural drawings	street signs

books related to building and construction

writing and drawing materials

DRAMATIC PLAY CENTER

kitchen furniture	cooking utensils, cookbooks, recipes	play money
dress-up clothes	paper, pencils, food coupons	telephone
telephone books	various dolls	

books, magazines, and newspapers about families

prop boxes containing other theme-related topics, such as restaurant, grocery store, transportation, post office

assorted print materials (maps, phone books, coupons) and writing and drawing materials

LIBRARY CENTER

a variety of teacher-made and child-made books, blank books, big books, books on tape, headphones, props to act out stories, pillows, soft chairs, magnetic board and letters, flannel board, flannel-board stories, puppets

MANIPULATIVES, PUZZLES, AND GAME CENTER

beads for stringing	pegboards and pegs	lacing cards
dressing frames	parquetry blocks	puzzles

construction toys (e.g., bristle blocks, star builders, Lincoln Logs, Tinkertoys, Legos)

sorting boards and games

a variety of teacher-made and commercial board and lotto games, concept games, collections

MATH CENTER

nesting cubes	geoboards and rubber bands	play money
abacus and rulers	counters and scales	cash register
playing cards	dice	yardstick
math manipulatives	parquetry blocks	Cuisenaire rods
interlocking cubes		

assortment of real objects (shells, rocks, buttons, leaves) for sorting and classifying

books about mathematics, counting, and math themes

MUSIC CENTER

drums and bells	rhythm sticks	record, tape, and CD players
toy instruments	graduated bottles	instrument-making materials
real instruments	child-made and teacher-made instruments	

books about music, musicians, and musical themes

SAND, SENSORY, AND WATER CENTER

wet and dry sand and water	sand or water table	bulb syringes, squirt bottles
assorted cups and molds	assorted sticks, strainers	pots and pans, shovels, scoops
colanders, sifters, funnels	small vehicles	flowerpots, flowers
small plastic animals	small garden tools	ice cubes, liquid soap
floating and sinking objects	straws	egg beater, ladle, sponges
rice,		
assorted paper		

SCIENCE CENTER

assorted bolts, nuts, washers, magnets, magnetic letters, buttons, fabric swatches, balls, paper, small magnifying lenses, empty plastic containers, droppers

assorted dried legumes, stones, pebbles, yarn, thread, cord, wire, pipe cleaners

variety of real insects and bugs in covered containers

pets appropriate for a classroom (gerbils, guinea pigs, fish)

plants with and without flowers, seeds, and gardening tools

things to take apart and put together and things to smell

paper, clapboard, and writing supplies

books, charts, posters, magazines, photo word cards about specific topics

instruction cards for completing experiments

small mirrors and flashlights

WOODWORKING CENTER

wooden wheels, spools	7-oz. claw hammers and plane	hand drill clamp
7-inch screwdrivers	woodworking bench	safety glasses

variety of rulers, protractors, tape measures

Styrofoam for sawing, hammering, and drilling

instruction cards to sequence actions such as hammering a nail into the wood, tools labeled with written words

posters and charts for building furniture, a deck, or shelves

paper and pencils to draw plans

WRITING CENTER

variety of types of paper	alphabet letter stamps	props to enact stories
stapler, hole punch, ink pads	scissors, erasers, glue	books and magazines
book of wallpaper samples	stationery, magic slates	tape recorder, tapes
old computer or keyboard		

Source: Adapted with permission of Terri Cardy, Laboratory School Faculty, Kent State University, Kent, Ohio.

APPENDIX E

Professional Resources for Teachers

EDUCATION RESOURCES INFORMATION CENTER (ERIC) CLEARINGHOUSES ERIC, sponsored by the Institute of Education Sciences (IES) of the U.S. Department of Education, produces the world's premiere database of journal and nonjournal education literature that can be accessed online at *www.eric.ed.gov*.

U.S. Department of Education
Special Collections:

What Works Clearinghouse *http://ies.ed.gov/ncee/wwc*

Regional Educational Laboratories (RELs) *http://ies.ed.gov/ncee/edlabs/*

Doing What Works *http://dww.ed.gov*

Disabilities and Gifted Education
The Council for Exceptional Children *www.cec.sped.org/ericec.html*

INTERSTATE NEW TEACHER ASSESSMENT AND SUPPORT CONSORTIUM (INTASC) STANDARDS The 10 INTASC standards and key indicators include knowledge, dispositions, and performance expectations for what all beginning teachers should be able to do to fulfill their professional responsibilities. All beginning teachers must be able to

1. understand the central concepts, tools of inquiry, and structures of the discipline(s) they teach and create meaningful learning experiences from them.

2. understand how children learn and develop, and provide learning opportunities to support each aspect of their development.

3. understand the many ways students learn and create learning opportunities that are adapted to learners from diverse cultural backgrounds and with exceptionalities.

4. understand and use a variety of instructional strategies.

5. create learning environments that encourage active engagement in learning, positive social interaction, and self-motivation.

6. use effective communication techniques that foster active inquiry in the classroom.

7. plan instruction based on knowledge of subject matter, children, the community, and curriculum goals.

8. use formal and informal assessment strategies to ensure continuous growth of the learner.

9. be reflective practitioners who continually evaluate choices and who actively seek out professional growth opportunities.

10. communicate and interact with families, colleagues, and the community to support student learning.

Source: The Interstate New Teacher Assessment and Support Consortium (INTASC) standards were developed by the Council of Chief State School Officers and member states. Copies may be downloaded from the Council's website at *http://www.ccsso.org*. Council of Chief State School Officers. (1992) *Model standards for beginning teacher licensing, assessment, and development: A resource for state dialogue.* Washington, DC: Author. *http://www.ccsso.org/content/pdfs/corestrd.pdf*.

PROFESSIONAL ASSOCIATIONS, ORGANIZATIONS, AND JOURNALS The following organizations provide information, services, and materials to early childhood teachers.

American Montessori Society (AMS) *www.amshq.org*

Association for Childhood Education International (ACEI) *www.acei.org*

   (Infancy through adolescence)

   Journal: *Childhood Education*

Canadian Association for Young Children www.cayc.ca/

Canadian Child Care Federation www.cccf-fcsge.ca

Newsletter: *Interaction*

Learning Through Play Tool Kit (Free while supplies last)

Council for Professional Recognition www.cdacouncil.org

CDA credentialing program, U.S. Military School-Age Child Care credential

National Association of Child Care Resource and Referral (NACCRRA) *www.naccrra.org*

National Association for the Education of Young Children (NAEYC) *www.naeyc.org*

Journals: *Young Children* focuses on teaching children birth through age 8; *Teaching Young Children* has general resources for teaching preschool children, including tip sheets as well as links to general preschool resources. Some resources are available in both English and Spanish. A collection of articles on a wide array of topics can be found online at http://www.naeyc.org/yc/pastissues.

Also available: programs supporting teachers and administrators, information resources, position papers, and standards

National Association for Family Child Care (NAFCC) *www.nafcc.org*

Provides technical assistance to Family Child Care Association

Newsletter: *National Perspectives*

U.S. National Committee of the World Organization for Early Childhood Education (OMEP) *http://omep-usnc.org*

Journal: *International Journal of Early Childhood*

CHILD ADVOCACY GROUPS

Action for Children's Television

Administration for Children, Youth, and Families

Canadian Day Care Advocacy Association

Child Health Alert

Child Trends

Child Welfare League of America

Children's Defense Fund

The Children's Foundation

Families and Work Institute

National Black Child Development Institute

National Child Care Information Center

Prevent Child Abuse America

Reading Is Fundamental

Save the Children

Society for Developmental Education and Behavioral Pediatrics

Stand for Children

United Nations International Children's Emergency Fund (UNICEF)

Zero to Three

OTHER PROFESSIONAL ASSOCIATIONS AND JOURNALS THAT PUBLISH SOME MATERIALS ABOUT EARLY CHILDHOOD

The Association for Supervision and Curriculum Development (ASCD) *www.ascd.org*

Journal: *Educational Leadership*

The Council for Exceptional Children (CEC) *www.cec.sped.org/*

Journal: *Exceptional Children*

Division for Early Childhood (DEC) *www.dec-sped.org/*

International Reading Association (IRA) *www.reading.org*

Journal: *The Reading Teacher*

National Art Education Association (Arts) (NAEA) *www.naea-reston.org*

Journal: *Art Education*

National Association for Bilingual Education (NABE) *www.nabe.org*

Journal: *Bilingual Research Journal*

National Association for Gifted Children (NAGC) *www.nagc.org*

Journal: *Gifted Child Quarterly*

National Council for the Social Studies (NCSS) *www.ncss.org*

Journal: *Social Studies and the Young Learner*

National Council of Teachers of Mathematics (NCTM) *www.nctm.org*

Journal: *Teaching Children Mathematics (PK–6)*

National Science Teachers Association (NSTA) *www.nsta.org*

Journal: *Science and Children (Elementary)*

OTHER JOURNALS AND PROFESSIONAL MAGAZINES DEDICATED TO EARLY CHILDHOOD EDUCATION

Beginnings

The Canadian Journal of Research in Early Childhood Education

Child Development

(Research journal of the Society for Research in Child Development)

Child Care Information Exchange

Children Today
> (Published by the U.S. Government Office of Human Development Services)

Dimensions of Early Childhood
> (Publication of the Southern Early Childhood Association)

Early Childhood Education Journal
> (Published by Springer International)

Early Childhood Research Quarterly
> (Research journal of the National Association for the Education of Young Children)

Early Childhood Today

Today's Child

OTHER JOURNALS THAT PUBLISH SOME ARTICLES ABOUT EARLY CHILDHOOD

American Journal of Orthopsychiatry

Children

Developmental Psychology

Journal of Research in Childhood Education
> (Published by the Association for Childhood Education International)

Language Arts
> (Publication of the National Council of Teachers of English)

Merrill-Palmer Quarterly of Behavior and Development

Peabody Journal of Education

Phi Delta Kappan
> (Journal of the National Honor Society, Phi Delta Kappa)

Review of Educational Research
> (Publication of the American Educational Research Association)

Teacher Research: The Journal of Classroom Inquiry

Topics in Early Childhood Special Education

BOOK PUBLISHERS/DISTRIBUTORS THAT FEATURE EARLY CHILDHOOD MATERIALS

Crystal Springs Books	Redleaf Press
Gryphon House	SkyLight
Modern Learning Press	Teacher Ideas Press
Pearson	Zero to Three

APPENDIX F

Organizing Professional Resources

As you create your own personal system for locating, gathering, and using professional resources, you will need a method for organizing them. Here we provide suggestions for organizing and finding materials and resources to include in your professional resource file.

To organize your resources, create a filing and record-keeping system that will work for you! Use either an electronic system on a hard drive or flash drive or a binder with tabbed dividers that contains hard copies of resources. Some suggestions for resource categories include:

assessments
calendars and schedules
curriculum area
forms
lesson plan file
children's portfolios
teaching strategies
thematic units

Finding Materials for a Good Resource File

- Materials distributed from instructors, leaders, and consultants
- Bulletins and publications from your local, state, and federal government; professional organizations; and commercial organizations
- Magazines, pictures, professional journal articles
- List of ideas shared by colleagues
- List of books from the public library
- Notes taken during workshops; coursework; national, state, and local conferences
- Your own growing file of activities, catalogs, and professional publications

Materials to Include in a Resource File

- Art suggestions (e.g., recipes for play dough, fingerpaints, materials collection)
- Before-school checklist (e.g., room arrangement, mailboxes and cubbies, laminate supplies, create day-of-the-week folders, substitute folder, welcome notes to children and families)
- Bulletin board and display ideas (e.g., pictures, themes, welcoming quotes or sayings, children's bulletin board creations)
- Drama (e.g., prop boxes, theme-related materials, Readers Theater)
- Equipment sources, catalogs, and teacher-made materials
- Field trips and excursions
- Fingerplays, songs, records, tapes, CDs, DVDs
- Health and safety information and learning activities
- Literacy information and learning activities
- Math and science suggestions
- Resources
  Children as resources
  Families as resources
  School resources
  Community resources
- Social studies (e.g., ideas for community, understanding the self, rights and responsibilities)
- Thematic unit topics appropriate for a particular age group
- Transition activities and ideas (e.g., between activities, early finishers, unexpected time)
- Other

APPENDIX G

Internet Resources

The following websites provide information and ideas about all areas of early childhood. Use this list as a beginning for your own list of useful sites.

BRAIN-BASED LEARNING

Dr. Nunley's website for educators
www.brains.org/
Provides practical classroom applications of current brain research

CHILD CARE

National Child Care Information Center
http://nccic.org
Lists A-to-Z index of topics on comprehensive child-care information and resources

CHILDREN'S BOOKS

Bank Street Children's Book Committee
www.bankstreet.edu/bookcom/best.html
Lists best children's books published each year by age level and special interests

Gryphon House Books
www.ghbooks.com
Offers free activities from resource and children's books by age and content area

CHILDREN WITH SPECIAL NEEDS

Children with ADD/ADHD
http://helpguide.org/mental/adhd_add_teaching_strategies.htm
Suggests teaching tips for teachers

Circle of Inclusion
www.circleofinclusion.org/
Has demonstrations of and information about effective practices of inclusive education for children birth through age 8

Cornucopia of Disability Information: Children with Disabilities
http://codi.buffalo.edu/children.htm
Provides activities for children with and without disabilities

Division for Early Childhood of the Council for Exceptional Children
www.dec-sped.org
Focuses on young children with disabilities—conferences, newsletters, journal *Young Exceptional Children*

Everything ESL
www.everythingesl.net/inservices/
Suggests teaching tips and resource picks for classroom teachers of English language learners

National Association for the Gifted and Talented
www.nsgt.org/articles/index.asp
Provides educational resources for children with gifts and talents and their families

New Horizons
http://education.jhu.edu/newhorizons/education-technology-resources-1/
Is a general resource for special education

Science Education for Students with Disabilities
www.sesd.info
Offers teacher resources in science for students at all levels and for specific disabilities

CURRICULUM

Curriculum Planning

www.inspiringteachers.com/
Has a teachers' toolbox and weekly teaching tips for beginning teachers, student teachers, and substitute teachers

www.teachernet.com
Provides a searchable database of classroom projects and bulletin board ideas

www.thinkport.org
Offers classroom activity kits, themes, and online field trips related to Maryland State curriculum

www.teachervision.com
Offers many lesson plans, graphic organizers, and themes from the Learning Network Teacher Channel

www.oz-teachernet.edu.au/projects
Provides online curriculum projects

Selected Subject Areas

Art
www.carlemuseum.org/
Eric Carle Museum of Picture Book Art
Lists books and art activities for children of all ages

Geography
www.nationalgeographic.com
Provides National Geographic for Kids videos and games as well as photography and information on the planet

Math
www.goenc.com
Eisenhower National Clearinghouse for Mathematics Lessons and activities by keyword, grade level, as well as standards and frameworks

Music
www.kididdles.com
Suggests a variety of songs, lyrics, and provides printables for children

Science
www.nasa.gov
Lists classroom materials organized by keywords, grade level, and subject as well as a wealth of links to further information

Spelling
www.spellingcity.com/
Provides online spelling practice, customized spelling lists, and spelling games and activities

DIVERSITY

National Education Association (NEA)
www.nea.org/tools/28978.htm
Click on "Promising Practices" for links to diversity toolkit, multicultural curriculum resources, culturally responsive teaching, and other web resources

Family Equality Council
www.familyequality.org/pdf/openingdoors.pdf
Offers information and educational materials, such as *Opening Doors and Opening More Doors*, to help teachers provide a safe and welcoming school environment for children of lesbian and gay parents

Multicultural Education Pavilion
www.edchange.org/handouts.html
Lists resources for educational equity, history and social studies, and class, poverty, and equity in education

National Association for the Education of Young Children
www.naeyc.org/yc/pastissues/2005/november
Offers an entire journal devoted to diversity issues and ideas

National Association for the Education of Young Children Code of Ethical Conduct and Statement of Commitment
www.naeyc.org/files/naeyc/file/positions/PSETH05.pdf
A position statement of the National Association for the Education of Young Children and Statement of Commitment, revised April, 2005; endorsed by the Association for Childhood Education International

Reading Is Fundamental
www.rif.org/educators/books/Bilingual_versions.mspx
Has an accessible list of bilingual versions of popular children's books

MISCELLANEOUS

Parents and Families
www.zerotothree.org/magic
Download a series of five booklets, endorsed by the Academy of Pediatrics, that tracks key developmental stages over the first 15 months of life

Library of Congress Information System Database for Teachers
www.loc.gov/teachers
Provides ready-to-use classroom materials created by teachers to bring the Library's resources into the classroom

The Smithsonian
www.smithsonianeducation.org/educators/
Offers access to educational resources by keyword, grade level, and subject area that are aligned to state standards

SOFTWARE EVALUATION CRITERIA

Technology has become an integral and accessible part of children's learning. Here are criteria for selecting and using software with young children.

Technical Features
Are the basic function keys (e.g., delete, return) used appropriately?

Can children easily start, stop, and move about in the program with little or no help?

Can children save or print their work?

Learning Features
Are there visual, auditory, and tactile features that make it easy for the child to understand?

Can the learner control the pace and path of the program (e.g., make it faster or slower)?

Do children receive quick feedback so they stay involved in learning?

Content Features
Do the activities help the child learn new content, processes, or skills?

Can the learner explore concepts on several levels of difficulty?

Developmentally Appropriate Features
Are the content, skills, or processes used appropriate to the age range suggested?

Does the program enable children to be playful or construct elements on their own (e.g., draw pictures, move characters, create stories)?

Is there a range of activities that differ in complexity (e.g., does a mathematics program have activities that include one-to-one correspondence, estimation, and simple addition)?

Do children experience success when using this program?

Sources: From "Thoughts on Technology and Education," by B. Bowman & E. Beyer, 1994, in J. Wright & D. Shade (Eds.), *Young Children: Active Learners in a Technological Age* (pp. 19–30), Washington, DC: National Association for the Education of Young Children; "Children and Technology," by J. Isenberg & T. Rosegrant, 1995, in J. Moyer (Ed.), *Selecting Educational Equipment and Materials for School and Home* (pp. 25–29), Wheaton, MD: Association for Childhood Education International; "Educational Technology in the Early and Primary Years," by S. Swaminathan & J. Wright, 2003, in J. Isenberg & M. Jalongo (Eds.), *Major Trends and Issues: Challenges, Controversies, and Insights* (2nd ed., pp. 136–150), New York, NY: Teachers College Press; and "Using Technology as a Teaching Tool," NAEYC, November 2003, *Young Children, 58*(6).

GLOSSARY

A

absorbent mind—a concept from the Montessori approach to education that considers children to be capable of retaining information long before it is formally taught to them (Chapter 3)

academic concerns—the teacher's awareness of the learning standards, subject matter, and student understanding of content (Chapter 1)

accommodation—the cognitive process of changing existing mental structures to incorporate new information (Chapter 6)

accountability—public demand for evidence from teachers and schools showing that the benefits of education are well worth the money invested (Chapter 3)

ACEI—Association for Childhood Education International; a professional organization dedicated to supporting the development and learning of children from birth through adolescence (Chapter 13)

achievement test—a formal assessment that is used to determine the extent to which a child has acquired certain information or skills that are identified as curricular objectives (Chapter 10)

active—one of the characteristics of reflective practice through which teachers search energetically for information that affects the quality of life in their classrooms (Chapter 1)

activities/lessons—specific learning experiences, designed by the teacher or together with a child or children, to meet the intended outcomes, goals, and objectives (Chapter 9)

adaptation—a principle of Piaget's cognitive developmental theory that looks at how the mind develops cognitive structures to make sense of the outside world and refines ways of categorizing and storing information (Chapter 6)

adult-guided experiences—activities that reflect the teacher's goal and are initiated and directed by the adult to promote the children's engagement (Chapter 6)

affective domain objectives—objectives that have more to do with attitudes, emotions, and values than with cognitive skills (Chapter 9)

alternative assessment—performance assessment task that emphasizes the practical application of skills, as it is more relevant to what children are likely to encounter outside the classroom (Chapter 10)

ambiance—the general feeling or tone of an environment; *ambiance* refers to sensory information that increases comfort, calm, understanding, and learning (Chapter 7)

anti-bias education—a perspective on education that respects the right of all children to learn, thrive, achieve their full potential, and become contributing members of a democratic society (Chapter 4)

assessment—formal and informal evidence to document that children have learned the stated objective (Chapter 8)

assessment in early childhood—methods of evaluation that document the individual child's progress, the achievements of a group, or the quality of the curriculum and program (Chapter 10)

assimilation—a principle from Piaget's cognitive developmental theory that refers to the process of taking in new information and incorporating it into existing structures in the brain (Chapter 6)

assistive technology—refers to any item or device that improves mobility and communication, particularly for children with special needs (Chapter 6)

association—a principle from the behavioral theory of learning that occurs when a person connects what was learned in one situation to another situation (Chapter 6)

attachment—a process in which infants establish one or more emotional ties to another human being; essential for children's mental health (Chapter 5)

authentic assessment—a performance assessment task that emphasizes the practical application of skills; as such, it is more relevant to what children are likely to encounter outside the classroom (Chapter 10)

authentic learning—generally resembles situations that children will encounter outside of the classroom; develops learners who see possibilities, want to know about things, and use what they are learning (Chapter 6)

autoeducation—learning activities chosen by the children that involve self-correcting materials so that children will know when a task has been completed correctly (Chapter 3)

autonomy—a fundamental human need; the need to exert an influence on decisions and events rather than feeling powerless and the victim of circumstance (Chapter 11)

B

Bank Street—an approach to education that follows John Dewey's Progressive philosophy and emphasizes respecting, understanding, and furthering young children's development (Chapter 3)

baseline—provides information on the starting point for the child before he or she begins a task, a curriculum, or the program (Chapter 10)

basic needs—part of Maslow's theory of human motivation based upon a hierarchy of universal needs; basic needs include both physiological needs (e.g., food and drink) and safety and survival needs (e.g., physical and psychological security) (Chapter 5)

behavioral perspective—view of curriculum that measures changes or tests students' achievement in particular skill areas; explicitly teaches and tests curriculum standards; and looks at the behaviors that children should learn (Chapter 8)

behavioral theory—identifies all learning in terms of behavior that can be observed, measured, and recorded (Chapter 6)

bi-directional social and cultural contexts—a key concept of Bronfenbrenner's ecological systems theory that the developing child is affected by the interrelated factors of the family, educational settings, community, and broader society (Chapter 5)

biological influences—factors that originate in the genes and determine things such as height, weight, metabolism, and brain development (Chapter 5)

bottom-up perspective—a program evaluation that focuses on the quality of the daily experience of the child in the program (Chapter 10)

C

caring—a genuine concern for and respect of others (Chapter 1)

caring community of learners—(Chapter 7); *See classroom community*

cephalocaudal development—a developmental principle that describes the direction maturation takes; it begins with the head and works its way down from the head to the neck, trunk, and so forth (Chapter 5)

child advocacy—action taken on behalf of children that supports families and argues for the cause of high-quality programs (Chapter 2)

child advocate—one who goes beyond common decency or expectations in defense of children, families, and the profession of education (Chapter 2)

child guidance—process of leading young children to more socially acceptable ways of handling powerful emotions and coping with the inevitable conflicts of interacting with others (Chapter 11)

child-guided experiences—planned happenings that enable children to pursue their interests and select activities with the teacher's support (Chapter 6)

chronosystem—part of Bronfenbrenner's ecological systems theory that includes the dimensions of time with ever-changing life events as they affect the child; can be external, such as a death or divorce, or internal, such as the child's growth process (Chapter 5)

classical conditioning—a principle from the behavioral theory of learning that occurs when a person generalizes between events to learn (Chapter 6)

classroom community—the positive group spirit that exists when all children's needs for autonomy, relatedness, and competence are met (Chapter 11)

climate—the feeling children get from the overall environment that dictates to what extent they will feel valued and be productive, engaged learners (Chapter 7)

cluster-style seating—arranging desks and tables so that small numbers of children can work face-to-face in small groups in the classroom setting (Chapter 7)

code of ethics—statement based on the core values of our profession that educators must adhere to in their work (Chapter 4)

cognitive domain objectives—one of Bloom's three domains of learning outcomes that focus on thinking and reasoning abilities, such as recalling or applying information (Chapter 9)

cognitive play—a type of organized play that developmentally reflects children's ages, understandings, and experiences (Chapter 6)

community of learners—(Chapter 7); *See classroom community*

competence—the human need to accomplish new things, acquire skills, and successfully put these things to use (Chapter 11)

computer drawing programs—software that allows children to create illustrations and manipulate shapes to make a picture or pictures (Chapter 6)

concept—a mental picture of a concept or idea that is formed by combining all of its aspects (Chapter 9)

concept web—a visual illustration of a big idea's connections and organization, often used as a curriculum planning tool (Chapter 9)

concrete operational stage—Piaget's third stage of cognitive development that occurs from 7–12 years; characterized by the ability to use logical thought to solve concrete problems related to concepts of space, time, causality, and numbers (Chapter 5)

construction of knowledge—the active process of making sense of experiences by building one's own knowledge (Chapter 6)

constructivist perspective—view that emphasizes the active role of the learner in building understanding; adults encourage children to explore their world, discover knowledge, reflect, and think critically (Chapter 8)

constructivist theory—a theory of learning that focuses on how people make meaning both on their own and in interaction with the environment and with others (Chapter 6)

content—what children are expected to learn (Chapter 8); the actual subject matter expected to be taught (Chapter 9)

content areas—the four basic subject areas of literacy, mathematics, science, and social studies (Chapter 8)

content standards—what learners should know and be able to do in the subject areas at specific grade levels, which includes the knowledge, skills, and dispositions toward learning that children need to develop (Chapter 8)

cooperative learning—learning that occurs when students work together to help each other learn (Chapter 7)

cultural capital—a person's access to relevant resources, power to effect positive changes in the environment, and esteem within the community that are necessary for success (Chapter 12)

cultural competence—understanding and appreciating varying cultures (Chapter 12)

cultural influences—factors of human development that include family, peers, community, and the media (Chapter 5)

cultural setting—the values, behaviors, languages, dialects, and feelings about being part of a group that form a particular context (Chapter 5)

culturally responsive—understanding and appreciating one's own backgrounds as well as the backgrounds of others (Chapter 4 and Chapter 7)

culturally responsive curriculum—a curriculum that acknowledges diversity in the classroom and takes cultural meanings and styles into account when developing curriculum and responding to students (Chapter 8)

curriculum—what children actually experience in schools from arrival to departure; reflects the philosophy, goals, objectives, and child outcomes of the program, classroom, or school district (Chapter 8)

D

daily plans—the schedule and activities for each school day, written by the teacher (Chapter 9)

development—the complex and dynamic cognitive, language, physical, motor, social, emotional, and moral processes that change throughout a lifetime (Chapter 5)

developmental considerations—the need to examine the learners' needs and motivations and match them to teaching strategies and learning activities (Chapter 1)

developmental delay—educational term used to describe a nonspecific disability that affects children's learning (Chapter 5)

developmental domains—areas of children's development that are associated with whole child learning and include the aesthetic, affective, cognitive, language, physical, and social domains (Chapter 8)

developmental screening—a simplified, quick scoring procedure designed to identify children who should receive further diagnostic assessment (Chapter 10)

developmentally appropriate practice (DAP)—set of principles that centers on what children know and can do (Chapter 8); practice that requires teachers to make decisions based on the knowledge of typical growth and development of children (Chapter 9)

diagnostic assessment—process used to identify those children with a disability or specific area of academic weakness (Chapter 10)

differentiation—practice of skillfully adapting curriculum to the needs of all learners in the classroom (Chapter 3 and Chapter 9)

digital literacy—having a working knowledge of technological skills (Chapter 6)

Direct Instruction—an approach to teaching that follows a predetermined, sequenced pattern of instruction; repetition, correction of errors, and praise are educationally beneficial (Chapter 3)

disability—an inability to do something specific, such as walk, hear, or see, or a diminished capacity, or impairment, to act in a specific way, such as pronouncing words clearly (Chapter 5)

discovery learning—a constructivist-based approach to education that uses inquiry-based instruction (Chapter 6)

disillusionment—the gap between what teaching is like ideally and in reality and the resulting disappointment when problems arise and are not quickly and easily resolved (Chapter 13)

disposition—one's inwardly motivated habits of mind and characteristic ways of approaching a situation; a person's inherent qualities of mind and character (Chapter 1)

diversity—important differences between and among individuals that contribute to their definition of self; includes, but is not limited to, such characteristics as race, gender, religious affiliation, and socioeconomic status (Chapter 4)

E

early childhood program—a planned way of supporting the care and education of young children from birth through age 8 that includes all domains of development—physical, cognitive, emotional, and social (Chapter 3)

early learning standards—a set of expectations for children's learning and development in all domains and developmental stages that provides the foundation for later learning (Chapter 8)

ecological contexts—environmental influences on development that are a major part of Bronfenbrenner's theory of development (Chapter 5)

e-learning—the act of acquiring knowledge and skills using electronic technologies such as the Internet (Chapter 6)

emergent curriculum—a curriculum that is responsive to children's interests, needs, prior knowledge, cultural backgrounds, and questions (Chapter 3 and Chapter 8)

emotion regulation—involves the human ability to start, change, or stop internal feelings and adjust emotion-related physical responses and goals accordingly (Chapter 11)

environmental influences—factors that are external and shape behavior, such as the effects of language, nutrition, and health care on human development (Chapter 5)

equilibration—a Piagetian cognitive process that creates a balance between a new bit of knowledge and the old information in order to understand the new information and integrate it into mental structures (Chapter 6)

equipment—refers to the large, more costly items in and around a classroom, such as classroom furniture and outdoor structures (Chapter 7)

ethic of care—Nel Noddings's concept that it is a teacher's responsibility and commitment to provide an appropriate amount of support to each child to increase his or her participation, achieve a sense of belonging, and help make learning meaningful (Chapter 7)

ethical teachers—educators who use moral principles to guide behavior and identify and empathize with the welfare of others beyond duty or common decency (Chapter 4)

exceptional learners—refers either to children with disabilities or children with gifts and talents (Chapter 5)

exceptionalities—a term that covers the entire ability spectrum; refers to children with disabilities or children with gifts and talents (Chapter 5 and Chapter 6)

exosystem—part of Bronfenbrenner's ecological systems theory that links two or more social settings, one of which does not include the child, but indirectly influences the child (e.g. the parent's workplace and the educational system) (Chapter 5)

experiential curriculum—an approach that emphasizes what children actually experience and learn; views knowledge as constantly changing and seeks to develop a curriculum that is relevant to each learner; in this approach, a teacher uses experience-based learning matched with students' needs and interests as the source of curriculum (Chapter 8)

F

family—an exclusive group of people who share a close relationship and are usually bound by similar attitudes, morals, and insights (Chapter 12)

family engagement—behavior with parents and families that goes beyond simply attending school conferences—it includes the family's decisions about children's care and education, sharing of information with school personnel, discussion and supervision within the home, teaching/learning activities at sites other than school, and interactions with school personnel through means other than the school context (Chapter 12)

family support—practice of the school reaching out to help the family unit; comes in three forms: informational (school calendar, classroom newsletter), material (links to intervention services), and emotional (telephone calls and individual meetings) (Chapter 12)

fine motor skills—also known as small muscle skills; refers to the process of acquiring greater control, dexterity, and coordination in tasks such as drawing and writing (Chapter 5)

formal operations stage—Piaget's fourth stage of cognitive development that occurs from 12 years and beyond; stage marks the beginning of logical and scientific thinking and is characterized by the ability to make predictions, think hypothetically, and handle abstract concepts (Chapter 5 and Chapter 6)

G

goals—the broad purposes for learning that are stated as outcomes (Chapter 9)

gross motor skills—also known as large muscle skills such as running, and kicking that prepare children for the more complex coordination needed to play organized sports (Chapter 5)

growth needs—part of Maslow's hierarchy of needs theory; growth needs emerge as children's basic needs are being met and include the need for *love and belonging* (e.g., being accepted and belonging to a group both in the family and in the school) and the need for *esteem* that comes from recognition, approval, and achievement from both peers and adults (Chapter 5)

H

Head Start—the only federally funded early childhood program in the United States that was originally part of the war on poverty in the 1960s; its mission is to promote school readiness by enhancing the social and cognitive development of children through the provision of educational, health, nutritional, social, and other services to enrolled children and families (Chapter 3)

heterogeneous—occurs when children are grouped with others of different backgrounds and abilities (Chapter 4)

hidden curriculum—unofficial procedures and the automatic responses that support or weaken student achievement and may reflect biases; also includes the lessons that are learned but not written down anywhere (Chapter 4)

High/Scope—a curriculum model based on Piaget's cognitive-developmental theory that believes children need to actively build their own understandings through hands-on activities (Chapter 3)

higher-order thinking skills—refers to more complex reasoning skills such as synthesizing, analyzing, reasoning, comprehending, application, and evaluation (Chapter 6)

history—the story of what preceded us; our chronological past (Chapter 2)

home visit—a face-to-face personal interview with one or more members of a child's family that takes place in their home, which can have goals in any/all developmental areas (Chapter 10)

homogeneous—when children are grouped with others of similar backgrounds and abilities (Chapter 4)

hundred languages of children—the Reggio Emilia philosophy reflected in the belief that children represent their knowledge in many, many different ways (Chapter 3)

I

inclusion—the idea that in a democratic society, every child merits and receives educational opportunities and experiences that other children get (Chapter 4 and Chapter 5)

inclusive learning environment—a classroom that has children with exceptionalities learning alongside their typically developing peers (Chapter 7)

Individuals with Disabilities Education Improvement Act (IDEIA)—federal law that identifies 11 different disabilities that qualify children for special education services (Chapter 5)

inside perspective—a view of program evaluation that deals with the working conditions experienced by teachers (Chapter 10)

instruction—a plan for teaching children content and processes; the way the teacher will teach the given material (content) (Chapter 8)

INTASC—acronym standing for "Interstate New Teacher Assessment and Support Consortium." A group that has created a set of performance standards for beginning teachers (Chapter 13)

integrated curriculum—a curriculum approach that joins learning in more than one developmental domain, more than one content area, or across domains and content areas (Chapter 8)

intentional teaching—method of teaching that does not wait for development to occur spontaneously; rather, it engages student interest, builds motivation, and encourages each child to become fully engaged in learning activities (Chapter 3)

intentionality—the deliberate decisions that adults make on children's behalf to promote children's learning and development (Chapter 8 and Chapter 9)

interdisciplinary approaches—approaches to education emphasizing the connections that exist between and among different subject areas (Chapter 3)

K

knowledge-centered perspective—a curriculum approach that focuses on the specific content knowledge (e.g., science, art, language) in which each subject area has its own way of conducting inquiry (Chapter 8)

K-W-L strategy—an advance organizer that asks children what they know (K) about the topic, what they want to know about it (W), and—after studying the topic—noting what they learned (L) (Chapter 9)

L

learner-centered focus—uses five principles of learning to plan curriculum: the learning needs of diverse learners, the impact of brain research on learning, lifelong learning, social and emotional learning as well as intellectual learning, and child-guided learning (Chapter 6)

learning—an act, process, or experience of gaining knowledge, skill, and insight (Chapter 6)

learning centers—the well-defined, organized areas of the classroom set aside for specific learning purposes, so that children can complete tasks without the teacher's constant presence and direction (Chapter 7)

learning cycle—a conceptualization of the learning process that begins with awareness, moves to exploration, then to inquiry, and finally to utilization (Chapter 6)

learning environment—all the influences that affect children and adults in early childhood classrooms (Chapter 7)

learning styles—how individuals process thoughts and feelings (Chapter 6)

lifelong learning—the disposition to become knowledgeable, responsible, and contributing adults throughout life (Chapter 6)

limited motor ability—a way of describing a child whose restricted ability to move his or her body has a negative effect on that child's participation in a given activity (Chapter 7)

long-term planning—very general plans that serve as a framework for overall planning; includes yearly, semester, quarterly, thematic unit, and project planning (Chapter 9)

M

macrosystem—part of Bronfenbrenner's ecological systems theory that includes the values, beliefs, laws, and customs of a child's culture and ethnicity that are transmitted from generation to generation and affect the interactions among the family, school, and community in the child's immediate world (Chapter 5)

materials—classroom items such as crayons, paints, and paper that are regularly replaced or replenished (Chapter 7)

maturation theory—a theoretical orientation that views development as a genetically determined process that, with proper support, unfolds naturally and follows a relatively predictable (Chapter 6)

meaningful curriculum—a curriculum that is relevant to a particular group of children and considers their developmental needs and interests, the environment, the culture in which they live, and ways to include each child in the learning process (Chapter 8)

mentoring programs—planned programs in which more experienced teachers become role models and a source of support and advice for less experienced teachers; new teachers often are assigned to a mentor in schools (Chapter 13)

mesosystem—part of Bronfenbrenner's ecological systems theory that links two or more of the child's microsystems, such as the connections between the family and school (Chapter 5)

microsystem—part of Bronfenbrenner's ecological systems theory where the child lives and experiences most of his or her activities and relationships, such as in the home, school, neighborhood, and with friends (Chapter 5)

Montessori—an approach to education designed by Maria Montessori that stresses a carefully structured environment with minimal interruptions and time to explore freely as a route to learning (Chapter 3)

multiple intelligences (MI)—the eight different frames of mind introduced by Howard Gardner: linguistic, logical/mathematical, musical, visual/spatial, bodily/kinesthetic, interpersonal, intrapersonal, and naturalist (Chapter 6)

N

NAEYC—National Association for the Education of Young Children; a large professional organization that promotes excellence in early childhood education (Chapter 1)

neurons—cells in the brain that send information to other cells (Chapter 5)

normative descriptions—systematic descriptions of children's development in all domains, including physical, language, intellectual, and social (Chapter 6)

O

objective—the specific behavior, skill, or concept the teacher wishes the child to attain as a result of the lessons and experiences (Chapter 9)

observation—the act of objectively watching and gathering data about a child in a particular setting; can be for a range of goals in any/all areas of development (Chapter 10)

observational learning—occurs when children watch the behaviors of peers and adults, form mental pictures of them, and later try to imitate those behaviors (Chapter 6)

open-ended materials—materials that lead to multiple uses, encourage thinking about possibilities, and invite a variety of children's responses through exploration, experimentation, and original thinking (Chapter 9)

open-ended software—a term that refers to computer software that encourages children to work together to create a quality digital product (Chapter 6)

operant conditioning—a form of learning in which a response either increases or decreases after being reinforced (Chapter 6)

outside-inside perspective—program evaluation that emphasizes the relationship between early childhood educators and the children's families (Chapter 10)

outside perspective—program evaluation that deals with the relationship between the educational program and the larger community/social context in which it operates (Chapter 10)

P

pedagogy—a teacher's specific knowledge about how to teach children effectively; the methods and practices associated with effective teaching (Chapter 1)

performance assessment—the use of a real-world task to evaluate what a student knows, understands, and can put to use (Chapter 10)

performance standards—goals that state what children can actually do in a particular subject area or a particular developmental domain (Chapter 8)

persistent—the disposition to think through difficult issues and pursue possible solutions even when the task may become challenging or tiring (Chapter 1)

physical environment—the actual classroom elements, such as the space, room arrangement, schedule, equipment, and materials of the classroom/school (Chapter 7)

physical health and safety needs—refers to environmental elements, such as having adequate space and appropriate entrances and exits in the classroom/school; also includes food, clothing, shelter, rest, medical care, and a balance between active and quiet activities (Chapter 7)

planning—a teacher's ability to think ahead and anticipate what is likely to make a learning experience run smoothly; involves making decisions about content, activities, grouping, materials needed, assessment, and management (Chapter 9)

plasticity—the brain's ability to change and be flexible (Chapter 5)

play—behavior that is symbolic, meaningful, active, pleasurable, voluntary, intrinsically motivating, rule-governed, and episodic (Chapter 6)

posttest—a test that is administered after the instruction has taken place; results of the posttest often are compared with pretest results as a way of documenting what was learned (Chapter 10)

predictable environments—settings with simple routines and rituals that help children to feel secure and safe, and to understand what behaviors are expected of them; predictable environments also have flexible structures that make it easy for everyone to work and be productive (Chapter 7)

preoperational stage—Piaget's second stage of cognitive development that occurs from 2–7 years; during this stage children typically have an increased ability to think symbolically and conceptually about objects and people outside of their immediate environment, which is evident through children's increasing use of language and imaginative play (Chapter 5 and Chapter 6)

prepared environment—a classroom setting that is carefully structured in advance by the teacher as a way to foster greater independence, encourage children's exploration, and promote self-evaluation (Chapter 3)

pretest—assessment of learner's performance before teaching a particular concept or skill to gauge the academic level of each child before teaching the new concept/skill (Chapter 10)

privacy—a principle of classroom design; the idea that children need private spaces within the classroom environment to nurture their emotional health (Chapter 7)

proactive—refers to a teacher's ability to "troubleshoot"; to anticipate questions from children and address issues within the classroom before problems occur (Chapter 1)

problem-solving and inquiry-oriented software—computer software that provides children with possibilities to gather information, make decisions, and test their solutions (Chapter 6)

procedures—specific mental processes; the steps a teacher plans to take to teach a lesson (Chapter 9)

processes—ways of thinking about and making sense of information (Chapter 9)

professional development—the knowledge and skills that promote personal development and career advancement; this is a cyclical process that should begin with preservice and continue through to retirement if the teacher is to become increasingly efficient and effective (Chapter 13)

professional disposition—a teacher's commitment to act in consistently responsible and ethical ways (Chapter 1)

professional growth cycle—the formal sequence of attaining professional development in order to become a more efficient teacher (Chapter 13)

professional teacher ethics—the personal, collective obligation to what is fair and just for all children, families, and colleagues (Chapter 4)

program model—a detailed approach to providing a high-quality program for young children that is supported by theory and research collected over an extended period of time (Chapter 3)

Progressive Education—an educational philosophy based on John Dewey's work. It contends that, in a democratic society, the overarching purpose of schooling is to prepare students to exert a positive influence on their world, both now and in the future (Chapter 6)

project approach—a strategy for organizing curriculum that revolves around the planned, in-depth investigations of a topic and that answers questions posed by the children or adults working with the children (Chapter 9)

project potential—the open-ended activities that have the possibility to emerge from the children's deepening understanding of the concept being studied (Chapter 9)

projects—focused, in-depth studies of something that children, in collaboration with teachers, initiate, direct, organize, and develop as part of the curriculum (Chapter 8)

prosocial skills—a set of interpersonal and intrapersonal skills that include the ability to cooperate and share in order to form and maintain healthy relationships with others (Chapter 4)

proximodistal development—a developmental principle that describes the direction maturation takes; it begins with the large trunk and arm muscles and works its way out to the smaller muscles in children's hands and fingers (Chapter 5)

psychological health and safety needs—refers to a child's need for a consistent, predictable relationship with a caring adult who has high, positive expectations, encourages strong peer acceptance, and builds children's self-respect (Chapter 7)

psychomotor domain objectives—objectives that refer to learning physical skills, such as holding a pencil or using science equipment appropriately (Chapter 9)

punishment—an act used in operant conditioning that consists of adverse consequences, such as the withdrawal of special privileges, as a way to stop/decrease inappropriate behaviors (Chapter 6)

R

rational—a characteristic of reflective practice; it refers to a person who does not blindly follow trends, act on impulses, or do whatever is most expedient; rather, he or she uses logic and ethical reasoning to guide professional practice (Chapter 1)

readiness test—a brief achievement test that is designed to determine a child's relative preparedness to participate in a particular classroom program or area of the curriculum (e.g., reading readiness test) (Chapter 10)

reflective practice—taking the time to rethink and rework teaching plans, strategies, words, and actions and scrutinizing them through the lens of ethical decision making and a teacher's careful consideration of the effects that her or his behavior may have on self and others (Chapter 1)

Reggio Emilia—a program model from an area of Italy that advocates the "emergent curriculum" and the "project approach"; values the potential of each child and each child's capabilities and the right to be part of and contribute to the community in which children are involved (Chapter 3)

reinforcement—a behaviorist principle that uses consequences—such as rewards—to change or strengthen behavior (Chapter 6)

reinforcers—the use of praise and other forms of encouragement (e.g. smiles, stickers) to continue/increase appropriate behaviors (Chapter 6)

relatedness—a human being's need for love, affirmation, a sense of connectedness with others, and belonging to a group (Chapter 11)

rote learning—learning that focuses mainly on memorization, imitation, and recitation of passive responses (Chapter 6)

routines—the regular and predictable activities that form the basis of the daily schedule and ensure effective use of time and space (e.g., cleanup time, starting the school day) (Chapter 7)

S

scaffolding—a support system that teachers and peers provide children to help them learn a new skill or to accomplish a task that they could not do on their own (Chapter 6)

schedule—a timeline for organizing who does what and when throughout the day (Chapter 7)

science process skills—skills of observing, comparing, classifying, measuring, communicating, inferring, and predicting that lead to the development of content knowledge and concept development in science (Chapter 8)

self-actualization—the human need to use one's abilities and talents to the fullest (Chapter 5)

self-concept—an individual's knowledge and beliefs about herself or himself that influence learning and interactions with others (Chapter 4)

self-regulation—a person's independent ability to start, change, or stop verbal or motor behaviors in varied contexts to achieve goals (Chapter 11)

sensitive periods—the particular times in a child's growth when certain concepts could be more readily learned and nurtured, as compared to other times; for example, young children often learn to speak a language without an accent, whereas adults rarely do (Chapter 3)

sensorimotor stage—Piaget's first stage of cognitive development that occurs from 0–2 years during which infants and toddlers use their senses and reflexes to respond to their immediate world, but do not think conceptually (Chapter 5 and Chapter 6)

short-term planning—specific and detailed planning that addresses the day-to-day decisions a teacher makes (Chapter 9)

skeptical—a characteristic of reflective practitioners, which enables them to realize that there are few absolutes in educational theories and practices and that they should use evidence to guide decision making (Chapter 1)

skilled dialogue—communication that embraces respect, reciprocity, and responsiveness when interacting with children and families from diverse cultural and linguistic backgrounds (Chapter 4)

social environment—the human interactions between and among children and adults that consist of content, experiences, values, goals, and daily organization that occur within the classroom (Chapter 7)

social learning environment—the relationships in the classroom that affect how children think, feel, and act (Chapter 7)

social learning theory—Bandura's theory that suggests children learn social behaviors primarily through observation and imitation, especially of their parents (Chapter 6)

social play—describes a category of children's play that is based on their social interactions with peers (Chapter 6)

social setting—refers to the significant people in children's lives who influence their development (Chapter 5)

sociocultural factors—the factors that include family, temperament, learning style, and experiences in specific social contexts (Chapter 5)

software—the instructions that make the computer do something specific (Chapter 6)

spiral curriculum—a curriculum approach that introduces children to "big ideas" or concepts in all subjects in the early childhood years and continues to revisit them more deeply in subsequent years (Chapter 6)

standards—the benchmarks that are used to guide curriculum development and plan for instruction and often are identified at the national, state, and local levels (Chapter 3)

standards-based curriculum—a curriculum that specifies what children are expected to learn; it focuses on practices that meet those standards, and continually assesses children to see if the given standards have been met (Chapter 8)

strategic thinking—the process of gathering information, forming ideas, and planning action (Chapter 6)

strategies—refers to how to teach content (Chapter 8)

student-led conference—a conference where children are active participants with their teachers and their families in talking about their educational progress (Chapter 10)

student work portfolio—a systematic, purposeful compilation of evidence that shows a child's development and learning over time through an organized collection of work samples (Chapter 10)

synapses—connections in the brain that carry messages between neurons (Chapter 5)

T

taught curriculum—what is actively observed as being taught; the teacher's way of delivering the program (Chapter 7 and Chapter 8)

teacher accountability to standards—a teacher who is knowledgeable about and uses the local, state, and national standards in his or her planning, teaching, and evaluation (Chapter 9)

teaching effectiveness—how teachers integrate research-based practices into their teaching and use careful analysis of student work to make data-driven decisions (Chapter 1)

teaching philosophy—a concise statement about the beliefs, values, and attitudes that influence a teacher's thoughts, actions, and interactions (Chapter 2)

temperament—a person's characteristic way of responding to a given situation (e.g., anxious, calm) (Chapter 5)

test—a sample of behavior in a particular area or domain that is used for assessment purposes (e.g., a reading achievement test) (Chapter 10)

testing—a systematic way that teachers elicit specific responses from children to evaluate their learning (Chapter 10)

thematic approach—planning that involves a variety of integrated learning experiences designed around a big idea, question, or problem that helps children make connections and furthers their understandings of the world around them. It has intellectual integrity, is relevant and

meaningful, and represents in-depth thinking and problem solving that can be studied at different age or grade levels (Chapter 9)

thematic units—long-term instructional plans that relate learning experiences to key concepts or ideas about a particular topic of study; last over a period of time (Chapter 8)

theory—an organized system of knowledge that describes, explains, and predicts behavior (Chapter 5)

timing—a teacher's decision about when children can best learn the material (Chapter 8)

top-down perspective—a view of program evaluation that examines easily observed and measured characteristics (Chapter 10)

traditional perspective—a curriculum perspective that focuses on a common body of knowledge and skills that teachers are obligated to transmit to children (Chapter 8)

U

universal prekindergarten—government-offered care and/or education programs for preschoolers that are free and available to everyone; common in, for example, Great Britain, Sweden, and Australia (Chapter 3)

universal rights of children—a government-given set of rights that states no child should be treated unfairly on any basis (Chapter 4)

W

webbing—a curriculum planning tool used to organize possible key concepts, ideas, and learning experiences and connections among them (Chapter 9)

WebQuests—an inquiry-oriented activity in which some or all of the information comes from resources on the Internet (Chapter 6)

weekly plans—a schedule for the planned activities for every day of the school week (Chapter 9)

whole child—an early childhood philosophy that considers all aspects (physical, cognitive, social, and emotional) of the child's development when planning activities (Chapter 5)

written curriculum—a comprehensive document for each grade level that contains the general goals, objectives, or outcomes that every child should meet; a sequence of study for selected topics and suggested learning activities (Chapter 7 and Chapter 8)

Y

yearly plans—very general plans that contain the overall knowledge, skills, and attitudes to be taught, topics of study, and cycles of the school year that will influence planning over the course of the year (Chapter 9)

Z

zone of proximal development (ZPD)—in Vygotsky's theory, the gap between what a child can do independently and what the child can do with the assistance of peers and adults; the ZPD is the place where a task is neither too easy nor too difficult and is the optimal situation for growth (Chapter 6)

REFERENCES

Preface

Hyson, M., & Biggar, H. (2006). NAEYC's standards for early childhood professional preparation: Getting from here to there. In M. Zaslow & I. Martinez-Beck (Eds.), *Critical issues in early childhood professional development* (pp. 283–308). Baltimore, MD: Paul H. Brookes.

Ingersoll, R., & Smith, T. (2003). The wrong solution to the teacher shortage. *Educational Leadership, 60*(8), 30–33.

Isenberg, J. P., & Jalongo, M. R. (2003). *Major trends and issues in early childhood education* (2nd ed.). New York, NY: Teachers College Press.

Johnson, S. M. (2006). *Finders and keepers: Helping new teachers survive and thrive in our schools.* San Francisco, CA: Jossey-Bass.

National Association for the Education of Young Children. (2001). *NAEYC standards for early childhood professional preparation: Initial licensure programs.* Washington, DC: Author.

National Association for the Education of Young Children. (2009). *NAEYC standards for early childhood professional preparation programs.* Washington, DC: Author.

Chapter 1

Ball, D. L. (2000). Bridging practices: Intertwining content and pedagogy in teaching and learning to teach. *Journal of Teacher Education, 51*(3), 241–247.

Belton, V., Thornbury Gould, H., & Scott, J. (2006). Developing the reflective practitioner—Designing an undergraduate class. *Interfaces, 36*(2), 150–164.

Berger, E. (2007). *Parents as partners in education: Families and schools working together* (7th ed.). Upper Saddle River, NJ: Pearson.

Birmingham, C. (2003). Practicing the virtue of reflection in an unfamiliar cultural context. *Theory into Practice, 42*(3), 188–194.

Blank, J. (2009). Life in the village: Teacher community and autonomy in an early childhood education center. *Early Childhood Education Journal, 36,* 373–380.

Bolton, G. (2001). *Reflective practice: Writing and professional development.* London, UK: Paul Chapman.

Boyer, E. L. (1995). *The basic school: A community for learning.* Princeton, NJ: The Carnegie Foundation.

Buchanan, A. M., Baldwin, S. C., & Rudisill, M. E. (2002). Service learning as scholarship in teacher education. *Educational Researcher, 30*(5), 28–34.

Bygdeson-Larsson, K. (2006). Educational Process Reflection (EPR): An evaluation of a model for professional development concerning social interaction and educational climate in the Swedish preschool. *Journal of In-Service Education, 32*(1), 13–31.

Carpenter-LaGattuta, A. (2002). Challenges in multicultural teacher education. *Multicultural Education, 9*(4), 27–29.

Chilvers, D. (2005). Re-thinking reflective practice in the early years. In K. Hirst & C. Nutbrown (Eds.), *Perspectives on early childhood education* (pp. 163–188). Stoke on Kent, UK: Trentham.

Cruickshank, D. (1987). *Reflective teaching.* Reston, VA: Association of Teacher Educators.

Darling-Hammond, L. (2006). *Powerful teacher education: Lessons from exemplary programs.* San Francisco, CA: Jossey-Bass.

Darling-Hammond, L., & Baratz-Snowden, J. (2005). *A good teacher in every classroom: Preparing the highly qualified teachers our children deserve.* San Francisco, CA: Jossey-Bass.

Davis, S. M. (2004). Early childhood student teachers, reflective practice through children's work. *Journal of Early Childhood Teacher Education, 25*(1), 49–59.

De Schipper, E. J., Riksen-Walraven, M. J., Geurts, S. A. E., & deWeerth, C. (2009). Cortisol levels of caregivers in child care centers as related to the quality of their caregiving. *Early Childhood Research Quarterly, 24,* 55–63.

Dewey, J. (1909). *How we think.* London, UK: Heath and Company.

Dewey, J. (1933). *How we think: A restatement of the relation of reflective thinking to the educative process.* Boston, MA: Heath and Company.

Early, D. M., Maxwell, K. L., Burchinal, M., Alva, S., Bender, R. H., Bryant, D., Cai, K., Clifford, R. M., Ebanks, C., Griffin, J. A., Henry, G. T., Howes, C., Iriondo-Perez, J., Jeon, H. J., Mashburn, A. J., Peisner-Feinberg, E., Pianta, R. C., Vandergrift, N., & Zill, N. (2007). Teachers' education, classroom quality, and young children's academic skills: Results from seven studies of preschool programs. *Child Development, 78*(2), 558–580.

Eby, J. W., Herrell, A. L., & Jordan, M. L. (2006). *Teaching in K–12 schools: A reflective action approach* (4th ed.). Upper Saddle River, NJ: Pearson.

Eliason, C., & Jenkins, L. (2007). *A practical guide to early childhood curriculum* (8th ed.). Upper Saddle River, NJ: Pearson.

Epstein, R. (2008). Reflection, perception, and the acquisition of wisdom. *Medical Education, 42*(11), 1048–1050.

Essa, E. (2002). *A practical guide to solving preschool behavior problems* (5th ed.). Belmont, CA: Delmar/Cengage.

Esslen, M., Metzler, S., Pascual-Marqui, R., & Jancke, L. (2008). Pre-reflective and reflective self-reference: A spatiotemporal EEG analysis. *NeuroImage, 42*(1), 437–449.

Falk, B. (2008). *Teaching the way children learn.* New York, NY: Teachers College Press.

Fukkink, R. G., & Lont, A. (2007). Does training matter? A meta-analysis and review of caregiver training studies. *Early Childhood Research Quarterly, 22,* 294–311.

Fuller, F. F., & Bown, O. H. (1975). Becoming a teacher. In K. Ryan (Ed.), *Teacher education: The 47th yearbook of the NSSE, Part II* (pp. 25–52). Chicago, IL: Rand McNally.

Glickman, C. D., & Alridge, D. P. (2001). Going public: The imperative of public education in the 21st century. In A. Lieberman & L. Miller (Eds.), *Teachers caught in the action: Professional development that matters* (pp. 12–22). New York, NY: Teachers College Press.

Gordon, A. M., & Browne, K. W. (2007). *Beginnings and beyond: Foundations of early childhood education* (7th ed.). Belmont, CA: Wadsworth.

Grant, C., & Zeichner, K. (1984). *Preparing for reflective teaching.* Boston, MA: Allyn & Bacon.

Harle, A., & Trudeau, K. (2006). Using reflection to increase children's learning in kindergarten. *Young Children, 61*(4), 101–104.

Helsing, D. (2006). Regarding uncertainty in teachers and teaching. *Teaching and Teacher Education, 23,* 1317–1333.

Jalongo, M. R., & Isenberg, J. P. (1995). *Teachers' stories: From personal narrative to professional insight.* New York, NY: Teachers College Press.

Jalongo, M. R., Rieg, S., & Helterbran, V. (2006). *Planning for learning: Collaborative approaches to lesson design and review.* New York, NY: Teachers College Press.

Jensen, E. (2006). *Enriching the brain: How to maximize every learner's potential.* San Francisco, CA: Jossey-Bass.

Kardos, S. M., Johnson, S. M., Peske, H. G., Kauffman, D., & Liu, E. (2001). Counting on colleagues: New teachers encounter the professional cultures of their schools. *Educational Administration Quarterly, 37*(2), 250–290.

Keiff, J. E. (2008). *Informed advocacy in early childhood care and education: Making a difference for young children and families.* Upper Saddle River, NJ: Pearson.

Kolb, A., & Kolb D. A. (2001) *Experiential learning theory bibliography 1971–2001.* Available online from http://trgmcber.haygroup.com/Products/learning/bibliography.htm.

Kostelnik, M. J., Soderman, A. K., & Whiren, A. P. (2010). *Developmentally appropriate curriculum: Best practices in early childhood education* (5th ed.). Upper Saddle River, NJ: Pearson.

Lampert, M. (2001). *Teaching problems and the problems of teaching.* New Haven, CT: Yale University Press.

Laverick, D. M., & Jalongo, M. R. (Eds.). (2011). *Transitions to early care and education: International perspectives on making schools ready for young children.* New York, NY: Springer.

Lee, H. (2005). Understanding and assessing preservice teachers' reflective thinking. *Teaching & Teacher Education, 21*(6), 699–715.

Li, Y. (2007). Teachers talking about effective practice: Understanding the knowledge and practice of teachers. *Journal of Early Childhood Teacher Education, 28*(3), 301–310.

LoCasale–Crouch, J., Konold, T., Pianta, R., Howes, C., Burchinal, M., Bryant, D., Clifford, R., Early, D., & Barbarin, O. (2007). Observed classroom quality profiles in state-funded pre-kindergarten programs and associations with teacher, program, and classroom characteristics. *Early Childhood Research Quarterly, 22,* 3–17.

Lowe Vandell, D., & Wolfe, B. (2000). *Child care quality: Does it matter and does it need to be improved?* Available online at http://aspe.hhs.gov/hsp/ccquality00/index.htm.

MacDonald, E. (2009). *The mindful teacher.* New York, NY: Teachers College Press.

Many, J., Howard, F., & Hoge, P. (2002). Epistemology and preservice teacher education: How do beliefs about knowledge affect our students' experiences? *English Education, 34*(4), 302–322.

Marotz, L. R., Cross, M. Z., & Rush, J. M. (2008). *Health, safety, and nutrition for the young child* (7th ed.). Belmont, CA: Wadsworth.

Marshall, N. L. (2004). The quality of early child care and children's development. *Current Direction in Psychological Science, 13*(4), 165–168.

Mastrilli, T., & Sardo-Brown, D. (2002). Novice teachers' cases: A vehicle for reflective practice. *Education, 123*(1), 56.

McDonald, J. P. (2001). Students' work and teachers' learning. In A. Lieberman & L. Miller (Eds.), *Teachers caught in the action: Professional development that matters* (pp. 209–235). New York, NY: Teachers College Press.

McGlamery, S., & Harrington, J. (2007). Developing reflective practitioners: The importance of field experience. *Delta Kappa Gamma Bulletin, 73*(3), 33–45.

McMullen, M. B., & Dixon, S. (2006). Research in review: Building on common ground: Unifying practice with infant/toddler specialists though a mindful, relationship-based approach. *Young Children, 61*(4), 46–52.

Nagle, J. F. (2009). Becoming a reflective practitioner in the age of accountability. *The Educational Forum, 73*(1), 76–86.

Nieto, S. (2005). *Why we teach.* New York, NY: Teachers College Press.

Noddings, N. (2006). *Critical lessons: What our schools should teach.* New York, NY: Cambridge University Press.

Ostorga, A. (2006). Developing teachers who are reflective practitioners: Complex process. *Issues in Teacher Education, 15*(2), 5–20.

Paris, C., & Lung, P. (2008). Agency and child-centered practices in novice teachers: Autonomy, efficacy, intentionality, and reflectivity. *Journal of Early Childhood Teacher Education, 29*(3), 253–268.

Perry, D. F., Kaufmann, R. K., & Knitzer, J. (Eds.)., (2007). *Social and emotional health in early childhood: Building bridges between services and systems.* Baltimore, MD: Paul H. Brookes.

Peters, W. H. (2000). Through the looking-glass portfolio: The journey of preservice teachers in becoming reflective practitioners. Urbana, IL: ERIC Clearinghouse. [ERIC Document Reproduction Service No. ED444950].

Poppe, J., & Clothier, S. (2007). The preschool promise: Going to preschool benefits children their entire lives. Can states afford to provide it to all kids? In K. Paciorek (Ed.), *Annual Editions: Early Childhood Education 06/07* (27th ed., pp. 14–17). Dubuque, IA: McGraw-Hill.

Schon, D. A. (1983). *The reflective practitioner: How professionals think in action.* New York, NY: Basic Books.

Schon, D. (1987). *Educating the reflective practitioner: Toward a new design for teaching and learning in the professions.* San Francisco, CA: Jossey-Bass.

Snow, C. E., Griffin, P., & Burns, M. S. (2005). *Knowledge to support the teaching of reading: Preparing teachers for a changing world.* New York, NY: John Wiley & Sons.

Sparks, L. D., & Edwards, J. (2010). *Anti-bias education for young children and ourselves.* Washington, DC: National Association for the Education of Young Children.

Stacey, M. (2009). *Teamwork and collaboration in early years settings.* Exeter, UK: Learning Matters.

Stronge, J. H. (2002). *Qualities of effective teachers.* Alexandria, VA: Association for Supervision and Curriculum Development.

Taggart, G. L., & Wilson, A. P. (2005). *Promoting reflective thinking in teachers: 50 action strategies* (2nd ed.). Thousand Oaks, CA: Corwin.

Tegano, D., & Moran, M. (2005). Conditions and contexts for teacher inquiry: Systematic approaches to preservice teacher collaborative experiences. *New Educator, 1*(4), 287–310.

Trawick-Smith, J. W. (2009). *Early childhood development: A multicultural perspective* (5th ed.). Upper Saddle River, NJ: Pearson.

Whitbeck, D. A. (2000). Born to be a teacher: What am I doing in a college of education? *Journal of Research in Education, 15*(1), 129–136.

Wortham, S. C. (2007). *Assessment in early childhood education* (5th ed.). Upper Saddle River, NJ: Pearson.

Zambo, D. (2007). Childcare workers' knowledge about the brain and developmentally appropriate practice. *Early Childhood Education Journal, 35*(6), 571–577.

Zull, J. (2006). Key aspects of how the brain learns. *New Directions for Adult & Continuing Education, 110,* 3–9.

Children's Books

Wilson, K., & Chapman, J. (2003). *Bear wants more.* New York, NY: Simon & Schuster.

Chapter 2

Addams, J. (1910). *Twenty years at Hull House.* Available online at http://books.google.com/books.

Anderson, C. (2010). Blocks: A versatile learning tool for yesterday, today, and tomorrow. *Young Children, 65*(2), 54–56.

Anderson, L. (1997). Argyris' and Schon's theory on congruence and learning. Available online at www.scu.edu.au/schools/sawd/arr/argyris.html.

Aries, P. (1962). *Centuries of childhood.* London, UK: Jonathan Cape.

Beaty, B. (1995). *Preschool education in America.* New Haven, CT: Yale University Press.

Bloch, M. N., & Price, G. G. (Eds.). (1994). *Essays on the history of early childhood education.* Norwood, NJ: Ablex.

Brosterman, N. (1997). *Inventing kindergarten.* New York, NY: Harry N. Abrams.

Brown, D. F., & Rose, T. D. (1995). Self-reported classroom impact of teachers' theories about learning and obstacles to implementation. *Action in Teacher Education, 17*(1), 20–29.

Buchanan, T. K., Burts, D. C., Bidner, J., White, V. F., & Charlesworth, R. (1998). Predictors of developmental appropriateness of the beliefs and practices of first, second, and third grade teachers. *Early Childhood Research Quarterly, 13*(2), 459–483.

Bullough, R. V., & Gitlin, A. D. (2001). *Becoming a student of teaching* (2nd ed.). New York, NY: RoutledgeFalmer.

Burt, J. L., Ortlieb, E. T., & Cheek Jr., E. H. (2009). An investigation of the impact of racially diverse teachers on the reading skills of fourth-grade students in a one race school. *Reading Improvement, 46*(1), 35–45.

Cassidy, D. J., & Lawrence, J. M. (2000). Teachers' beliefs: The "whys" behind the "how tos" in child care classrooms. *Journal of Research in Childhood Education, 14*(2), 193–204.

Chen, H. (2010). Formal writing assignment for ECED 215: Foundations of Early Childhood. Available online at www.salisbury.edu/wac/instructors/education/downloads/…/chen.doc.

Cleverley, J., & Phillips, D. C. (1986). *Visions of childhood: Influential models from Locke to Spock.* New York, NY: Teachers College Press.

Cooper, H., Allen, A. B., Patall, E. A., & Dent, A. L. (2010). Effects of full-day kindergarten on academic achievement and social development. *Review of Educational Research, 30*(1), 34–70.

DeMause, L. (Ed.). (1974). *The history of childhood.* New York, NY: The Psychohistory Press.

Fass, P. S., & Mason, M. A. (2000). *Childhood in America.* New York, NY: New York University Press.

Free the Slaves and Human Rights Center. (2004). *Hidden slaves: Forced labor in the United States.* Berkley, CA: Human Rights Center. Available online at www.hrcberkeley.org/download/hiddenslaves_report.pdf.

Goffin, S. G., & Lombardi, J. (1988). *Speaking out: Early childhood advocacy.* Washington, DC: National Association for the Education of Young Children.

Hatch J. A., & Freeman, E. B. (1988). Kindergarten philosophies and practices: Perspectives of teachers, principals, and supervisors. *Early Childhood Research Quarterly, 3,* 151–166.

Hewett, V. M. (2001). Examining the Reggio Emilia approach to early childhood education. *Early Childhood Education Journal, 29,* 95–100.

Holt, J. (1992). *How children learn.* Cambridge, MA: De Capo Press.

Hunter, R. (1905). *Poverty.* New York, NY: Macmillan. Available online at http://books.google.com/books.

Jalongo, M. R. (2005). Inspiration from the life of Cora Wilson Stewart, literacy educator. *Early Childhood Education Journal, 32*(5), 281–282.

Jalongo, M. R. (2006). The story of Mary Ellen Wilson: Tracing the origins of child protection in America. *Early Childhood Education Journal, 34*(1), 1–4.

Jalongo, M. R. (2008). "Enriching the brain"—The link between contemporary neuroscience and early childhood traditions. *Early Childhood Education Journal, 35*(6), 487–488.

Jalongo, M. R. (2009). "Little Italian slaves": Lessons Learned from the Padrone Boys. *Early Childhood Education Journal, 36*, 209–212.

Jalongo, M. R. (2010). From urban homelessness to rural work: International origins of the orphan trains. *Early Childhood Education Journal, 38*, 165–170.

Jensen, E. (2005). *Teaching with the brain in mind* (2nd ed.). Alexandria, VA: Association for Supervision and Curriculum Development.

Jensen, E. (2008). *Enriching the brain: How to maximize every learner's potential*. San Francisco, CA: Jossey-Bass.

Kowalski, K., Pretti-Fontczak, K., & Johnson, L. (2001). Preschool teachers' beliefs concerning the importance of various developmental skills and abilities. *Journal of Research in Childhood Education, 16*(1), 5–14.

Lascarides, V. C., & Hinitz, B. F. (2000). *History of early childhood education*. New York, NY: Falmer Press.

Liebovich, B. J., & Adler, S. M. (2009). Teaching advocacy in early years initial teacher education programmes. *Forum, 51*(1), 25–34.

May, H. (2006). "Being Froebelian": An antipodean analysis of the history of advocacy and early childhood. *History of Education, 35*(2), 245–262.

Meyer, R. J. (2005). Taking a stand: Strategies for activism. In K. Paciorek (Ed.), *Annual Editions: Early childhood education 06/07* (27th ed., pp. 28–31). Dubuque, IA: McGraw-Hill.

Mueller, A. (2003). Looking back and looking forward: Always becoming a teacher educator through self-study. *Reflective Practice, 4*(1), 67–84.

Nieto, S., & Bode, P. (2008). *Affirming diversity: The sociopolitical context of multicultural education* (5th ed.). New York, NY: Teachers College Press.

O'Connor, S. (2001). *Orphan trains: The story of Charles Loring Brace and the children he saved and failed*. Chicago, IL: University of Chicago Press.

Osborn, D. K. (1980). *Early childhood education in historical perspective* (2nd ed.). Atlanta, GA: Education Associates.

Pajares, M. F. (1992). Teacher beliefs and educational research: Cleaning up a messy construct. *Review of Educational Research, 62*(3), 307–332.

Patrick, M. D., & Trickel, E. G. (1997). *Orphan trains to Missouri*. Columbia, MO: University of Missouri Press.

Postman, N. (1982). *The disappearance of childhood*. New York, NY: Dell.

Quote DB. (2010). Available online at www.quotedb.com/quotes/2776.

Riis, J. A. (2000). The child-saving movement. In P. S. Fass & M. A. Mason (Eds.), *Childhood in America* (pp. 539–542). New York, NY: New York University Press.

Robinson, A., & Stark, D. R. (2002). *Advocates in action: Making a difference for young children*. Washington, DC: National Association for the Education of Young Children.

Rose, E. (2009). Poverty and parenting: Transforming early education's legacy in the 1960s. *History of Education Quarterly, 49*(2), 222–234.

Sadker, M., Sadker, D., & Zittleman, K. (2008). *Teachers, schools, and society* (8th ed.). New York, NY: McGraw-Hill.

Shapiro, M. S. (1983). *Child's garden: The kindergarten movement from Froebel to Dewey*. University Park, PA: Penn State Press.

Snyder, A. (1972). *Dauntless women in childhood education*. Washington, DC: Association for Childhood Education International.

Swick, K., & Brown, M. (1999). The caring ethic in early childhood teacher education. *Journal of Instructional Psychology, 26*(2), 116–121.

Tanner, L. N. (1997). *Dewey's Laboratory School: Lessons for today*. New York, NY: Teachers College Press.

Tuchman, B. (1978). *A distant mirror*. New York, NY: Alfred A. Knopf.

Vartulli, S. (1999). How early childhood teacher beliefs vary across grade level. *Early Childhood Research Quarterly, 14*(4), 489–514.

Weber, E. (1984). *Ideas influencing early childhood education. A theoretical analysis*. New York, NY: Teachers College Press.

Wiles, J. W., & Bondi, J. C. (2007). *Curriculum development: A guide to practice* (8th ed.). Upper Saddle River, NJ: Pearson.

Wortham, S. (1992). *Childhood: 1892–1992*. Olney, MD: Association for Childhood Education International.

Wyman, A. (1995). The earliest early childhood teachers: Women teachers of America's Dame Schools. *Young Children, 50*(2), 29–32.

Chapter 3

American Academy of Pediatrics, Committee on Early Childhood, Adoption, and Dependent Care. (2010). Quality early education and child care from birth to kindergarten. Available online at www.aap.org/healthtopics/childcare.cfm.

American Educational Research Association. (2005). Early childhood education: Investing in quality makes sense. Research points. Available online at www.aera.net/uploadedFiles/Journals_and_Publications/Research_Points/RPFall05.pdf.

Ball, D., & Cohen, D. (1996). Reform by the book: What is—or might be—the role of curriculum materials in teacher learning and instructional reform? *Educational Researcher, 25*(9), 6–8.

Bowman, B. T. (2006). Standards: At the heart of educational equity. *Beyond the Journal*. Available online at www.naeyc.org/btj/200609/BowmanBTJ.pdf.

Brandes, J., Ormsbee, C., & Haring, K. (2007). From early intervention to early childhood programs: Timeline for early successful transitions (TEST). *Intervention in School & Clinic, 42*(4), 204–211.

Cassidy, D. J., Mims, S., Rucker, L., & Boone, S. (2003). Emergent curriculum and kindergarten readiness. *Childhood Education, 79*(4), 345–360.

Center for the Child Care Workforce and Human Services Policy Center. (2008). *Estimating the size and components of the U.S. child care workforce and caregiving population* (p. 18). Washington, DC: Center for the Child Care Workforce; Seattle, WA: Human Services Policy Center, University of Washington.

Egertson, H. A. (2004). Achieving high standards and implementing developmentally appropriate practice: Both are possible. *Dimensions of Early Childhood, 32,* 3–9.

Estok, V. (2006). One district's study on the propriety of transition-grade classrooms. In K. Paciorek (Ed.), *Annual Editions: Early Childhood Education 06/07* (27th ed., pp. 92–95). Dubuque, IA: McGraw-Hill.

Evans, V. J. (2006). Economic perspectives on early care and education. In M. Zaslow & I. Martinez-Beck (Eds.), *Critical issues in early childhood professional development* (pp. 309–311). Baltimore, MD: Paul H. Brookes.

Frede, E., Jung, K., Barnett, W. S., & Figueras, A. (2009). The APPLES blossom: Abbott Preschool Program Longitudinal Effects Study (APPLES), preliminary results through second grade. Available online at http://nieer.org/pdf/apples_second_grade_results.pdf.

Fuller, B., Holloway, S. D., & Bozzi, L. (1997). Evaluating early childhood programs: Serving the interests of government, providers or parents? In B. Spodek & O. Saracho (eds.), *Issues in early childhood education: Yearbook in early childhood education* (pp. 7–27). New York, NY: Teachers College Press.

Gronlund, G. (2006). *Make early learning standards come alive: Connecting your practice and curriculum to state guidelines.* St Paul, MN: Redleaf Press.

Hale-Jinks, C., Knopf, H., & Kemple, K. (2006). Tackling teacher turnover in child care: Understanding causes and consequences, identifying solutions. *Childhood Education, 82*(4), 219–226.

Helm, J. H., & Beneke, S. (Eds.). (2003). *The power of projects: Meeting contemporary challenges in early childhood classrooms—Strategies and solutions.* Washington, DC: National Association for the Education of Young Children.

Johnson, S. M. (2006). *Finders and keepers: Helping new teachers survive and thrive in our schools.* San Francisco, CA: Jossey-Bass.

Kamerman, S. B., & Kahn, A. J. (1994). *A welcome for every child: Care, education and family support for infants and toddlers in Europe.* Arlington, VA: Zero to Three/National Center for Clinical Infant Programs.

Kuder, S. J. (2001). Effectiveness of the DISTAR reading program for children with learning disabilities. *Journal of Learning Disabilities, 23,* 69–71.

Lin, H.-L., Lawrence, F. R., & Gorrell, J. (2003). Kindergarten teachers' views of children's readiness for school. *Early Childhood Research Quarterly, 18,* 225–237.

Lynch, R. G. (2004). *Exceptional returns.* Washington, DC: Economic Policy Institute.

Malaguzzi, L. (1995). (interview with Gandini, L., trans.) History, ideas and philosophy. In C. Edwards, L. Gandini & G. Forman (Eds.), *The hundred languages of children.* Norwood, NJ: Ablex.

NAEYC & NAECS/SDE (National Association of Early Childhood Specialists in State Departments of Education). (2002). Joint position statement. Early learning standards: Creating the conditions for success. Available online at www.naeyc.org/resources/position_statements/earlylearn.pdf.

National Association of Child Care Resource and Referral Agencies (NACCRRA). (2010) Available online at www.naccrra.org.

National Center for Education Statistics (NCES). (2009). Home page. Available online at http://nces.ed.gov/programs/digest/d09/.

National Central Regional Laboratory. (2010). Organizing for effective early childhood programs and practices. Available online at www.ncrel.org/sdrs/areas/issues/students/earlycld/ea100.htm.

National Governors Association. (2005). *Building the foundation for bright futures.* Washington, DC: Author.

National Head Start Association. (2010). Home page. Available online at http://www.nhsa.org/about_nhsa.

National Institute for Early Education and Research (NIEER). (2009). *The state of preschool 2009.* New Brunswick, NJ: Rutgers University.

Pianta, R. C., & Howes, C. (Eds.). (2009). *The promise of pre-K.* Baltimore, MD: Paul H. Brookes.

Puckett, M., & Black, J. (2007). *The young child: Development from prebirth through age eight* (5th ed.). Upper Saddle River, NJ: Pearson.

Roopnarine, J. L., & Johnson, J. E. (2005). *Approaches to early childhood education* (4th ed.). Upper Saddle River, NJ: Pearson.

Sawchuck, S. (2010, June 1). Putting new standards into practice a tough job: Challenges on curricular and teaching fronts. *Education Week.* Available online at www.edweek.org/ew/contributors/stephen.sawchuk.html.

Schickendanz, J. A. (1995). Early education and care: Beginnings. *Journal of Education, 177*(3), 1–7.

Schweinhart, L. J. (2005). *The High/Scope Perry Preschool study through age 40: Summary, conclusions and frequently asked questions.* Ypsilanti, MI: High/Scope Educational Research Foundation.

Scott, E., London, A., & Hurst, A. (2005). Instability in patchworks of child care when moving from welfare to work. *Journal of Marriage and Family, 67*(2), 370–386.

Sexton, C. W. (2001). Effectiveness of the DISTAR Reading I program in developing first graders' language skills. *Journal of Educational Research, 82,* 291–293.

Swiniarski, L. B. (2006). Free universal preschool for all children [Guest Editorial]. *Early Childhood Education Journal, 33*(4), 201–202.

Wong, V. C., Cook, T. D., Barnett, W. S., & Jung, K. (2008). An effectiveness-based evaluation of five state pre-kindergarten programs. *Journal of Policy Analysis and Management, 27*(1), 122–154. Available online at www.sesp.northwestern.edu/docs/publications/16129652354859671644dba.pdf.

Yeh, H., & Barton, B. (2005). A cultural perspective on professional beliefs of childcare teachers. *Early Childhood Education Journal, 33*(3), 179–186.

Chapter 4

Achinstein, B., Ogawa, R. T., & Sexton, D. (2010). Retaining teachers of color: A pressing problem and a potential strategy for "hard-to-staff" schools. *Review of Educational Research, 80*(1), 71–107.

Banks, J. A. (2006). *Race, culture and education: The selected works of James A. Banks.* New York, NY: Routledge.

Barrera, I., & Corso, R. M. (2002). Cultural competency as skilled dialogue. *Topics in Early Childhood Special Education, 22*(2), 103–113.

Birmingham, C. (2003). Practicing the virtue of reflection in an unfamiliar cultural context. *Theory into Practice, 42*(3), 188–194.

Bishop, R., Berryman, M., Tiakiwai, S., & Richardson, C. (2003). *Te Kotahitanga: The experiences of Year 9 and 10 Maori students in mainstream classrooms.* Wellington, NZ: Ministry of Education.

Blue-Banning, M., Summers, J. A., Frankland, H. C., Nelson, L. L., & Beegle, G. (2004). Dimensions of family and professional partnership: Constructive guidelines for collaboration. *Exceptional Children, 70*(2), 167–184.

Bowman, N. A. (2010). College diversity experiences and cognitive development: A meta-analysis. *Review of Educational Research, 80*(1), 4–33.

Bruner, J. (1987). The transactional self. In J. Bruner & H. Haste (Eds.), *Making sense: The child's construction of the world* (pp. 81–96). New York, NY: Methuen.

Chak, A. (2006). Reflecting on the self: An experience in a preschool. *Reflective Practice, 7*(1), 31–42.

Charney, R. S. (2002). *Teaching children to care: Classroom management for ethical and academic growth, K–8* (rev. ed.). Turners Falls, MA: Northeast Foundation for Children.

Clawson, C., & Luze, G. (2008). Individual experiences of children with and without disabilities in early childhood settings. *Topics in Early Childhood Special Education, 28*(3), 132–147.

Copple, C., & Bredekamp, S. (Eds.). (2009). *Developmentally appropriate practice in early childhood programs serving children from birth through age eight* (rev. ed.) Washington, DC: National Association for the Education of Young Children.

Cushner, K., McClelland, A., & Safford, P. (2009). *Human diversity in education: An integrative approach* (6th ed.). Boston, MA: McGraw-Hill.

Delpit, L. (2006). *Other people's children: Conflict in the classroom.* New York, NY: New Press.

Derman-Sparks, L., & Edwards, J. O. (2010). *Anti-bias education: Empowering our children and ourselves.* Washington, DC: National Association for the Education of Young Children.

Division for Early Childhood (DEC). (2009). Code of Ethics. Available online at www.decsped.org/uploads/docs/about_dec/position_concept_papers/Code%20of%20Ethics.

Feeney. S. (2010). NAEYC Code of Ethical Conduct (Parts 1–7). [Video]. Available: wn.com/NAEYC_Code_of_Ethical_Conduct_Part_5_of_7_Official_Video.

Feeney, S., Freeman, N. K., & Moravcik, E. (2008). *Teaching the NAEYC code of ethical conduct* (rev. ed.). Washington, DC: National Association for the Education of Young Children.

Feeney, S., & Pizzolongo, P. (2010). Code of ethical conduct: Conversations with Stephanie Feeney and Peter Pizzolongo. Available online at www.naeyc.org/ecp/resources/ethics.

Fennimore, B. S., & Goodwin, A. L. (Eds.). (2011). *Promoting social justice for young children.* New York, NY: Springer.

Garcia, E. E., & Frede, E. C. (2010). *Young English language learners: Current research and emerging directions for practice and policy.* New York, NY: Teachers College Press.

Gay, G. (2010). *Culturally responsive teaching: Theory, research, and practice* (2nd ed.). New York, NY: Teachers College Press.

Genishi, C., & Dyson, A. H. (2009). *Children, language and literacy: Diverse learners in diverse times.* New York, NY: Teachers College Press.

Goode, T. (2005). Promoting cultural and linguistic competency [Checklist/Self-Assessment]. Available online at www.11.georgetown.edu/research/gucchd/nccc/documents/checklist.EIEC.doc.pdf.

Guthrie, C. (2009). Children's rights in Canada. *Transition, 39*(3), 10–12.

Han, H. S., & Thomas, M. S. (2010). No child misunderstood: Enhancing early childhood teachers' multicultural responsiveness to the social competence of diverse children. *Early Childhood Education Journal, 37*(6), 469–476.

Hanson, M. J., & Lynch, E. W. (2010). Working with families from diverse backgrounds. In R. A. McWilliam (Ed.), *Working with families of young children with special needs* (pp. 147–174). New York, NY: Guilford Press.

Harle, A., & Trudeau, K. (2006). Using reflection to increase children's learning in kindergarten. *Young Children, 61*(4), 101–104.

Herrera, S. (2010). *Biography-driven culturally responsive teaching.* New York, NY: Teachers College Press.

Hollins, E. R., & Guzman, M. R. (2005). Research on preparing teachers for diverse populations. In M. Cochran-Smith & K. M. Zeichner (Eds.), *Studying teacher education: The report of the AERA panel on research and teacher education* (pp. 477–548). Mahwah, NJ: Lawrence Erlbaum.

Ingersoll, R. M., & Connor, R. (2009, April). What the national data tell us about minority and Black teacher turnover. Paper presented at the annual meeting of the American Educational Research Association, San Diego, CA.

Jalongo, M. R. (2007). "I don't want to talk about" [Editorial]. *Early Childhood Education Journal, 35*(2), 95–96.

Keengwe, J. (2010). Fostering cross cultural competence in preservice teachers through multicultural education experiences. *Early Childhood Education Journal, 38*, 197–204.

Ladson-Billings, G. (2006). It's not the culture of poverty, it's the poverty of culture: The problem with teacher education. *Anthropology and Education Quarterly, 37*(2), 104–109.

Larrivee, B. (2008). Meeting the challenge of preparing reflective practitioners. *New Educator, 4*(2), 87–106.

Loreman, T. (2009). *Respecting childhood.* New York, NY: Continuum.

Lynch, R. G. (2004). *Exceptional returns.* Washington, DC: Economic Policy Institute.

Madrazo, G., & Motz, L. (2005). Brain research: Implications to diverse learners. *Science Educator, 14*(1), 56–60.

McClean, M., Wolery, M., & Bailey, D. (2004). *Assessing infants and preschoolers with special needs.* Upper Saddle River, NJ: Pearson.

McWilliam, R. A. (2010). Talking to families. In P. A. McWilliam (Ed.), *Working with families of young children with special needs* (pp. 127–146). New York, NY: Guilford.

Moll, L. C., Amanti, C., Nett, D., & Gonzalez, N. (1992). Funds of knowledge for teaching. *Theory into Practice, 31,* 132–141.

National Association for the Education of Young Children. (2005). *NAEYC early childhood program standards and accreditation criteria: The mark of quality in early childhood education.* Washington, DC: Author.

Nieto, S. (2009). *The light in their eyes: Creating multicultural learning communities* (10th anniversary ed.). New York, NY: Teachers College Press.

Nieto, S., & Bode, P. (2008). *Affirming diversity: The sociopolitical context of multicultural education* (5th ed.). Upper Saddle River, NJ: Pearson.

Noddings, N. (1984). *Caring: A feminine approach to ethics and moral education.* Berkeley, CA: University of California Press.

Ray, A., Bowman, B., & Robbins, J., (2006). *Preparing early childhood teachers to successfully educate all children: The contribution of state boards of higher education and national professional accreditation organizations, project on race, class and culture in early childhood.* Chicago, IL: Erikson Institute.

Sadker, M., Sadker, D., & Zittleman, K. (2008). *Teachers, schools, and society* (8th ed.). New York, NY: McGraw-Hill.

Seefeldt, C., Castle, S. D., & Falconer, R. (2010). *Social studies for the preschool/primary child.* Upper Saddle River, NJ: Pearson.

Strachota, B. (1996). *On their side: Helping children take charge of learning.* Turners Falls, MA: Northeast Foundation for Children.

Tennyson, W. W., & Strom, S. M. (1988). Beyond professional standards: Developing responsibilities. *Journal of Counseling and Development, 64*(5), 298–302.

U.S. Census Bureau. (2008a, August 14). *An older and more diverse nation by midcentury* [Press release]. Washington, DC: Author.

U.S. Census Bureau. (2008b, May 1). *U.S. Hispanic population surpasses 45 million: Now 15 percent of total* [Press release]. Washington, DC: Author.

Vaughn, W. (2005). Educating for diversity, social responsibility and action: Preservice teachers engage in immersion experiences. *Journal of Cultural Diversity 12*(1), 26–30.

Wiseman, A. M. (2009). Perceptions of community and experiences in school: Understanding the opportunities, resources, and education within one neighborhood. *Early Childhood Education Journal, 36*(4), 291–380.

Wyness, M. G. (2000). *Contesting childhood.* London, UK: The Falmer Press.

Xu, Y. (2007). Empowering culturally diverse families of young children with disabilities: The double ABCX model. *Early Childhood Education Journal, 34*(6), 431–437.

Chapter 5

Annie E. Casey Foundation (2009). *The 2009 Kids Count Data Book.* Baltimore, MD: Author.

Banks, J. A. (2006). *Cultural diversity and education: Foundations, curriculum, and teaching* (5th ed.). Boston, MA: Allyn & Bacon.

Berk, L. E. (2008). *Infants and children* (6th ed.). Boston, MA: Allyn & Bacon.

Berns, R. (2010). *Child, family, school, and community* (8th ed.). Belmont, CA: Wadsworth.

Brazleton, T. B., & Greenspan, S. I. (2001). *The irreducible needs of children: What every child must have to grow, learn, and flourish.* Cambridge, MA: Perseus.

Bronfenbrenner, U. (2004). *Making human beings human.* Thousand Oaks, CA: Sage.

Copple, C., & Bredekamp, S. (Eds.). (2009). *Developmentally appropriate practice in early childhood programs serving children from birth through age eight* (rev. ed.). Washington, DC: National Association for the Education of Young Children.

Copple, C., Sigel, I., & Saunders, R. (1984). *Educating the young thinker.* Mahwah, NJ: Lawrence Erlbaum.

deHaan, M., & Martinos, M. (2008). Brain function. In M. M. Haith & J. B. Benson (Eds.), *Encyclopaedia of infant and early childhood development* (pp. 106–177). Oxford, UK: Elsevier.

Diamond, A., Casey, B., & Munkata, V. (2010). *Developmental cognitive neuroscience.* New York, NY: Oxford University Press.

Division for Early Childhood (DEC) and National Association for the Education of Young Children (NAEYC). (2009). *Early childhood inclusion: A joint position statement of the Division for Early Childhood of the Council for Exceptional Children and the National Association for the Education of Young Children.* Chapel Hill, NC: Authors.

Erikson, E. H. (1993). *Childhood and society.* New York, NY: Norton. (Original work published 1963).

Gallagher, K. C. (2005). Brain research and early childhood development: A primer for developmentally appropriate practice. *Young Children, 60*(4), 12–21.

Goleman, D. (1998). *Working with emotional intelligence.* New York, NY: Bantam.

Hallahan, D., Kauffman, J., & Pullen, P. (2008). *Exceptional learners: An introduction to special education.* Boston, MA: Pearson Education.

Kamii, C., & DeVries, R. (1980). *Group games in early education* (p. vii). Washington, DC: National Association for the Education of Young Children.

Maslow, A. H. (1987). *Motivation and personality* (3rd ed.). New York, NY: Harper and Row.

National Association for the Education of Young Children. (2009). Where we stand on responding to linguistic and cultural diversity. Available online at www.naeyc.org/files/National_Association_for_the_Education_of_Young_Children/file/positions/diversity.pdf.

National Center for Health Statistics. (2010). *FastStats A to Z.* Hyattsville, MD. Available online at www.cdc.gov/nchs.

National Scientific Council on the Developing Child (2007). *The science of early childhood development: Closing the achievement gap between what we know and what we do.* Cambridge, MA: Center for the Developing Child at Harvard University.

Piaget, J. (1992). *The origins of intelligence in children.* Madison, CT: International Universities Press. (Original work published 1952).

Puckett, M., & Black, J. (2009). *The young child: Development from prebirth through age eight* (5th ed.). Upper Saddle River, NJ: Pearson.

Santrock, J. W. (2009). *Child development* (12th ed.). New York, NY: McGraw-Hill.

Shonkoff, J. P., & Phillips, D. A. (2001). *From neurons to neighborhoods: The science of early childhood development*. In Commission on Behavioral and Social Science and Education (Ed.), *Early childhood development and learning: New knowledge for policy* (pp. 1–20). Washington, DC: National Academy Press.

Vygotsky, L. (1978). *Mind in society: The development of higher psychological processes*. Cambridge, MA: Harvard University Press.

White, C. S., & Isenberg, J. P. (2003). Development issues affecting children. In J. P. Isenberg & M. R. Jalongo (Eds.), *Major trends and issues in early childhood education: Challenges, controversies, and insights* (pp. 13–29). New York, NY: Teachers College Press.

Wood, C. (2007). *Yardsticks* (3rd ed.). Turners Falls, MA: Northeast Foundation for Children.

Woolfolk, A. (2010). *Educational psychology* (10th ed.). Boston, MA: Allyn & Bacon.

Further Reading on Children with Diverse Backgrounds

Feng, J. (1994). *Asian-American children: What teachers should know*. ERIC Digest. EDO-PS-94-4. Urbana, IL: Clearinghouse on Elementary and Early Childhood Education.

Stewart, E. C., & Bennett, M. J. (1991). *American cultural patterns: A cross-cultural perspective* (rev. ed.). Yarmouth, ME: Intercultural Press.

Children's Books

Beaumont, K. (2004). *Baby danced the polka*. New York, NY: Dial.

Dewdney, A. (2005). *Llama, llama red pajama*. New York, NY: Viking.

English, K. (2004). *Hot day on Abbott Avenue*. New York, NY: Clarion.

Henkes, K. (2004). *Kitten's first full moon*. New York, NY: Greenwillow.

Hesse, K. (2004). *The cats in Krasinski Square*. New York, NY: Scholastic.

Hillman, E. (1992). *Min-Yo and the moon dragon*. Dallas, TX: Harcourt Brace.

Hooks, W. (1987). *Moss gown*. New York, NY: Clarion.

Matas, C. (1993). *Daniel's story*. New York, NY: Scholastic.

O'Dell, S. (1960). *Island of the blue dolphins*. Boston, MA: Houghton Mifflin.

Sendak, M. (1964). *Where the wild things are*. New York, NY: Harper.

Chapter 6

Allen, K. E., & Cowdery, G. E. (2009). *The exceptional child: Inclusion in early childhood education* (6th ed.). Clifton Park, NY: Thomson Delmar Learning.

Alliance for Technology Access. (2004). *Computer resources for people with disabilities: A guide to assistive technologies, tools, and resources for people of all ages* (4th ed.). Alameda, CA: Hunter House. Available online at www.ataccess.org.

American Psychological Association. (2005). *Learner centered psychological principles: Guidelines for school redesign and reform* [Electronic version]. Washington, DC: American Psychological Association. Available online at www.apa.org/ed/cpnewtext.html.

Armstrong, T. (2000). *Multiple intelligences in the classroom* (2nd ed.). Alexandria, VA: Association for Supervision and Curriculum Development.

Bandura, A. (1997). *Self-efficacy: The exercise of control*. New York, NY: Freeman.

Bandura, A. (2001). Social cognitive theory. *Annual Review of Psychology, 52*. Palo Alto, CA: Annual Review.

Banks J. A., (2008). *Introduction to multicultural education* (4th ed.). Boston, MA: Allyn & Bacon.

Berns, R. M. (2010). *Child, family, school and community. Socialization and support* (8th ed.). Belmont, CA: Thomson Wadsworth.

Bodrova, E., & Leong, D. (1996). *Tools of the mind: The Vygotskian approach to early childhood education*. Upper Saddle River, NJ: Pearson.

Bodrova, E., & Leong, D. (2005). Uniquely preschool. *Educational Leadership, 63*(1), 44–47.

Bransford, J. D., Brown, A. I., & Cocking, R. R. (Eds.). (2000). *How people learn: Brain, mind, experience, and school* (exp. ed.). Washington, DC: National Academy Press.

Bredekamp, S., & Rosegrant, T. (Eds.). (1992). *Reaching potentials: Appropriate curriculum and assessment for young children* (Vol. 1). Washington, DC: National Association for the Education of Young Children.

Bruner, J. (1966). *Toward a theory of instruction*. New York, NY: Norton.

Campbell, L., Campbell, B., & Dickinson, D. (2004). *Teaching and learning through multiple intelligences* (3rd ed.). Boston, MA: Pearson.

Clements, D., & Sarama, J. (2003). Young children and technology: What does the research say? *Young Children, 58*(6), 34–40.

Commission on Behavioral and Social Sciences and Education. (2001). *Early childhood development and learning: New knowledge for policy*. Washington, DC: National Academy Press.

Copple, C., & Bredekamp, S. (2009), *Developmentally appropriate practice in early childhood programs* (3rd ed.). Washington, DC: National Association for the Education of Young Children.

Daniels, D. H., Kalkman, D. L., & McCombs, B. L. (2001). Individual differences in young children's learning and teacher practices: Effects of learner-centered contexts on motivations. *Early Education Development, 12*(2), 253–273.

Denton, P. (2005). *Learning through academic choice*. Turners Falls, MA: Northeast Foundation for Children.

Dewey, J. (1916). *Democracy and education*. New York, NY: Macmillan.

Donovan, M. S., & Bransford, J. D. (2005). *How students learn history, mathematics, and science in the classroom*. Washington, DC: National Academy Press.

Elkind, D. (2007). *The power of play: How spontaneous imaginative activities lead to happier, healthier children.* Cambridge, MA: Da Capo Press.

Epstein, A. S. (2007). *The intentional teacher. Choosing the best strategies for young children's learning.* Washington, DC: National Association for the Education of Young Children.

Espinosa, L. (2010). *Getting it RIGHT for young children from diverse backgrounds; Applying research to improve practice.* Washington, DC: National Association for the Education of Young Children.

Fromberg, D. P., & Bergen, D. (2006). *Play from birth to twelve* (2nd ed.). New York, NY: Routledge.

Frost, J., Wortham, S., & Reifel, S. (2008). *Play and child development* (3rd ed.). Upper Saddle River, NJ: Pearson.

Fulghum, R. (1986). *All I really needed to know I learned in kindergarten.* New York, NY: Ballantine Books.

Gallagher, K. C. (2005). Brain research and early childhood development: A primer for developmentally appropriate practice. *Young Children, 60*(4), 12–21.

Gallagher, K. C., & Mayer, K. (2008). Enhancing development and learning through teacher–child relationships. *Young Children 63*(6), 80–87.

Gardner, H. (1993). *Frames of mind. The theory of multiple intelligences* (2nd ed.). New York, NY: Basic Books.

Gardner, H. (2000). *The disciplined mind.* New York, NY: Penguin/Putnam.

Gesell, A. (1933). Maturation and patterning of behavior. In C. Murchison (Ed.), *A handbook of child psychology.* Worcester, MA: Clark University Press.

Halfon, N., Shulman, E., & Hochstein, M. (2001). Brain development in early childhood. Policy Briefs 13:1–4. Los Angeles, CA: UCLA Center for Healthier Children, Families, and Communities, California Policy Research Center.

Hannaford, C. (2005). *Smart moves: Why learning is not all in your head.* Salt Lake City, UT: Great River Books.

Henniger, M. L. (2009). *Teaching young children: An introduction* (4th ed.). Upper Saddle River, NJ: Pearson.

Hyson, M. (2008). *Enthusiastic and engaged learners: Approaches to learning in the early childhood classroom.* Washington, DC: National Association for the Education of Young Children.

International Society for Technology in Education (ISTE). (2007). The National Educational Technology Standards (NETS-S) and Performance Indicators for Students. Available online at www/iste.org.

Isenberg, J. P., & Jalongo, M. R. (2010). *Creative thinking and arts-based learning: Preschool through fourth grade* (5th ed.). Upper Saddle River, NJ: Pearson.

Jacobsen, D., Eggen, P., & Kauchak, D. (2009). *Methods for teaching: Promoting student learning in K–12 classrooms.* Boston, MA: Allyn & Bacon.

Jensen, E. (2008). *Brain-based learning: The new paradigm of teaching.* Thousand Oaks, CA: Corwin Press.

Liess, E., & Ritchie, G. (1995). Using multiple intelligence theory to transform a first-grade health curriculum. *Early Childhood Education Journal, 23*(2), 71–79.

Lynch, R. G. (2005). *Early childhood investment yields big payoff.* San Francisco, CA: WestEd. Available online at www.wested/org/online_pubs/pp-05-02.pdf.

McCombs, B. L., & Miller, L. (2007). *Learner-centered classroom practices and assessment: Maximizing student motivation, learning, and achievement.* Thousand Oaks, CA: Corwin Press.

McCombs, B. L., & Whisler, J. S. (1997). *The learner-centered classroom and school: Strategies for increasing student motivation and achievement.* San Francisco, CA: Jossey-Bass.

National Association for the Education of Young Children (NAEYC) Technology and Young Children Interest Forum. (2008). *On Our Minds: Meaningful Technology Integration in Early Learning Environments.* Technology and Young Children Interest Forum Members, Young Children, September 2008, Vol. 63, No. 5. Available online at http://www.naeyc.org/.files/yc/files/yc/file/200809/OnnOurMinds.pdf.

National Association for the Education of Young Children. (1996). *Position statement on technology and young children—Ages three through eight.* Washington, DC: Author.

National Research Council (2009). *Mathematics learning in early childhood: Paths toward excellence and equity.* Washington, DC: National Academics Press.

Parten, M. (1932). Social participation among preschool children. *Journal of Abnormal and Social Psychology, 27*(2), 243–269.

Piaget, J. (1970). Piaget's theory. In P. Mussen (Ed.), *Carmichael's manual of child psychology* (3rd ed., Vol. 1, pp. 703–732). New York, NY: Wiley.

Piaget, J. (1980). Foreword. In C. Kamii & R. Devries (Eds.), *Group games in early education* (p. vii). Washington, DC: National Association for the Education of Young Children.

Pica, R. (2008). Learning by leaps and bounds: In defense of learning. *Young Children 63*(6), 52–53.

Riley, J., & Jones, R. (2010). Acknowledging learning through play in the primary grades. *Childhood Education, 86*(3), 146–149.

Santrock, J. W. (2009). *Children* (11th ed.). Boston, MA: McGraw-Hill.

Sawyer, K. (2006). The new science of learning. In R. K. Sawyer (Ed.), *The Cambridge handbook of the learning sciences* (p. 4). New York, NY: The Cambridge University Press.

Shonkoff, J., & Phillips, D. (Eds.). (2001). *Neurons to neighborhoods: The science of early childhood development.* Washington, DC: National Academy Press.

Smilansky, S., & Shefatya, L. (1990). *Facilitating play: A medium for promoting cognitive, socio-emotional, and academic development in young children.* Gaithersburg, MD: Psychosocial and Educational Publications.

Stipek, D. (2002). *Motivation to learn: Integrating theory and practice* (4th ed). Boston, MA: Allyn & Bacon.

Swaminathan, S., & Wright, J. (2003). Educational technology in the early and primary years. In J. P. Isenberg & M. R. Jalongo (Eds.), *Major trends and issues in early childhood education: Challenges, controversies, and insights* (2nd ed., pp. 136–149). New York, NY: Teachers College Press.

Vygotsky, L. (1978). *Mind in society.* Cambridge, MA: Harvard University Press.

Woolfolk, A. (2010). *Educational psychology* (11th ed.). Boston, MA: Allyn & Bacon.

Additional References

Dana Alliance for Brain Initiatives. (2006). Brainwork. Available online at www.dana.org/books/press/brainwork.

Hechinger Institute on Education and the Media. (2005). New York, NY: Teachers College Press.

Silver, H. F., Strong, R. W., & Perini, M. J. (2000). *So each may learn: Integrating learning styles and multiple intelligences*. Alexandria, VA: Association for Supervision and Curriculum Development.

Children's Books

Mora, P. (1992). *A birthday basket for Tia*. New York, NY: Simon & Schuster.

Zak, M. (1992). *Save my rain forest*. Volcano, CA: Volcano Press.

Software and Websites

www.techandyoungchildren.org/.

www.netc.org/earlyconnections/index.html.

Kidspiration. (2000). Inspiration Software.

Chapter 7

American Alliance for Health, Physical Education, Recreation, and Dance. (2006a). *Active start: A statement of physical activity guidelines for children birth to five years*. Reston, VA: Author.

American Alliance for Health, Physical Education, Recreation, and Dance. (2006b). *Physical activity for children: A statement of guidelines for children 5–12* (2nd ed.). Reston, VA: Author.

Allen, K. E., & Cowdery, G. E. (2009). *The exceptional child: Inclusion in early childhood education* (6th ed.). Clifton Park, NY: Thomson Delmar Learning.

Association for Supervision and Curriculum Development. (1997). Making a good start. *Education Update, 39*(6), 6.

Bransford, J. D., Brown, A. I., & Cocking, R. R. (Eds.). (1999). *How people learn: Brain, mind, experience, and school*. Washington, DC: National Academy Press.

Bullard, J. (2010). *Creative environments for learning*. Upper Saddle River, NJ: Pearson.

Carnegie Task Force on Meeting the Needs of Young Children. (1994). *Starting points: Meeting the needs of our youngest children*. New York, NY: Carnegie Corporation of New York.

Carter, M. (2006). Rethinking our use of resources part 2: Space, attitude, and attention. *Exchange, 16*(7), 18–20.

Clayton, M. K. (2001). *Classroom spaces that work*. Turners Falls, MA: Northeast Foundation for Children.

Colker, L. J. (2005). *The cooking book: Fostering young children's learning and delight*. Washington, DC: National Association for the Education of Young Children.

Copple, C., & Bredekamp, S. (2006). *Basics of developmentally appropriate practices: An introduction for teachers of children 3 to 6*. Washington, DC: National Association for the Education of Young Children.

Copple, C., & Bredekamp, S. (2009). *Developmentally appropriate practice in early childhood programs* (3rd ed.). Washington, DC: National Association for the Education of Young Children.

Corson, D. (2001). *Language, diversity, and education*. Mahwah, NJ: Lawrence Erlbaum.

Crumpacker, S. (1995). Using cultural information to create schools that work. In A. Meek (Ed.), *Designing places for learning* (pp. 31–42). Alexandria, VA: Association for Supervision and Curriculum Development.

Cryer, D., & Phillipsen, L. (1997). Quality details: A close-up look at child care program strengths and weaknesses. *Young Children, 52*(5), 51–61.

Curtis, D., & Carter, M. (2005). Rethinking early childhood environments to inform learning. *Young Children, 6*(63), 34–38.

Derman-Sparks, L., & Edwards, J. O. (2010). *Anti-bias education for young children and ourselves*. Washington, DC: National Association for the Education of Young Children.

Deiner, P. L. (2010). *Resources for educating children with diverse abilities* (5th ed.). Belmont, CA: Wadsworth/Cengage.

Division for Early Childhood (DEC) and the National Association for the Education of Young Children (NAEYC). (2009). Early childhood inclusion: A joint position statement of the Division for Early Childhood (DEC) and the National Association for the Education of Young Children (NAEYC). Available online at www.dec-sped.org.

Early, D. M., Barbarin, O., Bryant, D., Burchenal, M., Chang, F., Clifford, R., Crawford, G., & Weaver, W. (2005). Pre-kindergarten in eleven states: NCEDCS Multi-state study of pre-kindergarten and study of statewide early education programs (SWEEP): Preliminary descriptive report. New York, NY: Foundation for Child Development. Available online at www.fcd-us.org/usi_doc/Prekindergarten//states.pdf.

Edwards, C., Gandini, L., & Forman, G. (Eds.). (1998). *The hundred languages of children: The Reggio Emilia approach—Advanced reflections* (2nd ed.). Norwood, NJ: Ablex.

Falk, B. (2009). *Teaching the way children learn*. New York, NY: Teachers College Press.

Firlik, R. (2006). Preparing school and classroom environments for active learning. *ACEI Focus on Elementary, 18*(3), 1–4.

Fraser, S., & Gestwicki, C. (2002). *Authentic childhood: Exploring Reggio Emilia in the classroom*. Albany, NY: Delmar.

Frost, J. L., Wortham, S., & Riefel, S. (2008). *Play and child development* (3rd ed.). Upper Saddle River, NJ: Pearson.

Frye, M. A., & Mumpower, J. O. (2001). Lost in space? Design learning areas for today. *Dimensions of Early Childhood, 29*(2), 16–22.

Gargiulo, R., & Metcalf, D. (2010). *Teaching in today's inclusive classrooms*. Belmont, CA: Wadsworth/Cengage.

Garreau, M., & Kennedy, C. (1991). Structure time and space to promote pursuit of learning in the primary grades. *Young Children, 64*(4), 46–51.

Gay, G. (2000). *Culturally responsive teaching: Theory, research, and practice*. New York, NY: Teachers College Press.

Gronlund, G. (2006). *Make early learning standards come alive: Connecting your practice and curriculum to state guidelines*. St. Paul, MN: Redleaf Press.

Harms, T., Clifford, R., & Cryer, D. (2004). *Early childhood environment rating scale (ECRS)* (rev. ed.). New York, NY: Teachers College Press.

Hendrick, J., & Weissman, P. (2006). *The whole child: Developmental education for the early years* (8th ed.). Upper Saddle River, NJ: Pearson.

Hohman, M., & Weikart, D. (1995). *Educating young children: Active learning practices for preschool and child care programs.* Ypsilanti, MI: High/ScopePress.

Hyson, M. (2008). *Enthusiastic and engaged learners: Approaches to learning in the early childhood classroom.* New York, NY: Teachers College Press.

Isbell, R., & Exelby, B. (2001). *Early learning environments that work.* Beltsville, MD: Gryphon House.

Isenberg, J., & Jalongo, M. (2010). *Creative thinking and arts-based learning: Preschool through fourth grade* (5th ed.). Upper Saddle River, NJ: Pearson.

Jacobs, G., & Crowley, K. (2010). *Reaching standards and beyond in kindergarten.* Thousand Oaks, CA: Corwin Press.

Jalongo, M. R. (2007). "I don't want to talk about" [Editorial]. *Early Childhood Education Journal, 35*(2), 95–96.

Jones, E., & Prescott, E. (1978). *Dimensions of teaching—learning environments II: Focus on day care.* Pasadena, CA: Pacific Oaks College.

Kontos, S., & Wilcox-Herzog, A. (1997). Influences on children's competence in early childhood classrooms. *Early Childhood Research Quarterly, 12*(3), 247–262.

Kritchevsky, S., Prescott, E., & Walling, C. (1977). *Planning environments for young children: Physical space.* Washington, DC: National Association for the Education of Young Children.

Martinez-Beck, I., & Zaslow, M. (2006). *Critical issues in early childhood professional development.* Baltimore, MD: Paul H. Brookes.

Maslow, A. H. (1987). *Motivation and personality* (3rd ed.). New York, NY: Harper and Row.

McWilliams, R., Wolery, M., & Odom, S. (2001). Instructional perspectives in inclusive preschool classrooms. In M. J. Guralnick (Ed.), *Early childhood inclusion: Focus on change.* Baltimore, MD: Paul H. Brookes.

Montgomery, W. (2001). Creating culturally responsive, inclusive classrooms. *Teaching Exceptional Children, 33*(1), 4–9.

Moore, G. T., & Lackney, J. A. (1995). Design patterns for American schools: Responding to the reform movement. In A. Meek (Ed.), *Designing places for learning* (pp. 11–22). Alexandria, VA: Association for Supervision and Curriculum Development.

National Association for the Education of Young Children. (2005a). Embracing diversity in early childhood settings. *Young Children, 60*(6). Entire issue.

National Association for the Education of Young Children. (2005b). Environments. *Young Children, 60*(3). Entire issue.

National Association for the Education of Young Children. (2006). Nutrition and fitness. *Young Children, 61*(3), 10–58.

National Institute of Child Health and Human Development, Early Child Care Research Network (2002). The relation of first grade classroom environment to structural classroom features, teacher, and student behaviors. *The Elementary School Journal, 102*, 367–387.

National Scientific Council on the Developing Child. (2004). Children's emotional development is built into the architecture of their brains. Working Paper No. 2. Available online at www.developingchild.net/pubs/wp/childrens_emotional_development_architecture_brains.pdf.

Noddings, N. (1992). *The challenge to care in schools.* New York, NY: Teachers College Press.

Noddings, N. (2002). *Educating moral people. A caring alternative to character education.* New York, NY: Teachers College Press.

Pecaski-McLennan, D. M. (2009). Ten ways to create a more democratic classroom. *Young Children, 64*(4), 100–101.

Pianta, R. C., LaParo, K. M., & Hamre, B. K. (2005). Classroom assessment scoring system (CLASS). Baltimore, MD: Paul H. Brookes.

Picar, R. (2006). Physical fitness and the early childhood curriculum. *Young Children, 61*(3), 12–18.

Read, M. A. (2007). A sense of place in child care environments. *Early Childhood Education Journal, 34*, 387–392.

Readdick, C. A. (2006). Managing noise in early childhood settings. *Dimensions of Early Childhood, 34*(1), 17–22.

Rivkin, M. (2002). Outdoor settings for play and learning. *Young Children, 57*(3), 8–9.

Sanoff, H. (1995). *Creating environments for young children.* Mansfield, OH: BookMasters.

Shonkoff, J. P., & Phillips, D. (2000). *From neurons to neighborhoods: The science of early childhood development.* In Commission on Behavioral and Social Science and Education (Ed.), *Early childhood development and learning: New knowledge for policy* (pp. 1–20). Washington, DC: National Academy Press.

Strong-Wilson, T., & Ellis, J. (2007). Children and place: Reggio Emilia environment as third teacher. *Theory into Practice, 46*(1), 40–47.

Swiniarski, L., & Breitborde, M. (2003). *Educating the global village: Including the young child in the world* (2nd ed.). Upper Saddle River, NJ: Pearson.

Tegano, D., Moran, J., DeLong, A., Brickman, J., & Ramsisini, K. (1996). Designing classroom spaces: Making the most of time. *Early Childhood Education Journal, 24*(3), 191–194.

Tiedt, P., & Tiedt, I. (2010). *Multicultural teaching* (8th ed.). Boston, MA: Allyn & Bacon.

U.S. Department of Education. (1994). *Goals 2000: Educate America Act.* Washington, DC: Author.

Villegas, A. M., & Lucas, T. (2002). *Educating culturally responsive teachers: A cohort approach.* Albany, NY: State University of New York.

Wassermann, S. (2000). *Serious players in the early childhood classroom* (2nd ed.). New York, NY: Teachers College Press.

Wellhousen, K. (2002). *Outdoor play every day.* Albany, NY: Delmar.

Williams, K. C., & Cooney, M. H. (2006). Young children and social justice. *Young Children, 61*(2), 75–82.

Wortham, S. (2010). *Early childhood curriculum: Developmental bases for learning and teaching* (5th ed.). Upper Saddle River, NJ: Pearson.

Chapter 8

Allen, K. E., & Cowdery, G. E. (2009). *The exceptional child: Inclusion in early childhood education* (6th ed.). Clifton Park, NY: Thomson Delmar Learning.

Allington, R. (2002). What I've learned about effective reading instruction. *Phi Delta Kappan, 83*(10), 740–747.

ASCD Advisory Panel on Improving Student Achievement. (1995). Barriers to good instruction. In R. W. Cole (Ed.), *Educating everybody's children: Diverse teaching strategies for diverse learners* (pp. 9–20). Alexandria, VA: Association for Supervision and Curriculum Development.

Bandura, A. (1997). *Self-efficacy: The exercise of control.* New York, NY: Freeman.

Banks, J., & Banks, C. (2005). *Multicultural education: Issues and perspectives* (5th ed.). New York, NY: John Wiley & Sons.

Barnett, W. S. (2008). *Preschool education and its lasting effects: Research and policy implications.* Boulder, CO: Education and the Public Interest Center and Education Policy Research Unit.

Bowman, B. T. (2006). Standards at the heart of educational equity. *Young Children, 61*(5), 42–48.

Bredekamp, S. (2009). Early learning standards and developmentally appropriate practice: Contradictory or compatible? In S. Feeney, A. Galper, & C. Seefeldt (Eds.), *Continuing issues in early childhood education* (pp. 258–271). Upper Saddle River, NJ: Pearson.

Center on the Developing Child. (2007). *A science-based framework for early childhood policy: Using evidence to improve outcomes in learning, behavior, and health for vulnerable children.* Cambridge, MA: Harvard.

Chaille, C., & Britain, L. (2003). *The young child as scientist: A constructivist approach to early childhood science education* (3rd ed.). White Plains, NY: Longman.

Charlesworth, R., & Lind, K. (2007). *Math and science for young children* (5th ed.). Clifton Park, NY: Delmar Cengage.

Commission on Behavioral and Social Sciences and Education. (2001). *Early childhood development and learning: New knowledge for policy.* Washington, DC: National Academy Press.

Copple, C., & Bredekamp, S. (2006). *Basics of developmentally appropriate practice. An introduction for teachers of children 3 to 6.* Washington, DC: National Association for the Education of Young Children.

Copple, C., & Bredekamp, S. (2009). *Developmentally appropriate practice in early childhood programs serving children from birth through age 8.* Washington, DC: National Association for the Education of Young Children.

Deiner, P. L. (2010). *Inclusive early childhood education* (5th ed.). Belmont, CA: Wadsworth.

Denton, P. (2007). *The power of our words: Teacher language that helps children learn.* Turners Falls, MA: Northeast Foundation for Children.

Dewey, J. (1938). *Experience and education.* New York, NY: Collier Books.

Dodge, D., Colker, L., & Heroman, C. (2002). *The creative curriculum for preschool* (4th ed.). Washington, DC: Teaching Strategies.

Edwards, C., Gandini, L., & Forman, G. (Eds.). (1998). *The hundred languages of children: The Reggio Emilia approach—Advanced reflections* (2nd ed.). Norwood, NJ: Ablex.

Eggen, P., & Kauchak, D. (2010). *Educational psychology: Windows on classrooms* (8th ed.). Boston, MA: Allyn & Bacon.

Espinosa, L. (2009). *Getting it right for young children from diverse backgrounds.* Washington, DC: National Association for The Education of Young Children.

Fleener, C. E., & Bucher, K. T. (2003/2004). Linking reading, science, and fiction books. *Childhood Education, 80*(2), 76–83.

Gay, G. (2004). The importance of multicultural education. *Educational Leadership, 61*(4), 30–35.

Gronlund, G. (2006). *Make early learning standards come alive: Connecting your practice and curriculum to state guidelines.* St. Paul, MN: Redleaf Press.

Hendrick, J., & Weissman, P. (2011). *Total learning: Developmental curriculum for the young child* (8th ed.). Upper Saddle River, NJ: Pearson.

Henson, K. (2010). *Curriculum planning: Integrating multiculturalism, conservatism and education reform* (4th ed.). Long Grove, IL: Waveland Press.

Hyson, M. (2008). *Enthusiastic and engaged learners.* New York, NY: Teachers College Press.

Jackman, H. L. (2009). *Early childhood curriculum: A child's connection to the world* (4th ed.). Clifton Park, NY: Delmar/Cengage.

Jensen, E. (2005). *Teaching with the brain in mind* (2nd ed.). Alexandria, VA: Association for Supervision and Curriculum Development.

Jones, E., & Nimmo, J. (1994). *Emergent curriculum.* Washington, DC: National Association for the Education of Young Children.

Katz, L. G., & Chard, S. C. (2000). *Engaging children's minds: The project approach* (2nd ed.). Norwood, NJ: Ablex.

Kilpatrick, W. H. (1936). *Remaking the curriculum.* New York, NY: Newson & Co.

Kostelnik, M., Soderman, A., & Whiren, A. (2011). *Developmentally appropriate curriculum: Best practices in early childhood education* (5th ed.). Upper Saddle River, NJ: Pearson.

Landry, S. H. (2005). *Effective early childhood programs: Turning knowledge into action.* Houston, TX: University of Texas, Health Series Center.

Lazar, L., & Darlington, R. (1982). Lasting effects of early childhood education: A report from the consortium for longitudinal studies. *Monographs of the Society for Research in Child Development, 47*(2–3, Serial No. 195). Chicago, IL: University of Chicago Press.

Lewin-Benham, A. (2006). One teacher, 20 preschoolers, and a goldfish: Environmental awareness, emergent curriculum, and documentation. *Young Children, 61*(2), 28–34.

Miller, E., & Almon, J. (2009). *Crisis in the kindergarten: Why children need to play in school.* College Park, MD: Alliance for Childhood.

Morrow, L. M. (2005). *Literacy development in the early years: Helping children read and write* (5th ed.). Boston, MA: Allyn & Bacon.

National Association for the Education of Young Children. (2001). *NAEYC standards for early childhood professional preparation: Initial licensure programs.* Washington, DC: Author.

National Association for the Education of Young Children. (2003). *Early learning standards creating the conditions for success.* Joint position statement of National Association for the Education of Young Children and the National Association of Early Childhood Specialists in State Departments of Education. Executive summary. *Young Children, 58*(1), 69–70.

National Association for the Education of Young Children. (2009). *NAEYC standards for early childhood professional preparation programs.* Washington, DC: Author.

National Board for Professional Teaching Standards. (2001). *Early childhood generalist standards for National Board certification* (2nd ed.). Arlington, VA: Author.

National Center for Education Statistics (2009). *The children born in 2001 at kindergarten entry: First findings from the kindergarten data collections of the early childhood longitudinal study, birth cohort (ECLS-B).* Washington, DC: Author. [Publication # 2010005].

National Study Group for the Affirmative Development of Academic Ability. (2004). *All students reaching the top: Strategies for closing the achievement gap.* Naperville, IL: Learning Point Associates. Available online at www.ncrel.org/gap/studies/allstudents.pdf.

Palmer, P. (1998). *The courage to teach: Exploring the inner landscape of a teacher's life.* San Francisco, CA: Jossey-Bass.

Piaget, J. (1965). *The moral judgment of the child.* New York, NY: Free Press.

Posner, G. (2004). *Analyzing the curriculum* (3rd ed.). New York, NY: McGraw-Hill.

Raines, S. R., & Johnston, J. (2003). Developmental appropriateness: New contexts and challenges. In J. P. Isenberg & M. R. Jalongo (Eds.), *Major trends and issues in early childhood education. Challenges, controversies, and insights* (2nd ed., pp. 83–96). New York, NY: Teachers College Press.

Rosenthal, R. and Jacobson, L. (1968). *Pygmalion in the classroom: Teacher expectation and pupils' intellectual development.* New York, NY: Holt, Rinehart, & Winston. Expanded edition, 1992.

Schweinhart, L. J., & Weikart, D. P. (1996). *Lasting differences: The High/Scope preschool curriculum comparison study through age 23.* Monographs of the High/Scope Educational Research Foundation, no. 12. Ypsilanti, MI: High Scope Press.

Seefeldt, C. (2005a). *How to work with standards in the early childhood classroom.* New York, NY: Teachers College Press.

Seefeldt, C. (2005b). *Social studies for the preschool/primary child* (7th ed.). Upper Saddle River, NJ: Pearson.

Shonkoff, J., & Phillips, D. (Eds.). (2000). *From neurons to neighborhoods: The science of early childhood development.* Washington, DC: National Academy Press.

Squires, D. (2005). *Aligning and balancing the standards-based curriculum.* Thousand Oaks, CA: Corwin Press.

Stacey, S. (2009). *Emergent curriculum in early childhood education: From theory to practice.* St. Paul, MN: Redleaf Press.

Sternberg, R. (2008). Excellence for all. *Education Leadership, 66*(2) 14–19.

Tiedt, P., & Tiedt, I. (2010). *Multicultural teaching: A handbook of activities, information, and resources* (8th ed.). Boston, MA: Allyn & Bacon.

Vygotsky, L. (1978). *Mind in society. The development of higher order psychological processes.* Cambridge, MA: Harvard University Press.

Wolfe, P. (2001). *Brain matters: Translating research into classroom practice.* Alexandria, VA: Association for Supervision and Curriculum Development.

Wortham, S. C. (2010). *Early childhood curriculum: Developmental bases for learning and teaching* (5th ed.). Upper Saddle River, NJ: Pearson.

Children's Books

Burns, D. (1995). *Trees, leaves, and bark.* Minnetonka, MN: Northwood Press.

Gibbons, G. (2002). *Tell me tree: All about trees for kids.* Boston, MA: Little Brown.

Grifalconi, A. (1986). *The village of round and square houses.* Boston, MA: Little Brown.

Hoban, T. (1986). *Shapes, shapes, shapes.* New York, NY: Greenwillow.

Hoberman, M. A. (1978). *A house is a house for me.* New York, NY: Scholastic.

Hutchins, P. (1968). *Rosie's walk.* New York, NY: Simon & Schuster.

Chapter 9

Anderson, L., & Krathwol, D. (2001). (Eds.). *A taxonomy for learning, teaching, and assessing: A revision of Bloom's taxonomy of educational objectives.* New York, NY: Longman.

Arends, R. (2009). *Learning to teach* (8th ed.). New York, NY: McGraw-Hill.

Berliner, D. C. (1986). In pursuit of the expert pedagogue. *Educational Researcher, 15*(7), 5–13.

Borko, H., Bellamy, M. L., & Sanders, L. (1992). A cognitive analysis in science instruction by expert and novice teachers. In T. Russell & H. Mundby (Eds.), *Teachers and teaching: From classrooms to reflection* (pp. 49–70). London, UK: Falmer Press.

Bowman, B. (2010). State funded preschools. In V. Washington & J. P. Andrews (Eds.), *Children of 2020: Creating a better tomorrow* (pp. 105–109). Washington, DC: Council for Professional Recognition and National Association for the Education of Young Children.

Chaille, C. (2008). *Constructivism across the curriculum in early childhood education: Big ideas of inspiration.* Boston, MA: Pearson.

Clark, C., & Dunn, S. (1991). Second generation research on teacher planning. In H. C. Waxman & H. J. Walberg (Eds.), *Effective teaching: Current research* (pp. 183–210). Berkeley, CA: McCutchan.

Clark, C. M., & Peterson, P. L. (1986). Teachers' thought processes. In M. C. Wittrock (Ed.), *Handbook of research on teaching* (3rd ed., pp. 198–243). Berkeley, CA: McCutchan.

Copple, C., & Bredekamp, S. (2009). *Developmentally appropriate practice in early childhood programs* (3rd ed.). Washington, DC: National Association for the Education of Young Children.

Copple, C., & Bredekamp, S. (Eds.) (2006). *Developmentally appropriate practice: An introduction for teachers of children 3 to 6.* Washington, DC: National Association for the Education of Young Children.

Derman-Sparks, L., & Edwards, J. (2010). *Anti-bias education for young children and ourselves.* Washington, DC: National Association for the Education of Young Children.

Epstein, A. (2007). *The intentional teacher: Choosing the best strategies for young children.* Washington, DC: National Association for the Education of Young Children.

Espinosa, L. (2010). *Getting it RIGHT for young children from diverse backgrounds.* Upper Saddle River, NJ: Pearson.

Freiberg, H. J., & Driscoll, A. (2005). *Universal teaching strategies* (4th ed.). Boston MA: Allyn & Bacon.

Gardner, H. (1993). *Frames of mind: The theory of multiple intelligences* (2nd ed.). New York, NY: Basic Books.

Gordon, A., & Williams-Browne, K. (2011). *Beginnings and beyond. Foundations of early childhood education* (8th ed.). Belmont, CA: Delmar Cengage.

Gronlund, G. (2006). *Make early learning standards come alive: Connecting your practice to state guidelines.* St. Paul, MN: Redleaf Press.

Henson, K. (2010). *Curriculum planning: Integrating multiculturalism, constructivism, and education reform.* Long Grove, IL: Waveland Press.

Hiebert, J., Morris, A., Berk, D., & Jansen, A. (2007). Preparing teachers to learn from teaching. *Journal of Teacher Education, 58*(1), 47–61.

Katz, L., & Chard, S. (2000). *Engaging children's minds: The project approach* (2nd ed.). Norwood, NJ: Ablex.

Jacobsen, D., Kauchak, D. P., & Eggen, P. D. (2009). *Methods for teaching: Promoting student learning in K–12 classrooms* (8th ed.). Boston, MA: Allyn & Bacon.

Keefe, J., & Jenkins, J. (2002). Personalized instruction. *Phi Delta Kappan, 83*(6), 440–448.

Kostelnik, M. (2008). On teaching young children using thematic units. In M. Jalongo & J. Isenberg, *Exploring your role: An introduction to early childhood education,* (3rd ed., pp. 298–299). Upper Saddle River, NJ: Pearson.

Kostelnik, M., Soderman, A., & Whiren, A. (2011). *Developmentally appropriate curriculum: Best practices in early childhood education* (5th ed.). Upper Saddle River, NJ: Pearson.

Lawler-Prince, D., & Jones, C. (1997). Development of pre-service early childhood education teachers' instructional planning. *Journal of Early Childhood Teacher Education, 18*(3), 77–85.

Morine-Dershimer, G. (2009). Instructional planning. In J. M. Cooper (Ed.), *Classroom teaching skills* (9th ed., pp. 45–81). Belmont, CA: Wadsworth.

National Council for the Social Studies. (1994). *Expectations of excellence: Curriculum standards for social studies.* Washington, DC: Author.

Ogle, D. (1986). K W L: A teaching method that develops active reading of expository text. *The Reading Teacher, 39*(6), 564–570.

Perkins, D., & Blythe, T. (1994). Putting understanding up front. *Educational Leadership, 51,* 4–7.

Price, K. M., & Nelson, K. L. (2011). *Planning effective instruction* (4th ed.). Belmont, CA: Wadsworth.

Salend, S. (2010). *Creating inclusive classrooms; Effective and reflective practices* (7th ed.). Upper Saddle River, NJ: Pearson.

Schoenfeldt, M., & Salsbury, D. (2009). *Lesson planning: A research-based model for K–12 classrooms.* Upper Saddle River, NJ: Pearson.

Seefeldt, C., Castle, S., & Falconer, R. (2010). *Social studies for the preschool/primary child* (8th ed.). Upper Saddle River, NJ: Pearson.

Seefeldt, C., & Galper, A. (2006). *Active experiences for active children: Social studies* (2nd ed.). Upper Saddle River, NJ: Pearson.

Shambaugh, N., & Magliaro, S. (2006). *Instructional design.* Boston, MA: Allyn & Bacon.

Silver, H. F., Strong, R. W., & Perini, M. J. (2000). *So each may learn.* Alexandria, VA: Association for Supervision and Curriculum Development.

Tiedt, P., & Tiedt, I. (2010). *Multicultural teaching: A handbook of activities, information, and resources* (8th ed) Boston, MA: Allyn & Bacon.

Tomlinson, C., & Cunningham-Eidson, C. (2003). *Differentiation in practice: A resource guide for differentiating curriculum. Grades K–5.* Alexandria, VA: Association for Supervision and Curriculum Development.

Trelease, J. (2006). *The read aloud handbook* (6th ed.). New York, NY: Penguin Group.

Woolfolk, A. (2010). *Educational psychology* (11th ed.). Boston, MA: Allyn & Bacon.

Children's Books

Beal, K. (1991). *I love my family.* Reading, MA: Addison-Wesley.

Curtis, J. L. (1996). *Tell me again about the night I was born.* New York, NY: HarperCollins.

Jossee, B. (2005). *Papa, do you love me?* San Francisco, CA: Chronicle Books.

Mora, P. (2010). *Gracias, thanks.* New York, NY: Lee & Low. [Bilingual edition in Spanish and English].

Polacco, P. (1998). *The keeping quilt.* New York, NY: Simon & Schuster.

Prelutsky, J. (2007). *Me I am.* New York, NY: Random House.

Chapter 10

Bowman, B., Donovan, S., & Burns, M. S. (Eds.). (2001). *Eager to learn: Educating our preschoolers.* Washington, DC: National Academy Press.

Bredekamp, S., & Rosegrant, T. (Eds.). (1992). *Reaching potentials: Appropriate curriculum and assessment for young children* (Vol. 1). Washington, DC: National Association for the Education of Young Children.

Carter, M., & Curtis, D. (1996). *Spreading the news: Sharing stories of early childhood education.* St. Paul, MN: Redleaf Press.

Chard, S. C. (1996). Documentation: Displaying children's learning. *Scholastic Early Childhood Today, 11*(1), 56–58.

Colker, L. (2008, March). Twelve characteristics of effective early childhood educators. *Beyond the Journal: Young Children on the Web*. Available at www.naeyc.org/files/yc/file/200803/BTJ_Colker.pdf.

Curtis, D., & Carter, M. (2000). *The art of awareness: How observation can transform your teaching*. St. Paul, MN: Redleaf.

Dale-Easley, S., & Mitchell, K. (2003). *Portfolios matter: What, where, when, why and how to use them*. Markham, Ontario, Canada: Pembroke.

Educational Testing Service (ETS). (2003). *Understanding standards-based assessment*. Pathwise series. Princeton, NJ: Author.

Falk, B. (2000). *The heart of the matter: Using standards and assessment to learn*. Portsmouth, NH: Heinemann.

Fleet, A., Patterson, C., & Robertson, J. (2006). *Insights: Behind early childhood pedagogical documentation*. Castle Hill, New South Wales, Australia: Pademelon.

Gandini, L., & Kaminsky, J. A. (2004). Reflections on the relationship between documentation and assessment in the American context: An interview with Brenda Fyfe. *Innovations in Early Education: The International Reggio Exchange, 11*(1), 5–17.

Groark, C. J., Mehaffie, K. E., McCall, R., & Greenberg, M. T. (2006). *Evidence-based practices and programs for early childhood care and education*. Thousand Oaks, CA: Corwin Press.

Gullo, D. F. (2006a). Alternative means of assessing children's learning in early childhood classrooms. In B. Spodek & O. N. Saracho (Eds.), *Handbook of research on the education of young children* (2nd ed., pp. 443–456). Mahwah, NJ: Erlbaum.

Gullo, D. F. (2006b). Assessment in kindergarten. In D. F. Gullo (Ed.), *K today: Teaching and learning in the kindergarten year* (pp. 138–147). Washington, DC: National Association for the Education of Young Children.

Helm, J. H., & Helm, A. (2006). *Building support for your school: How to use children's work to show learning*. New York, NY: Teachers College Press.

Hirsh-Pasek, K., Kochanoff, A., Newcombe, N., & de Villiers, J. (2005). Using scientific knowledge to inform preschool assessment: Making the case for "empirical validity." *Social Policy Report, 19*(1). Available online at http://bearcenter.berkeley.edu/measurement/pubs/CommentarySmith_Schweingruber.pdf.

International Reading Association/National Council of Teachers of English. (1995). *Standards for the assessment of reading and writing*. Newark, DE: International Reading Association.

Jewiss, J., & Clark-Keefe, K. (2007). On a personal note: Practical pedagogical activities to foster the development of "reflective practitioners." *American Journal of Evaluation, 28*(3), 334–347.

Johnston, P. H., & Rogers, R. (2001). Early literacy development: The case for "informed assessment." In S. B. Neuman & D. K. Dickinson (Eds.), *Handbook of early literacy research* (pp. 377–389). New York, NY: The Guilford Press.

Kagan, S. L., Carroll, J., Comer, J. P., & Scott-Little, C. (2006). Alignment: A missing link in early childhood transitions? *Young Children, 61*(5), 26–32.

Katz, L. (1993). *Five perspectives on quality in early childhood programs*. Urbana, IL: ERIC Clearinghouse on Elementary and Early Childhood Education. [ERIC Document Reproduction Service No. ED 351–148].

Kroeger, J., & Cardy, T. (2006). Documentation: A hard to reach place. *Early Childhood Education Journal, 33*, 389–398.

La Paro, K. M., Pianta, R. C., & Stuhlman, M. (2004). The classroom assessment scoring system: Findings from the prekindergarten year. *The Elementary School Journal, 104*, 409–426.

Lee, B. Y. (2010). Investigating toddlers' and parents' storybook reading during morning transition. *Early Childhood Education Journal, 38*, 213–221.

Lin, M., & Bates, A. B. (2010). Home visits: How do they affect teachers' beliefs about teaching and diversity? *Early Childhood Education Journal, 38*, 179–185.

Litty, C. G., & Hatch, J. A. (2006). Hurry up and wait: Rethinking special education identification in kindergarten. *Early Childhood Education Journal, 33*(4), 203–208.

Mathers, S., Linskey, F., Seddon, J., & Sylva, K. (2007). Using quality rating scales for professional development: Experiences from the UK. *International Journal of Early Years Education, 15*(3), 261–274.

McAfee, O., & Leong, D. J. (2011). *Assessing and guiding young children's development and learning* (5th edition). Upper Saddle River, NJ: Pearson.

McTighe, J. (1997). What happens between assessment? *Educational Leadership, 54*(4), 6–12.

Meisels, S. J., Bickel, D. D., Nicholson, J., Xue, Y., & Atkins-Burnett, S. (2001). Trusting teachers' judgments: A validity study of a curriculum-embedded performance assessment in kindergarten to grade 3. *American Educational Research Journal, 38*(1), 73–95.

Mindes, G. (2007). *Assessing young children* (3rd ed.). Upper Saddle River, NJ: Pearson.

Myers, R. G. (2004). *In search of quality in programmes of early childhood care and education (ECCE)*. Paper commissioned for the EFA Global Monitoring Report 2005, The Quality Imperative. Available online at http://portal.unesco.org/education/en/files/36353/11002676193Myers.doc/Myers.doc.

National Association for the Education of Young Children (NAEYC) and National Association of Early Childhood Specialists in State Departments of Education (NAECS/SDE). (2003). *Joint position statement: Early childhood curriculum, assessment, and program evaluation building an effective, accountable system in programs for children birth through age 8*. Washington, DC: National Association for the Education of Young Children.

National Early Childhood Accountability Task Force (NECATF). (2008). *Taking stock: assessing and improving early childhood learning and program quality* (Report No. 1). Washington, DC: The National Academies Press.

New, R. (2003). Reggio Emilia: New ways to think about schooling. *Educational Leadership, 60*(7), 34–38.

Perrone, V. (1997). Toward an education of consequence: Connecting assessment, teaching, and learning. In A. L. Goodman (Ed.), *Assessment for equity and inclusion* (pp. 305–315). New York, NY: Routledge.

Project Zero. (2003). *Making teaching visible: Documenting individual and group learning as professional development*. Cambridge, MA: Project Zero.

Rinaldi, C. (2004). *In dialogue with Reggio Emilia: Listening, researching, and learning*. New York, NY: Routledge.

Rose, L. C., & Gallup, A. M. (2007). 38th Annual Phi Delta Kappa/Gallup Poll of the public's attitudes toward the public schools. Available online at www.pdkintl.org/kappan/k0609pol.htm#teachers.

Scott-Little, C., Kagan, S. L., & Frelow, V. S. (2006). Conceptualization of readiness and the content of early learning standards: The intersection of policy and research? *Early Childhood Research Quarterly, 21*(2), 153–173.

Seidel, S. (2003). Appendix D: Collaborative assessment protocol. In Project Zero, Cambridgeport Children's Center, Ezra H. Baker School & John Simpkins School (Eds.)., *Making teaching visible: Documenting individual and group learning as professional development.* Cambridge, MA: Project Zero.

Seitz, H., & Bartholomew, C. (2008). Powerful portfolios in early childhood. *Early Childhood Education Journal, 36*(1), 63–68.

Sheets, R. H. (2005). *Diversity pedagogy: Examining the role of culture in the teaching-learning process.* Upper Saddle River, NJ: Pearson.

Smith, Y., & Goodwin, A. L. (1997). The democratic, child-centered classroom: Provisioning for a vision. In A. L. Goodwin (Ed.), *Assessment for equity and inclusion* (pp. 101–120). New York, NY: Routledge.

Snow, C. E., & Van Hemel, S. B. (Eds). (2008). *Early childhood assessment: Why, what, and how.* Committee on Developmental Outcomes and Assessments for Young Children. Washington, DC: The National Academies Press.

Strickland, D. S. (2006). Language and literacy in kindergarten. In D. F. Gullo (Ed.), *K today: Teaching and learning in the kindergarten year* (pp. 73–84). Washington, DC: National Association for the Education of Young Children.

Tolbert, L., & Theobald, P. (2006). Finding their place in the community: Urban education outside the classroom. *Childhood Education, 82*(5), 271–274.

Vecchi, V. (2001). The curiosity to understand. In C. Guidici, C. Rinaldi, & M. Krechevsky (Eds.), *Making learning visible: Children as individual and group learners in Italy.* Rome, Italy: Reggio Children.

Wiggins, G. (1998). *Educative assessment: Designing assessments to inform and improve student performance.* San Francisco, CA: Jossey-Bass.

Wiggins, G., & McTighe, J. (2005). *Understanding by design* (2nd ed.). Alexandria, VA: Association for Supervision and Curriculum.

Children's Books

Carle, E. *The very hungry caterpillar.* New York, NY: Penguin Group.

Chapter 11

Adams, S. K., & Baronberg, J. (2005). *Promoting positive behavior: Guidance strategies for early childhood settings.* Upper Saddle River, NJ: Pearson.

Bagner, D. M., Boggs, S. R., & Eyberg, S. M. (2010). Evidence-based school behavior assessment of externalizing behavior in young children. *Education and Treatment of Children, 33*(1), 65–83.

Barrera, I., & Corso, R. M. (2003). *Skilled dialogue: Strategies for responding to cultural diversity in early childhood.* Baltimore, MD: Paul H. Brookes.

Beaty, J. J. (2006). *50 early childhood guidance strategies.* Upper Saddle River, NJ: Pearson.

Boyer, E. (1995). *The basic school: A community for learning.* Carnegie Foundation for the Advancement of Teaching.

Brazelton, T. B., & Greenspan, S. I. (2000). *The irreducible needs of children: What every child must have to grow.* Cambridge, MA: Merloyd Lawrence.

Bronson, M. B. (2006). Developing social and emotional competence. In D. F. Gullo (Ed.), *K today: Teaching and learning in the kindergarten year* (pp. 47–56). Washington, DC: National Association for the Education of Young Children.

Carlsson-Paige, N. (2009). *Taking back childhood: A proven roadmap for raising confident, creative and compassionate kids.* New York, NY: Plume.

Church, E. B. (1997). Group time: Resources for teacing around the circle. New York, NY: Scholastic.

Deci, E. L., & Ryan, R. M. (1985). *Intrinsic motivation and self-determination in human behavior.* New York, NY: Plenum.

Diamond, K. E., Reagan, A. J., & Bandyk, J. E. (2000). Parents' conceptions of kindergarten readiness: Relationships with race, ethnicity, and development. *Journal of Educational Research, 94,* 93–100.

Dinkmeyer, D., & McKay, G. (1989). *Systematic training for effective parenting* (3rd ed.). Minneapolis, MN: American Guidance Service.

Dunlap, G., Strain, P. S., Fox, L., Carta, J., Conroy, M., Smith, B. J., et al. (2006). Prevention and intervention with young children's challenging behavior: A summary of current knowledge. *Behavioral Disorders, 32,* 29–45.

Elementary Educators. (2006). *Creating a safe and friendly school.* Turners Falls, MA: Northeast Foundation for Children.

Gannon, B., & Mncayi, P. (1996). You *can* get there from here. *Reaching Today's Youth, 1*(1), 55–57.

Ganz, J. B., & Flores, M. M. (2010). Implementing visual cues for young children with Autism spectrum disorders and their classmates. *Young Children, 65*(3), 78–83.

Gartrell, D. (2006). Guidance matters: Boys and men teachers. *Young Children, 61*(3), 92–93.

Gilliam, W. S. (2005). Prekindergartners left behind: Expulsion rates in state prekindergarten systems. Available online at www.fcd-us.org/PDFs/NationalPreKExpulsionPaper03.02_new.pdf.

Glasser, W. (1999). *Choice theory: A new psychology of personal freedom.* New York, NY: Harper Paperbacks.

Gurian, M., & Stevens, K. (2005). *The mind of boys: Saving our sons from falling behind in school and life.* San Francisco, CA: Jossey-Bass.

Henley, M. (1996). Teaching self-control to young children. *Reaching Today's Youth, 1*(1), 13–16.

Heroman, C., & Copple, C. (2006). Teaching in the kindergarten year. In D. F. Gullo (Ed.), *K today: Teaching and learning in the kindergarten year* (pp. 59–72). Washington, DC: National Association for the Education of Young Children.

Hewitt, D. (1995). *So this is normal too? Teachers and parents working out developmental issues in young children.* St. Paul, MN: Redleaf Press.

Isenberg, J. P., & Jalongo, M. R. (2010). *Creative thinking and arts-based learning: Preschool through fourth grade* (5th ed.). Upper Saddle River, NJ: Pearson.

Kaiser, B., & Rasminsky, J. S. (2006). *Challenging behavior in young children: Understanding, preventing, and responding effectively* (2nd ed.). Boston, MA: Allyn & Bacon.

Kohn, A. (1996). *Beyond discipline: From compliance to community.* Alexandria, VA: Association for Supervision and Curriculum Development.

Korthagen, F., & Vasalos, A. (2005). Levels in reflection: Core reflection as a means to enhance professional growth. *Teachers and Teaching: Theory and Practice, 11*(1), 47–71.

Krahl, C., & Jalongo, M. R. (1998). Creating caring classroom communities: Advice from an intervention specialist. *Childhood Education, 75*(2), 83–89.

Lewis, R. (2001). Classroom discipline and student responsibility: The students' view. *Teaching and Teacher Education, 17*(3), 307–319.

Maag, J. W. (2001). Rewarded by punishment: Reflections on the disuse of positive reinforcement in schools. *Teaching Exceptional Children, 67*(2), 173–186.

Marion, M. (2007). *Guidance of young children* (7th ed.). Upper Saddle River, NJ: Pearson.

Martin, L. A., Chiodo, J. J., & Chang, L. (2001). First year teachers: Looking back after three years. *Action in Teacher Education, 23*(1), 55–63.

Maslow, A. (1968). *Toward a psychology of being* (2nd ed.). Princeton, NJ: Van Nostrand.

McFarland, L., Saunders, R., & Allen, S. (2009). Reflective practice and self-evaluation in learning positive guidance: Experiences of early childhood practicum students. *Early Childhood Education Journal, 36*(6), 505–511.

Mindes, G. (2006). Social studies in kindergarten. In D. F. Gullo (Ed.), *K today: Teaching and learning in the kindergarten year* (pp. 107–115). Washington, DC: National Association for the Education of Young Children.

National Association for the Education of Young Children. (1996). *Early years are learning years: Teaching children not to be—Or be victims of—Bullies.* Washington, DC: Author.

Nelsen, J., Erwin, C., & Duffy, R. (1995). *Positive discipline for preschoolers: For their early years—Raising children who are responsible and resourceful.* Rocklin, CA: Prima Publishing.

Nissen, H., & Hawkins, C. J. (2010). Promoting emotional competence in the preschool classroom. *Childhood Education, 86*(4), 255–259.

Ostrosky, M. M., & Jung, E. Y. (2006). Building positive teacher–child relationships. *Early Childhood Education Journal, 28*, 144–146.

Paley, V. (1992). *You can't say you can't play.* Cambridge, MA: Harvard University Press.

Preusse, K. (2006). Fostering prosocial behavior in young children. In K. Paciorek (Ed.), *Annual editions: Early Childhood Education 06/07* (27th ed., pp. 181–184). Dubuque, IA: McGraw-Hill.

Rief, S. F. (1993). *How to reach and teach ADD/ADHD children: Practical techniques, strategies, and interventions for helping children with attention problems and hyperactivity.* West Nyack, NJ: The Center for Applied Research in Education.

Rodgers, D. B. (1998). Research in review: Supporting autonomy in young children. *Young Children, 53*(3), 75–80.

Saifer, S. (2003). *Practical solutions to practically every problem: The early childhood teachers' manual.* St. Paul, MN: Redleaf.

Severson, H., & Walker, H. (2002). Proactive approaches for identifying children at risk for sociobehavioral problems. In K. Lane, F. M. Gresham, & T. O'Shaughnessy (Eds.), *Interventions for children with or at-risk for emotional and behavioral disorders* (pp. 33–53). Boston, MA: Allyn & Bacon.

Shore, C. (2003). *The many faces of childhood: Diversity in development.* Boston, MA: Allyn & Bacon.

Silvestri, L. (2001). Pre-service teachers' self-reported knowledge of classroom management. *Education, 121*(3), 575–580.

Sowers, J. (2004). *Creating a community of learners: Solving the puzzle of classroom management.* Portland, OR: Northwest Regional Educational Laboratory.

Strachota, B. (1996). *On their side: Helping children take charge of learning.* Turners Falls, MA: Northeast Foundation for Children.

Tobin, L. (1991). *What do you do with a child like this?* Duluth, MN: Whole Person Associates.

Walker, H. M., Ramsey, E., & Gresham, F. M. (2003/2004). Heading off disruptive behavior: How early intervention can reduce defiant behavior—And win back teaching time. *American Educator, 29*, pp. 6, 8–21, 46.

Wein, C. A. (2006). From policing to participation: Overturning the rules and creating amiable classrooms. In K. Paciorek (Ed.), *Annual editions: Early Childhood Education 06/07* (27th ed., pp. 133–139). Dubuque, IA: McGraw-Hill.

Weinstein C., Tomlinson-Clarke S., & Curran M. (2004). Toward a conception of culturally responsive classroom management. *Journal of Teacher Education, 55*(1), 25–38.

Zaslow, M., & Martinez-Beck, I. (Eds.). (2006). *Critical issues in early childhood professional development.* Baltimore, MD: Paul H. Brookes.

Chapter 12

Anderson, S., & Sabatelli, R. (2007). *Family interaction: A multigenerational perspective* (4th ed.). Boston, MA: Allyn & Bacon.

Barnett, M. A. (2008). Economic disadvantage in complex family systems: Expansion of family stress models. *Clinical Child Family Psychological Review, 11*, 145–161.

Baum, A. C., & Swick, K. J. (2008). Dispositions towards families and family involvement: Supporting preservice teacher development. *Early Childhood Education Journal, 35*, 579–584.

Berger, E. H. (2007). *Parents as partners in education: Families and schools working together* (7th ed.). Upper Saddle River, NJ: Pearson.

Berry, C. F., & Mindes, G. (1993). *Theme-based curriculum: Goals, themes, activities and planning guides for 4's and 5's.* Glenview, IL: GoodYear.

Berthelsen, D., & Walker, S. (2008). Parents' involvement in their children's education. *Family Matters, 79,* 34–41.

Bouffard, S., & Weiss, H. (2008). Thinking big: A new framework for family involvement policy, practice, and research. *The Evaluation Exchange, 14*(1&2), 2–5.

Boyer, E. L. (1995). *The basic school: A community for learning.* Princeton, NJ: Carnegie Foundation for the Advancement of Teaching.

Bronfenbrenner, U. (2005). *Making human beings human: Bioecological perspectives on human development.* Thousand Oaks, CA: Sage.

Bullough, R. V., & Gitlin, A. D. (2001). *Becoming a student of teaching: Linking knowledge production and practice* (2nd ed.). New York, NY: Routledge Falmer.

Ceglowski, D., & Bacigalupa, C. (2002). Four perspectives on child care quality. *Early Childhood Education Journal, 30*(2), 87–92.

Cheadle, J. E. (2008). Educational investment, family context, and children's math and reading growth from kindergarten through the third grade. *Sociology of Education, 81*(1), 1–31.

Christenson, S. L., & Sheridan, S. M. (2001). *Schools and families: Creating essential connections for learning.* New York, NY: The Guilford Press.

Clawson, C., & Luze, G. (2008). Individual experiences of children with and without disabilities in early childhood settings. *Topics in Early Childhood Special Education, 28*(3), 132–147.

Comer, J. P., & Ben-Avie, M. (2010). Promoting community in early childhood programs: A comparison of two programs, *Early Childhood Education Journal, 38,* 87–94.

Copple, C., & Bredekamp, S. (Eds.). (2009). *Developmentally appropriate practice in early childhood programs serving children from birth through age eight* (rev. ed.). Washington, DC: National Association for the Education of Young Children.

Dimock, C., O'Donoghue, T., & Robb, A. (1996). Parent involvement in schooling: An emerging research agenda. *Compare, 26,* 5–20.

Division for Early Childhood (DEC). (2009). Code of Ethics. Available online at www.decsped.org/uploads/docs/about_dec/position_concept_papers/Code%20of%20Ethics.

Dunst, C. J., Raab, M., Trivette, C. A., & Swanson, J. (2010). Community based everyday child learning opportunities. In R. A. McWilliam (Ed.), *Working with families of children with special needs* (pp. 60–92). New York, NY: Guilford Press.

Elkind, D. (1995). School and family in the postmodern world. *Phi Delta Kappan, 77*(1), 8–14.

Fantuzzo, J., McWayne, C., Perry, M. A., & Childs, S. (2004). Multiple dimensions of family involvement and their relations to behavioral and learning competencies for urban, low-income children. *School Psychology Review, 33*(4), 467–480.

Garmston, R. J. (2005). *The presenter's fieldbook: A practical guide.* Norwood, MA: Christopher-Gordon.

Gennarelli, C. (2004). Family ties: Communicating with families: Children lead the way. *Young Children, 59*(1), 98.

Gestwicki, C. (2009). *Home, school and community relations: A guide to working with families.* Belmont, CA: Wadsworth.

González, N., Moll, L., & Amanti, C. (2005). *Funds of knowledge: Theorizing practices in households, communities, and classrooms.* Mahwah, NJ: Lawrence Erlbaum.

Gonzalez-Mena, J. (2006). *The young child in the family and the community* (4th ed.). Upper Saddle River, NJ: Pearson.

Griebel, W., & Niesel, R. (2009). A developmental psychology perspective in Germany: Co-construction of transitions between family and education system by the child, parents, and pedagogues. *Early Years, 29*(1), 59–68.

Hanson, M. J., & Lynch, E. W. (2010). Working with families from diverse backgrounds. In R. A. McWilliam (Ed.), *Working with families of young children with special needs* (pp. 147–174). New York, NY: The Guilford Press.

Henderson, A. T., & Mapp, K. L. (2002). *A new wave of evidence: The impact of school, family, and community connections on student achievement.* Austin, TX: National Center for Family & Community Connections with Schools, Southwest Educational Development Laboratory. Available online at www.sedl.org/connections/resources/evidence.pdf.

Henderson, A. T., Marburger, C. L., & Ooms, T. (1992). *Beyond the bake sale: An education guide to working with parents.* Washington, DC: National Committee for Citizens in Education.

Ho, S. C., & Willims, J. D. (1996). Effects of parental involvement on eight-grade achievement. *Sociology of Education, 96*(2), 126–141.

Isik-Ercan, Z. (2010). Looking at school from the house window: Learning from Turkish-American parents' experiences with early elementary education in the United States. *Early Childhood Education Journal, 38,* 133–142.

Kendall, F. E. (1996). *Diversity in the classroom: New approaches to the education of young children* (2nd ed.). New York, NY: Teachers College Press.

Knopf, H. T., & Swick, K. J. (2007). How parents feel about their child's teacher/school: Implications for early childhood professionals. *Early Childhood Education Journal, 34*(4), 291–296.

Lareau, A. (2003). *Unequal childhoods: Race, class and family life.* Berkeley, CA: University of California Press.

Laverick, D. M., & Jalongo, M. R. (Eds.). (2011). *Transitions to early care and education: International perspectives on making schools ready for young children.* New York, NY: Springer.

Lawrence-Lightfoot, S. (2003). *The essential conversation: What parents and teachers can learn from each other.* New York, NY: Random House.

Lawson, M. (2003). School–family relations in context: Parent and teacher perceptions of parent involvement. *Urban Education, 38*(1), 77–133.

Lester, B. M., & Sparrow, J. D. (Eds.). (2010). *Nurturing children and families: Building on the legacy of T. Berry Brazelton.* Hoboken, NJ: Wiley-Blackwell.

Liess, E., & Ritchie, G. (1995). Using multiple intelligence theory to transform a first-grade health curriculum. *Early Childhood Education Journal, 23*(2), 71–79.

Lopez, M. E., Kreider, H., & Caspe, M. (2004). Co-constructing family involvement. *Evaluation Exchange, 10*(4), 2–3.

McBride, B. A., & Rane, T. R. (1997). Father/male involvement in early childhood programs: Issues and challenges. *Early Childhood Education Journal, 25*(1), 11–15.

McDevitt, T., & Ormrod, J. E. (2009). *Child development and education* (4th ed.). Upper Saddle River, NJ: Pearson.

Mensing, J. F., French, D., Fuller, B., & Kagan, S. L. (2000). Child care selection under welfare reform: How mothers balance work requirements and parenting. *Early Education & Development, 11*, 573–595.

Murray, J. (2007). The cycle of punishment: Social exclusion of prisoners and their children. *Criminology and Social Justice, 7*(1), 55–81.

National Center for Children in Poverty. (2010). Who are America's poor children? Available online at www.nccp.org/publications/pub_912.html.

Pew Center on the States. (2010). State of the states 2010. Available online at www.pewcenteronthestates.org/.

Powers-Costello, E., & Swick, K. J. (2008). Exploring the dynamics of teacher perceptions of homeless children and families during the early years. *Early Childhood Education Journal, 36*, 241–245.

Raab, M., & Dunst, C. J. (2004). Early intervention practitioner approaches to natural environment interventions. *Journal of Early Intervention, 27*(1), 15–26.

Reynolds, A., & Clements, M. (2005). Parent involvement and children's school success. In E. N. Patrikalou, R. P. Weissberg, S. Redding, & H. J. Walberg (Eds.), *School–family partnerships: Promotion of the social, emotional, and academic growth of children* (pp. 109–127). New York, NY: Teachers College Press.

Rinaldi, C. (2000). Values in education. Speech presented at Mills College, Oakland, CA, March.

Sachs, J. (2005). *The end of poverty: Possibilities for our time.* New York, NY: Penguin.

Seplocha, H. (2004). Partnerships for learning: Conferencing with families. *Young Children, 59*(5), 96–99.

Souto-Manning, M. (2010). Family involvement: Challenges to consider, strengths to build on. *Young Children, 65*(2), 82–88.

Swick, K. (2004a). Communicating effectively with parents and families who are homeless. *Early Childhood Education Journal, 32*(3), 211–216.

Swick, K. (2004b). *Empowering parents, families, schools, and communities during the early childhood years.* Champaign, IL: Stipes.

Swick, K. (2004c). What parents seek in relations with early childhood family helpers. *Early Childhood Education Journal, 32*(3), 217–220.

Swick, K., & Hooks, L. (2005). Parental experiences and beliefs regarding inclusive placements of their special needs children. *Early Childhood Education Journal, 32*(6), 1–6.

Zuna, N. I., Selig, J. P., Summers, J. A., & Turnbull, A. P. (2009). Confirmatory factor analysis of a family quality of life scale for families of kindergarten children without disabilities. *Journal of Early Intervention, 31*(2), 111–125.

Chapter 13

Berliner, D. C. (1994). Expertise: The wonder of exemplary performances. In C. C. Block & J. Mangieri (Eds.), *Creating powerful thinking in teachers and students: Diverse perspectives* (pp. 161–186). Fort Worth, TX: Harcourt Brace.

Bodie, G. D., & Burleson, B. R. (2008). Explaining variations in the effects of supportive messages: A dual-process framework. In C. Beck (Ed.), *Communication yearbook 32* (pp. 354–398). New York, NY: Routledge.

Britzman, D. (2003). *Practice makes practice: A critical study of learning to teach* (2nd ed.). Albany, NY: SUNY Press.

Buysee, V., Winton, P. J., & Rous, B. (2009). Reaching consensus on a definition of professional development for the early childhood field. *Topics in Early Childhood Special Education, 28*(4), 235–243.

Colker, L. (2008). Twelve characteristics of effective early childhood educators. *Beyond the Journal: Young Children on the Web.* Available online at www.naeyc.org/files/yc/file/200803/BTJ_Colker.pdf.

Darling-Hammond, L. (2006). *Powerful teacher education: Lessons from exemplary programs.* San Francisco, CA: Jossey-Bass.

Darling-Hammond, L., & Bransford, J. (2005). *Preparing teachers for a changing world: What teachers should learn and be able to do.* San Francisco, CA: Jossey-Bass.

Division for Early Childhood (DEC). (2009). *Code of Ethics.* Available online at www.decsped.org/uploads/docs/about_dec/position_concept_papers/Code%20of%20Ethics.

Drago-Severson, E. (2009). *Leading adult learning: Supporting adult development in our schools.* Thousand Oaks, CA: Corwin.

Editors of *Education Week*. (2002, January 10). *Quality counts 2002: Building blocks for success* [Special issue].

Essa, E. (2002). *A practical guide to solving preschool behavior problems* (5th ed.). Belmont, CA: Delmar/Cengage.

Fullan, M. (2007). *Leading in a culture of change.* San Francisco, CA: Jossey-Bass.

Graves, D. (2001). Build energy with colleagues. *Language Arts, 79*(1), 12–19.

Jalongo, M. R., Fennimore, B., Laverick, D., Pattnaik, J., Mutuku, M., & Brewster, J. (2004). Blended perspectives: A global vision for high-quality early childhood education. *Early Childhood Education Journal, 32*(3), 143–155.

Katz, L. (1977). *Talks with teachers.* Washington, DC: National Association for the Education of Young Children.

Kern, P., Wolery, M., & Aldridge, D. (2007). Use of songs to promote independence in morning greeting routines for young children with autism. *Journal of Autism Development Disorders, 37*, 1264–1271.

Korthagen, F. (2004). In search of the essence of a good teacher: Towards a more holistic approach in teacher education. *Teaching and Teacher Education, 20*, 77–97.

Lee, W. (2008). Teachers as powerful learners. Available online at elp.co.nz/Wendy_Lee_Article_Education_Gazette.pdf.

Little, J. W. (2001). Professional development in pursuit of school reform. In A. Lieberman & L. Miller (Eds.), *Teachers caught in the action: Professional development that matters* (pp. 23–44). New York, NY: Teachers College Press.

MacDonald, R. E. (1991). *A handbook of basic skills and strategies for beginning teachers: Facing the challenge of teaching in today's schools*. White Plains, NY: Longman.

National Association for the Education of Young Children (NAEYC). (2004). Code of ethical conduct: Supplement for early childhood adult educators. A joint position statement of NAEYC, NAECTE (National Association of Early Childhood Teacher Educators), & ACCESS (American Associate Degree Early Childhood Teacher Educators). Available online at http://208.118.177.216/about/positions/pdf/ethics04.pdf.

Nieto, S. (2003). *What keeps teachers going?* New York, NY: Teachers College Press.

Ryan, K., & Cooper, J. M. (2006). *Those who can, teach* (11th ed.). Belmont, CA: Wadsworth.

Smith, R. G. (2007). Developing professional identities and knowledge: Becoming primary teachers. *Teachers and Teaching: Theory and Practice, 13*(4), 377–397.

Swick, K. J., & Hanes, M. L. (1987). *The developing teacher.* Champaign, IL: Stipes.

The Work Buzz. (2010). The future's 15 most wanted workers. Available online at www.theworkbuzz.com/employment-trends/most-wanted-workers/.

Zaslow, M., & Martinez-Beck, I. (Eds.). (2005). *Critical issues in early childhood professional development*. Baltimore, MD: Paul H. Brookes.

NAME
Index

Kochanoff, A., 270b
Kohn, A., 296
Kontos, K., 176
Korthagen, F., 306, 308, 358f
Kostelnik, M., 5, 212, 213f, 214, 236, 240, 247, 251
Kowalski, K., 28
Krahl, C., 298
Krathwol, D., 240
Kreider, H., 324
Kritchevsky, S., 170
Kroeger, J., 287f
Kuder, S.J., 65

L
Lackney, J.A., 178
Ladson-Billings, G., 84
Landry, S.H., 201
LaParo, K.M., 186, 286
Lareau, A., 320
Larrivee, B., 77
Lascarides, V.C., 33, 39f
Laverick, D.M., 3, 321f
Lawler-Prince, D., 237
Lawrence, F.R., 60
Lawrence, J.M., 28
Lawrence-Lightfoot, S., 327
Lawson, M., 325
Lazar, L., 203
Lee, B.Y., 269
Lee, W., 344
Leong, D.J., 30, 135, 139, 271f, 272
Lester, B.M., 325
Lewin-Benham, A., 216
Lewis, R., 294b
Liebovich, B.J., 28
Liess, E., 162
Lin, H.L., 60
Lin, M., 283
Lind, K., 213, 214
Linskey, F., 286
Little, J.W., 346b
Litty, C.G., 277
Locke, J., 32, 149, 156t
Lombardi, J., 45
London, A., 50
Lont, A., 5
Lopez, M.E., 324
Loreman, T., 79
Lucas, T., 182
Luther, M., 32
Luze, G., 76
Lynch, E.W., 75, 321
Lynch, R.G., 54, 75, 77, 84, 133

M
Maag, J.W., 294b
MacDonald, R.E., 349
Madrazo, G., 74
Magliaro, S., 234
Malaguzzi, L., 63
Mapp, K.L., 325
Marburger, C.L., 324
Marion, M., 306
Martin, L.A., 294b
Martinez-Beck, I., 166, 294b, 305
Mashburn, A.J., 5
Maslow, A., 96–97, 124–125, 168, 294
Mason, M.A., 24, 29, 31, 32, 33, 35, 36
Matas, C., 119
Mathers, S., 286
Maxwell, K.L., 5
May, H., 26, 33, 36, 39
Mayer, K., 135
McAfee, O., 271f
McBride, B.A., 324
McCall, R., 276
McClanahan, S., 255
McClean, M., 76
McClelland, A., 75
McCombs, B.L., 135, 136, 139
McDevitt, T., 320b
McDonald, J.P., 5
McFarland, L., 298
McGee, C.A., 31
McGee, J.A., 31
McKay, G., 296
McMillen, M., 54
McMillen, R., 54
McTighe, J., 270, 281
McWayne, C., 325
McWilliam, R.A., 90
McWilliams, R., 191
Mehaffee, K.E., 276
Meisels, S.J., 280
Mensing, J.F., 326
Metcalf, D., 191, 192
Metzler, S., 5
Meyer, R.J., 40
Miller, E., 204
Miller, L., 139
Mims, S., 57
Mindes, G., 282, 303f, 321b
Mistral, G., 19
Mitchell, K., 281
Mitchell, L.S., 30, 62
Mncayi, P., 296

Moll, L.C., 85
Montessori, M., 31, 34f, 35, 41f, 42f, 61
Montgomery, W., 182
Moore, G.T., 178
Mora, P., 139
Moran, J., 22, 181, 241
Moravcik, E., 81
Morine-Dershimer, G., 234, 239, 240
Morris, A., 246
Morrow, L.M., 213
Motz, L., 74
Mueller, A., 26
Mumpower, J.O., 176, 178
Munkata, V., 109
Murray, J., 331

N
Naumburg, M., 30
Nelsen, J., 303f
Nelson, K.L., 236, 237, 239, 240, 243, 245
Nelson, L.L., 90
Nett, D., 85
New, R., 287
Newcombe, N., 270b
Nicholson. J., 280
Niesel, R., 321f
Nieto, S., 6, 26, 74b, 75, 76, 77, 84, 350
Nimmo, J., 216
Nissen, H., 305
Noddings, N., 2, 81, 175, 184

O
O'Connor, A., 39f
O'Connor, S., 38f
O'Dell, S., 119
Odom, S., 191
O'Donoghue, T., 322
Ogawa, R.T., 74b
Ogle, D., 242, 244f, 245
Ooms, T., 324
Ormrod, J.E., 320b
Ormsbee, C., 55
Ornstein, M., 255
Ortlieb, E.T., 26
Osborn, D.K., 26, 29, 32, 39f, 43
Ostrosky, M.M., 303f
Owen, R., 31, 33, 53

P
Pajares, M.F., 28
Paley, V., 310
Palmer, P., 205

SUBJECT Index

After page numbers, b indicates box, f indicates figure, and t indicates table.

Strategies and Tools to Take into the Classroom

This information is designed to highlight resources that have immediate applicability to the early childhood classroom. The following categories correspond with the main topics in the 2010 draft standards of the Interstate Teachers Assessment and Support Consortium (INTASC) that outline what all teachers should know and be able to do to help all learners be successful, and the Association for Childhood Education International (ACEI) standards that are used to accredit programs. More detailed information about the standards is in the Learning Outcomes listed at the start of each chapter.